THE MITCHELL/McGRAW-HILL TITLES IN INFORMATION SYSTEMS

FOURTH E

BUSINESS
COMPUTER SYSTEMS

AN INTRODUCTION

BUSINESS COMPUTER SYSTEMS
AN INTRODUCTION

David M. Kroenke

Kathleen A. Dolan

 Mitchell **McGRAW-HILL**

New York St. Louis San Francisco Auckland Bogotá Caracas
Hamburg Lisbon London Madrid Mexico Milan Montreal
New Delhi Oklahoma City Paris San Juan SãoPaulo Singapore
Sydney Tokyo Toronto Watsonville

BUSINESS COMPUTER SYSTEMS:
An Introduction, 4th Edition

Copyright © 1990, by McGraw-Hill, Inc. All rights reserved. Printed in the United States of America. Except as permitted under the United States Copyright Act of 1976, no part of this publication may be reproduced or distributed in any form or by any means, or stored in a data base or retrieval system, without the prior written permission of the publisher.

2 3 4 5 6 7 8 9 0   DOW DOW   9 5 4 3 2 1 0

ISBN: 0-07-035604-1

The sponsoring editor was Erika Berg.
The designer was John Edeen.
The production manager was Betty Drury.
The cover design was by John Edeen.
The production was supervised by Greg Hubit.
Graphic Typesetting Service was the typesetter.
R. R. Donnelley & Sons Company was the printer and binder.

Library of Congress Card Catalog No.: 89-62071

The Support Package

Using Application Software in Business: VP-Planner PLUS, dBASE III PLUS, and WordPerfect 4.2, *by Kathleen Dolan and Keiko Pitter*

This manual combines Pitter's popular step-by-step tutorials with Dolan's real-world scenarios from *Business Computer Systems*, 4th Edition. Students learn how to use the most popular commercial packages to increase their productivity. A data disk is included. The educational version of all three packages is available either shrink-wrapped with the manual or as a master from which to make copies for student use.

Other Application Software Manuals

A wealth of other lab manuals—with or without software—covering full-power commercial, limited commercial, or full-power shareware is available shrink-wrapped with the text at a discounted package price.

Student Study Guide/Casebook, *by Diana Stark*

Over the past three editions, this popular supplement has been required by more than 50 percent of the schools using the text.

Instructor's Guide, *by David Kroenke and Kathleen Dolan*

Complete with detailed lecture outlines, a summary of changes to ease the transition from the third to the fourth edition, sample course syllabi, teaching tips for part-time instructors and TAs, and "emergency lectures," this comprehensive manual was written entirely by the authors of the text.

Computerized Test Bank

Class-tested and -developed over three editions, this test generator gives instructors the power to add, delete, or modify more than 1,500 true/false, multiple-choice, and fill-in-the-blank questions. Also available in printed form.

Color Transparencies and Black and White Masters

Two sets of transparencies accompany the text: a set of masters based on text figures and a set of full-color transparencies designed to enhance the text with original art.

Broadcast-Quality Videotapes

Computers at Work has been revised to illustrate the most current computer concepts and applications. Thirteen documentary-style videotapes are included. Ask about our Adopter's Policy.

Brief Contents

Complete Contents

Preface to the Instructor

The introductory computer information systems course can be one of the most difficult courses to teach. For one reason, students' expectations often are different from our own. The difference results, in part, from another challenge in teaching this course. Students usually have little real-world business experience. Thus, they do not yet appreciate, firsthand, the need for information systems and the problems that poorly developed systems can create.

RESPONDING TO THE CHALLENGES

We have found a number of strategies effective in responding to the challenges facing introductory information systems instructors.

A Conceptual Framework

First, we take the bull by the horns and demonstrate from the beginning of the text to the end that a computer information system consists of five components: hardware, software, data, procedures, and personnel. This five-component model, which has been the backbone of each edition of this text, illustrates to students that data, procedures, and personnel—the components most often overshadowed by hardware and programs—are often the source of information systems problems in the business world.

Personal to Multiuser Information Systems

Second, we think it is important to meet students at their level of expectation and then expand the discussion to ours. Since many students expect this course to be a microcomputer applications course, we begin with personal computer applications. We capture the students' attention with the concepts that they expect, then gradually broaden the concepts to multiuser information systems.

Real-World Examples

Third, we believe it is essential to illustrate the use of information systems in practical settings. Without real-world applications, students learn only isolated terms and concepts, and rarely learn what to do with that information once the course is over. Thus, this text includes many short vignettes written to illustrate why and how users and organizations employ information systems technology. These examples do not assume any previous business experience.

Why? What? How?

In light of these challenges and because the introductory course threatens to become a thousand loose definitions heading in many different directions, we balance coverage of the *what* with the *why* and the *how*. For instance, *why* is a database management system needed to improve the productivity of an individual user or organization? *What* are the components of a local area network? *How* is a spreadsheet designed, a desktop publishing package purchased, any other type of information system developed?

WHAT'S NEW IN THE FOURTH EDITION?

The major difference between the fourth edition and prior editions of **Business Computer Systems** is the shift in emphasis from computer specialists to end users. Previous editions emphasized large-scale systems, and responded to the needs of students who would become programmers or systems analysts. The fourth edition responds to the needs of today's students, tomorrow's users. To accomplish this goal, we have:

- Adopted an **end-user perspective** to emphasize how information systems technology can and should be employed by end users to increase productivity, solve business problems, and make decisions.
- **Consolidated** into a new Chapter 2 what today's students need to know about the **five components** of every user's computer system: hardware, programs, data, procedures, and personnel.
- Progressed from **personal information systems** (Part II) to **multi-user information systems** (Part III); that is, we have built on the students' level of experience to illustrate the various roles played by users in the development and use of systems.
- Added a new Part II (Chapters 4–8) on the concepts and applications of **spreadsheets, graphics, databases, word processing**, and **desktop publishing,** equipping students to use these productivity tools to solve problems.
- Replaced the coverage of sequential and direct access file processing, and changed the orientation of the database coverage to become more **relevant and useful** to end users.
- Broken down the coverage of **systems development** into two chapters, to differentiate between what users need to know about their role in developing each personal information system (Chapter 8) and multiuser information systems (Chapter 12).
- Added **current coverage** of these increasingly important topics: ethics, hypermedia, OS/2, networking, expert systems, AI, proto-

typing, CASE tools, 4GLs, end-user computing, and information centers.

- Completely rewritten the **Microsoft BASIC** programming appendix, stepping students through seven hands-on lessons, from loading BASIC to arrays.

FULL-COLOR PHOTO ESSAYS

Full-color photo essays, popular in the previous editions of *Business Computer Systems*, are designed to graphically illustrate topics of emerging importance in the information systems industry. This edition includes five photo essays:

- **Computer Systems Extending Human Capabilities. . .** depicts some of the many ways that computer systems have extended the range of human intellect—in space, in science, in medicine, in education, with artificial intelligence, and in the arts.
- **Hardware: More and More for Less and Less. . .** shows hardware devices that students are most likely to encounter in personal, departmental, and multiuser environments.
- **The Chip: The Heart of the Computer. . .** tours a semiconductor factory and shows how the chip is developed—from silicon rocks to finished computer.
- **Communicating with Computer Systems. . .** illustrates the role of information systems in facilitating communication, human-to-human as well as computer-to-computer. Includes graphics, telecommunications, and international business.
- **Information Systems for a Competitive Advantage. . .** shows ways information systems enable users and organizations to develop, produce, and deliver better products. Includes product marketing, conceptualization, design, manufacturing, and customer support.

USING APPLICATION SOFTWARE?

An application software manual has been specially designed to accompany *Business Computer Systems*. ***Using Application Software in Business,*** by Keiko Pitter and Kathleen Dolan, is a step-by-step, hands-on tutorial for the educational versions of three of the most popular commercial packages: VP-Planner Plus, a Lotus "clone"; dBASE III PLUS; and WordPerfect 4.2.

Included with the manual is a disk containing data from scenerios in this text. Hands-on exercises, practice sessions, and projects in the manual cast students as end users. Using the accompanying packages to solve real-world problems posed in the text—such as changing spreadsheet figures and evaluating the results—gives students an opportunity to integrate and apply concepts in a business setting and increase their productivity.

EXTENSIVE SUPPORT PACKAGE

A variety of supporting materials is available, including:

- **Using Application Software in Business**, by Kathleen Dolan and Keiko Pitter with data disk.
- Educational version of **VP-Planner Plus, dBASE III PLUS,** and **WordPerfect 4.2** (four disks).
- Many **other tutorial manuals**—with or without software, for full-power commercial, limited commercial, or full-power "shareware."
- *Student Study Guide/Casebook,* by Diana Stark. Over the past three editions, this popular supplement has been ordered by 50 percent of adopters.
- *Instructor's Manual,* by David Kroenke and Kathleen Dolan. Includes lecture outlines, a summary of changes to ease the transition from the third to the fourth edition, teaching tips, answers to review questions, guidelines for using *Using Application Software in Business* with the text.
- Color **transparencies** and black and white masters.
- *Test Bank,* printed and on disk with computer test generator.
- Thirteen documentary-style, broadcast-quality **videotapes.**

ACKNOWLEDGMENTS

We gratefully acknowledge the assistance of many people in the development of this text. First and foremost, we are grateful for the support and guidance of Erika Berg, who has been an editor and supporter of this text for many years. We also appreciate the hard work of Raleigh Wilson, Marianne Taflinger, Denise Nickeson, and Rich DeVitto, also of Mitchell Publishing, who helped us publish this edition.

Comments and suggestions for changes in this edition were received from many people. We would like to thank the following:

William Amadio,
Rider College

Gary Armstrong,
Shippensburg University

Tonya Barrier,
University of Texas at Arlington

Bill Barth,
Cayuga Community College

Eli Boyd Cohen,
Bradley University

Caroline Curtis,
Lorain County Community College

Jay Davis,
DeVry Institute of Technology

John DeNisco,
Buffalo State College

Dennis Emmerich,
Community College of Aurora

Lucian Endicott, Jr.,
Central Texas College

Paul Fitzer,
Central State University

Barry Floyd,
New York University

Michael Gourey,
Central State University

Michael Graves,
Portland Community College

Richard Hatch,
San Diego State University

Roger Hayen,
Central Michigan University

C. Brian Honess,
University of South Carolina at
Columbia

Gary Huston,
Arizona State University

Peter Irwin,
Richland College

S. W. Joshi,
Slippery Rock University

Jerry Joyce,
Keene State College

John Krobock,
Sacramento State University

Thom Luce,
Ohio University

Gerald Mackey,
Georgia Institute of Technology

Charles McNichols,
Florida Institute of Technology

Carolyn Meinhardt

Dick Meyer,
Hartnell College

R. Nickerson,
San Francisco State University

John Palipchak,
Pennsylvania State University

Keiko Pitter,
Truckee Meadows Community
College

R. K. Raja,
University of Texas at Arlington

Eugene Rathswohl,
Shippensburg University

Ted Robinson,
Central Texas College

John Schillak,
University of Wisconsin at
Eau Claire

Leonard Schwab,
California State University at
Hayward

Noel Smith,
University of Texas at Arlington

David Stamper,
University of Northern Colorado

Margaret Thomas,
Ohio University

Diane Visor,
Central State University

Steve Watson,
Washington State University

David Whitney,
San Francisco State University

Samual Wiley,
LaSalle University

Ken Wilson,
Algonquin College

Jim Wood,
University of Texas at Arlington

David M. Kroenke
Seattle, Washington

Kathleen A. Dolan
Vernon, Connecticut

FOURTH EDITION

BUSINESS COMPUTER SYSTEMS

AN INTRODUCTION

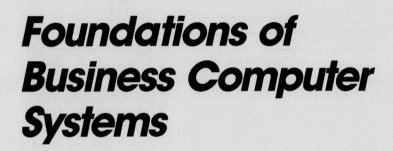

Foundations of Business Computer Systems

In Part One, you will learn the basics about business computer systems, or, as they are sometimes called, information systems. You will find out why people use business computer systems (to increase productivity), what business computer systems are (the five components), and how business computer systems are used in real applications (a survey of computer systems in business).

Throughout this text, you will be discovering how you can put information systems to work for you. In Chapter 1 we present four situations in which an information system could help an ordinary businessperson do his or her job better. We also illustrate how important it is for users—like you—to know that a system is more than just a computer and some programs. Developing an effective information system takes time and dedication. Neither Rome nor an effective system was built in a day.

In Chapter 2 you will learn about the five components that make up every business computer system. Besides equipment and programs, a system includes the data that must be collected, entered, and stored; it includes people, who must be trained to use, develop, and operate the system effectively; and it includes written procedures that every system user, developer, and operator must follow for the system to function.

In Chapter 3 you will learn how business computer systems are put to use. First you will become acquainted with five types of business information systems, and the characteristics of each one. Then you will learn how information systems are used in functional areas of business, such as accounting and manufacturing.

As you study these first foundation chapters, think about computer systems you have already encountered, such as the system that issues monthly telephone bills or the system your school uses for class registration. How does what you learn in this course relate to computer systems such as these?

CHAPTER 1

Using Business Computer Systems to Increase Productivity

You may have enrolled in this course thinking that you are going to study computers and programs. In part, you will. But, as a future business person, it is not enough for you to know how to turn on a computer and what keys to push to run a word processing program or a spreadsheet application. You need to know more.

You need to know how to integrate computers and programs into the work that you will do. You need to know how to use computer technology to increase your productivity and the productivity of the department and organization in which you work. To do this, you need to learn about information systems, which include computers and programs, but which also involve data, procedures, and people. You need to know why information systems are important, what they are composed of, and how you should go about developing them.

The purpose of this chapter is to introduce the major themes of this text:

- What business information systems are
- Why business information systems are important to you, the end user
- How to develop effective information systems
- The differences between single-user and multiuser systems

To introduce those themes, we will consider the experiences of an example company.

We frequently will use examples like the following in this text. Their purpose is to show you how to apply the concepts you are learning to the business environment. Mathematicians use equations to express their thoughts; electrical engineers use circuit diagrams to express theirs. In information systems, we often use vignettes to show how concepts and technology can be applied. Consider these vignettes in the same way that you would consider a technical diagram in an engineering text.

Questions

1.1 Explain what you need to learn about computer systems besides how to turn on a computer and what keys to push.

1.2 What is the major purpose of using information systems?

1.3 What are the three dimensions of information systems that we will study in this text?

1.4 Why does this text make use of vignettes?

Jenson-Kehrwald Company

Jenson-Kehrwald Company (JKC) is a partnership that designs and develops interior landscapes for hotels, restaurants, condominiums, and large private estates. In its designs it uses a mixture of commonly available plants, flowers, and shrubs, imported rare and exotic plants, silk and dried flowers, pottery, and other materials. JKC employs 25 people and has gross sales of $3.6 million with a before-tax profit of $648,000.

Elizabeth Jenson and Chip Kehrwald own the partnership equally. Elizabeth, a designer, has won many awards for her innovative landscapes and gardens. Chip is an experienced businessperson. Although Elizabeth and Chip have never developed formal job descriptions, their partnership has evolved over the last ten years such that Elizabeth manages the artistic side of the business, including not only supervision of the design activity, but also plant purchases, job production, and the selection of vendors; Chip is the general manager and supervises the sales and financial activities.

The Order Process

The typical job proceeds as follows. One of the JKC salespeople calls upon an existing or potential customer and identifies an opportunity. Sometimes these calls are unsolicited, but more often they are made in response to a customer request. Once the salespeople identify a real prospect, they introduce one or more of the designers to the customer. The designers meet with the customer, determine the customer's needs, and then develop a design. The design is reviewed with the customer, adjusted as needed, and then approved (or rejected). If approved, the project is turned over to the production department for implementation. Accounts receivable then follows up for payment.

The Design Process

There are nine people in the design group: six full-time designers, an administrative assistant, a botanist, and the group manager, Cheryl Poy. Cheryl works closely with Elizabeth, who remains the firm's chief designer. This arrangement could be problematical except that Cheryl and Elizabeth have worked together for many years and they have established a relationship in which Cheryl manages the more administrative concerns of the design group while Elizabeth oversees and contributes to the major design activities.

As stated, designers meet with the customer to determine the customer's requirements. Depending on the size and complexity of the project, the designers may produce one or more preliminary sketches. Once they have settled on the basics of a design, they then develop more formal sketches and blueprints. They also prepare a written bid that contains a general description of the project, a list of plants and materials, and a detailed listing of both material and labor costs. The written bid is prepared by the administrative assistant.

What Are the Components of an Information System?

To understand the components of an information system, consider the following conversation between Michelle Jackson, a new employee at JKC, and one of her friends.

"Hey, Michelle, I heard you got a new job!"

"Hi, Jason. Yeah, I do. It's with a landscape design company called Jenson-Kehrwald."

"That's terrific. You like plants—you must really enjoy it. What do you do?"

"I'm an administrative assistant. Which means I do just about anything that needs to be done. I work for the partners and take care of whatever comes up. We've got so many different projects, something's always happening. I don't think I'll ever be bored."

"Like the people?"

"Yeah, a lot. Everyone's real friendly and helpful. But I'm not sure they like me."

"What do you mean? Everybody likes you."

"Well, thanks; but I goofed last week. I mean I really goofed. Elizabeth, one of the two partners, and Cheryl, the manager of the design department, had to cancel their plans last Thursday night and help me get a proposal done. I felt like such a jerk. Elizabeth had some meeting she had to cancel and Cheryl missed her son's basketball game."

"They can't expect miracles. You've just started."

"Yeah. But, well . . . I might as well tell you what happened.

"Part of my job is to prepare the written proposals. The salespeople develop a proposal, present it to the customer, and if it's accepted, they make a few changes and give it to me to put into the format of a contract. They have a word processing computer and I use it to make the changes and then print the contract."

"So? You've used computers before. That shouldn't be a problem."

"Well, no, it shouldn't. But you see, I've never used this kind of computer before, or this type of program. Though that's not really the problem, either.

"Anyway, the first week, Kathleen, the woman they promoted from the job I have, showed me how to use the computer, how to use the program, how to load paper in the printer, things like that. It's pretty easy to do, and as you said, I've used computers before.

"The problem is I have to do several different jobs, sometimes at the same time, and it gets kind of complicated. What's worse is, nothing's written down. And I had a lot of things to learn, all at once.

"Well, we have to deal with all these Latin names for plants, like *Laccospadix australasica* palm, *Arenga pinnata* palm, and *Chamaedorea falcifera* palm. They're pretty confusing and hard to type correctly. Also, the salespeople don't spell all of these out in the draft contracts. They'll write, 'One 18-inch *Lacc. aus.* palm,' for example, and I have to type '*Laccospadix australasica* palm' into the contract.

"To help me, Kathleen gave me a disk that had all of the plant names. She said I could use it to check the names and copy them into the contract. She also gave me a disk that has all of the customer names and addresses, and a third disk that had all of the contracts they had sent out this month.

"The idea is that to prepare a new contract, I use the format of one already sent out, copy the correct customer name from the customer disk, and get the correct plant names from the plant disk."

"That sounds pretty complicated, Michelle."

"Well, it isn't really. Anyway, I'm in the middle of this and Elizabeth comes in and asks me to help her carry about a hundred begonias out to her van to take to the Winter Garden opening. Then the phone rings. Then we get a delivery of the new pots from Italy (which, by the way, are so beautiful). Then a couple of other things happen. Finally, I go back to work on the contract.

"Well, I've forgotten where I am, and I make some mistake, I don't really know what it was, and the system says, 'Insert new disk in drive *a*.' So I think I'm supposed to put the plant inventory disk into drive *a*, because that's what Kathleen showed me to do. And I do that.

"Well, the disk starts churning away and pretty soon I realize that something's not right. It never did that before. I start to panic and I take the disk out of the drive. And I put the other disk, the one with the old contracts, into the drive. The system gives me some kind of error message, and now I don't know what to do. So I type 'OK' and let it churn away.

"Meanwhile, I can't find Kathleen. She's out on a sales call. And I'm supposed to have this contract done by 4:30. And I'm getting more and more panicky because I really like this job and I want to make a good impression.

"It turns out that I somehow wiped out both of the disks. When I looked at the directories, there was nothing on either of them. It was horrible. I went to Cheryl and showed her what was going on and about then Elizabeth came back and then Kathleen showed up and then the salesperson came by to pick up the contract. I had nothing to show. Nothing.

"We all sat there sort of stunned and pretty soon Elizabeth said, 'We've got to get this contract in by 9:00 tomorrow. We'll just have to key in all of the data and the contract from scratch tonight.'

"By now it was about 5:30 and she canceled her dinner and Cheryl backed out on the basketball game and we all sat there until about 9:30 to finish the contract for the meeting on Friday. It was horrible. Everybody was really angry and upset but they were trying not to let it show. I'm surprised I wasn't fired on the spot.

"I know I made a mistake. But the thing is, nothing's written down. It would be so much easier if they had the basic steps written somewhere. Where I worked before, they had a book that had basic procedures in it. Also, shouldn't the company have another copy of all that data somewhere? I mean, am I the only one to ever make a mistake like that? It really doesn't seem fair. But then again, I did goof. Ugh, it was awful, Jason!"

Michelle is right. It is not fair. And it is not entirely her fault. Whoever designed the word processing application at JKC did a poor job. They developed only a portion of the system.

As you will learn in the next chapter, an information system consists of hardware, programs, data, procedures, and people. The designer of JKC's word processing application did not pay enough attention to either the procedure or the people component. Michelle's intuition is correct; there should have been written procedures that described how to use the system. There should also have been procedures for making backup copies of the data to be used when mistakes are made. A well-designed system would include backup data so that the cost of Michelle's error would not be so great. Michelle probably also deserved better training than she received.

One of the major themes of this book is to explain what an information system is, and that an effective information system includes all

Questions

1.5 What are the five components of an information system?

1.6 Describe the problem that Michelle had in using her word processing application. What was lacking in the system that she used?

five components. When you finish this course, you will know what comprises a well-designed information system, and you should be able to protect yourself from problems like the one Michelle encountered. If you become a manager, you should be able to ensure that systems are developed properly, so that your employees are not subject to problems like this.

Why Use Information Systems?

Another of the major themes of this text concerns the reasons for which information systems are developed. We believe that people develop information systems to improve productivity—their own and that of their organization. To understand this better, consider the following discussion between Michelle and Elizabeth several weeks after the incident described above.

"Michelle, I need your help. Every weekend I spend three or four hours developing a report about our sales activity. There's no reason that you can't make the report for me, and I want to show you how. OK with you?"

"Sure, I'd like to learn."

"All right. Every Friday by 3:00, the salespeople turn in a copy of all of the proposals they have submitted that week. [An example proposal is shown in Figure 1-1.] I add the amounts of all orders for each salesperson for that week and write the total here, in this report. [A copy of Elizabeth's report is shown in Figure 1-2.] I also compute the total for the month and the total for the year. Then I compute grand totals for the company. Got it so far?"

"Yes, I think so."

"Now, once a proposal is accepted, the salespeople generate a work order [shown in Figure 1-3]. The work order describes the amount of plant stock, silk and dried flowers, pottery, and labor for the accepted bid. Michael brings me a copy of all the work orders for the week late on Friday. Then, what I do is to add up the amount of sales for each of the four categories for each salesperson and a grand total for the company. [See Figure 1-2.]

"The last thing I do is to plot the data on this graph. [See Figure 1-4.] I plot the grand total of proposals submitted for the company as well as the grand total of committed sales. I'd like to graph the numbers for each of the salespeople, but I never have enough time to do that.

"Does this make sense?"

"Yes. I think I can do that, Elizabeth. It doesn't seem too hard."

"No, it really isn't. The biggest problem is doing all the addition correctly. I don't expect you to do this over the weekend, but why don't you see if you can have it done by the end of the day on Monday? Thanks."

In this scenario, Elizabeth is developing a report about the sales activities at JKC. She wants this report for a number of reasons. For

Computer Systems Extend Human Capabilities

1 *Astrophysicists study the formation and growth of galaxies using a large mainframe computer.*

Computer systems extend the range and power of human capabilities. Computer systems increase our ability to perceive, to visualize, to conceptualize, to learn, to reason, to work, and to play.

Exploration of the Natural Environment (photos 1–6)
Computer systems expand our ability to probe, explore, and discover natural phenomena on all scales—from the origin of galaxies to the surface of a molecule. Computer systems direct, control, monitor, and interpret signals from both manned and unmanned space flights. They can be used to learn about physical processes on our own planet. Such systems are also used to model the structures of molecules and atoms. These systems enable humans to visualize objects that they cannot see directly.

Study and Exploration of the Human Body (photos 7–17)
Computer systems extend our ability to understand our own bodies. Computer-based medical systems facilitate the development of treatment plans, they enable medical personnel to examine tissues and organs without physical intervention, and they can be used to understand and improve human performance.

Education (photos 18–20)
With the proliferation of computers on campus and in the public schools, computer systems can be used to increase our capacity to learn. Educational programs can be tailored to the needs of individuals, rote learning can be conducted in the context of computer games, and expensive, messy, or dangerous experiments can be simulated on the computer screen.

Artificial Intelligence (photos 21–31)
The term *artificial intelligence* (AI) refers to a group of related activities that are normally associated with intelligent human behavior. Some AI systems *reason.* *Expert systems* attempt to capture the essence of human knowledge of a domain and to apply that knowledge to solve real-world problems. *Natural language* is concerned with the development of human language computer interfaces and with the translation of human languages. *Vision systems* address the technology required for computer systems to "see." *Robotics* primarily concerns the development of industrial robots. Robotics and vision can be combined, as shown in the accompanying photos.

Computer Systems and Art (photos 32–40)
Computer systems are used for both commercial and fine art. Images for commercial applications are developed and even printed using

personal and other computer systems. Some computer art, such as the portrait by the CRAY supercomputer shown on page 14 of this photo essay, can have very high resolution and quality. Computer systems can use mathematics to construct seemingly realistic artificial worlds.

Even fine artists are beginning to use computer systems. Interesting and enjoyable still art can be created, as well as displays for games and animated entertainment. Computer systems can be combined with synthesizers to create and perform music. Some of the most beautiful and complicated computer art has been developed for fantasy space movies such as *Star Wars.*

10

MOON OF JUPITER

Image captured on 9400 by JPL, transformed to 6214 data and printed on Ramtek's 4100 Colorgraphic Printer (pat.pend.)

⊚ RAMTEK CORPORATION 1981

2 Computer systems played a pivotal role in controlling Voyager spacecraft, in causing Voyager equipment to generate appropriate signals, and in interpreting the signals as they arrived on Earth.

3 Computer systems were critical to the Apollo space program, even in 1969!

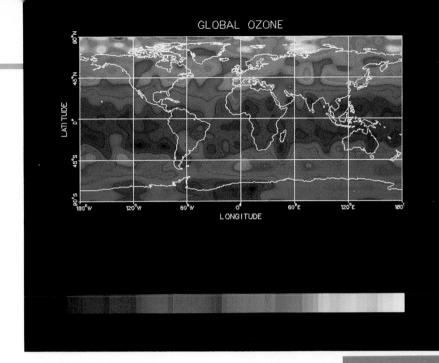

4 Computer systems interpret satellite-generated data and create images and graphics that show the distribution of ozone in the atmosphere.

5 Computer simulation of the effects of erosion on the future terrain of the Sandia, N.M., mountains.

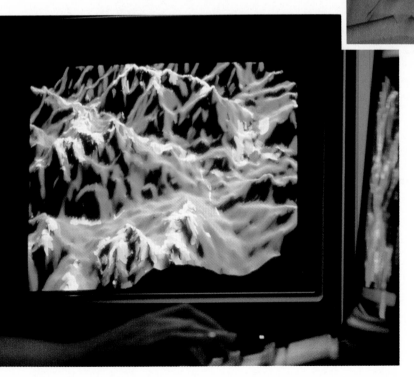

6 Computer-generated graphics of images produced by an electron microscope.

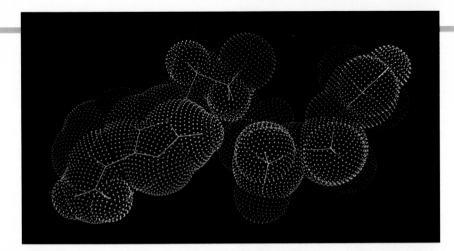

7 A chemical modeling system used to generate a visualization of an adenosine triphosphate (ATP) molecule.

8 A molecular modeling system extends the capabilities of the Apple Macintosh to create three-dimensional chemical models.

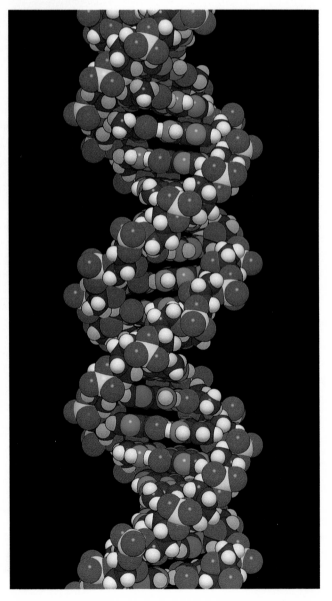

9 A model of a portion of human DNA.

10 An image system used to prepare an orthodontics treatment plan.

11 A magnetic resonance imaging (MRI) system portrays a human liver without surgery or other physical invasion or disruption.

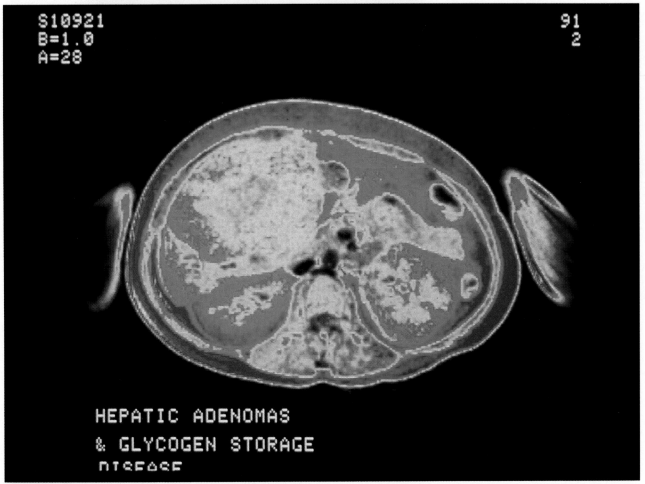

S10921
B=1.0
A=28

91
2

HEPATIC ADENOMAS
& GLYCOGEN STORAGE
DISEASE

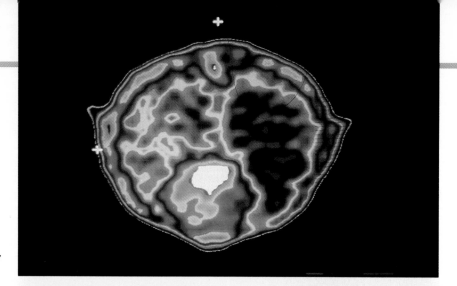

12 A computerized axial tomography (CAT) scan image of a human brain.

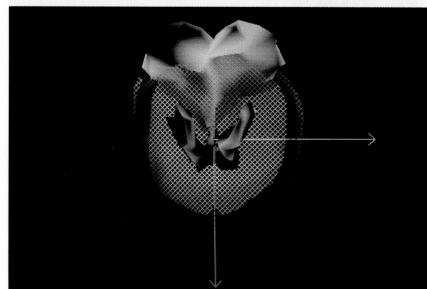

13 A three-dimensional portrayal of a human brain shows the extent and impact of diseases and injury and helps surgeons plan operations.

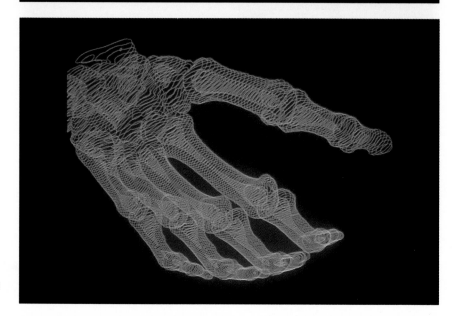

14 An image of a human hand bone structure is used to determine the extent of injury or disease—it can also be used to develop a treatment plan.

15, 16, 17 A computer system is used to record and analyze body movements of U.S. athletes in preparation for the Olympic Games.

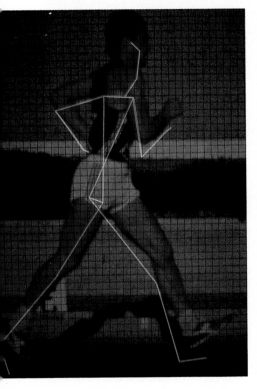

18 Prevalence of microcomputers in student life is changing the delivery of education.

19 Computer educational games can make rote learning enjoyable.

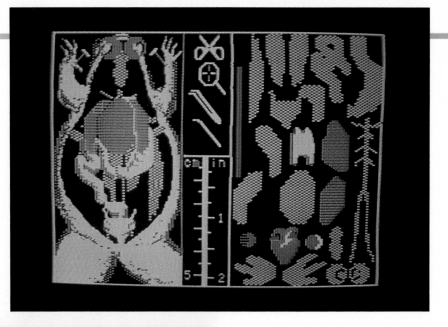

20 Computer-based simulation of frog dissection simplifies lab activities and saves frogs.

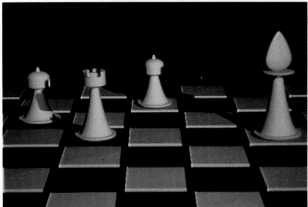

21 The development of chess-playing computer programs was far more difficult than initially thought, and the struggle revealed the power and complexity of the human mind. Some programs today play at the master's level.

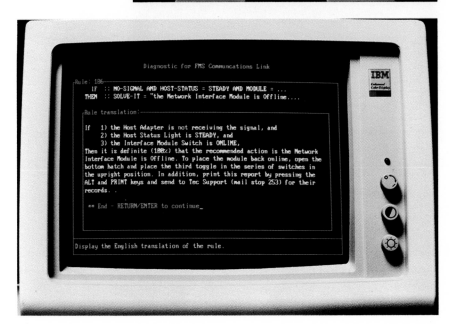

22 An expert system is a computer system that processes a knowledge base to make conclusions, recommendations, or diagnoses. This system diagnoses problems in a communications network.

23 An expert system that diagnoses faults in the electronic controls of a large land-based gas turbine.

24 An expert system that diagnoses reactor faults.

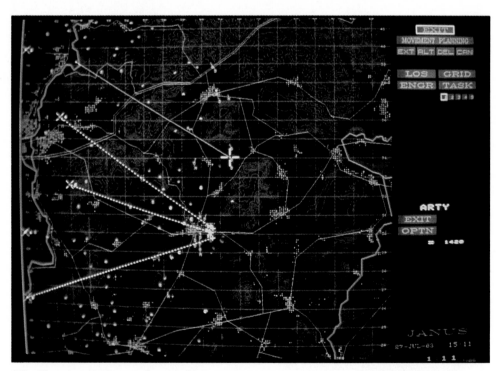

25 Expert systems are also used to configure military communications and control systems in response to a rapidly changing environment.

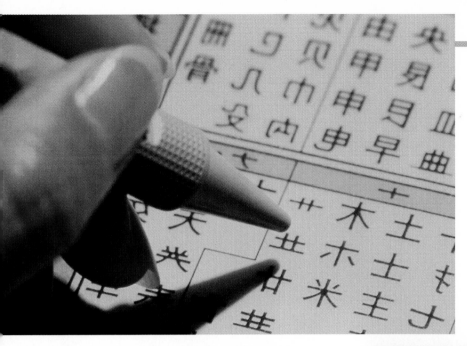

26 Research has been under way since the 1950s on machine translation of human languages. So far, only limited success has been achieved.

27 A robot used by Woods Hole Oceanographic Institution enables exploration of an environment too hostile for humans to survive in.

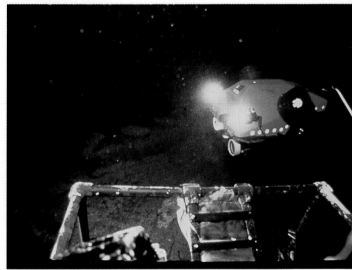

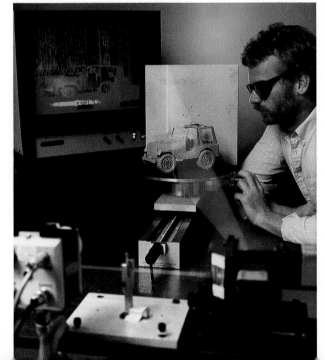

28 Machine vision systems with cameras for eyes can recognize objects they "see."

29 *This robot runs on its own vision system and avoids many obstacles. Such robots can be used in hostile environments such as those contaminated by radioactivity.*

30 *This robot uses vision to select objects from a bin.*

31 A vision robot that can identify and select objects by color.

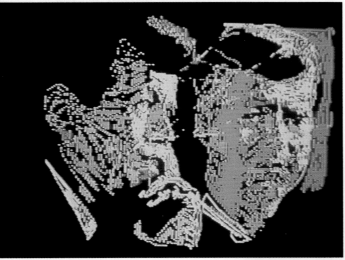

32 A computer-drawn portrait of John F. Kennedy.

33 Increasingly, computer systems are used to produce art for marketing and other industrial applications.

34 A self-portrait—this photo is an image of a CRAY supercomputer that was drawn by programs running on that computer.

35 This picture of an artificial world was generated by a computer program that calculated values for color and color intensities from sine and polynomial equations.

36 Computers have become one of the tools used by fine artists.

37 *Fish and chips—art produced using computer systems.*

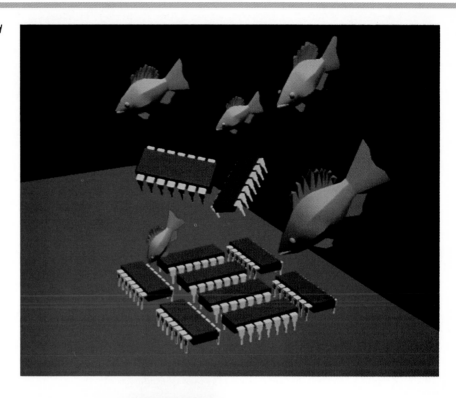

38 *Computers combined with synthesizers are revolutionizing musical composition and performance.*

39 *Computer animation greatly reduces the cost of animated movies.*

40 *A "star fighter" produced by a computer graphics system.*

Figure 1-1
Example proposal

Jenson-Kehrwald Company

To: **Fitzroy and Alsop, Architects**
1721 Fourteenth Avenue North
Seattle, Washington 98109

Attn: **Michael Foote**

Subject: Proposal and Price Quotation for Exterior Landscape Redesign at Bay Vista

Description of Materials

Location: Exterior of china and crystal store and nail salon

2 each 28" #1 Italian terra-cotta containers (existing)
Each to be planted with:
1 each 7' to 8' Hollywood Torulosa
base planted with summer annuals and ivy

Location: Under Vista Office Group sign

2 each 32" #1 Italian terra-cotta containers
Each to be planted with:
1 each 7' to 8' Hollywood Torulosa
base planted with summer annuals and ivy

2 each 24" #1 Italian terra-cotta containers (existing)
Each to be planted with:
5-gallon Acanthus and summer annuals

2 each 20" #1 Italian terra-cotta containers
Each to be planted with:
Liriope and summer annuals

Location: Under residential awning

2 each 24" #1 Italian terra-cotta containers (existing)
Each to be planted with:
6' to 7' Topiary Ligustrum japonica
base planted with summer annuals and ivy

4 each 20" #1 Italian terra-cotta containers
Each to be planted with:
Liriope and trailing summer annuals

Price Quotation

Additional Italian terra-cotta containers	$ 510.00
Additional plants and annuals	1,115.00
Installation and delivery	195.00
Total price	$1,820.00
Monthly maintenance fee	$ 85.00

Terms

50 percent deposit required on order
Balance due net 10 days after installation

Week of 4/23/90   *Sales Effectiveness Report*

Name	Proposal Dollars			Committed Sales Dollars			
	Week	Month	Year	Plants	Silk	Pottery	Labor
Jess	42,387	105,467	387,659	19,558	0	8,446	4,978
Michael	27,654	97,588	355,782	14,345	3,285	1,866	2,788
Robin	42,337	157,889	667,118	23,119	4,233	7,756	6,543
Total	112,378	360,944	1,410,559	57,022	7,518	18,068	14,309

Figure 1-2
Manually prepared report

one, she wants to know how the company is doing, overall. She also wants to know how each salesperson is doing, and how they are doing in comparison to each other. She also uses this report to motivate the salespeople; they know she is computing the dollar amounts of their proposals and their sales. Knowing this, they pay close attention to those numbers as well. In this way, Elizabeth can motivate the sales people to focus on the activities on which she wants them to focus.

The system described by Elizabeth is a manual information system. It has three components: data, procedures, and people. Elizabeth (or Michelle) follows the procedures described above, processing the data on the proposal and work orders to produce the information shown in Figure 1-2.

Using a Computer-based System

The information in this report could readily be produced by a computer-based information system. Figure 1-5 shows results from what is called an *electronic spreadsheet application* that produces this information. A clerk enters proposal and sales data as shown in Figure 1-5a. The spreadsheet application adds the data items together to produce the summarized spreadsheet in Figure 1-5b. The information system also produces the graphs shown in Figure 1-5c.

When Elizabeth develops this information herself, it takes her about three hours. It will probably take Michelle at least that long, perhaps longer. Using the system that generated the data in Figure 1-5, either of them could produce the reports and graphs in about fifteen minutes. Further, once the data is entered, there are a number of other reports and graphs that can be developed. The graph of performance by salespeople—which Elizabeth never has time to do—is an example.

Using a computer-based system would enable Elizabeth to increase *productivity*. A measure of productivity is the ratio of outputs to inputs. To improve productivity, we increase this ratio. The increase can be achieved in three ways: we can obtain more output for the same input; we can obtain the same output for less input; or we can do both. In the JKC example, a computer-based system would enable Elizabeth to do

Figure 1-3
Example work order

Jenson-Kehrwald Company
Work Order

Work Order number 1876-43

Bill To: **Fitzroy and Alsop, Architects**
1721 Fourteenth Avenue North
Seattle, Washington 98109
Attn: **Michael Foote**

Quantity	Description	Price
4	7' Hollywood Torulosa	$ 540.00
2	5-gallon Acanthus	$ 60.00
2	6' Topiary Ligustrum japonica	$ 375.00
14	Summer annuals, ivy, Liriope	$ 140.00
2	32-inch #1 Italian terra-cotta	$ 100.00
2	28-inch #1 Italian terra-cotta	$ 90.00
4	24-inch #1 Italian terra-cotta	$ 140.00
6	20-inch #1 Italian terra-cotta	$ 180.00
	Installation and delivery	$ 195.00
	Subtotal	$1,820.00
	Tax	$ 132.86
	Total amount	$1,952.86

Figure 1-4
Graph of monthly proposal and sales
data (prepared manually)

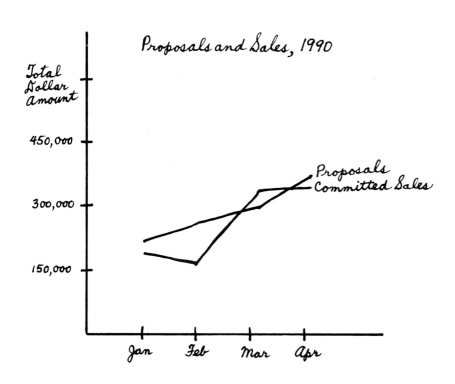

Figure 1-5
Results from an electronic
spreadsheet

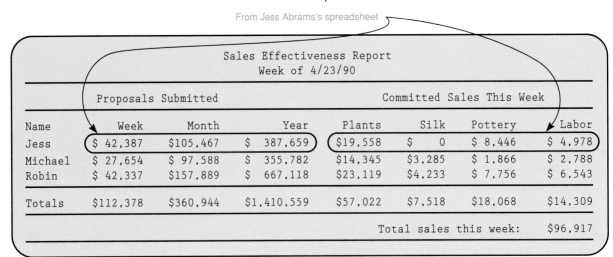

```
                    Proposals Generated by Jess Abrams
                                April 1990

                                                         Year-to-date
      Date      Amount    Weekly Total    Monthly Total       Total

      Week of 4/2/90
      4/2/90    $13,456
      4/5/90    $ 9,232      $22,688         $ 22,688      $304,880

      Week of 4/9/90
      4/9/90    $8,367
      4/11/90   $7,880
      4/12/90   $9,787       $26,034         $ 48,722      $330,914

      Week of 4/16/90
      4/16/90   $5,567
      4/20/90   $8,791       $14,358         $ 63,080      $345,272

      Week of 4/23/90
      4/23/90   $29,792
      4/26/90   $12,595      $42,387         $105,467      $387,659
```

Fed to
summarized
spreadsheet

```
                    Sales Generated by Jess Abrams
                                April 1990

      Date      WO#    Plants    Silk    Pottery    Labor      Total

      4/3/90   1876-41 $ 8,567  $    0  $ 8,876  $ 3,423  $ 20,866
      4/6/90   1876-37 $ 1,787  $  779  $   324  $   198  $  3,088
      4/10/90  1876-40 $12,459  $    0  $ 3,409  $ 8,889  $ 24,757
      4/16/90  1876-47 $11,556  $3,356  $ 1,658  $ 4,433  $ 21,003
      4/23/90  1876-51 $10,058  $    0  $ 4,246  $ 2,200  $ 16,504
      4/25/90  1876-52 $ 9,500  $    0  $ 4,200  $ 2,778  $ 16,478

      Totals           $53,927  $4,135  $22,713  $21,921  $102,696
```

Fed to
summarized
spreadsheet

a. Proposal and sales data for Jess Abrams

From Jess Abrams's spreadsheet

```
                    Sales Effectiveness Report
                          Week of 4/23/90

            Proposals Submitted                Committed Sales This Week

 Name       Week      Month       Year     Plants    Silk    Pottery     Labor
 Jess     $ 42,387  $105,467  $ 387,659   $19,558  $    0  $ 8,446   $ 4,978
 Michael  $ 27,654  $ 97,588  $ 355,782   $14,345  $3,285  $ 1,866   $ 2,788
 Robin    $ 42,337  $157,889  $ 667,118   $23,119  $4,233  $ 7,756   $ 6,543

 Totals   $112,378  $360,944  $1,410,559  $57,022  $7,518  $18,068   $14,309

                                      Total sales this week:   $96,917
```

b. Summarized spreadsheet

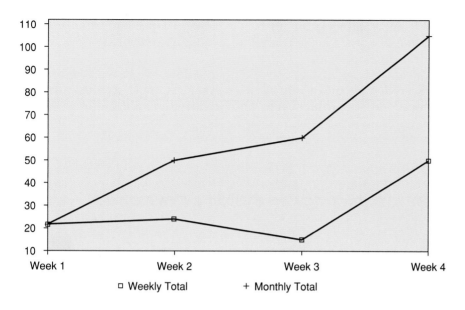

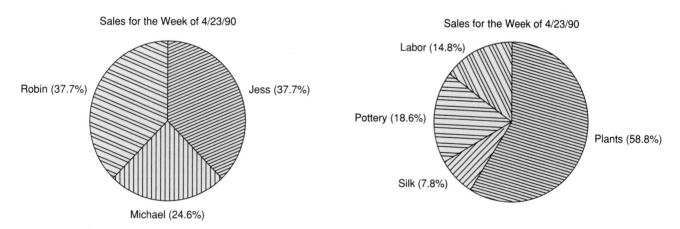

c. Graphs generated by spreadsheet program

both. She would get more information for less of her (or Michelle's) time.

In addition to the savings in Elizabeth's time, there is another way in which an information system can increase productivity. Elizabeth wants the information because she wants to increase the productivity of the sales staff. Before she developed this report, Elizabeth had the sense that the salespeople were unfocused. She believed they sometimes spent their time in activities not directly related to the acquisition of new sales. By producing this report she caused the salespeople to focus on their sales results. As they did this, they began to become more productive.

This second type of productivity increase occurs because information is being created that measures some aspect of the outputs or the inputs of the business. This increase occurs with either the manual or the computer-based system. Often, however, computer-based systems

Questions

1.7 Explain how a spreadsheet program could increase Elizabeth's or Michelle's productivity in developing the sales effectiveness report.

1.8 Define one way to measure productivity.

1.9 What are three ways that productivity can be increased?

1.10   Explain how the information in the sales effectiveness report can be used to increase the productivity of the sales force.

1.11   In general, what are the two ways that information systems can be used to increase productivity?

enable more information to be developed than could otherwise be developed; or they make it feasible to develop information that could not be developed by a manual system.

Thus, when we say that computer-based information systems increase productivity, we mean this in two ways. First, these systems increase the productivity of the people who produce the information. Second, such systems produce information that enables the people, departments, or organizations involved to increase their productivity.

How are Information Systems Developed?

The third major theme of this text concerns the development of information systems. Such systems do not arise spontaneously; they must be created. In some cases, businesspeople can develop their own information systems. In other cases, they hire others to do it, but maintain control over the project. In still other cases, businesspeople are participants in a development activity that is managed by someone else, usually an information systems professional from the company's management information system (MIS) department.

One of the goals of this text is to help you learn how to distinguish between the various situations. When is it appropriate for you to develop your own system, and when should you call in a professional? Another goal is to teach you the roles that you should play and the expectations that you should have. Even when you do not do the work yourself, you should know what kind of work is supposed to be done. You need to be an informed consumer of others' services. Consider another scenario at JKC. This one involves Chip, one of the partners, and Thomas Boston, an accountant at JKC.

The Computerization Project

"Chip, sorry to bother you. I wonder if we could talk for a minute."

"Sure, Thomas. What's up?"

"Well, I've only been here six months, but I've heard you say a couple of times that you have an open-door policy and that if we want to talk with you about something, we should."

"Yeah, both Elizabeth and I feel that way. Tell me what's bothering you."

"It isn't bothering me exactly, and in some ways it's none of my business, but I think we've got the cart before the horse on our computer project for plant maintenance billing."

"Really. Hmmm. It could be. None of us knows much about computers around here. We've got that word processor, but not much else. You know something about computers?"

"A little. I took a course at the university and I worked with them some in my first job."

"What do you mean we have the cart before the horse?"

"In my opinion, we're being driven by a pushy salesperson from the computer dealer. We're about to buy hardware and I'm not certain we know what we want. I'm not even sure we understand the whole problem. And I'm convinced the salesperson doesn't understand our problem. What he understands is selling hardware. And I doubt we've even got the best price on the hardware that we are buying."

"That's interesting. I'm glad you've brought this up. I don't have a lot of time right now and I'd like Elizabeth to hear this. Hmmm. We have our partner's lunch tomorrow. Why don't you come and tell us what you think we should be doing. Could you meet at noon at the City Club?"

"Sure. I'd be happy to."

"OK, see you then. And, Thomas, thanks for stopping by."

Thomas went back to his desk wondering if he hadn't made a mistake. Chip seemed pleased and open to listening, but Thomas was no professional at developing information systems. Still, he seemed to know more than anyone else at Jenson-Kehrwald.

Thomas spent several hours that afternoon thinking about what he would say. He had learned a process for developing information systems in his class, and he recalled the stages in that process. These are shown in Figure 1-6.

As he looked at the stages, he realized what was bothering him. He remembered that buying hardware is supposed to occur in the last stage, implementation. But the people at JKC were about to buy hardware when they were just getting started. They hadn't really thought about what hardware they would need, they hadn't given any attention to programs, and they hadn't looked at alternatives. In fact, they had omitted the first four stages entirely.

That night, at home, Thomas dug out his old course lectures and made notes for the meeting. First, he considered the basic stages of the development process (listed in Figure 1-6), and then he thought about how those tasks would apply to the development of the plant maintenance billing system. Finally, he prepared the recommendations for action shown in Figure 1-7. He decided to go in to work early the next morning and type these notes (as well as others not shown here) into a handout he could give to Chip and Elizabeth for the discussion over lunch.

He planned to describe each stage as follows:

Definition   During the definition stage, the problem to be solved is investigated. This involves a number of tasks (as you will learn in Chap-

---

1. Define the problem

2. Establish specific requirements

3. Evaluate alternatives

4. Design

5. Implement

Figure 1-6

Stages in the systems development process

Figure 1-7
Recommended near-term actions for
development of the maintenance
billing system

1. Stop the purchase of the new equipment

2. Assign the involved employees to a project team

3. Define the problem, including estimates of costs and benefits

4. Meet with the partners to develop the next steps

ter 8), but for the purpose of the luncheon, Thomas decided to focus on just one of them: problem definition. So far, JKC had not really defined the problem.

Requirements   From his course, Thomas knew that the next step should be to establish requirements—what the new system is to do. JKC had done none of this work. It had its existing bills, but beyond that, no one had thought about what the system should do. Thomas thought that JKC should consider questions like: What is the system to produce? What inputs (ingredients) are necessary for the system to produce them? And finally, How big is the system going to be?

Evaluation   The third step is to evaluate alternatives. It bothered Thomas that everyone assumed that a computer system was the answer. But no one had investigated other alternatives. Maybe it would be better just to have the clerk photocopy the bills each month. Maybe there was a company that could provide a billing service far cheaper than JKC could provide its own. Even if a computer system was necessary, no one had thought about how the new system would fit with existing systems. JKC not only does billing for the recurring monthly maintenance, it also does billing for landscape work. Should the two billing problems be addressed together? Maybe customers would object to receiving two separate bills. Again, no one had thought about these things.

Design   If JKC decided that a computer-based system was needed, then Thomas knew that it would need to develop specifications for each of the five components. What hardware? How much capacity should it have? What types of programs? What program products? What data will they need to store? In what format? What will be the procedures and which personnel will be needed? What training should those people have?

Implementation   Finally, after all of this other work had been done, Thomas thought JKC would be in a position to implement. Implementation involves purchasing hardware and programs, obtaining the data, documenting procedures, and training personnel. JKC could then test the system, and install it for operational use. Thomas thought that if the company followed this course of action, it would be far more likely to obtain a system that would meet its needs, and at a fair price.

Plan of Action

Thomas didn't want to leave the luncheon on a negative note, so he developed the plan of action shown in Figure 1-7. As you can see, he recommended that JKC stop the hardware purchase, form a team, and define the problem. He then suggested that the team meet with the partners to determine the next steps to take. It was impossible to know what those steps should be until the problem had been defined.

The Luncheon

Thomas went to work early the next morning and typed out discussion notes to take to the luncheon.

After the social amenities were over, Thomas began by saying that he made no claim to be a systems developer. He had no experience in developing systems himself and he did not want to leave the impression that he did. What he did have, he said, was a notion of what should be done. He knew, he said, how to be a consumer of other people's systems development expertise.

He then discussed his ideas and concerns with Elizabeth and Chip. They were open to his comments and seemed more than willing to consider his thoughts. (In fact, although he didn't know it, they were exceedingly impressed with his thinking, initiative, and organization. They also were very glad that they had hired him.)

At the end of the luncheon, Chip said, "Thomas, this is excellent. Why don't you to head up this project? What do you think, Elizabeth?"

"Makes sense to me. I understand, Thomas, that you don't feel qualified to do the development work yourself. But you know more than anyone else in our company. I say, go ahead and take the actions you recommend, and if we decide to proceed with the project, we'll see about hiring a consultant or someone to help us build a system."

This scenario illustrates one way in which you might be involved in the development of an information system. Like Thomas, you may not know how to accomplish the development tasks; but when you've finished this text, you should know what fundamental tasks need to be done. With this knowledge, you will be better able to participate in and possibly oversee development projects.

Questions

1.12 List three ways in which users can be involved in the development of information systems.

1.13 Explain the statement, in the third vignette, that Thomas did not know how to perform the systems development but did know what tasks should be performed.

1.14 List the five stages of the development process that Thomas presented to the partners at JKC.

1.15 Describe briefly the nature of each of the stages in your answer to question 1.14.

1.16 In the third vignette, why did Thomas think it was inappropriate for JKC to be purchasing computer hardware?

Multiuser Systems

"Our inventory system was working just fine as long as we had only one computer. But as our business grew, we just couldn't get all of the work done on one machine. The designers weren't willing to wait for one another. At the same time, we needed to input data about purchases and plant arrivals, and to generate bills for the inventory stock we had sold. So we bought a system that had four microcomputers tied together in something called a *local area network*. The microcomputers all shared a common pool of data that was processed by a fifth microcomputer called the *file server*.

1.1   INCREASING YOUR PERSONAL PRODUCTIVITY

Who Are the Power Users?

Power users. You'll find them in every organization, easily recognizable by having the latest and greatest technology on their desks. Often such people have developed a reputation for possessing a level of technical expertise that surpasses even the professional support staff—and as a result they can wield an inordinate amount of power and resources within the end-user community.

Power users are often a godsend—providing help, suggestions, support, and testing at a level of sophistication difficult to find outside of hiring high-priced independent consultants. But they can also be a source of tension and discord: demanding too much, contributing too little, and even tempting other users to stray down technical paths in the opposite direction from the corporate computing strategy.

For these and other reasons, the ways in which a PC professional defines and deals with power users is critical to a successful systems strategy. More specifically, PC managers need to be aware that power users often serve as role models for others within an organization. Rewarding or encouraging a power user to develop technically in an inappropriate manner, therefore, can lead to problems with and misuse of technology that extends far beyond that one individual.

Perhaps because of their growing influence, power users can also be a source of headaches for PC managers, who are quick to run down a list of "pitfalls." First, these employees can lead fellow PC users astray by purchasing, installing, and then training them to use products not supported by the corporate systems division. The other pitfall is that some power users get too intensely involved in the technical issues—neglecting their "real" jobs.

Another problem that can arise from depending informally on a power user to support his or her colleagues—without it being in the power user's job description or included in the salary—is that so-called power users can get demanding, requesting unreasonable technology in return for their rendered expertise and services.

Balancing the assistance power users can provide with the potential problems they may cause is only going to get more difficult. As symbiotic as the relationship between PC managers and power users is now, it is likely to become more so in the 1990s.

No longer can a PC manager alone develop an innovative systems strategy that benefits the business needs of the corporation. Because of this, they're increasingly relying on steering committees and management teams—containing both systems professionals *and* end-users—to decide such issues.

While this approach will inevitably result in better decisions regarding the acquisition and use of computers, it also shifts the balance of power between PC managers and their hard-core users. And although PC managers recognize the value of leveraging the knowledge of power users, they still find themselves grappling with the ramifications of relying on the very users they're paid to support.

"We had some real growing pains. It turns out it's quite a bit harder than you would expect to have several computers sharing the same data. We were really surprised, first by how much more difficult (and expensive) it was to get the system up and running, and then by the kinds of procedures we needed to develop for ourselves."

This statement was made by Thomas Boston at JKC about a year after he had the luncheon with Elizabeth and Chip. During the intervening period, Thomas had become the resident information systems specialist. He had been instrumental in developing the maintenance billing system discussed at the luncheon, and then he had led the development of a new inventory system. As Thomas stated, at first the system was processed by one computer; but over time, the company needed more keyboard space and it developed a multiuser system.

Thomas's statement about the difficulty in going from a single-user to a multiuser system would be echoed by hundreds of businesspeople today. There are a number of challenges in multiuser processing that do not exist in single-user processing.

For one, multiuser systems are more complicated. They involve more hardware and the programs that process the hardware must be more sophisticated. Figure 1-8 shows the general structure of the inventory system at JKC. Each of the microcomputers must be connected to a communications line. This requires considerable amounts of special-purpose hardware. Also, the messages that pass among the computers must be carefully managed; otherwise messages will collide and interfere with one another.

Still another complication arises because different users may attempt to process the same data at the same time. Two designers may decide to access the inventory data for *Chamaedorea falcifera* palms at the same time. Suppose there is only one palm left. Without controls, each designer might think that he or she got the last palm from inventory. No one will know that this has happened until the production department tries to obtain materials for the two jobs. Then there will be considerable confusion. No matter what the inventory system said, there is only one palm. Problems like this can be solved, but the solution takes time and is complicated.

Other problems concern the use of the data. Consider the following conversation between Thomas and April, one of the designers.

"Thomas, something's wrong. I access the inventory data, trying to find out the number of *Arenga pinnata* palms in inventory. The system says it can't find any, but I know they're there. I saw three sitting in the showroom this morning."

"Hmmm." (Thomas sits down at April's computer and tries for himself.) "Sure enough, they're not there. There's not even a record of them. I wonder what's happened? I'll look into it."

Late that afternoon, Thomas investigated the problem. He determined that the data for Arenga palms was deleted, and that there was

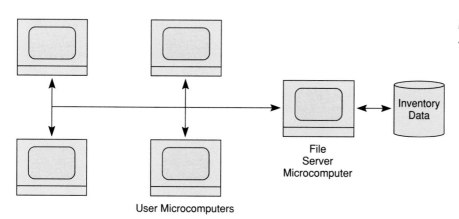

Figure 1-8
JKC's multiuser system architecture

User Microcomputers

File
Server
Microcomputer

Inventory
Data

1.2   INCREASING YOUR PERSONAL PRODUCTIVITY

Ten Ways to Get Ahead Using Information Technology

Telemarketing Testing cold leads by telephone first—using computer runs to ferret out the best prospects—helps slash sales-force expenses and boost productivity.

Customer Service By letting customers tap into your data base to track their orders and shipments, you build loyalty and smooth relations.

Training Training or retraining workers lets them learn at their own speed—and lets you cut training costs.

Sales Giving salespeople portable computers so they can get messages faster and enter orders directly adds up to quicker deliveries, better cash flow, and less paperwork.

Better Financial Management By setting up computer links between the treasurer's office and your banks, you can obtain financial information faster.

Product Development By providing a toll-free number for consumer questions and complaints, you get ideas for product improvements and new products. In-house electronic publishing can help turn out product manuals faster.

Market Intelligence By assembling and manipulating data on demographics and competitors, you can spot untapped niches, develop new products, and avoid inventory crunches.

New Businesses Information technologies make whole new operations possible. Federal Express, for one, could not work without computer-equipped trucks and facilities.

Locking In Customers By creating exclusive computer communications with customers for order entry and exchange of product and service data, you can help thwart competitors.

Selling Extra Processing Power You can use off-peak processing power to develop completely new services for outsiders. That way, you can transfer some of the high costs of building your information network.

no apparent disruption in service or other problem that might have caused the loss of data. Using a backup copy of the data, he restored the Arenga palm record and informed April. She finished her work.

The next week, the same thing happened. Again, one of the designers was trying to access the Arenga palm record and it had disappeared! Thomas became concerned and he called the vendor that supports JKC's system. Later that day, one of the vendor's support personnel looked into the problem and determined that the data was deleted by someone on another microcomputer. The support person told Thomas which computer did the deletion and when.

With that knowledge, Thomas worked backward to determine who was using the computer at that time. It turned out to be Elizabeth!

Thomas walked over to Elizabeth's office and knocked on her door.

"Elizabeth," said Thomas cautiously, "did you delete the Arenga palm data?"

"What? Oh, hi, Thomas. What did you say?"

"Did you by chance delete the Arenga palm data from our inventory?"

"Yeah, I did. The price of those things has gone wild. I'm not buying any more of them. I took them out of the inventory so they wouldn't show up on the purchase sheets for Cheryl or me to worry about. Funny, though—I had to do it twice. I took them out last week, but somehow they got back in."

This scenario points out the need for coordination and control of shared databases. No matter how sophisticated the hardware or how capable the programs, they cannot keep users from performing valid operations that interfere with one another. Elizabeth, viewing the data from the purchasing perspective, does not want the data in inventory any longer. She deletes the data, not thinking about the problems this will cause both for the design department and for billing.

This is just one example of the kinds of coordination procedures needed for multiuser systems. There are many more, as you will learn in Part Three of this text.

Overview of the Text

This chapter has presented an overview of the four major themes of this text. In the next chapter, we will address the first theme presented in this chapter, the WHAT theme. We will describe each of the five components of a business computer system. In Chapter 3 we will describe, in a broad overview, the roles and functions played by information systems in business. Then, in Part Two, we will address single-user information systems. We will consider the WHY and the WHAT of different types of personal information systems in Chapters 4–7, and HOW to develop such systems in Chapter 8. In Part Three we will address multiuser systems. We will consider the WHY and the WHAT of such systems in Chapters 9–11. We will address your role in the development of multiuser systems in Chapter 12. Finally, we will present several specialized topics in Part Four.

Summary

This text deals with the use of computer technology to increase personal and organizational productivity. This involves the application of information systems to business activities.

This chapter introduced the major themes of this text. It described three dimensions of information systems: what, why, and how. It also illustrated several of the important differences between single-user and multiuser systems.

Often we will use business cases or vignettes to show the relevance and application of concepts and technology to business situations. These vignettes are important for learning how to apply technology in a pragmatic and practical way in your career.

The first vignette addressed the WHAT dimension by illustrating the need for all five components of an information system. In the situation described, considerable effort was required to recover from a problem that occurred because insufficient attention had been paid to the data,

Questions

1.17 According to Thomas's statement, what reasons caused JKC to build a multiuser system?

1.18 What growing pains did Thomas describe in the transition from a single-user to a multiuser system?

1.19 Why are multiuser systems more complicated than single-user systems?

1.20 Explain the reason for the loss of the Arenga palm data in the fourth vignette.

1.21 Refer to question 1.20. How could the problem have been prevented?

procedure, and personnel components. The point was to show, in part, why information systems are more than just computers and programs.

The next vignette addressed the WHY dimension. It showed how one type of information system, called an electronic spreadsheet, can be used to increase productivity in two ways. First, the spreadsheet allowed information to be produced more quickly with less effort than was required to produce the information manually. Second, the information itself was then used to allow management to increase the productivity of the sales staff.

We then considered the HOW dimension. In some cases, users can serve as their own developers; in others, like the situation described in the third vignette, users manage and direct the activities of professional developers. It is important for you to learn how to distinguish one situation from the other, and to know how to proceed in either case.

The last section discussed some of the ways that multiuser systems differ from single-user systems. The fourth vignette illustrated one type of problem that can arise with a multiuser system. In crossing the boundary from a single-user to a multiuser system, a number of significant challenges will arise; you will learn about those challenges and the users' responsibility with regard to them in Part Three of this text.

Word List

electronic spreadsheet application

local area network

file server

Discussion Questions and Exercises

A. Do you agree that a knowledge of computers and programs is insufficient for you to take advantage of computer technology in your business career? If not, why not? If so, what other knowledge do you think you will need?

B. The text mentions three roles for users in developing systems: Users can develop systems themselves, they can manage the work of others, or they can participate as team members in projects managed by others. Under what conditions do you think each of these roles is appropriate? How would you decide which role to take on a particular project?

The Components of a Business Computer System

Throughout this course you will learn how business computer systems can help you be more productive. Business computer systems vary in size, features, capabilities, and price. They can be used by individuals and by groups of people. They are used in thousands of applications. And it is difficult to imagine anyone—like you—beginning a career at the threshold of the 21st century without seeing that person as a computer user. So what do you—a future user—need to know about business computer systems? You need to know what a business computer system is, what your role as a user will be in developing one, and how you can use computer technology to help solve business problems.

By the end of this chapter you will have a framework you can use to examine any business computer system, no matter how big or small, simple or complex. This framework is called the *five-component model*.

The Five-Component Model

A system is a collection of components that interact to achieve some goal. A *computer system* is a collection of components, including a computer, that interact to achieve some goal. Note that a computer system is not merely a computer. Rather, a computer is one part of the computer system. A **business computer system** is a collection of components, including a computer, that interact to satisfy some business need. For example, some business computer systems manage inventory, some issue invoices, some compute taxes, and so forth.

Many businesspeople incorrectly believe that a business computer system is merely a computer, and that if they simply buy a computer all their business problems will be solved. Actually, the computer is only one of five components of a business computer system. The other four components are important and often expensive, and integrating all five components into a working system can be a challenging task.

The five components of a business computer system are *hardware, programs, data, procedures,* and *trained personnel*. All five are required for an effective business computer system; take away any component and the business needs which the system was supposed to satisfy cannot be met. Let's consider each of the five components in turn.

Hardware

The first and most obvious component of a business computer system is computer equipment, or **hardware**. Figure 2-1 shows examples of computer equipment. As you can see in the figure, the equipment used in an insurance company is very large (and expensive). The computer equipment used by a real estate agent is considerably smaller, less powerful, and less expensive than that of the insurance company. But it serves the business needs of only a few people, and does that very well.

Figure 2-1
Examples of computer equipment

a. Equipment used in a large insurance company

b. Equipment used in a real estate agent's office

Programs

The second component of a business computer system is **programs**. Most computers are general-purpose machines, which means that they can perform fundamental operations like adding, subtracting, and

Figure 2-2

Parts of sample programs

```
1000 REM PROGRAM TO CONVERT MILES TO KILOMETERS
1010 '
1020 '          PROGRAM VARIABLES
1030 '          MILES           DISTANCE IN MILES
1040 '          KM              DISTANCE IN KILOMETERS
1060 '
2000 '*************** PROGRAM MAINLINE ********************
2010 CLS
2020 GOSUB 3000                    'INPUT MILES
2030 WHILE MILES >= 0
2050     GOSUB 4000                'CONVERT
2060     GOSUB 5000                'PRINT RESULTS
2070     GOSUB 3000                'INPUT MILES
2080 WEND
2090 END
```

a. Sample BASIC program

```
43    PROCEDURE DIVISION.
44    MAIN-ROUTINE.
45        PERFORM INITIALIZE-ROUTINE
46        PERFORM PROCESS-ROUTINE UNTIL END-OF-FILE = "YES"
47        PERFORM TERMINATION-ROUTINE
48        STOP RUN.
49
50    INITIALIZE-ROUTINE.
51        OPEN INPUT INVEN-FILE
52        OPEN OUTPUT REPORT-FILE
53        READ INVEN-FILE,
54          AT END
55            MOVE "YES" TO END-OF-FILE
56        END-READ.
```

b. Sample COBOL program

comparing, but they are not designed to suit any specific needs. In order to perform a particular task a computer must follow a sequence of instructions—a program. Depending on the instructions, one program might control access to a centralized database, while other programs produced payroll, processed insurance claims, and designed airplane engines. The same computer could be used to run all four programs. Figure 2-2 shows parts of two different programs.

Data

The third component of a business computer system is **data**. Data means simply the facts that go into a computer to be processed or stored for later retrieval. Hardware, programs, and data all work together to produce *information*, or knowledge derived from facts.

Complete and correct data is essential for the successful operation of a business computer system. Computers are fast, but they have no intuition or judgment. With gibberish for input, they will work diligently and produce output of the same kind. "Garbage in, garbage out" is an old but appropriate saying in the computer business.

Procedures

The last two components of a business computer system, procedures and trained personnel, go hand in hand. **Procedures** are instructions for people on the use and operation of a system. Procedures describe how to prepare input data and how to use the results. Procedures also explain what to do when errors occur and need to be corrected. Further, procedures explain to people how to operate the computer hardware. They describe what programs to run, what data to use, and what to do with the results. Procedures also describe what to do when the system fails, or **crashes**.

Trained Personnel

Trained personnel is the final component of a business computer system. People bring together the other four components and integrate the computer system into the business environment. People are needed to develop business computer systems, to operate them, to enter data, and to use the results.

Figure 2-3 summarizes the five components, which we will now examine in more detail.

- Hardware
- Programs
- Data
- Procedures
- Trained personnel

Figure 2-3
The five-component model of a business computer system

Questions

2.1 Which of the five components of a business computer system is optional?

2.2 Briefly describe the purpose of each of the five components.

Hardware

A computer is a configuration of four types of devices, connected by cables. The heart of the configuration is the *central processing unit.* Attached to it are *input devices, output devices,* and *storage devices.* (See Figure 2-4.)

The Central Processing Unit

The **central processing unit** (also known as the **CPU**, or simply the *processor*) holds programs and data awaiting processing, interprets and carries out program instructions, and communicates with the other devices.

The CPU comprises three distinct devices, all packaged in the same box: the control unit, the arithmetic/logic unit, and main memory (see Figure 2-5).

The **control unit** interprets program instructions and communicates with the input, output, and storage devices attached to the CPU. The **arithmetic/logic unit** performs arithmetic and logic operations when the control unit tells it to do so. **Main memory** holds data to be processed, programs to be executed, and program results waiting to be issued. Main memory is also called *temporary storage*, because whatever is

Figure 2-4
Generic computer configuration

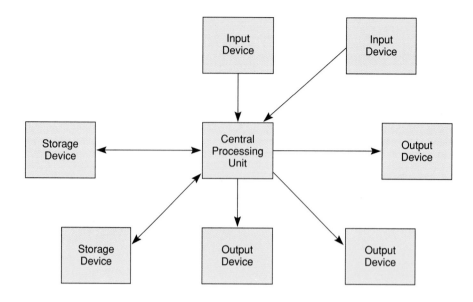

there is lost when the power is turned off (unlike magnetic tape and magnetic disk; we'll talk about them later). A computer's size is stated in terms of the amount of main memory it has, measured in **bytes**. In the simplest terms, a byte can hold one letter or one digit. Personal computers (also called microcomputers) usually have between 64,000 bytes (64K) and 16 million bytes (16 megabytes or 16 MB) of memory. Mainframe computers contain between 4MB and 1024MB of memory.

Input Devices

Input devices are used to enter program instructions and data into the computer's main memory for processing. Instructions not in the computer's memory (for example, programs written on paper) cannot be executed until they are **loaded**, or entered into main memory. Data not in the computer's memory (for example, data written on insurance forms) cannot be processed. Examples of input devices are terminals, scanning devices, and voice recognition devices.

Terminals   The primary input device for a computer is the **terminal** (see Figure 2-6). A terminal really is two devices in one: a keyboard for input and a video display (or monitor) for output. Here we will look at keyboards. We will examine monitors later, when we discuss output devices.

Computer *keyboards* contain alphanumeric keys, function keys, and a numeric keypad (see Figure 2-7). A terminal operator enters data by typing it on the keyboard. This is a widely used but relatively slow and error-prone technique for data entry.

In addition to the full-keyboard terminal, other specialized terminals can be used as input devices. For example, *point-of-sale (POS) ter-*

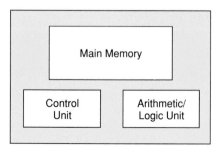

Figure 2-5
The central processing unit

Figure 2-6
Terminals

minals have replaced cash registers in many stores. Information keyed on the terminal is transmitted to a mainframe computer for storage or processing. These are called point-of-sale terminals because transaction data is entered at the point the sale is made to a customer. This approach enables companies to keep their records current.

Another specialized terminal is the *automated teller machine*, or *ATM*. An ATM screen is usually very small: just large enough to display instructions or answers to the customer. The keyboard also is limited: it contains a small number of function keys (labeled, for example, "Withdraw," "Deposit," or "Transfer") and a numeric keypad for entering a transaction amount. Data entered through an ATM is captured and transmitted to the bank's mainframe computer where it is used to update account balances.

Figure 2-7
Computer keyboard

Scanning Devices   **Scanning devices**, or **scanners**, are cameras that read a printed document and transform the reflected light into digital codes, then transmit the codes to the computer for displaying, storage, or further processing. Scanners can input text typed on a page, photographs, and line drawings. The advantage of using a scanner to input data is that it is faster and usually more error-free than traditional keyed data entry. Scanning devices eliminate the manual conversion of source data into digital format.

Various scanners are used for different types of source documents. The *mark-sense reader* scans a page like the one in Figure 2-8 and detects and interprets the existence of marks, made usually with a number two pencil. You probably have used such forms when taking standardized tests, or when registering for courses.

An *optical character reader (OCR)* is an input device that scans a document and interprets symbols as numbers or letters of the alphabet. Optical character readers are used in many applications; for example, in some department stores the clerk passes a pistol-shaped scanner over the price tag, and the OCR interprets the letters and numbers on the tag. To eliminate ambiguity between similar characters, a special type font is used.

The *laser bar-code scanner* is familiar to almost anyone who shops in a major grocery store chain. The clerk passes an item over a laser scanner which reads and interprets the bar code printed on the item package. The ubiquitous bar code, called the *Universal Product Code (UPC)* is printed on everything from soup to nuts, from clothing to record albums. Deli and bakery departments have scales that print price tags in the form of bar codes to be read by the scanner at the checkout.

A *digital scanner* scans a page and copies the image into the computer as a single entity. The page might contain printed text, photographic images, line drawings, or combinations. Digital scanners frequently are used in desktop publishing applications (see Chapter 7).

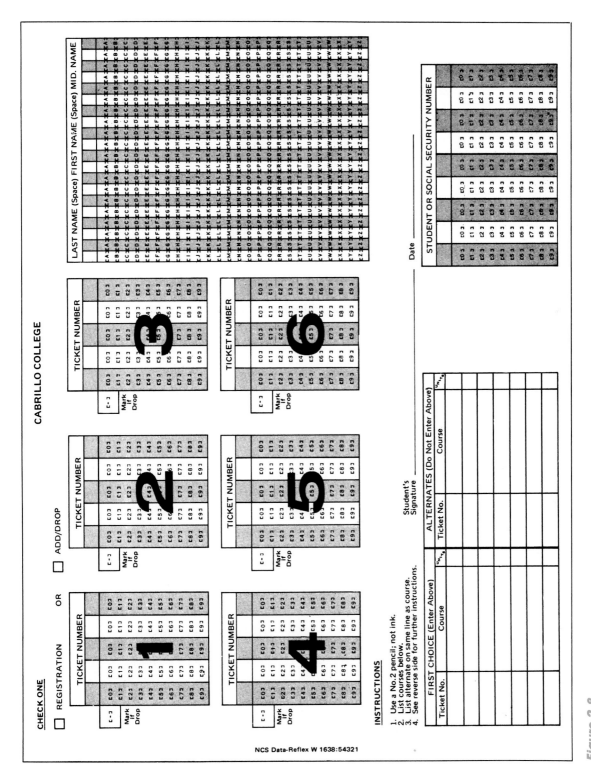

Figure 2-8
Mark-sense form

Voice Recognition Devices   Voice recognition devices are not widely used, but they hold the promise of even easier computer input. With a voice recognition device, you can speak commands into a computer microphone. The sound is digitized and input to the processor. There, a program compares the digital pattern of your command and a file of commands you already "taught" it, that is, commands you already spoke into the microphone for storage. When the system finds a match, it performs the appropriate programmed function. Voice recognition technology is still in the development stages.

Output Devices

The results of computer processing are developed in the CPU. To be useful to people, they must be presented in a human-readable format, for example, printed on paper or displayed on a computer monitor. A variety of computer **output devices** exist. One of the most widely used is the display screen, or monitor. Another type of output device produces **hard copy,** or printed output. The third type of output device that we will examine here is the speech synthesizer. Other examples of computer output equipment can be found in the Hardware photo essay.

Computer Monitors   **Computer monitors** are known by many other names, including *screens* and **video display terminals (VDTs).** A typical computer monitor displays 80 characters across the screen and 24 lines down the screen. See Figure 2-9. Various video technologies are employed in computer monitors, but they all accomplish essentially the same thing: they display output (numbers, text, graphs, pictures) to the user.

Figure 2-9
Computer monitor

Figure 2-10
Dot-matrix printer

One family of computer monitors uses technology similar to that used in television screens, called the *cathode-ray tube,* or *CRT.* A CRT employs an electronic gun to shoot beams at the back of the screen, creating tiny points of light. Each point is called a picture element, or **pixel**. Patterns of light and dark pixels create a visible image.

Resolution refers to the sharpness of the screen display. This is determined by the density of pixels used in the display technology. The higher the number of pixels, the sharper the image.

CRT monitors can be monochrome or color monitors. Monochrome monitors display one color against a contrasting background, for example, green on black or amber on black. Color monitors are not so limited; depending on the sophistication of the equipment, a color monitor can display hundreds of shades of color.

Monitors that use CRT technology are relatively bulky, thus not very useful for portable computers. Consequently, other display technologies are used in the flat monitors of laptop computers, for example, *liquid crystal display (LCD),* and *plasma.* LCDs are widely used—in calculators, watches, and microwave ovens, as well as in laptop computer monitors. They do not produce as high resolution as CRTs, though. Plasma screens sandwich between two sheets of glass a gas that turns amber colored when energized. Plasma screens produce excellent resolution, but are relatively expensive.

Hard-Copy Output Devices   Computer devices that produce paper output include printers, plotters, and typesetters.

Printers   Three popular types of computer printer are the dot-matrix printer, the line printer, and the laser printer. A **dot-matrix printer** (see Figure 2-10) is an impact printer. This means that a device bearing a character image strikes a ribbon against the paper, leaving the ink-impression of the symbol on the page. Dot-matrix printers have a print head containing a cluster of pins. Each pin produces a tiny dot; each character has a specific configuration of dots that make up its shape. To print a page of text, the printer produces one character at a time, changing the pin configuration for every symbol. Dot-matrix printers

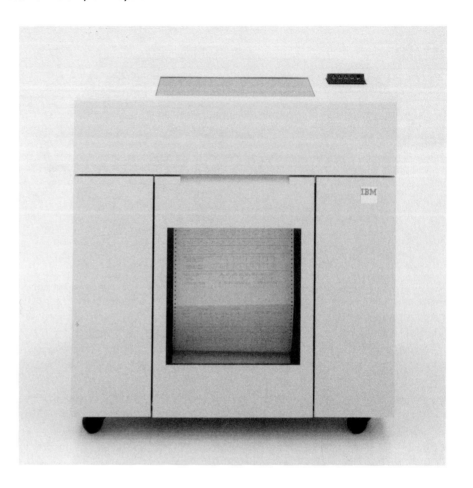

vary in the number of pins that make up the matrix. The more pins, the higher the quality of the resulting printed output. Dot-matrix printers are used in microcomputer-based systems.

A **line printer** (see Figure 2-11) is an impact printer that produces an entire line of text at once. Line printers are used primarily in mainframe computer systems. Some can print as many as 3,000 lines per minute. However, line printers are not capable of printing graphics.

A **laser printer** is a nonimpact printer (see Figure 2-12). Consequently, it is almost silent. Also, a laser printer produces an entire page at a time. It uses a laser beam to form the image to be printed onto a print drum, which attracts toner (like that used in photocopying machines). A sheet of paper rolls around the drum, and the toner image is transferred to the paper. Laser printers produce high-quality output, and are widely used in text processing applications (see Chapter 7), both on microcomputers and mainframes. Laser printers can print graphics; and they are very fast, some producing 100 pages per minute.

Plotters   *Plotters* also are output devices that produce hard copy output (see Figure 2-13). Plotters employ pens that actually draw lines on the paper to form letters, numbers, and other symbols, as well as graphical

Figure 2-12
Laser printer

Figure 2-13
Plotters

output such as diagrams, charts, and maps. They are used especially for graphical output. Some plotters use multicolored pens to produce color graphics.

Typesetters   Some applications require high-quality, volume printing. Examples include newspaper and magazine publishing, textbook publishing, advertising brochures, and corporate publications such as annual reports. In these cases, ordinary printers cannot produce the volume of documents needed. In fact, they cannot produce a high enough qual-

Figure 2-14
Linotype typesetter

ity output even for photocopying or offset printing. The only satisfactory output is that produced by a typesetting machine. Before typesetters became available as output devices, material to be typeset needed to be rekeyed into the typesetter. This manual process was slow, costly, and redundant, and was a source of typographical errors. With typesetters that can accept computer output directly (see Figure 2-14), the typesetting process is much faster and much more error-free.

Speech Synthesizers   *Speech synthesizers* produce audible computer output by speaking words and numbers to the user. Speech synthesis is used in various applications, such as electronic message centers, telephone sales, elevator announcements, and computers for the blind and visually impaired. The technology has improved over the years, so computer voices no longer need to be flat and mechanical. They can sound like men, women, or children, and the rate at which they speak can be slowed or speeded up without the "chipmunk" distortion that once occurred.

Storage Devices

Storage devices exist to save programs and data for future processing. As we noted earlier, only program instructions in the CPU's memory can be executed; when the computer is turned off, all programs and data in the CPU are lost. So if you want to use a program or data again, you must store them before turning the computer off.

Storage devices record data and programs on various media. Most storage media can be reused. That is, when stored data or programs become obsolete, other data or programs can be recorded over them. The data or programs remain until they are erased or until something else overwrites them. We will discuss three computer storage media: magnetic disk, magnetic tape, and optical disk (or CD-ROM).

Magnetic Disk   **Magnetic disks** are circular platters coated with a substance that can be magnetized. One or several platters attached to a central hub are placed in a disk drive. The drive rotates the stack of platters, called a *volume*, at very high speed—up to about 3600 revolutions per minute—and read/write heads attached to access arms read or record information on the disk surfaces. See Figure 2-15. Information is recorded as a series of magnetic spots—bits—in concentric tracks (see Figure 2-16). Mainframe computers use only hard disk, while microcomputers use both hard disk and diskette (see Chapter 4 for a discussion of disk storage for microcomputers).

Disk storage capacity depends on the number of platters, the diameter of the platters, and the density of bits, that is, how close the magnetic spots are to each other. Some mainframe disks can hold several

Figure 2-15
Hard disk

Figure 2-16
Recording data on disk

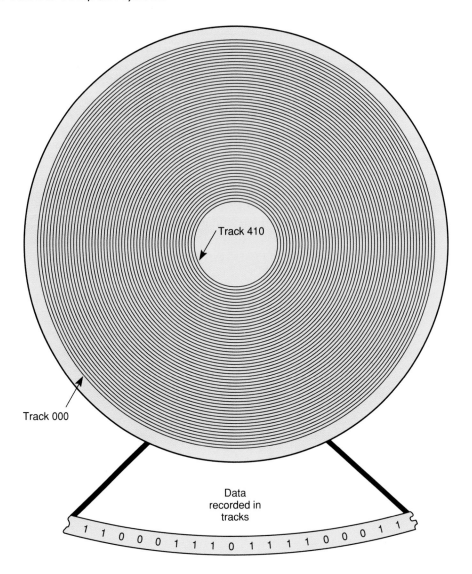

Track 410

Track 000

Data
recorded in
tracks

1 1 0 0 0 1 1 1 0 1 1 1 1 0 0 0 1 1

billion bytes of data. Mainframe computer disks like the ones in Figure 2-15 are the precursors of the scaled-down versions used in microcomputer systems. While most microcomputers have one hard disk permanently installed, most mainframe computers have dozens (even hundreds) of disk drives on-line at once, giving the mainframe computer ready access to an enormous amount of data.

The most common storage medium used with personal computers is **diskette,** also known as *floppy disk.* A diskette is a flexible plastic disk coated with a substance that can be magnetized. Each diskette holds a fixed number of tracks, and every track has the capacity to record a specific number of characters. For example, a dual-sided, double-density 5¼-inch diskette (still the most popular) holds exactly 362,496 bytes of data. Diskettes come in two sizes: 3½ inch and 5¼ inch. See Figure 2-17.

Figure 2-17
Diskettes

Magnetic Tape   Once used as a primary storage medium, magnetic tape now is used mainly for permanently storing records, called archives, and for making **backups**—copies of data and programs stored on hard disk. See Figure 2-18. Backups are made periodically in anticipation of accidental data loss. For example, if one of the read/write heads in your disk drive malfunctioned (called a *head crash*—fortunately a fairly unusual occurrence) some or all of the data on the disk in that drive could be destroyed. However, you could recover from this potential disaster by repairing the drive, then restoring the lost data to a new disk from backup copies.

Backups in personal computer systems can be made on diskette or cassette tape. The advantage of tape is that data can be recorded at very high speed, and the tape itself can hold more information than a diskette. Consequently, it is possible to insert a single tape and backup an entire database stored on hard disk very quickly, say a few minutes. Accomplishing the same thing with diskette might require inserting, removing, and labeling several diskettes, a slow and tedious process. For example, approximately 56 3½-inch, 720K diskettes are required to backup one 40MB hard disk.

Magnetic tape is relatively cheap as well as easily transportable (neither of these characteristics is true of hard disk). Accessing data on magnetic tape, however, is much slower than disk access. Consequently, magnetic tape is better suited for archival use and for file backup than it is for daily data processing.

Optical Disk   Optical disk technology for computer data storage is the same technology used in audio compact disks (CDs); that is, data is recorded and read with light energy (a laser beam) rather than with electrical and magnetic energy. The acronym **CD-ROM** stands for *compact disk read-only memory*. Data on optical disks is written permanently (unlike that on magnetic tape and disk, which are reusable); once recorded, it can only be read—whence the descriptor *read-only*.

Figure 2-18
Magnetic tape

CD-ROMs have very high storage capacity, measured in *gigabytes*—one billion bytes, or a thousand megabytes. CD-ROMs can be used for storing reference works (encyclopedias, for example) and for archiving documents, among other things. CD-ROMs are sometimes called *WORM* devices, an acronym that stands for *write once, read many times*. The NeXT personal computer is based on CD-ROM technology, while most other personal computers are magnetic-disk-based.

Communications Devices

Communications devices enable two or more computers to communicate with each other. With communications equipment, computers can share programs and data. Some configurations involve as few as two computers, but other complex networks—such as airline reservations systems—involve thousands of computers.

Two computers that need to communicate with each other—say for the purpose of sharing stored data—require special communications equipment. For example, a microcomputer user who uses an information utility on a mainframe computer (such as Prodigy, The Source, or the Dow Jones News/Retrieval Service) requires a special piece of equipment. The device that allows such computer-to-computer dialogue is called a **modem.** *Modem* stands for *modulator-demodulator;* this

Hardware: More and More for Less and Less

1   The keyboard is the most common data entry device.

The processing of data involves four fundamental functions: data is input to the computer, it is processed, results are output, and data is stored in machine-readable form. Computer equipment can be classified according to these four primary functions.

Input equipment is used to transform data from a physical format (often human readable) into a machine-readable format. *Processing equipment* manipulates the data to produce the desired results. *Output equipment* transforms results from machine-readable format into a human-readable format. Finally, *storage equipment* saves data, in some machine-readable format, for subsequent processing.

Keyboard Input (photos 1–5)
Keyboard input hardware requires that a person key data using a keyboard or some other key device. The keying of data may be done by a user of a personal computer, as part of a job task,

such as by a bank teller, or as a full-time job by production data entry personnel, such as an order-entry or airline reservation clerk.

Nonkey Input (photos 6–15)
The keying of data is time consuming and prone to errors. Further, not everyone can or is willing to key data. Consequently, a number of alternative means have been developed to enter data. Cards with magnetic stripes, bar code scanners, image scanners, digitizers, and even the human voice are alternatives that are used in business today. The most common alternative to the keyboard, however, is the mouse.

Processing Hardware (photos 16–31)
In this text, we consider two categories of processing hardware: single-user and multiuser systems. A single-user system is employed by an individual to perform his or her job. Personal micro-

computers and microcomputer workstations are used for such applications. Two personal computer types have become standard: The IBM and IBM-compatible computer family and the Apple Macintosh computer family. Microcomputers are portable—especially laptop micros. Engineering workstations can also be stand-alone systems; they provide sophisticated graphics and extended math processing capabilities.

As discussed in Chapter 9, two types of multiuser processing hardware are common. Multiple computers (normally microcomputers) can be connected via local area networks. Alternatively, a large and powerful centralized computer can support multiple "dumb" terminals in a teleprocessing system.

Local area networks are flexible and can be used in many different environments; possibilities are offices, retail stores, and manufacturing plants. Teleprocessing systems vary substantially in size. On one end of the spectrum, a teleprocessing system could support a few terminals in a departmental setting. On the other end of this spectrum, a centralized computer could support thousands of terminals all over the world. Supercomputers are very fast (and expensive) computers used for specialized processing such as weather prediction.

Output Hardware (photos 32–39)
The computer display screen is the most common output device. Not all screens are equal. Some are two color with low resolution; others have hundreds of colors with exceedingly high resolution and clarity. The latter are often used for engineering and publishing applications. A variety of specialized technologies are used to provide high-quality output in small computers such as laptops.

Laser-based page printers provide high-quality text and graphical output in a single color. Dot matrix printers form characters by an arrangement of dots produced by pins that strike a computer ribbon. Line printers have been used for many years to produce high-volume output; they print a line at a time. They are gradually being replaced by laser printers. Color printers produce both text and graphics in color, while color plotters can produce very high quality, sophisticated graphics.

Storage Hardware (photos 40–44)
Disks and tape are the most common storage media. Disks vary from the lower-capacity $5\frac{1}{4}$-inch floppies to very large capacity fixed disks used in mainframe applications. Magnetic tape requires sequential data access and is gradually being displaced by disk storage for most applications. Optical disk provides very high capacity storage, but most such devices allow only reading. Such optical disks are written at the factory, and no data can be added or changed.

2   End users use a keyboard for data input.

3   Keyboard data is input by bank tellers.

5 Production data is input for airline reservations.

4 An order-entry clerk keys order data.

6 Data is input via a magnetic stripe on a retail card.

7 Using a banking card with a magnetic stripe at an automated teller machine (ATM).

8 Data is input via a hand-held scanner.

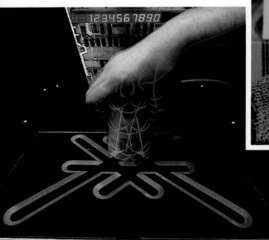

9 Scanner input at a grocery store checkout.

10 Scanning a photo for use in desktop publishing applications.

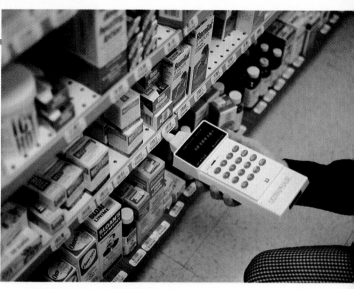

12 Data is input via a portable keypad.

11 Using a light pen to enter data.

13 Entering graphical data using a digitizer.

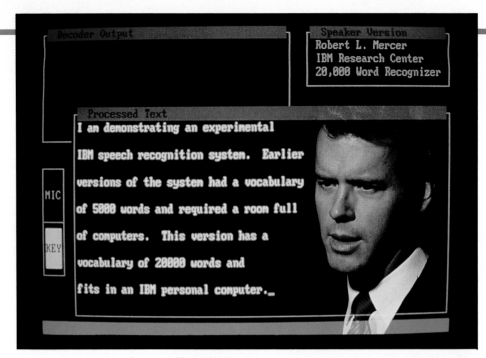

14   *Input via a speech recognition system.*

16   *A Macintosh personal computer.*

15   *Entering data with a mouse.*

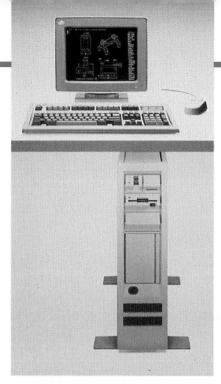

17 *An IBM PS/2 personal computer.*

18 *Personal computers are movable and portable.*

19 *Laptop computers can be taken to meetings.*

20 In the office, laptops can be connected to printers and other devices.

21 Business professionals use stand-alone personal computers.

22 Engineering workstations are personal computers with extended graphics and math processing capabilities.

23 A local area network links personal computers together in an office environment.

24 A local area network links personal computers in a retail environment.

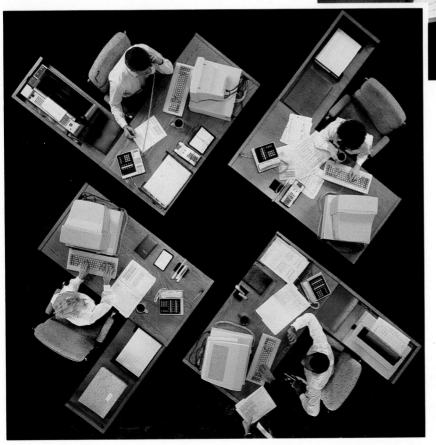

25 A local area network ring configuration.

26 *A small teleprocessing system connects local terminals in an office environment.*

27 *This teleprocessing system connects both local and remote terminals.*

28 *A centralized computer supports both a small teleprocessing system and local batch processing.*

29 *A large mainframe computer supports hundreds of terminals in an organizational teleprocessing system.*

30 *A Cray Y-MP supercomputer— one of the world's fastest computers.*

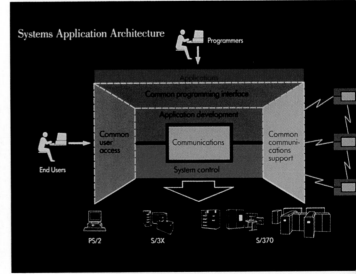

31 *Systems application architecture is one standard for connecting many different types of computers.*

32 A computer display serves as an output device.

33 An engineering workstation provides sophisticated graphical output on its display.

34 A gas plasma display used for a laptop computer.

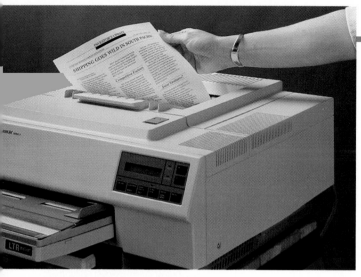

35 A laser-based page printer can produce both text and graphics.

36 A dot matrix printer composes characters from dots—as does a sports scoreboard.

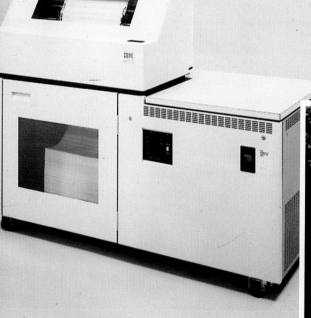

37 A line printer is fast and prints a line at a time.

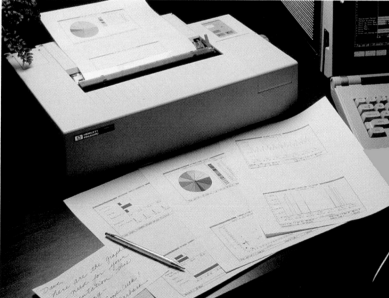

38 A color graphics printer produces both text and graphics.

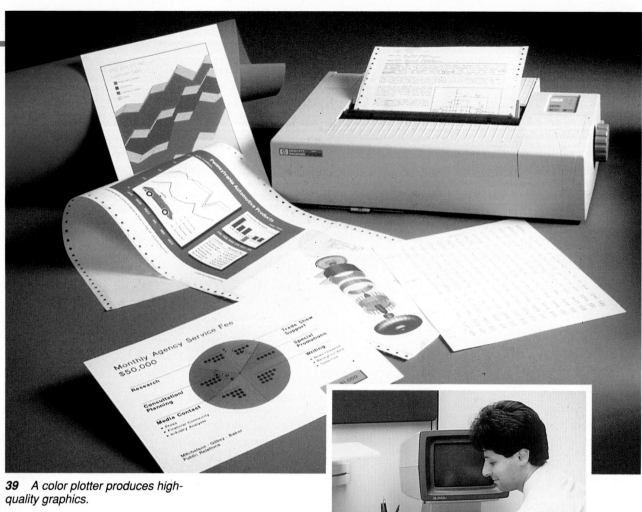

39 A color plotter produces high-quality graphics.

40 A user inserts a $3\frac{1}{2}$-inch disk into a PS/2 personal computer.

41 *A user inserts a $5\frac{1}{4}$-inch floppy disk into a personal computer.*

42 *A large capacity fixed disk used in a mainframe computer system.*

43 *Using magnetic tape storage.*

44 *An optical disk provides very high capacity storage.*

Figure 2-19
Modems

a. External modem

b. Internal modem

refers to the technique used for translating computer codes (called digital signals) into codes used in telephone transmission (called analog signals). Two computers communicating with a modem actually transfer messages over telephone lines.

Some modems are external and some are built into the same chassis as the CPU (see Figure 2-19). All modems use a phone jack to connect with the telephone system. Modems are one example of specialized communications equipment. Other communications hardware will be discussed in Chapter 9.

Questions

2.3 Name five types of equipment that make a computer. Briefly describe the purpose of each type.

2.4 Name and describe the three parts of the central processing unit.

2.5 Where must programs be loaded to be executed?

2.6 What device is used to input diagrams to a computer?

2.7 Compare and contrast diskettes and hard disks.

2.8 Describe two applications for CD-ROM.

2.9 What is the primary use of cassette tape in microcomputer-based systems?

2.10 What is the function of a modem?

2.11 What two devices make up a terminal?

2.12 List and briefly describe four scanning devices.

2.13 Why do scanning devices result in fewer data-entry errors than keyed data-entry?

2.14 What does the acronym UPC stand for?

2.15 Describe three types of hard-copy output devices.

2.16 Why is magnetic tape used for archiving and for file backups?

Programs

Programs are the instructions that make computers work. As a user, you will need to understand the types of programs that exist, where to obtain them, and how to use them within your own computer system. As an end user it is highly unlikely that you will ever develop a program from scratch yourself (although you might write a few programs in BASIC or Pascal, just to see how it's done). Despite that, learning about programs is important. Understanding programs will help you to participate as an end user in the development of large mainframe-based systems by enabling you to better articulate your needs to systems analysts and programmers building the system. Understanding programs also will help you to configure your own personal information system, or to articulate your needs to a consultant who is configuring the system for you. And finally, the more you know about how computer systems actually work, the less mystical they appear. Knowledge gives you more control over your system.

A program is a series of instructions, understandable to the computer, that makes it perform desired functions. Just as computer equipment is called *hardware* because it is tangible, programs are called **software,** because they are not tangible. Yet programs are vital to the operation of a computer system. Without programs, computer equipment—such as the central processing unit—is just so much electronic junk. But directed by programs, that electronic equipment can scan millions of records looking for specific ones, can monitor the heartbeat of a patient in intensive care, can help design fuel-efficient automobiles, and can print refund checks for the Internal Revenue Service, to name just a few functions.

Because a computer understands only its own *machine language*, and because machine language code is very tedious and time-consuming to write, almost all programs are written in a *programming language*—such as C, BASIC, or COBOL—then translated into machine language by a special program called a *compiler* (more about that later).

Essentially there are two types of computer programs, system programs and application programs (see Figure 2-20). **System programs** operate the computer equipment and establish the general computing environment. **Application programs** solve specific user problems or satisfy specific user needs. Application programs are of two types: packaged, and custom-developed.

System Programs

System programs exist to provide general computing services to anyone who wants to use the computer. We will discuss five types of system programs: operating systems, utilities, language translators, database management systems, and communications programs (see Figure 2-21).

Operating Systems   An **operating system** is a program (or set of programs) that coordinates the execution of all other programs. It is the system's traffic cop. See Figure 2-22. An operating system also is the

Figure 2-20
The two types of programs

- System programs

  —Operate the equipment

  —Establish the general computing environment

- Application programs

  —Solve specific problems

  —Can be packaged or custom-developed

interface between each application program and the input, output, and storage devices the program uses. Because the operating system coordinates and services the system's activity, it determines the environment for the information system. It is not the hardware so much as the operating system that gives your system a distinct look and feel, a distinct way of interfacing with you.

When a computer is powered on, the first thing it does is give control to the operating system. The operating system then takes over, and remains active until the computer is shut off. (The portion of main memory not used by the operating system is used by application programs.) When it takes over, the operating system provides three important services: job management, task management, and data management.

The function of the *job management* portion of the operating system is to schedule jobs and allocate computer resources to them. Most large computer systems (and some personal systems) support multitasking, that is, they allow several application programs to be loaded into the CPU at once for execution. Each program—or *job*—contends for resources, such as computer equipment (disk drives, the printer, and so forth). Using algorithms to minimize contention, job management determines which of all the programs waiting should be loaded.

The *task management* portion of the operating system takes over once an application program has been loaded into the CPU's main memory for execution. Although the CPU executes instructions at a phenomenal rate—such as 10 million instructions per second—it can execute only one instruction at a time. To take advantage of CPU speed, and to accommodate for other relatively slow operations within a program (such as printing a line or waiting for the user to type a response on a keyboard), task management gives each loaded application program a little slice of the CPU's time, in round-robin fashion. For instance, if five programs vie for CPU time, task management lets the first one use the CPU for, say, one-tenth of a second, then it lets the second one do the same, then the third, and so forth. Eventually the first program gets another chance to execute for a tenth of a second, as would all the others. As each program finishes, it is replaced (by job management routines) with another program waiting to be loaded. Spreading the expensive CPU resources this way is called *time slicing*.

- Operating systems

- Utilities

- Language translators

- Database management systems

- Communications software

Figure 2-21
System programs

Figure 2-22
Operating system functions in main
memory

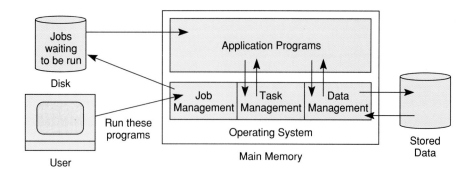

Another function of task management is to allocate additional main memory to programs that need it, and to keep track of where all the programs are located. Some programs are larger than the amount of main memory available. Task management resolves this apparent problem by temporarily removing unused portions of programs to temporary disk storage (called *virtual memory*), thus freeing up valuable main memory. When those program pieces are needed, task management retrieves them from disk and loads them into available main memory for execution.

The *data management* portion of the operating system provides services to create, process, and administer data. For example, when an application program issues a command such as READ (an instruction that retrieves data from a disk file), the data management portion of the operating system processes the command. It determines where the data is located and issues commands to the various hardware components (such as the disk drive) to cause the data to be transmitted from disk to main memory. When data arrives, data management routines check to see that it arrived in good condition. If not, the data management routines take corrective action. Similar actions occur when output is produced, such as displaying words and numbers on a computer screen. Data management routines help the data get to where it is supposed to go.

Data management routines also are used to maintain catalogs of stored data, such as a tape or disk library. A catalog, or directory as it is sometimes called, records who created the data, when it was created, when it was last processed, and so forth.

The operating system functions are summarized in Figure 2-23.

Utilities The second type of system program is the **utility.** A utility program satisfies a common need. For example, utilities exist that perform the following functions:

- Backup an entire database onto tape or disk
- Convert a file from one format to another
- Print the contents of a disk file
- Prepare a new disk for use

Figure 2-23
Summary of operating system functions

- Job management

    —Schedules and loads application programs

    —Allocates computer resources to application programs

- Task management

    —Allocates CPU time to each program in memory

    —Allocates main memory to application programs

- Data management

    —Creates, processes, and administers stored data

    —Maintains catalogs of stored data

- Rename a file
- Delete a group of files
- Sort a group of records

These and other commonly used routines are ones that users do not want to be bothered with writing on their own. For both mainframe and personal computers, utilities can be obtained from the operating system vendor and from third parties.

Compilers   A computer understands only machine code. But writing machine code—strings of 1s and 0s—is error-prone and tedious. As a result, programs are written in programming languages, which are codes that people understand more easily. Compilers are language translation programs that translate program code (called *source code*) into machine instructions (called *object code*). A program written in the language C must be translated by a C compiler; a program written in COBOL is translated by a COBOL compiler; and a program written in ADA is translated by an ADA compiler. Dozens of programming languages exist. Some popular ones are listed in Figure 2-24.

As a user, you will not have to know any programming languages. You might learn how to write some programs in BASIC, in this or other courses—perhaps you learned some BASIC in high school. But to be a programmer you would need to learn much more about the computer, the operating system, data storage, programming languages, and so forth.

Mainframe compilers are obtained from computer manufacturers (such as IBM or DEC) and from third parties. Personal computer compilers are obtained from a computer retailer or from mail-order companies. Most personal computers come with a version of BASIC. But many other languages, such as Pascal, C, and COBOL, are available for personal computers as well.

Figure 2-24
Comparison of programming
languages

Language	Primary Uses	Comments
ADA	Systems, Scientific	Derivative of Pascal; developed for U.S. Dept. of Defense
ALGOL	Scientific	Popular in Europe, not in North America
APL	Scientific	Requires special keyboard; primarily available on IBM computers
Assembler	Systems	Highly efficient; system dependent; difficult to read and understand
BASIC	Education, Simple programs	Simple to learn; limited functions
C	Systems	Developed by Bell Laboratories as part of the UNIX operating system
COBOL	Business	Old language; wordy; extensive file-handling capability; durable
FORTRAN	Scientific	Old language; has limitations, but very popular in science
Pascal	Education, Systems, Scientific	Excellent structured language; limited I/O
PL/I	General purpose	Rich language, but complex
RPG	Business report writing	Parameter driven; quick way to generate reports

Database Management Systems   Another type of system program, the **database management system (DBMS),** is a program that provides special data management capabilities, beyond the ordinary file handling provided by an operating system. A DBMS provides an interface between a user or an application program and the operating system's data management routines (see Figure 2-25). As you will learn in Chapter 10, a database includes not only application data (such as customer names and addresses, sales receipts, and inventory records), but also much information about the application data (such as the customer to whom a sale was made and which inventory items were sold in that transaction). Juggling not only the data itself but also information about the data requires special instructions, provided by DBMS software. DBMSs are available for both mainframe and personal computers. For mainframe computers they can be obtained from a computer manufacturer (for example, IBM licenses DB/2, a mainframe DBMS), or from third parties (for example, Cullinet licenses IDMS, another mainframe DBMS). The price of such software usually runs into the tens of thousands of dollars. DBMSs for personal computers are obtained from

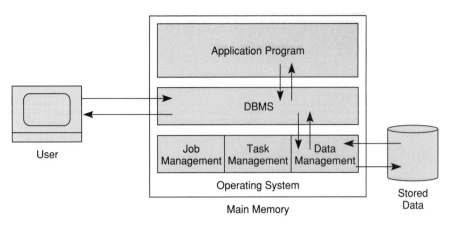

Figure 2-25
DBMS interface with the operating system

local or mail-order computer software retailers. Examples include dBase, Foxbase, Oracle, Paradox, and RBase. Personal computer DBMSs cost only hundreds of dollars, usually between $200 and $1,000.

Communications Software   Like database management software, **communications software** provides system functions beyond those of the operating system. In the case of communications software, this means allowing two computers to talk to one another, a surprisingly complex activity (see Figure 2-26). You will learn about telecommunications in Chapter 9, so a brief introduction will suffice at this point.

Each computer system has its way of doing things: of formatting, storing, and retrieving data; of executing instructions; of accepting electronic signals for input; and of producing electronic signals for output. If the entire world were made up of, say, Apple Macintosh computers, communications would be easy. But just as the United Nations employs people to provide interfaces between representatives of countries that have different languages, cultures, and customs, telecommunications systems use software to enable computers with different backgrounds to send messages to each other.

Also, computers that communicate with each other often do so by sending messages across telephone lines and between satellites. Communications software is needed to package the message, address it to a destination computer, and send it on its way. Communications software in the receiving computer accepts the message, unpackages it, verifies that it was received in good condition, and acknowledges that it was received. Communications software controls the fairly straightforward dialogue between two computers as well as communication among an entire network of computers, maybe thousands in all.

System Programs—Summary   System programs enable you to use the computer system. They provide you with an interface to the computer itself, and give you an operating environment. They provide you with useful utility programs and language translators. And they give your system additional power with optional database management and communications capabilities.

Figure 2-26
Communications software

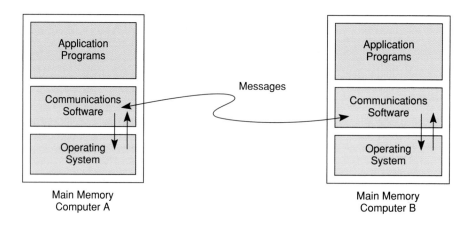

Application Programs

For all that system programs do, they do not solve your business problems. No system program will tell you who to send bills to this month, or how much money you have left in the household account, or which salespeople will receive bonuses this week. All of those specific business-oriented problems are handled by the second category of programs, application programs. Application programs can be purchased ready-made (packaged programs), or they can be custom developed.

Packaged Application Programs   Some business problems are common to many users. Depending on the nature of the problem, it may be common to many different types of users (for example, lots of businesses use electronic spreadsheet programs to do budgets) or many users of the same type (for example, most retail stores use some sort of computer-based inventory control system). Consequently, packaged application software has two possible markets: the horizontal market and the vertical market. These are discussed below.

The advantages of using packaged application programs are that they are immediately available, so development time is nil; programs are less expensive to purchase than they are to build; and if the product has been around for a while, it has been thoroughly tested and probably is very reliable.

The risk of using packaged application programs is that the developer might go out of business. The developer usually provides customer service, program upgrades, and, to some extent, training. If the developer suddenly no longer is available, then you no longer have customer support. However, if you choose popular packages from reputable developers, this should not be a problem.

Horizontal market programs provide general business functions to a variety of users (see Figure 2-27). Some widely-used business applications include accounts receivable, accounts payable, general ledger, and payroll functions. So many accounting packages exist that it is inconceivable that anyone would custom develop such software nowadays.

Figure 2-27
Characteristics of horizontal-market
application programs

- General business functions

- Obtained from the developer or software retailer

- Read computer magazines for information about these programs

- Benefits:
  Minimum development time
  Cheaper than custom-developed programs

- Risks:
  Vendor might go out of business

Figure 2-27
Characteristics of horizontal-market
application programs

Other horizontal market software includes the personal productivity software, such as electronic spreadsheet programs, word processing programs, and graphics software. All of these programs provide general business tools that can be employed in many industries.

Whereas horizontal market programs provide general business functions to diverse users, *vertical market programs* provide industry-specific functions to one type of user (see Figure 2-28). For example, a software developer might write a package of programs to be used in a dentist's office that includes features such as appointment scheduling, consultation summary writing, and insurance processing. Dentists of all types have needs like these. Designed properly—and with provisions for minor tailoring for each user—one package can be sold to many users within the same industry.

Vertical market programs are obtained either from consultants who develop and market products on their own or from **value-added resellers, or VARs.** A VAR obtains authorization from another software vendor to build an application based on the other vendor's product. In doing so, the developer adds value to the original product by making it more usable. For example, a VAR might use a database program such as Oracle as the backbone for a dental office package. The user will not even see the DBMS, but it is buried in the package, providing database

- Industry-specific functions

- Obtained from consultants or VARs

- Read industry literature for information about these programs

- Benefits:
  Minimum development time
  Close fit to user needs
  Cheaper than custom-developed programs

- Risks:
  Vendor could go out of business
  Might not be a perfect requirements fit

Figure 2-28
Characteristics of vertical-market
application programs

management services for the other application software that deals with dental office business problems. Whereas no ordinary dentist would bother to obtain a DBMS and develop his or her own application, he or she might purchase an entire office application package that happened to include a DBMS.

Custom-Developed Application Programs Custom-developed application programs are developed by computer professionals on behalf of one company (see Figure 2-29). To accomplish this, the developer must identify specific user requirements, then build and test computer programs that will satisfy the requirements. It is a long, tedious, and expensive process. Custom development is necessary in those instances where no software already exists to address the user's needs.

Application programs are written in languages such as those mentioned earlier—Pascal, C, COBOL, and BASIC, to name a few. Each program must be designed, coded, tested, debugged (a bug is a program error), retested, and so forth. Eventually all the programs are tested together to be sure they complement one another correctly. When all works well, the programs can be employed by the user.

Some companies have entire staffs of computer programmers, analysts, and other technicians to develop custom software. Other users hire contractors or consultants to develop applications. In either case, the job is labor intensive. Because the application is custom tailored, it can be used only in that organization. Consequently, that company must bear all the development costs. Contrast custom developing an accounting package with purchasing one ready-made. Assume each costs $100,000 to develop. The entire cost of the custom-developed application is borne by the company that developed it, while the cost of developing the packaged software is shared by each of the (say) 500 companies that purchase it.

Despite the high cost of custom-developed software, there is one benefit: it can fit the user's requirements like a glove. And in some instances, a perfect fit is required, regardless of cost. Just as a suit bought off the rack never fits as well as a tailored one, packaged application programs seldom satisfy every user requirement. But just as your budget or willingness to compromise may lead you to buy most

Questions

2.17 What is a program?

2.18 What is machine language?

2.19 What is the difference between system programs and application programs?

2.20 Name five types of system programs.

2.21 What does an operating system do?

2.22 Once it is loaded, why does an operating system stay in main memory as long as the computer is on?

2.23 Describe the job management function.

2.24 Describe the task management function.

2.25 What is time-slicing?

2.26 Describe the data management function.

2.27 What is a utility program?

2.28 What is a compiler?

2.29 What is a database management system?

2.30 What is an application program?

2.31 What is a packaged application program?

Figure 2-29
Characteristics of traditional custom-developed programs

- Developed by programmer using traditional programming language
- Lengthy and expensive development process
- Risks:
  High expense
  Requires skilled personnel
- Benefits:
  Satisfies user requirements perfectly

of your wardrobe ready-made, so most users find the convenience, price, and availability of packaged software reason enough to compromise on some of their requirements.

Conclusion   If another alternative exists, do not custom develop programs. The costs are very high, and the corresponding benefits seldom merit the expenditure. As a user, you will probably never develop programs, at least not using the traditional method of writing code in a programming language. You might develop some applications using application-development software like that which you will learn in Part II. But for the most part, software exists to meet ordinary business needs. Take advantage of such packaged software, and you'll have more time and money to devote to your business.

2.32 Describe and contrast two types of packaged application program.

2.33 What is a VAR?

2.34 Name two risks associated with packaged application programs. Name two benefits.

2.35 What are custom-developed application programs?

2.36 Why are custom-developed application programs so costly?

Data

The facts that go into a computer system are called *data*. Data used in an accounting system, for example, includes account numbers, names, addresses, payments made, purchase amounts, and the date payment is due. In a school administration system the data would include each student's identification number, name, address, year of graduation, date of birth, and major field of study.

Business computer systems help people by generating *information*. In fact, we use the terms *business computer system* and *business information system* interchangeably. Information is knowledge derived from facts. For example, we might store certain facts about a softball player, including all the times she was at bat, how many singles, doubles, triples, and home runs she got, how many times she struck out, and so forth. Those bits of data are facts. Some of the information we might derive from those facts include her batting average, her performance in early versus late innings, and her performance against left-handed pitchers. The information is more useful to the coach than a report of all her batting activity would be.

Types of Data

Data can be classified in the same way as computer equipment is: there is input, processing, output, and stored data (see Figure 2-30).

Input data is the raw facts that are fed into the computer system by means of some input device, such as a keyboard or a scanner.

Processing data is data that has been loaded into the main memory of the central processing unit for processing. For example, a list of today's sales might be loaded into the processor to determine a salesperson's commission. Processing data is processed by one of the programs that also has been loaded into the computer's main memory.

Output data is the information produced for human consumption. Examples include a graph showing sales trends displayed on a computer screen, an employee's paycheck, and a list of graduates who donated money to the college scholarship fund. Output data is issued by an output device such as a printer or a computer monitor.

Finally, *stored data* is facts being saved on a computer-readable medium such as disk or magnetic tape. Stored data cannot be read by a person, but it can be read by the computer if some program needs it.

Computer Representation of Data

In this section we will examine how data is represented in the computer.

Bits   The basic building block for representing computer data is called a **bit.** The term *bit* is an abbreviation for *binary digit.* You know what a decimal digit is. It is one of the symbols 0, 1, 2, 3, 4, 5, 6, 7, 8, or 9. A binary digit is similar, but there are only two symbols: 0 and 1.

Bits are used to describe computer data because they easily represent the electronics that computers are based on. Bits represent things that are either on or off. For example, we can say that when a light is on, we will represent it as a 1; when it is off we will represent it as 0. Figure 2-31 shows a panel of light switches. If we define up as 1 and down as 0, then this panel can be represented by the bit pattern 1101. Computers are not composed of panels of light switches, but they do contain millions of electronic switches that can be off or on.

Bits are recorded in various ways, depending on the computer device. In the central processing unit, for instance, a bit is recorded as a direc-

Figure 2-30
Input, stored, processing, and output data

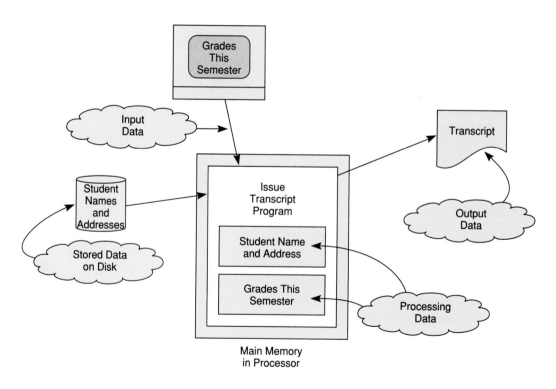

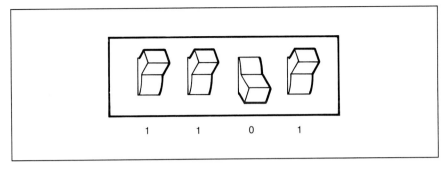

Figure 2-31
Panel of light switches corresponding
to bit pattern 1101

tion of flow of electricity or as a voltage at a particular location. On magnetic media, such as tape or disk, a bit is recorded as a direction of magnetization; one direction indicates a 1 and the other direction indicates a 0.

In the simplest terms, patterns of bits, or *configurations*, are used to represent characters—the letters A to Z, the digits 0 to 9, and special symbols such as #, &, {, and %. For example, the pattern 1100 0001 might represent an A; the pattern 1100 0010, a B; and so forth. The word *might* is used here because there is no single code. The code varies, depending on the type of computer system and the type of equipment. Two popular codes are EBCDIC and ASCII.

EBCDIC and ASCII Codes   One of the most common ways of representing data is the *Extended Binary Coded Decimal Interchange Code*, or **EBCDIC** (pronounced eb-sa-dick). EBCDIC is used to represent data on magnetic tape, on magnetic disk, and in main memory, especially on mainframe computers.

This code uses eight bits to represent each character. Figure 2-32 shows a portion of EBCDIC. There is no particular magic about the bit patterns. The fact that 1100 0001 represents an *A* and 1000 0001 represents an *a* has nothing to do with the names of the letters. The assignment of patterns to letters was arbitrary, and the designers of EBCDIC happened to choose these.

Numbers also are represented in EBCDIC. When put in this coded form, numbers are considered by the computer to be text. They can be read, stored, and printed. But in this form, numbers cannot be used in arithmetic. For example, no arithmetic can be done with the number in *95th Street*.

Computers can store numbers in a form that permits arithmetic to be done. In fact, several such forms are available. Numbers can be stored as decimals, as binary integers (whole numbers), and as binary fractions. These formats are described in Module B in Part Four. As a user, you will not be concerned with the particulars of internal data representation.

A second popular code for representing computer data is the *American Standard Code for Information Interchange*, or **ASCII** (pronounced

Figure 2-32
Portions of the EBCDIC and ASCII codes

Character	EBCDIC Bit Pattern	ASCII Bit Pattern
$	0101 1011	010 0100
*	0101 1100	010 1010
)	0101 1101	010 1001
.		
.		
.		
a	1000 0001	110 0001
b	1000 0010	110 0010
c	1000 0011	110 0011
d	1000 0100	110 0100
.		
.		
.		
A	1100 0001	100 0001
B	1100 0010	100 0010
C	1100 0011	100 0011
D	1100 0100	100 0100

ask-key). Whereas EBCDIC uses eight bits, ASCII uses only seven. Figure 2-32 also shows a portion of the ASCII codes. ASCII is used widely in personal computer systems. It is considered a standard in data communications, and therefore is used more widely than EBCDIC in those applications.

Data Hierarchy As described above, a group of bits in a particular pattern represents a character, such as *Q* or *5*. A character is sometimes referred to as a *byte*. Although almost synonymous, the terms *character* and *byte* usually are used in different contexts. When describing data, such as a customer's name, we might say it is 25 *characters* long. But when describing the physical capacity of computer hardware, such as main memory, we would say it holds 1.2 million *bytes* of data. That said, many people use the terms interchangeably. In any event, a group of bits (usually seven or eight) makes a byte (or character).

A group of related characters is called a **field.** Fields usually have logical meanings; they represent some item of data, some fact. Thus, the five characters in a zip code are the Zip Code field; the nine characters in a social security number are the Social Security Number field.

A collection of related fields is called a **record.** A collection of fields about a student, for example, is called the student record. Figure 2-33 depicts a student status record that might be used in a university's administrative system. The numbers across the top refer to character positions or columns. They are in the figure just for reference. If an image of this record were printed, the student number would appear

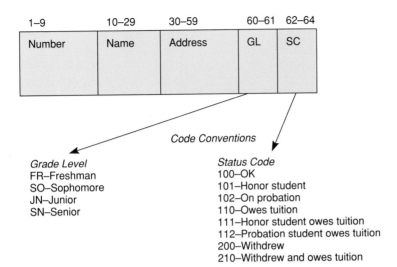

Figure 2-33
Format of the student status record

in positions 1 through 9, the name would appear in positions 10 through 29, and so forth. A field needs to be as long as the longest possible entry. Thus, the name *Susan Butcher* would use only 13 of the allowable 20 positions in the Name field; the rest would be filled with spaces. The name *Pauline Papadopolous* would just fit. A name longer than 20 characters would be *truncated,* or chopped off, to fit in the defined space.

Note the use in the student status record of abbreviations and special codes. Rather than write (or key) lengthy grade levels like *sophomore,* abbreviations are used. Furthermore, the Status Code field contains numbers that are assigned meanings as shown in Figure 2-33. These codes are set up as *conventions* when the system is designed. Thus, a 101 in the Code field is understood to mean the student is an honor student who owes no tuition. When codes like these are used, they must be explained in procedures documentation (we'll get to that later in this chapter) so people know what they are.

A collection of related records is called a **file.** All student status records together might be referred to as the *student status file* (see Figure 2-34). The schedule file might contain all of the class schedule records. Figure 2-34 illustrates the terminology: *characters* are grouped into *fields;* fields are grouped into *records;* and related records are grouped into a *file.*

File Storage

Data stored in a business computer system can reside in a file or in a database. In this section we will discuss files. In the next section we will briefly consider databases. They will be addressed more thoroughly in subsequent chapters.

A business computer system might use dozens—even hundreds—of files. Each file contains data about one aspect of the business. For exam-

Figure 2-34
Part of the student status file

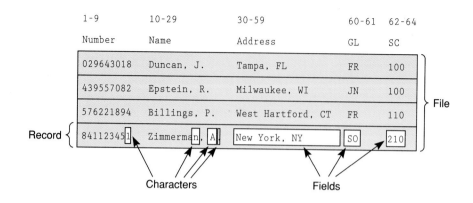

ple, there might be a file with vendor names and addresses, a file for customer accounts, a price file, an employee file, and so forth. To process the data in those files (that is, update the file data and retrieve data for manipulation) requires knowledge of file structures and access methods. Such skills are usually practiced by professional programmers.

There are two primary file access methods, called *sequential access* and *direct access*. As a user, you should know the difference because the method used will affect the cost, development schedule, and responsiveness of your system.

In a **sequential** file, records are stored physically next to one another, end-to-end, like songs recorded on a cassette tape (see Figure 2-35). In order to get to the 20th record, the program processing this file needs to access the first 19 records. In order to get to the 4,000th record, the program needs to access the first 3,999 records. Processing a file sequentially can be slow. Sequential files can be stored on tape and on disk.

In contrast, **direct access** is a method employed on certain disk files only (not tape). If the file is set up properly, any record in it can be accessed almost directly, without accessing any preceding records. This is possible due to the mechanics of disk. Its read/write heads can be positioned rapidly at any disk location. Just as you can directly locate a song on a compact disk, you can directly access a record on a magnetic disk.

Still, whether you use sequential or direct access, you need to depend on a programmer (or a programming staff) to write programs to access the data. If related data needs to be gotten from, say, five different files, the programmer needs to custom design a program to do just that.

Database Storage

In contrast to file processing systems, database processing systems allow much more user flexibility with data storage and access. A **database** is a collection of related files, plus overhead data that tells the database management software how various records are related, where they are stored on disk, and what user policies govern them. A database management system (DBMS) is a set of programs that stores and retrieves

Questions

2.37 What is the difference, if any, between data and information?

2.38 Describe four classifications of data in a business information system. Give an example of each.

2.39 What is a bit? Why are bits used to represent computer data?

Abel	$200	Baker	$1000	Charles	$500 ...

Figure 2-35
Sequential file

database data (and does a lot more that you'll learn about later). When you use a DBMS, the software does most of the work. Many times, programmers are unnecessary. Some users, especially those who use personal DBMSs, build and maintain their own databases.

When employing a DBMS (versus a file management system), a user can pose questions such as, "Which customers purchased more than $2,000 worth of goods in Store #1 between January 1 and June 30 last year?" and can receive an answer in a few seconds. Answering that same question using a file management system would more than likely require some custom programming. Instead of receiving the information in seconds, the user might have to wait days. As you will learn later, database systems often are more expensive than file systems, but their benefits frequently outweigh their costs.

2.40 What are EBCDIC and ASCII? What is their purpose?

2.41 Define the following terms: character, byte, field, record, file. How do they relate to one another?

2.42 What is the difference, if any, between a byte and a character?

2.43 What does *truncate* mean?

2.44 What is the difference between sequential file access and direct file access?

Trained Personnel

The fourth component of a business computer system is *trained personnel*. There are four types of people involved: systems development personnel (systems analysts and programmers), operations personnel, system users, and system clientele.

Systems Analysts

Systems analysts are people who know both business and computing. When a system is being developed, systems analysts interview users and with them determine the requirements for the new system. When developing a personal computer system, the system owner often hires a consultant to play the role of the systems analyst. Analysts also design computer systems to satisfy the users' requirements.

Good systems analysts possess a rare combination of skills. They must be good at communicating with people; they must understand at least one business specialty; and they must know computer technology. The same skills should be found in a skilled consultant. As a user, you will probably have occasion to work with both analysts and consultants.

Programmers

Programmers are computer specialists who write programs. Programmers do not need to be as good as analysts in dealing with people, nor do they need to know business as well. However, they must know more about computer technology. Specifically, a programmer needs to know one or more programming languages, various data storage techniques, and the technical details of computing.

Figure 2-36
Examples of training needs of systems
personnel

Personnel	Training Requirements
System developers	Communication skills
	Business fundamentals and principles
	Programming languages
	Software packages
	Computer hardware
	Computer technology
	Project management
Operations personnel	How to operate computers
	How to handle failures
	How to run business computer systems
	Preventive maintenance
	Operations staff supervision
Users	How to prepare inputs
	How to interpret outputs
	Duties and responsibilities
	Forthcoming changes to systems

Once a system is implemented, development personnel are no longer responsible for it. Responsibility for using systems lies only with users and operations personnel. Most systems at some point require changes to be made. This is called **system maintenance.** Maintenance might be done by some of the development personnel, or it might be done by a group of technicians who specialize in maintenance. Changes can be made to any of the five components.

To do their jobs properly, system development personnel need to know the latest in computer technology. Training is thus a recurring need (see Figure 2-36). One month a year is not an unusual amount of training time.

Operations Personnel

Operations personnel (operators) run the computer. They need to know how to start the computer, how to stop it, and how to run programs. They also need to know how to operate equipment like printers and disk drives. When the computer fails, operations personnel need to know what to do to minimize the damage, and they need to know how to restart the computer. This is true of operators in a large mainframe installation, and it is equally true for the user/operator of a single-user personal computer system.

In a well-run data processing center, the majority of the processing is done according to a schedule. In addition, everything the operators need to know about running a system is documented. Therefore, neither system developers nor users need to be in the computer room. To enforce this measure, many companies control access to the computer room with security systems that allow in only operations personnel.

Operators need to know how to run computer systems. They do not need in-depth knowledge of computing technology, nor even of how the computer works. Consequently, operations personnel usually have less technical knowledge than systems developers do. A typical computer operator has three to six months of formal training followed by about the same amount of on-the-job training.

Clientele

The third group of personnel is **system clientele.** These are the people who ultimately benefit from a system, although they may not directly interact with it. As a student, you are a member of the clientele of a class enrollment system, a grade posting system, a billing system, and many others.

Some system clientele do interact with a system. Because they receive absolutely no formal training, procedures for using the system must be explicit and unambiguous. An example is the bank customer using an automatic teller machine. Initially, the miniature screen contains one instruction: Insert bank card. A drawing above the slot shows how the card should be inserted. The next instruction is equally direct: Enter personal identification number. In fact, at any time only one simple instruction is displayed on the screen. Only after that instruction is successfully completed does the system prompt the client/user with another one. One step at a time, the system leads the client/user through the procedure to perform the desired banking transaction.

Users

The final category of personnel is *system users.* These people generally have little or no formal training in computing technology. Users have expertise in some business specialty, and they use the computer system as a tool to do their jobs. Many users—and the number grows each day—employ personal productivity software on personal computers as part of the job. We will address personal productivity software in Part Two.

The need for trained personnel is so obvious it is often overlooked. When users do not receive adequate training, system implementation is delayed until they learn by experience—a slow and costly process. Users of personal computer systems need to learn how to use the hardware and software effectively. When personnel are not properly trained, they often use the system ineffectively or inefficiently. They may take two hours to accomplish a task that would take only a few minutes if done properly.

Users have a right to be trained during system development, either by system development personnel or by other professional trainers. As a future user, you should insist on proper training. Plan into your budget and schedule the cost and time for training programs.

Questions

2.45 What are four types of trained personnel associated with a business computer system?

2.46 Describe the skills and responsibilities of a systems analyst, a computer programmer, and a computer operator.

2.47 Describe the difference, if any, between system users and system clientele.

2.1 INCREASING YOUR PERSONAL PRODUCTIVITY

What Do You Do When the System Shuts Down?

Wal-Mart founder Sam Walton pitched in to help checkout clerks at his store in Fort Walton Beach, Fla., when an electronic problem shut down the cash registers. The 71-year-old Walton, one of the world's richest men, grabbed a note pad Tuesday night and started hand-writing merchandise prices for customers so their bills could be tallied more quickly on calculators. "People began recognizing him and coming up and greeting him," store manager Paul Sively said. "He shook their hands and talked to everyone he could. The registers were out for about 45 minutes, and I don't think we had one customer complain."

Procedures

Consider this situation. At Megalopolis University, George arrived at the registrar's office at the appointed time to register for classes. When he submitted his class request form and the data was fed into the computer system, George discovered that the college thought he owed money. Although George knew he had paid all his fees, the registrar clerk would not allow him to register until his account was resolved. So he went to the finance office. The finance office agreed with George; he owed no money. They didn't know what to do, so they sent him to the computer center. The computer center told him they couldn't change his records, and sent him back to finance. In desperation, George went to his advisor, who was sympathetic but unable to help. George went back to his room wondering if college was worth the hassle.

Why is George having this problem? Obviously an error has been made, but why can't it be corrected? Is the hardware incapable of changing George's record? No. Can programs be written to change the errant data? Certainly. George has a problem because of a lack of procedures. No one knows what to do.

The Need for Procedures

Procedures are needed by many people associated with a system, including developers, operators, and users.

Procedures for Developers   System developers need procedures that specify a standard way of building business computer systems. These procedures explain how to determine requirements, how to develop system designs, how to write and test programs, and how to implement new systems (see Figure 2-37). Later in this course you will learn a standard way of doing system development.

To appreciate how important development procedures are (and they often are called *development standards* within an organization), you need to understand how large development projects can be. Some companies have hundreds of systems analysts and programmers working on projects that might take years to complete and cost hundreds of thousands (or millions) of dollars. Development standards help keep projects on track, enable easier communication among project members, and provide a record of what has been (and needs to be) done in the event a team member leaves the project team.

Whereas system developers need standards they can follow to develop systems, operators and users need procedures to follow once the system has been developed and installed. In fact, each group needs two sets of standards: one set that describes what to do under normal operating conditions, and another set that describes what to do in case of system failure.

How to determine requirements
Standards for system design
How to write and test programs
How to implement new systems

Figure 2-37
Examples of procedures for developers

Procedures for Operators As you can see from Figure 2-38, one set of procedures for operators explains how to run the system under normal conditions. Operators need to know who is authorized to make entries, what entries to expect, how often to run jobs, where output goes, how often to make backups, and so forth. Operators also need to know the mechanics of running jobs, such as which tapes and disks are to be read and what sort of paper should be in each printer.

In addition to normal operating procedures, operators need to know what to do in case of any system failure. They need to know how to quickly and correctly restore the system to its proper status when the system crashes (stops midstream), when communications failures occur (for instance, suddenly a terminal is unable to send data over the communications network), when equipment fails (for example, a disk drive or printer malfunctions), or when a database is rendered unusable and must be restored from backups. Other failures for which procedures are needed can occur—this is by no means an exhaustive list.

Procedures for Users System users need to know how to employ the computer system under normal conditions. They need to know how to activate each available function, how to enter data, and how to interpret results. Users also need to know any special responsibilities they

Figure 2-38
Examples of procedures for operators

Normal Operating Procedures	***Failure Recovery Procedures***
Who is authorized to provide inputs	System crash
What format inputs should have	Communications failure
When to run jobs	Equipment failure
Where output goes	Restoring data from backups
Making backups	
How to run jobs—tapes to use, forms to mount, etc.	

Figure 2-39
Examples of procedures for users

Normal Operating Procedures	Failure Recovery Procedures
Activating system features	Error correction
Entering data	Processing during system crash
Interpreting screens	Resuming processing after system
Interpreting reports	is restored
Duties and responsibilities	Who to contact in emergency

have; for example, bank tellers need to know whether they should rectify an incorrect deposit slip or return it to the customer. (See Figure 2-39.)

In addition to normal operating procedures, users need to know how to correct minor errors that may occur. They need to know what to do if the system becomes inoperable—are there manual procedures to follow, or do they hang a Gone Fishing sign on the terminal until the system is up again? When the system is returned to normal, what does the user do? Start from the beginning or resume where he left off? Procedures answer these and other questions which users may have regarding the use of the system. Finally, when all else fails, the user needs to know who to contact. A list of emergency telephone numbers can prove exceedingly helpful to an anxious or frustrated user.

Documentation

Procedures are ineffective if they are lost or forgotten; consequently they must be documented. **Documentation** consists of written procedures, which should be evaluated by concerned personnel and approved by management. Documentation is extremely important, not only as a way to preserve procedures, but also as a way of ensuring that procedures are complete and comprehensible. Most large computer installations have three volumes of documentation for each system: one for users, one for operators, and one for developers.

Procedure documentation serves several important functions. First, personnel training can be more efficient and effective if new people read documentation before, during, and after training sessions. Second, written documentation helps to standardize processing and thus improve the quality of service. Without documentation, someone like George trying to register for university courses might not happen to find a knowledgeable clerk. That student will receive poor service, which can lead to ill will among the system's clientele. Finally, documentation serves as a system memory. Procedures that are seldom used are quickly forgotten.

Questions

2.48 Why are procedures needed?

2.49 What do procedures for system developers describe?

2.50 For what two types of situation do system operators and system users need procedures?

Summary

If you have learned the material in this chapter, you understand more about business computer systems than most businesspeople do. Knowing that a business computer system consists of hardware, programs, data, procedures, and people, you have a framework in which to evaluate any system, large or small. You will never be duped into thinking that if you buy a computer your problems will be over.

Hardware is computer equipment. Computer hardware is classified into five categories: input, processing, storage, output, and communications equipment. Programs, also called software, are instructions that direct the hardware. System programs provide general computing functions; application programs solve specific business problems.

Data is the facts used in programs. Data, like hardware, is classified by the role it plays: input, stored, processing, or output. Computers are electronic devices. Consequently, data is recorded internally as groups of bits, or binary digits, which are equivalent to switches that are on or off. Several bits (seven or eight, depending on the code being used) represent one byte, or character. Logical groups of characters are called a field. Several related fields constitute a record. And a group of related records is a file. A database is a collection of integrated data that is accessed by special database management programs.

Just as computer equipment follows instructions in programs, people follow written procedures. Trained personnel are an integral part of any computer system. System developers, computer operators, and users all need to know how to interact with the system. Developers follow standard procedures for system development. Operators and users follow procedures for both normal system operation and for failure recovery.

All business computer systems incorporate the five components. But what can business computer systems do for you, the user? In the next chapter you will learn about various business applications in which business computer systems will help improve your productivity.

Word List

Many terms are introduced in this chapter. Terms that you should be sure you understand are listed here in the order in which they appear in the text.

business computer system	arithmetic/logic unit	hard copy
hardware	main memory	computer monitor
program	byte	pixel
data	input device	video display terminal (VDT)
procedure	load	dot-matrix printer
crash	terminal	line printer
central processing unit (CPU)	scanning device (scanner)	laser printer
control unit	output device	magnetic disk

diskette
backup
CD-ROM
communications device
modem
software
system program
application program
operating system
utility

database management system
 (DBMS)
communications software
value-added reseller (VAR)
bit
EBCDIC code
ASCII code
field
record
file

sequential access
direct access
database
systems analyst
programmer
system maintenance
operations personnel (operators)
system clientele
documentation

Discussion Questions and Exercises

A. Why are storage devices sometimes called input/output, or I/O, devices?

B. Develop a list of hardware components for any computer system on campus; for example, your own (or a classmate's) system, a school administrative system, the computer lab, or computers used for research. Classify the hardware according to the categories of input, processing, storage, output, and communications. For each device, identify the manufacturer, the make, and the model. For example, you might have a NEC Pinwriter P/6 dot-matrix printer. Compare your answer with that of another student.

C. In what language is a compiler written?

D. Research programming languages in your school library. Photocopy from textbooks or technical manuals sample programs in at least three programming languages.

E. Interview a computer user: a business person, a school administrator, or a working graduate. What has been their experience with packaged software? What has been their experience with custom-developed software? Do they agree with the assertion that whenever possible packaged programs are preferred to custom-developed ones? Why or why not?

F. Suppose a generous benefactor offered you any personal computer system (hardware and software) you wanted. Given your current situation and your career goals, describe the system you would want.

G. Describe a situation in which you were told, "The computer made a mistake and nothing can be done about it," or in which you were given the runaround. What explicit procedures would have resolved that situation?

Survey of Business Computer Systems

This chapter introduces you to five fundamental types of information systems. **Transaction processing systems (TPSs)** support the operational, day-to-day activity of the organization. **Management information systems (MISs)** are used to facilitate the management of those day-to-day activities. **Decision support systems (DSSs)** are special-purpose applications that exist to support decision making in unstructured environments. **Office automation systems (OASs)** facilitate office activities such as the preparation and communication of correspondence. Finally, **executive support systems (ESSs)** are systems employed by very senior managers to keep abreast of the organization in broad, overview terms.

We will examine each of these system types in turn, with a brief description of each type's characteristics and general architecture, and an example of that type. After the five types have been discussed, we will consider the use of information systems in the functional areas of business.

The goal of this chapter is to illustrate and discuss fundamental, generic types of information systems. The goal is to get a broad view of the forest, before we look closely at the trees (in Parts Two and Three). When you finish this chapter, you should have a general understanding of the role of information systems in organizations.

Transaction Processing Systems (TPSs)

Transaction processing systems support day-to-day operations. A few examples are: ticket reservation systems, order entry systems, check processing systems, accounts payable systems, accounts receivable systems, and payroll systems. All of these systems help a company conduct its operations and keep track of its activities.

TPSs are the oldest type of information system. They were first developed in the 1950s in the accounting departments of major corporations. They have been the workhorse of the information systems industry for the last thirty years.

Architecture of a TPS

Figure 3-1 shows the typical architecture of a transaction processing system. The graphical symbols in this figure represent various components of a TPS. These symbols are not arbitrary; they have standardized meanings—see Figure 3-2.

Consider Figure 3-1. An event occurs in the business world; this could be a request for a concert ticket (order entry), the presentation of a check for payment (check processing), or the completion of a certain number of hours of work (payroll). Data about the event is keyed into the computer system as a **transaction:** a representation of the event. A computer program, called a **transaction processing program,** processes the transaction against stored TPS data.

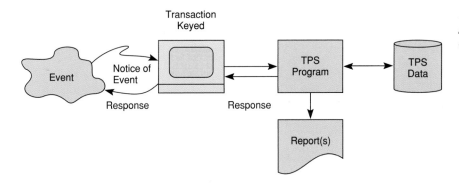

Figure 3-1
Architecture of a generic TPS
application

The nature of TPS data depends on the application. In a ticket reservation system, the TPS data contains the location of available seats. In the case of check processing, the TPS data contains account information such as the account balance. In the case of payroll, the TPS data includes the employee's pay rate, accrued pay and taxes, and so forth.

The transaction processing program generates two types of outputs. It sends messages back to the terminal operator and it generates printed documents. For a ticket reservation system, for example, the program would display a message on the terminal that indicates which seats have been sold to the customer; it also would print the tickets and, perhaps, a mailing label for sending them.

On-Line Transaction Processing   There are two fundamental types of TPS, on-line systems and batch systems. **On-line** systems involve a direct connection between the operator and the transaction processing program. On-line systems provide immediate results. They are used to process a single transaction at a time. Let's say an order arrives by telephone. The on-line TPS processes it at once and produces results immediately. The system shown in Figure 3-1 is an on-line TPS since the operator has a direct connection to the transaction processing program.

The direct access storage unit in Figure 3-1 represents a computer storage device that allows data to be accessed directly, in any order, as described in the last chapter. This allows, for example, the transaction processing program to read data about ticket reservations in the order that customers inquire about reservations, not in the order in which they are stored on the file.

Batch Transaction Processing   **Batch** systems are the second type of TPS. In batch systems, transactions are grouped together and processed as a unit. For example, in a check processing system, all of the checks received in a particular time period such as a day are grouped together. Then they are sorted by account number and processed in a batch.

The architecture of a typical batch processing application is shown in Figure 3-3. The transactions are grouped into a **transaction file** and sorted. The batch is then read in order by the transaction processing program. This program reads the stored data, often called the **old mas-**

Figure 3-2

Symbols used in systems architecture diagrams

Symbol	Name	Comments
	Computer Program	Program runs on a computer, which is usually not shown
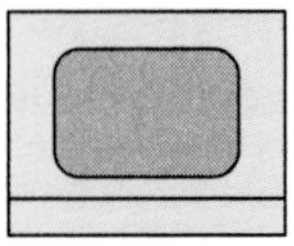	User Workstation	Keyboard and screen Can be terminal or microcomputer connected to computer
	Direct Access Storage Device (DASD)	Data repository Data can be read or written in any order
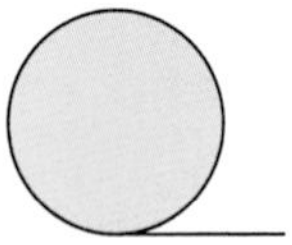	Tape-Sequential Access Device	Data repository Data must be read and written sequentially
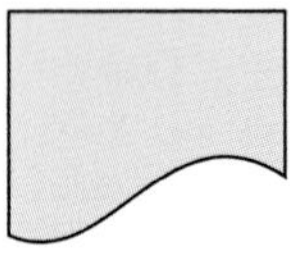	Document	Report or form
	Telecommunications Link	Telephone line or similar connection
	Manual Process	Activity performed off-line by a person such as key-to-disk operator

ter file data, processes the transactions, and creates **new master file** data. As it does so it generates reports. To match transaction records with master file records, the transaction records are sorted in the same way that the master file is sorted, for example, in ascending sequence on account number. Although tape units are shown in this figure, the master file can reside on either direct access hardware (disk) or sequential access hardware (tape).

In a check processing system, as mentioned above, the checks are batched and sorted by account number. The old master file, which is also sorted by account number, contains customer checking account data from the prior time period. This data is updated to create the new customer master file. Reports produced include lists of overdrawn accounts, monthly summaries, lists of suspicious activities, and so forth.

An Example TPS: Hourly Payroll

Now, consider a familiar accounting system, **hourly payroll.** The major functions and features of such a system are listed in Figure 3-4. Keep in mind that this system concerns only employees who are paid on an hourly basis.

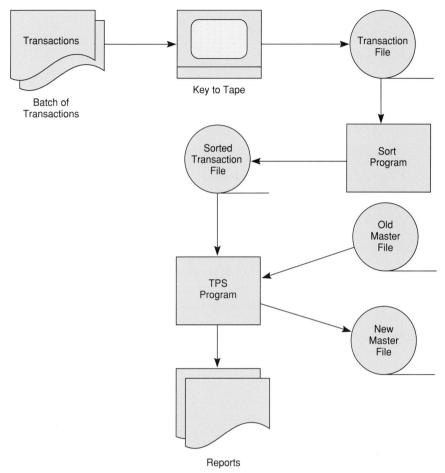

Figure 3-3
Architecture of a batch transaction processing application

The first two requirements are self-explanatory. The third requirement refers to the **general ledger**, or company accounts. Payroll systems generate entries for accounting. These entries reduce cash by the amount of payroll, accrued taxes and FICA payments; and make other necessary bookkeeping adjustments.

Accounting for sick leave and vacation time requires the system to accumulate the time earned in each pay period, reducing it by the amount of leave or vacation actually taken. The requirement to print W-2 tax forms at year end means that the system must keep track of each employee's total pay to date, total taxes to date, total FICA payments, and total of any other taxable income. This data must be kept even for employees who leave the organization.

The next two requirements refer to changes that will be made to the TPS stored data, that is, the employee master file. As employees are hired, data for them must be added to the master file. Also, since pay rates are in the master file, changes must be made when employees receive pay increases. When an employee leaves the company, his or her record must be marked so that no further paychecks will be issued. The record cannot be deleted, however, until the W-2 form is printed

Figure 3-4
Major functions of hourly payroll

- Compute pay, taxes, deductions

- Print paychecks

- Produce entries for general ledger

- Account for sick leave and vacation time

- Print W-2 tax forms at year end

- Accommodate new employees and changes to employee data

- Account for ex-employees until year end

- Minimize risk of error or unauthorized activity

at the end of the year. Finally, all of these requirements must be met in a way that minimizes the risk of errors and unauthorized activity.

Payroll can be processed by either an on-line or a batch system, though batch is more common. If a batch system is used, the payroll master file can be stored on either tape or disk. Figure 3-5 shows a system flowchart of a batch payroll system that maintains the master file on a direct access device.

The system shown in Figure 3-5 divides processing into phases. This **phased processing** provides checks and balances between the payroll department and the MIS department. During phase 1, the changes to the master file are keyed (to disk) and then edited by one of the payroll programs. **Editing** means the program will check the input to be sure it has the correct format, is plausible, and so forth. No changes actually are made to the master file during phase 1. The file of changes is now called *Edited* Master File Changes.

The report produced in the first phase is called an **edit report**. The users check this report, and if they are satisfied that the changes are correct, they authorize the changes to be made to the master file in phase 2. If there are errors in the edit report, then phase 1 is repeated until all of the input data is correct (or at least believed to be correct).

An example edit report is shown in Figure 3-6. The first two proposed master file changes appear to be correct. The edit program, however, detected an error in the third entry. This company has a convention that all employee numbers begin with a 1. This employee number does not, so it is flagged as an error. The new employee data for Joy Johnson must be verified by payroll personnel. Additionally, the pay change for employee 17281 also appears to contain an error; the pay change probably should be 9.87 not 98.70. The program has not flagged this record as an error, so the responsibility lies with the payroll department to detect this possible problem.

These discrepancies point out the need for procedures and trained personnel. Without them, an error may go undetected. Perhaps, too, you can see why *all* business people need some knowledge about information systems.

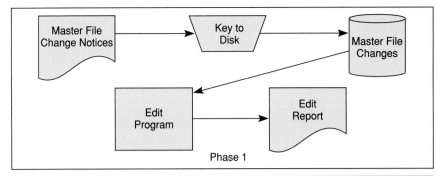

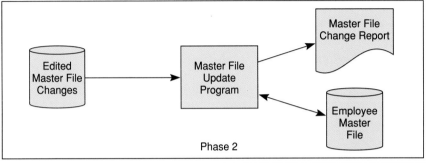

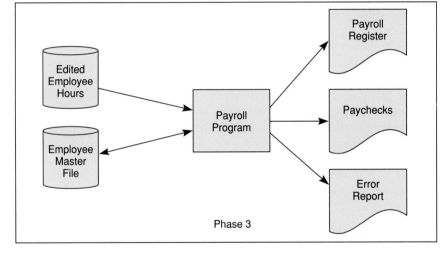

Figure 3-5
System flowchart for hourly payroll system

During phase 2, the edited changes are applied to the employee master file. To provide checks and balances, the processing in phase 2 is often directed by a second party—perhaps by someone in the MIS department, or perhaps by a manager within the payroll department.

At this point, a second report, called the **master file change report**, is produced. This report shows changes actually made to the employee master file. The payroll department reconciles this report with the edit report to ensure accuracy. If the phase 2 report is correct, payroll authorizes MIS to perform phase 3 (or performs phase 3 itself, depending on the particular system). If the phase 2 report is not correct, phases 1 and 2 are repeated.

Questions

3.1 List the five types of information systems described in this chapter.

3.2 Describe the general nature of transaction processing systems.

3.3 Explain each of the elements in Figure 3-1.

```
        EMPLOYEE
        NUMBER        EMPLOYEE NAME              TYPE OF CHANGE

        12481         FRED PARKS                 PAY CHANGE TO 8.73
        14618         SALLY BATTS                PAY CHANGE TO 7.50
        *** ERROR IN NEXT CHANGE-INCORRECT EMPLOYEE NUMBER ***
        02800         JOY JOHNSON                NEW EMPLOYEE
                      ADDRESS                    1418 S. TAMARACK
                                                 ALEXANDRIA, VA 01042
                      DATE OF BIRTH              DECEMBER 11, 1944
                      TITLE                      PRODUCTION ASSISTANT
                      PAY RATE                   7.52
                      DEPENDENTS                 3
                      SOCIAL SECURITY NUMBER     522-00-1841
        17281         ELMER NILSON               PAY CHANGE TO 98.70
        16415         DOROTHY SUHM               PAY CHANGE TO 21.50
```

Figure 3-6
Payroll master file edit report

3.4 Explain each of the symbols in Figure 3-2.

3.5 What is a transaction?

3.6 Describe the general nature of an on-line transaction processing system.

3.7 Describe the general nature of a batch transaction processing system.

3.8 Define the terms *old master file* and *new master file*.

3.9 List the major functions of hourly payroll.

3.10 Why are the phases shown in Figure 3-5 necessary?

3.11 What is the purpose of the edit report in Figure 3-5?

3.12 What is the purpose of the change report in Figure 3-5?

3.13 What is the purpose of the payroll register in Figure 3-5?

3.14 List the key characteristics of transaction processing systems.

In phase 3, a file of employee hours is entered as input into the payroll program along with the employee master file. The hourly data has gone through an edit similar to that shown in phase 1. For the sake of brevity, it is not shown here. The payroll program computes pay, taxes, and deductions; it accounts for time off; and it updates the employee master file to show the new year-to-date totals.

The payroll program also produces three reports. The **payroll register** contains the entries to be made to the general ledger and a list of every check written. Payroll uses this list to verify amounts before signing the paychecks. The second report consists of the paychecks (an example is shown in Figure 3-7). The last report lists any errors that the payroll program detected—for example, a report of hourly work performed by a nonexistent or terminated employee.

Characteristics of TPSs

Payroll is a typical transaction processing system. Such systems are the oldest computer-based information systems and are common in accounting applications. Such systems generally are multiuser systems supported by mainframe computers.

Key characteristics of a transaction processing system are:

- Supports day-to-day operations
- High volume of data
- Needs high performance (because of large amount of data)
- Logic of processing is relatively simple
- High degree of accuracy required
- Data processed repetitively
- Supports many users
- Vulnerable to unauthorized or criminal activity

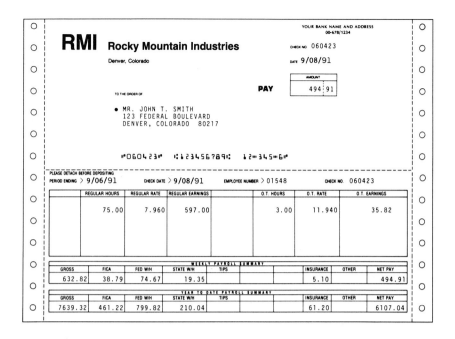

Figure 3-7
Printed payroll check

Management Information Systems (MISs)

The term **Management Information System** (MIS) has two very different meanings. The first is a broad and encompassing meaning that refers to the general application of information systems in business. In this sense, MIS is defined as the development and use of effective information systems in organizations. (It is this broad definition that company data processing departments use when they call themselves the MIS department.) The second definition, and the one that concerns us here, is much more narrow. The second definition identifies a particular type of MIS.

Narrowly defined, an MIS is an information system that facilitates management control by producing structured, summarized reports on a regular and recurring basis. The outputs of such MISs are produced routinely and used primarily for applications that involve the acquisition and productive use of resources.

Such MISs are conceptually a level above transaction processing applications. They are not concerned with day-to-day operations but rather with the management of resources involved in operations. Such resources include labor, money, materials, equipment, and the like.

Consider the example of ticket reservations. A **TPS** is used to take orders and print tickets. An MIS is used to measure and report the performance of each of the agents who sell tickets. Such an MIS keeps track of the number and dollar amount of sales by each agent, and regularly produces reports about agent effectiveness. An example report is shown in Figure 3-8. This report is used by the sales office manager to track agent performance, identify problems, and reward exceptional sales activity.

Sales for the Week of 8 August

Salesperson	Hours Worked	Number of Sales	Dollar Sales	Dollar Sales/Hour
Jane Adams	40	486	$10,692	$267
Mark Baker	40	654	$16,350	$409
Michelle Johnson	20	392	$10,192	$510
Bill McIntyre	40	441	$10,143	$254

Figure 3-8
Example MIS report for ticket sales activity

Architecture of an MIS

Usually, MIS applications process data that is generated by a TPS or other internal information source. Figure 3-9 shows a typical MIS system architecture. The user submits a request for a report to an MIS program. The MIS program processes the TPS data by aggregating and reformatting it to produce a report. The report is either printed or displayed on the user's workstation.

In some cases, reports are automatically generated. For example, the MIS programs may be written to produce a certain series of reports every Monday morning, or at the close of every business day, or at the end of some other period. Sometimes the MIS application programs are written to look for exceptional conditions in the data and produce reports if and when those conditions occur. A ticket agency, for example, might have an MIS application that prints the artist, date, and location of any concert that is not at least one-third sold out three weeks prior to the event. Such reports are called **exception reports**.

In some cases, the MIS application does not read the operational TPS data directly. Instead, an extract of the TPS data is made, and the MIS application processes the extract. This is done for a variety of reasons—to provide security for the TPS data, to transfer data across computers when the TPS and the MIS operate on different machines, or to consolidate data to make MIS processing more efficient.

The MIS may also store and maintain data of its own. Some MIS applications have simple models of business activity that they use for processing data to generate information for the manager. If such models exist, they are static, so that the manager gets the same report every period. You will see an example of such a static model in the next section.

An Example MIS Application Concerning Labor Effectiveness

MISs (narrow definition) provide information to facilitate the acquisition and use of resources. In this section, we will consider an MIS application concerning labor effectiveness. This MIS uses, in part, data that is produced by the payroll transaction processing system described earlier in this chapter.

Figure 3-10 shows the architecture of this MIS. Observe that this system is a special case of the general architecture shown in Figure 3-9. Data is extracted from the payroll transaction processing system.

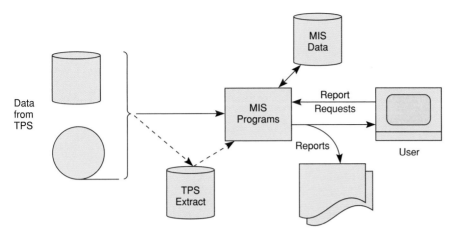

Figure 3-9
Architecture of a generic MIS application

This system, which resides on a mainframe computer, transmits data to the MIS, which resides on a microcomputer. (We will consider such transmission in more detail in Chapter 9.) The MIS programs process the extracted payroll data along with budget data that is part of the MIS and produce reports for management regarding labor and labor effectiveness.

Figure 3-11 shows an example of the extracted data that is input to the MIS. For brevity, just a few records are shown. In a real application, it is likely there would be hundreds or thousands of such records. Observe that the data includes each employee's payroll data for the week—job code, project number, pay, and vacation and sick days taken.

The MIS produces a number of standard reports, as shown in Figure 3-12. First is a summary report that shows the total payroll and the total vacation and sick days taken. Then, the data is divided and analyzed in three dimensions: by department, by job code, and by project. Finally, actual hourly payroll data is compared to budgeted data for each project.

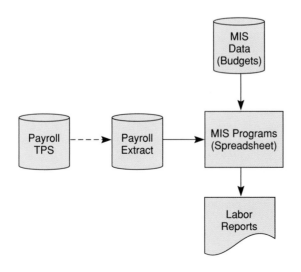

Figure 3-10
Architecture of labor effectiveness MIS

Hourly Payroll Data
Week of April 23, 1990

Emp#	Dept	Job-code	Project#	Tot-pay	Vac-days	Sick-days
100	Acct	1010	P1200	$1,459	0	0
200	Acct	1010	P2000	$2,099	0	2
250	Marketing	2070	P1200	$2,889	2	1
300	Marketing	2070	P1200	$3,257	0	2
400	Marketing	1010	P2000	$3,321	0	3
450	Marketing	2100	P2000	$2,765	2	0
500	Sales	2100	P1200	$2,340	0	0
550	Sales	2100	P1200	$3,550	1	0

Figure 3-11

Example of payroll data extracted from the payroll TPS

A general manager of this company might use this data as follows. The summary report indicates that, on average, each employee took one day of sick leave last week. The manager is concerned about this high rate of absenteeism and so examines the more detailed reports to see if there is an explanation. The report showing payroll data by department indicates that an unusually high number of sick leave days was taken by employees in the marketing department. Looking further, the highest number of sick days was taken by employees having job code 1010 and employees on project P2000. Using this information, the manager could then follow up to determine what factors have caused this situation.

Managers also can use the report of budget versus actual payroll expense to assess the status of projects. Whereas the other MIS reports can be prepared using only data extracted from the payroll TPS, the budget report requires additional budgetary data, which is stored as part of the MIS data.

This MIS is most likely a single-user system. For example, an analyst in the finance and administration department may employ this MIS to

Questions

3.15 Explain the two meanings of the term *management information system*. Which meaning is used in this chapter?

3.16 Explain each of the elements in Figure 3-9.

3.17 What is an exception report?

3.18 Explain how a manager might use the reports shown in Figure 3-12.

Figure 3-12

Labor effectiveness MIS reports

Hourly Payroll Summary
Week of April 23, 1990

Total hourly payroll	$21,680
Average paycheck	$2,710
Total vacation days	5
Average vacation days	0.625
Total sick days	8
Average sick days	1

a. Summary report

Hourly Payroll Statistics
by Department

Dept	Tot-pay	Avg-pay	Tot-vac	Avg-vac	Tot-sick	Avg-sick
Acct	$3,558	$1,779	0	0	2	1
Marketing	$12,232	$3,058	4	1	6	1.5
Sales	$5,890	$2,945	1	0.5	0	0

Hourly Payroll Statistics
by Job Code

Job-code	Avg-pay	Avg-vac	Avg-sick
1010	$2,293	1.00	1.67
2070	$3,073	1.00	1.50
2100	$2,885	1.00	0.00

Hourly Payroll Statistics
by Project

Project#	Tot-pay	Avg-pay	Avg-vac	Avg-sick
P1200	$13,495	$2,699	0.60	0.60
P2000	$8,185	$2,728	0.67	1.67

b. Payroll statistics by department, job code, and project

Hourly Payroll
Project Labor Dollars: Budget vs. Actual
Week of April 23, 1990

	Project P1200	Project P2000	Total
Week			
Budget	$12,000	$9,000	$21,000
Actual	$13,495	$8,185	$21,680
Month			
Budget	$48,000	$36,000	$84,000
Actual	$55,987	$33,787	$89,774
Year			
Budget	$107,800	$36,000	$143,800
Actual	$127,800	$33,787	$161,587

c. Labor costs: budget vs. actual

prepare the reports shown in Figure 3-12. These reports are then sent to management. In this case, the system's user is the financial analyst; the clientele are the managers who receive the report.

Decision Support Systems (DSSs)

Decision support systems are interactive (on-line) computer-based facilities for assisting human decision making. DSSs differ from TPSs and MISs in that they support the solution of problems that are less structured than those of an MIS or TPS. In fact, DSSs in many ways are not formalized, closed systems, but rather are a set of facilities for helping people make decisions. Further, unlike TPSs and MISs, DSSs do not always support an ongoing process. Often, DSSs are created to solve particular problems on an ad hoc processing basis. Unlike MISs, which are regular and recurring, the need for a DSS can be irregular.

Consider the need for a DSS in the ticket reservation setting. As stated earlier, TPSs are used to support operations; MISs are used to facilitate the management of operations. A DSS could be used to study unique, unstructured, possibly one-of-a-kind problems or opportunities.

For example, suppose a strike by the musicians' union forces the cancellation of opera performances. The management of the opera association wants to know the impact on revenue of each performance cancellation. A DSS could be used to process the ticket agencies' data to produce this information.

Actually, the term *decision support facility* would be more accurate than *decision support system*. A DSS is not a structured, finished system as a TPS or MIS is. Rather, a DSS is a collection of data and data processing tools used to creatively manipulate data to answer unknown and often unexpected questions. Also, the users of a DSS often do not have the assistance of professional information systems personnel. Instead, they employ the tools on their own.

Like MISs, DSSs involve models of business activity. Unlike an MIS, however, DSS models often are quite complex. They also are dynamic. The DSS user frequently changes the models to adapt them to changing understandings and needs. For example, the ticket agency may have a series of equations that predicts ticket sales on the basis of type of performance, day of the week, time of year, and so forth. As the musicians' strike progresses, the DSS users may add to or otherwise modify these equations to produce information that is important for negotiating a resolution to the strike. These models become part of the DSS stored data.

Architecture of a DSS

Figure 3-13 shows the architecture of a DSS. Data from the organization's TPS and MIS applications is input to the DSS programs along with data from external sources, such as independent data utilities. As stated, the DSS may store and later reprocess its own model data as

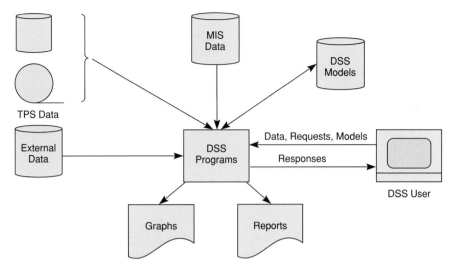

Figure 3-13
Architecture of a generic DSS
application

well. The user interacts with the DSS on-line, making requests, creating or adjusting models, manipulating data, and so forth. DSS program output can be text, structured reports, or graphics.

A variety of programs support the DSS, including spreadsheet programs, personal DBMSs, word processing packages, graphics generators, statistical packages, and other, special-purpose programs. (You will learn more about such programs in Part Two. For now, just be aware that a typical DSS includes many different types of programs.)

Types of Decision Support Systems

There are a number of different types of decision support systems. They all provide support for decision making in unstructured environments, but they differ in the way that they do it. We will consider four different types in this section.

Financial and Other Modeling Applications   Probably the most common type of decision support system involves use of **financial models** and other types of business models. The applications most frequently involve the use of electronic spreadsheets. In these applications, TPS, MIS, and external data is input to spreadsheet models. Such models are composed of a series of equations that relate outputs to values of input data.

For example, one company has a model containing equations that predict sales based on the number of salespeople, the dollars spent on advertising, and the size of the market. These equations were developed by analyzing TPS data from past periods. Using the equations, the decision makers vary the inputs (number of salespeople, dollars spent on advertising, assumed size of market) and obtain different sales projections. Figure 3-14 shows several examples. Such an analysis is sometimes called a *what-if* analysis because it shows what is expected to occur if different courses of action are taken.

Figure 3-14
Results from what-if analysis

Number of Sales-people	Advertising Budget (millions of $)	Assumed Market Size	Projected Sales (millions of $)
50	1.3	100,000	22
50	1.7	100,000	27
75	1.7	200,000	35
75	2.0	200,000	38
100	2.0	300,000	41
100	2.5	300,000	49

Observe that the DSS does not make any decisions. People use DSSs to approximate results for different assumed conditions. Then the people make decisions based on those results.

Database Query Applications   Another type of DSS, the **database query application,** involves the ad hoc querying of databases. These databases may contain TPS data, MIS data, external data, or some combination thereof. The decision maker processes the data using a *query language*. Although there are a number of different query languages, the American National Standards Institute has established a language known as *SQL*, or *structured query language*, as a national standard.

Consider an example. Suppose a quality control analyst is attempting to determine the cause of a large number of rejected products. Assume the analyst is able to obtain the following two tables of data from manufacturing transaction processing systems:

PROD-QUAL (Product#, Batch#, Inspector, Reject%)
BATCH-PROD (Batch#, Date, Plant-location)

Example data for these two tables is shown in Figure 3-15. The analyst is uncertain about the cause of the high number of rejects. First she wonders if it might be due to an overzealous inspector. Consequently, she queries the PROD-QUAL table to see if there are substantial differences in reject percentages among inspectors. Using SQL, the analyst would issue the following instruction to the program that processes the database (called the DBMS, or database management system):

SELECT Inspector, AVG(Reject%)
FROM PROD-QUAL
GROUP BY Inspector

The particular form and syntax of this statement is unimportant at this point. You should just understand the general format of a query command.

The result of this query is shown in Figure 3-16*a*. The analyst examines this result and decides that there do not appear to be significant

PROD-QUAL Table

Product #	Batch #	Inspector	Reject %
100	1000	Jones	2.30
101	1500	Jones	15.70
102	2000	Parks	3.05
104	1500	Smith	15.00
105	1500	Parks	17.50
106	1000	Parks	3.40
107	2000	Smith	2.20
108	1700	Jones	12.40

BATCH-PROD Table

Batch #	Date	Plant-location
1500	04/23/90	Bldg A
1000	04/23/90	Bldg B
1700	04/23/90	Bldg A
2000	04/25/90	Bldg B

Figure 3-15
Example quality control data

differences among inspectors. Next, she considers the possibility that there was a problem with one or more production batches. To study that, she issues another, similar query command that produces the data shown in Figure 3-16b.

Examining this data, the analyst decides that there are significant differences among the batches. Some of the batches seem to have much higher reject percentages than others. She now decides to determine when and where the batches with the highest reject rates were produced. She issues a query on data in both of the tables and obtains the results shown in Figure 3-16c. At this point, the analyst has determined that batches produced at a particular plant (building A) on a particular day (4/23/90) have been the source of most of the problem.

Here again, the DSS has played a supporting role in identifying the source of a problem. The DSS did not solve the problem, but it provided a facility to identify the source of the problem.

Expert Systems   A third type of decision support system is **expert systems**. An expert system is a computer-based system in which knowledge about some problem domain is represented in data and is processed systematically so as to make a diagnosis, make a recommendation, create a design, or produce some similar output. Figure 3-17 lists the kinds of activities that are addressed by expert systems.

The term *expert system* may be misleading. The development of systems that provide the capabilities of a true human expert has proven to be difficult and expensive. Thus, most of the expert systems that you will encounter in business are less ambitious in scope; they possess expertise in a limited problem domain. Examples are the expertise to process an insurance claim or the expertise to troubleshoot problems in the installation of computer software.

Figure 3-16
Results from database query

Inspector	Average Reject %
Jones	10.13
Smith	8.60
Parks	7.98

a. Average reject percentage by inspector

Batch #	Average Reject %
1000	2.85
1500	16.07
1700	12.40
2000	2.63

b. Average reject percentage by batch number

Batch #	Date	Plant-location	Reject %
1000	4/23/90	Bldg B	2.85
1500	4/23/90	Bldg A	16.07
1700	4/23/90	Bldg A	12.40
2000	4/25/90	Bldg B	2.63

c. Batch date and location reject percentages

Questions

3.19 Define *decision support systems*.

3.20 In what two ways do DSSs differ from MISs and TPSs?

3.21 Why would the term *decision support facility* be more appropriate than *decision support system*?

Consider an illustration. A steel manufacturer developed an expert system to diagnose potential causes of imperfections in molten steel. In the production of high-quality steel, materials must be carefully blended at certain temperatures for specific periods of time. Sometimes the process goes awry. Often when this occurs, the batch can be saved if the appropriate corrective action is taken at the appropriate time. This company developed an expert system in which production workers enter into the system parameters that describe the problem and the expert system identifies possible causes and suggests courses of action. You will learn more about expert systems in Chapter 11.

Figure 3-17
Types of problems addressed by
expert systems

- Procedures

- Diagnoses

- Monitoring

- Configuration and design

- Scheduling and planning

Group Decision Support Systems   A fourth type of DSS is **group decision support systems** or **GDSSs.** Initially DSSs were seen as tools for individual decision makers or analysts. The notion was that the results from an individual's DSS session or sessions would be printed, graphed, or otherwise documented. Those results either would be used by the individual or would be taken to a meeting in which the results would be discussed.

Recent work in DSS, however, has expanded DSS applications into the group decision environment. Here, members of the group employ the DSS together. They communicate with the DSS or with other members of the group via their computers. If the group meets in the same physical location, they share a public screen for input and output. If they are geographically dispersed, their computers are connected via communications lines. From their computers they each have access to the shared screen and to DSS data and programs.

The intention of GDSS applications is to allow people to process, produce, and interpret information together, as a group. Members can observe the group proceedings while processing information on their own. They can create information privately while the group process is under way and examine their results. If they desire, they can move private data to public files and displays, and so forth. In a sense, a GDSS is a computer-augmented meeting.

As stated, decision support systems are interactive computer-based facilities for assisting human decision making. As these examples have shown, a wide variety of systems fall in this category. Common to all of these applications is that they address unstructured problem domains, and that they facilitate solutions but do not actually solve.

3.22   Explain each of the elements in Figure 3-13.

3.23   Describe the nature of a financial modeling DSS. Briefly describe an application for such a system.

3.24   Describe the nature of a database query DSS. Briefly describe an application for such a system.

3.25   What is SQL?

3.26   Describe the nature of an expert system. Briefly describe an application for such a system.

3.27   Describe the nature of a group decision support system. Briefly describe an application for such a system.

Office Automation Systems (OASs)

The fourth category of information system we will discuss is office automation systems (OASs). OASs are information systems that create, store, modify, display, and communicate business correspondence, whether in written, verbal, or video form.

The prevalence of microcomputers in the office, along with a veritable explosion in communications, computer, and storage products, are causing fundamental changes in the ways that offices conduct their business. At first, computer systems were used just for **stand-alone word processing**, that is, the creation, editing, storing, and printing of documents on separate, unconnected computers. Over time, however, computers were connected to one another, and could not only share word processing files, but also send messages to one another.

With these developments, **electronic mail (E-mail)** systems were created, in which office personnel generate and send messages to one another. Also, since a company's office workers could all access the same files, they began to create **electronic bulletin boards**. These are computer files in which people can leave public messages. All of these capabilities became even more exciting as high-quality graphics printers became affordable, so that most people could utilize illustrations and graphics as well as text. Additionally, **facsimile machines** were improved and reduced in cost, so that documents with text, illustrations, and graphics, could be communicated inexpensively over telephone lines.

In parallel with these developments, computer technology was used to improve office voice systems. Office telephones were connected to more sophisticated **private branch exchange (PBX)** systems. (You will learn about this technology in Chapter 9. For now, think of a PBX as a computer-based switchboard.) Such systems allow workers to have *voice mailboxes* in which they can leave voice messages for one another.

Finally, video systems also were developed. Large organizations developed **video conferencing** capabilities so that people could communicate face-to-face without traveling. At first, such capabilities were used to connect a few executives in two or three locations. Recently, however, such systems have been used to connect thousands of people to the same presentation. IBM, for example, has connected over 100,000 people in a video conference to announce new products.

OASs and New Human Capacities

Doug Englebart, one of the pioneers in OAS, states that the real power of OAS will not be realized by improving the productivity of existing office work. Rather, he believes the greatest benefit will be to enable people to think, communicate, and work together in new ways. OAS has the potential to change the way people view, conceptualize, and solve problems.

Hypertext systems are an example. With such systems, text, illustrations, graphics, data, and programs (and, in the long run, even audio and video segments) are integrated into an electronic document. Users can read such a document sequentially or at random, just as books can be read. Users also can follow many different preestablished paths, or *threads*, through the document, or they can establish their own paths. Thus, for example, multiple threads could be created for reading a repair manual. Each thread would be used for a different purpose; one might be used to make a particular repair, while another would be used to learn a given skill.

Hypertext versions of encyclopedias and dictionaries also are being created. With these, the *see also* references are replaced by links to the actual text. Thus, if a reader wants to follow the see-also link, he or she just touches a key and the material is immediately presented. Paging through multiple volumes no longer is necessary.

Architecture of an OAS

Figure 3-18 shows the general architecture of an office automation system. Not every system has all of these components. In fact, most systems today have only the computer and telephone components, with segregated copying machines. The other components presently are rare.

Unfortunately, there are today two important limitations in the development and use of OASs. First, much of the required equipment has been developed by different vendors, working independently and using different standards. Because of this, machines often cannot communicate with one another. For example, it is difficult to connect computers to copying machines.

Part of the problem is technology, and part is the fact that vendors sometimes have a negative incentive to connect to each other's equipment. IBM and AT&T, for example, are competitors. Neither company wants to operate on a common standard, for fear that its equipment would be readily replaceable by the other company's equipment.

The upshot of this situation is that today OASs are divided into islands of capability: an island of computers linked together, an island of copying equipment, an island of telephones, and an island of video-conferencing capabilities. Over time, these islands undoubtedly will be integrated as customers demand standardization and connectivity.

Questions

3.28 Define *office automation systems*.

3.29 List three different types of OAS.

3.30 Explain why some people think that OAS will lead to new human capabilities.

3.31 Explain each of the elements in Figure 3-18.

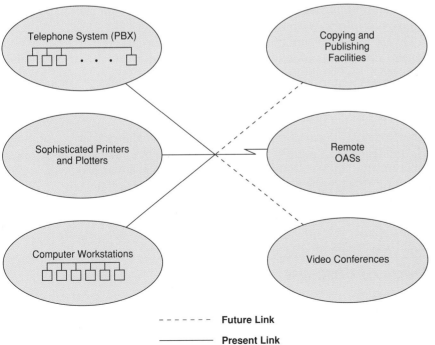

Figure 3-18
Architecture of a generic OAS application

Telephone System (PBX)

Copying and Publishing Facilities

Sophisticated Printers and Plotters

Remote OASs

Computer Workstations

Video Conferences

- - - - - Future Link

——— Present Link

The second limitation concerns storage. Nontext data such as graphs and illustrations requires substantially more storage than does text data. Voice and video data require even more. Consequently, with today's technology it is not possible to store large volumes of typical office documents in electronic form. Optical disk storage (see Chapter 2—if you had a hypertext version of this textbook, you could touch a key and the discussion about optical disks would appear, right here and now) may provide a solution. Certainly some solution may be expected to appear during your career.

Executive Support Systems (ESSs)

The fifth and last category of information systems is executive support systems (ESSs). ESSs are information systems that support the information needs of very senior executives. They summarize and present data at the highest levels of aggregation. Usually, they produce reports in standard formats, and often they involve graphics.

Because ESSs support very senior executives, these systems incorporate very high-quality user interfaces. Often, the most expensive color monitors with the highest resolution and clarity are used, as are the best plotters and cameras.

ESSs are the newest of the five categories. To date, they have had less acceptance than the other types. One reason for this is that most executives started their careers prior to the widespread use of computer-based information systems. They did not study information systems in college, and they are reluctant users. Many, in fact, still consider using a keyboard to be secretarial work. Furthermore, most executives have a staff of assistants who can produce written reports to meet the executive's information needs.

This situation is changing, and, during your career, computer-experienced business professionals will rise to senior executive positions. They most likely will be more open to, and even expect, support from computer-based systems.

Figure 3-19 shows the generic architecture of an ESS application. The ESS accepts data from all the other types of information systems. Also it accepts inputs from those who support the executive, such as administrative assistants. As you can see, the primary goal of an ESS is to obtain data from a variety of sources, integrate and aggregate the data, and display the resulting information in an easy-to-use, comprehensible format.

Questions

3.32 Define *executive support systems*.

3.33 Explain each of the elements in Figure 3-19.

Information Systems in the Functional Areas of Business

In prior sections of this chapter we considered the different types of information systems and addressed the nature and character of those types. That is one way to classify information systems.

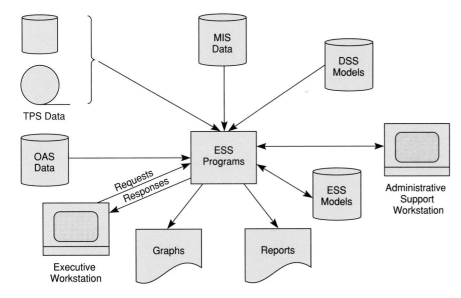

Figure 3-19
Architecture of a generic ESS application

Another way of looking at them is to consider their use in the functional areas of business. In this section we will consider the use of information systems in accounting, finance, sales and marketing, and manufacturing.

Information Systems in Accounting

A wide variety of information systems are used in accounting. Most of these systems support day-to-day operations and thus are transaction processing systems. In addition, however, many such systems also produce MIS reports from the TPS data that they generate and process.

We already have studied one type of accounting system, hourly payroll. In addition, there are systems that process salaried and executive payrolls. **Billing systems** generate bills or statements to customers. Figure 3-20 shows an example of a billing statement. **Accounts receivable systems** keep track of debts owed to the company. Reports generated by this system are used for bill collection, for checking customer credit when processing orders, and for monitoring potential bad debts. Figure 3-21 shows a sample accounts receivable report.

Accounts payable systems produce checks to pay the organization's bills. Since accounts payable systems generate checks, they usually have the same controls and phased processing as payroll systems. A common accounts payable problem concerns discounts. Suppliers often offer price reductions if payment is made within a certain time period. The company may or may not want to take the discount, depending on its available cash, the amount of the debt, and the size of the discount. Some accounts payable systems use these factors to determine the best time to pay debts.

General ledger systems maintain the company accounts. They perform bookkeeping for the company. Balance sheets and income state-

```
                        CONSOLIDATED INDUSTRIES

                      STATEMENT OF ACCOUNT WITH

TAYLOR CONSTRUCTION PRODUCTS                           DECEMBER 3, 1990

INVOICE            SHIPMENT DATE        DESCRIPTION             COST

11046              10/22/90             ALUMINUM SIDING       $1148.12
11982              11/05/90             FASTENERS                37.15
12257              11/20/90             ROOFING MATERIALS      3894.84

TOTAL DUE                                                    $5080.11
```

Figure 3-20
Billing statement

ments usually are produced, as well as other types of reports. (Figure 3-22 shows an example of a balance statement.)

Inventory accounting systems maintain records of the amounts of finished goods or raw materials added to or taken from stock. Information systems often are used for inventory accounting because some accounting techniques (such as last in, first out, or LIFO) have sizable tax advantages but are complex. Without a computer-based system, many companies cannot cope with the computational requirements of the more sophisticated accounting techniques.

Information Systems in Finance

Finance, the science of managing funds, provides management control over the financial resources of an organization. Finance is primarily concerned with the acquisition and use of cash and other assets. Since management control is the purpose of MIS applications, it is not surprising that information systems used in finance tend to have more the character of MIS applications than the character of TPS applications. Additionally, DSS applications are used for unstructured decisions and problems.

Financial calculations tend to be more complex than those involved in typical accounting or other TPS applications. If you have taken a finance course, you know that the calculations for determining the rate of return on an investment, or those for computing the present value of a stream of expenditures and receipts, can be complicated. These calculations are commonly done by computer programs.

Further, in finance, alternatives to be evaluated often involve complex interactions among variables. For example, suppose a financial analyst estimates earnings of $30,000 for a $300,000 machine. The analyst might want to know what the impact will be on the earning potential of the machine if sales go up by, say, 20 percent. If sales go up that much, the machine will be used more. If the machine is used more, expenses will go up, maintenance will increase, and the amount of time

CONSOLIDATED INDUSTRIES

AGED ACCOUNTS RECEIVABLE   DECEMBER 3, 1990

CUSTOMER NUMBER	CUSTOMER NAME	CURRENT BALANCE	BALANCE OVER 30 DAYS LATE	BALANCE OVER 60 DAYS LATE	TOTAL BALANCE
37842	TAYLOR CONST.	$5080.11	$ 0.00	$ 0.00	$5080.11
39148	ABC SUPPLIES	0.00	438.10	300.14	738.24
40418	SHAKEWELL INC.	127.13	541.27	1384.17	2052.57
41183	ZAVASKY INC.	2312.47	0.00	0.00	2312.47
44817	ABLE ENTERPRISE	1497.12	348.97	0.00	1846.09

Figure 3-21
Accounts receivable report

the machine is available for use will decrease. If the availability of the machine decreases, a backlog will develop, orders may be lost, and so forth. Electronic spreadsheet programs can easily perform the calculations involved in situations like this.

Using spreadsheets is particularly helpful because financial analyses often involve what-if questions. Recalculating is frequently necessary to determine the effects of changing certain variables. For example, the financial analyst in the previous example might also want to know the outcome of the machine investment if sales decrease by 5 percent, increase by 10 percent, or increase by 15 percent. With an electronic spreadsheet, the analyst may need to change only one or two input values and instruct the spreadsheet program to recalculate the results. When done by hand, such recalculations would require almost as much time as the original calculations. Because of the time saved, many more possibilities can be examined.

There are a number of different applications for computer-based systems in finance. **Capital expenditure analysis** is done to determine whether large, complex, or expensive investments are worthwhile. Examples are analyzing costs and benefits for building a new manufacturing plant, introducing a new line of products, or adding a new division to a corporation.

Financial planning is another application. The purpose of financial planning is to project revenue and expenses over some future time period. **Cash planning** is a similar application. Usually money must be spent on a project for some time before revenue is generated. The situation can lead to a cash shortage—the long-run financial situation is good, but bills can't be paid in the short run. Cash planning applications identify these situations before they occur and allow management to find supplementary sources of cash as needed. Similarly, cash planning can identify when cash will not be needed, so that it can be invested in longer-term, better-paying investments.

Another application is **financial contingency planning**. Here, the financial situation of the organization is projected assuming some con-

```
                    FRONTIER IRONWORKS

              BALANCE STATEMENT          DECEMBER 31, 1990
             (THOUSANDS OF DOLLARS)

         ASSETS                              LIABILITIES


  CASH                    $   127     ACCOUNTS PAYABLE       $   197
  ACCOUNTS RECEIVABLE         583     ACCRUED EXPENSES
  INVENTORY                   317        EMPLOYEE BENEFITS       349
  PREPAID EXPENSES             53        OTHER                    23
  MACHINERY                 1,483     PREFERRED STOCK          987
  FURNITURE AND FIXTURES      275     COMMON STOCK           2,384
  LAND AND BUILDINGS        1,788     RETAINED EARNINGS         686


  TOTAL ASSETS            $4,626      TOTAL LIABILITIES      $4,626
```

Figure 3-22
Balance statement

tingency occurs. Examples are the acquisition of other companies, the divesture of certain divisions, the raising of capital through the sale of stocks and bonds, and so forth. As stated, any of these applications can be supported by either MIS or DSS systems.

Information Systems in Sales and Marketing

Sales and marketing are two closely related fields that involve the generation of revenue through the sale of goods and services. People who work in these departments have widely varying responsibilities that include planning, management, and operations. TPS, MIS, DSS, and OAS applications all support sales and marketing activities.

The primary function of sales is to identify potential customers, to present products and services to them, to generate sales, and to provide customer support. Since most of these activities involve day-to-day operations, sales is supported principally with TPS applications.

However, the sales force does need to be managed. Sales territories must be defined, quotas established, sales performance monitored, and corrective action taken when necessary. For these sales functions, MIS and DSS applications are used more frequently than TPS applications are.

The function of marketing is to manage products from "cradle to grave." This includes determining the need for the product, developing product specifications, working with engineering to build the product, creating demand for the product through promotional activities, establishing product pricing, developing product sales plans, and, finally, at the end of the product's life, managing the withdrawal of the product from the market. Since most of these activities involve unstructured decision making, DSS applications are the most common. MIS applications are also used.

Sales and marketing can use OAS applications to coordinate their activities. This is especially important during the product planning and rollout phases.

Considering specific systems, the most common sales systems are concerned with **order entry** and **order processing**. These systems, which are transaction processing systems, receive order requests, check inventory levels, prepare picking slips for use in the warehouse, generate shipping lists, and create invoices. Often they interface directly with accounts receivable, purchasing, and manufacturing systems.

The TPS data from these systems can be used to generate MIS reports for sales management activities. For example, salespeople use **customer profile reports** (Figure 3-23) to identify sales opportunities and to plan sales calls. **Salesperson performance reports** (Figure 3-24) show the sales of products by each salesperson. These reports help salespeople and their managers analyze sales effectiveness in selling different products. Salesperson performance reports also can show commissions and bonuses earned. Sometimes they compare current sales to performance in prior periods.

Customer support systems allow personnel to verify and check the status of orders and to provide other information to customers. Sometimes customer support systems are combined with order processing systems.

The most common marketing systems are those that track product sales performance and compare it to the product plan. These are often

Figure 3-23
Customer profile report

```
                         CUSTOMER PROFILES

                         SOUTHWEST REGION

                      PERIOD ENDING MARCH 1990

          CUSTOMER                  PRODUCT                 PURCHASES
 NAME               NUMBER    NAME               NUMBER    UNITS      AMOUNT

 ACE BILLIARD       10043     DISPLAY CASE       P1040       4       $1287.50
                             EXECUTIVE DESK     Q3877       1       $1150.99

 AJ ARCHITECT       70089     DRAWING TABLES     J8897      12       $4588.85
                             72-INCH TABLES     J9789       4       $1768.04
                             SECRETARY DESK     Q0446       4       $1238.79
                             EXECUTIVE DESK     Q3877       3       $3452.97

 DR. PAUL A AZURE   33879     EXECUTIVE DESK     Q3877       1       $1150.99

                                    •
                                    •
                                    •
```

```
                    SALES AGENT EFFECTIVENESS REPORT

                        FALL QUARTER, 1990

   SALES AGENT              PRODUCT                      SALES
   NAME              NAME            NUMBER       UNITS     AMOUNT

   MARY PITTS        ZANSEN BOOTS    14327         319     $47,340
                     JET IV SKIS     36575         412      38,415
                     LAMBRETH POLES  55478         127       1,270


   LENNY PORTZ       ZANSEN BOOTS    14327         450      66,780
                     NORDIC BOOTS    13788         139      27,845
                     JET IV SKIS     36575           7         653
                     K-3 SKIS        37782         539      73,422

                                              .
                                              .
                                              .
```

Figure 3-24
Sales agent effectiveness report

MIS applications based on order entry TPS data. Other marketing systems are used to manage marketing projects (advertising, public relations, product rollouts), to analyze market data, and to track product quality and service.

In summary, sales and marketing activities are supported by TPS, MIS, DSS, and OAS applications. TPS applications directly support the sales function. MIS applications support both sales management and marketing management. DSSs are used primarily by marketing. OASs are used by both sales and marketing to coordinate their activities.

Information Systems in Manufacturing

Manufacturing is a broad and complicated subject. Some companies make toothpicks, some build office buildings, some build computers, and some build airplane engines. Obviously, the process used to manufacture toothpicks differs substantially from that of building computers, which differs substantially again from building jet engines. Further, there are many different activities involved in each type of manufacturing, including inventory management, facility scheduling, labor management, robotics and factory automation, quality control, and other subjects.

The complex task of manufacturing is composed of four distinct activities. The first is *engineering*. The design of new parts or new machines is an engineering responsibility, as is the incorporation of new materials or new technology into existing products. Engineering is a creative endeavor that involves many what-if type questions.

The second major activity is *procurement*. Manufacturing personnel must order sufficient raw materials to produce the desired quantity of finished goods. The task may seem simple, but consider the great variety and vast number of components needed to produce a television set, a computer, or an automobile. Often the lead time for ordering raw materials is long—six months or more. Manufacturing must determine its needs at least that far in advance so that the raw materials will be available when needed.

The third activity is *production scheduling*. Manufacturing personnel want to schedule the use of their facilities to maximize productivity while meeting the needs for finished products. Work should be scheduled and routed through the manufacturing process in a way that prevents bottlenecks. Also, machine setup time should be minimized. Suppose it takes 10 minutes to set up a saw to cut table legs and 15 minutes to set up the saw to cut table tops. If five tables are to be produced, it makes sense to cut all the legs and then all the tops. Otherwise, if the saw first cuts the legs for one table, then the top, then cuts the legs for the next table, then the top, and so forth, much time will be wasted changing the saw setup. In this simple example, the proper course of action is clear; in a more complicated and realistic situation, it often is not easy to know how work should be scheduled.

The fourth and perhaps most familiar manufacturing activity is *fabrication*. Fabrication means making components and assembling them into finished products. Quality control is considered part of the fabrication task.

Computer systems are used to support all four of these activities. Some systems, particularly those supporting procurement and fabrication, are TPS in nature. Others, especially those supporting scheduling, are more likely to be DSS and MIS in nature.

There are a number of important information systems that support manufacturing. **Material requirements planning (MRP)** is an information system that facilitates the purchasing of raw materials. With MRP, an overall production plan, called the master production schedule, is developed. This schedule concerns production for an extended period of time, perhaps six months to a year or more. It is input to MRP programs, along with descriptions of the materials needed to make products (an example of such a *bill of materials* is shown in Figure 3-25) and data about vendor lead times. The result is a schedule of raw materials purchases that will enable materials to be available when needed while reducing the cost of raw materials inventory.

Sometimes MRP is combined with an inventory management strategy called **just in time (JIT)**. With JIT, ideally, raw materials or components arrive at the production line just as they are needed. The manufacturer has a blanket purchase agreement with each vendor that details the prices and terms of materials purchases. As materials are needed, the manufacturer orders a certain number of items under the blanket purchase agreement.

MRP and JIT can be combined. In that case, the manufacturer makes its production schedule known to its vendors. Since each vendor knows when the various products will be produced, it can determine when the components that it supplies will be needed. Each vendor can then plan its own production schedule more effectively. In a sense, the combination of MRP and JIT reduces two inventory management problems

Questions

3.34 Describe the general nature of information systems in accounting.

3.35 List four different accounting information systems.

3.36 Describe the general nature of information systems in finance.

Figure 3-25
Bill of materials example

```
BILL OF MATERIALS FOR

HIKER BACKPACK

PRODUCT NUMBER 14356

MATERIAL                QUANTITY        DIMENSIONS (INCHES)

CLOTH TOP                  1                20x12
CLOTH SIDES                4                8x22
LEATHER BOTTOM             1                8x14
VELCRO HOOK TAPE           1                6x1/2
LEATHER TIEDOWN            3                3x2
WEB STRAPS                 2                2x35
PADDED BELT                1                3x40
THREAD                     1                400(FEET)
```

3.37 List four different information systems in finance.

3.38 Describe the general nature of information systems in sales.

3.39 List four different information systems in sales.

3.40 Describe the general nature of information systems in marketing.

3.41 List four different information systems in marketing.

3.42 Describe the general nature of information systems in manufacturing.

3.43 List four different information systems in manufacturing.

(finished goods at the vendor and raw materials at the manufacturer) into one (finished goods at the vendor). In this way, there is one stocking problem, not two.

Facility scheduling systems are another category of computer applications in manufacturing. Systems are used to help balance the use of machines and to minimize the amount of time wasted by machine setup or schedule conflicts. A specialty known as **operations research** uses mathematics to compute optimum solutions to such problems. Another category of applications is **process control**, in which computer systems control and operate machines. **Robotics** is an extension of process control systems. A robot is a programmable manipulator designed to move materials, parts, tools, or other devices in a predefined way. Robots are especially useful for performing boring and repetitive tasks and for working in uncomfortable or dangerous environments.

CAD/CAM, or **computer assisted design/computer assisted manufacturing** is another information system used in manufacturing. In CAD/CAM, designs from engineering are transformed by an information system into instructions for machines and robots. Thus, a design can be transformed from a drawing into commands directing a drill press to make certain holes in certain locations, or directing a saw to cut material in certain ways. Robots can be directed in a similar way.

Summary

This chapter introduced five fundamental types of information systems: transaction processing systems (TPS), management information systems (MIS), decision support systems (DSS), office automation systems (OAS), and executive support systems (ESS). The chapter concluded with a discussion of the role of information systems in the business functions of accounting, finance, sales and marketing, and manufacturing.

Transaction processing systems support day-to-day operations. They are the oldest type of information system. Two types of TPS are on-line systems and batch systems. Hourly payroll is an example of a transaction processing program.

The term *management information system* has two meanings. One is broad and refers to the general application of information systems in business. The second, and the one that is used in this chapter, is more narrow. It refers to information systems that produce structured, summarized reports on a regular and recurring basis. MISs, in this sense, support management control functions.

DSS is the third type of information system. DSSs are interactive, computer-based facilities that assist human decision making. DSSs address problems that are less structured than those addressed by TPS and MIS applications. The chapter described four types of DSS: financial and other modeling applications, database query applications, expert systems, and group decision support systems.

OASs are information systems that create, store, modify, display, and communicate business correspondence, whether in written, verbal, or video form. OAS includes word processing, electronic mail, video conferencing, hypertext, and other applications.

The fifth type of information system, ESS, consists of systems that support the information needs of senior executives. ESSs summarize and present data at the highest levels of aggregation, usually with high quality and sophisticated graphics and other displays.

Information systems used in accounting tend to be TPS in character, though MIS applications also are common. Typical systems include payroll, billing, accounts receivable, accounts payable, general ledger, and inventory accounting.

Finance is primarily concerned with the acquisition and use of an organization's capital resources. Information systems that support finance tend to be either MIS or DSS applications. Spreadsheet applications are common. Typical systems include those that address capital expenditure analysis, financial planning, cash planning, and financial contingency planning.

Sales and marketing activities involve the generation of revenue through the sale of goods and services. Information systems that support sales tend to be primarily TPS, though MIS are used to support sales management. Marketing systems tend to be DSS applications. Sales and marketing also use OAS applications to coordinate their activities.

Common systems in sales are order entry and order processing systems, and customer support systems. MIS reports, such as customer profiles and salesperson performance reports, often are produced from order entry TPS data. Information systems in marketing track product performance, facilitate the management of marketing projects, analyze market data, and track product quality and service.

Manufacturing is a complicated process that includes four major activities: engineering, procurement, manufacturing scheduling, and fabrication. Information systems used in manufacturing include material requirements planning (MRP), possibly with just-in-time (JIT) inventory management, facility scheduling, process control, robotics, and CAD/CAM.

Word List

transaction processing system (TPS)
management information system (MIS)
decision support system (DSS)
office automation system (OAS)
executive support system (ESS)
transaction
transaction processing program
on-line transaction processing
batch transaction processing
transaction file
old master file
new master file
hourly payroll
general ledger
phased processing
editing
edit report
master file change report
payroll register

management information system (two meanings)
exception report
financial model application
database query application
expert system
group decision support system (GDSS)
stand-alone word processing
electronic mail (E-mail)
electronic bulletin board
facsimile machine
private branch exchange (PBX)
video conferencing
hypertext
billing system
accounts receivable system
accounts payable system
general ledger system
inventory accounting system

capital expenditure analysis
financial planning
cash planning
financial contingency planning
order entry
order processing
customer profile report
salesperson performance report
customer support system
material requirements planning (MRP)
just-in-time (JIT) inventory management
facility scheduling system
operations research
process control
robotics
CAD/CAM (computer-assisted design/computer-assisted manufacturing)

Discussion Questions and Exercises

A. Suppose that you operate a small summer business that provides swimming instruction at three different pools. You have three instructors who work for you.
1. Describe a possible application for a TPS. What transactions would it process? What data would it maintain?
2. Describe an application for an MIS. What reports would be generated?
3. Describe an application for a DSS. What kinds of questions would the system help you answer? What facilities would the DSS need to have?
4. Describe an application for an OAS. What systems would the OAS include?

B. If you are interested in accounting:
1. What are the potential dangers of using computers for accounting purposes? What steps can be taken to reduce these dangers?
2. Interview one of your accounting professors and ask how computers have changed accounting. How do CPAs treat computer systems during an audit? Find out what SAS-3 is and why it is important to both information systems and accounting professionals.
C. If you are interested in finance:
1. Interview one of your finance professors or someone at your computer lab. Find out what types of computer programs are available for financial analysis and describe their functions.

2. A venture capitalist once remarked that spreadsheet programs can generate so many analyses so readily that far too many projections are included in most proposals. Consequently, he does not pay much attention to them. Comment on this situation. How would you deal with it if you were preparing a business proposal for a venture capitalist?

D. If you are interested in sales and marketing:

1. How are computer systems used to support direct mail marketing? How can such systems reduce the cost of direct mail while increasing its effectiveness?
2. Describe ways that you think a field salesperson could best take advantage of a personal computer.
3. Describe ways that you think a product manager could best take advantage of a personal computer.

E. If you are interested in manufacturing:

1. Define *MRP*. Do MRP systems require a computer? Why or why not? What do you suppose are the chief requirements for a computer in an MRP system?
2. Investigate just-in-time inventory policy. How can information systems facilitate the use of this policy? Explain the statement in the text that just-in-time transforms two inventory problems into one inventory problem.
3. Investigate the application of robotics in manufacturing. How many robots exist? Which industries are using them? What types of work do robots perform? Who are the major vendors? What posture have labor unions taken toward robots?

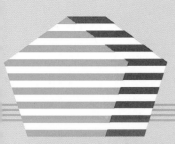

Personal Information Systems

Nowhere has the productivity power of the computer been more visible than in the use of personal computers. Large computer systems have always been expensive to buy, use, and maintain; their use by a single individual is almost never cost-effective. But during the 1980s the personal computer came into its own, and the way people do business was forever changed. The personal computer is cheap and small, and there is a growing pool of inexpensive software available. Personal computers are now standard business equipment in large and small companies alike.

In Part Two you will learn about personal information systems. Chapter 4 lays the groundwork. It builds on the five-component model you learned in Chapter 2, to define the unique characteristics of a personal information system. As a user, you probably will obtain a personal information system sometime soon—say within the next five years. The material in this chapter will prove useful when you undertake that task.

In Chapters 5 through 7 you will learn about three personal computer applications: electronic spreadsheets, personal databases, and word processing and desktop publishing programs. We describe what each of these applications is, why you would use it, and how to develop a system using it. Each chapter also includes case studies based on situations we have encountered in the business world.

Chapter 8 takes you through the steps you should follow in developing your own personal information system. We describe the five-stage system development process, and relate the stages to the five system components (hardware, programs, data, people, and procedures). Most importantly, we describe your role—as the system owner and primary user—in the system development process.

As you study the material in Part Two, think about how the productivity tools being presented could be used in your own academic or business situation. How could you use them? How might your employer use them? Also think about business situations in which a personal information system would *not* be appropriate. It is important for you to realize not only the power but also the limitations of personal information systems.

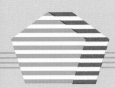

CHAPTER 4

An Introduction to Personal Information Systems

Personal information systems are business computer systems used by individuals to increase their productivity. In this chapter we will examine the need for personal information systems, the components of such systems, and—briefly—how to develop them. In the next three chapters we will study three applications—electronic spreadsheets, personal databases, and text processing—in some depth. Finally, we will look at a formal process for developing personal systems in Chapter 8.

Why Use a Personal Information System? To Increase Productivity

Increasing productivity seems to be one goal of most business people. But what does it mean to increase productivity? **Productivity** can be defined as the use of time and resources to get results. All three factors can be quantified. For example, a clerk might use 2 hours of time, an electric typewriter, 100 sheets of letterhead, and some correction fluid to produce 100 invitations to a store opening.

Increasing productivity means getting either more output or better results with the same amount of time and resources. For example, if the clerk figures out a way to produce 150 invitations in 2 hours then he's increased his productivity. Another way to describe an increase in productivity is to say you get the same results using less time or fewer resources. For example, the clerk might be able to produce 100 invitations in 30 minutes. Thus, increasing productivity means:

- Getting better (or more) results with the same time and resources, or
- Getting the same results with less time or fewer resources, or
- Getting better results with less time or fewer resources.

Questions

4.1 What is productivity?

4.2 How can productivity be increased?

To increase his productivity, the clerk might type faster, make fewer mistakes, or use a faster or more accurate technology, such as a personal word processing system. In the next several chapters you will see many applications in which personal information systems help individuals increase their personal productivity by enabling them to do more in less time.

What Are the Components of a Personal Information System?

Like any business computer system, a personal information system has five components: hardware, programs, data, people, and procedures. In this section we will discuss only those aspects of each component that pertain specifically to personal information systems. You can review other material about the five components in Chapter 2.

Hardware

A personal information system has at its center a **microcomputer** (also called a personal computer, or PC). A microcomputer incorporates all five types of hardware: input, processing, output, storage, and communications equipment. Many types of hardware were presented in Chapter 2 and in the Hardware photo essay. In this section we will highlight only certain input, processing, and storage equipment particular to microcomputers.

Input Hardware   A **mouse** is a device that controls the position of an on-screen pointer, usually on a microcomputer. When the computer user rolls the hand-held mouse device on a table surface, the pointer moves on the screen (see Figure 4-1). When it is properly located (for example, pointing to a symbol that means you want to erase a file), you push one of the two or three mouse buttons to activate that function. Such user interfaces are sometimes called **point-and-click interfaces.** They are simple to learn and to use. They usually incorporate graphical symbols—called **icons**—to represent functions. The pictures serve as mnemonics, so you do not need to memorize a lot of computer commands or terminology.

With the other type of user interface, called a **character-based interface,** you need to type commands on the keyboard. Thus, to erase a file you might need to type "DEL C:\MM\TAXES\F1991." With a character-based interface, you need to memorize commands and their formats. With a point-and-click interface, you just select the appropriate function from the list of options displayed on the screen.

Processing Hardware   A microcomputer consists of a **microprocessor,** various types of memory, and a pathway to connect the microprocessor with the memory and peripheral devices (printers, disks, a mouse, and so forth).

Figure 4-1
Point-and-click interface

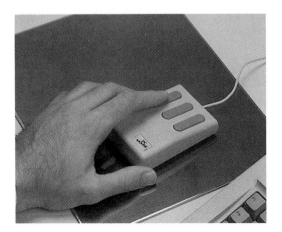

a. Mouse

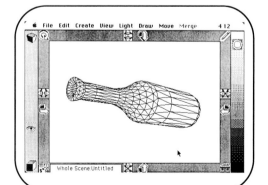

b. Pointing to an on-screen image

Figure 4-2
Popular microprocessors and the
computers that use them

Microprocessor	Computer
MOS Technology 6502	Commodore PET, Apple II
Zilog Z-80	Radio Shack TRS-80
Intel 8088	IBM (and IBM-compatible) PC
Intel 80286	IBM (and IBM-compatible) PC
Intel 80386	IBM PS/2
Intel 80486	IBM PS/2
Motorola 68000	Apple Macintosh

The Microprocessor   The microprocessor is the brain of the computer. It contains the arithmetic/logic unit (ALU), a clock to sequence events, and other components. The microprocessor is located on a chip (see the photo essay on chips), which itself is attached to one of the many circuit boards in the computer—this particular one is called the **mother board.**

Many different microprocessors have been invented since the mid-1970s. But two families of microprocessors dominate the market, those developed by Intel and by Motorola. A brief list of types of microprocessors can be seen in Figure 4-2.

Activities in a microprocessor are organized in terms of **cycles.** A cycle is a unit of time required for the various components of the microprocessor to complete a certain amount of work. Some operations take more cycles to complete than others. For instance, it might take 4 cycles to add two numbers together. But dividing two numbers involving fractions might require 8 or 10 cycles.

Microprocessor capacities are measured in terms of their speed (the number of cycles per second), and in terms of the amount of data that can be manipulated in the arithmetic/logic unit in one cycle. Processor speed is measured in millions of cycles per second (called **megahertz**). A slow microprocessor might perform at the rate of 1 million cycles per second, or 1 megahertz, while a fast one might process 20 megahertz. Note that the number of instructions per second is less than the number of cycles per second, because some instructions require more than one cycle. Instruction speed often is expressed in **MIPS,** or millions of instructions per second. When you purchase a computer, remember that megahertz and MIPS are not the same.

The amount of data manipulated by the ALU in one cycle is measured in bits. Some of the early microprocessors manipulated chunks of data 8 bits wide. More recent technology has resulted in processors that can handle data that is 16 or 32 bits wide. You can liken microprocessor capacity to a gardener shoveling dirt from a pile into a wheelbarrow. Suppose a cycle is the amount of time it takes to move one shovelful of dirt from the pile to the wheelbarrow and return the shovel to the pile. Speed refers to the number of cycles made in, say, one hour. Amount of data is like the width of the shovel. You can have an 8-inch, 16-inch, or 32-inch shovel. The wider the shovel, the more dirt can be moved at once. The gardener can increase throughput by shortening the cycle time (shoveling faster), increasing the amount of dirt moved at one time (getting a wider shovel), or both.

Microcomputer Memory   Main memory in a microcomputer is made up of two types, random access memory and read-only memory. **Random access memory (RAM)** is used for user-defined programs and data. When you load a new program into RAM you erase the one that was originally there, just like recording over a song on a cassette tape. The amount of RAM varies from computer to computer, ranging from about 500K to 16MB. When you purchase a microcomputer, you specify the amount of RAM you want, which depends on the programs you will be running: some programs require more memory than others.

In contrast to RAM, **read-only memory (ROM)** contains unalterable programs and data. Consequently, ROM is used by manufacturers to permanently store programs such as the operating system and the BASIC language translator. Programs stored on ROM chips are called **firmware.**

Attaching Peripheral Devices   The microprocessor contains instructions that activate the **peripheral devices,** that is, all of the input, storage, and output devices connected to the CPU. Consequently, those devices must be connected somehow to the microprocessor. This is accomplished by means of a device called a **channel.** The channel usually has built-in **ports** for connecting the keyboard, monitor, printer(s), and mouse. In addition, **expansion slots** also are attached to the channel. The purpose of an expansion slot is to accept optional add-on equipment, such as the hardware needed to drive a plotter, a disk drive, or a scanner.

Storage Hardware   Microcomputers use disk as their primary storage medium. All have at least one diskette drive (as described in Chapter 2); most have a hard disk installed as well. Some have a special removable mass-storage device. In this section we will discuss hard disks and removable mass-storage devices.

4.1   INCREASING YOUR PERSONAL PRODUCTIVITY

Did You Know?

The careless use and storage of your floppy disks can damage them. If this happens, data on the damaged disk is lost forever. You'll have to retype that term paper or ask friends for their telephone numbers again. By following a few simple procedures, you can minimize the chances of accidentally damaging your disks.

1. Always keep your disks in their paper jackets.
2. Always hold a disk by its label. Don't touch the oval access opening used by the disk drive.
3. Always use a felt-tip pen when writing on a disk label.
4. Always insert a disk into the disk drive gently and carefully.
5. Don't bend or fold disks.
6. Don't take a disk out of the disk drive when the red light is on.
7. Don't leave disks out in the sun, in a hot car, or in the cold.
8. Don't put disks on top of a working television, telephone, stereo, or any appliance which generates a magnetic field.

Figure 4-3
Winchester disk

Hard Disk   Hard disks for microcomputers are also called **Winchester disks** (see Figure 4-3). Like mainframe hard disks, they store data magnetically. Most often, a Winchester disk is built into the same chassis that holds the circuit boards, and therefore is not visible. Microcomputer hard disks, like their mainframe cousins, are made of several rigid disks attached to a central hub. All the disks rotate together, and special read/write heads record and read information on the disk. Winchester disk storage capacity varies; 10MB, 20MB, and 40MB disks are common.

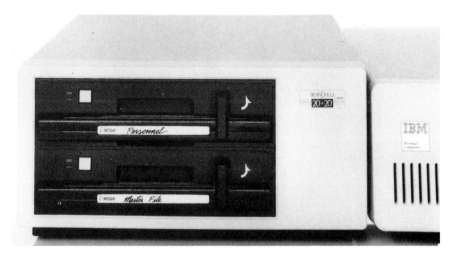

Figure 4-4
Bernoulli box—one PC mass-storage device

Whereas mainframe computers have both fixed and removable hard disks, microcomputer hard disks are fixed. Thus, information stored on microcomputer hard disk is accessible by anyone using the computer—a potential problem. The advantage of using hard disk rather than diskettes as the primary storage medium is that all of your stored data and programs are instantly available: you do not need to search file boxes for the correct diskette and put it in the disk drive. However, hard disks are more expensive than diskette drives.

Removable Mass-Storage Devices   A **removable mass-storage device** is a disk cartridge that combines the portability of floppy disks with the high storage capacity of hard disks (see Figure 4-4). The flexible disk inside the cartridge spins rapidly, and the device's aerodynamic design minimizes the possibility of **head crashes.** A head crash occurs in a disk device when a contaminant, such as dust or a fingerprint, lands on the disk surface and contacts the read/write head. The result is the equivalent of scratching a vinyl record: it renders the platter unusable, and can damage the recording device as well.

Programs

A wide spectrum of system programs and packaged application programs is available for microcomputer users. Of all programs, it is the operating system that gives your system its feel, its personality. The operating system dictates how you interact with the computer. When you select an operating system you should know what options are available, and what you can reasonably expect the software to do for you.

Operating Systems for Personal Computers   Most personal computers used for business applications are IBM-compatibles. This means they either are IBM personal computers or are manufactured by someone else but capable of running all the software that can be run on an IBM personal computer. Examples include Compaq, Leading Edge, AT&T,

Questions

4.3   What is a mouse?

4.4   Describe the difference between a point-and-click interface and a character-based interface.

4.5   What is a mother board?

4.6   Name and describe the two characteristics of a microprocessor used to measure its capacity.

4.7   Why does a microprocessor usually complete more cycles per second than instructions per second?

4.8   What does MIPS mean? Of what is it a measurement?

4.9   Describe two ways in which the processing capacity of a microprocessor can be increased.

4.10   What is the difference between ROM and RAM?

4.11   Is firmware stored on RAM or ROM? Why?

4.12   Describe the purpose of the following devices: channel, port, expansion slot.

4.13   What is a Winchester disk?

Figure 4-5
MS-DOS is a single-user, single-task operating system

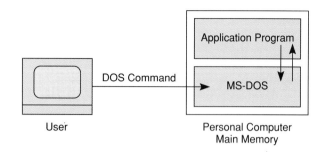

and some Tandy computers. Most IBM-compatible computers in use today run under an operating system called MS-DOS, developed by Microsoft. The same operating system, when licensed and marketed by IBM, is called PC-DOS. (*DOS* simply stands for *disk-based operating system*, meaning the operating system is stored on either hard disk or diskette.)

MS-DOS is a single-user, single-task operating system (see Figure 4-5). This means that it can support only one user at a time, running only one program at a time. MS-DOS can manage up to 640K of main memory. It employs a command-driven interface. A typical command might be:

COPY C:\MM\LETTERS\RESUME.DOC A:RESUME

It is not important for you to decipher or understand that command at this stage. The point is that to use MS-DOS, you would need to learn a cryptic language. It can be done, of course. After all, there are millions of MS-DOS users in this hemisphere.

To make communicating with DOS a little more palatable, you can obtain a program called a **shell.** A shell is loaded along with the operating system (see Figure 4-6). It serves as an interface between you and DOS by accepting your keyboard input and translating it into DOS commands. The value of shells lies in the fact that instead of waiting for you to type commands onto a blank screen, they display **menus,** that is, lists of available options from which you can choose a desired activity. Thus, a shell menu might offer these options:

File functions
Run program
Display disk directory
DOS

Figure 4-6
Using a shell with MS-DOS

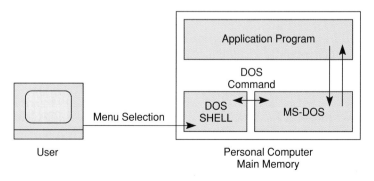

If you wanted to see the directory for the diskette in drive B, you would simply select the *Display disk directory* option, perhaps by typing "Di" or by pointing to it with your mouse and clicking (pushing a mouse button). Using a shell eliminates the need to memorize lengthy and cryptic DOS commands.

Although the use of shells makes DOS more user-friendly, the operating system itself is limited to running only one application program at a time—a problem for some users.

Developments on the Path to Multitasking   **Multitasking** means having two (or more) application programs in memory at one time. This requires RAM enough to hold all the programs, plus an operating system capable of supporting the flip-flop between (or among) them. Let's consider the evolution of personal multitasking systems.

For some people, loading and running one program at a time is satisfactory. But personal computer users often demand more than that. For example, it often is tedious to exit from one program in order to load the next one, even if you need only to peek at one word processor page or one spreadsheet before returning to the original program (reloading the first one also is time-consuming and tedious.) **Context switching** refers to early attempts to simulate multitasking on personal computer systems (see Figure 4-7). As long as there was enough RAM to hold at least two programs, the user was able to press a few keys

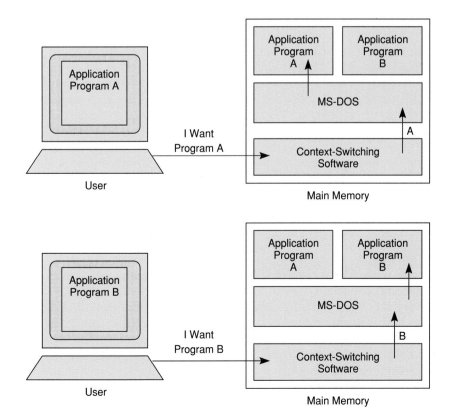

Figure 4-7
Context switching

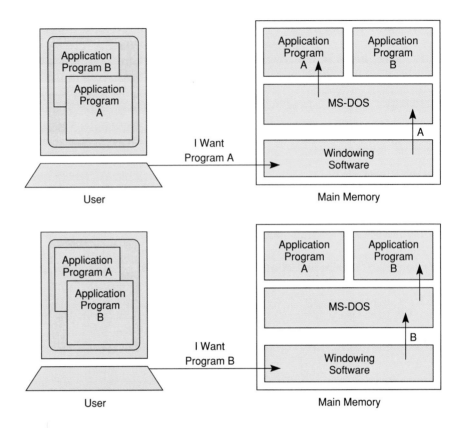

Figure 4-8
Use of windowing software with
MS-DOS

and switch between one program and another. The 640K memory limitation was somewhat overcome by memory enhancement techniques, such as expansion boards that contained additional RAM chips. Context switching was not, of course, multitasking, as only one application could run at a time. In fact, only one application appeared on the computer screen at a time. The convenience to the user came from not having to constantly unload and reload programs.

The next refinement on the way to multitasking is called **windowing.** Windowing allows the user to see several applications on the screen at the same time (see Figure 4-8). To understand how windowing works, imagine that you are working on a pile of papers at your desk, with notes on one sheet of paper, an outline on another sheet, and a chart on a third sheet. As you look at your desk, the paper on top—the one you're working on—is the only one completely visible. The other papers are only partly visible, if at all—you can see perhaps an edge or a corner of each page. The windowing environment replicates this situation on a personal computer.

On the computer screen, one window is in the **foreground.** This contains the program the user is currently running. Other windows, only partly visible, are in the **background.** They contain programs that are in a state of suspended animation. By pressing a few keys, the user can instantly bring any background program into the foreground and run it. When he does this, the program that was in the foreground becomes suspended. Programs such as Microsoft Windows make switching from one program to another very easy. They are loaded into RAM along with the operating system, and interface with it.

Multitasking Achieved   Eventually a microprocessor was developed which can execute instructions very quickly (millions of instructions per second) and can support vast amounts of RAM (millions of bytes versus the 640,000-byte limitation of the chip used in earlier CPUs). With this microprocessor came the ability to perform real multitasking on personal computers. By definition, multitasking means that several programs can be running at once. Remember that the windowing approach merely made switching from one program to another faster and easier—but only the foreground program could be running. With multitasking, background programs can run at the same time as the foreground program. The difference between background and foreground programs is that only the foreground program can receive input from the keyboard.

Although MS-DOS does not support multitasking, you can procure special programs that sit on top of DOS and bolster it with multitasking

4.2   INCREASING YOUR PERSONAL PRODUCTIVITY

How Computers Can Help You Solve Problems

As general-purpose tools suited to a variety of tasks, word processors, spreadsheets and data bases are fundamental. In simplest terms, word processors are for writing, spreadsheets are for manipulating numbers and data bases combine qualities of the two, arranging information made up of both words and numbers. Sometimes these tools are used as stand-alone programs; other times you'll find them as part of an integrated package.

For many businesses, accounting software can be just as basic. And then there are two common business tasks—personalizing form letters and tracking appointments—with two specialized software solutions: mailmerge programs and desk-top accessories.

Spreadsheets   Spreadsheet software can be the single most versatile tool for many businesses. It will take you from making appoint-

ments to bookkeeping and from tracking small inventories to financial projections. The ability to link various spreadsheets to exchange data makes accounting, for one, easier, because the "books" can then be constructed in modular form.

Personal Databases   One key feature to look for in a database manager is the ability to sort by date as well as by alphabetical order. The database manager should have a complete, built-in report function, which allows you to extract only the information you need from a mass of data. And "complete" means the ability to perform arithmetic calculations on your numeric data, such as totals or averages. That's useful in tracking inventories, printing invoices, and more.

Word Processors   Beyond its use for writing itself (letters, reports, etc.), a business-class word processor

should have a "macro" feature, sometimes called a "glossary." With this function, you make one or two keystrokes represent a large number of keystrokes (i.e., a paragraph or a complicated set of commands). Then, by pressing the key(s) you've coded for your macro, the program will automatically insert all the words or perform all the commands assigned to it.

For example, you could set up the letter "C" on a macro to insert a standard closing of a letter. Not only does this make it easy to insert pieces of standard text (often called "boilerplate") into your documents, it also allows you to automate many of the word processor's other functions (such as mailmerge or cataloging disks), a time- and memory-saver. Mailmerge capacities usually are built into sophisticated business word processors.

capabilities. Two examples are DESQview and Windows/386. Using these add-on programs means that users who have lots of programs written under DOS will be able to use them in the multitasking environment without making program changes.

Alternatively, you can purchase a personal computer operating system that fully supports multitasking, thus eliminating the need for add-on software like DESQview. For example, PC-MOS/386 is a multiuser, multitasking operating system that allows up to 25 simultaneous users. Programs written in DOS can be used with PC-MOS/386 without any difficulty. Even data stored on hard disk under DOS does not need to be converted. IBM has taken a different approach.

OS/2   **OS/2** is an operating system licensed by IBM for use with its PS/2 family of personal computers. These computers are based on a different microchip (the Intel 80286, 80386, and 80486 family) than the older DOS-based machines. As a result, PS/2s can execute instructions much faster than the IBM-PC-compatibles, and can address millions of bytes of main memory, way beyond the 640K restriction of DOS. Because of the speed of the PS/2 CPU and the design of OS/2, this operating system can support multitasking. Programs to be run in the multitasking environment must be written specially for this operating system. Although OS/2 will run programs written under DOS (an important marketing feature for IBM, which does not want to abandon MS-DOS users), it will run only one DOS program at a time.

The user can run invisible programs in the background while employing the entire screen for the foreground program, or can open up multiple windows on the screen with an OS/2 feature called the Presentation Manager. With multiple windows, the user can observe changes on the visible portions of each miniscreen. As in other multitasking systems, only the foreground window can receive keyboard input. Thus, programs running in the background that need the user to key in data or responses must wait until they are pulled into the foreground to get the input and continue executing.

UNIX   A version of the operating system **UNIX** also is available on personal computers. Because UNIX (and UNIX-based operating systems such as XENIX) was designed from the start to be a multiuser, multitasking operating system, it has more features and is generally more powerful than any of the DOS-based operating systems. A favorite among users of DEC computers, UNIX is only now beginning to make its way into the personal computer market in any substantial way. This has been made possible by the development of microprocessors that are faster and address much more memory, two UNIX requirements; and partly by the fact that DOS programs now can run as tasks under UNIX, so that users who have invested much money and effort in developing DOS applications are not necessarily faced with abandoning them and starting from scratch. However, the investment in a UNIX system is relatively high. Therefore, using UNIX only for multitasking is probably not cost-effective. However, using it for multiuser processing would make a lot of sense.

Operating System	Environment
MS-DOS (PC-DOS)	Single-user, single-task
OS/2	Single-user, multitask
Mac OS	Single-user, multitask
PC-MOS/386	Multiuser, multitask
UNIX (XENIX)	Multiuser, multitask

Figure 4-9
Some operating systems for personal computers

Mac OS   Although most personal business computers are IBMs or IBM-compatibles, one notable exception is the Apple Macintosh computer. The Macintosh is a highly respected computer that has established graphic user interfaces as standard. Its operating system, **Mac OS,** is capable of supporting multitasking, and it employs a point-and-click interface.

The Mac operating system is stored on ROM (read-only memory), and is purchased as part of the computer hardware package. By placing the operating system on ROM, Apple is able to free up almost all of the Mac's RAM for application programs.

Operating Systems—Summary   Operating systems for personal computers may support single-user, single-task; single-user, multitask; or multiuser applications (see Figure 4-9). They are available from many vendors, and usually are obtained at a computer retail store or through mail order. They range in price from about $150 to $1,000. In addition to operating systems, add-on software can be used to provide additional services, such as windows, that are not available from the operating system. This add-on software works with the operating system; it does not replace it. To find out about operating systems and related software, you should read magazines such as *Personal Computing, PC Today,* and *PC Magazine.*

Data

Miriam is a social worker. She followed all the system development steps, just as she had learned in her computer systems course. She determined her business needs, found the software that would help her do her work faster and better, got a good deal on a computer that would support the software, and took classes in word processing and database management at her local college. At the time, she couldn't wait to get her new system up and running. How easy it would soon be to compile case statistics, scan her case load looking for trends, compare actual to budgeted expenditures, write follow-up reports, and so forth. She had been so excited. So after two weeks why did she look so worn out? Why wasn't she gleefully churning out reports? The reason was simple: before she could use all that data, she needed to get it into her computer, then check it for accuracy. And that was taking a lot of time.

Questions

4.14   What does it mean to say that MS-DOS is a single-user, single-task operating system?

4.15   What is a shell?

4.16   Compare and contrast context switching and windowing.

4.17   Define foreground and background windows.

4.18   Under MS-DOS, which window(s) can contain active programs?

4.19   Under a multitasking operating system, which window(s) can contain active programs?

4.20   Is there any difference between the programs in the foreground and background windows under multitasking?

4.21   Where does one obtain a personal computer operating system?

4.3   *INCREASING YOUR PERSONAL PRODUCTIVITY*

Just What Is HyperCard?

HyperCard has been called everything from "an erector set of information" (creator Bill Atkinson) to "a French restaurant that can also clean your Peugeot" (Apple Product Development V.P. Jean-Louis Gassée).

Clearly, it's a little difficult to correctly assess the importance and impact of a product that can be viewed in such a variety of ways. Just what *is* HyperCard?

The Basics   The first step toward profiting from the possibilities that HyperCard offers is learning enough about the product to be able to examine those possibilities.

Basically, HyperCard is software that allows you to manipulate information in the form of text, graphics, video, voice, and animation, and to access large amounts of this information quickly and efficiently through the creation of logical linkages.

These broad capabilities suggest a number of possibilities for higher education. And these possibilities are made even more attractive by the software's ease of use, which can vastly reduce development time and costs.

The Possibilities   First, a HyperCard stack could be used in conjunction with a textbook as an interactive index. Such a product would allow students to move through the information freely, following their own trends of thought and making their own logical connections.

The second possibility is the opposite of the first; a HyperCard stack could present the main body of information, supplemented by a printed text.

Third, HyperCard can be used as an authoring tool to create courseware—that is, software for use in instruction. This courseware could range from the very simple—a conventional drill-and-practice program that mirrors the lessons in a text—to the very complex—a standalone simulation involving animation, video, or even a combination of visual technologies.

Fourth, the ability of HyperCard to be used in conjunction with CD-ROMs makes it possible to distribute massive amounts of information on a single compact disc, along with a HyperCard "front end" that makes all of this information readily accessible. Encyclopedias, atlases, and other large reference works are naturals for this approach.

Programs Without Programmers
One of the beauties of HyperCard is that it makes creating software possible for people who know little about conventional programming (though a technical background or some knowledge of design can be very helpful).

Managing Data   Gathering, entering, verifying, and protecting data requires both time and resources. Miriam had 500 clients, and she needed to get together data on all of them from file folders, reports, and so forth. Then she needed to type it into her computer via a database application—a time-consuming job. After she typed each client's data, she got a printout of it. It was absolutely essential that the data be correct. What if a client lost custody of a child because her computer data was incorrect? What if funding to a needy family was suddenly terminated because one of her computer reports showed too many zeros in an income field? And so, laboriously, she plodded through the printouts, hoping to catch most, if not all, of her mistakes.

Finally, because the data Miriam was using was confidential, she needed to lock her diskettes in a file cabinet each evening before she left the office. Data on diskette, she learned, is almost as easily read as printed reports, so it merited the same level of security as the clients' file folders.

Eventually, all the case data was entered. Soon Miriam was able to use the system to do her work much faster. When she got a new client, his or her data was easily entered and verified. And instead of taking hours to pore through file folders looking for, say, the names of all the clients she had served in Winsted between 1984 and 1986, she could tap a request on the computer keyboard and get the answer in a few minutes. The personal information system made her much more productive, but it cost time and effort up front. Miriam never forgot those first few weeks of typing. She hoped she'd never have to do that again.

Data Compatibility   A friend had a copy of a statistics package that he no longer used, so he gave it to Miriam for her system. With this tool she could more easily analyze her case load, looking for trends, similarities, recurring situations, and the like. This surely would make her job even easier, enabling her to spend more time working with clients, and less time fussing with the numbers. This would be great.

Only it didn't work. The friend didn't understand why. After all, he had used that software on an identical computer the week before. But when he compared their systems, he discovered that they were using different database programs. As it happened, Miriam's software stored data in a format that was not understood by the statistics package. The data was not **compatible.**

Software packages—such as spreadsheets, word processors, graphics generators, and database management systems—all produce and read data. When they create records on disk, they use a particular format. All software packages do not necessarily use a standard format. For example, a word processor produces output in the form of documents—strings of words and punctuation. The bit configuration used by one word processor to indicate that a word is underlined (or boldfaced, or indented, etc.) may not be identical to the one used by another word processor. Their data formats are different. As a result, you might not be able to write a document with one word processor and then read or edit it with another one.

Similarly, the format of data produced by an electronic spreadsheet program may or may not be understandable to, say, a particular word processor. So what? you may say. What difference does it make? Well, it can make a great deal of difference. You might want to copy into a report (written with a word processor) a table from a spreadsheet program. If the data formats aren't compatible, the process is difficult, maybe impossible.

Fortunately for Miriam, she was given the statistical software as a gift. When it did not work with her existing data, she had lost nothing. But if you develop a personal information system of your own and you need to share data among various packages, be sure their data is compatible. Ask the salesperson to confirm that before you buy any software.

Trained Personnel

People are an important component of business computer systems. In this section we'll discuss the roles that are played and the training needed.

Roles   The roles described in Chapter 2 for the people component all exist in personal information systems: developer, operator, clientele, and user. However, in a personal information system the user/owner may fill several of these roles, or all of them.

The operator of a personal information system is invariably the user. After all, a personal information system is, by definition, a system used by an individual to improve productivity. And the system clientele usually is the user also. The user reads and interprets the output, and enjoys the benefits of the system.

The role of system developer may or may not be played by the user. In a large corporation with an MIS department, one or several professional system developers might analyze, build, and implement a user's personal information system. Another option is for the user to hire a consultant to perform one or more of the system development steps.

A third option, for those users who have the time, interest, and skills, is to develop their own personal information systems. Because a personal computer system can cost $10,000 or more, such a project should not be undertaken lightly. You, or any user, should know what you are doing before spending that kind of money. We will discuss a system development methodology in Chapter 8.

Training   Effectively using a personal information system requires training. You need to understand how each application works, how to use it to achieve the maximum benefit from it, and how to add new applications to your existing system. You can learn about your system, and about the productivity software you run on it, from a variety of sources. We will survey some of the sources here.

First, every piece of computer equipment and every software package comes with documentation. You should familiarize yourself with this, although it can be pretty dry reading. Software, such as electronic spreadsheets and graphics packages, also usually comes with a **tutorial program.** A tutorial program introduces you to the basic operation and features of the software; you should, of course, run the tutorial program for any new software you acquire.

Second, almost all popular software packages eventually become the subject of books. A trip to your local big-chain bookstore will show you dozens of titles in the computer section, many of them how-to guides for application software. Much valuable information can be found in such texts. They often are a good investment.

Third, for those who learn more effectively in a formal classroom setting, three further options are available. One of these options is application software or system courses at a local college or university. Some schools also offer intensive workshops or adult education courses teaching the keystrokes, that is, the use of a particular package. Another option is courses offered by a local computer retail store. When you purchase hardware or software, get the store's course schedule from the salesperson. The cost of computer store courses varies, but it will probably range from $50 to $150, depending on the length of the course. The third option is courses offered by independent companies or consultants—usually professional trainers who teach such courses for a fee. Often the courses are thorough, intensive, and worthwhile. They also can be expensive, costing from $250 to $1,000 or more, depending on the length of the course.

4.4 INCREASING YOUR PERSONAL PRODUCTIVITY

Backup Software: For the Moment After   by Edward Mendelson

Nothing is certain but death, taxes, and lost files. But while death permanently removes you from the earth and taxes part you from your money forever, lost files can be recovered—if you've been backing them up.

With backups, irreplaceable data can survive disasters, like corrupted hard drive files, crashed disks, stolen computers, even fire and flood. If you lead a charmed life and disasters never happen to you or your data, you will still find backups useful for preserving older versions of crucial files.

You can also use backups as temporary storage for your files when updating your hard disk from an older version of DOS, or you can use them simply as a way of transferring a group of files between two computers. If a file is larger than a single floppy disk, a backup is almost always the most efficient way to move it from one computer to another—unless you're willing to tie up the phone lines for a few hours.

Most users in corporate and private offices use backup software to transfer files from hard disks of moderate size—up to 40MB—to floppy disks. When your data expands beyond 40MB, it's time to consider a tape drive so you won't have to spend a whole afternoon feeding floppies to an insatiable backup program.

But even in the age of 600MB hard disks and gigabyte tape drives, programs that primarily back up to floppy disk drives still have their place. Provided that they're not limited to backing up to floppy disks only, they can be used in a network to let each user make a personal set of backups on floppy disks; they also can back up the user's hard disk to the hard disk in the server, then back up the files backed up to the server to a giant tape or WORM [write once, read many times] drive.

As you can see, a variety of training options exists, ranging from the inexpensive to the costly. But remember that training really is an investment. If you spend $10,000 on a system that you hope will help increase your productivity by, say, 40 percent (resulting in more income), then spending an additional $750 on the training that will enable you more quickly to achieve that goal is probably cost-effective.

Procedures

With a caseload of 500 clients, Miriam needed a routine, just to keep up with all the work. So she set aside every Monday morning to update her computer records, print reports, and do other paperwork. Also, the first Monday of every month she made backup copies on cassette tape of her client files. She rotated three tapes, so that she always had backups of the last three months' data. Without realizing it, Miriam had established procedures for her information system, just by using common sense. This paid off when her office was vandalized one night, and the computer was damaged. It was repaired, but the hard disk, on which all her data was stored, had to be replaced. Using her backups, she reinstalled her database in a few hours. It would have taken her days to type everything out again, as she had done in the beginning.

In multiuser systems it is obvious that procedures are vital; it is often not so obvious in a personal information system. After all, when the system fails, only one person is inconvenienced or suffers in any way. Also, procedures often are established so groups of people can communicate and can coordinate their activities, but in a single-user system

Figure 4-10
Examples of procedures for personal information systems

Normal Processing	Failure Recovery
Format for file names	Undeleting lost files
Format for diskette labels	Restoring lost data from
Preparing new storage media	backups
File and database backup	Phone numbers for computer
Directories and subdirectories	store's service department and
Loading new software	software vendors' customer
Changing AUTOEXEC.BAT file	service departments

Questions

4.22   What is meant by data compatibility? Is data compatibility an important factor when you run only one software package?

4.23   Name three groups of individuals who develop personal information systems.

4.24   Describe four sources of training for personal computer software packages.

4.25   Describe three normal operating procedures and three failure recovery procedures for a personal information system.

4.26   Why are procedures for personal information systems often informal?

there is no group requiring coordination. The temptation to dispense with procedures in a single-user system is great.

Many personal information system users incorrectly assume that they are—and always will be—the system's only users. Yet frequently someone else eventually needs to learn the system. Consider the office worker in Chapter 1 who inherited from another employee several diskettes containing plant names and client information. If the original user of that system had had—and followed—written procedures, then the second one probably would not have accidentally erased the only copy of those important files.

Every personal computer user ought to adopt standard procedures, if only to make his or her life easier. Some examples are listed in Figure 4-10.

Notice that users of personal computer systems, like the users of multiuser systems, need procedures both for normal processing and for failure recovery. Writing those procedures in a notebook you keep on your desk will serve as your documentation. Notes like these prove very helpful, especially when you perform a task infrequently. For example, writing down how to backup your database, or how to produce a pie chart, or how to type an envelope, makes doing it easier than it would be if you had to dig through the computer manuals every time. Notes also are vital if anyone else needs to learn your system.

How to Develop a Personal Information System

Developing a personal information system can be straightforward, as long as a reasonable methodology is followed. Most first-time buyers make the mistake of rushing out to buy hardware without considering what they *really* need or what software they are likely to be running. The five steps in developing an information system are:

1.   Identify your problem
2.   Define your needs (or requirements)
3.   Identify alternative solutions
4.   Design the five components of your system
5.   Implement your new system

These steps will be explained briefly here, and more thoroughly in Chapter 8.

The first step, *identify your problem*, puts you on the right track. Once you know your problem (for example, customer bills aren't being mailed out soon enough), then you can focus all your energy and resources on solving it. (You might identify several problems, of course.)

During the second step, *define your needs*, you determine precisely what the new system needs to accomplish so you can solve your problem. For example, maybe the new system needs to print and mail 500 customer bills every two weeks. Notice that at this point we talk in general terms: we haven't decided yet to build a *computer* system to send bills, just a system. Maybe it will be a manual one.

During the third step, *identify alternative solutions*, you consider various ways to solve your problem. Maybe you can hire a part-time clerk to do billing. Perhaps there is a local service bureau that would do your billing for a small fee. Or maybe you want to have a personal information system that you can use to do the billing yourself. Comparing the costs and benefits of the various alternatives enables you to select the most appropriate one.

Assuming you decide to develop a business computer system, during the fourth step you lay out all your plans. This step is called the *design stage*. You need to consider each of the five system components—hardware, programs, data, people, and procedures—during this step. You will need to plan for each component.

During the fifth step, *implementation*, you acquire, build, or install each of the five components. Then you put together all the pieces and test them as one entity, being sure that all the parts fit with one another. Satisfied that everything works as it should, you can begin using the system for your work. As we saw with the social worker earlier in this chapter, it is unrealistic to think you will reap the benefits of a new system immediately. Much preparation needs to be done. You will benefit from your system more quickly if all five steps are performed properly.

Question

4.27   What are the five steps in developing a personal information system?

Summary

Personal information systems are business computer systems used by individuals to increase their productivity. Productivity can be increased by using less time or resources to get the same results as before, or by getting more or better results with the same time or resources.

Personal information systems have five components: hardware, programs, data, procedures, and trained personnel. A microprocessor is at the center of a microcomputer, the heart of a personal information system. Personal computer operating systems control your interface with the machine. Operating systems exist that support one or more users, and that support one or more active programs at a time. You should select an operating system according to your processing needs.

Because many personal computer user/owners are also system developers, a step-by-step process for system development should be followed. The five-step process was defined briefly in this chapter. It will be described and illustrated more thoroughly in Chapter 8. The five steps are:

1. Identify your problem
2. Define your needs (or requirements)
3. Identify alternative solutions
4. Design the five components of your system
5. Implement your new system

Word List

personal information system	random access memory (RAM)	menu
productivity	read-only memory (ROM)	multitasking
microcomputer	firmware	context switching
mouse	peripheral device	windowing
point-and-click interface	channel	foreground
icon	port	background
character-based interface	expansion slot	OS/2
microprocessor	Winchester disk	UNIX
mother board	removable mass-storage device	Mac OS
cycle	head-crash	data compatibility
megahertz	MS-DOS	tutorial program
MIPS	shell	

Discussion Questions and Exercises

A. A young entrepreneur was negotiating with the owner of a florist shop who wanted to sell the business—shop, inventory, computer, client accounts, everything. They were having trouble agreeing on a price for the computer system. The hardware was adequate, and the previous owner had had a consultant custom-tailor an accounting package for him. The problem was that there was no documentation for the system (i.e., no written procedures), and the consultant had left the area. The owner insisted that the software was simple enough to run without documentation, and wanted $15,000 for it, half the price it had cost to develop. The prospective buyer was wary of the claim. What would you do?

B. Visit a computer store or your campus computer lab and use MS-DOS (or another personal computer operating system) both by itself and with a shell. Which is easier to use? What is the advantage—if any—of using an operating system without a shell?

C. Visit a computer store or your campus computer lab and use an Apple Macintosh computer. Compare the Mac interface with that of MS-DOS, or another character-based one. Which do you prefer? Which do you think most users would prefer? Why are point-and-click graphical interfaces usually more costly than character-based ones? (Note: Cost includes not only the price of the software itself, but also of the RAM or ROM it occupies and any other resources it requires.)

D. Using current periodicals in your school library, determine the cost, storage capacity, and system requirements for a Winchester hard disk (any manufacturer), and a 3½-inch diskette drive. Compare the advantages and disadvantages of each.

E. If you were configuring a personal information system of your own, would you choose a 3½-inch or 5¼-inch diskette drive? Defend your decision.

F. Find as many sources of training in your area as you can for the following software: Lotus 1-2-3; Excel; Ventura Publisher or Pagemaker; dBase III+; dBase IV.

CHAPTER 5

Electronic Spreadsheet Applications

CHAPTER OUTLINE

Tom had worked out all the details. He knew just how much money the new house was going to cost, and the spreadsheet told the story. He knew the cost of the land and how much it would take to develop it: road, sewer, water, gas line, and so forth. He had a beautiful house design, and had developed the materials list—including prices, sales tax, delivery charges, and discounts—right down to the last pound of nails. Tom was on a tight budget, so he scheduled work according to his finances. He arranged for a loan that he needed to begin payments on immediately. He anticipated a nice bonus this year that would be a cushion in case unanticipated expenses arose. If everything went according to plan, he would just be able to make the payments to the bank, the general contractor, the subcontractors, and the lumber supply store.

Everything did not go as planned. After the site had been prepared and the foundation had been excavated, the general contractor got delayed with another construction job. Everything needed to be pushed back by three months. When this happened, Tom discovered that the prices of some of the materials were going up. As he had no place to store the materials, he was afraid he'd have buy them three months later at the higher prices. What effect would this have on his overall budget? Would it be cheaper, he wondered, to rent storage space at $1,000 per month and buy materials at the lower price? Tom would have to recalculate the prices and total everything up again. That would take hours. Or would it? Tom was using an electronic spreadsheet program. He changed some figures on the computer screen and instantly saw the new totals. In Figure 5-1 you can see the part of Tom's spreadsheet that summarizes some of his material costs, both before and after the price change. (His entire spreadsheet is actually much larger.) Aha! It actually would be cheaper to buy now and pay $3,000 for storage.

Now Tom would need to take out a short-term loan to cover the new expense. He'd pay off the loan when he got his bonus. How much would that loan cost in interest? He needed to add that to the cost of storage. Would it still be cheaper? Once again, Tom entered new figures into the electronic spreadsheet, and immediately saw the answers. Although he was not happy about this change in events, he was happy that he could get right to the problem and not waste time refiguring everything with a calculator.

An Introduction to Spreadsheet Systems

The first electronic spreadsheet program, VisiCalc, was sold in 1979. Since then, millions of electronic spreadsheet programs, such as Lotus 1-2-3, Excel, SuperCalc, and VisiCalc, have been purchased for use on personal computers. Electronic spreadsheet programs are the most widely used personal computer software. With prices ranging from under $100 to over $500, hundreds of millions of dollars have been spent on these programs. Why are electronic spreadsheets so popular?

```
MATERIALS

LUMBER

           Board feet                Type            Cost/ft          Total

                 6000                2 × 4             1.25         7500.00
                 4000                2 × 6             2.30         9200.00
                15000         3/4" ext plywood         0.70        10500.00


INSULATION

               Unit                  Type            Cost/unit        Total

             180 Roll           16" R23 Kraft         12.00         2160.00
              50 Roll           16" R16                8.50          425.00
             200 Lb.            loose fibergl          0.28           56.00


FASTENERS

               Unit                  Type            Cost/unit        Total

                100           #10d common              3.40          340.00
                 20           #8d finish               4.20           84.00
                 50           #6d roofing              6.15          307.50
                 50           Box #8 wood              3.00          150.00
                 20           Box #4 wood              2.75           55.00
                540           Joist hanger             0.18           97.20

                                                                 $30,874.70
```

a. Before price changes

Figure 5-1
Part of spreadsheet showing building
material costs (*continued*)

An **electronic spreadsheet** program enables a user, like Tom, to quickly and easily manipulate numerical data in tabular format. The electronic spreadsheet is an automated version of the ledger paper used by accountants. Figure 5-2 shows an example of a paper spreadsheet. The paper spreadsheet is simple in its concept and in its design: it consists of rows and columns in which data—usually numbers—is written and summarized. The electronic spreadsheet is equally simple, both in concept and design; but it is far more powerful than the paper version.

What Is a Spreadsheet?

The spreadsheet illustrated on ledger paper in Figure 5-2 is a typical one. Each **column** in this case represents a time period: a month or the entire quarter. Each **row** in this case represents a source of sales income or an expense. Rows are totaled (under the heading 1ST QTR TOTAL),

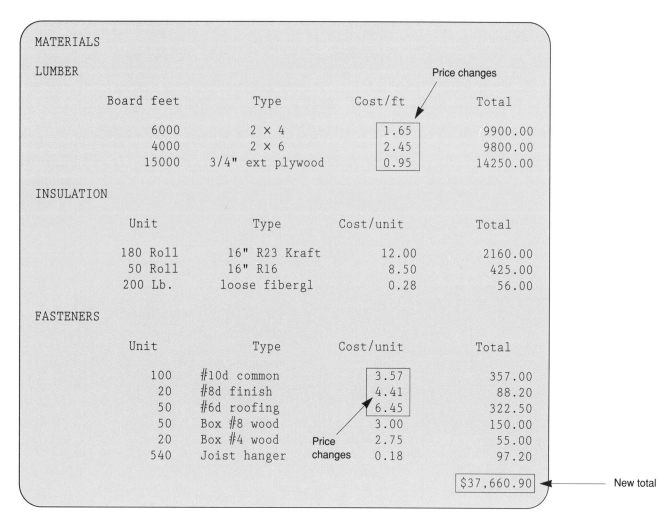

```
MATERIALS

LUMBER
                                                    Price changes

        Board feet          Type          Cost/ft          Total

             6000          2 × 4          ┌──────┐         9900.00
             4000          2 × 6          │ 1.65 │         9800.00
            15000     3/4" ext plywood    │ 2.45 │        14250.00
                                          │ 0.95 │
                                          └──────┘

INSULATION

          Unit              Type          Cost/unit        Total

        180 Roll      16" R23 Kraft        12.00          2160.00
         50 Roll      16" R16               8.50           425.00
        200 Lb.       loose fibergl         0.28            56.00

FASTENERS

          Unit              Type          Cost/unit        Total

            100      #10d common          ┌──────┐          357.00
             20      #8d finish           │ 3.57 │           88.20
             50      #6d roofing          │ 4.41 │          322.50
             50      Box #8 wood          │ 6.45 │          150.00
             20      Box #4 wood    Price   3.00             55.00
            540      Joist hanger  changes  2.75             97.20
                                            0.18
                                          ┌──────────────┐
                                          │ $37,660.90   │  ◄──── New total
                                          └──────────────┘
```

Figure 5-1
(Continued)

b. After price changes

and columns are totaled (beside the heading NET BEFORE TAXES at the bottom of the page). Thus, many details about this company's financial status have been captured on a single page; for example, the income from each source for each month, the income from each source for the first quarter, the expenses for each month, the total income for the entire period, and the net income (income minus expenses) for each month and for the quarter. This kind of financial information is important to businesspeople in large and small companies alike.

What Is an Electronic Spreadsheet?

Now examine the electronic spreadsheet in Figure 5-3. It uses the same format and presents the same data that appears in Figure 5-2. Parts of the spreadsheet have been highlighted and labeled for use in this text, although they would not appear that way on a computer screen. Notice that the electronic spreadsheet also is made up of rows and columns.

Elliot Bay Electronics
First Quarter Summary

		JAN	FEB	MAR	1ST QTR TOTAL	
1	SALES					
2						
3	St. Louis	18000	7605	12953	38558	
4	Portland	21600	14900	6500	43000	
5	Appleton	11750	8800	17040	37590	
6						
7	TOTAL SALES	51350	31305	36493	119148	
8						
9	EXPENSES					
10						
11	Advertising	5000	2000	2000	9000	
12	Salaries	11200	11200	11200	33600	
13	Bonuses	650	1000	1300	2950	
14	Travel & Entertain.	8400	8000	8600	25000	
15						
16	TOTAL EXPENSES	25250	22200	23100	70550	
17						
18						
19	NET BEFORE TAXES	26100	9105	13393	48598	
20						

Figure 5-2
Paper spreadsheet

The intersection of a row and a column is called a **cell**. Each cell has an address which is defined by that cell's row and column, referred to as its **coordinates**. Columns are identified with letters (A–Z for the first 26 columns, then AA, AB, and so forth), and the rows are numbered. Thus, A1 is the address of the cell in the first column, first row; D16 is the address of the cell in the fourth column (D), 16th row.

Electronic spreadsheet programs offer some very interesting and powerful features. Among them are formulas, automatic recalculation, size, and graphics capabilities.

Formulas and Automatic Recalculation   By far the most powerful aspect of electronic spreadsheet programs is the user's ability to define **for-**

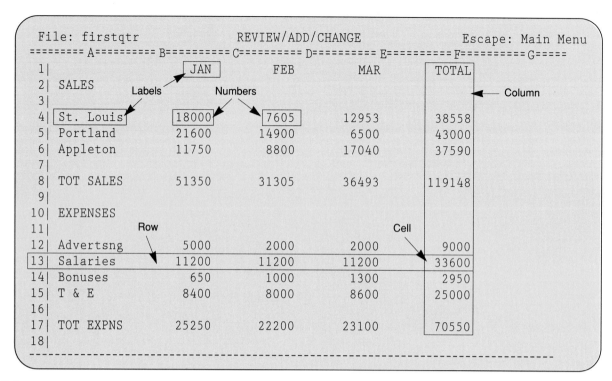

```
 File: firstqtr              REVIEW/ADD/CHANGE              Escape: Main Menu
========= A========== B========== C========== D========== E========== F========== G=====
 1|                     JAN         FEB          MAR          TOTAL
 2| SALES        Labels          Numbers                                     Column
 3|
 4| St. Louis       18000        7605        12953        38558
 5| Portland        21600       14900         6500        43000
 6| Appleton        11750        8800        17040        37590
 7|
 8| TOT SALES       51350       31305        36493       119148
 9|
10| EXPENSES
11|            Row                                  Cell
12| Advertsng        5000        2000         2000         9000
13| Salaries        11200       11200        11200        33600
14| Bonuses           650        1000         1300         2950
15| T & E            8400        8000         8600        25000
16|
17| TOT EXPNS       25250       22200        23100        70550
18|
```

Figure 5-3
Electronic spreadsheet

mulas in the spreadsheet, thereby directing the computer to do calculations that the user might otherwise need to do with paper and pencil. To learn how this works, take a sheet of paper and follow this example manually.

Suppose you worked for a lumberyard. A customer buys items from you at a certain price. Contractors customarily receive a 5 percent discount on their purchases. Everyone pays 8 percent state sales tax. Thus, to issue an itemized invoice to a customer you need to complete a form like the one in Figure 5-4. We have filled in some of the figures. Now you fill in the columns headed DISCOUNT (assume a 5 percent rate), DISCOUNTED PRICE, SALES TAX and ITEM TOTAL; and fill in the INVOICE TOTAL. Notice the process you follow.

For each item, you first multiply the item price by the number ordered; this gives you the nondiscounted price (which is not written on the spreadsheet). Then you multiply the nondiscounted price by .05 to get the discount. Subtracting the discount from the nondiscounted price gives the discounted price. Then you multiply the discounted price by .08 to compute the sales tax. The item total is equal to the discounted price plus the sales tax. The invoice total is equal to the sum of all the item totals.

With a calculator and some patience, this process can be done manually (as you have demonstrated). But how tedious it would be if there were, say, fifty items. And what happens if, just as you complete this invoice, the lumberyard owner appears and recognizes the customer as an old college buddy? "Give him a 12 percent discount," the boss says. Now you have to refigure everything. Let's see how an electronic

	A	B	C	D	E	F	G
49	ITEM	ITEM	NUMBER	DISCOUNT	DISCOUNTED	SALES	ITEM
50		PRICE	ORDERED		PRICE	TAX	TOTAL
51							
52	QUICKRETE	1.69	18				
53	6×8 STOCKADE FENCE	16.99	40				
54	4×4×4' POST PT	5.99	82				
55	2×8×12 PT	7.59	75				
56					INVOICE TOTAL		
57							
58							
59							
60							
61							
62							
63							
64							
65							
66							
67							
68							

Figure 5-4
Partial spreadsheet for lumberyard invoice

spreadsheet would help. First, we'll look at the basic formulas you could use. Then we'll see how easily you can make adjustments and get fast results.

Let's start by placing this spreadsheet on the electronic screen (see Figure 5-5). We will arbitrarily place the upper left corner at cell A49. Thus, the item price for Quickrete is at B52, and the number ordered is at C52. If the discount rate is 5 percent, the discount for Quickrete (cell D52), is given by this formula:

D52 = (B52 * C52) * .05

(The asterisk (*) means multiplication.) The discounted price (E52) is computed this way:

E52 = (B52 * C52) − D52

That is, the discounted price equals the nondiscounted price minus the discount. Similarly, the sales tax is computed using this formula:

F52 = E52 * .08

That is, the sales tax equals the discounted price times 8 percent. Finally, the item total is computed:

G52 = E52 + F52

Using that row as an example, fill in the formulas for rows 53 through 55.

	A	B	C	D	E	F	G
49	ITEM	ITEM	NUMBER	DISCOUNT	DISCOUNTED	SALES	ITEM
50		PRICE	ORDERED		PRICE	TAX	TOTAL
51							
52	QUICKRETE	1.69	18	(B52*C52*0.05)	(B52*C52-D52)	(E52*0.08)	(E52+F52)
53	6×8 STOCKADE FENCE	16.99	40				
54	4×4×4' POST PT	5.99	82				
55	2×8×12 PT	7.59	75				
56							
57					INVOICE TOTAL		
58							
59							
60							
61							
62							
63							
64							
65							
66							
67							
68							

Figure 5-5
Lumberyard invoice formulas

Notice the pattern that developed. Each row of formulas used the same relative structure. For example, to compute the discount for any row, multiply the product of the two cells to the left by .05. Patterns like these occur so frequently in spreadsheets that electronic spreadsheet programs allow you to write formulas in one row, then copy the formulas to other rows. As they are copied, the appropriate relative cell addresses are used. Thus, you could enter just the formulas for row 52, then press a few keys to copy them into rows 53, 54, and 55. (This feature is even more impressive when you are dealing with a larger number of rows. And the same technique can be used to copy columns of formulas, although we will not illustrate it here.)

This feature makes developing the spreadsheet relatively easy. Now consider the formula for computing the invoice total in cell G57. The invoice total is the sum of all the item totals. We can write the formula in two ways. We can name each addend; or we can describe a range, that is, a contiguous group of cells—in this case from G52 through G55. Here are the alternatives:

$$G57 = G52 + G53 + G54 + G55$$

or

$$G57 = @SUM(G52 . . G55)$$

The first alternative uses a simple algebraic expression. The second alternative uses an electronic spreadsheet feature called a **function**. A function is a built-in mathematical formula. The symbols @SUM (used in Lotus 1-2-3 and its clones) indicate the sum function. Other spreadsheet programs might use slightly different symbols, such as !SUM or

%SUM. If there were, say, fifty rows to be summed, the first alternative would not be feasible. The sum function would be vastly easier to enter than the cell locations of fifty addends.

At this point, you have seen an example of entering formulas into the spreadsheet. But the real power of an electronic spreadsheet becomes apparent when changes to values or to formulas need to be made. When values change—say the price of Quickrete goes up to $2.39—you need only type the new price over the old one. The spreadsheet program **automatically recalculates** every entry on the page affected by the change. Similarly, if a formula changes—say the boss tells you to give his college buddy a 12 percent discount—then all you need to do is enter a new formula into cell D52 and copy it into cells D53 through D55. All the affected figures on the spreadsheet are automatically recalculated with the new data.

To truly appreciate what we've just discussed, you should try it out with an electronic spreadsheet program. There are many available, and your instructor probably has selected one for the class to use. The symbols used in your spreadsheet might differ slightly from the ones in this text, but the principles will be the same. Once you learn the principles, you can apply them to any spreadsheet program.

Size   One difference between a paper spreadsheet and its electronic counterpart is its size, that is, the number of columns and rows it can contain. Whereas a paper spreadsheet's size is limited by the dimensions of the paper, an electronic spreadsheet has much larger dimensions. Most electronic spreadsheets are at least 250 columns wide and 250 rows long, although some are much bigger—up to 8192 rows, for example. Of course, the entire spreadsheet cannot fit onto a computer screen at once, so at any given time you see only a piece of the entire form. This piece is called a **window** (Figure 5-6), and you can position

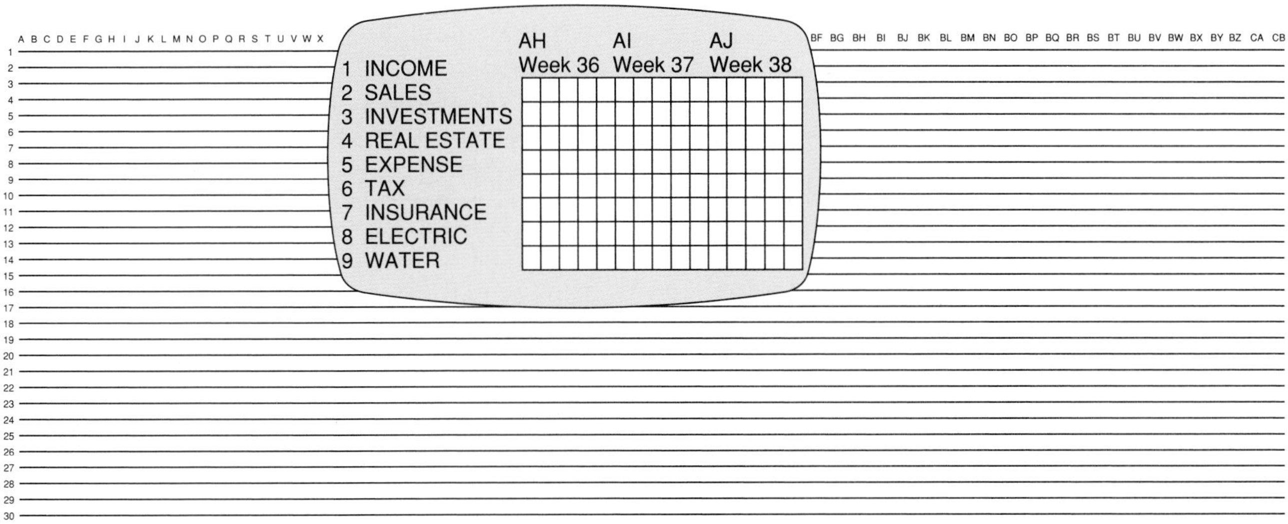

Figure 5-6
A computer screen is a window into the spreadsheet

it on the form anywhere you want to. It is as if you have a magnifying glass that can take in only so much of an object at a time; to see another part of the object, you move the magnifying glass.

When working with a large spreadsheet it might be helpful to view two parts of the spreadsheet at the same time. For example, you might want to see the effect on a total when one or several of its components are changed. Some electronic spreadsheet programs provide a **split screen** feature in which each half of the computer screen is a window displaying a different part of the spreadsheet. Figure 5-7*a* shows the part of the spreadsheet that fits on one screen. The totals, however, are located in row 57, which does not fit on the screen. Figure 5-7*b* shows how the split screen feature works. In one part of the screen the user sees rows 1 through 14; in the other part of the screen, the user sees rows 56 and 57. When the user changes figures in the top window, any effects on the totals can be observed instantly in the lower window. Screens that are split vertically work in a similar way.

Charts and Graphs Another powerful feature of electronic spreadsheet programs is the ability to produce graphs based on data extracted from a spreadsheet. Graphs are used extensively in business, especially to increase the visual impact of summary information. The example graphs in Figure 5-8 were derived from spreadsheet data. Although the use of such graphs is nothing new to business, having a software product instantly draw them from electronic data is exceedingly timesaving.

Why Use Spreadsheets in Business?

Managers use spreadsheets to summarize numerical data. They manipulate the data and observe the results such changes have on the overall

Figure 5-7
Use of split screen

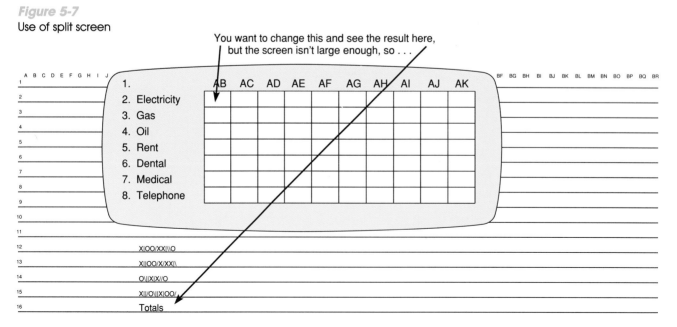

a. Single screen

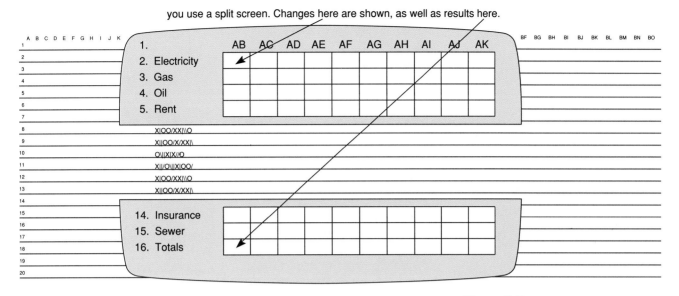

b. Split screen

Figure 5-7
(Continued)

spreadsheet. They use spreadsheets to help them generate the information necessary for making sound business decisions. Electronic spreadsheets are used for numerical summaries, for financial models and simulation, and for record keeping. This is by no means an exhaustive catalogue; as you become familiar with electronic spreadsheets and with business (and business problems), more applications will become apparent to you.

Numerical Summaries   Some applications are simple and straightforward in that they record financial facts which the user enters. Calculations allow various subtotals and totals to be quickly determined and displayed. Examples include a summary of one student's college expenses (Figure 5-9), and a statement of income and expenses for the campus ski club (Figure 5-10).

Financial Models and Simulation   Electronic spreadsheet programs are used extensively to build financial models in which variables can be changed and the results observed, such as in sales forecasting. A *model* describes the relationships between things in the real business world. A **financial model**, as we saw in Chapter 3, describes the relationships between various monetary aspects of a company, such as income sources and amounts, cost centers, payroll, and other expenditures. Thus, the spreadsheet provides a model of the company's finances.

By altering variables, the user effectively poses what-if questions. Often such simulation involves calculations more complex than simple summaries. For instance, a spreadsheet program can be used to determine the return on an investment such as a 12-month certificate of deposit, as illustrated in Figure 5-11. The user can vary both the initial

Figure 5-8
Examples of graphs

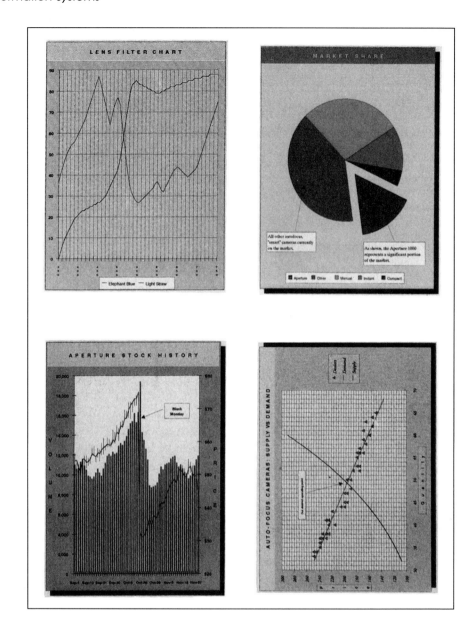

deposit (in the example it is $1,000) and the interest rate (in this case, it is 10.5 percent).

Another example of a financial model is loan analysis. For example, consider a company that plans to finance the construction of a $200-million assembly plant. The company will probably consider several variables, including how much of the $200 million it will borrow, the time period over which it will pay off the loan, and the rate at which the loans will be financed. The company's financial planners build several financial models, changing variables and examining the results to assist in their decisions.

```
          A                B      C       D        E        F
 1  SUMMARY OF YEARLY COLLEGE EXPENSES
 2
 3   Tuition                2800
 4   Books                   400
 5   Supplies                150
 6   Lab/studio fees         200
 7   Student activity fees   250
 8
 9   Living Expenses
10     Apt. rent            2700
11     Food/other           1800
12     Phone                 500
13     Entertainment         900
14
15   Car Expenses
16     Insurance            1000
17     Gas/oil               600
18     Parking                50
19                          -------
20   Total                 11350
```

Figure 5-9
Summary of college expenses

On a smaller scale, a college graduate who has worked for a couple of years and saved money for the down payment on a new car might want to consider how much money to borrow for a car loan as well as the terms of the loan. One factor she considers is that interest rates for short-term loans are usually lower than those for longer-term ones. But she also needs to consider her monthly payment.

A comparison of two different loan structures appears in Figure 5-12. The user enters the principal, interest rate, and number of payments. Then the spreadsheet program computes both the monthly payment on the loan and the total interest that will be paid over the life of the loan. Like the company financing a multimillion dollar construction project, our car buyer needs these financial models (and maybe others) to help her decide which scenario best suits her financial situation. Working these figures with a calculator is possible, but it is time-consuming and prone to error. Using a spreadsheet program, only a few seconds are required to compare an $8\frac{1}{2}$ percent, 12-month loan with a $13\frac{1}{2}$ percent, 24-month loan. And with just a few more keystrokes, our car buyer could see the results of borrowing more (or less) money.

Record Keeping   Electronic spreadsheet programs also can be used for limited record keeping. For instance, a table of employee personnel records can be stored, retrieved, and manipulated with an electronic spreadsheet program. An example is shown in Figure 5-13.

	A	B	C	D	E	F	G	H
1				SKI CLUB				
2								
3		INCOME				EXPENSES		
4								
5	Membership dues		1500		Trips			
6	Event fees		1200		Buses		1180	
7	Student activity		500		Lodging		1200	
8	Trust fund		200		Trail fees &		400	
9	Ski-a-thon		125		lift tickets			
10	Car wash		200		Insurance		1000	
11			-------		Flyers		25	
12	Total income		3725		Postage		100	
13					Phone		100	
14							-------	
15					Total expenses		4005	
16								
17								
18	Ending balance this year			($280.00)				
19								
20								

Figure 5-10
Ski club income and expenses

Calculations can be performed on the data in the spreadsheet. For example, we could determine the annual base pay for each employee (assuming, say, a 40-hour work week) by multiplying the hourly rate by 40 hours by 52 weeks. In addition to performing calculations, many electronic spreadsheet packages provide functions which assist the user in searching the table for records that meet certain criteria. For instance, the program could find all employees who were hired before 1975, or all employees who earn more than $20.00 per hour.

Although the ability to search a spreadsheet can be useful, other software products are designed specifically for rapid data access, especially for large groups of records. Consequently, a user who needs that accessing ability would probably create and maintain the data using another software product (for example, a database management system—see Chapter 6), and then would **import** pertinent data from those files to the spreadsheet program for further manipulation. Importing files means using data produced by another program. With this approach the user employs the best tool for each task: an electronic spreadsheet for financial analysis, and database management software for data storage and retrieval.

Let us summarize what has been described so far. Electronic spreadsheet programs allow a user to store and manipulate tabular data. Electronic spreadsheets are used extensively for numerical analysis because users can easily build a numerical model, modify variables to

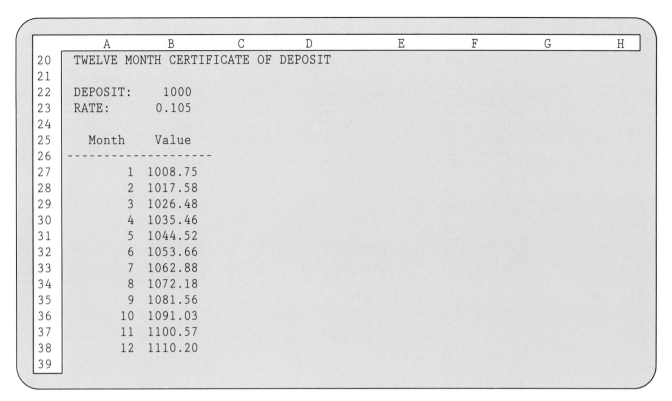

```
          A          B          C        D        E        F        G        H
20   TWELVE MONTH CERTIFICATE OF DEPOSIT
21
22   DEPOSIT:      1000
23   RATE:         0.105
24
25      Month     Value
26   --------------------
27          1   1008.75
28          2   1017.58
29          3   1026.48
30          4   1035.46
31          5   1044.52
32          6   1053.66
33          7   1062.88
34          8   1072.18
35          9   1081.56
36         10   1091.03
37         11   1100.57
38         12   1110.20
39
```

Figure 5-11

Return on a 12-month certificate of deposit

simulate changes, and instantly observe the results. Electronic spreadsheet programs also can be used for data storage and retrieval, but other tools available for personal computing might perform those tasks more flexibly and efficiently.

A Word of Caution   Prior to the age of the electronic spreadsheet, some business decisions were made on instinct alone. Now, with electronic spreadsheets, users can rely more on financial facts. Building very complex financial models is relatively easy, and comparing many different scenarios can help people make sound decisions. Used carefully, an electronic spreadsheet can help increase profitability. However, like any other tool, the electronic spreadsheet can be misused; consequently, using this powerful software is not without some risk.

One problem is that users can easily lose sight of the fact that when they manipulate a financial model, they are working with a make-believe company. A financial model is just numbers inside a computer, merely an electronic image of a real company or even of an imagined one. Spurred by the excitement of playing with the numbers, users can forget that a company is more than the figures—it also includes people, a corporate image and mission, corporate and individual values and ethics, and many other intangibles. Decisions that affect a company certainly should be supported by facts from a computer, but not to the exclusion of other factors.

Questions

5.1   How long have electronic spreadsheets been commercially available?

5.2   Describe the physical structure of a spreadsheet.

5.3   What is a cell?

5.4   How does a user refer to a specific cell?

5.5   Name three types of entries you can make in a cell. Give an example of each.

5.6   What is a window?

5.7   Describe the split-screen feature.

5.8   What is a formula?

5.9   Describe the automatic recalculation feature.

```
          A            B          C         D         E         F         G
 1  Principal    Interest    Number of            Monthly
 2               rate        payments             payment
 3      4000         8.50%      12                 348.88
 4  -------------------------------------------------------------------
 5  Payment #  Balance    Interest  Principal    New
 6                         paid       paid      balance
 7  ---------------------------------------------------------------
 8          1   4000.00    28.33    320.55    3679.45
 9          2   3679.45    26.06    322.82    3356.64
10          3   3356.64    23.78    325.10    3031.53
11          4   3031.53    21.47    327.41    2704.13
12          5   2704.13    19.15    329.72    2374.40
13          6   2374.40    16.82    332.06    2042.34
14          7   2042.34    14.47    334.41    1707.93
15          8   1707.93    12.10    336.78    1371.15
16          9   1371.15     9.71    339.17    1031.98
17         10   1031.98     7.31    341.57     690.41
18         11    690.41     4.89    343.99     346.43
19         12    346.43     2.45    346.43       0.00
20
21      Interest paid $186.55
22
23
```

Figure 5-12
Comparison of two loan structures

a. $8\frac{1}{2}$% for 12 months

5.10 Why is the automatic recalculation feature so helpful to users?

5.11 Describe three applications of electronic spreadsheets.

5.12 How might an electronic spreadsheet program and a database management program be used together?

5.13 Are the numbers on an electronic spreadsheet always correct? Should they always be accepted as true?

A second problem is that computers have a tendency to legitimize things. You will realize after taking this course that the output from an electronic spreadsheet program (or from any other program) is only as accurate and realistic as the formulas and input entered by the user. But some people do not realize that. It is easy to present true and accurate figures with an electronic spreadsheet; it is just as easy to present incorrect, incomplete or misleading information with one. The problem here is a societal one—we tend to believe that what the computer tells us is true. It is perhaps more important than ever to question the spreadsheet author about the source of his or her input, the formulas used, the assumptions that were made, and so forth. Computer printouts look so authoritative that we often accept them with complacency. We must instead question their authority.

Inside an Electronic Spreadsheet

In this text, our presentation of electronic spreadsheets is both generic and fundamental. The principles you learn here apply to all electronic spreadsheet products. Furthermore, electronic spreadsheet programs

	A	B	C	D	E	F	G
1	Principal	Interest	Number of		Monthly		
2		rate	payments		payment		
3	4000	13.50%	24		191.11		
4	--						
5	Payment #	Balance	Interest	Principal	New		
6			paid	paid	balance		
7	---						
8	1	4000.00	45.00	146.11	3853.89		
9	2	3853.89	43.36	147.75	3706.14		
10	3	3706.14	41.69	149.41	3556.73		
11	4	3556.73	40.01	151.09	3405.63		
12	5	3405.63	38.31	152.79	3252.84		
13	6	3252.84	36.59	154.51	3098.32		
14	7	3098.32	34.86	156.25	2942.07		
15	8	2942.07	33.10	158.01	2784.06		
16	9	2784.06	31.32	159.79	2624.27		
17	10	2624.27	29.52	161.58	2462.69		
18	11	2462.69	27.71	163.40	2299.29		
19	12	2299.29	25.87	165.24	2134.05		
20	13	2134.05	24.01	167.10	1966.94		
21	14	1966.94	22.13	168.98	1797.97		
22	15	1797.97	20.23	170.88	1627.08		
23	16	1627.08	18.30	172.80	1454.28		
24	17	1454.28	16.36	174.75	1279.53		
25	18	1279.53	14.39	176.71	1102.82		
26	19	1102.82	12.41	178.70	924.12		
27	20	924.12	10.40	180.71	743.41		
28	21	743.41	8.36	182.74	560.66		
29	22	560.66	6.31	184.80	375.86		
30	23	375.86	4.23	186.88	188.98		
31	24	188.98	2.13	188.98	0.00		
32							
33		Interest paid $586.59					
34							
35							
36							
37							
38							
39							

b. $13\frac{1}{2}$% for 24 months

provide enough material to fill several textbooks (in fact, many exist). In this single chapter, we focus on the fundamentals. When you become experienced in the use of a spreadsheet product, you will be in a good position to explore many of the other features the product offers you.

	A	B	C	D	E	F	G	H
1			ACME GAGS, INC.		PERSONNEL			
2								
3		Hourly	Date	Insur.	Vacation	Sick	Dept.	
4		Rate	Hired	Plan	Days	Days		
5								
6	Chico	20.00	10/20/80	C-90	1098	47	Sales	
7	Groucho	22.00	05/18/87	C-90	2786	99	Cust.Serv.	
8	Harpo	18.50	09/08/73	C-96	1500	108	Sales	
9	Zeppo	15.00	05/14/88	HMO	11	45	R&D	
10								
11								
12								
13								
14								
15								
16								
17								
18								
19								
20								

Figure 5-13
Using a spreadsheet to store personnel data

The Spreadsheet Screen

When you load an electronic spreadsheet program you see a screen like the one in Figure 5-14. Part of the spreadsheet appears on the screen (the whole thing cannot fit, of course) starting in cell A1, called the **home** position. At the top or bottom of your screen is a special area used by the spreadsheet program to give you information, accept your input, or display processing options available to you. This area is called the **control panel**.

The **cursor** is a highlighted rectangle that indicates where you can enter data. The location at which the cursor is located is called the **current cell**. You can move the cursor to any position on the spreadsheet by making use of the arrow keys (up, down, left, right), the mouse, or the Home key. Pressing the Home key always returns you to cell A1. Most electronic spreadsheet programs allow you to place the cursor at a specific cell location by using a special function key called the Go To key. In Lotus 1-2-3 and its clones, the Go To key is F5. When you press F5 the cursor temporarily jumps to the control panel where you are prompted to type a cell location. When you do that and press Return, the cursor jumps back to the spreadsheet and positions itself at the location you specified.

Command Structure

Most spreadsheet programs are built around a command structure, a

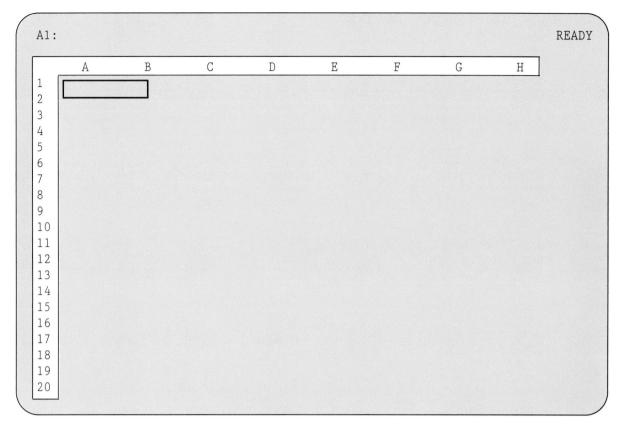

A1:   READY

	A	B	C	D	E	F	G	H
1								
2								
3								
4								
5								
6								
7								
8								
9								
10								
11								
12								
13								
14								
15								
16								
17								
18								
19								
20								

Figure 5-14
Sample electronic spreadsheet screen

series of menus and submenus that enable you to indicate which of dozens of options you want to invoke. As long as your cursor is located in a spreadsheet cell, you can enter a numeric value, a formula, or a label (more about this in the next section). But if you want to do anything else, such as copy some formulas, go to another spreadsheet location, print the spreadsheet, or exit from the program, you need to invoke a command. Literally dozens of commands exist. To spare the user the trouble of memorizing the commands, spreadsheet program engineers cleverly grouped related commands together into a meaningful structure of menus. By selecting an option from one menu, you gain access to another menu of options where you make another selection, continuing the process until finally you get to the specific command you want.

To get into the command mode, you press a special key—Lotus 1-2-3 and its clones use the slash key (/). The cursor immediately jumps to the control panel, where you can choose from the first menu of options. The horizontal menu might look like this:

Worksheet Range Copy Move File Print Graph Data Quit

Each option represents a major group of subcommands. The cursor can be moved—either by pointing with the mouse, or by pressing the right arrow, the space bar, or the first letter of an option—to indicate your choice of options. When you press Return a new menu of options spe-

5.1 INCREASING YOUR PERSONAL PRODUCTIVITY

Tips for Better Spreadsheets

There is no one way to design a spreadsheet. But some tips collected from a variety of users, industry observers, and instructors can be helpful in simplifying design and eliminating errors.

- *Isolate variables:* Group the key parameters that will be frequently changed in one area of the spreadsheet. Have all references to that variable address that single cell. This simplifies changes, reduces errors, and makes the spreadsheet more readable.
- *Focus on key ratios:* Plan the spreadsheet around those parameters that you believe drive your business. Those will be the values you'll want to manipulate or on which you'll want to see the impact of manipulating other values.
- *Use English:* English is a wonderful language. Use it freely. It may take a few more keystrokes to type "West Coast Sales" than "WCS" but the spreadsheet will be much easier to use and read, both for yourself and for anyone else with whom you share the matrix.
- *Keep it simple:* Mammoth equations are difficult to understand. Errors in using them are hard to trace and their logic is difficult to decipher. Break equations up by using intermediate variables.
- *Use modules:* An entire spreadsheet doesn't have to be built at once. Create a working spreadsheet for one month or one department, then copy that to other sections of the spreadsheet. Finding errors in logic is easier in the smaller subsections.
- *Use hash totals:* Spreadsheets created with paper and pencil invariably add numbers both horizontally and vertically across columns to double-check accuracy. The same approach can be of assistance for spreadsheets created with software.
- *Check equations:* It is easy to assume that anything printed out by a computer is infallible, but spreadsheets are only as accurate as the logic, and the typing, that created the equations. Check them carefully and recheck them.
- *Save models:* The value of saving copies of spreadsheets goes beyond the requirement for backup in case of disk failure or damage. As changes are made in the model and it becomes ever more complex, retracing your steps can become extremely difficult. Save copies of the model at each step, particularly if the spreadsheet is shared with other individuals who will be modifying it themselves.
- *Build in checks:* Use If statements, macros, comparisons with known ratios—anything you can think of to build in checks and safeguards against errors in either data entry or logic.
- *Have fun:* Lastly, remember that using personal computers is fun. In concentrating on the productivity-enhancing power of computers, it is easy to forget this fact. If you've become jaded, remember what it was like when you first switched from struggling for hours with a pencil and a calculator to using a personal computer, or waiting months for the data-processing department to run figures for you. That feeling alone is worth the switch.

cific to your first choice appears. For example, if you want to save a spreadsheet in a file, you choose *File* from the first-level menu. The next menu you see might look like this:

Retrieve Save Combine Xtract Erase List Import

This menu represents all the functions you can perform on a file. You highlight *Save* and press Return again. At this point, a prompt asks you to enter the file name you want to use. When you type the file name and press Return the spreadsheet is saved with that name on disk.

5.2   INCREASING YOUR PERSONAL PRODUCTIVITY

Graphics Service Bureaus or In-House?

by Tracey Capen

How do you decide between in-house production of your presentation graphics or the use of an outside service bureau? It needn't be an either-or decision, according to Jerry Cohn, president of Brilliant Image services. Almost all businesses needing presentation graphics on 35mm slides will use outside services, regardless of whether they have in-house facilities, he said. Start-up businesses turn to an outside graphics service when they are putting together their first visual presentations, and Fortune 500 businesses continue to depend on outside graphics services even after investing hundreds of thousands of dollars on in-house presentation graphics facilities, Cohn said.

Small companies are most likely to turn to a service bureau for generating slides. They normally have small volume, limited personnel, and limited equipment capital. As the business grows and volume increases, the yearly expenditures rise. For high-volume users of presentation materials, such as training companies, these costs can run up into the tens or hundreds of thousands of dollars, Cohn said. At this point, some businesses may consider in-house production to cut costs and add more internal control.

The attraction of creating in-house services is based on the per-slide costs. High-volume service bureaus charge in the range of $10 to $15 per slide. In-house production, not including labor or equipment costs, can be about 50 cents to $1.50 per slide, depending on the type of film used.

The investment costs for in-house presentation graphics production vary greatly. Single-user, desktop film recorders range from $3,000 to $10,000. Producing one slide every half minute to 13 minutes, they are suitable for low-volume production.

High-end systems can range from $25,000 to over $200,000. These units produce the highest quality images, at rates of up to 1,000 slides a day.

The investment in presentation slide production goes well beyond simply buying a film recorder. In addition to hardware costs, buyers must take into account the investment in training and personnel. Training involves more than just learning how to operate a film recorder, since learning how to operate the hardware is only a small part of the total training cost. The larger portion involves learning one or more presentation graphics applications and the basics of graphics design. Depending on who is assigned the job, the business may face a long and expensive learning process.

Additional cost questions include: Will additional personnel need to be hired or will these new responsibilities be given to a present employee? Will the person assigned to use the film recorder be able to produce the level of quality expected by management?

For businesses committed to in-house production, a service bureau can still supply valuable support. Most service bureaus provide overnight or over-the-weekend processing.

Other services provided by outside service bureaus include consulting and training for a business's in-house staff; specialized graphics design work; and backup when the in-house staff becomes overloaded, personnel are on vacation, or the hardware needs servicing.

Because you can highlight a menu selection by typing the first letter of the option (for example, "F" for *File*), you can string together several keystrokes to invoke the function you want without looking at the menus. To save a file, then, you could type:

/FS *filename* [Return]

which speeds you through all the menus and prompts. Experienced users learn how to do this with time. In effect, they memorize frequently used keystroke sequences.

Cell Entries

With the cursor on a cell you are able to make one of three kinds of entries: a **label**, which is used to identify row or column contents; a number (also called a constant); or a formula. When you type a label or a number, you see displayed in the cell the value you entered. When you type a formula, you see the formula displayed in the control panel, but on the spreadsheet itself you see the value derived by the formula.

Labels   Labels identify row or column contents for the user; the electronic spreadsheet program uses cell addresses. It is better to use full words for labels than to use abbreviations or codes. Thus, "Sales Tax" is a more understandable column heading than "Slstx." All spreadsheet programs allow you to adjust the width of a column, so make each one wide enough to accommodate a meaningful title.

Labels are made up of alphanumeric characters. Most labels start with a letter—this tells the program that the entry is a label. However, some labels start with a numeric character; this makes the program want to treat them as numbers (which makes a difference in the way the data is displayed and in the way it is processed). Thus, a label such as *1991* needs to be preceded by a special character to identify it as a label. Lotus 1-2-3 and its clones use a single apostrophe (') for this purpose. A caret (^), which centers the label in its column, will also identify the entry as a label.

Numbers   When you enter a number, you can use only the numeric characters, a decimal point, and the minus sign. Do not use dollar signs, commas, or any other punctuation. You need to enter only the *value*.

Spreadsheet programs offer a variety of numeric **display formats** from which you can choose. For instance, you might want the figures in one column to be displayed as integers with commas inserted every three positions. You might want the figures in another column displayed in currency format, that is, with a leading dollar sign, commas in appropriate places, and two digits to the right of the decimal point. Many other formats are available, and you (the user) control which one is used in each cell. Just remember that specifying the display format is different from entering the numeric value.

Formulas   As you saw earlier, formulas are placed in cells so that the spreadsheet program will derive values to display there. With the cursor positioned on a cell, you can enter a formula. The formula appears in the control panel. When you press Return, a value is derived and displayed on the spreadsheet at that cell location. Any time you want to check a formula, you simply place the cursor on the appropriate cell, and the formula will appear in the control panel.

Spreadsheet programs feature a variety of operations, including addition, subtraction, multiplication, division, and exponentiation (see Figure 5-15). They also feature built-in statistical functions such as finding the sum, average, count, and standard deviation of a range of figures. Common financial functions also are available, such as calculating the future value of an annuity or the mortgage payment per

```
          A         B
  1
  2    TEST #     SCORE
  3
  4    Test1       100
  5    Test2        80
  6    Test3        90
  7    Test4        70
  8    Test5       100
```

Figure 5-15
Sample formulas

OPERATION	FORMULA	RESULT
Add Test1 and Test2	B4+B5	180
Add Test1, Test3, and Test 5	B4+B6+B8	290
Divide Test1 by 2	B4/2	50
Divide Test1 by 2 and add 10	B4/2+10	60
Find 5% of Test1	B4*.05	5
Divide Test1 by the difference of Test3 minus Test4	B4/(B6-B7)	5
Square Test1	B4^2	10000
Find the sum of all test scores	SUM(B4,B5,B6,B7,B8) or	
	SUM(B4..B8)	440
Find the average score	AVG(B4..B8)	88
Find the low score	MIN(B4..B8)	70

period. Although it is not important that you understand right now what each of those functions is, it is important that you realize how many useful features spreadsheet programs provide.

The spreadsheet program evaluates formulas starting in the top row and moving to the right. Then it drops to the second row and repeats the process, all the way to the bottom of the spreadsheet.

Printing a Spreadsheet

Several options are available for printing a spreadsheet. A relatively small spreadsheet can be printed on a page measuring $8\frac{1}{2}$ by 11 inches. That approach is fine as long as the spreadsheet itself actually fits in that space. If the spreadsheet is just a little too big, you can print it using **condensed print**, meaning all the letters and numbers are a bit smaller so they'll fit on the page.

Some spreadsheets are wider than they are long. Thus, another printing option is to reorient the data 90 degrees and print it on the page sideways. This is called **landscape printing**. Landscape printing can be combined with condensed printing. Utility programs also are available that allow you to print a very wide spreadsheet on continuous-form

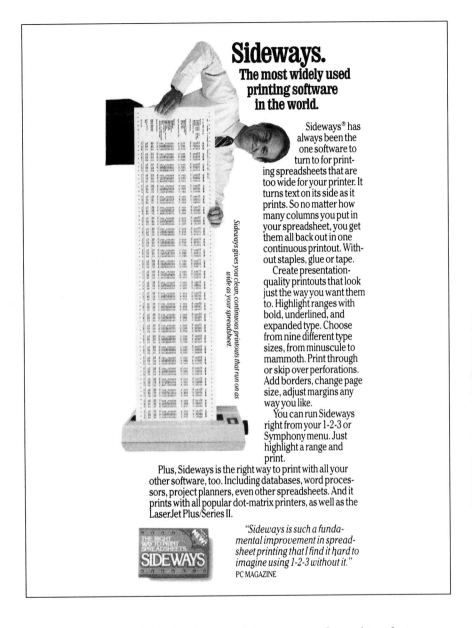

paper (see Figure 5-16). Such spreadsheets are awkward to photocopy, though.

Printing a very large spreadsheet can be done in sections; this process is sometimes called cut-and-paste. For example, you might print the part of the spreadsheet that summarizes the first year's budget on one page, the second year's budget on another page, and so on for all the years described in your spreadsheet. A separate page might contain a summary of the yearly totals along with the grand totals. This set of documents is easy to photocopy, and easy to comprehend because each page contains a cohesive chunk of information.

In all of the techniques mentioned above, the spreadsheet is printed as displayed on the computer screen. This means that derived values appear in all cells that contain formulas. However, spreadsheet pro-

grams also can print the actual contents of each cell, that is, the formulas rather than the derived values. Figure 5-17 illustrates these two methods of printing. Printing the cell contents allows you to make a hard-copy record of all your formulas. In fact, whenever you develop a spreadsheet application, you should print your formulas as part of your documentation. More about that later.

Macros

A **macro** is a series of keystrokes that you define and name. Thereafter you can invoke the macro by its name. Macros are useful particularly

Figure 5-17
Two ways of printing a spreadsheet

	A	B	C	D	E	F	G
48							
49	ITEM	ITEM	NUMBER	DISCOUNT	DISCOUNTED	SALES	ITEM
50		PRICE	ORDERED		PRICE	TAX	TOTAL
51							
52	QUICKRETE	1.69	18	1.52	28.90	2.31	31.21
53	6×8 STOCKADE FENCE	16.99	40	33.98	645.62	51.65	697.27
54	4×4×4' POST PT	5.99	82	24.56	466.62	37.33	503.95
55	2×8×12 PT	7.59	75	28.46	540.79	43.26	584.05
56							
57					INVOICE TOTAL		$1,816.48
58							
59							
60							
61							

a. Display values are printed

	A	B	C	D	E	F	G
48							
49	ITEM	ITEM	NUMBER	DISCOUNT	DISCOUNTED	SALES	ITEM
50		PRICE	ORDERED		PRICE	TAX	TOTAL
51							
52	QUICKRETE	1.69	18	(B52*C52*0.05)	(B52*C52-D52)	(E52*0.08)	(E52+F52)
53	6×8 STOCKADE FENCE	16.99	40	(B53*C53*0.05)	(B53*C53-D53)	(E53*0.08)	(E53+F53)
54	4×4×4' POST PT	5.99	82	(B54*C54*0.05)	(B54*C54-D54)	(E54*0.08)	(E54+F54)
55	2×8×12 PT	7.59	75	(B55*C55*0.05)	(B55*C55-D55)	(E55*0.08)	(E55+F55)
56							
57					INVOICE TOTAL		@SUM(G52..G55)
58							
59							
60							
61							

b. Cell contents are printed

in situations where you find yourself typing the same string of keystrokes over and over again.

For example, suppose you frequently save on disk different versions of a spreadsheet. Let's say that you are building a five-year financial plan, and each year some of the figures change (the formulas all stay the same, only the values change). After you fill the spreadsheet with the data for the first year, you save it, then erase some of the figures (say from cell B50 through cell D75) so you can fill in the second year's data. After you fill in the data for the second year, you repeat the procedure, and so on for each successive year. One set of keystrokes you use frequently is the set that invokes the File command, then the Save command, then erases several columns of data. The key sequence might look like this:

/FS *filename* [Return] /RE b50.d75 [Return]

Don't worry if you do not completely understand that series of commands. It is just an illustration. Rather than typing in that sequence every time you wanted to perform those functions, you could build a miniprogram called a macro, give it a name—for example, F for "file"—then invoke it with a single keystroke each time you wanted to save a file. Lotus 1-2-3 and its clones use the alternate key and the single-letter macro name to invoke a macro. In this example, then, Alt-F invokes the file-save macro.

When you invoke a macro, you are telling the program to get the "keystrokes" from a section of the spreadsheet rather than wait for you to type them at the keyboard. Your macro might look like this:

/FS
{?}~
/RE
b50.d75
~

Notice that some macro symbols are different from the actual keystrokes they represent. For instance, {?} tells the spreadsheet program to wait until you type an entry from the keyboard (in this case, the file name you want to use). The tilde (~) represents a Return key within a macro.

It is not important for you to understand the specifics of macro programming at this point. But you should know that you can develop macros within your spreadsheets, and that they can be very useful to you. You will more fully appreciate applications for macros when you become familiar with an electronic spreadsheet program.

Presentation Graphics

Spreadsheet programs offer a powerful feature that enables you to produce **presentation graphics** with very little effort. Presentation graphics are charts that summarize information visually. Examples include pie graphs, bar graphs, and line graphs.

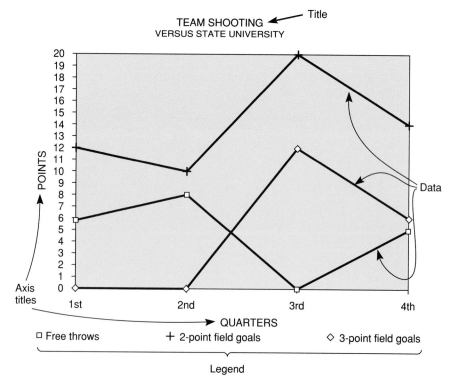

	A	B	C	D	E	F	G	H
1			QUARTER					
2								
3	TEAM TOTALS		1st	2nd	3rd	4th	Total	
4								
5	FREE THROWS		6	8	0	5	19	
6	2-PT FIELD GOALS		12	10	20	14	56	
7	3-PT FIELD GOALS		0	0	12	6	18	
8								
9			18	18	32	25	93	
10								
11								
12								
13								
14								
15								
16								
17								
18								
19								
20								

a. Spreadsheet containing basketball scores by quarter

Figure 5-18
An example of spreadsheet graphing

b. Line graph of basketball scores

Questions

5.14 Define these terms: control panel, home, cursor, current cell.

5.15 Describe a spreadsheet command structure.

5.16 Ordinarily what is displayed in a cell that contains a formula?

5.17 Write the formula to find the average of the sum of values in cells B17 through B20.

5.18 Describe three techniques you can use to print a spreadsheet that does not fit on a single sheet of printer paper.

5.19 What is a macro?

5.20 What kind of information is conveyed with a line graph? A bar graph? A pie graph?

5.21 To show the portion of each tax dollar spent on medical expenses versus other types of expenditures, what type of presentation graph would you use?

When deciding on a type of graph, you need to consider the concepts you want your picture to convey to the reader. A line graph shows performance over a period of time. For example, the line graph in Figure 5-18 shows how a basketball team fared each quarter in terms of the types of points it scored. The graph tells us that the team's performance in both types of field goals improved dramatically in the third quarter, but it scored no free throw points, a big drop from the second quarter.

In contrast, a bar graph and a pie graph both show the relative contribution made by various factors. Look at the same basketball scoring data illustrated as a bar graph (Figure 5-19). In this diagram you can more easily see the relative contribution made by each type of scoring during each quarter.

Now look at the pie graph in Figure 5-20. This pie graph (showing only the fourth-quarter scores) even more dramatically illustrates how each type of scoring contributed to the fourth-quarter effort. This is done by presenting each type of scoring as a part of the total fourth-quarter score. Each wedge of the pie represents the portion of total points made in a scoring category.

Having decided on the type of graph, you use various spreadsheet commands to define the title, axis titles, and legend (see Figure 5-18), and the data range. The data ranges indicate the spreadsheet locations at which the program will find the data values it is supposed to graph.

When you have defined all the graph components you can view the graph on the computer screen, print it on paper, or save it for future use. The particulars of graphing depend on the electronic spreadsheet product you are using.

Figure 5-19
Bar graph of basketball scores

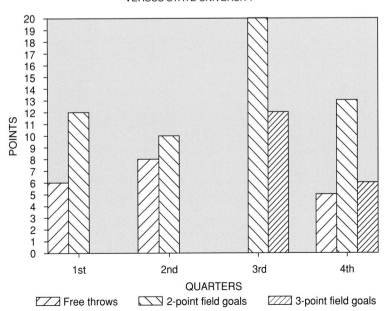

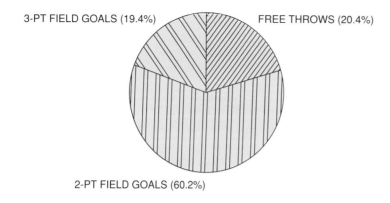

Figure 5-20
Pie graph of basketball scores

How to Develop a Spreadsheet Application

Before undertaking any project—building a deck, writing a résumé, preparing a four-course dinner—you need a plan. Without blueprints, an outline, a chart of cooking times for each course, you would have difficulty doing any of those three projects effectively. You might muddle through somehow, but the results probably will not be as good as they would be with some careful planning. The same is true for spreadsheet applications (and for *any* computerized business application). Planning before building is essential. In fact, we can break the process of developing a spreadsheet application into four steps: logical design, physical design, implementation, and testing. These steps are summarized in Figure 5-21.

Logical Design

During this step, you need to *define the problem* you are trying to solve with the spreadsheet program. Some problems are really simple, such as developing your own budget for the school year. Others require research. Consider the lumberyard invoice we examined earlier. Suppose the company charges 6 percent for delivery. Turn back to Figure 5-4 and determine the formula for computing delivery charges.

Did you have enough information to do that correctly? Did you realize that delivery charges are based on the price before sales tax, that is, on the total of the discounted prices? Or did you assume we meant that the delivery charge was 6 percent of the invoice total? The point here is not to trick you. It is simply to emphasize the importance of knowing what you are doing before you do it.

If you are developing a spreadsheet for your own application over which you have complete control, then you'll know most if not all of the answers up front. If you are developing a spreadsheet for someone else, or there are factors you don't know offhand, then some investigation is in order.

Also during this step you *identify the outputs* you want, so you can in turn *identify the inputs* you need. For example, in order to compute an

5.3   *INCREASING YOUR PERSONAL PRODUCTIVITY*

Spreadsheets Suffer from On-the-Fly Design and Misuse

by Alex Kask

Spreadsheet design begins before you turn the computer on. Deciding what you want to accomplish, and a general plan of how you expect to accomplish it, should be the first step in designing any program. Yet most spreadsheets seem to be designed on the fly. The result is a haphazard collection of schedules and sub-schedules with no clear plan and no easy way to figure out what is being done.

What do I look for when I'm given a Lotus or Supercalc document to dissect? I look for basic features to identify the file: a short descriptive title, the date of preparation (as distinct from the current date), the developer's name, and the file name—all as part of the printout area. I like to see a title in cell A1 because the contents of that cell pop up on the Supercalc directory screen when loading a file; of course, the title should differentiate the file from others on the disk. If a spreadsheet is large, I expect a table of contents to identify significant areas: data input, calculation formulas, output range, instructions, and error checks.

I expect to see those areas clearly segregated. All inputs should go to a specific area, and no other parts of the spreadsheets should have to be modified by the user. Therefore, the entire spreadsheet can be protected, except for those cells where user input is expected. The user should not have to hunt over 10,000 cells to find assumption or input blocks in different places.

Instructions are an important element. Even the developer cannot always explain how to use a spreadsheet a week after it's supposedly finished. Any macros must be identified, labeled, and fully commented, with instructions for running them.

I like to see spreadsheets designed and laid out with a diagonal structure, so each block or section starts at the bottom right corner of the previous block. In this way, rows or columns can be inserted within a block without changing the structure of other blocks—very important if macros are included within the spreadsheet.

Control procedures are essential. Software like The Spreadsheet Auditor can be useful, but controls really start with the use of cross-checks on calculations: footing and cross-footing checks to determine that row totals and column totals agree; reasonableness checks to see that unusual data are flagged or that numbers are within a specified range; verification that details do not add up to more than the total population. I often use the graphics features of Supercalc to make it easier to eyeball data for reasonableness; you can spot an "outlier" a lot easier when your data are shown as a bar chart or line plot.

Of course, user review of the out-put is always needed. "The computer did it so it must be right" attitude too often leads to the acceptance of ridiculous conclusions. The famous instance of the inserted row in a bid-estimate spreadsheet, which was not included in the Sum range and therefore resulted in a low—and unfortunately successful—bid on a job, should have been caught by a user review.

Quite often, my critique of a spreadsheet presented to me for review is: Why? Why was this project put on a spreadsheet in the first place? Spreadsheets are powerful tools, and the better ones can be used for almost any purpose. But when I see a 45K file that contains five-year schedules for hundreds of accounts, and the only formula in the entire spreadsheet is a Sum function that foots the Total column, I wonder what persuaded the developer to waste all that time typing in data that can't even be checked (except manually). Many spreadsheets are really database projects, and database work is really done best by database managers.

Current versions of spreadsheet software make it easier to use small files and link them together, so we don't really need those 2,000-row-by-75 column monsters any more. But using some of these techniques makes it a lot easier to create, work with, debug, and document spreadsheets and makes the quality reviewer's work a lot easier.

invoice total, you need not only each item's price, but also the number of items the customer bought.

Having identified the data, you can *list your assumptions and decisions.* An **assumption** is the allocation of a value, which you suppose to be accurate, to a variable over which you have no real control. For

- Logical design
    - Define problem
    - Identify outputs
    - Identify inputs
    - List assumptions and decisions
    - Document formulas

- Physical design
    - Develop spreadsheet map

- Implementation
    - Write internal documentation
    - Enter spreadsheet data and formulas
    - Build macros
    - Write external documentation

- Testing
    - Develop test cases
    - Calculate results manually
    - Run test cases
    - Compare actual results with expected results
    - Debug if necessary

Figure 5-21
Steps in developing a spreadsheet application

example, if you were doing sales projections you might assume that you would increase sales next year by 5 percent. If you were doing a yearly household budget, you might base it on the assumption that you will receive a 3 percent raise in July, and that the price of home heating oil will be $1.69 per gallon. Those assumptions may or may not prove to be accurate.

A **decision** is the allocation of a value to a variable over which you have complete control. For example, at the lumberyard the owner decided to give contractors a 5 percent discount. At any time the owner can change that to zero or 6 or 10 percent.

Finally, before you ever load your spreadsheet software you must *document the formulas* you plan to use. Write them in English in algebraic format. For example, the formula for computing the contractor's discount might be written:

Contractor's Discount = (Item Price $\times$ Number Ordered) $\times$ 5%

Physical Design

The next step is to lay out your spreadsheet on paper. You make a physical design for the spreadsheet by deciding where all the groups of spreadsheet entries will be. Figure 5-22 shows a spreadsheet format, adapted from one described by Jack Holt in *Cases and Applications in Lotus 1-2-3* (Homewood, Ill.: Irwin, 1988).

This chapter has focused on the group of spreadsheet entries called Calculations in Figure 5-22. Notice that many other sections exist as well.

Documentation   Start the internal documentation in cell A1. By locating documentation here you ensure that when the spreadsheet is loaded

Figure 5-22
Suggested format for physical layout
of spreadsheet

Documentation	Macros
Independent Variables (assumptions and decisions)	Scratch Area (graphs, data tables, etc.)
Calculations (formulas)	Summary Area

the first thing you (or any other user) will see is the documentation. It describes the name and general purpose of the spreadsheet, the author, the date it was created, and any assumptions or limitations of the spreadsheet. Documentation also can list the names and functions of any macros used. It *must* contain a *spreadsheet map* indicating the locations of the spreadsheet sections, for example, where calculations begin, where macros are found, and where assumptions and decisions are located.

Documentation also can be placed at the beginning of each section, explaining features of the entries in the section.

External documentation is kept in a notebook. It describes the spreadsheet in more detail than the internal documentation does. Also it contains a list of the contents of every cell, including a list of all formulas. This is especially valuable documentation. Often you (or a user, auditor, or someone else) need to check the validity and accuracy of various formulas. Having a listing of formulas is more desirable than having to load the spreadsheet and examine each cell, one by one.

Macros   Not all spreadsheet applications require macros. If used at all, they should be used sparingly and should be as simple as possible.

Macros are built in columns of the spreadsheet. They should be located in an area of the spreadsheet into which new rows are unlikely to be inserted. (New rows might be inserted into an invoice, for example, if the customer purchases further items. The new rows would go between the existing line items and the invoice total.) A row extends the entire width of the spreadsheet, filling the unused cells to the right with blanks. Many spreadsheet programs interpret a blank cell in the column as indicating the end of the macro. Consequently, if you build a macro from, say, Z50 through Z57, and then insert a new row Z54 (in the calculations section), cell Z54 will become blank and the rest of the macro will be pushed down one cell. Subsequent executions of the macro will be incorrect because only part of it will be executed—the program will stop each time at the blank cell Z54.

One appropriate location for macros is opposite the documentation section, starting, say, in column AA. The documentation section is unlikely to have new rows inserted into it, so the macro section will be fairly stable.

Independent Variables   In the **independent variables** section, you define the variables whose values the user can modify. (For example, in Figure

5-11 the user could vary the starting value of the 12-month certificate of deposit as well as the interest rate.) Independent variables are defined in this section, and then referenced in the formulas in the calculations section.

As an illustration of the use of independent variables, consider the spreadsheet for the lumberyard invoice. In Figure 5-23*a* the formulas are displayed in the appropriate cells. Notice that in column D the numeric constant .05 appears in all the formulas (the discount rate is 5 percent), and in column F the sales tax rate (currently 8 percent) appears in all the formulas.

Now consider the alternative design shown in Figure 5-23*b*. In this case the discount rate and sales tax rate are defined as independent variables, placed at C44 and C45, respectively. Now the formulas for computing the discount and the sales tax can refer to cells C44 and C45 instead of using raw numeric values. What is the advantage of this design over the previous one? If the discount rate or sales tax rate changes, the only cells that need to be modified are C44 and C45. Thus, if the sales tax rate is raised to $8\frac{1}{2}$ percent, the user simply changes the value of cell C45 to .085. The formulas that use the sales tax rate do not have to be updated; the program will automatically use the new value in computing the sales tax.

If you try implementing the same change in the spreadsheet in Figure 5-23*a*, you will understand the benefits of defining independent variables separate from the formulas that use them. In summary, whenever possible, define independent variables in an area separate from the calculations, and then reference them in your formulas.

Scratch Area   A scratch area can be used for temporary values used in the spreadsheet, such as graphs and data tables. As you become more experienced with spreadsheet programs, you will learn about their applications. Keep in mind that the sections you use in a spreadsheet are determined by the spreadsheet application. Consequently, not all spreadsheets need macros, scratch areas, or independent variables. Use what is right for the application.

Calculations   The calculations section contains the formulas that make up the lion's share of the spreadsheet. Whenever possible, avoid hard-coding constant values into formulas (that's what we did in the example in Figure 5-23*a*). Formulas should reference locations at which appropriate values can be found.

Summary Area   The summary area can be used for a one-page (or larger) summary of the results of calculations. For example, if the calculations generate figures for 100 monthly expenses for a four-year period (a large spreadsheet), you could place a summary of expenses and totals in the summary area. When you change any of the data in the calculations, the corresponding changes are made in the summary area. The summary area is an excellent place to format an output report.

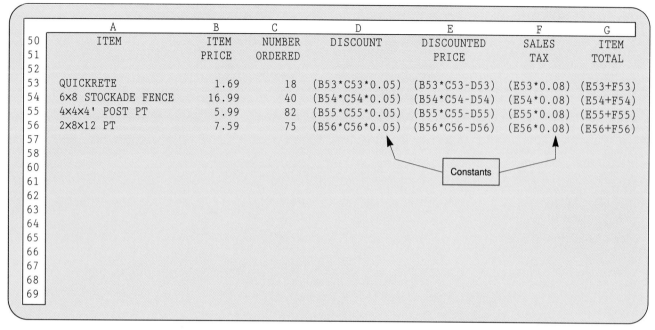

a. Formulas for discount and sales tax contain numeric constants

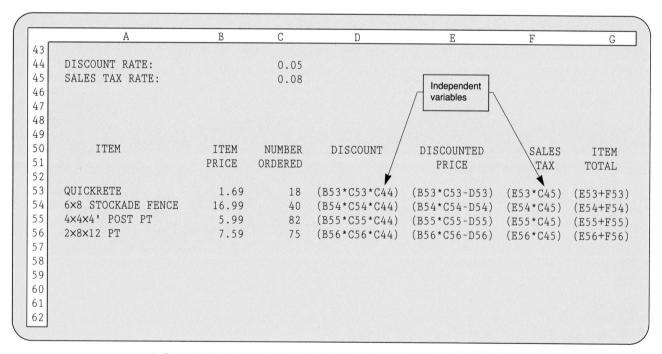

b. Formulas for discount and sales tax refer to independent variables

Figure 5-23
Alternative designs for lumberyard
invoice

Implementation

During the implementation stage of spreadsheet application development you make concrete the logical and physical design you developed in previous stages. This is the point at which you load your electronic spreadsheet program and construct the spreadsheet: write internal documentation, build macros (if you have any—when you are just beginning it is unlikely you will), and enter spreadsheet data and formulas, carefully following your design.

This stage may take only a few minutes or hours for a simple spreadsheet application. It might take several days for a large and complex application. What is important is not the amount of time you take, but carefully adhering to your design. If you vary from your original design, you should update your documentation accordingly. Also, develop external documentation during this stage.

Testing

Testing a spreadsheet application (or any computerized application) is an important stage. Too often it is overlooked or done poorly. Testing can be time-consuming, but it almost certainly will take less time if done systematically. Use this five-step process:

1. *Develop a set of test cases.* Use values only near the edges of valid ranges. For example, a program computing the returns on certificates of deposit needs to be tested only with one or two values near the minimum deposit (say $1,000 and $1,005) and the maximum deposit (say $24,999 and $25,000). If the computations work for the edges of the range, they are almost sure to work for the values in the middle.

   Write all test cases on paper. Do not "shoot from the hip," creating them at the keyboard.
2. *Calculate the results manually.* Using paper and pencil, figure out the results the program *should* produce with the test data. Write these results down.
3. *Run the program with the test data* that you decided on in step 1.
4. *Compare the actual results* (the ones produced by the program) *with the expected results* (the ones produced manually in step 2). If any discrepancies exist, investigate the problem and find an explanation.
5. *Debug the program if necessary.* **Debugging** means modifying the program to remove any bugs, or flaws. When you believe you have the problem resolved, go back to step 3 and try again. Repeat this process until you get the results you expect.

When you are satisfied that your spreadsheet produces correct output, you can begin to use it with "real" data. If you ever modify the spreadsheet (say by changing formulas or by inserting new columns or writing a macro), then rerun the application with the test cases that you developed and documented. Having a set of test cases available can be very helpful and timesaving.

Questions

5.22 Describe the process of developing a spreadsheet application.

5.23 What is a spreadsheet map?

5.24 Describe internal documentation and external documentation.

5.25 What is an assumption? What is a decision?

5.26 Describe the process of testing a spreadsheet application.

Solving Problems with an Electronic Spreadsheet Program

In this section we will see how an electronic spreadsheet program helped solve some of the problems faced by a basketball team statistician.

The Problem

"Oh, brother, this time I think I've bitten off more than I can chew," Victor groaned. "It was okay to do some simple record keeping for the coach, but this is going to take too much time. I'm stretching myself pretty thin as it is between work and school. I just don't have time to come up with all the stats the coach needs after every game. They oughta be able to do this with a computer."

Victor's audience listened quietly. Chris didn't like basketball, probably because she never really learned much about it. But she liked Victor and she had used a computer while working for her mother's firm during the summer. Chris was no expert, but she thought she might be able to help.

"Okay, Vic, settle down. What is it the coach wants that you don't think you can deliver?"

It turned out that until now the coach, who was working diligently to introduce a basketball program to this small college on a shoestring budget, had been happy to receive *any* statistics on the team after a game. Victor was one of the few volunteers the coach could count on. Vic would go to a game and keep a tally on how many shots each player took and how many he made. After the game, Victor needed about half an hour to summarize the numbers and gave the coach his results. The coach had to work with the limited information Victor could generate, such as team-wide statistics on field goal and free throw percentages. Although it was helpful to know, for example, that during a game the team had completed 22 out of 30 free throws (or 73 percent), the coach really wanted that type of data on each individual. And so, after tonight's game, the coach had asked Victor to come up with the stats on each player from now on. Without thinking about it, Victor had said okay.

Victor and Chris talked a while longer, Chris asking questions about the numbers that needed to be derived, and Victor explaining what the coach wanted. The next day they met at the computer lab.

The Spreadsheet Solution

Chris had worked up a sample report on paper to be sure she understood what Victor had in mind. The report listed each player's performance in each of three categories: 3-point field goals, 2-point field goals, and free throws. Performance was to be calculated by dividing the number of completions by the number of shots taken, with the answer presented as a percentage. The sample report is shown in Figure 5-24. That was the right idea, Victor agreed, but could she include team totals in all the categories? No problem. Chris loaded the spreadsheet

Player	3-Point Field Goals			2-Point Field Goals			Free Throws		
	Att.	Comp.	%	Att.	Comp.	%	Att.	Comp.	%
Rocky	1	1	100	14	8	57.1	5	4	80
Bullwinkle	2	1	50	6	2	33.3	11	8	72.7
Quickdraw	22	14	63.6	28	17	60.7	13	2	15.4
Augie	0	0	0	0	0	0	6	6	100
Yogi	4	2	50	12	9	75	16	15	93.7

Figure 5-24
Prototype of player statistics report

program and began to develop an application that would enable Victor to generate more information than before and in less time.

It turned out to be even simpler than Chris had anticipated. The formula for each category was the same, that is, the number of completions divided by the number of attempts. Chris had the spreadsheet done in about ten minutes (see Figure 5-25). The hardest part was typing the names of all the team members. Chris entered the stats for the previous night's game, and compared her results with the ones Victor had done manually. Not surprisingly, they were identical. (Well, not quite. In two instances Victor had made a calculation error.) "So," Chris explained, "all you have to do is enter the new facts for each player after a game, and the program will automatically come up with all the player statistics for you."

"Just like that?" Victor asked hopefully.

"Just like that."

Needless to say, the coach thought this was terrific. In fact, he wondered if the figures could be broken down by the quarter as well. He wanted to see how each player and the team did as a game wore on. And could Victor also tell him what portion of the total score was represented by each type of shot? If Victor hadn't needed the productivity power of the spreadsheet program before, he certainly needed it now. Another conference with Chris in the computer lab yielded a spreadsheet similar to the one in Figure 5-25, but showing the stats

	A	B	C	D	E	F	G	H	I	J
1			3pt FG				2pt FG			FT
2		Att	Made	Percent	Att	Made	Percent	Att	Made	Percent
3		- - - - - - - - - - - - - - - - -			==========			===========		- - - - - - - - - - - - - - - - -
4	Beres	1	1	100.0	14	8	57.1	5	4	80.0
5	Davita	2	1	50.0	6	2	33.3	11	8	72.7
6	Fournier	22	14	63.6	28	17	60.7	13	2	15.4
7	Falk							6	6	100.0
8	Kitsock	4	2	50.0	12	9	75.0	16	15	93.7
9	Miranda				3	1	33.3			
10	Russell				2	0	0.0	1	1	100.0
11	Wentworth									
12	Pietras									
13	Pratt									
14	St. Gean				5	2	40.0			
15	Conrad									
16	Vasquez	3	1	33.3	6	2	33.3	2	1	50.0
17	Church									
18	Leonard									
19										
20	Team	32	19	59.4	76	41	53.9	54	37	68.5

Figure 5-25
Player stats for the game

	A	B	C	D	E	F	G	H
28								
29								
30								
31								
32	Game Totals		Score:	131				
33			3-pt	24	18.3%			
34			2-pt	72	55.0%			
35			FT	35	26.7%			
36								
37								
38								
39								
40								
41								
42								
43								
44								
45								
46								
47								

Figure 5-26
Game totals summary

during each quarter for each player and for the team. The formulas remained the same, but this new spreadsheet would require Victor to enter four sets of figures for each player. Even that would take only a couple of minutes after a game. With a few more keystrokes, Chris produced the game totals summary shown in Figure 5-26.

Tracking Player Stats for the Season

When people discover what a computer system can do, they naturally begin to explore new applications, asking for information they never would have dreamed about if they had to do all the calculations by hand. So it came as no surprise to Victor or Chris that the coach wanted to know if they might be able to chart each player's progress in each category throughout the season. This would require saving game statistics to date and then combining them into a summary. An example of one player's graph appears in Figure 5-27. Although it took Chris and Victor a while to figure out how to do this, after they added the format for the graph to the existing spreadsheet, all Victor had to do was enter the players' numbers after each game and then print the graphs. All calculations and plotting were accomplished automatically.

Figure 5-27
Summary of one player's performance in several games

	A	B	C	D	E	F	G
1							
2		PERCENTAGE OF SHOTS COMPLETED					
3	PLAYER:	BERES					
4							
5	Game	1	2	3	4	5	6
6							
7							
8	Free throw	52	48	45	51	66	37
9	2-pt field goal	18	22	40	33	28	65
10	3-pt field goal	0	0	0	50	75	33
11							
12							
13							
14							
15							
16							
17							
18							
19							
20							

a. Spreadsheet data

Figure 5-27
(Continued)

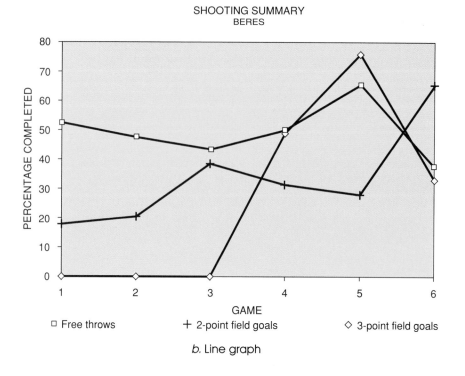

b. Line graph

By the end of the season, the team had improved considerably, at least partly due to the information Victor was able to provide the coach the day after each game. By then, Victor had learned enough about the spreadsheet program to offer the coach other reports of his own design. And producing the game statistics did not interfere with Victor's job or with his studies. The spreadsheet program had proven to be a valuable productivity tool for him.

Summary

An electronic spreadsheet is a program that enables you to use the power of a personal computer to manipulate data in a spreadsheet format. Electronic spreadsheets are the single most popular personal software products used in business.

The real power of a spreadsheet program lies in the fact that you can define formulas so the computer performs all your calculations. And when any data on the spreadsheet changes, all the figures affected by the change are automatically recalculated.

Spreadsheets are used extensively for numerical summaries and for financial modeling. They also can be used for record keeping, although that is not their primary strength. Electronic spreadsheet programs also produce presentation graphics—charts that summarize and compare data visually.

Learning how to use an electronic spreadsheet program requires working with one on your computer. Once you become familiar with the basic features and functions of the program you can develop some of your own applications.

Developing a spreadsheet application should be done systematically. Most people who do not take the time to carefully define their problems and design a solution are disappointed with the results. Following a step-by-step development process might seem time-consuming in the short run, but putting in the required planning effort can pay off handsomely in the long run. As the saying goes, if you don't have time to do it right, you don't have time to do it over.

Word List

electronic spreadsheet	split screen	condensed print
column	financial model	landscape printing
row	import	macro
cell	home	presentation graphics
coordinates	control panel	assumption
formula	cursor	decision
function	current cell	independent variable
automatic recalculation	label	debug
window	display format	

Discussion Questions and Exercises

A. It has been said that the electronic spreadsheet changed the way Americans do business. Comment on that statement.

B. It has been said that electronic spreadsheets made microcomputers popular. It has also been said that personal computers made electronic spreadsheets possible. Both have enjoyed enormous popularity in the past ten years. Why do you suppose they both "came of age" at the same time?

C. Design on paper a small spreadsheet. Use a graphical-based spreadsheet program, such as Excel, to develop it. Now use a character-based program, such as Lotus 1-2-3, to develop it. Compare the results. How easy/difficult was each to learn? How easy/difficult was each to use?

D. Suppose you were given an electronic spreadsheet program as a gift. Describe the first application you would develop for it. Be specific. If you have access to a spreadsheet program, develop that application.

E. Design a spreadsheet application to track your personal income and school-related expenses for the next two years. Follow the steps for spreadsheet application development described in this chapter.

F. If you have access to an electronic spreadsheet program, implement and test the application you designed in exercise E.

Personal Database Applications

The Director of Giving for your alma mater has planned a special invitation-only dinner theater as part of the scholarship fund-raising campaign. The color brochure she plans to send to graduates will be expensive, as will the long-distance phone calls and personal follow-up. Consequently, she needs to target from her list of 100,000 graduates the names of those most likely to attend such an event. She loads her Fund Raising application into her desktop computer, grabs the mouse, at the first menu points to the option *Select names,* and clicks once.

On the next screen several lists of selection criteria appear. Under *Giving history* she points to *At least every two years;* under *Amount of gift* she points to *At least $250;* under *Gender* she selects *Both;* under *Other* she types "Involved in drama club or chorus." Finally she points to the *Run* option on the screen and clicks the mouse again. Very soon names appear on the screen: names of graduates who consistently have contributed gifts of at least $250 to the scholarship fund-raiser, and who were involved in the drama club or the chorus at school.

Satisfied that this is the right subset of grads, the director saves the names and addresses in a file. Then she goes back to the first menu, points to *Print mailing labels,* identifies the file she just created, sets up the printer, and begins printing. What might have required countless hours of searching through old records took only a few minutes using a database application.

An Introduction to Personal Database Systems

In the scenario just described, the Director of Giving was faced with a business problem: how to minimize the cost of the fund-raising effort while maximizing the likelihood of response from graduates. If expenses were no problem, then brochures could be sent to all grads, regardless of their past contributions or potential interest in this particular event. But expenses do matter. So the director decided to send literature only to a select subset of graduates.

How the director decided on the subset is not relevant here. What is relevant is that once the criteria were determined, a database application was used to find graduates who fit the criteria, and then to produce mailing labels. The same database application might interface with a word processing program to generate call-back lists, personalized letters, and follow-up letters.

You can imagine how difficult that job would be if the director had had only manual (paper) records to work with. The record-keeping skills of a computer certainly were necessary in this office. Several years ago a file management system (not a database system) had been installed. At the time it was an improvement over the manual one— but it had its drawbacks. Using the file management system to accomplish the objectives described above, the director would have contacted the manager of the school's administrative computing services department, described her needs to a computer programmer; then waited until the programmer developed the program(s) to search the appropriate files for the data, consolidate it, and print mailing labels. Sometimes this took weeks because the programmers were busy writing programs for many campus users.

With file management systems, one often is dependent on a skilled technician who knows how the data records actually are stored and how to retrieve them. Although such a file management system was a big improvement over the paper file method, the Director of Giving is much happier now that she is in control of some of her own computing. Her database management system knows how and where the data is stored, so all she needs to do is describe what records she wants. She no longer is dependent on the administrative computing services department for all her information needs.

What Is a . . .

To understand how database management systems can be used to solve data storage and retrieval problems you need to learn what a database, a database management system, and a database application are.

Database   A **database** is a self-describing collection of integrated records. Unlike files, whose physical structures must be known by the programmers who write code to process them, a database contains its own description, a description that can be read by the database management software. The net result is that less effort needs to be spent on writing code, so that more effort can be spent on solving business problems. A database contains integrated records; this means that the records contain data about real-world entities that are associated with one another. For example, an insurance agent handles a customer's policy—the agent and the policy are associated with one another. This relationship would be stored within the database.

A database is *not* an electronic spreadsheet. A database is *not* a box filled with all the diskettes you own. Rather, a database is a collection of *related* data stored in a particular way and accessed with specialized database management software. Let's consider an example.

Imagine a small retailer who needs to keep track of customers, salespeople, and sales. He might have a file cabinet filled with customer records, another file cabinet filled with file folders on sales personnel, and a third file cabinet filled with sales receipts (see Figure 6-1). As you can surmise, each customer's record contains the same kind of data: account number, name, address, telephone number, and balance. Similarly, appropriate details are saved about each salesperson, and about each sale. You will notice by studying the sales receipt shown in the example that it contains the name of the customer who made the purchase (Johnson, Inc.) as well as the name of the salesperson who closed the deal (Ofir Katz).

Figure 6-2 shows the same data stored in tables. The CUSTOMERS table (we write database table names in capital letters) contains columns for account number, name, address, telephone number, and bal-

Figure 6-1
Data used by a retailer

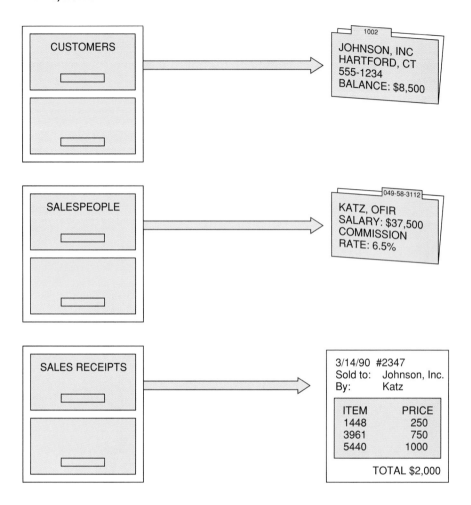

Figure 6-1
Data used by a retailer

ance. Likewise, the SALESPERSONS and SALES tables contain columns for appropriate details. A column corresponds to a field, as defined in Chapter 2. Each row in the CUSTOMERS table describes a customer; each row in the SALESPERSONS table describes a salesperson; and so on. Thus, a row corresponds to a record. A table corresponds roughly to a file. In the CUSTOMERS table, the Account Number field will have a unique value for each customer. In the SALESPERSONS table, the Social Security Number field will have a unique value for each salesperson. Such identifying fields are called **key fields**.

Notice that no matter how the retailer stores his data—in file cabinets or in computerized tables—the data is essentially the same. In either case, he is keeping track of three related things: customers, salespeople, and sales. Look at the diagram in Figure 6-3. Each rectangle represents an entity that is important to the retailer. A line between two rectangles means that the two entities are related. For example, a sale occurs when a customer purchases something; therefore, customer and sale are related.

CUSTOMERS

Account Number	Name	Address	Phone Number	Balance
1002	Johnson, Inc.	Hartford, CT	555-1234	8,500

Figure 6-2
The retailer's data in table form

SALESPERSONS

Social Security Number	Name	Salary	Commission Rate
049-58-3112	Katz, Ofir	37,500	6.5

SALES

Sale Number	Date	Amount	Customer Account Number	Salesperson Social Security Number
2347	03/14/90	2,000	1002	049-58-3112

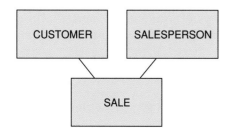

Figure 6-3
Relationships

By storing his data in a database, the retailer can employ powerful database software to retrieve and manipulate the data. He can answer questions like:

- Which customers made purchases on August 1?
- What did Akim Associates buy this month?
- Did Bob Asbury sell anything to customers in Wethersfield last week?

Notice how a database differs from an electronic spreadsheet. Although both use a tabular format, the similarity ends there. In a spreadsheet, numerical data is related *within* a table by means of formulas that refer to various cells in the spreadsheet. The relationship between one cell and another is purely arithmetic. In contrast, a database usually consists of multiple tables, and relationships exist *between* tables. A row in one table represents one item, such as a salesperson (in the SALES-PERSONS table) or a sale (in the SALES table). We represent the relationship between a certain salesperson and a certain sale, for example, by placing the salesperson's social security number in the appropriate sale record. For example, we know from examining the SALES table in Figure 6-2 that Ofir Katz closed sale number 2347, because his social security number is recorded in the record for that sale. (We know from the SALESPERSONS table that social security number 049-58-3112 belongs to Ofir Katz.)

Databases can be far more complex than the example we have been discussing. And as you will learn in Chapter 10, database management software is very complex and very powerful. But to the user, a database is relatively simple and straightforward. When all the dust settles, to the user it's just a collection of related tables. And if designed properly, a database application, such as the one described at the beginning of this chapter, is exceedingly easy to use.

Database Application   A **database application** provides the user with the means to add, delete, modify, sort, print, and otherwise manipulate database data. An application is an organized set of menus, forms, reports, and programs, plus the database it manipulates.

To perform database functions such as adding and deleting records, the user runs the application and chooses from a predefined list of options to carry out tasks supported by the application. The user does not need to know the structure of the database, how the application works, or how to write program code. As described earlier in the chapter, the Director of Giving used a fund-raising application to search her database for a subset of graduates. Doing that required no intimate knowledge of the database, of the application, or of programming.

Consider the customers-salespersons-sales example in Figure 6-4. The retailer who owns this database might need to perform the following business functions:

- Add new customers, salespeople, and sales
- Change data about customers, salespeople, and sales
- Delete unwanted customers, salespeople, and sales

CUSTOMERS

Account Number	Name	Address	Phone Number	Balance
1002	Johnson, Inc.	Hartford, CT	555-1234	8,500
1009	Akim Assoc.	Wethersfield, CT	555-6901	7,000
1028	M. Dane	Springfield, MA	555-1977	5,200
2402	E. Annino	Clinton, CT	555-0652	4,900

Figure 6-4
Customers, salespersons, and sales

SALESPERSONS

Social Security Number	Name	Salary	Commission Rate
049-58-3112	Katz, Ofir	37,500	6.5
286-00-0552	Asbury, Bob	42,900	7.2
111-22-3333	Trask, Judy	38,000	6.9

SALES

Sale Number	Date	Amount	Customer Account Number	Salesperson Social Security Number
2347	03/14/90	2,000	1002	049-58-3112
2348	03/14/90	2,500	1028	111-22-3333
2349	03/14/90	6,000	1009	049-58-3112
2350	03/15/90	1,000	1002	286-00-0552
2351	03/15/90	2,500	2402	111-22-3333

- Extract information from the database to answer ad hoc (unanticipated) questions
- Print reports containing data extracted from the tables
- Issue salespeople's paychecks
- Tell the computer which of the above options to perform

An application provides the interfaces that enable the user to perform those functions. In the following we show how the user can invoke those functions with different types of interfaces.

Figure 6-5
Menus for a retail application

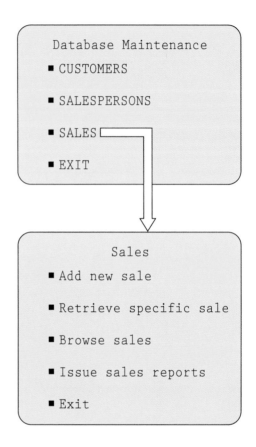

Menus **Menus** are lists of actions with which the user can tell the computer which application function to perform. Sometimes choosing an option on one menu causes the application to display another menu, and so forth, for several levels. An example of a menu for the retailer appears in Figure 6-5. As you can see, selecting *Sales* in the first menu causes another menu to be displayed.

Data Entry Forms **Data entry forms** are video displays used to enter and change database data. In Figure 6-6 you can see a data entry form for entering a sale receipt. A video form can resemble the hard-copy paper forms of the business, and thus facilitate interaction with the database. Some of the data in Figure 6-6 is entered by the user (for example, sale number and customer account number). Some of it (such as customer name) is looked up by the database management system (DBMS) and displayed on the computer screen. Look back at the CUS-TOMERS table in Figure 6-4. Once the user enters the account number, the DBMS automatically can retrieve the customer name. And some of the data on the form is computed and displayed (for example, the total).

This form can be used to display, and possibly change, sales data already stored in the table. Suppose a clerk mistakenly entered Ofir Katz's social security number for a sale instead of Bob Asbury's. By bringing up the sale record in this form, the clerk could change the "Sold by" entry. This form also can be used to delete unwanted data

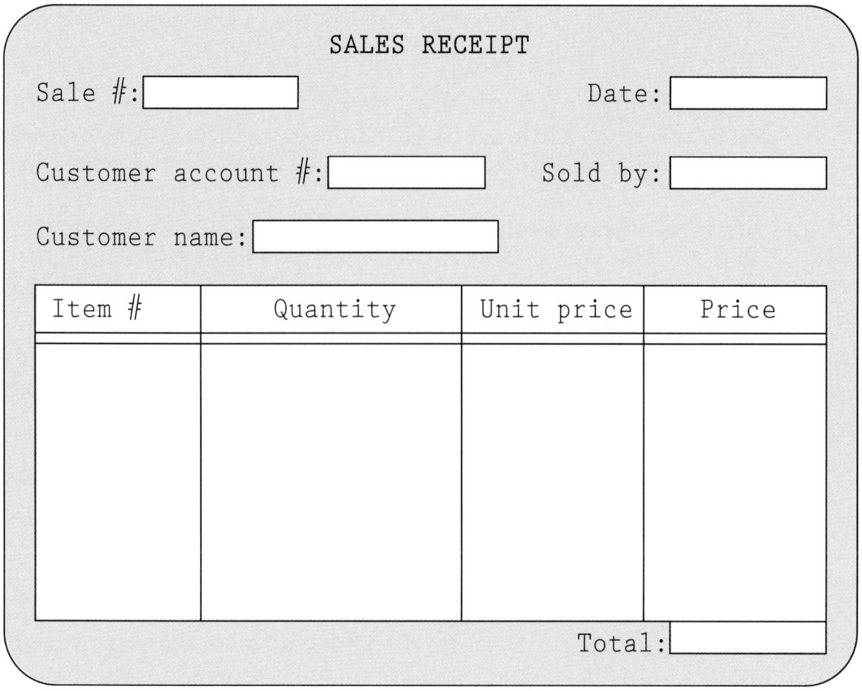

```
                    SALES RECEIPT
  Sale #:[          ]           Date:[        ]

  Customer account #:[        ]  Sold by:[        ]

  Customer name:[              ]

  ┌────────┬────────────┬────────────┬──────────┐
  │ Item # │  Quantity  │ Unit price │  Price   │
  ├────────┼────────────┼────────────┼──────────┤
  │        │            │            │          │
  │        │            │            │          │
  │        │            │            │          │
  │        │            │            │          │
  │        │            │            │          │
  │        │            │            │          │
  │        │            │     Total:[          ]│
  └────────┴────────────┴────────────┴──────────┘
```

Figure 6-6
Data entry form for sale receipt

from the tables. This might be necessary, for example, if a customer returns a purchase.

Reports   A **report** is a hard-copy output of database data, by far the most common way of displaying database data. Reports can contain data from one or several tables. When developing an application, take the time to design useful and readable reports. A report should be nicely formatted with report and page headings, the date, page numbers, column headings, summary lines, and totals. The actual data should be printed with numeric fields in alignment, and should be formatted with appropriate punctuation (dollar signs, commas, decimal points, and so forth). We'll talk more about design later.

Query Languages   Another way to produce output is by using a **query language**, which is a general-purpose language for obtaining data from the database. Query languages frequently are used to answer questions that were not anticipated when the application was being developed. These are called ad hoc questions; when expressed in a query language, they are called **ad hoc queries.** Query languages can be learned by people who have no background in computer programming.

To phrase an ad hoc query, you must understand how your database data is linked together, that is, how to use data from one table to look up data in another table. For instance, using the data in Figure 6-4, answer the following questions:

- Which customers did Judy Trask make sales to?
- Which salesperson(s) did Johnson, Inc., do business with?
- Did any salespeople make sales in Springfield, Mass.? If so, who?

■ How much money did Ofir Katz make in commissions in March, 1990?

Your answers should have been: M. Dane and E. Annino; Ofir Katz and Bob Asbury; yes, Judy Trask; and $520. If those were not your answers, keep working on the questions until you figure out how to use the data to answer them.

The important aspect of that exercise was for you to see how to find desired data by going from one table to another. For instance, to figure out how much money Ofir Katz made in commissions, you first look up Ofir's row in the SALESPERSONS table and determine his social security number and commission rate. Then you look for all the sales containing his social security number. (There are two.) You next sum the amounts for the two sales (the total is $8,000), and multiply the sum by Ofir's commission rate (6.5%). The answer is $520.

Imagine how difficult that task would have been if all the data were stored on paper in file cabinets. The beauty of storing such data in a database and using a personal DBMS to access it, is that such questions (and many others) can be answered quickly and easily with just a few keystrokes, because the data is stored with the relationships maintained. Of course, in the exercise you maneuvered your own way through the tables. If you used an actual database management system to answer, say, the second question above (Which salespersons did Johnson, Inc. do business with?) you would enter a query language instruction such as:

SELECT NAME OF SALESPERSONS WHERE
CUSTOMER-ACCOUNT-NUMBER OF SALES = 1002
AND
SOCIAL-SECURITY-NUMBER OF SALESPERSONS =
SALESPERSON-SOCIAL-SECURITY-NUMBER OF SALES

The DBMS's response to the query would be:

Katz, Ofir
Asbury, Bob

Right now, the query might seem pretty cryptic. It is written in SQL (Structured Query Language), the standard language for database queries. But even if it takes a while to learn how to pose questions in a way understandable to the DBMS, once you learn how to do it you can ask a wide range of questions and get rapid-fire answers. Also, most personal DBMSs provide tools that make working with the database relatively easy. We will take a closer look at those tools later in this chapter.

Application Programs   Sometimes you need to process database data in a way that built-in database functions—such as add, edit, delete, and sort—cannot handle. Database management systems are designed to make the storage and retrieval of data easy. And they provide features that make simple report writing and data maintenance straightforward. However, some business problems are not easily solved with the data retrieval features of a DBMS. Some require further programming. In such cases you may need to develop **application programs**.

For example, suppose the retailer wants his application to compute salespersons' paychecks, automatically deposit them in the salespersons' bank accounts, write a summary report, and record all the transactions on disk. Some of the data required to compute paychecks is found in the database (for example, salary and commission rate are part of the SALESPERSONS table, and total sales for each salesperson can be derived from the SALES table). But other details used in the computations (such as deductions, withholding tax rates, federal insurance rates, and so forth) are found elsewhere. In addition, the retailer's database management system does not have communications abilities (for transferring the funds to the bank accounts), it cannot perform the necessary calculations, and it cannot write the resulting data to disk (it could write a report to disk, but this is not a report). Thus, an application program would be needed to extract data from the database, and then to perform the calculations and issue the required output.

As you review the application components—menus, data entry forms, reports, query languages, and application programs—think of which ones were used by the Director of Giving in the opening section of this chapter. Which ones were mentioned explicitly? Which ones might have been used? Which ones would you have wanted if you were the Director of Giving?

Database Management System (DBMS) A **database management system (DBMS)** is a program (or set of programs) that you use to develop and use databases and database applications. A DBMS provides the user with three sets of tools. First, it provides a means of defining the database itself. This is done with a data definition language, or DDL. Second, a DBMS provides a means of accessing (storing, retrieving, and changing) database data. This is done via the data manipulation language, or DML. Third, the more user-friendly DBMSs also provide easy-to-use tools to define the database and database application components, including menus, reports, and data entry forms.

Most personal DBMSs include application development tools. Consequently, you will not have to learn database DDL or DML. Instead, you will load your personal DBMS software into your computer and use the application development tools provided. Unknown to you, the development software constructs appropriate DDL or DML commands, while you define your database and application interfaces either with pictures or by answering prompts that appear on the screen. In other words, you let the software do the hard work for you. We will look more closely at the application development tools in a later section.

Why Use a Personal DBMS?

Personal database applications are used by people who need to keep track of something. Consequently, the types of problems that a personal DBMS helps solve involve record keeping of one sort or another. Because

Questions

6.1 What kinds of problems are database applications used to solve?

6.2 What is a database?

6.3 How does a database system differ from a file management system?

6.4 What is a database application?

6.5 How does a database resemble an electronic spreadsheet? How does it differ from one?

6.6 In a database, how is a row in one table related to rows in other tables?

6.7 List four user interfaces and give an original example of each.

6.8 What is a menu?

6.9 What is a data entry form used for?

6.10 How does a report differ from an ad hoc query?

6.11 What is the name of the standard language for database queries?

6.12 What is an application program? Why are application programs needed?

6.13 What do *DDL* and *DML* stand for? Which one is used to establish table structure? Which is used to access database data?

6.1 INCREASING YOUR PERSONAL PRODUCTIVITY

Life by 2001 P.C.

By the turn of the century, John Sculley, Apple's Chairman of the Board, predicts personal computers will house the type of technology and interface design that will seem like descendants of today's UNIX and Macintosh systems. He calls this futuristic PC the *Knowledge Navigator* and has described in several recent speeches the five key technologies crucial to its success.

The first feature is advanced communications technology that can link processors and databases around the world, thus providing better vehicles and broader infor-

mation pathways. Secondly, real-time, 3-D color animations will become commonplace as users rely more on graphic simulations. Such capabilities will allow scientists to visualize complex numerical models with the same ease with which they now graph a column on a spreadsheet.

Improved database technology —element number three—is the key to creating intuitive and responsive information systems. One approach that Sculley claims shows great promise involves mapping and

storing information into object-oriented structures.

Fourth is hypermedia which will give future PC users more intuitive ways of navigating through enormous collections of information: combining text, graphics, sound, and motion. Rounding out the essentials is artificial intelligence technology—critical to the future vision of personal computing. AI will allow future users to create agents that can recognize and anticipate strategies and preferences as well as increase productivity.

personal DBMS software is relatively inexpensive and easy to use, many people purchase it to keep track of just a few simple files. On the other hand, because personal DBMS software is relatively versatile and powerful, other people use it to address complex applications involving dozens of interrelated tables containing thousands of rows and hundreds of columns. Finally, DBMS software is employed by people who need to scan stored data looking for answers to questions they just thought of asking—ad hoc questions. We will discuss each of these uses in turn.

Simple Record Keeping

Taking advantage of its user-friendly definition and manipulation functions, some people store just a few simple, unrelated files in a "database." Examples include a salesperson's telephone list, a club's mailing list, a caterer's recipes, and personal book, videocassette, audio tape, or compact disk libraries. Although using DBMS software for such record keeping might seem like overkill, the relatively low cost (if the user already has a computer) and ease of use make it cost-effective.

What DBMS features would such an individual use? Consider a club's mailing list. For starters, the club secretary would use the DBMS application definition tools to define a NAMES AND ADDRESSES table, to define a data entry form, to define a membership report, and to define a menu listing all the processing options. He might use a query language to search the table for all the club members who live in a certain town, or who joined more than three years ago. The fact that the user does not need (therefore does not use) some of the other more powerful

DBMS features needn't prevent him from using those features that solve his particular (if limited) problems. The important thing is that using the DBMS makes his job easier because it makes him more productive.

Manipulating Data in Related Tables

Unlike the application just described, which involved only one table, some personal database applications involve several tables of related data. For example, consider the Director of Giving, who opened this chapter. She probably is dealing with (at least) a table of graduates and a table of donations; they are two different entities, yet they are related. The tables might look like those in Figure 6-7.

Questions like the following can be answered by consulting only one of the two tables:

- Who are all the people in the class of 1972?
- How much money was donated in 1989?
- How many donors were from the class of 1973?
- Which graduates live in the Midwest?

GRADUATES

Class	Name	City	Phone
72	O'Connell, P.	Bethesda, MD	301-233-6745
72	O'Connell, N.	Boston, MA	617-399-7111
72	Zitnik, D.	Park Ridge, IL	312-963-0138
73	Carmen, R.	Tulsa, OK	918-895-0344
73	McElduff, S.	Teaneck, NJ	201-438-6655
73	Ruller, D.	Topeka, KS	913-639-2741
73	Arbona, C.	San Juan, PR	809-921-1411

DONATIONS

Class	Name	Date	Amount
72	O'Connell, P.	10/89	100
72	O'Connell, N.	06/89	250
73	Carmen, R.	06/89	25
73	Ruller, D.	10/89	500
73	McElduff, S.	10/89	300

Figure 6-7

Tables used in fund-raising application

But in other instances, both tables (or more, if they exist) are needed:

- Mail thank you letters to everyone who donated in 1989.
- Mail letters to those who gave less than $50.00, to encourage them to increase their donation next time.
- Print cards the volunteer callers can use during the annual phonathon. Each card contains the graduate's name, class, address, telephone number, and amount of last donation.
- Calculate the percentage of donors in each class.

In such a situation, a database application would be very effective. Once developed and tested, the application enables the user to efficiently address those problems.

Enforcing Constraints One aspect of DBMS applications we have not yet discussed is the ability to define and enforce **constraints** on database data. A constraint is a limitation imposed on database data. For example, a salesperson keeping track of customers and sales might establish the constraint that any sale added to his table must be for one of his customers. Thus, if his customers' account numbers were 12, 45, 64, 99, and 104, the DBMS application would prevent him from entering a sale for customer #401. The benefit of such constraint enforcement is that the software automatically checks the data as it is entered. For example, the salesperson would discover immediately that he typed 401 rather than 104, and could correct it right away.

In the fund-raising example above, the Director of Giving might consider placing a constraint on the data such that every donation *must* be associated with a graduate. But could donations come from other sources? What do you think the director should decide to do?

Answering Ad Hoc Questions

By definition, ad hoc questions are questions no one anticipated, and therefore no plan (that is, no program or application) exists to answer them. When data is stored in a database, though, it can be searched easily. Thus, in a short time the user can answer ad hoc questions that might have taken hours (or days) to answer if a database were not used. As mentioned earlier, query languages often are used for this purpose.

For example, consider a caterer who stores recipes in a database. A bad storm on the east coast suddenly drives sky high the price of quahogs (pronounced "co-hogs"—they are a type of saltwater clam). The caterer knows he'll be serving lots of seafood in the next few weeks, but will lose his shirt if he doesn't selectively raise his prices. He figures he can do one of three things: either substitute another ingredient for fresh quahogs (such as canned clams or sea clams), substitute another dish for the clam dish, or charge customers more for clam dishes.

Suppose the same caterer maintains a table of upcoming events (weddings, banquets, bar mitzvahs, and so forth). He might first use the DBMS to pull his clam recipes, hoping to substitute another ingredient for the clams. The query might be:

SELECT RECIPE WHERE INGREDIENT = "QUAHOG"

Then he might look for all events in the next two weeks where he'll be serving dishes that require fresh clams. The query might be:

```
SELECT CUSTOMER-NAME, PHONE OF EVENT
WHERE DATE IS LESS THAN 07/01/90
AND
DISH-SERVED  =  "CLAMS CASINO" OR
                "CLAMS ON THE HALF SHELL" OR
                "NEW ENGLAND CLAM CHOWDER" OR
                "RHODE ISLAND CLAM CHOWDER"
```

Now he can call each of the appropriate customers, explain the price increase, and offer the customer some options. (Note: this caterer also has a spreadsheet program with which he computes the total cost of each dish, based on the variable costs of ingredients, preparation labor, and serving. He plugs the higher cost of quahogs into his spreadsheet to determine the new per-serving price to quote to each customer.) The end results are that the caterer earns the money he expects to, and each customer is given reasonable options from which to choose. The caterer is a good businessman and probably would be one if he never saw a computer; but in this case, the DBMS helped him solve a business problem quickly and easily, and to his customers' satisfaction.

As you have seen, personal database management systems can be used to maintain simple lists as well as integrated tables of data. And regardless of the complexity of the data, a DBMS can be used to answer ad hoc questions. If you discover you have business problems like these, then you might consider getting a personal DBMS. Figure 6-8 lists some factors to consider if you do decide to purchase a personal DBMS.

Questions

6.14 List three types of problems that can be solved using a personal DBMS. Give an example of each.

6.15 What is a database constraint? Give an example of one.

- Number of tables allowed at one time
- Maximum number of columns in a table
- Maximum number of records (rows) in a table
- Data types allowed (character, integer, date, etc.)
- Compatibility with other software (e.g., word processor, electronic spreadsheet)
- Sort feature
- Built-in features such as subtotaling, finding highest and lowest values in a table
- Compatibility with your present hardware
- Price
- Customer support availability

Figure 6-8
Factors to consider when buying a personal DBMS

How to Develop a Personal Database Application

Developing a personal database application requires a generous amount of planning and designing. Just as we discussed in the chapter on electronic spreadsheets, time well spent up front yields big payoffs later on. In this section we will discuss a process you can follow to design and implement your own database applications. But first, let's consider your role in this process.

We distinguish among several roles when discussing personal database applications. The *application user* is an individual who makes hands-on use of the application to accomplish job-related tasks. Thus, the Director of Giving earlier in this chapter is an application user. She is concerned primarily with what features the application offers her and how to use them. She does not need to know about the structure of the database or of the application.

The *database owner* is responsible for the database data. Its integrity and security must be ensured, and the database owner does just that.

The *application developer* decides how the user, the application, and the database interact. The application developer might also be the owner (and the user); or the developer might be a consultant. If the developer does not own the database, then he or she needs to consult with the owner to develop an acceptable design. After getting the owner's approval, the developer builds all the components: the database tables, menus, reports, and so forth.

In this chapter we assume that you are the user, owner, and developer. If you someday hire someone to develop an application, remember that you must participate fully in the process. After all, only you know what the system should do for you.

In this section we will describe the steps you should take to develop a database application. In the next section we will illustrate the process with an example. The steps in developing a personal database application are summarized in Figure 6-9.

Figure 6-9
Designing and building a personal database application

- Design the Database
    Identify output
    Determine necessary input
    Design tables

- Build the Database
    Define tables

- Test the Database
    Load small amount of data into each table

- Design the Application
    Design menus, data-entry forms, reports

- Build the Application

- Test the Application
    Try out each form, report, and menu
    Modify, if necessary, and test again

Design the Database

Generally, when you design your database you start with your desired output, work backwards to the input you need, and then decide how to organize that data into tables. For example, suppose you are the retailer mentioned earlier in this chapter (Figures 6-1 through 6-6). What you need from the computer is answers to questions such as: How did each salesperson do this month? How did sales go this week? How much did customer so-and-so buy in the last 30 days? Each of these questions is answered with a report (see Figures 6-10*a* through 6-10*c*).

The next task is to determine from the outputs all the facts you will need to store in the database. For example, you can tell from the Customer Recap report (Figure 6-10*c*) that you'll need to store the customer's account number, name, address, and balance. (Other reports might demonstrate a need for the customer's telephone number, credit limit, or other facts.) From the same report you can see that for each sale you'll need to save the sale number, date, amount of sale, and sales-

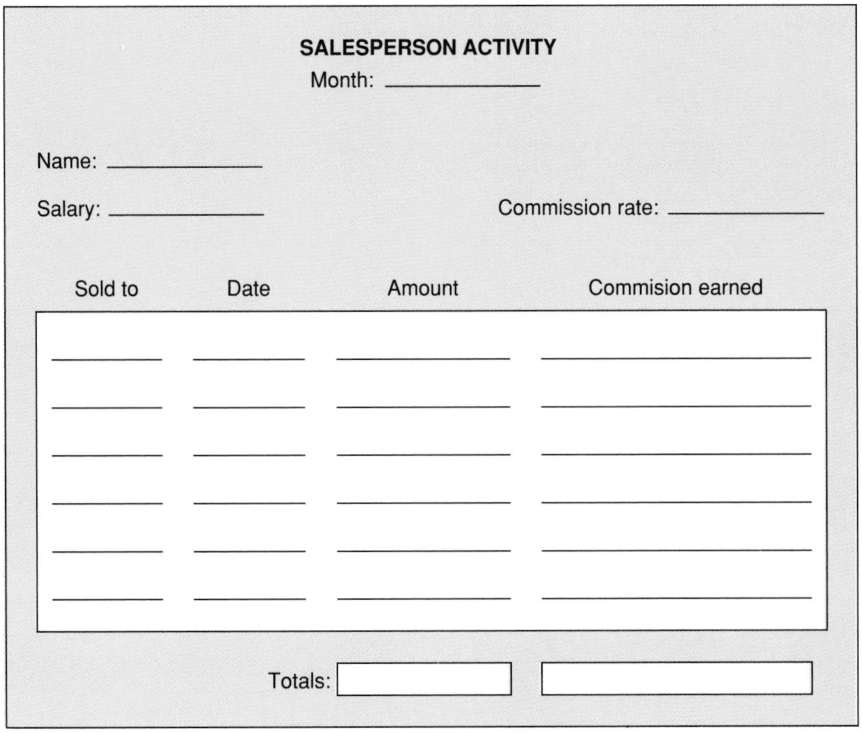

SALESPERSON ACTIVITY
Month: _____

Name: _____

Salary: _____   Commission rate: _____

Sold to	Date	Amount	Commision earned
_____	_____	_____	_____
_____	_____	_____	_____
_____	_____	_____	_____
_____	_____	_____	_____
_____	_____	_____	_____
_____	_____	_____	_____

Totals: [_____] [_____]

a. Salesperson activity report

Figure 6-10
Sample reports
(continued)

Figure 6-10
(Continued)

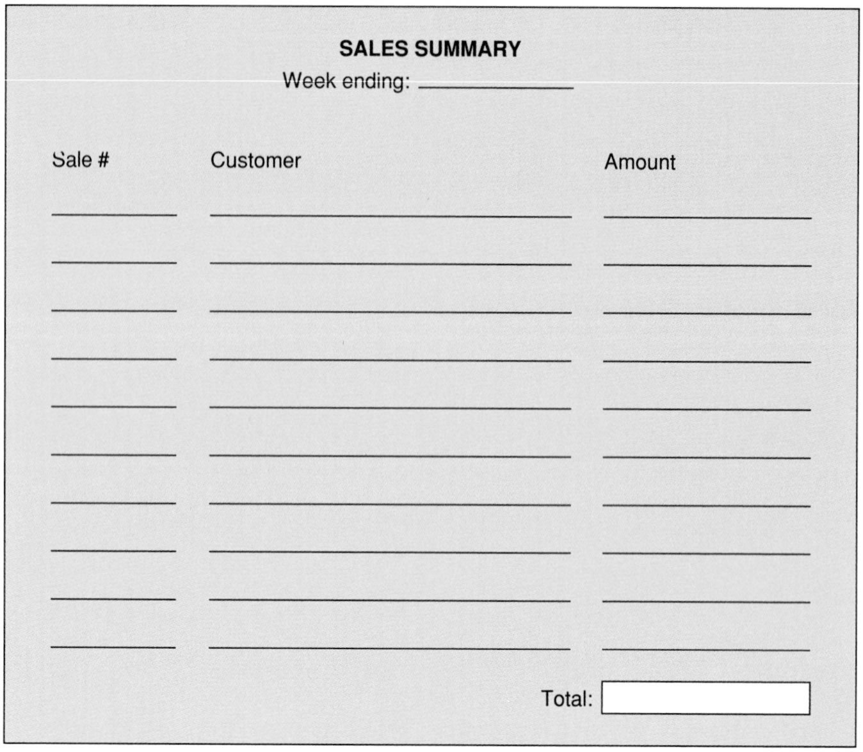

SALES SUMMARY

Week ending: _____

Sale #	Customer	Amount
_____	_____	_____
_____	_____	_____
_____	_____	_____
_____	_____	_____
_____	_____	_____
_____	_____	_____
_____	_____	_____
_____	_____	_____
_____	_____	_____
_____	_____	_____

Total: [_____]

b. Weekly sales summary report

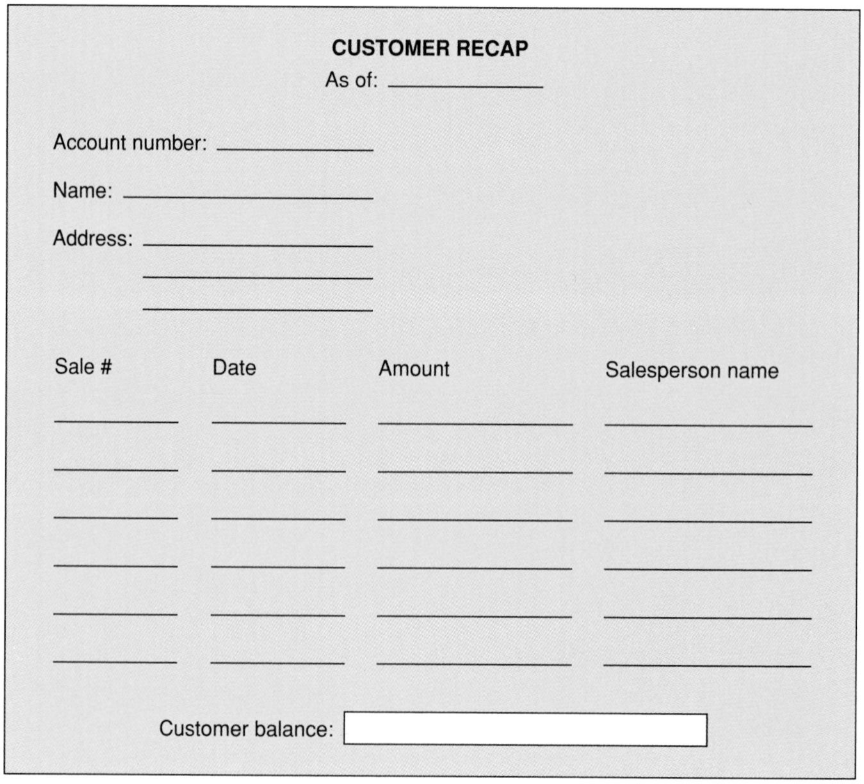

CUSTOMER RECAP

As of: _____

Account number: _____

Name: _____

Address: _____
_____
_____

Sale #	Date	Amount	Salesperson name
_____	_____	_____	_____
_____	_____	_____	_____
_____	_____	_____	_____
_____	_____	_____	_____
_____	_____	_____	_____
_____	_____	_____	_____

Customer balance: [_____]

c. Customer recap report

person who closed the sale. Examining each report, you determine the input you will need to place in your database.

The third task is to design the database tables in which your data will be stored. Each table should support a single theme. In this example there are three tables: CUSTOMERS, SALESPERSONS, and SALES. Each table should have a column used for a key (such as account number, social security number, sale number). Having decided the composition of each table, you must determine the size (length) of each data item and the type of data contained in it (see Figure 6-11).

Computers are choosy about how they process data, and if you will be doing any arithmetic with a data item it must be defined as numeric. Some DBMSs ask you to further define numeric fields as integer, decimal, dollar, or scientific. If you will not use the field for arithmetic, then you can define it as text, or character, data. Some DBMSs allow you to select special formats, such as date formats (mm/dd/yyyy).

Finally, you need to be sure you have noted any constraints on data items. For example, if customer credit limits were being stored (they are not in this example), then you might decide that no credit limit may exceed $5,000. Also, you need to note all inter-table constraints. One example is that the salesperson social security number on any sale being entered must belong to one of the salespeople already in the database. By deciding these policies during design you will make the next step—building the database—straightforward.

Figure 6-11

Defining field lengths and data types

Table/Field	Length	Data Type
CUSTOMERS		
Account number	4	integer
Name	38	character
Address	55	character
Telephone number	8	character
Balance	9	dollar
SALESPERSONS		
Social security number	11	character
Name	38	character
Salary	7	dollar
Commission rate	3	decimal
SALES		
Sale number	4	integer
Date	8	date
Amount	7	dollar
Account number	–	–
Social security number	–	–

Build the Database

To do this step you load the DBMS software into your personal computer and activate the database definition feature. Notice that the previous step, design, was done without the benefit of computer technology: it was mostly thinking and writing notes.

Although the specifics of DBMS software vary from vendor to vendor, in most cases you are expected to name a table, name each column in the table, and define the size, type of data, and constraints of each column. Figure 6-12 shows how the computer screen might appear when you define the CUSTOMERS table. Most DBMS products limit the length of table and column names, so abbreviations are often used (such as *acctnum* for account number). Consequently, it would be wise to build a glossary of column names as you go along.

Test the Database

When you finish defining the structure of the database (that's what all the table definitions are), then load a few records into each table. Don't load all your data before you have tested your application. With just a few records in each table, browse the tables to be sure everything is stored as it should be. (You might want to postpone this step until you develop your database application. Then you'll have data entry forms and reports to make the testing process a little easier.)

Design the Application

With the structure of the database tables complete you can move on to designing the application. In this step you use paper and pencil to decide on the format of your menus, data entry forms, and reports.

Designing menus means sketching a tree. The first menu, sometimes called the **main menu**, is the first one the user will see when loading the application. This menu offers the first set of processing options. The menu tree illustrated in Figure 6-13 matches the menus we saw in Figure 6-5.

Next, decide on an action for each menu option. In some cases, the action is to display another menu. In other cases you will add a record to a table, delete a record, change data, sort data, select data, print a

Figure 6-12
Defining CUSTOMERS table (R:Base format)

```
┌──────────────┐
│ customers    │
└──────────────┘

= = = = = = = = = = = = = = = = = = = = = = = = = = =
acctnum       name        addr        phone       balance
- - - - - - - - - - - - - - - - - - - - - - - - - - - -
NUMERIC 4     TEXT 38     TEXT 55     TEXT 8      DOLLAR 9
```

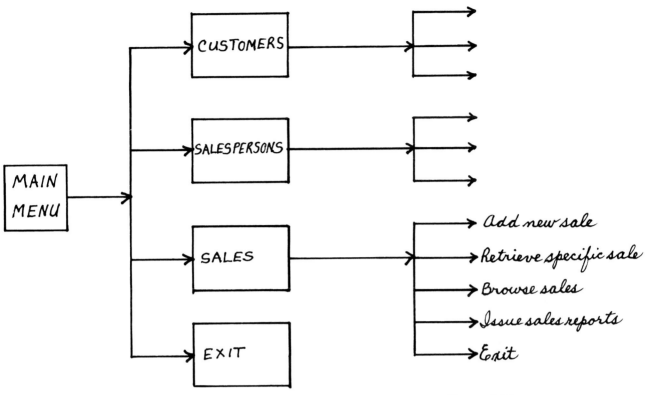

Figure 6-13
Partial menu tree (corresponding to
Figure 6-5)

report, and so forth. Write the actions next to the appropriate menu
selections on the menu design form.

Designing data entry forms means choosing the form layout (the
location of the prompts and the field entry areas) as well as the actual
prompts. What do you want the user to see on the computer screen
when he or she is supposed to add a new customer to the database, for
example? This can be sketched on paper, then used in the next step to
actually build the form.

Finally, you need to design your output reports. You may already
have done this step (or at least started it). If during the first step (designing the database) you considered your output needs, then at least some
of your report designs may already exist. (See Figures 6-10*a* through
6-10*c*.) Add to them any other reports your application will issue.

Build the Application

At this point you load the DBMS software once again, and this time
use the application definition feature. Using the designs you developed,
build all the menus, data entry forms, and report formats.

An example of a data entry form for the CUSTOMERS table is shown
in Figure 6-14. Notice that the words used as prompts on the data entry
form are not necessarily the same as the column names for the CUS-
TOMERS table, as shown in Figure 6-12. As you define a data entry
form, you indicate the prompt (such as "Account number:"), the screen

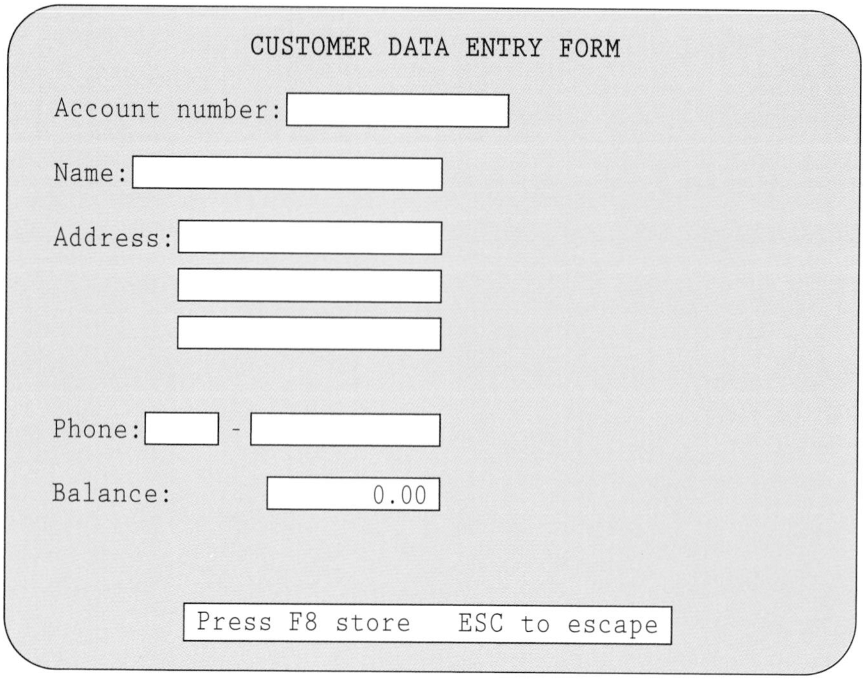

Figure 6-14
Data entry form for CUSTOMERS table

```
┌──────────────────────────────────────────────────────┐
│              CUSTOMER DATA ENTRY FORM                  │
│                                                        │
│   Account number:┌──────────────────┐                 │
│                  └──────────────────┘                 │
│   Name:┌──────────────────────────┐                   │
│        └──────────────────────────┘                   │
│   Address:┌──────────────────────┐                    │
│           └──────────────────────┘                    │
│           ┌──────────────────────┐                    │
│           └──────────────────────┘                    │
│           ┌──────────────────────┐                    │
│           └──────────────────────┘                    │
│                                                        │
│   Phone:┌──────┐ - ┌────────────┐                     │
│         └──────┘   └────────────┘                     │
│   Balance:      ┌──────────────┐                      │
│                 │         0.00 │                      │
│                 └──────────────┘                      │
│                                                        │
│         ┌──────────────────────────────────┐         │
│         │ Press F8 store    ESC to escape   │         │
│         └──────────────────────────────────┘         │
└──────────────────────────────────────────────────────┘
```

Questions

6.16 List the steps in developing a personal database application.

6.17 How are database tables designed?

6.18 Design a table to hold data on your classmates. Include name, date of birth, major field of study, and eye color.

6.19 Can building a table be accomplished before design? Why or why not? Are there any risks associated with building before designing?

6.20 What must be defined during the application design step?

6.21 Design a data entry form to input data for the table you designed in question 6.18.

6.22 Design a report to print a list of your classmates showing the data you described for the table in question 6.18.

location where the data will be entered, and the name of the table and column the data will be stored in (such as CUSTOMERS acctnum).

If your database software enforces constraints (not all do), then it is here that you describe them. For instance, if no acctnum value could be less than 0500, then that rule would be stated in the data entry form for the CUSTOMERS table. Thereafter, when this data entry form is used, an attempted entry of a number less than 0500 in the acctnum field will be rejected by the DBMS software.

With all data entry forms defined, you might next define your reports. In defining a report you need to name the report and define its layout. The layout includes constants—such as report title and column headings—and variables. Variables either are extracted from the database or are derived arithmetically from numbers in the database. The glossary of table names and their composition will come in handy here, because you need to use the variable names you used when defining the tables. Now is not the time to wonder, "Did I name it 'acctnum' or 'acctno'?"

The remaining step in building the application is to define the menus. When defining a menu, you name it and then specify the list of menu options. For each option you specify the action to be taken: perhaps display a data entry form, issue a report, invoke another menu, or exit. Follow the design for your menus, and this step can go very quickly.

Test the Application

The final step is to test the application. Load the application—you should see displayed on the computer screen the main menu. Choose the option you need to add data to your tables. Then, using the data entry forms, load a little data into each table. Attempt to add data that violates your established constraints, to be sure it is rejected correctly.

Next, try each report. Are the results what you expected? Are all totals correct? Is the right data being displayed? Are any records left out that were supposed to be there? Attempt to add, change, and delete entries in every table. Can you perform all these functions? If anything is not correct, load the DBMS definition programs again and fix the problem areas. Then load the application and test it again. Do this until you eliminate all the bugs.

When you are satisfied that your application produces the anticipated results, you can install the system by loading all the data into the appropriate tables. Then you can use your personal database application.

6.23 Design a menu showing the options of adding, deleting, changing, and reading the classmate data described in question 6.18, as well as exiting from the application.

6.24 How are applications tested?

6.25 Why do we bother testing an application?

6.26 Do you think that the effort put into design will have any effect on testing? Why or why not?

Solving Problems with a Personal Database

In this section you will see how one user solved some of his data management problems by developing and using a personal database application. The user-owner-developer in this example is a baseball league commissioner who develops an application to keep track of the umpire schedule for the season.

Defining the Problem

One of the more difficult and tedious tasks Jeff had as the league baseball commissioner was scheduling umpires for all the games in the regular season. He had to get the master game schedule agreed to by the school coaches' committee. Then he had to contact the league umpires to find out their availability—although most were flexible, some could umpire only night games, others were not free on certain days of the week or certain dates.

Filling the schedule with an umpire for every game was an exercise in itself. Jeff tried to keep their schedules balanced and to assign umpires to games near their homes, though this was not always possible. Umpires were paid by the home team for services rendered, and at the end of the season, each one paid Jeff a stipend of a few dollars per game. Jeff clearly was doing this out of his love for the game, not for the money.

Jeff was getting writer's cramp writing the same information over and over again. After he established the umpiring schedule on a big wall chart, he sent to each coach a list of the school's home games and the names and phone numbers of the umpires assigned (see Figure 6-15). Having been a coach, Jeff knew how helpful it was to have the umpire's phone number in case a game was cancelled or postponed due to bad weather.

Then he wrote each umpire's schedule, indicating the date, time, and location of each game assigned (see Figure 6-16). Finally, he sent a list of the umpires to the state umpires' association (see Figure 6-17).

While massaging his writing hand during a preseason planning session, Jeff wondered if he couldn't use his desktop computer to help him

Figure 6-15
School's home schedule

```
HOME SCHEDULE FOR        HAMDEN HIGH SCHOOL
                         14 VINE ST
                         HAMDEN, CT 06944

COACH:  C. JOHN

DATE               UMPIRE              PHONE
4/25               J. MEE              872-1144
4/28               R. BILLINGS         669-4412
```

```
SCHEDULE FOR: J. MEE

DATE      TIME       HOME TEAM      VISITING TEAM      LOCATION
4/17      3:00 p.    GUILFORD       HAMDEN             GUILFORD H.S.
4/20      3:00 p.    W. HAVEN       E. HAVEN           TOWN PARK #3
4/25      4:00 p.    HAMDEN         CLINTON            HAMDEN H.S.
```

Figure 6-16
Umpire's schedule

```
UMPIRES  1990 SEASON

Name         Street        City        State    ZIP      Certified

J. Mee       17 Main St.   West Haven  CT       06059    X
M. Adamczyk  43 Olive Ln.  Middletown  CT       06457
K. Lentieri  RFD3 #7       Colchester  CT       06049    X
```

Figure 6-17
Report to state umpires' association

out. He had bought it with a lot of software to do some household budgeting, financial planning, and record keeping. Jeff had used his DBMS for some other—more business-like—applications. Still, the more he thought about it, the better he liked the idea of getting some computer help. He didn't figure the computer could do his scheduling, but why couldn't it write the various schedules once they were established? He collected the three reports he'd been working on and started to develop his system.

Designing Tables

From the reports Jeff could see that three things were important to him: schools, umpires, and games. On a sheet of paper, Jeff wrote the facts he thought he needed to keep about each entity (see Figure 6-18). Then he decided on table names, column names, and the definition of each table (see Figure 6-19). The only constraint he wanted the DBMS to enforce was that any umpire scheduled for a game had to be in the UMPIRE table.

Designing Menus

Jeff decided that he wanted to be able to perform the functions listed in Figure 6-20, and he organized the functions into four cohesive menus. He named this the Baseball Scheduling application.

Building the Database and the Application

Jeff loaded his DBMS software and selected the option to create the components of his application. He started with the three tables, virtually copying the information from the designs shown in Figure 6-19. With the tables defined, he turned to his three reports. To format a report, Jeff needed to indicate

- Report and column headings
- The name of each database item to be included
- The location of each database item to be printed
- The source of each data item (that is, the table it came from)

Figure 6-18
Facts needed for each entity

SCHOOL: Name, address, coach
UMPIRE: Name, address, phone number, certification
GAME: Date, time, home team, visiting team,
        location, umpire

Figure 6-19
Jeff's table designs

SCHOOL

Name	20	Character
Street	20	Character
City	20	Character
State	2	Character
Zip	5	Character
Coach	15	Character

UMPIRE

Name	20	Character
Street	20	Character
City	20	Character
State	2	Character
Zip	5	Character
Phone	8	Character
Certif	1	Character (Y/N)

GAME

Date	5	Character	(mm/dd)
Time	6	Character	(e.g., 04:30p)
Hometeam	20	Character	
Visitor	20	Character	
Location	20	Character	
Umpire	20	Character	Rule: Must match any name in UMPIRE table

One of the report definitions can be seen in Figure 6-21; the others follow a similar format.

Jeff's next step was to create a data entry form for each of the three tables. His software used an approach called **WYSIWYG** (pronounced "wissy-wig"), meaning "What you see is what you get." Thus, he *painted* an exact image of the form on his computer screen by typing labels and prompts, then indicating the screen location into which he would eventually enter each data item.

Figure 6-20
Menus in the Baseball Scheduling Application

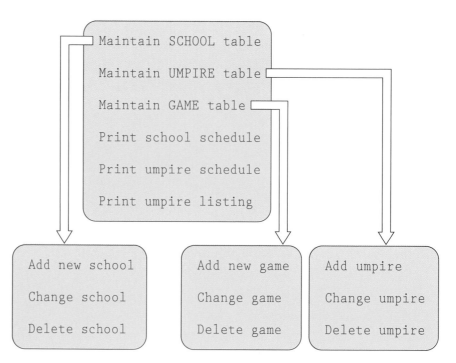

```
Maintain SCHOOL table

Maintain UMPIRE table

Maintain GAME table

Print school schedule

Print umpire schedule

Print umpire listing
```

```
Add new school

Change school

Delete school
```

```
Add new game

Change game

Delete game
```

```
Add umpire

Change umpire

Delete umpire
```

His last step in building the baseball scheduling application was to create the four menus shown in Figure 6-20. Starting with the first menu, Jeff typed each option, then indicated what the DBMS was supposed to do when this option was selected. For example, for the first option on that menu, *Maintain SCHOOL table,* the action was to display another menu. And for the fourth option on the main menu, *Print school schedule,* the action was to print a report. On the lower-level menu for maintaining the SCHOOL table, for the first option, *Add new school,* the action was to enter data using the school data entry form Jeff had already defined.

With his tables, forms, reports, and menus created, Jeff could test his application. He loaded the application and examined the main menu, choosing option 1, *Maintain SCHOOL table.* The next screen showed a second menu, just as it was supposed to; he chose *Add new school.* The next screen showed the data entry form Jeff had created for the SCHOOL table, and he typed the first school's data and saved it. Then he typed in another school's data and exited from that screen, returning to the main menu.

He followed a similar procedure to enter two umpires into the UMPIRE table, and four games into the GAME table. While adding a game he tried to enter an umpire he hadn't yet put in the UMPIRE table. The DBMS rejected it, just the way he had planned. Jeff felt pretty smug about how well this was working out.

The last thing Jeff had to test was report writing. He returned to the main menu and chose *Print school schedule.* He didn't like the way this report turned out. The school data wasn't located properly (his design flaw, he admitted), and he had forgotten to indicate that each schedule had to start on a new page. He left the application, returned to the database definition mode, and modified the report format. Then he loaded the application and tested it again. This time it worked (see Figure 6-22). After testing the other reports in a similar fashion, Jeff was satisfied that the application was sound. Now it was time to use it.

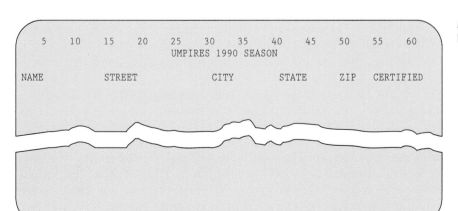

Figure 6-21
Report layout for umpire schedule

Figure 6-22
Jeff's first school schedule report

```
         HOME SCHEDULE FOR

        Hamden High School
           14 Vine Street
        Hamden, CT    06944

           Coach: C. John

 DATE      UMPIRE        PHONE

 4/25      J. Mee        872-1144
 4/28      R. Billings   669-4412
 5/1       M. Dolan      653-0000
 5/2       B. Kohler     433-1104
 5/4       J. Murphy     400-7639
```

Using the Application

The next night, Jeff got organized. He compiled lists of all the schools and all the umpires he would be dealing with in the upcoming season. He set aside any schools or umpires for whom he did not have complete data. He needed to research them before entering them into his database.

It took a couple of hours to enter all the data. Before long, Jeff realized that all the schools and most of the umpires lived in Connecticut, so the value in the State field was almost always "CT". He consulted his user manual and discovered that he could modify the data entry form so all fields except State would be cleared each time he entered new data. It took a few minutes to do that, but Jeff thought it was worthwhile. Now, every screen automatically had "CT" in the State field; he could accept it or type over it, if he chose to.

To verify his new data, Jeff used a database function that enabled him to browse through each table, visually editing it. He identified several typos, so he went into the table maintenance functions he had defined and fixed them. The next several nights Jeff spent finding the data he was missing on several schools and umpires. Later, he added them to his database. Finally, the master game schedule arrived.

It had never been Jeff's intention to automate the scheduling process. He did it by hand this year, just as he had done every year. But when he was through, he entered the umpire assignments into his database (in the GAME table, of course). This is the step that then enabled him to print the school schedules, the umpires' schedules, and the umpire roster.

With all the data entered, Jeff made a backup copy of his database: tables, report formats, forms, and so forth. He did not want to start from square one if anything happened to it. Throughout the season Jeff updated his database. Games were rescheduled frequently (it was a rainy season), and often he would need to assign a different umpire to the newly scheduled game. Two umpires moved out of state. One school was suspended from the league. And every once in a while a coach would call and let him know that the assigned umpire just wouldn't do. Jeff still had to scramble to shift people around; but at least once he made a change he could easily record it and issue revised schedules.

Jeff was happy with his new system—but like most users, he was already thinking about expanding it for next year. "When an umpire calls in sick at the last minute I have to go digging through all my papers to find a substitute. Why can't I have the DBMS tell me that? Hmmm, I'd have to save each umpire's availability in the database. That would probably mean another table . . ."

Summary

Personal database applications exist to help people keep track of things. In essence, they are computerized record-keeping systems. A database is a self-defining collection of integrated data. A database application is a group of user interfaces that enable a user to easily retrieve and manipulate database data. A database management system (DBMS) is a program or group of programs that you use to develop and use databases and database applications.

DBMS software provides tools that enable a user to define the database application (with the data definition language) and to access the database (with the data manipulation language). Most personal DBMS products include a user-friendly set of tools that enable a user to define and use databases and applications without needing an intimate knowledge of the database structure.

Developing a personal database application takes time and effort, especially in the area of design. Consequently, some user-owners hire consultants to do database development. But anyone who can put in the time to carefully design an application and learn how to use DBMS functions to define it can develop his or her own applications.

In fact, the user friendliness of personal DBMS products convinces many people to buy DBMS software even if they need only simple file-handling capabilities. And the power and versatility of personal DBMS software make it equally attractive to people whose data storage and retrieval needs are more complex. Whereas at one time only wealthy companies with vast computer systems could afford database technology, now individuals with a $3,000 desktop computer and a $400 DBMS package can enjoy many of the benefits of that technology.

Word List

database	query language	main menu
key field	ad hoc query	WYSIWYG
database application	application program	
menu	database management system	
data entry form	(DBMS)	
report	constraint	

Discussion Questions and Exercises

A. Each student lives in a dormitory, and a student can be assigned a permit to park in one of the campus parking lots. Design the database tables needed in an application that keeps track of students, dormitories, and student parking lots. Name each column, and determine its length and data type. Also, establish a link between each student and his or her dorm, and between each student and his or her parking lot.

B. Pick a classmate to work on this exercise with you. One of you will use electronic spreadsheet software and the other will use a DBMS.

Build the tables described in exercise A. Enter ten students, three dormitories, and two parking lots. Be sure that each student lives in a dormitory, that each dormitory has at least one student, and that each parking lot has at least one student. A student can live in only one dorm, and can park in only one lot (although not all students use parking facilities).

Now use the means at your disposal to write a report showing where all the students live, and who parks in lot #1.

Discuss with your partner the ease or difficulty encountered in doing this exercise. Which software is more suited for this exercise, the spreadsheet or the DBMS? Or are they both equally effective?

C. In response to a recent survey, the majority of top executives polled named an electronic spreadsheet program when asked for the name of their favorite database software. In light of exercise B, how would you explain the differences between the two types of programs? Why do you suppose the executives responded the way they did?

D. If you were given a personal DBMS as a gift, what one application would you design and implement? Be specific and creative. Would you catalog your audio library, build an address/birthday/telephone list, file your favorite recipes? Define your table(s), including field names and definitions, and establish links between related tables.

Design data entry forms and menus. What reports will you produce? Do you have the right data to produce them? What ad hoc queries might you pose?

E. If you have access to personal DBMS software, build the application you designed in exercise D.

CHAPTER 7

Word Processing and Desktop Publishing Systems

CHAPTER OUTLINE

Murray didn't think he'd ever finish his graduate school applications. In addition to his school records, he had to submit a letter to the admissions officer of each university. It was practically the same letter to all the schools: all that was different was the university's name and address and a few facts about each school he included to personalize the cover letter. It seemed to Murray that he could not get through even one letter without making a typing error, and he was reluctant to use correction fluid on such important documents. After several frustrating days of editing, proofreading, and retyping he finally got the applications into the mail.

Linda had been called at the last minute to make a presentation at a prestigious conference about a solar heating product she had developed. A self-employed engineering consultant, she had no staff to fall back on to prepare materials. But she did have a Macintosh computer with some great desktop publishing software. In just two days she handed to her local printer handouts that included her presentation outline, several graphs and diagrams, price lists, and a four-color marketing brochure. On her own printer, Linda produced masters for the overhead transparencies she would use. Without her computer, Linda would have had to settle for pretty ordinary presentation materials, or would have paid a high price for a professional to do the job. With her system she was able to produce first-class materials at a fraction of the cost of a professional. These two stories illustrate the need for text processing systems. In the first instance, Murray could have used a word processor to produce error-free letters in a fraction of the time it took him to do it with a typewriter. In the second example, using a desktop publishing system Linda did for herself what would have been very costly to have done professionally.

Text processing simply means preparing, storing, and printing documents. The documents can be simple text, like Murray's graduate school applications, or they can contain varied type fonts and graphics, like Linda's presentation materials. Your study of text processing will include word processing, desktop publishing, and graphics.

An Introduction to Word Processing Systems

Word processing systems grew out of a need for a faster, more efficient way to create, store, and retrieve documents. With word processing, documents are entered via a computer workstation, stored, and subsequently printed. A good word processing package for a personal computer might cost between $200 and $600. Many word processing programs exist, and some of them are listed in Figure 7-1. The manuscript for this text was prepared using MultiMate and XyWrite on IBM-compatible microcomputers.

With word processing, composing and printing a document are separate steps. When a document is entered it is stored on disk. Later the

Personal Word Processors

Personal (or low-end) word processors usually cost under $200 and are designed primarily for schools, homes, and small businesses. Popular personal word processors include the following (listed in alphabetical order):

- *Ami, Samna Corp.*, 2700 NE Expwy, Suite C-700, Atlanta, GA 30345, 800-831-9679, $199.
- *Bank Street Writer Plus*, Broderbund Software Inc., 17 Paul Dr., San Rafael, CA 94903-2101, 415-492-3200, $79.95.
- *Celebrity Write*, Good Software Corp., 13601 Preston Road, Suite 500W LB 226, Dallas TX 75240, 214-239-6085, $129.95.
- *Dac Easy Word II*, Dac Software Inc., 4810 Spring Valley Rd., Bldg. 110B, Dallas, TX 75244, 800-992-7779, $49.95.
- *Display Write Assistant*, IBM Corp., Old Orchard Rd., Armonk, NY 10504, 800-447-4700, $195.
- *Easy Extra*, MicroPro International Corp., 33 San Pablo Ave., San Rafael, CA 94903, 800-227-5609, $99.
- *Executive Writer*, Paperback Software International, 2830 Ninth St., Berkeley, CA 94710, 800-225-3242, $69.95.
- *Microsoft Windows Write*, Microsoft Corp., 16011 NE 36th Way, Redmond, WA 98073-9717, 206-882-8088, $99.
- *Paperback Writer*, Paperback Software International, 2830 Ninth St., Berkeley, CA 94710, 800-225-3242, $39.95.
- *Personal WordPerfect* WordPerfect Corp, 1555 N. Technology Way, Orem, UT 84057, 801-225-5000, $195.
- *PFS: Professional Write*, Software Publishing Corp., 1901 Landings Dr., Mountain View, CA 94043, 415-962-8910, $199.
- *Textra*, Ann Arbor Software, 345 S. Division, Ann Arbor, MI 84104, 313-769-9088, $29.95.
- *Volkswriter Deluxe*, Lifetree Software Inc., 411 Pacific St., Monterey, CA 93940, 408-373-4718, $99.

Professional Word Processors

Professional (or high-end) word processors cost from $200 to $600 and are designed for serious writers, publishers, and large businesses. The most popular professional word processors include the following (listed in alphabetical order):

- *Ami Professional*, Samna Corp., 2700 NE Expwy, Suite C-700, Atlanta, GA 30345, 800-831-9679, $495.
- *DisplayWrite 4*, IBM Corp., Old Orchard R., Armonk, NY 10504, 800-447-4700, $495.
- *Microsoft Word*, Microsoft Corp., 16011 NE 36th Way, Redmond, WA 98073-9717, 206-882-8088, $450.
- *MultiMate Advantage*, Ashton-Tate, 20101 Hamilton Ave., Torrance, CA 90502-1319, 213-329-8000, $565.
- *Nota Bene*, Dragonfly Software, 285 W. Broadway #500, New York, NY 10013, 212-334-0445, $495.
- *Samna Plus IV*, Samna Corp., 2700 NE Expwy, Suite C-700, Atlanta, GA 30345, 800-831-9679, $695.
- *WordPerfect*, WordPerfect Corp., 1555 N. Technology Way, Orem, UT 84057, 801-225-5000, $495.
- *WordStar 2000 Plus*, MicroPro International Corp., 33 San Pablo Ave., San Rafael, CA 94903, 800-227-5609, $595.
- *XyWrite III Plus*, XyQuest Inc., 44 Manning Rd., Billerica, MA 01821, 617-671-0888, $445.

Figure 7-1

A sample of word processing programs for personal computers

user can direct the word processing program to print the document. The printed document can be sent directly to the printer, saved on another file, transmitted to another workstation via electronic mail, or faxed to another machine via telephone lines.

Because a document is stored electronically, word processing is more efficient than typing. First, mistakes are easily corrected. A typographical error can be rekeyed, missing text can be inserted, and unwanted text can be removed easily. Second, word processors can move and copy blocks of text, search a document for particular letters, words, or phrases, and replace automatically one group of characters with another. These are all examples of editing options, which we will discuss later. Third, print formatting options such as spacing, margin widths, and page numbering are specified only when the document is about to be printed. Thus, the typist is not concerned with those document characteristics while typing.

Basic Word Processing Functions

Word processing programs offer many options and features. Generally, you get what you pay for. But all word processors include four categories of functions: document handling, document retrieval and editing, document formatting, and document printing. We will describe briefly each of these functions.

Document Handling   The unit of work for a word processor is called a **document**, a named unit of text that can be one or many pages long. Documents are stored on either hard disk or diskette. Backup copies of documents usually are stored on diskette.

Document handling options include creating, saving, deleting, copying, and renaming a document. A word processing program generally presents a menu of functions from which you select the one you want performed. In the example in Figure 7-2, several of the available main menu options are document handling functions. In other word processing products the document handling functions might have different names or be presented in a different way.

The first step in developing a document is to create it. Creating a document means giving it a unique name, and entering text.

You enter text just as if you were typing. As you type, the cursor indicates the position on the screen where the next character will be entered. Word processors have a feature called **wraparound** that lets you type past the end of a line. Words that do not fit on one line are automatically dropped to the next line. The cursor also drops automatically to the next line, so there is no need to use the Return key except at the end of a paragraph. Some word processors have an automatic hyphenation feature. If a word does not fit entirely on one line, then the program hyphenates it. (If the word cannot be hyphenated, it is dropped to the next line.)

When you complete a session you must save your document on disk. Should you turn off your computer or load another program without saving the document, the document would be erased from the computer's memory.

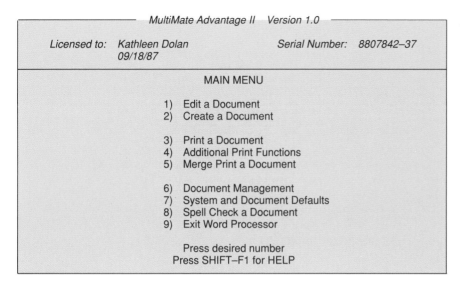

Figure 7-2
Menu of word processing functions

Document Retrieval and Editing   To retrieve a document from disk so you can edit it, you simply select from the menu the option for editing, then indicate the document name. The program searches the disk for that document and makes it available on the computer monitor.

One of the greatest strengths of word processors is the ease with which you can edit a document. Unlike Murray, who had to retype every application in which he made a typographical error, you can use the rich editing features of a word processing program and get excellent results much faster. For example, to fix small mistakes, simply type over them. You also can insert, delete, move, and copy text. Moving blocks of text in the document is known as **cut and paste**.

Word processors can search a document for all occurrences of a particular letter combination (such as a word or phrase) and replace it with one you want. For instance, you might change "Acme Trucking Company" wherever it appears in a document to "ATC." For some examples of a document before and after editing, see Figure 7-3.

Document Formatting   The **format** of a document specifies its physical appearance. Format includes the length of each line (or the width of the margins, if you prefer to think of it that way), the number of lines on a page, and the tab settings, if any. You need to format a document whether you use a typewriter or a word processor. One of the marvelous features of word processors, though, is that you can change one or several format characteristics, and the program electronically shifts everything around to fit the new format. For example, increasing the size of your right margin by half an inch can be done by pressing a few keys. The next time you print the document, the text will have been rearranged so that every line has the desired margin size.

Most word processors include an automatic centering feature, useful for titles and page headers. Most also include a feature that allows you to indent an entire block of text with one or two keystrokes. Using a typewriter, you would have to tab every line.

Figure 7-3
Word processor editing features

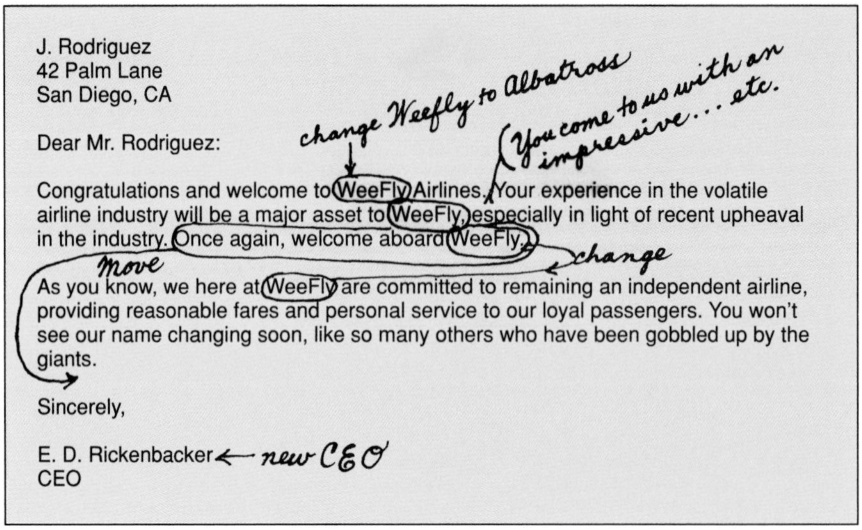

J. Rodriguez
42 Palm Lane
San Diego, CA

Dear Mr. Rodriguez:

change Weefly to Albatross
(You come to us with an impressive... etc.

Congratulations and welcome to WeeFly Airlines. Your experience in the volatile airline industry will be a major asset to WeeFly, especially in light of recent upheaval in the industry. Once again, welcome aboard WeeFly.
change

move
As you know, we here at WeeFly are committed to remaining an independent airline, providing reasonable fares and personal service to our loyal passengers. You won't see our name changing soon, like so many others who have been gobbled up by the giants.

Sincerely,

E. D. Rickenbacker *← new CEO*
CEO

a. Before editing

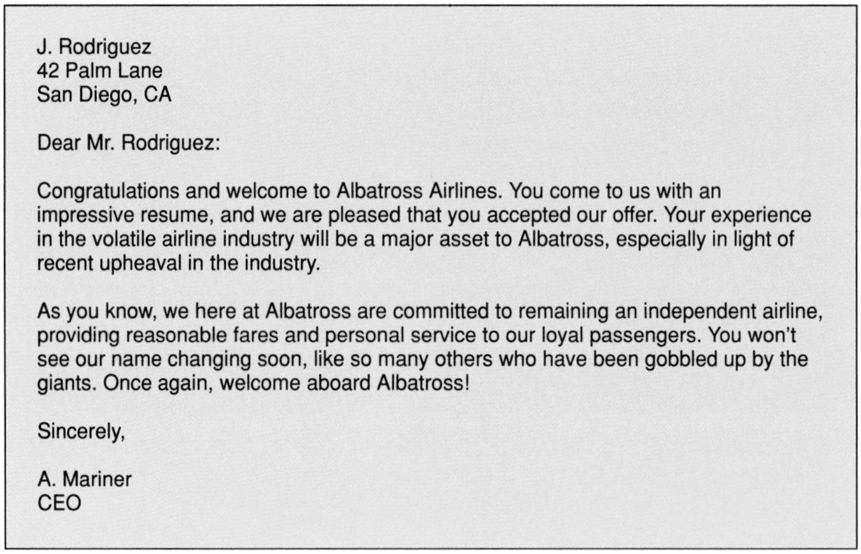

J. Rodriguez
42 Palm Lane
San Diego, CA

Dear Mr. Rodriguez:

Congratulations and welcome to Albatross Airlines. You come to us with an impressive resume, and we are pleased that you accepted our offer. Your experience in the volatile airline industry will be a major asset to Albatross, especially in light of recent upheaval in the industry.

As you know, we here at Albatross are committed to remaining an independent airline, providing reasonable fares and personal service to our loyal passengers. You won't see our name changing soon, like so many others who have been gobbled up by the giants. Once again, welcome aboard Albatross!

Sincerely,

A. Mariner
CEO

b. After editing

One feature available with word processors that is almost non-existent in typewriting is **justification**, that is, varying the spacing between words so that all lines are the same length. With a typewriter the text is aligned along the left margin; the text along the right margin is ragged. Most word processors can automatically justify the text, so that it is aligned on the right side as well (see Figure 7-4). They do this by varying the amount of space between words; some may also vary the amount of space between letters. Other formatting features allow

When the spacing between words is fixed, the lines are of different lengths and the right margin is ragged. When the spacing between words is varied, the lines can be made equal in length so that the right edge is straight. Compare the two versions of this paragraph to see the difference.

When the spacing between words is fixed, the lines are of different lengths and the right margin is ragged. When the spacing between words is varied, the lines can be made equal in length so that the right edge is straight. Compare the two versions of this paragraph to see the difference.

a. Not justified

b. Justified

Figure 7-4 Justification

Figure 7-5
Some formatting options

This example contains illustrations of various formatting options available in most word processing programs.

For example, words and sentences can be <u>underlined</u>, and <u>double underlined</u>.

Words can be printed in **boldface**, which makes them stand out from the rest of the document.

Shadow printing makes words and sections stand out visually from the rest of the page.

Many word processors allow you to indent entire paragraphs without tabbing each line of the indented text. Consider this excerpt from a word processing user manual:
> Use the Indent function to temporarily change the left margin of a section of text. Indent levels are indicated by tab stops in the format line. Simply move the cursor to any position in a line before a tab stop, press F4, type the text to be indented, and end the section by pressing RETURN.

Other formatting options might be available—find out what they are by reading the user documentation or by taking a class.

you to underscore, double underscore, and print in boldface. See Figure 7-5.

A useful and timesaving feature is repagination. The **repagination** feature automatically moves lines of text so that every page has the same number of lines. This is a handy feature if you have inserted blocks on some pages (so they exceed the number of lines you can print on a sheet of paper) and deleted blocks on others, leaving large gaps at the bottoms of some pages. Repagination evens out the pages before you print.

Document Printing   Some powerful, timesaving printing features are available, including ones that print only selected pages of a document (you tell the program which ones), print more than one "original" copy (you tell the program how many), adjust the type font, and automatically number pages.

Type font refers to the size and style of printed characters (see Figure 7-6). Many word processors allow the user to determine the type font for a document. Some allow you to vary type fonts within a document;

TYPE TO GO

A collection of yesterday's lunch-counter terms in today's PostScript typefaces.

BLT DOWN
BACON, LETTUCE, TOMATO ON TOAST
BAUER BODONI BOLD: BITSTREAM

STRETCH ONE
A LARGE COKE
GIOTTO:CASADY & GREENE

A BOWL OF BIRD SEED
A BOWL OF CEREAL
GILL: THE FONT COMPANY

REPEATERS
BAKED BEANS
BERNHARD FASHION: KINGSLEY/ATF

BURN THE VAN
A VANILLA MALT
BODONI ULTRA: CASADY & GREENE

LOOSENERS
A DISH OF STEWED PRUNES
FLOURISH: JUDY SUTCLIFFE

ADAM & EVE ON A RAFT
TWO POACHED EGGS ON TOAST
GARAMOND: ADOBE ORIGINAL SERIES

WRECK A PAIR
TWO SCRAMBLED EGGS
CHINA: OLDUVAI

HOLD THE HAIL
WITHOUT ICE
GARAMOND TITLING: ADOBE ORIGINAL SERIES

PUT OUT THE LIGHTS AND CRY
LIVER AND ONIONS
BODONI ULTRA CONDENSED ITALIC: CASADY & GREENE

HOUSEBOAT
A BANANA SPLIT
BAUER BODONI: BITSTREAM

PAINT IT RED
WITH KETCHUP
SIMONCINI GARAMOND: THE FONT COMPANY

CLINKERS
AN ORDER OF BISCUITS
BERNHARD FASHION: KINGSLEY/ATF

BOSSY IN A BOWL
BEEF STEW
BEMBO: THE FONT COMPANY

Compiled from Stuart Berg Flexner's Listening To America.

Figure 7-6
Samples of type fonts

The Chip: The Heart of the Computer

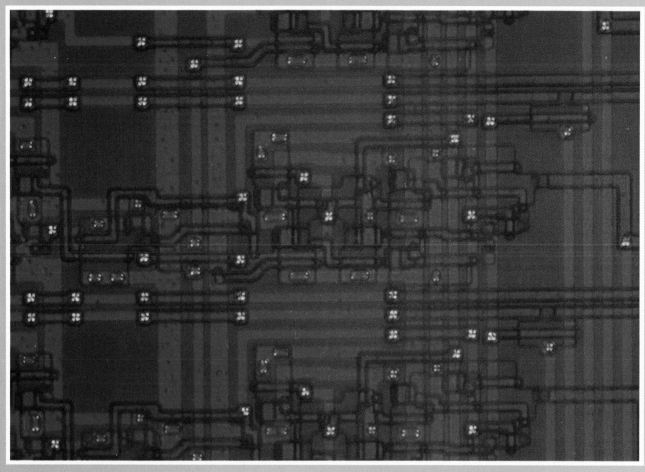

1   Metallic lines connect transistors and other electronic components into circuits that perform arithmetic and logic.

Some called it the gold rush of the 1980s, others called it magic, some even referred to alchemy; by whatever name, the semiconductor industry has worked miracles in miniaturization in the past decade. The result has been incredible reductions in computer prices with equally incredible increases in computer performance. By the standards of 1960, today we can buy a Rolls Royce for the price of a toy car.

And there is no end in sight. The latest microprocessor, the Intel i486, has more than a million transistors on a 1/4-inch-square chip. Processors with several million transistors are on the drawing boards.

Drawing boards is only a figure of speech. Although early processors were drawn by hand on drafting tables, today's chips are far too complex for such an approach. In fact, chips have become so complicated that most new chips are designed, in large measure, by computer program.

The use of such software is also speeding the pace of processor design and shortening the time it takes for new designs to reach the market. Ten years ago, two dozen engineers and technicians took three years to design the Intel 80186 microprocessor, a processor with only 40,000 transistors. Today, two designers could accomplish the same task in less than a year. Thus, we can expect new chips to become available at an ever-increasing rate.

In this photo essay, we show some of the more than 300 steps required to produce a microprocessor chip. It is a process that embeds one of the most advanced accomplishments of the human mind into the humble substance of silicon, thus turning rocks into thought processors. On reflection, perhaps the term *alchemy* is not too strong at all.

2   *Silicon rocks are crushed . . .*

3   *and melted . . .*

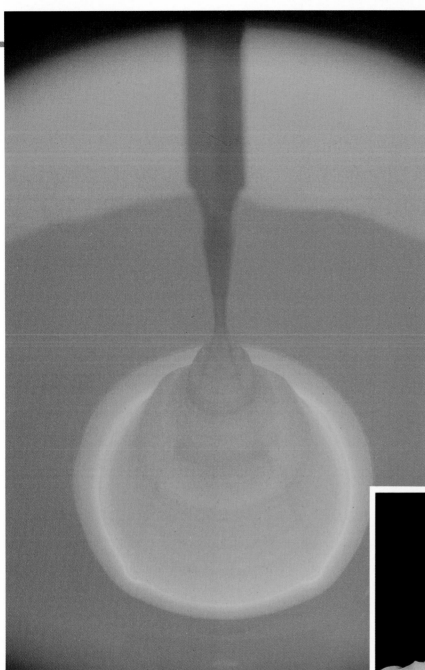

4   *into a nearly pure silicon liquid . . .*

5   *from which silicon crystals, or ingots, are made. Ingots vary from two to six inches in diameter.*

6 *A microprocessor embedded in a cradle of wires connecting it to other components in the microcomputer.*

7 *Microprocessors—the gold rush of the late 20th century?*

8 *Fabricating a chip.*

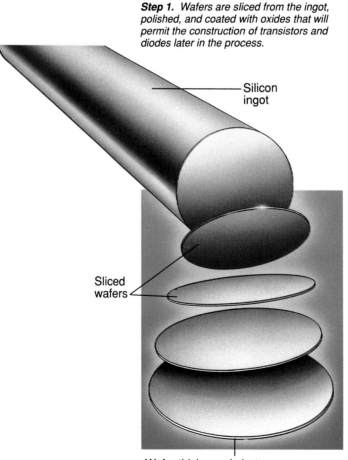

Step 1. *Wafers are sliced from the ingot, polished, and coated with oxides that will permit the construction of transistors and diodes later in the process.*

Step 2. *The processor circuit is reduced and replicated on the surface of a photomask. Photoresist is added to the wafer's surface to sensitize it to accept an image of the circuit on the photomask. The photomask is placed on top of the coated wafer.*

Silicon ingot

Sliced wafers

Photomask with circuit design

Wafer thickness is between 9 and 20 one-thousandths of an inch.

Wafer thickness is between 9 and 20 one-thousandths of an inch.

Photoresist
Oxide layer
Silicon wafer

Step 3. *The wafer is exposed to light and an image of the circuit is transferred in a process similar to that used for everyday photographic film.*

Step 4. *The photomask is removed and the wafer is exposed to acids and other chemicals. These etch the circuit in areas where the photomask has been printed.*

Ultraviolet light

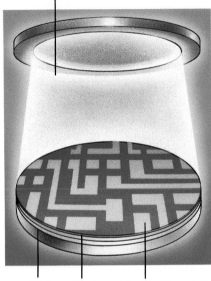

Wafer Photoresist Masking plate with circuit design

Mask blueprint imprints on photoresist

Step 5. *Ions of boron, phosphorus, and arsenic (the dopants) are implanted in the wafer to create transistors, diodes, and other components.*

Chemical dopants are embedded to create transistors and diodes.

Step 6. *A finished wafer is examined under a microscope and with other techniques. Defective wafers are discarded.*

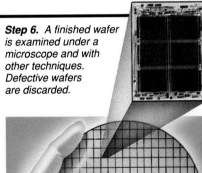

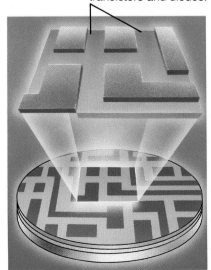

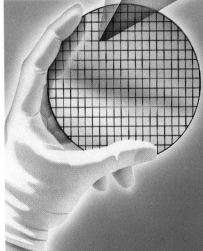

Steps 3 through 6 may be repeated a dozen or more times to build up layers of circuits.

9 *Engineers develop the circuitry of the microprocessor with the assistance of computer software.*

10 *Circuits are transformed to photographic images.*

11 *Connections among components must be painstakingly checked and errors corrected.*

12 *An engineer lays out the design of a competitor's chip. In this way, designers learn and sometimes borrow from one another.*

13 The production of silicon chips requires a "clean room" environment. A single speck of dust can ruin a wafer; specks of dust appear as boulders when shown on the scale of a microprocessor circuit.

14 A processor circuit is reduced and replicated on a photomask.

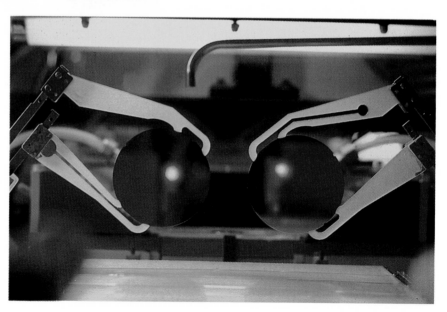

15 A photomask and a wafer are combined; the photomask lies on top of the wafer. Yellow light is used in rooms where photo processes are under way and serves a function similar to that of darkroom lights in normal photography.

16 Wafers and photomasks are exposed to ultraviolet light. The image of the circuit is exposed on the wafers.

17 Acids and other chemicals etch the circuit on the wafer.

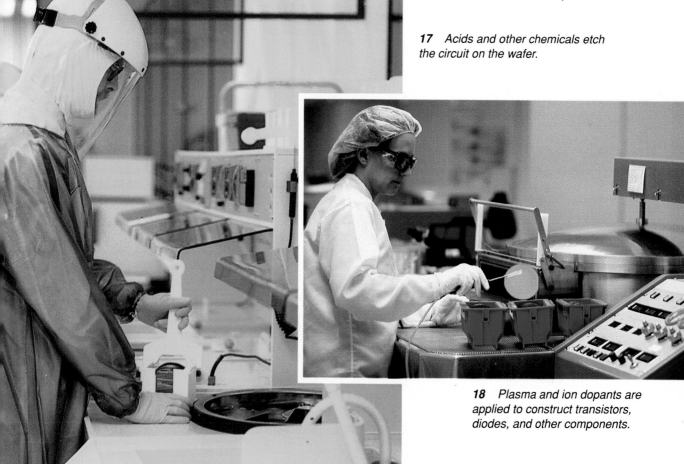

18 Plasma and ion dopants are applied to construct transistors, diodes, and other components.

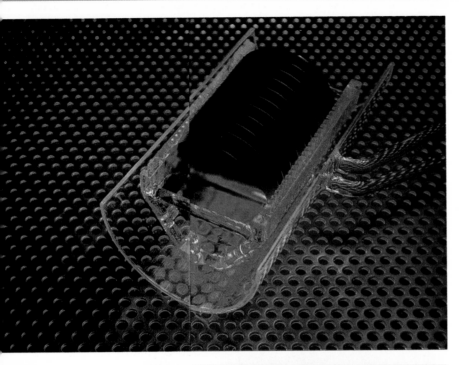

19 The wafers are loaded into a crystal glass boat before entering a diffusion furnace.

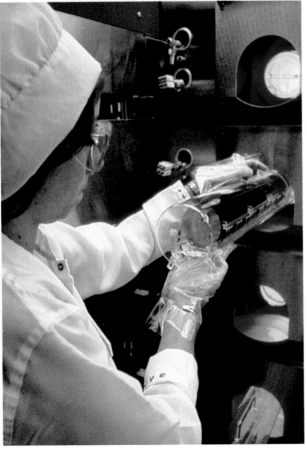

21 In order to build up layers of circuits, the wafers may be exposed to light through many different photomasks. The light exposure/chemical/heat process is repeated for each exposure.

20 Some wafers are exposed to temperatures as high as 1400 degrees Celsius.

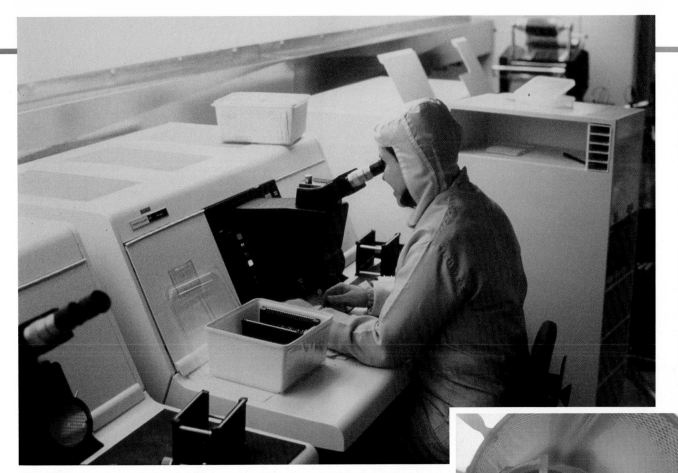

22 Wafers are inspected and defects removed from production.

23 A wafer is exposed to ultraviolet light with another photomask.

24 More chemicals etch out an additional layer of circuit.

25 *The wafers may be heated again.*

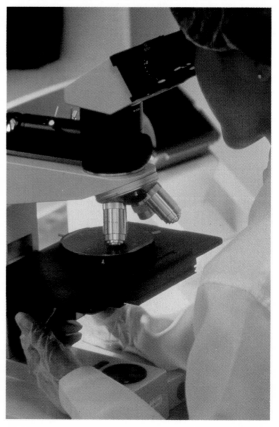

26 *The wafers are inspected again.*

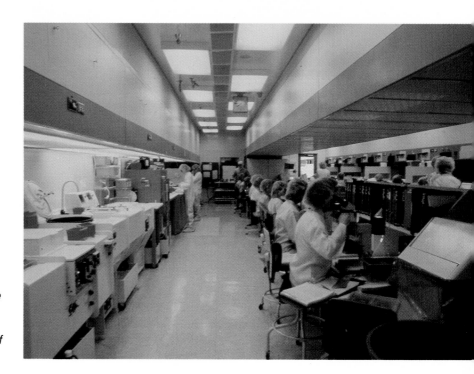

27 *The wafers progress through the production facility. The photomasking process is repeated a dozen or more times, depending on the complexity of the chip.*

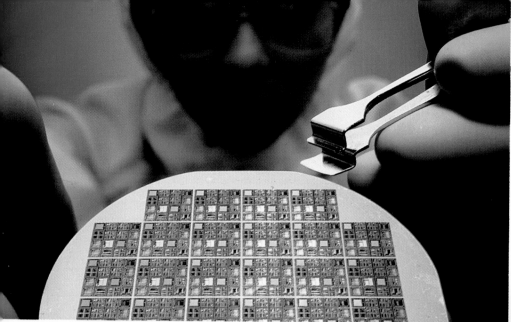

28 A finished wafer.

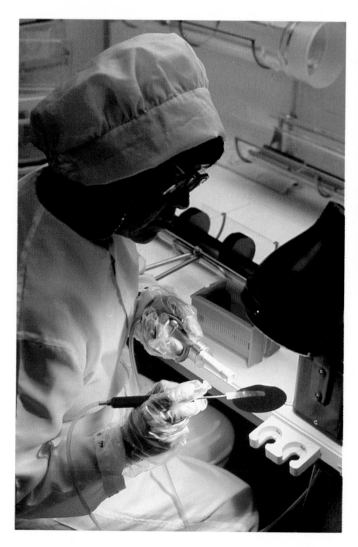

29 Finished wafers are examined through a microscope.

30 The finished wafers are electronically tested.

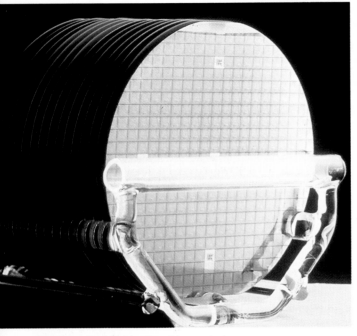

31 *A rack of finished and inspected wafers on the way to the cutting facility.*

32 *The wafers are cut . . .*

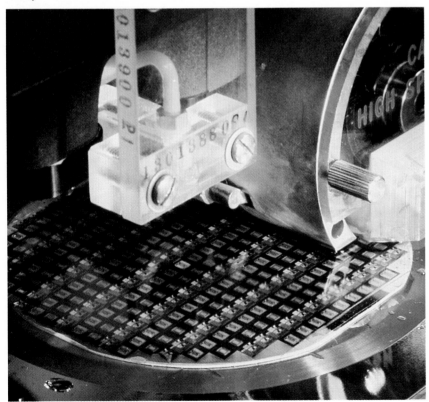

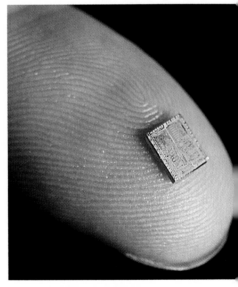

34 *to produce individual chips.*

33 *with precision diamond saws . . .*

35 Some chips are used in specialized applications, such as prosthetic devices.

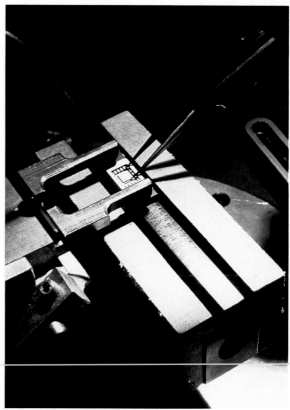

36 Microcomputer chips, however, are bonded and wired to frames.

37 The chips in frames are then combined . . .

38 to form microcomputer boards.

39 *The microcomputer boards are assembled with keyboards and other components . . .*

40 *to produce a finished microcomputer.*

7.1   INCREASING YOUR PERSONAL PRODUCTIVITY

Mr. Computer, Take a Letter—Please

Business forms software is one of the hottest new product categories around, as the feature "Forms Software Fills in the Blanks," in this issue, attests. Fine new programs let any modern-day Huck Finn with access to a laser printer and scanner create signed copies of your company's purchase order and open a personal loading dock. Clever *dBASE* mavens can buy mailing lists to automate the process. It's what the Chinese used to call a great leap forward.

Yet a similar product remains in the shadows: form-letter software. Every year or so, some bright entrepreneur comes up with dozens of prewritten letter forms, lets you hook them into your mail-merge program, and eliminates the drudgery of having minimum-wage drones try to produce snappy, grammatically correct correspondence. Every year or so, the world yawns.

Why? Because they're too general, that's why. Here's some of what you get on the *Microsoft Bookshelf* disk:

- Follow-up presentation
- General response to inquiry
- Letter of introduction
- Letter requesting a sales interview
- Request for references
- Salesperson motivation letter
- Welcome to new employee

Real Direct Mail   It's a case of missed opportunity. The problem isn't general letters; the problem is indus-try-specific letters, missives on topics the clerical and temporary help simply can't be expected to understand. That's why Dee Murre of Murresoft has introduced her first vertical-market application, Computer Correspondence. It offers forms for our real world:

- Announcement of earnings decline
- Apology for late payment
- Explanation of CEO's stock sale
- Industry analyst's correction
- Notice of decrease in support hours
- Programmer's motivation letter
- Technical writer's excuse note

Now that's more like it!

for example, you might use italics for emphasis or a special typeface for headings. This feature is available in most desktop publishing programs, and is becoming more popular in word processors.

In summary, all word processing programs feature document handling, document retrieval and editing, document formatting, and document printing functions. These features are incorporated into even the most basic, inexpensive word processing software. In the next section we will look at other word processing features you might find useful.

Other Word Processing Functions

Many word processing systems include additional functions and features that businesspeople find useful. Here we will examine five of them: spelling checker, on-line thesaurus, column format, sorting, and importing and exporting files.

Spelling Checker   Word processors with spelling checker capabilities incorporate an on-line dictionary. You can check the spelling of a single word or of a block of text (from a few words to many pages in length). The spelling checker software compares each word to entries in its dictionary. A word not found is flagged as a misspelling. You have the option of correcting it or leaving it as it is. Some properly spelled words might not appear in the dictionary, and so would mistakenly be flagged

》
Word processors with spelling checker capabilities incorporate an on-line dictionary. You can check the spelling of a single word or of a block of text (from a few words to many pages in length). The spelling checker software compares each word to entries in its dictionary. A word not found is flagged as a mispelling. You have the option of correcting it or leaving it as it is. Some properly spelled words might not appear in the dictionary, and so would mistakenly be flagged as errors, such as proper names (e.g., Hiram Valier), intentional misspellings (e.g., *Pet Sematary*), or newly-coined terms (e.g., WYSIWYG). Often spelling checkers allow the user to add new words to the dictionary. Use of an on-line spelling checker helps produce a more professional, error-free document.》
》

                    Please enter desired function
        0)   Add this word to the Custom Dictionary
        1)   Ignore this place mark and find the next mark
        2)   Clear this place mark and find the next mark
        3)   List possible correct spellings
        4)   Type replacement spelling
        5)   Delete a word from the Custom Dictionary
        ESC) End Spell Edit and resume Document Edit

a. A misspelled word is flagged

》
Word processors with spelling checker capabilities incorporate an on-line dictionary. You can check the spelling of a single word or of a block of text (from a few words to many pages in length). The spelling checker software compares each word to entries in its dictionary. A word not found is flagged as a mispelling. You have the option of correcting it or leaving it as it is. Some properly spelled words might not appear in the dictionary, and so would mistakenly be flagged as errors, such as proper names (e.g., Hiram Valier), intentional misspellings (e.g., *Pet Sematary*), or newly-coined terms (e.g., WYSIWYG). Often spelling checkers allow the user to add new words to the dictionary. Use of an on-line spelling checker helps produce a more professional, error-free document.》
》

       Enter the number of the word to replace the misspelled word
                or press ESC to return to Spell Edit menu.
    1) misspelling.   4) misshaping.   7) misshapenly.
    2) misapplying.   5) misspend.   8) misshapen.
    3) misspellings.   6) misspent.   9) misplacing.

b. Possible correct spellings are listed

Figure 7-7
Using a spelling checker

as errors, such as proper names (e.g., Hiram Valier), intentional mis-spellings (e.g., *Pet Sematary*), or newly coined terms (e.g., WYSIWYG). Often spelling checkers allow the user to add new words to the dictionary. Use of an on-line spelling checker helps produce a more professional, error-free document. (See Figure 7-7.)

Thesaurus   As you know, a thesaurus is a reference book containing synonyms and antonyms. Many writers spend time thumbing through a thesaurus to find "just the right word." Writers using a word processor that has a thesaurus can do the same thing, only faster and on the computer screen. To invoke this useful option you simply indicate the word for which you need synonyms, then activate the thesaurus function. The result is a list of synonyms from which you might choose a replacement. See Figure 7-8.

Column Format   Some word processors allow you to enter text in columns on a page, rather than only between the left- and right-hand margins. Of course, that effect can be achieved if you simply set tabs across the page, then type words at appropriate tab settings. The tabbing technique is useful for documents such as address and phone lists. But for a newsletter or similar document you want to produce **snake columns**, in which the text "snakes" from the bottom of the first column to the top of the next one, and so forth. Examples of tab and snake columns can be seen in Figure 7-9.

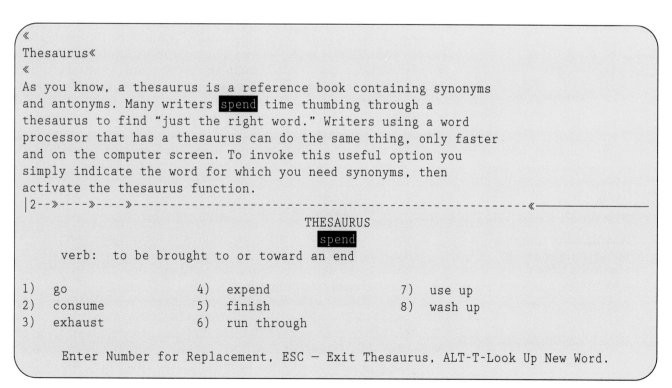

Figure 7-8
Using an on-line thesaurus

```
Smith, Joe           3 Elm Street        (203) 555-6789
Quinlon, Alison      1 Maple Ave.        (203) 999-0000
Hurlbert, Rich       19 Grove St.        (203) 582-4159
Barlowski, Phil      322 Bristol La.     (203) 589-3884
Barlowski, Mary      322 Bristol La.     (203) 589-3884
Wey, M. B.           221 Northway        (301) 555-2378
Schuler, Beth        Bridgeman Terr.     (301) 999-1874
```

a. Tab columns

This document uses the snake column format. The columns of text wrap from one column to the next as if each column were a skinny page and you put three of the skinny pages side by side.

Snake columns are frequently referred to as newspaper format.

If you prepare an office or club newsletter, you may want to use this format for the articles you write. The snake column format gives you narrow columns of text which can be easily read.

By using multiple columns of text, you also have more flexibility when it comes to positioning artwork or photographs you may want to include with your articles.

This particular format includes three columns of text. This means that you could include photos that were one, two, or three columns wide.

Usually, a photo of a single individual is one column wide. A small group shot is frequently two columns wide. Large group shots—like the annual photo of the field hockey team—are often three columns wide. By using a word processor, you can produce a simple newsletter complete with photos, which you paste into the final page layout.

b. Snake columns

Figure 7-9
Two types of columns

Questions

7.1   What is text processing?

7.2   Describe four differences between word processing and typing.

7.3   Describe three similarities between word processing and typing.

7.4   What is a document?

7.5   What does the wraparound word processing feature accomplish? How does it differ from typing?

7.6   What does the term *cut and paste* mean?

7.7   What is a document's format?

7.8   What is justification?

7.9   What is a type font?

Sorting   A useful word processing feature available with some products is sorting, that is, arranging column entries in alphabetical or numerical order. For example, suppose your document contains a list of names and telephone numbers. By sorting them into alphabetical order, you get a more readable and useful list. See Figure 7-10.

Sorting can be helpful when used in conjunction with an electronic spreadsheet program. For example, if your spreadsheet program does not have a sorting feature, you might use the following procedure to sort a group of employee personnel records into sequence based on the date they were hired.

1. Transfer the employee records from the spreadsheet to the word processor.
2. Using the word processing program, sort the employee records on the Date Hired field.
3. Transfer the sorted data from the word processor back to the electronic spreadsheet program.
4. Bring the newly arranged list of employee records up on the spreadsheet screen and continue manipulating them.

Importing and Exporting Files   As we just mentioned, some word processing programs are able to import and export files. Most programs are capable of producing and accepting **ASCII** files, that is, straight

Figure 7-10
Alphabetical sorting

Telephone List

Smith, Joe	3 Elm Street	(203) 555-6789
Quinlon, Alison	1 Maple Ave.	(203) 999-0000
Hurlbert, Rich	19 Grove St.	(203) 582-4159
Barlowski, Phil	322 Bristol La.	(203) 589-3884
Barlowski, Mary	322 Bristol La.	(203) 589-3884
Wey, M. B.	221 Northway	(301) 555-2378
Schuler, Beth	Bridgeman Terr.	(301) 999-1874

a. Before sorting

Telephone List

Barlowski, Mary	322 Bristol La.	(203) 589-3884
Barlowski, Phil	322 Bristol La.	(203) 589-3884
Hurlbert, Rich	19 Grove St.	(203) 582-4159
Quinlon, Alison	1 Maple Ave.	(203) 999-0000
Schuler, Beth	Bridgeman Terr.	(301) 999-1874
Smith, Joe	3 Elm Street	(203) 555-6789
Wey, M. B.	221 Northway	(301) 555-2378

b. After sorting

text files with no embedded characters to control format, underscoring, tab settings, and so forth. Thus, if you produce a document using one word processing program and then want to edit it with a different one, you can first put it in ASCII format, import it, then reinsert control codes appropriate to the second word processing program.

Some word processing programs accept output directly from another word processor and automatically replace the other program's control codes with its own. This approach is faster, but it is not available with all programs.

Will Word Processing Make You a Better Writer?

A standard marketing approach is to claim that a word processing program can "make writing easier." Do not be fooled by this claim. Writing, whether a letter, a report, a thesis, or a textbook, involves much more than pressing some keys on a keyboard. If you have nothing to say, a word processor will not help you. However, since editing is so easy with a word processor, it is more likely that you will make several drafts of a document, each one (hopefully) a little better than the previous one. Most writers are more willing to incorporate improvements if they can do so without extensive retyping. The result is often a better product.

7.10 Describe the spelling checker feature of a word processing program. What are its advantages? Are there any disadvantages or costs associated with such a feature?

7.11 Describe the on-line thesaurus feature of a word processing program. Do all word processing programs include this feature? Describe two situations in which such a feature would be useful to you.

7.12 What is the difference between a tab column and a snake column?

7.13 Describe an application (not in the text) for tab columns. Describe an application (not in the text) for snake columns.

7.14 How can the word processing sort feature be used in conjunction with an electronic spreadsheet (or DBMS) program?

7.2 INCREASING YOUR PERSONAL PRODUCTIVITY

Questionnaire: Do you really need a word processor?

How often do you (or would you like to) do the following? (3 = three or more times a week, 2 = about once or twice a week, 1 = about once a week or less, 0 = never):

_____ Type a letter or memo?

_____ Type an article, essay, or research paper?

_____ Type a report, brochure, or catalog?

_____ Type a book or manual?

_____ Type tables or charts?

_____ Create a family or company newsletter?

_____ Check your spelling in a dictionary?

_____ Type the same information in different documents?

_____ Make copies of your written work?

_____ Change or revise what you write?

_____ Need help with hyphenation?

_____ Use a thesaurus?

_____ Use specialized words in your vocabulary?

_____ Use a multiple-column format?

_____ Address envelopes or use a mailing label?

_____ Need specialized characters in your document?

_____ Underline, bold, or italicize words in your writing?

_____ Demand perfection in everything you write or type?

_____ Own or are planning to buy a computer?

_____ Own a small business?

_____ **Score** *(Sum of all the points)*

If your score is:

40 or more	Drop everything and buy a word processor—now!
25 to 39	You would definitely benefit from a word processor.
10 to 24	If you have the money, buy a word processor.
9 or less	Save your money or go buy a new stereo system.

Desktop Publishing

The second category of text processing technology is called desktop publishing. **Desktop publishing (DTP)** is a computer-based application that enables you to produce professional-quality page layouts. In essence, desktop publishing software is page composition software.

The output you produce with a desktop publishing system can be equivalent in quality to those produced by typographers, graphic artists, and graphics professionals. You can print your final document on paper—this is called **camera-ready copy**—and use it as the master for offset printing. Figure 7-11a shows a brochure produced by this method. DTP output also can be transmitted electronically to a typesetting machine for high-quality, high-volume printing such as book printing. The brochure shown in Figure 7-11b was produced by this method. A summary of the uses of desktop publishing in business can be seen in Figure 7-12. They include newsletters, fliers, annual reports, and books, to name a few.

The unit you work with in page layout is the page. Pages can have multiple columns, various type sizes and styles, rules, bars, boxes, and other graphical symbols that are standard in the publishing industry. In addition, page layouts often combine text with artwork (see the section on graphics, below). Thus, desktop publishing software must enable you to combine words and pictures on the same page.

To make page layout easier, most DTP systems display on the computer screen an exact image of how the printed page will look. This is known in the industry as what-you-see-is-what-you-get, or WYSIWYG ("wissy-wig"). WYSIWYG allows quick and easy page formatting because the results of design changes can be seen and evaluated immediately.

In the introduction to this chapter you met Linda, the solar engineer who put together various handouts in a couple of days with the help of her desktop publishing system. The handouts contained several graphs

Figure 7-11
Two examples of desktop publishing output (*continued*)

a. Using WordPerfect and laser printer

Figure 7-11
(Continued)

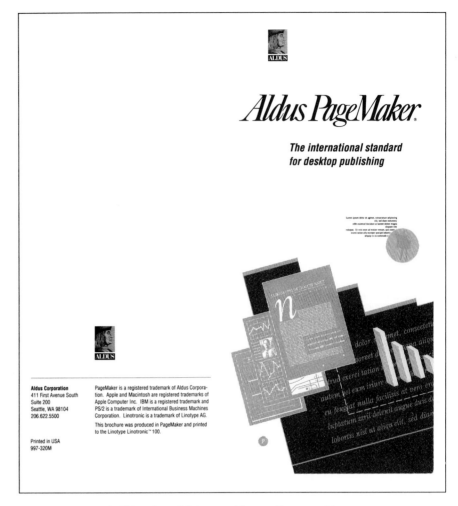

b. Using PageMaker and typesetting machine

and diagrams interspersed throughout the printed text. Figure 7-13 illustrates the process she used to develop her presentation materials. Linda needed to draw pictures (using freehand drawing software—described later in this chapter) and store them in disk files. Then she typed and stored the text, using a word processor. Finally, she used DTP software to merge the graphics and text by indicating the location and size of each picture and column of text within each page, producing the final document. Let's look at how DTP software handles text and graphics.

Text Handling

Desktop publishing products allow you to enter text directly, using the DTP product. But most DTP users enter and edit their text with a word processing program, then import the document into the desktop publisher for page layout. Once they get the text onto the layout screen, they can use DTP software to format it appropriately for printing. For

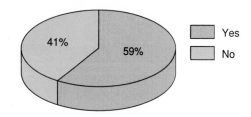

Do you use or have you selected for your company a desktop publishing program?

41%   59%   Yes / No

When *PC Magazine* checked into desktop publishing use, it found that *PageMaker* and *Ventura Publisher* are dividing the largest part of the market, and standard office projects, like newsletters and brochures, are the main tasks.

Of the 41 percent who said they don't currently use a desktop publishing program, 59 percent said they planned to get one.

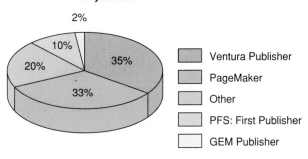

Which desktop publishing program do you use?

2%, 10%, 20%, 33%, 35%

Ventura Publisher / PageMaker / Other / PFS: First Publisher / GEM Publisher

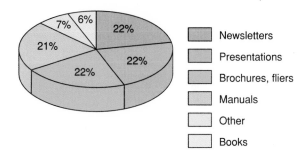

What kinds of projects do you use desktop publishing software for?

6%, 7%, 21%, 22%, 22%, 22%

Newsletters / Presentations / Brochures, fliers / Manuals / Other / Books

Figure 7-12
Desktop publishing in business

example, they might insert paragraph or section headings, headlines, and bylines. The typeface for certain words or blocks of text might be changed on the screen. What the original author wrote as an ordinary document might be laid out in columns, as in a newspaper. Thus, it must be changed to look like a newspaper.

Newspaper columns (and book pages) are justified—the spaces between words are adjusted so that all lines are the same length. In addition, varying the amount of space between the letters within each word can make the overall appearance of the document more consistent. For example, an *l* doesn't need as much space as an *m* (though a typewriter will give them both the same space). Varying the space between letters is called **kerning**. An illustration of kerning can be seen in Figure 7-14. DTP software can automatically adjust the letter spacing to achieve good visual results.

Another feature that is useful to page compositors is automatic **leading**. Leading (pronounced "led-ding") means varying the amount of blank space between lines to achieve overall consistency. Typesetters used to use strips of lead between lines of type to achieve this effect, and the term *leading* is still used although the technology has changed. DTP software can automatically adjust line spacing, even fractionally, to achieve a visually consistent image.

When laying out text for publication, you should avoid *widows* and *orphans*. A **widow** occurs when the last line of a paragraph appears at the top of a page or column. An **orphan** exists when the first line of a paragraph appears at the bottom of a page or column. In such cases,

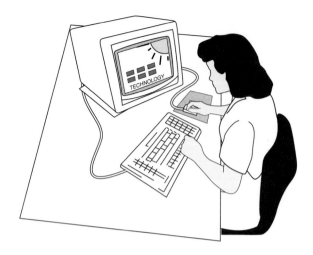

Step 1: Build graphics file using drawing program.

Step 2: Build text file using word processing program.

Step 3: Merge text and art into page layouts using desktop publishing program.

Figure 7-13
Steps in producing Linda's handouts

the dangling line must be moved backward or forward (as appropriate) or one or more related lines of text must be moved ahead or backward to join it. DTP software automatically detects and resolves widow and orphan problems.

Graphics Handling

Graphics that are to be incorporated into a document can get there from three sources. First, the document can be printed on paper with blank space where the graphic should appear. The printer can then paste the graphic to the page for shooting (literally cut and paste). In this case, the DTP software only needs to be able to leave blank space on a page.

Second, graphics also can be drawn into the document directly, using the freehand drawing capabilities of the desktop publishing software. This is a reasonable option for simple line drawings.

Third, pictures, photographs, and drawings can be developed and stored in files (we'll discuss graphics later), and then the DTP software can incorporate them into the page layout wherever the user wants them to be.

Once a graphic is on the screen, several options are available for manipulating it. For example, the image can be increased or decreased in size. It can be rotated. Some products allow you to retouch graphics once the images have been entered into the system. You can change colors (assuming your system can handle colors), for example, changing the background in a photograph from blue to beige. Of course, not all DTP products incorporate all these features. But these are examples of the kinds of page layout functions you can find in desktop publishing software.

Although desktop publishing software is reasonably user-friendly, you should remember that it is merely a tool for designing and laying out printed matter. To produce a good document, it is at least as important to understand the principles behind graphic design as it is to know how to use a desktop publishing program. Just as a word processing system will not make you a writer, neither will a desktop publishing system make you a layout artist. A visit to your local library or even a computer store can help you find reference materials on design and page layouts (for example, *The Aldus Guide to Basic Design* by Roger C. Parker, and *The Illustrated Handbook of Desktop Publishing and Typesetting* by Michael L. Kleper). A desktop publishing program can help you improve your productivity. But first you need to understand the job you are doing.

Figure 7-14
Kerning

In this figure you see the same paragraph typeset two different ways. In the first example, the amount of space between the letters within words is always the same. In the second example, the typesetter adjusted the space between letters, giving a more consistent overall appearance.

a. Without kerning

In this figure you see the same paragraph typeset two different ways. In the first example, the amount of space between the letters within words is always the same. In the second example, the typesetter adjusted the space between letters, giving a more consistent overall appearance.

b. With kerning

7.3   INCREASING YOUR PERSONAL PRODUCTIVITY

How to Decide Between a Desktop Publisher and a Word Processor

Needs Analysis Managers throughout the microcomputing world are increasingly being asked to perform the same sort of analysis as Kalemmack, as users seek more control over their finished documents.

One of the first things managers need to ask their users is what kind of work they want to do, said Amy Wohl, president of Wohl Associates in Bala Cynwyd, Pennsylvania, which does consulting in end-user computing.

High-End Word Processing vs. Desktop Publishing "If you were mainly looking to add fonts, type sizes, and imported graphics to a document, I'd probably suggest that you don't really need desktop publishing because you can do all of those things with high-end word processors now," Wohl said. "If you wanted to do a lot of layout, especially complicated layout, I'd probably be more inclined to think that you need desktop publishing."

Another way to look at the issue is in terms of typographic sophistication, Cline said. "A lot of the word processors today will give you the ability to justify text, and some will even hyphenate for you automatically and do multiple columns and so forth," he said. "But overall, you just don't have the same range of typographic control [on a word processor] as with a desktop publishing package."

User Skill Level Another important consideration is the user's level of experience with word processing. "If you are a skilled word processing user, asking you to use the facilities in, say, WordPerfect 5.0 to do fancier output is a reasonable thing to do," Wohl said. "But if you are a new user, that is really asking you to do quite a lot." Word processing novices might as well go straight to a desktop publishing package if that's what they need, despite the extra time and expense it would entail, she added.

If the user's experience is with a word processing package that does not offer a high-end version with desktop publishing features, the user may have to face another hard choice, Wohl said. "Should I buy a desktop publishing product to use in addition to the word processor I am using now, or is this the signal that I need to move to a different kind of [word processing] product?"

Training But the single most critical issue in this whole process is training, according to Chad Canty, founder of Seattle Micropublishing, a publishing consultant service. Managers should always ask their users about how much training they have had in desktop publishing and how much they are willing to undergo, Canty said.

Graphics: Art for Business Publications

When discussing desktop publishing, we separate the components of a document into two categories: text and art. Text refers to printed words, entered (usually) via a word processing program, and stored as a text file. Anything that is not text is art. The art you incorporate in a page layout can be entered directly via the DTP program (as mentioned above), or it can come from a disk file. How art gets into disk files is the subject of this section.

Basically, there are two kinds of art: line art and continuous-tone art. **Line art**, such as line drawings and bar charts, consists simply of black lines on a white background. **Continuous-tone art**, such as photographs, is made up of many shades of gray. Continuous-tone art can be entered into a computer system via a scanner, a camera that digitizes the printed image (these were discussed in Chapter 2). A desktop scan-

7.4 INCREASING YOUR PERSONAL PRODUCTIVITY

A Quick Guide to PC Graphics

The world of graphics is a complicated one. Here are its seven main continents.

Paint Programs Paint programs are for rough sketches, freehand drawings, or modification of scanned (TIFF) images for desktop publishing. They produce bitmapped images, which degrade when enlarged and have device-dependent resolution. Images are easily editable at the pixel level, and file size grows with image size. Most of these programs generate files in .PCX format. Examples: *PC Paintbrush, Publisher's Paintbrush, Windows Paint.*

Illustration/Design Software This type of software produces vector-based images. Curved line-drawing tools are an advantage found in these programs. Sophisticated color models are often available for the creation of camera-ready color separations. The popularity of these packages is growing relative to that of paint programs, because output is device-independent (image resolution can be as high as the output device allows). Programs generate a number of proprietary file formats. .CGM (Computer Graphics Metafile) is a strong candidate for the object-based standard image file format. Examples: *Adobe Illustrator, Corel Draw!, GEM Artline, MASS-11 Draw, Micrografx Designer.*

Presentation Graphics Software Presentation graphics packages help the nonartist create good-looking text, data-driven graphs, and simple diagrams. Charting is linked to numeric data (often imported from spreadsheets). Some packages include graphics primitives (arrows, boxes, lines), and some offer clip-art libraries to supplement diagrams and charts. Editing, moving, and resizing is easy. Packages support a variety of output devices, including film recorders, plotters, laser printers, color printers, and slide service bureaus. Examples: *Freelance Plus, Graph Plus, Harvard Graphics.*

Desktop presentation packages are offshoots of presentation graphics that stress the concept of a total presentation. They include the ability to sequence slide shows on a monitor and to prepare speaker notes and audience handouts. Some graphics packages (*Freelance Plus, Harvard Graphics*) are addressing this need with slide-show utilities, but right now, with the exception of *Xerox Presents,* the Mac's *Microsoft Powerpoint* and *Aldus Persuasion* have no PC peers.

Animation Software These programs link, chain, and sequence multiple graphics to create desktop videos. All have transitional screen dissolves (wipes, fades) that you can design and direct. Packages include scripting languages that let you create the illusion of movement; they also include simple graphics tools to create images. Screen captures from other sources can be modified and sequenced as well. The results are shown on a monitor, sent as a demo or tutorial disk, or used on a laptop during a sales call. Examples: *PC Storyboard Plus, Show Partner F/X, VCN Concorde.*

CADD Software As technical cousins of vector-based design software, CADD (computer-aided design and drafting) packages are primarily used in the fields of architecture, engineering, industrial design, and facilities management. Auto-dimensioning, 3-D capabilities, shading, and solid modeling are some of the high-end features that make CADD stand apart from illustration packages, though many CADD images can be exported to illustration packages for further editing, or to desktop publishing documents. Examples: *AutoCAD, Cadkey, Generic CAD.*

Desktop Publishing DTP packages import graphical images created elsewhere and surround them with text to create complete fliers, newsletters, advertisements, and books. These packages can import all common graphics types, and they have some ability to modify and size graphics directly. Examples: *IBM Interleaf Publisher* (which includes built-in charting and illustration tools), *PageMaker, Ventura Publisher.*

Other Graphics Tools **Clip-art libraries** contain files of professionally created illustrations and are available in both bitmapped and object-based formats from a number of vendors. Some packages, like Computer Support's *Arts & Letters* offer extensive editing capabilities, while others, like *ImageBase*, offer images that aren't meant to be edited.

Screen capture software grabs the image on-screen from video memory for insertion into a document, for output to a high-quality device, or for modification. Examples: *Collage, Hotshot, Pixel Pop.*

File conversion software translates one graphics format into another to move images among graphics programs—for instance, between vector-based and pixel-based packages. Examples: *HiJaak, Passport.*

Questions

7.15 What is desktop publishing?

7.16 What is the output of a desktop publishing system?

7.17 What is camera-ready copy?

7.18 Describe the difference between word processing and desktop publishing in terms of the output of each.

7.19 What does the acronym *WYSIWYG* stand for? What does it mean in terms of desktop publishing?

7.20 What is kerning? What is leading?

7.21 Describe the difference between a widow and an orphan in a document.

7.22 Name two kinds of art used in desktop publishing. Give an example of each.

7.23 Describe four methods for placing graphics in a library.

ner looks much like a photocopying machine, but instead of copying an image to paper, it feeds it into a computer so it can be displayed on a screen, edited, and stored in a file.

Several options are available for entering line art. For example, you can produce business graphs with an electronic spreadsheet program and store them in files. Various files or libraries of commercially produced **clip art** also are available at most computer stores (see Figure 7-15). The advantages of clip art are that it is relatively inexpensive and is immediately available. For those reasons, clip art is used frequently in newsletters. The primary disadvantage of commercial clip art is that you are limited to the pictures someone else decided to draw. If you want pictures not in the library, you need to create them yourself.

You can create your own line drawings by using one of the many electronic freehand drawing programs available, such as MacDraw and MacPaint, Adobe Illustrator and Microsoft Paintbrush. See Figure 7-16. Such graphics editing programs let you use a mouse to draw lines on the computer screen. Then you can add color, invert shapes on the screen, create mirror images of shapes, and perform many other functions. When satisfied with the drawing, you save it in a file for further editing or for inclusion in a page layout. This approach takes longer than clip art, but the result is custom artwork.

Finally, line drawings also can be entered into your computer system via a scanner. Professional illustrators often begin design work with pencil and paper, called a *pencil rough*. When satisfied with a design concept, they scan the rough into the computer, call the image up on the screen, and use the graphics program to work with it.

As you can see, you can build graphics files in a variety of ways. No matter how it got there, once a graphic is stored in a file it can be incorporated into a page layout by means of a desktop publishing program.

Why Use Text Processing Programs?

Many applications exist for text processing systems. We will consider four categories: professional writing, mail/merge applications, boilerplate document production, and corporate document production.

Professional Writing

The opening scene of the television program "Murder, She Wrote" shows the leading character, an author of bestselling murder mysteries, typing on a vintage-1945 typewriter. It is easier to believe that no matter where this lady goes a murder somehow occurs than to believe that a prolific late-20th-century bestselling author is not using a word processor. In fact, most publishers expect their authors—even ones from Cabot Cove, Maine—to submit manuscripts not only in printed form but also on diskette.

Of course, most businesspeople are not professional writers in the sense of writing books. But producing written documents is a part of

Clip Art 3-D

CD-ROM
Software

Over 2500 Three Dimensional Images

Now you can access over 2500 three-dimensional images on one CD-ROM disc for use in Desktop Publishing, Design and Presentation Graphics. Categories include: geography, human figures, transportation, buildings, food, equipment and 3-D fonts to name just a few.

Image Manipulation Capabilities

Change any image to suit your needs with a variety of editing tools that let you change the position, perspective and size of the image. You can even change the location of the image and the lighting and color with eight custom light sources that give you maximum flexibility.

Composite Building

Even though the Clip Art 3-D program provides you 500 pre-made composites, you can build your own composite images when-

ever and wherever you like. The graphic possibilities are endless.

Easy Exportation System

After the image you have selected has been edited to your specifications and you're ready to insert it into your presentation, simply export it via .PIC, .WMF or Postscript graphics file formats. Image manipulation and implementation have never been easier or more efficient.

Endless Possibilities

The possibilities for Clip Art 3-D are endless. Use them whenever and wherever you wish to make a strong graphic impression.

NEC Home Electronics (U.S.A.) Inc.

NEC is a registered trademark of NEC Corporation

Postscript is a registered trademark of Adobe Systems Incorporated.

Macintosh System Requirements: Macintosh Plus, • Macintosh II, or • Macintosh SE •1 Megabyte of RAM • CD-ROM Reader Supporting Apple Format • Hard Disk Drive

IBM System Requirements: IBM Personal Computers and 100% Compatibles • 640K Memory • DOS 3.1 or above • Color Graphics Adapter or above • CD-ROM Reader Supporting ISO 9660 Format • MS-DOS CD-ROM Extensions • Microsoft Mouse or Compatible • Hard Disk Drive

Figure 7-15
Clip art

many people's jobs. Some have a clerical staff to type and print documents, while others do it themselves. But by and large, professional writers have turned to word processing rather than typing. Entering text, formatting it, printing it, and archiving it are so easy with a word processing system that personal computers with word processing software are rapidly replacing typewriters as standard business equipment.

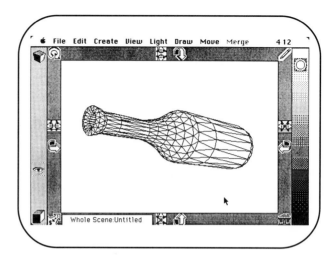

Figure 7-16
Examples of output from drawing programs

Mail/Merge Applications

Many individuals and businesses use direct mail marketing. Environmental groups, manufacturers, consumer advocates, magazine clearing houses, political lobbyists, school development directors, and candidates for public office sell themselves, their product, or their cause via direct mail. To accomplish this, these individuals and groups produce and mail *personalized form letters* (an obvious contradiction in terms).

Personalized form letters (an example is shown in Figure 7-17) contain text that is identical for all recipients; they are personalized by filling in the addressee's name, address, company name, and so forth, in the appropriate locations. Some of these letters include personalized data both in the address and in the body of the letter.

As shown in Figure 7-18, two files are needed to produce such letters. One file contains the form letter while the other one contains the personalizing data, such as name, address, and anything else to be inserted. Data from these files is merged, and the result mailed to each recipient—hence the term **mail/merge**.

The exact technique used depends on the particular word processor. In general, each item to be inserted from the addressee file is assigned a label, for example, *T1*, *T2*, *T3*, and so on. When creating the form letter, the typist keys a code such as "@@T1" in the document location where line T1 should be inserted. That tells the word processing program how to merge the two files. One letter is produced for each set of lines in the addressee file. Figure 7-18 shows an example of this process. The result is a letter that the recipient is supposed to believe was carefully hand-typed just for him or her.

Figure 7-19 illustrates the use of a mail/merge application for a direct-mail sale campaign. Notice that this application employs both database functions and word processing functions. It is an example of integrating the two technologies to solve a business problem. Let's say that the customer database contains the names, addresses, and buying histories

If you return the grand-prize winning number

KATHLEEN A DOLAN IS THE
WINNER OF $1,000,000.00 CASH

Be sure to return your sweepstakes numbers at once. Each of these prize claim numbers has been selected by computer and registered in the name of one person only -- **Kathleen A Dolan of Vernon, Connecticut.** If any of the **Kathleen A Dolan numbers** is the grand-prize winning number, YOU HAVE ALREADY WON $1,000,000.00 IN CASH. PLUS YOU COULD ALSO WIN THE **SURPRISE SUPER BONUS PRIZE** YOU HAVE SCRATCHED OFF!

But you **must** return your sweepstakes numbers. If you are holding the winning number and you **fail to return it,** your **$1,000,000.00 and your SUPER BONUS PRIZE will be lost forever!** Please don't let that happen, Kathleen A Dolan. Send in your **FREE ISSUE/ENTRY CERTIFICATE** with all your prize claim numbers today!

And that's just the beginning of the good news the Vernon postman has just brought to 85 Old Town Rd 24.

Figure 7-17
Example of personalized form letter produced by a mail/merge application

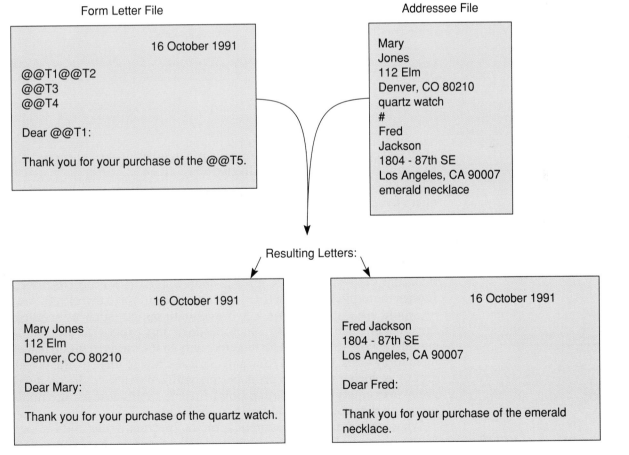

Figure 7-18
Example of personalized form letter preparation

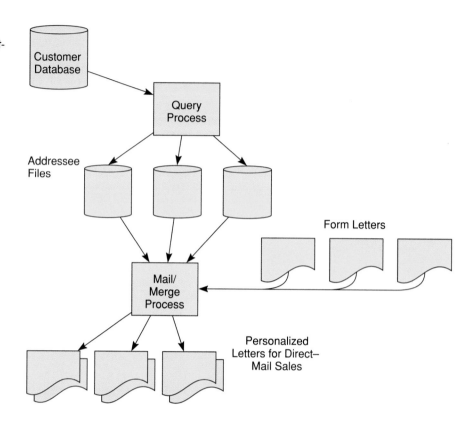

of 10,000 customers. The salesman wants to offer a particular product to a subset of customers most likely to buy it.

He targets three specific types of customers, then uses his **DBMS** query facility to build address files for each of the groups. Next, he uses his word processor to create three form letters, one for each group. Finally, he uses the mail/merge features of his word processor to print the personalized form letters. Using this approach, the salesman makes many carefully focused customer contacts in less than a day. Without the computerized functions, the salesman would be severely impaired. Rather than quickly contacting just the people most likely to respond, he would have to settle for a less adequate option, such as sending impersonal form letters to everyone (fast, but expensive and unfocused), sending impersonal form letters only to the targeted group (saves on mailing costs, but takes time and clerical effort to identify the target group), or hiring typists to produce personalized letters to the targeted group (extremely expensive and slow). Clearly, in this case using a mail/merge application is a good business decision.

Whereas in a mail/merge application the "personalizing" data comes from a file and a high volume of output is produced, in the text processing application we will discuss next, the personalizing data is entered by an operator, and only one or two documents at a time are produced.

Automated Document Production

Another word processing application is the production of **boilerplate** documents. Boilerplate is standardized language in a document. This can be combined with specific data to produce an individual document, analogous to a personalized form letter.

For example, an insurance policy consists of many paragraphs of standard legal language—boilerplate—that describes the basic contract between the insurance company and any insured. At various places in the document, an agent or clerk fills in appropriate individual data, such as the insured's name, address, amount of coverage, and beneficiary.

Another example is mortgage documents. Standard forms are used in most states, and information specific to the mortgagor is ordinarily penned in by the real estate agent, banker, or attorney.

Word processing systems can be used to easily create such documents. The process is similar to the one used for form letters, except in this case the individual data is entered manually, not automatically. The standard form is brought up on the screen, and the typist keys in the appropriate data. Murray (at the beginning of this chapter) could have used this approach when typing cover letters to the admissions officers at several graduate schools. It would have enabled him to easily produce a "personal" letter to each one, while sparing him the chore of typing the same letter over and over.

Additionally, libraries of standard forms exist. For example, you can purchase a library of boilerplate documents used, say, in real estate. This would be a collection of the forms and documents a real estate broker would need. The forms would already by stored on disk. Purchasing such a library frees real estate brokers from generating the blank forms themselves with a word processing program.

Corporate Document Production

The cost to companies of large-scale document production is staggering. Consider an insurance company about to increase its rates for certain types of insurance. Management wants each affected customer to receive a handsome brochure describing the benefits to him or her of this change, the rationale behind it, the legal changes that necessitated it, and so forth. In essence, management wants each customer to feel good about paying a higher insurance premium.

The director of this public relations campaign sketches his ideas for the pamphlet and accompanying cover letter. He gets two of the company's graphic artists to start on the graphics, while enlisting the aid of a researcher to find the figures he needs for various charts in the brochure. After a few days (or weeks, depending on the workload), the researcher and the artists have some results. The PR officer likes most of what he sees but suggests some changes. Everyone returns to the drawing board (some literally) and reemerges a few days or weeks later with some more proposals. This time, it looks good.

Now the public relations officer takes the hand-drawn brochure design and text to the print shop where another crew takes over, this time laying out each page, setting the type, deciding on colors and shading to be used, and producing page proofs—images of actual pages used for proofreading. Proofreaders identify and correct several typographical errors, and send the pages back to the print shop for correction. Another, corrected, set of proofs is produced and passes inspection, and the brochure is actually printed.

The remarkable aspects of this scenario are the number of people and the amount of time required to produce a pamphlet. Before the introduction of desktop publishing systems, corporations that produced large-volume printed documents had to support a staff of specialists, like the one described above. Furthermore, because that staff produced documents company-wide, a long turnaround time often was tolerated. However, since the advent of desktop publishing more and more corporations have greatly reduced their publishing staffs and accelerated the development process, all the while either maintaining or increasing the quality of the documents produced.

With a desktop publishing system, the insurance company's public relations officer might have collaborated with one graphic artist (or he might become skilled himself) on the brochure design, making design changes in a few seconds on the computer screen. With access to a database, he could have gotten the figures he needed in a matter of minutes rather than waiting days for a researcher to get them.

Depending on the system he used, he could have determined color and shading. He could have printed a proof copy and had it proofread, and corrected it at his own workstation. Finally, he could have transmitted the final design electronically to the typesetting machine in the print shop where it could go directly into production. The entire process could be performed in a fraction of the time needed previously, with fewer people, and at a lower overall cost to the company.

Once the brochures were completed, the insurance company would scan its database to find those individuals to whom the brochure must be mailed, and use a mail/merge program to personalize the cover letters. Text processing systems can greatly increase the productivity of people who handle documents for a living.

How to Produce a Document with a Text Processing System

People adopt different styles to produce written documents. Some begin with detailed outlines and write meticulous notes before they strike the first key. Others create at the keyboard. Still other people—such as typists—use a text processing system to transcribe someone else's words and ideas from paper or cassette tape. Regardless of what you did *prior* to loading your text processing software into your microcomputer, following the steps described below will help you get the printed output you want. (The steps are summarized in Figure 7-20).

Begin by *entering the first draft* of your document, whether it is a letter, a memo, a price list, a report, or a job application. For an important document, many people find it helpful to set the first draft aside for a period of time, such as a day or a week, then go back to it.

The next step is *editing*. Editing includes correcting errors and revising the material. You might move sentences or paragraphs around, rephrase some sections, clarify with examples, and delete passages. One easy editing step is using the word processor's built-in spelling checker, if your software provides it. Editing might take a few minutes or several days.

If you are doing desktop publishing, then you need to *establish the graphics* you will incorporate. You draw them (using a graphics software package, or the drawing options of the DTP program), import them from other programs, or digitize them with the help of a scanner. In any event, you build your file of graphics.

Next you *lay out each page*, establishing exactly what it will look like, and placing the art in its proper locations. You probably will experiment with several page layouts before you achieve the results you want.

When you are satisfied that the document is correct, *print a draft copy*. If you are working with a lengthy document (say five or more pages), then print only the first two or three pages. Check the format. If you see anything you need to *revise*, bring the document up on your computer screen and make the necessary changes.

When everything looks good, *print the final document*.

A system for naming documents is usually a good idea. Consider a salesperson who sends various pieces of sales literature to potential customers. He sends form letters, price lists, special promotion announcements, and discount schedules. To keep all these documents organized, he might use a scheme like this to name his documents:

- Form letters: FL#x
- Price lists: PL#x
- Promotions: PR#x
- Discount schedules: DS#x

where *x* represents a number. In a notebook, he could keep a printed copy of each piece, along with its number. This would give him quick reference to all his mailing pieces.

Important documents should be copied onto diskette for backup. In case you encounter problems using the program, you should be familiar with the vendor-supplied documentation. Most problems can be resolved easily, just from the information in the documentation. You should be prepared also for major problems, which will require contacting the vendor's customer service department or the retailer from whom you purchased your software. Unless you have a customer service agreement, the vendor or retailer probably will charge a fee.

- Enter first draft
- Edit draft copy
- Build or acquire art work in graphics file
- Lay out each page
- Print draft copy
- Revise, if necessary
- Print final document

Figure 7-20
Steps in producing a document using a text processing system

Solving Problems with a Text Processing System

In this section you will learn about one business in which word processing and desktop publishing were found to be cost-effective solutions to the owner's problems.

Problem 1: Writing Proposals

Art Fox had been in the landscaping business for years, and had established both a good reputation and a good client base. By many he was considered an artist. Right now, he thought of himself as a typist.

With so many office buildings going up, business was really booming. He was making bids and proposals every week, submitting them to corporate committees that compared his design and planting list to all the others they'd received. Often, as was now the case, he would wind up competing with just one other landscaper. The committee would ask him to change a few plantings here and there and resubmit the bid. The trouble was that he couldn't just cross out a line or two and pencil in some new information. To make a good impression, Art had to submit a brand new proposal. And that meant typing long Latin plant names over and over (see Figure 7-21). The time he spent typing he *could* be out landscaping or meeting more potential customers. He figured there had to be a better way.

Art contacted a local computer consultant who spent some time with him defining Art's current and future business requirements. The prob-

Figure 7-21
One of Art's landscaping proposals

Landscaping proposal prepared for

RIVERSIDE BUSINESS PARK
111 Riverside Drive
Glastonbury, CT

Submitted by ART FOX LANDSCAPING AND DESIGN
Hartford, CT
June 1

Species	Common name	Quantity
Cornus florida	Flowering Dogwood	15
Forsythia × intermedia	Forsythia	40
Hydrangea paniculata	Hydrangea	18
Tsuga canadensis	Hemlock	6
Pinus mugo mughus	Mugo Pine	50
Juniperus horizontalis wiltoni	Blue Rug Juniper	35
Magnolia soulangeana	Magnolia	12
Betula papyrifera	White Birch	24
Lonicera tartarica	Honeysuckle	60

Total cost for purchase, delivery, and planting of items listed above, based on current market prices, is $16,500. Market price variations at time of delivery can affect cost. All plants are warranted for 12 months, if cared for according to instructions provided. Unacceptable plants will be replaced free of charge.

lem that needed immediate attention, they agreed, was proposal writing. And for that, the consultant said, Art would need a word processing system. Art was ready to move quickly.

In a few days, the consultant had configured a good word processing system, using a popular and powerful microcomputer and a word processing program that had been around for years. It was a favorite among microcomputer users, and could interface with many other programs. Though Art was not ready to plunge into any more technology at the moment, he was pleased that the system was one that could be easily expanded if necessary.

The consultant installed Art's new system, tested it out, and pronounced it ready. He handed Art the bill for his services, the documentation for the computer and the word processing programs, and the schedule for word processing classes at the computer store where he'd bought the system. The next day, Art signed up for three half-day classes.

In a very short time, Art had all but abandoned his typewriter. (He still didn't know how to address envelopes with his word processor, but he knew it was just a matter of time before he figured that out.) Now when he developed a proposal, he could type, edit, and print it very quickly. When changes needed to be made, he simply modified the document on the screen, then printed a new original. What used to take hours now took only minutes. Already, Art felt that he had made a wise investment.

Browsing through the vendor documentation one day, Art discovered that there was a way for him to more easily enter the lengthy Latin names for the plants in his proposals. He could build a list—a file, the documentation called it—of the plant names, and assign each one a code. Then he could type his proposal, but insert the appropriate codes instead of plant names. Finally, he could merge the names into the document, producing a proposal with all the Latin names.

Art considered this for a while. Of the several hundred plants he used in his business, about 20 appeared in almost every proposal. He decided to try this new idea with just those 20 plants, and continue typing the rest of the names, as usual. It worked like a charm. Instead of typing *"Pinus mugo mughus"*, he typed *"%%18"*; instead of typing *"Syringa vulgaris"*, Art entered *"%%15"*. When he printed the document, the codes were replaced by the Latin names. Pleased, Art taped the list of plant names and their codes (see Figure 7-22) on the wall next to his computer. Typing proposals was becoming less of a hassle. Art was feeling more productive.

Problem 2: Customer Support

Part of Art's success in his landscaping business was his dedication to customer support. All customers, from a homeowner with a small garden to an office complex on acres of land, received special follow-up attention from Art or from one of his few employees. Art knew that his business would thrive as long as his plants did. Unfortunately, many factors could affect the vitality of the plants, such as water, nutrition, insects, acid rain and pollution, and fungus. Art had little control over

Figure 7-22

Codes for Art's most frequently used plants

CODE	COMMON	LATIN
%%1	Arborvitae	*Thuja occidentalis*
%%2	Azalea	*Azalea*
%%3	Blue Rug Juniper	*Juniperus horizontalis wiltoni*
%%4	Burkwood Viburnum	*Viburnum × burkwoodii*
%%5	Burning Bush	*Euonymus alatus*
%%6	Cinquefoil	*Potentilla fruticosa*
%%7	Cotoneaster	*Cotoneaster*
%%8	Flowering Dogwood	*Cornus florida*
%%9	Forsythia	*Forsythia × intermedia*
%%10	Hemlock	*Tsuga canadensis*
%%11	Honey Locust	*Gleditsia triacanthos*
%%12	Japanese Andromeda	*Pieris japonica*
%%13	Japanese Garden Juniper	*Juniperus procumbens nana*
%%14	Japanese Maple	*Acer japonicum*
%%15	Lilac	*Syringa vulgaris*
%%16	Magnolia	*Magnolia soulangeana*
%%17	Mountain Laurel	*Kalmia latifolia*
%%18	Mugo Pine	*Pinus mugo mughus*
%%19	Norway Spruce	*Picea abies*
%%20	Rhododendron	*Rhododendron*
%%21	Spreading Yew	*Taxus × media*
%%22	Sugar Maple	*Acer saccharum*
%%23	White Pine	*Pinus strobus*

these factors, but tried to advise customers about the care of their plants, and help solve problems when they arose.

Lately, for example, one popular plant in the region was being attacked by a tiny mite. Art used his word processor to write a pamphlet describing the mite infestation and what to do about it. He mailed the pamphlet to all customers he'd sold that plant to, offering to answer questions if customers wanted to call. The phone hardly stopped ringing. It took a while to explain how to tell this mite from other plant diseases, and Art or one of his staff often ended up going to the customer site to see if there truly was a problem.

Customer service, Art was beginning to realize, was a two-edged sword. Providing it when he had a small clientele had been easy, and had enabled his business to grow; but providing it to everyone now was really cutting into the time and resources he needed to do business. If only he could send pictures to his customers, he wouldn't need to tie up his employees with visiting customer sites so frequently. Maybe a newsletter would do the trick, he thought.

Art called his computer consultant again, and was introduced to the world of desktop publishing. The computer he had would support such an application just fine. He needed a mouse (that cost only $100), a desktop publishing program (they chose PageMaker for $895), and a desktop scanner to input line drawings and photographs (another $3,000). Rather than buying a scanner outright, Art decided to lease one until he decided if the newsletter was cost-effective.

In the meantime, one of Art's employees expressed an interest in working part-time in the field and part-time in the office. She was comfortable with computers; as an undergraduate in horticulture she had used computers to sketch designs and produce cost estimates. With no further prompting, Art turned the newsletter project over to her and got back to the business of landscaping. The first couple of newsletters were pretty simple. They were mailed to all customers, along with an evaluation form the customer could use to make comments and suggestions. Customer response was very positive.

With the help of several excellent books on desktop publishing she got at the computer store, the editor soon had designed an attractive, easy-to-read newsletter. It featured regular articles on plants, newly-completed landscaping jobs (complete with photographs of happy customers), a question and answer column, and finally—Art's favorite—a feature called "Disease of the Month." The Disease of the Month column featured the latest information on a particular plant infestation. It contained a narrative description of the problem, and supplemented it with photographs of both normal and sick plants. In cases where the customer might mistake a similar disease for this one, Art included line drawings, pointing out distinguishing characteristics. Additionally, the column told the reader how to treat the problem. And, like the pamphlet that had started this whole thing, the column invited readers to call if they needed help.

Fortunately, now most of the calls were just to say thanks. The photographs and line drawings made problems easier to identify. Consequently, customers could treat them faster. And the sooner the infestations were under control, the sooner the plants recovered. It was clear to Art that the newsletter was a great idea: it provided important information to customers, it kept his company's name visible, and it provided an added dimension to customer support by helping customers keep their plants healthy. As Art knew, healthy plants made for a healthy business.

Epilogue

The story of Art's landscaping and design business could end here. Or you could learn that Art finally did buy a scanner. He also gained more customers and before long tripled his staff. And it will come as no surprise that Art added several other functions to his personal computer system, such as a spreadsheet (for budgets, etc.) and a DBMS (for mailing lists and vendor data). But the exciting development revolved around the newsletter.

It seems that Art's customers shared the newsletter with their friends, many of whom also were interested in horticulture and landscape design. So many requests came in for copies that Art decided to publish the newsletter for wider consumption. At first, Art's subscribers were concentrated in just four states. But because of the overwhelming response, Art purchased national mailing lists and sent out thousands of complimentary copies to potential subscribers. Once again, the response was remarkable.

Questions

7.24 What is a mail/merge word processing application? Give an example of one.

7.25 What is boilerplate? Give an example (not one described in the chapter).

7.26 In what ways can a company realize savings when it uses desktop publishing rather than traditional document production techniques?

7.27 Suppose you won a gift certificate for a word processing system. Describe the components (all five of them) of your system.

7.28 Suppose you won a gift certificate for a desktop publishing system. Describe the components (all five of them) of your DTP system.

7.29 Based on your current situation, would you realize more benefit from a word processing system or a desktop publishing system?

7.30 In the text we said that to do desktop publishing it is as important to learn graphic design as to know how to use DTP software. Why do you think that is true?

7.31 Describe the procedures needed to produce a document using a text processing system.

Now Art publishes five regional versions of the newsletter to thousands of subscribers across the United States and Canada, and a quarterly magazine whose subscribers and list of paid advertisers are increasing every day. To no one's surprise, his editors all use desktop publishing software to do their layouts. The publications represent a significant—and growing—part of Art's business.

Summary

More and more individuals and businesses are turning to computer technology to handle text processing, including word processing and desktop publishing. Word processing deals almost exclusively with textual information: streams of letters typed into the computer system via a keyboard. In addition to being an electronic typewriter, the word processor is also an electronic filer and a high-speed printer.

Because creating a document and printing a document are separate functions, a word processor can offer the advantages of speedy on-screen editing and control over format changes. Changing margin width, tab locations, type font, line spacing, and other document characteristics are accomplished without rekeying the document. Other features, such as the spelling checker and the on-line thesaurus, put until-now manual functions literally at the user's fingertips. Word processing is used widely by those who produce typewritten documents.

Desktop publishing allows you to produce page layouts for printing magazines, brochures, and other documents. With a desktop publishing program you define the page layout, then merge text (usually from word processing files) and artwork (usually from graphics files) onto the page. Program features allow you to manage the artwork, to change the size and style of text, and perform a host of other page composition tasks. The final product is the image of a page exactly as it will be printed. Desktop publishing is used by people who produce high-quality (and often high-volume) documents that contain both text and art.

Building a graphics library for use in desktop publishing is an ongoing process. Some graphics can be purchased in the form of clip art libraries. Other graphics are built by the user, such as business graphs, freehand drawings, or photographs whose images are scanned and digitized by special cameras. All such graphic images can be incorporated into a DTP document.

At present, word processing is a fairly well-established technology. Desktop publishing is increasing in popularity, due, at least in part, to improvements in computer graphics capabilities, and to the availability of reasonably priced, user-friendly software, fast and powerful microcomputers, and printers capable of producing exceptionally sharp copy. Distinctions between the two areas of text processing will probably become blurred in the future.

Word List

document	snake column	orphan
wraparound	desktop publishing (DTP)	line art
cut and paste	camera-ready copy	continuous-tone art
format	kerning	clip art
justification	leading	mail/merge
repagination	widow	boilerplate
type font		

Discussion Questions and Exercises

A. Direct mail (such as "personalized" form letters) is sent to millions of potential consumers every day. The idea, of course, is to get the recipient to respond to the "personal" approach (by ordering something, making a donation, etc.), at least partly because the item is addressed to that individual. What is your opinion of personalized form letters?

B. Desktop publishing allows people to produce beautiful, professional-looking documents that are impressive to look at. Many critics have said that the quality of output has gone way up, but the content hasn't improved. Respond to this in terms of your own experience. Do you compare two books, for example, more on the basis of their content or the quality of production? Does the existence of shiny presentation materials—say in a sales pitch—necessarily mean that something worthwhile is being said, or can it mask a lack of content? How critical do you, as a consumer, need to be?

C. In terms of your present situation, what applications do you have for a word processing system? What applications do you have for a desktop publishing system? What would be the source of graphics for your DTP documents?

D. In some way, make teams of five students in your class. Using systems available at your school, develop a two-page newsletter for the class (each team produces a different one). If possible, include at least one line drawing or photograph. The newsletter should be formatted with at least two columns on a page. Although there are many techniques you could use, one way of distributing the team's work is to designate one individual as the editor, while the others each produce one article. The editor specifies article length, then puts the newsletter together.

If you have both word processing and DTP software, each team should produce two newsletters. Discuss the relative merits of doing this with a word processor and with a DTP program.

Developing Personal Information Systems

A careful buyer all his life, Herb was baffled by the white elephant perched on his desk. The salesman had promised an end to his record-keeping woes if he bought this system. He had told Herb that his was one of the most versatile printers for the money. And this integrated software would let him do not only spreadsheets and word processing, but also graphics and desktop publishing. Unfortunately, the system never delivered on those promises. Response time was painfully long, the "database" system did not allow any queries with multiple conditions (such as "Who are the customers in the Southwest with yearly purchases over $10,000?"), and although graphics looked great on the screen, they were muddy and blurred when printed.

Herb was just beginning to realize that he'd been had. He paid over $12,000 of his hard-earned cash for what he believed would be a first-class system. Instead it was turning into a first-class headache. Although he was angry at himself for letting this happen, at this point he simply needed a way to make the best of this very bad investment.

The Systems Development Process

Herb's lament could be repeated by thousands of disappointed consumers across the country. Lots of people buy personal computer systems with expectations reaching far beyond what the system actually delivers. Part of the problem is that many people are first-time buyers, so they do not know what to expect. Another part of the problem is that many people simply are unprepared to determine systematically (1) whether they actually need a personal information system, (2) what present and future needs a personal information system might help address, and (3) what the best configuration is *for their specific needs*. A system that your sister the lawyer thinks is great might be a poor investment for your jewelry store.

In the previous three chapters you learned how to develop applications with certain types of computer software. Those chapters presumed that you had a system (hardware, software, etc.) in place. In this chapter you will learn an approach you can use to develop a personal information system. Keep in mind that a system is made up of all five components.

Consider the life cycle of a system (see Figure 8-1). The life of a system begins when someone, often a user, recognizes a need for one. With that need in mind, and with a knowledge of the resources available to address that need, the system can be developed and put to use. After the system has been in use for a while, its effectiveness is evaluated and changes might be made.

Changes may need to be made because (1) the user's needs have changed, either because he now recognizes new needs or his business changed, or both, (2) the system did not actually meet the user's needs in the first place, or (3) technology has changed, offering new ways to

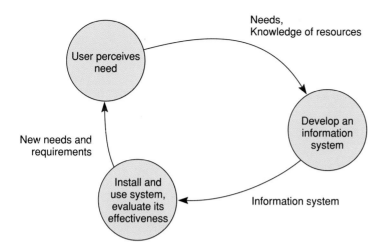

Figure 8-1
System life cycle

address the user's needs. Whenever system changes are needed, the cycle begins again. Developing an information system is an ongoing, iterative process, for small and large systems alike. Each new version of a system solves some problems for the moment. But developing information systems to solve business problems is like trying to hit a moving target. The business continues to change, so the information system must change, too. In this chapter, you will learn how to improve your chances of success by using a five-stage system development process.

Your Role in the Process

As the owner of the personal information system under consideration, you play two roles during system development. You will probably be the only user—therefore you must define your needs. And very often you will be the developer. This means that you need to decide which programs to use, which hardware to buy, how to structure your database, and so forth, for all five system components. If you have access to someone skilled in system development—such as a paid consultant—then by all means enlist professional help. For the purposes of this chapter, we will assume you are the developer.

The Stages of System Development

The five stages are listed in Figure 8-2. As you might imagine, the process of developing a large-scale computerized information system—say for a bank or an airline—is likely to take longer and to cost more money than developing a personal information system, for many reasons: the nature of the problems being solved, the number of people involved, various regulations and corporate policies to consider, and so forth. However, the approach described here, if applied correctly, can make system development relatively organized and straightforward, regardless of the magnitude of the problem.

Figure 8-2
The five stages of system
development

- Problem definition
    Define the problem
    Assess feasibility
    Create a development plan

- Requirements definition
    Identify output requirements
    Identify input requirements
    Estimate amount of data and make processing projections
    Determine constraints

- Requirements evaluation
    Evaluate requirements
    Compare alternative system approaches
    Select approach

- Design
    Determine hardware specifications
    Determine software specifications; perform program and macro design
    Design data structures, forms, reports, menus
    Document procedures
    Determine sources of training

- Implementation
    Obtain components and test them
    Integrate components and test the system
    Install system

During the first stage, *problem definition*, you define the problem, determine the feasibility of using computer technology to solve the problem, and develop a plan for the rest of the development process. The major goals during this stage are to determine exactly what your business problem is and to determine whether or not it makes sense to develop a computer-based system to solve the problem. Remember, computer-based information systems are expensive. If developing one is not a feasible solution to the problem, then the earlier you find that out the better.

The second stage is called *requirements definition*. During this stage you identify specific requirements for the system. A functional requirement describes something the system must do, such as produce a report or perform a calculation. During this stage you might develop **prototypes**—examples of reports and forms that the system will use or produce. Using prototypes can help you evaluate the accuracy and completeness of your requirements. An operational requirement describes an operating characteristic of the system. For example, the system might be required to produce 2,000 personalized form letters every Thursday.

The third stage is *requirements evaluation*. During this stage you consider each of the requirements in light of the cost of satisfying it. Some requirements might greatly complicate the system or increase its cost. Should your list contain requirements of that nature, you might decide to forego some of them. The next step during this stage is to compare different system alternatives and to choose one of them. For example, you might consider using a file-based system versus a database system.

The result of the evaluation stage is a firm set of requirements along with a definition of the technology to be used.

The fourth stage is called *design*. During this stage you specify each of the five system components. For example, at this point you decide which software packages you will use; you select the specific brand and model of each piece of hardware; you determine how your data will be stored; and you figure out how, where, and when you—or other users— will receive training.

The fifth and last stage in system development is *implementation and follow-up*. During this stage you acquire, integrate, test, and install the system components. Once the system is up and running, you need to look back and see if it actually is solving the problems you defined at the very beginning. Fine-tuning sometimes is needed.

The Importance of Adhering to the Five-Stage Process

Most people, when they feel they are ready for a computer, take their checkbook down to the local computer store, talk to a salesperson for a little while, maybe try some of the software and computers on display, and in a few hours or days, buy a "system." All too often, after living with the system for a while, they, like Herb who opened this chapter, discover the shortcomings of the system and complain about the computer, the software, or the vendor. Most consumers, if they follow the five-stage process, can have the system they really want.

As a society we tend to be impulse buyers. But when it comes to an information system, we need to be much more structured in our approach. Each stage is important. For example, it is vital for you to identify the problem you are trying to solve. Rushing into buying a computer (the stage where most disappointed consumers start) is likely to generate a solution to the wrong problem, or to be more expensive than it needs to be. The guideline here is take your time. Perform each step.

You will be much happier with the end result.

Questions

8.1 Describe the system life cycle.

8.2 What are three reasons why changes might need to be made to an existing information system? Give an example of each.

8.3 In the text we state, "Developing information systems to solve business problems is like trying to hit a moving target." Explain that statement.

8.4 What is the role of the user during development of a personal information system?

8.5 Name the five stages of system development.

8.6 What is the major goal of each stage?

8.7 Why is it important to follow the five-stage process of system development?

Problem Definition Stage

Figure 8-3 summarizes the tasks you need to accomplish during the problem definition stage. First, you need to define the problem. This sounds easy, even obvious. But many people don't do it and consequently are shooting in the dark when putting together their systems. A problem is a perceived difference between what is and what ought to be. You might perceive a problem in your business's current performance, cost, or effectiveness.

Performance problems exist when the business is not doing the volume of work (or profits) you believe it should. For example, suppose you are a consultant doing one to two weeks of billable work each month. You believe you should be doing billable work two to three weeks each month. You perceive a performance problem: you are not doing enough business.

- Define the problem
  Perception of difference between what is and what ought to be

- Assess feasibility
  Cost
  Schedule
  Technical

- Create a plan
  Completion dates
  Costs

Figure 8-3
Tasks in the problem definition stage

Cost problems exist when the cost of doing business exceeds what you believe it should be. For example, suppose you examine your business expenses (travel, telephone, clerical, copy center, and so forth) for the past six months. You discover that travel expenses have increased each month, but without a commensurate increase in sales. You perceive that you have a cost problem.

Effectiveness problems exist when you believe you are not performing your business functions well enough. One clue here might be a high number of customer complaints or returns. For instance, suppose that as a consultant you advise clients how to prevent water from seeping into their basements. You examine a site, take soil samples, study local geological and hydrological data, and make recommendations, for which you are paid. Unexpectedly, one-third of your clients contact you within six months indicating that, despite following your recommendations, water seepage problems still exist. You perceive that you have an effectiveness problem: you are not doing your job well.

Zeroing in on a problem (or problems) is crucial. When you know the nature of the problem, then you can decide between alternative ways of proceeding to a goal. The goal, of course, is to solve the problem.

When defining a problem, it is tempting to be vague, using phrases like "poor quality," or "dissatisfied customers," or "error-prone data entry." Be specific in setting a goal that technology will help you reach. What is your target? How will you know when you've hit it? How will you measure your success? Phrases like "increase sales by 20 percent," "reduce travel costs by 15 percent," or "reduce customer complaints to no more than 1 in 20" are much clearer and therefore more useful in helping you to find a solution.

Problem Definition at Herb's Herbal Teas

In this section, we will consider two scenarios involving Herb. One describes what happened. The other describes what might have happened if Herb had known about the five-stage development process.

What Happened   Herb decided one day that his problem was that he needed a computer. He had read in some magazines how entrepreneurs like himself used them for everything, from budgets to proposal writing to solar house design. If he had a computer, then maybe he could spend his time more productively and increase his herbal tea packing and distribution business. He talked to his brother-in-law, whose architectural firm had dozens of computers. Impressed with the firm's extensive use of computers, and convinced this was the right thing to do, Herb went to one of the computer retailers in town to select a computer.

What Could Have Happened   Herb studied his sales figures and operating costs for the past three years. He was doing fairly well financially, but he thought business could be better. On examining his sales data, he noticed that most of his business came from mail orders. Sales increased significantly each time he issued a new catalog. At the time, he was mailing them five times a year. He estimated how much sales would increase if he doubled that to ten times per year, but was very concerned about production cost. Each catalog was expensive to produce.

In addition, Herb felt he could depend on a loyal customer base only so much. Doubling the number of catalogs per year probably would not double sales. He estimated that he needed to increase his customer base by 20 percent. Herb jotted these notes:

- Problem: Need to increase sales.
  Solution: Issue mail-order catalog 10 times per year (increase of 100%).
- Problem: Catalog production costs too high.
  Solution: Don't know. Need to study production costs to see where they can be reduced. Goal is to reduce production cost by 10%.
- Problem: Current customer base cannot support desired growth.
  Solution: Increase customer base by 20%.

With a clearer understanding of his problems, Herb thought he'd pay a visit to a few computer retailers in the next few days.

Feasibility Assessment

Feasibility measures the likelihood that you can solve your problem with existing technology, and within your own financial and time constraints. During this step you need to consider three aspects of feasibility: cost, schedule, and technical.

Cost Feasibility The first aspect is **cost feasibility**. Here you must decide if an information system is likely to provide a cost-effective solution to the problem. Although this stage is too early for precise figures, you can consider gross estimates. The goal is to determine whether or not the project makes sense from a financial standpoint. If a system costs $20,000 and it solves a $5,000 problem, then it is not cost feasible. If a system costs $10,000 and it brings in $50,000 in business, then it is cost feasible.

Consider the problems at Herb's Herbal Teas. If present production costs for a catalog are $0.75 and Herb issues 20,000 of them five times per year, then his catalog costs are $75,000 per year. If he develops a system that reduces his per catalog cost to $0.68 (a 10 percent reduction), then he'll spend only $68,000 on catalogs, or $7,000 less. Herb wants the system to pay for itself in three years or less. Assuming that catalog costs were Herb's only problem, then a system costing $21,000 or less (ignoring interest he would pay to finance his purchase) would be cost feasible.

Schedule Feasibility **Schedule feasibility** concerns whether or not the system will be available in time. For many personal information systems, the time frame for development is fairly loose—often described in terms of "as soon as possible." Most of the time, individuals have in place an existing information system—usually manual—that they will use until a new system is developed.

Figure 8-4

Plan for system development at Herb's Herbal Teas

TASK	COMPLETION DATE
• Requirements definition Identify output requirements Identify input requirements Estimate amount of data and make processing projections Determine constraints	30 Apr
• Requirements evaluation Evaluate requirements Compare alternative system approaches Select approach	14 May
• Design Determine hardware specifications Determine software specifications; perform program and macro design Design data structures, forms, reports, menus Document procedures Determine sources of training	15 Jun
• Implementation Obtain components and test them Integrate components and test them Test system Install system	15 Jul

Questions

8.8 What is a problem?

8.9 Give an example of a problem that you have that might be addressed with a personal information system.

8.10 What were Herb's problems?

8.11 Describe the three aspects of feasibility, and give an original example of each.

Schedule feasibility problems often involve external agencies. For example, if Herb needs a system to report annual earnings to the state by January 31, then it is schedule infeasible if it's not available until February 15.

Technical Feasibility When considering **technical feasibility**, you determine whether or not existing technology can provide a solution to the problem. In Herb's case, current technology can be used to solve the problems he identified. In fact, most record keeping, text processing, and "number crunching" problems found in personal information systems can be handled by today's personal computers. (The same cannot always be said of multiuser information systems.)

Some examples of problems that cannot as yet be solved with computer technology are near-perfect natural language translations (such as English to Greek) and accessing 100 trillion bytes of data in a personal computer.

Development Plan

After the problem is defined and feasibility is assessed, the last step is to build a development plan. A development plan identifies each step, estimates the time each step will take, and often indicates how much money is needed and at what points. A plan will help you with your own scheduling and budgeting processes. See Figure 8-4.

Figure 8-5
Tasks in the requirements definition stage

- Determine output required
  - Reports
  - Graphs
  - Files

- Determine input needed (and sources of each)
  - Manual forms
  - Other data

- Estimate system size
  - Amount of data
  - Frequency of data change
  - Frequency of report production

- Determine constraints
  - Hardware
  - Programs
  - Data
  - Procedures
  - People

Figure 8-5

Tasks in the requirements definition stage

Requirements Definition Stage

The objective of the requirements definition stage is to identify and document, as completely as possible, the requirements for the information system. Since the requirements are used in subsequent stages to build the system, they must be written or otherwise documented in prototypes and sketches. As you can see in Figure 8-5, you will need to determine the output you expect the system to produce, identify the input needed, estimate the size of the system in terms of data, and identify constraints you will place on the development of your system.

Identifying Output Requirements

The three types of output you consider are reports, graphical output, and export files. *Reports* are by far the most common type of output. For example, consider Herb's Herbal Teas. One problem he wanted to address involved increasing his customer base by 20 percent. Thus, he might want a monthly report like the one in Figure 8-6 to help him track his company's progress toward its goal.

Another type of output, *graphical output*, includes charts used within a company, such as the line graphs for Herb's Herbal Teas in Figure 8-7, and pie charts and bar charts like the ones you studied in Chapter 5. Graphical output also includes desktop publishing. One of the options Herb should consider to reduce his production costs is developing a desktop publishing system to design his own catalogs in-house (see Figure 8-8).

The third type of output is *export files*. Export files are needed when one system produces data to be used by another system. For example, Herb may want to export some database data (such as price data) into

Figure 8-6
Sample customer base report for
Herb's Herbal Teas

Customer Base Report

	Jan	Feb	Mar	Apr	Total
Number of sales	250	200	280	250	980
New customers	50	45	63	62	220
% new customers	20%	22.5%	22.5%	24.8%	22.4%
Change	—	+2.5%	0%	+2.3%	—

Figure 8-7
Example of graph to be issued by
Herb's system

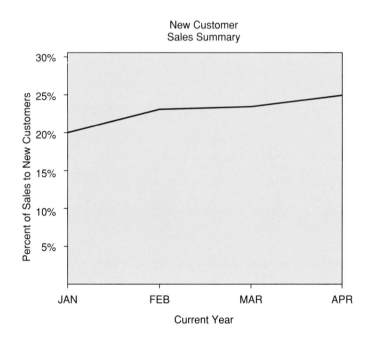

a word processing system (to develop his catalog). During this stage, requirements for data compatibility need to be identified and documented.

Identifying Input Requirements

The next step is to determine the input data needed to produce the desired output. You can proceed in two ways: by looking at the output and working your way backward to input requirements, or by looking at your existing system (even if it is manual) to discover what input data you currently use. Many people combine the two approaches.

Let's consider Herb's situation for some examples. In order to determine the input he needs to capture to produce his mail-order catalog, he can examine his current catalog. He will discover such facts as item number, item name, description, package quantity, and unit cost. And when examining the monthly customer base report in Figure 8-6, Herb realizes that he will need to track each customer's purchasing history in order to determine if a sale is to a first-time buyer or not.

Figure 8-8
Examples from Herb's catalog

```
#809LE      Lemon Delight    Tasty, tangy lift for midafternoon
                             spirits.  Secret blend of lemon and
                             spices guaranteed to perk you
                             up--but with no caffeine.  100 bags:
                             $4.50

#235RH      Rose Hip Tea     An old favorite, especially for
                             crisp autumn mornings at the shore.
                             In fact, that's where we harvest our
                             tea.  A sure winner.  Loose: $6.00
                             per lb.  Bags: 50 for $3.00

#433AT      Licorice Bomb    If you've never tried licorice tea,
                             you're in for a taste surprise.  No
                             mere hint of licorice here--this tea
                             packs a wallop that will leave your
                             mouth begging for more.  Loose only:
                             $4.50 per half pound.
```

a. Herb's current catalog

b. Herb's catalog produced with DTP technology.

On the other hand, to determine the input required to send catalogs, Herb can turn to his existing system. Each mailing label contains a customer's name, mailing address, and the date the customer last placed an order. Herb will use that data in his new system as well.

Estimates of System Size

One of the first questions Herb was asked when he entered the computer store was "How much data do you have?" Unprepared as he was (remember, in reality Herb did not follow the process you are learning. He was not in a good position to procure an information system), Herb

8.1   *INCREASING YOUR PERSONAL PRODUCTIVITY*

What Is Upgrading?

What do you do when your computer becomes "too slow?" When you desire to add more memory? When you wish to have graphics capabilities?

These are typical questions asked by individual users. These types of questions have a single, rather simple answer. You take out the old and bring in the new. Computer manufacturers, from the beginning, have developed techniques to "upgrade" user systems. No matter what computer you may be using, design features are built in so that you can replace old components with new parts that will increase computer system capabilities and, in turn, your personal and professional productivity.

Years ago, upgrading hardware was quite expensive. However, with the advent of microcomputers built from standard components, a new breed of manufacturers, known as "third-party vendors," have entered the marketplace. These companies specialize in providing components designed to add new features and to upgrade capabilities of existing systems. The presence of third-party vendors assures you that there is a group of companies trying to think up ways to enhance the value of your computer. A few examples of how to upgrade your computer:

Need more memory? Purchase an expansion board.

Want to add graphics capabilities? Add a graphics card and a high-resolution monitor, either color or monochrome.

Looking for increased processing speed? You need a co-processor, or accelerator card.

The more knowledgeable you become as a user, the more conscious you will be of potential benefits from added hardware features, and of the need to shop with caution. Ask some critical questions, such as the following:

Is the upgrade you are considering fully compatible with your existing computer system? You may find that you have to buy special connecting devices to use a given component with the system you have. You also may find that the manufacturer has neglected to state that an upgrade device is not compatible with your system.

Will service be available both for your computer and for the attachment? If your system has a mix of parts from different vendors, who will be responsible for service? Will any of the parties refuse service because you have attached "foreign" devices?

Look out for yourself! You are the customer. Know what you are buying.

said he thought he had about 8,000 customers. What more should Herb have been able to say about his data?

He should have known the *amount of data* (number of customers, number of items in his catalog, and the size of his mailing list); the frequency with which data is *added or changed* (for example, how many sales are processed per day, how many new customers are added to the mailing list, how many people ask to be removed from the mailing list, how often products are added or discontinued, and how often item prices change); and the frequency with which *reports are produced* (in this case, Herb knew his catalogs came out five times per year. But he also needed to define how often he wanted his new reports to be issued: daily? weekly? monthly?). To more accurately assess the size of his system, Herb should have produced a chart like the one in Figure 8-9. Such information helps a developer to determine the processing speed and capacity requirements for the system.

Possible Constraints

In addition to knowing what you want the system to do, you often need to define those conditions or situations that will **constrain**, or limit, the system. Consider each of the five components.

Figure 8-9
Estimates of system size for Herb's
Herbal Teas

- Data storage requirements

  Mailing list
  20,000 at 170 bytes each = 3,400,000 bytes of mailing list data

  Active customers
  8,000 at 200 bytes each = 1,600,000 bytes of active customer data

  Purchases
  250 per month for 3 years = 9,000 purchase records
  30 bytes each = 270,000 bytes of purchase data

  Total storage for current data = 5,270,000 bytes

- Data update requirements

  Annual increase is
  300 new active customers at 200 bytes each = 60,000 bytes
  10,000 new names on mailing list at 170 bytes each = 1,700,000 bytes
  600 new purchases at 30 bytes each = 9,000 bytes
  400 purchases over three years old deleted each year at 30 bytes each =
  −1,200 bytes

  Total projected annual growth is 1,767,800 bytes

- Report generation requirements
  Catalog produced 10 times per year
  Customer base reports produced monthly

First, there might be hardware constraints. If you already own a computer, then you may not want to (or have the money to) buy another one. Or perhaps you are willing to upgrade your existing computer, but you haven't yet finished paying for your printer. Furthermore, if you are developing a personal information system for use within a larger company, the company might have policies governing the make and model of personal computers used.

Software constraints might exist also. For example, you might already own a database management program, or a word processor (although programs for personal computers are relatively inexpensive, so you might consider replacing ones that no longer satisfy your needs). In a company, standards may exist governing the software that can be used.

Hardware and software often impose constraints on one another. For example, certain hard disk drives are supported only by some operating systems. And all personal computers do not support all software. For example, if you consider using the database management system called R:BASE, then you can consider only those computers that support it—thus you could use an IBM PC or IBM-PC-compatible, but not an Apple Macintosh. Similarly, some programs can produce output only on certain printers. Thus, deciding on software limits your choices of hardware, and vice versa.

Data constraints are more often found in large, multiuser systems. But certainly the data characteristics defined above (such as the number of records and the size of each record) could constrain your choices of hardware and software.

Questions

8.12 What is the purpose of the requirements definition stage?

8.13 Name three types of output, and give an original example of each.

8.14 Describe two ways for determining input requirements.

8.15 Why are estimates of system size important?

8.16 Describe system constraints in terms of each of the five components.

Finally, for a personal information system, constraints are not likely to be imposed by either of the two remaining components, procedures and people.

Constraints for the Herb's Herbal Teas System

Herb did not as yet own a computer, so he faced no hardware or software constraints. His mailing labels were being produced by a local service company, and Herb was told he could get the mailing list from the company in whatever format his new system required. His only constraints, then, had to do with the amount of data and the anticipated increase, as described in Figure 8-9.

Requirements Evaluation Stage

The objective of the requirements evaluation stage is to establish a general strategy for selecting a system that meets the requirements defined in the previous stage. During this evaluation, first the requirements are considered and, if necessary, some are eliminated. Then a number of basic system alternatives are identified. These alternatives are evaluated, and one is selected.

Evaluate Requirements

The first step during this stage is to critically evaluate each requirement identified earlier. You may discover that one or two or even several requirements make the system more complex or costly than is appropriate. For example, Herb might have wanted to track sales for all customers for the past ten years, without considering the amount of data involved or the expense of entering it into a database. During requirements evaluation (if he had performed it), Herb would have compared the cost of that requirement to the potential value he expected to gain from it. As a result, he probably would have scaled back the requirement, say to the previous two or three years.

Whereas the requirements identified during requirements definition reflected an ideal system, during this step "reality sets in." The result is a list of realistic system requirements that will be the target document for the remaining system development stages.

Compare Alternative System Approaches

The second task during requirements evaluation is to compare alternative system approaches. Your goal is to consider different approaches or technologies that will be used as the basis of the system. For example, consider Herb's goal of reducing the cost of catalog production by 10 percent. He could use less expensive paper and binding techniques. Or he could reduce the number of pages by using smaller print. Or he could do his own page layouts with a desktop publisher, in which case

SOFTWARE

Type *Graphics*   Delivery date *Immediately*

Name *Adobe Illustrator 88*   Training *Tutorial Only*

Vendor *Adobe Systems*   Customer support *No*

Price *$195.00*

SYSTEM REQUIREMENTS

Hardware

Computer *Macintosh Plus, SE or II*

Disk *Hard disk*

Printer *Postscript printer or typesetter*

Monitor *Color*

Graphics card *(standard)*

Mouse *(standard)*

Other *Scanner (optional)*

Other Software

Operating system *Apple System Software (Ver. 4.2 or greater)*

Other *Adobe Collector's Edition I; Adobe type library; Mac Draw; Mac Paint*

Figure 8-10
Alternative comparison chart

he must consider various hardware and software configurations. Each of these is an alternative.

The purpose of this task is to create a number of reasonable alternatives, and to resist the temptation to latch on to one approach, vendor, or set of programs without considering others. Sometimes a non-computerized alternative will be the best one. Our emphasis here, of course, is on computer-based alternatives.

For each alternative, you should consider the five components and build a chart like the one in Figure 8-10. When complete, the stack of forms will help you to identify the most appropriate alternative (or alternatives). With the help of a computer salesperson and industry literature, you should develop various system configurations. Start with software packages, because they will limit your hardware options. When considering software, keep in mind factors besides cost, such as ease of use, availability of training materials, the reputation of the publisher, and the length of time the software has been around.

For each component, write the price and the delivery date. Also determine if the dealer offers discounts for purchasing an entire package—hardware and software—at once.

Be sure to determine the training available for the products you are considering. Does the retailer offer classes? Do self-paced tutorials exist? Is someone at the computer store familiar with the package to help you if you get stuck? Examine the documentation to determine if it is professionally done, easy to use, and helpful. Remember, once you get the system home, you are pretty much on your own.

Finally, take the comparison charts for several attractive alternatives to at least one other dealer. Get price quotes, talk to the sales staff, and find out about service and training. Just as you comparison shop for an automobile, you should comparison shop for a personal information system. Be sure to compare oranges to oranges, though. Get dealer quotes on identical configurations, or it will be difficult to determine the best one.

Select an Approach

At this point you need to select the approach that best suits your situation. Ultimately, you are trying to choose a cost-effective system solution to your problem. Thus, you need to weigh the cost of the system against its potential benefits. You have identified costs already. Even if one system's cost is significantly lower than the others, it may not be the best option. You probably will want to consider benefits of each candidate system beyond simple cost comparison.

Some benefits are tangible. For instance, you might be able to learn how to use a system with a graphical interface much faster than one with a command interface. Consequently, you could be using your new system productively sooner. That is a tangible benefit. You might have a home computer that is compatible with one of the configurations you are considering for your office. Choosing a compatible system would enable you to do some work at home instead of staying at your office at night, another tangible benefit.

Some benefits are intangible: more subjective and less easily measured. For example, you might feel more comfortable with one of the vendors than with the others. Or one system might offer leading-edge technology that you hope to build on in the future.

The Evaluation Stage at Herb's Herbal Teas

Herb never performed this stage; but if he had, this is what might have happened.

Herb considered his system requirements (see Figure 8-11). He did not believe that any requirements could be pared from the list, although he decided that customer purchasing history would be useful to him for only the most recent three years.

After discussing his requirements with a salesperson (recommended to him by a friend) at a computer retail store, and after trying out several computers and software packages on display, Herb and the salesperson narrowed his system alternatives to three.

The first alternative would be a "bare bones" approach, using the least expensive components that could meet Herb's immediate needs.

- Do page layouts in-house using word processing, desktop publishing, or both; not necessary to incorporate graphics at this point—line drawings and photos can be pasted onto pages

- Manage mailing list of 20,000 to 30,000 names, catalog of 1,000 items, and customer purchasing history for ten years

- Produce reports, charts, and graphs showing change (increase) in customer base

- Issue catalog ten times per year

Figure 8-11
Herb's system requirements

The second alternative would include a graphical user interface based on an IBM-compatible computer. It would include a desktop publishing program. The third alternative would be similar to the second one, but it would be based on an Apple Macintosh computer, known for its excellent desktop publishing features and user-friendly graphical interface. With three broad system alternatives in mind, Herb's salesperson developed three configurations for Herb's consideration (Figure 8-12).

The first system alternative included a word processor that could be used not only to write catalog text, but also to arrange text in columns and to draw boxes on a page. It also included a relational database product that was fully compatible with the word processor. The DBMS would enable him to track customer purchasing history and to produce mailing labels (via the word processor). This configuration also included an electronic spreadsheet program that could accept numbers stored in the DBMS and produce line, bar, and pie charts. In terms of hardware, this alternative used an IBM-compatible computer with a hard

Figure 8-12
Three system alternatives for Herb's Herbal Teas

Alternative #1

   Software: Word processor, DBMS, electronic spreadsheet, MS-DOS operating system

   Hardware: IBM-compatible with 40MB hard disk, monochrome monitor, keyboard, dot-matrix printer

Alternative #2

   Software: Word processor, DBMS, electronic spreadsheet, DTP, OS/2 operating system, windows-type program

   Hardware: IBM-compatible (PS/2) with 60MB hard disk, high-resolution color monitor, keyboard, mouse, laser printer

Alternative #3

   Software: Word processor, DBMS, electronic spreadsheet, graphics package, DTP, operating system

   Hardware: Apple Macintosh with hard disk, high-resolution color monitor, keyboard, mouse, laser printer, scanner

disk, a monochrome monitor, and a dot-matrix printer. The operating system used a command interface requiring only a keyboard, not a mouse.

Herb's second alternative also included a word processor, a DBMS, and an electronic spreadsheet program. Additionally, it included a desktop publishing program to do page layouts. It was more expensive than the first alternative, but it would allow Herb in the future to do more than draw boxes—which is all that the word processor in the first system alternative would be able to do. Furthermore, the second alternative was based on different hardware: it was IBM-compatible, like the first alternative, but used a high-resolution color monitor (useful for future expansion of DTP) and a laser printer. The laser printer quietly and rapidly produced sharp copy. The user interface was a graphical one, so a mouse was required.

The third alternative that Herb considered was based on a personal computer different from the IBM variety. It employed an Apple Macintosh, which had impressive graphical interfaces. The DTP software accepted text from almost any word processing program, and graphics could be incorporated from a variety of sources. Although Herb was not planning to do graphics yet, the salesperson configured the system as if he were, just to give him a point of comparison. Thus, this system included a graphics program and an inexpensive scanner, as well as the more usual business equipment and software.

With these alternatives in mind, Herb compared the costs, expected benefits, advantages, and disadvantages of each. He decided against the first alternative, because it left no room for expansion. He felt that his desktop publishing needs would quickly outgrow the limitations imposed by using a word processor to accomplish that function.

Of the remaining system alternatives, both used a graphical interface, so Herb wasn't worried about having to memorize a lot of "computer mumbo jumbo," as he put it. He finally decided on the second alternative. He found the DTP features of both systems impressive, and was sure he could become proficient fairly quickly. But he was especially impressed with the DBMS in the second alternative, which, unfortunately, was not available for the Macintosh computer. The query capabilities were such that Herb could see himself producing special mailings targeted at certain groups of customers, once he got his system established. In addition, the salesperson assured him that the second alternative was highly expandable, and that graphics packages and scanners were available for it whenever he wished to add them.

Questions

8.17 What are the major tasks of the requirements evaluation stage?

8.18 What is the difference between tangible and intangible benefits? Give an original example of each.

Design Stage

The objective of the design stage is to specify precisely whatever is needed to procure each of the five components of the information system. We will discuss each of the five system components, and then consider what Herb could have done during the design stage.

Determine Hardware Specifications

Specifications for computer hardware include factors such as the amount of computer memory, the amount of disk storage, the type and resolution of the monitor, the type and speed of the printer, and so forth. Typical considerations for personal system hardware are listed in Figure 8-13.

At this point you should decide where your computer will be located. You might need to have an electrical outlet installed, buy some computer furniture, change the lighting in your work area, and so forth.

Determine Software Specifications

In personal information systems, programs usually are acquired from computer retailers or software vendors. You need to accomplish several tasks related to programs during the design stage.

First, you need to select specific software products, if you did not do so already during the alternative-selection step in the requirements stage. Thus, if you decided then to buy an electronic spreadsheet program, now you need to decide which one. Keep in mind that your various programs need to be compatible: they need to run under your operating system, and you may need to transfer data files between them.

Second, you need to plan the installation of the software on your system. For example, if you are using an MS-DOS-based system, you need to determine your directories and subdirectories and to design the main menu, the first screen you will see when you boot your system. This may require the design of an AUTOEXEC.BAT file as well as other .BAT files used to invoke the various software packages. Instructions on performing this task are found in the user documentation for your operating system.

Third, the program design stage includes planning a sequence for building your information system. For example, if you are going to use

---

- Personal computer
    Brand
    Processor type
    Speed
    Amount of memory

- Disk storage
    Type of disk
    Amount of storage

- Monitor
    Brand
    Resolution
    Color or monochrome
    Display adaptor type and
    brand

- Printer
    Brand
    Type
    Speed
    Graphics capability
    Color or black and white

- Miscellaneous
    Plotter
    Scanner
    Mouse
    Communications hardware

Figure 8-13

Personal system hardware specification requirements

word processing and database programs to do mail/merge functions, then you need to orchestrate the tasks of building your database application, building your library of form letters, and merging the two.

Finally, in some cases, actual program design needs to be performed. The normal functions of software packages might not be able to solve all your business problems. In those instances, custom programs might be written, say in a language such as BASIC or C. Unless you are a proficient programmer, you would probably be better off hiring a professional to develop such software. Your responsibility is to establish program requirements before hiring a contractor.

Similarly, you may need to write some macros, "programs" within a software product that perform commonly-used tasks (see Chapter 5). Before writing a macro, you need to design it, deciding on the steps within the macro and the sequence in which the steps will be performed.

Design the Data Component

Tasks in data design vary depending on the type of system. In the case of nondatabase applications (spreadsheets, word processing, and desktop publishing, for example), most of the work involves establishing standards you will use in your system. For example, during this stage you develop standards for naming files, creating directories and allocating files to them, and for formatting screen forms, reports, and other output.

You need to do more for database applications. A database is a collection of tables (or files) and during the design stage you need to determine the number, identity, and contents of each table. Also, databases normally involve data forms, menus, and reports. You need to design each of these also. For a refresher on developing personal DBMS applications, review Chapter 6.

Develop Document Procedures

In Chapter 4 you learned that four types of procedures exist in information systems: user procedures for normal processing and for failure recovery, and operator procedures for normal processing and for failure recovery. Usually in a personal information system the user and operator are the same person. Consequently, the four sets of procedures are often reduced to two: normal processing and failure recovery.

For normal processing, you need to establish procedures for starting the system, entering and editing data, producing reports, and ending the session. You also must establish procedures for periodically making backup copies of your data.

For failure recovery you need to know how to identify and correct a problem, and how to restore the application's data once the problem is fixed. One approach is to write down the name and telephone number of someone who can help diagnose problems. Although failure recovery procedures for a personal information system are somewhat informal, it is important to consider the possibility of failure before it occurs. In later chapters you will learn how vital failure recovery procedures are for multiuser information systems.

Determine Sources of Training

During this stage, you need to determine how, where, and when you are going to learn how to use your new system productively. You need to schedule time for classes, set aside time for self-paced tutorials, develop a reading list, and so forth. If you do not learn how to use your new system, you will have wasted time and money.

The Design Stage at Herb's Herbal Teas

If Herb had followed the system development procedure described in this chapter, he would have worked with the salesperson to identify the hardware and software that would best meet his needs, budget, schedule, and future requirements. Let's look at how it might have happened, starting with hardware and software.

Hardware and Software Design   During this stage, Herb's consultant selected Herb's hardware and software. He ensured that the programs were compatible and could share data if necessary. He also double-checked the entire configuration to make certain that the hardware would support the programs he picked. Through the computer retailer, the consultant got the name of a local person who had a similar configuration. He visited her and tried the system out. As a result of this visit, the consultant convinced Herb to purchase a more expensive printer than they originally had planned on. The consultant believed that the original printer would not produce copy of high enough quality for Herb's needs.

Following this, the consultant designed the directories and subdirectories that would allow the most efficient access to the software products. He also laid out the master menu in such a way that the cursor automatically would be positioned at the option Herb would select most often, allowing Herb to simply turn on the system, then click the mouse without moving it anywhere.

The consultant and Herb worked out a plan by which Herb would build his information system, beginning with the database application, then generating the analysis charts with the electronic spreadsheet program, followed by designing the catalog in-house.

Data Design for Herb's Herbal Teas   Designing Herb's data component was quite straightforward. At this point he needed only to (1) maintain a mailing list, (2) track customers' purchasing histories so he could determine for each order whether or not the buyer was a new customer, and (3) maintain a list of items, descriptions, and prices for inclusion in the catalog. As you can see in Figure 8-14, Herb at first needed only three tables, one for customer data, one for purchase history data, and

Figure 8-14
Database tables for Herb's Herbal
Teas

Table	Data type	Length
CUSTOMER		
Customer #	Integer	6
Name	Char	34
Street	Char	34
Apartment	Char	4
City	Char	12
State/province	Char	2
Postal code	Char	8
PURCHASE		
Order #	Integer	8
Customer #	—	—
Total	Currency	6.2
Date received	Date	8
Date shipped	Date	8
CATALOG-ITEM		
Item #	Char	5
Description	Char	50
Unit	Char	8
Price	Currency	3.2

one for catalog item data. Purchases are linked to customers by including the customer's number on a purchase record.

When Herb begins to add demographic data to his database it will become more complex, but for now, his database needs can be met by manipulating the data in just those three tables.

Designing Procedures Herb needed to establish procedures for several activities: maintaining the database, producing the catalog, printing mailing labels, and backing up his files.

To maintain the database, for example, Herb needed to decide when to delete a customer from the mailing list. He decided to do that whenever a customer requested it or when a customer had not placed an order in 24 months. He also established a procedure for eliminating duplicate (or near duplicate) mailing labels.

In order to produce a catalog, Herb established procedures for producing camera-ready copy (including page size, margins, overall design, typefaces used, type size, borders, placement of photos and drawings, and other standards), for matching photos and drawings to page locations, and for delivering copy to the printer.

Herb needed mailing labels as soon as the catalogs arrived from the printer, and scheduled their printing accordingly. Furthermore, he needed to add customers to and delete customers from the mailing list *before* he printed labels.

Finally, Herb decided that he would backup his database once each week (on Friday), and that he would keep three week's worth of backups at his home. In addition, Herb purchased a customer service agreement from the vendors of his word processing program and his desktop publishing program. This arrangement, though it cost a few hundred dollars more, would allow him to call the vendors' customer service engineers and get immediate answers to any problems he encountered.

Herb wrote all these procedures in a notebook that he kept near the computer. When he needs it, his documentation is readily available.

Training   The last thing Herb did during the design stage was to set aside time for learning how to use his new system. This was not easy, because he needed to keep up with all the work associated with running his own business. He decided to first use the tutorials provided with each software package, including the computer and operating system, the database management system, the word processor, the electronic spreadsheet, and the desktop publisher. He set aside three hours a day plus all of Saturday for two weeks to introduce himself to the system.

Then, with that background, Herb planned to take some of the courses offered by the computer retailer. The dealer had included ten hours of training in the agreement, so Herb would choose the courses he thought he needed most after he used the self-paced tutorials. He suspected that desktop publishing was more involved than the other system functions, so he tentatively signed up for the next DTP course.

Implementation Stage

During the implementation stage the five components are acquired, installed, and tested. Generally, each component is tested by itself and then an *integrated test*, a test of the system as a whole, is performed. Finally, the system is installed in the operating environment. (See Figure 8-15.)

Install Hardware

At this stage, you purchase, install, and test the hardware. Generally, microcomputers and related equipment are available from the dealer's inventory. Consequently, hardware can be received within a week or two of the order. If this is not the case, then you may need to place your order sooner in the system development process.

Once you receive the hardware you need to unpack, assemble, connect and test it. Some dealers will perform this task, but often you will do it yourself. This generally is not too difficult *as long as you follow the instructions*. Be sure to have a backup source of expertise in case you encounter difficulties. Usually, the dealer's service department can help you out. If you are installing a personal information system in a large company, then someone from the organization's MIS department can fill this role.

Questions

8.19 What are hardware specifications, and why are they necessary?

8.20 What needs to be done during the design stage for the program component?

8.21 What needs to be accomplished during the design stage for the procedures component?

8.22 What do you do during the design stage with respect to the people component?

8.23 How can you prepare for failure recovery?

- Obtain components and test them

    Acquire, install, and test hardware

    Acquire, install, and test programs
    Operating system
    Application software
    Tutorials

    Enter and verify data

    Document and test procedures

    Learn how to use the system

- Integrate and test the system as a unit

- Install the system

Figure 8-15
Tasks in implementing a system

Install Programs

After the hardware is installed, the programs are next. First you must install the operating system. Usually the operating system has utility programs and special commands that make the process straightforward. If the operating system does not install according to the documentation, then do not continue. Fix any problems in the operating system before proceeding. The operating system provides an environment for the other software. If it does not function properly then the results from your system will be unpredictable, at best.

Next, install application software. Software publishers generally provide installation instructions. This documentation usually is helpful and accurate. Sometimes the vendor will include a READ ME file on the installation disk. That file might contain modifications to the printed documentation, so read it first.

Better software products have utility programs that lead you through the installation process. Often questions regarding the hardware in use will be asked. Examples include the type of monitor, type of printer, number, type, and size of disk storage, and miscellaneous facts such as the country of use (for proper interpretation of the keyboard and display of special characters and the currency symbol). When you acquire your system hardware, complete (or have the computer retailer complete) a chart like the one in Figure 8-16. Even if you do not understand every entry, you will have on one page the data you need to respond to software installation prompts. Keep the form in your documentation notebook, and change it whenever you update your system.

As mentioned earlier, almost all software products today include a tutorial—a set of hands-on lessons that illustrate the major features and functions of the product. By all means, run the tutorial. This not only will acquaint you with the product, but it also will help you verify that the product is installed properly and operating correctly. This is good practice even for sophisticated computer users.

Enter and Verify Data

With the hardware and software installed, you are ready to enter data and verify it for correctness. Specific steps depend upon the nature of the application. In general, it is necessary to obtain the data from its current sources, enter it from the keyboard, and then carefully review it for correctness. This review is very important. Bad input data will produce incorrect results, and it is discouraging and frustrating to produce bad reports, especially at the start.

Document and Test Procedures

During the implementation stage you document and test procedures. Do not depend on your memory—write them down. As you use them, you may discover they need to be modified according to lessons you've learned and problems you've discovered.

Testing procedures is important for two reasons. First, you may not be the only one who ever uses this system. Consider Herb: as his com-

Software Installation Checklist

Computer:
    _____ XT (8088 or 8086)   _____ AT (80286)   _____ 80386   _____ 80486

Memory Capacity:
    _____ K RAM
    Expanded Memory: _____ (K or Megabytes)
    Extended Memory: _____ (K or Megabytes)

Monitor:
    Color: _____ Yes   _____ No
    Type: _____ Monochrome/Text only   _____ EGA
        _____ Monochrome/Graphics   _____ VGA (Monochrome or Gray Scale)
        _____ CGA   _____ VGA (Color)
            _____ Multisync

Communication Ports:
    Number of Serial Ports   _____
    Connected to:
        COM1   _____   COM3   _____
        COM2   _____   COM4   _____
    Number of Parallel Ports   _____
    Connected to:
        LPT1   _____   LPT3   _____
        LPT2   _____   LPT4   _____

Printers:
    Manufacturer: _____
    Model: _____
    Type: _____ 9 Pin Dot Matrix   _____ Laser Printer
        _____ 24 Pin Dot Matrix   _____ Other (inkjet, thermal)
    Connected to Communications Port: _____
    (COM 1,2,3 or 4 for Serial Printer,   LPT 1,2,3 or 4 for Parallel Printer)
    Emulates the following printers:
        1. _____   3. _____
        2. _____   4. _____

Disk Drives:
    Hard Disk(s):
        Manufacturer: _____
        Model(s):   _____
        Capacity: _____ megabytes
    Floppy Disk Drives:
        Enter number of drives at each capacity:
        5 $\frac{1}{4}$" 360 K   _____   3 $\frac{1}{2}$" 720 K   _____
        5 $\frac{1}{4}$" 1.2 MB   _____   3 $\frac{1}{2}$" 1.44 MB   _____

Mouse:
    Manufacturer: _____
    Type: _____ Bus   _____ Serial Port
    If Serial Mouse:
        Connected to Serial Port: _____
        (COM 1,2,3 or 4)
    Emulates the following model(s):
        _____ Mouse Systems   _____ Microsoft Mouse

Modem:
    Manufacturer   _____
    Model   _____
    Maximum Baud Rate   _____ (2400/1200/300)
    Connected to Communications (Serial) Port:
        _____ (COM1/COM2/COM3/COM4)

Figure 8-16
Software installation checklist
(Reprinted from *PC Today*, September 1989, p. 91.)

pany grows, he undoubtedly will hire some help, perhaps to perform some of the record-keeping chores. The procedures must be documented clearly and accurately. (Do you remember the employee in Chapter 1 who accidentally erased two very important diskettes, partly because the previous user never wrote down any of her procedures?)

Second, you can make mistakes when establishing procedures. Until all the processes have been worked through, there is always the possibility, for example, that you will try to use data that is not yet entered, that the product will not work quite the way you expect it to, or that it will take you much longer to do something than you anticipated.

Learn How to Use the System

During the implementation stage, you (or others who will use the new system) need to learn how to use it. As you know, several training options are available. You need to select the approach that will be most cost-effective in your circumstances. You may want to explore all facets of the system. Or you may want to learn only what you need to know at the time. How much and how quickly you learn depends on your own situation.

Integrate and Test the System

The final step is to integrate all the components and test the system as a unit. This activity is the system's dress rehearsal. Before becoming dependent on the system, you want to be sure it lives up to your expectations.

You need to invoke all the major functions of the system, including backup and recovery. If you find any discrepancies between your expectations and the system's behavior then document them and get them fixed.

Install the System

The four major installation styles are listed in Figure 8-17. **Parallel installation** means that you run the new system in parallel with the old one until the new system proves itself effective and reliable. For example, Herb might decide to continue to use the service bureau to produce mailing labels until he is sure that his own mailing label process is accurate.

Piecemeal installation (sometimes called phased installation) occurs when one portion of the system is installed at a time. If that portion functions properly, then other pieces are added until the entire system is installed. For example, Herb might install only the mailing list maintenance functions at first. When that works perfectly, he might add the analysis of new versus repeat buyers, and so forth.

Pilot installation means implementing the entire system, but in only one part of an organization. For example, if Herb's Herbal Teas consisted of four branch operations, Herb could install the entire system

- Parallel
- Piecemeal
- Pilot
- Plunge

Figure 8-17
Four styles of system installation

in just one branch. If problems are encountered, vulnerability is limited to that one branch.

Finally, **plunge installation** means completely abandoning the old system and immediately putting the new system in place. This is a very dangerous approach, because virtually no backup exists if and when problems are encountered. The plunge approach is the most risky one and generally should be avoided.

System Implementation at Herb's Herbal Teas

In reality, installation at Herb's Herbal Teas was haphazard. The dealer had assembled the hardware at the store, and had installed the software on Herb's hard disk. When Herb got it to his office, he was baffled. He did not know where to begin to learn about this new system. After glancing through some of the user reference manuals, he felt over-whelmed. Finally, he stumbled upon a booklet with "READ ME FIRST" stamped on the cover. It told him how to get started with the word processing program. After several frustrating days, Herb signed up for an introduction course at the computer store.

Herb's installation, if planned and prepared for, could have gone much smoother. It could have gone like this:

> The dealer assembled Herb's hardware in the store and tested the configuration, which was fine. Then, with Herb present, the dealer installed the software as well, pointing out important details to Herb each step of the way. As each product was installed, Herb reviewed the documentation and noted the tutorials and "Getting Started" sections. Before leaving, Herb got an updated class schedule and the business card of the service manager.
>
> At his office, Herb unpacked his equipment and reassembled it, according to instructions. Over the next several days, Herb resisted the temptation to begin building the rest of his information system; instead he concentrated on learning about the features of his new hardware and software. When he felt he had a handle on that, he moved on.
>
> He followed the process described in this section, building his data-base application, getting a copy of his mailing list from the service bureau in the format his DBMS required, and doing page layouts for sample pages of his catalog. He decided to implement his system piecemeal, starting with the analysis of purchases, then printing his own mailing labels, and finally producing the catalog.

Although he encountered some problems along the way, at no point was any problem devastating. It was always contained and, in most cases, Herb could resolve it himself. When difficult problems arose, Herb had no qualms about making use of his customer service agreements, deciding to work on a problem only for so long before calling for help.

Epilogue

Within four months, Herb's system was satisfying the requirements he'd established at the very beginning of the system development process. He was doing his own catalog page layouts, as planned. His goal had

Questions

8.24   Can a user install hardware, or must it be done by a technician?

8.25   Can a user install software, or must it be done by a technician?

8.26   Name two reasons for running tutorials.

8.27   What are two reasons you should test your procedures?

8.28   Name the four styles of system installation. What are the advantages and disadvantages of each?

been to decrease catalog production costs by 10 percent, but after four issues, Herb discovered that his new system had enabled him to slash costs in half.

Herb also increased his mailing list by purchasing some other lists and merging them with his own. Sales increased accordingly.

The discovery that surprised Herb the most was that his customer base was exceedingly loyal. Over 90 percent of his sales were to repeat customers. He had grossly underestimated this figure in the past, but now he had the facts before him. Such knowledge would very useful when planning marketing strategies.

Summary

Information systems exist within a life cycle. A user perceives a need, then a system is developed to address that need, and the resulting system is installed, monitored, and evaluated. When new needs are identified the cycle begins again. To develop a system, you follow a five-stage system development process.

The five stages are: problem definition, requirements definition, requirements evaluation, design, and implementation. Each stage is made up of certain specific tasks. Because each stage produces information needed for the next stage, they all must be performed.

During the first two stages, problem definition and requirements definition, you focus on the problem(s) you need to solve and the requirements your system *must* satisfy to help you solve the problem(s). During the third stage, requirements evaluation, you establish a hard-and-fast list of system requirements, then determine the best system approach to take. "Best," of course, refers to your own needs, finances, time frame, comfort level with computer technology, and many other factors. Only you can decide what's best for you.

During the design stage, you make all your choices regarding hardware and software, plan your database, document procedures for normal processing and failure recovery, and plan your own training schedule. Finally, during implementation you put all the pieces together into an integrated system. Implementation might take a while to accomplish, especially if you install your system in pieces. Learning how to use the system, installing the hardware and software, entering your data and checking it for correctness, and so forth, all take time. It might be a few weeks or a few months before your new system is completely installed.

Once it is, look at it critically. If it does not yet address your needs, determine why not and modify the system. If your needs have changed (and often they do), then go through the system development process again, beginning with problem definition. Initial system development usually takes longer and requires more effort than system modification, but the five-stage process still should be followed. Although it is no guarantee for success, following it can greatly improve your chances of developing a useful and satisfying system.

Word List

prototype	technical feasibility	piecemeal installation
cost feasibility	constraint	pilot installation
schedule feasibility	parallel installation	plunge installation

Discussion Questions and Exercises

A. System development, when performed using the method described in this chapter, can take a relatively long time. If you were truly pressed for time, which stages or steps within stages would you skip? What risks are associated with your decisions? What benefits? In light of your decisions, comment on the statement: "If you don't have time to do it right, you don't have time to do it over."

B. Describe three of Herb's biggest mistakes. Why did he make them? How could he have avoided them? You will almost certainly be a personal information system developer in the future. How will you ensure that you don't fall into Herb's traps?

C. Many personal information system buyers depend on the advice of a salesperson at a computer store to make some very expensive decisions. What are the risks of depending on a salesperson for such advice? How can you protect yourself from buying hardware and software that is not best for you?

D. You must configure a computer system (hardware and software) for your finance department at work. The system must meet the following criteria:

1. Total cost cannot exceed $8,000.
2. The computer must be an IBM or IBM-compatible.
3. It must include a hard drive of at least 50 megabytes. It also must include a 3½-inch floppy disk drive.
4. The machine must have an 80386 microprocessor.
5. It must have a color monitor.
6. Two printers—a dot-matrix and a laser printer—must be included.
7. Software must include:
   a) a database management system
   b) an electronic spreadsheet program, compatible with the DBMS
   c) an operating system

Submit a report detailing your recommendation. The report must include:

1. A detailed list of selected hardware and software.
2. For each item, the vendor (or publisher), cost, and warranty information.
3. Justification for the selection of the microcomputer.
4. Constraints of the system.
5. A profile of the microcomputer manufacturer: location of headquarters, length of time in business, summary of product line, reputation, and so on.

Write your report using a word processor. Include a spreadsheet that summarizes and totals the system configuration. Write the report as if your job depended on it.

Multiuser Information Systems

The personal information systems you studied in Part Two play an important role in business. But despite the proliferation of personal information systems, most of the computing done worldwide is accomplished by larger, more complex, and more expensive multiuser systems—systems in which many people are on-line at once. In such systems, as few as three or four users—or as many as thousands—can access the same database or use the same computer resources concurrently. As you might imagine, more problems exist with multiuser information systems than with isolated personal computer systems. In Part Three you will learn what these problems are and how they are addressed.

Chapter 9 is a foundation for the remaining chapters in this part. By definition, all multiuser systems allow more than one user to be connected to the system at once. Chapter 9 covers the two types of environments in which this can occur: teleprocessing systems and local area networks.

In Chapters 10 and 11 we discuss, from the end user's perspective, two primary applications of multiuser systems. In Chapter 10 you will learn about systems in which multiple users share the same data, usually stored in a common database. You will learn what must be done to make a shared database work, as well as your eventual role as a user of a shared database.

Chapter 11 deals with another major application for multiuser information systems: providing timely and accurate information to people who make business decisions. Such systems are called management information systems (MISs) and decision support systems (DSSs). You will learn how MISs and DSSs are used to gain a competitive advantage in business—the ultimate goal in productivity. You will learn the difference between an MIS and a DSS (a DSS is used for less structured problem solving). And you will learn where the MIS department belongs in a company's organizational hierarchy.

As a future end user, you need to know what multiuser systems are and what you can gain from them. You also need to know their limitations. And you need to know what your role will be when your company or organization develops a multiuser system. A multiuser system is developed in a five-stage process, just as a personal information system is; but the entire process is more complex, as you will learn in Chapter 12. You also will learn about some of the tools currently used in system development, such as prototyping and CASE methodology.

As you study Part Three, think about how you as a user fit into the larger scheme of things. What role will you play if you take a job at a bank, an insurance company, a manufacturer, an accounting firm, or a school? How will you use teleprocessing or a local area network? How do you see yourself using a common database? What are the kinds of business decisions for which you will need computer-generated information?

Teleprocessing Systems and Local Area Networks

CHAPTER OUTLINE

The personal information systems you studied in the last five chapters provide important services and benefits to individual businesspeople. However, these systems have a serious limitation: they are stand-alone systems—independent of one another and thus isolated. Business often involves the coordinated activity of several (or many) people. For these situations, multiuser systems, which allow users to communicate and to share resources, are needed.

In this chapter, we will address the components of two environments that support communication and resources sharing among several users. We begin with a brief introduction to the purposes served by multiuser systems. Then we describe three fundamental multiuser architectures. Next we discuss the hardware and program components of teleprocessing systems, and finally, the hardware and program components of one type of distributed system, local area networks.

Be aware that this chapter does not describe business information *systems*. Instead, it describes two environments, teleprocessing and distributed processing, that support business information systems. Thus, in this chapter we discuss only two of the five system components, hardware and programs. In Chapters 10 and 11, we will discuss the business information systems that use the processing environments described here. Those two chapters will consider all five components.

The Need for Multiuser Information Systems

Multiuser information systems serve three fundamental purposes: to share hardware, to facilitate communication, and to share data. In this section we will briefly describe each.

Hardware Sharing Systems

The simplest type of multiuser system is a **hardware sharing system**. Such a system allows a group of users to share access to computer hardware devices. This is usually done so that multiple users can have access to an expensive hardware device that they could not justify for their own applications alone. For example, the members of a department may each operate one or more personal information systems. While some of these applications require the occasional use of a laser printer, it may be that none of them can justify the expense of such a printer by itself. However, if several applications can share the printer, those applications can also share the expense.

Expensive printers, plotters, cameras, and other output hardware are often shared this way. In addition, fast, large-capacity disks also can be shared. In this case, the disk is divided into separate regions and each user is allocated one or more of the regions. This differs from data sharing applications, to be described below, in which users share the same data at the same disk locations.

Disk sharing allows for **diskless workstations**. These are not only cheaper; the absence of a disk reduces the likelihood that data will be stolen or otherwise compromised by copying it via local disks.

Figure 9-1 shows two ways that hardware can be shared. The system in Figure 9-1*a* is primitive; users copy data onto floppy diskettes and physically carry it to the plotter, printer, or other device. This is sometimes called the **Nike method** (put on your Nikes, grab the diskette, and run down the hall). Figure 9-1*b* shows a more sophisticated system. Here, the computers are connected via a **local area network** (LAN), which is a system that allows the computers to communicate with one another and with shared hardware. A LAN consists of cables and processor cards that are inserted in the expansion slots of the microcomputers. You will learn more about LANs later in this chapter.

Hardware sharing systems are, in many ways, the simplest type of multiuser computer system. There is minimal need for coordination and cooperation. Users may need to coordinate their use of the hardware, just as they need to coordinate their use of a copying machine. But this is easy to do. And, with some devices, the hardware itself will queue user requests and perform the coordination. Again, the major goal of a hardware sharing system is to enable applications to share access to expensive hardware that they could not cost justify on their own.

Communications Systems

A large number of multiuser systems facilitate human communication. In this section we will discuss **electronic mail (E-mail)**, the most common one. Technology is developing rapidly in this field, and in the course of your career it is likely that new forms of computer-based multiuser communication will evolve. Group conferencing and group

Figure 9-1
Hardware-sharing alternatives
(continued)

a. Sharing hardware via Nike method

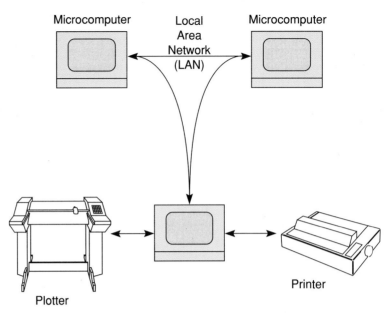

b. Sharing hardware via LAN

Figure 9-1
(Continued)

decision support are two such possibilities. See Kraemer and King for a survey of current research activities.[1]

The purpose of E-mail systems is to provide a means for creating, editing, and disseminating messages electronically. With electronic mail, each person connected to the system is allocated a **mailbox** and a set of programs for creating, transmitting, and reading mail. The mailbox is simply a file into which the electronic mail system deposits electronic correspondence.

Figure 9-2 shows a schematic of a typical E-mail application. This system consists of a group of microcomputers connected together via communications lines in a local area network. E-mail also can reside on concurrently accessed mini- and mainframe computers, but this is less common. For the system in Figure 9-2, each computer owns a mailbox on a centralized disk where the E-mail system deposits mail. Periodically, the microcomputer users examine their mailboxes (via the LAN) to see if they have mail.

Figure 9-3 shows a screen that is typical of those used to create mail. The originator specifies his or her identity and the identity of those to whom the mail is to be directed. The originator then keys in the message and directs the system to send the mail. Addressees can be specified by name or by distribution list. For example, a user could direct that a message be sent to all employees in a particular department, to all employees connected to the E-mail system, or to some other predefined group of users.

1. Kenneth L. Kraemer and John Leslie King, "Computer-based Systems for Cooperative Work and Group Decision Making," *Computing Surveys* Vol. 20, No. 2 (June 1988).

Communicating with Computer Systems

1   International keyboard symbolizes the computer's role in communication.

Computer Systems and Communications

Computer systems facilitate communication in many ways. The outputs of information systems are used to communicate the status of situations, problems, and opportunities among a group of workers. Computers communicate with one another to facilitate remote operations and to support other geographically distributed information system applications. International business relies heavily upon computer-based communication systems.

Communicating via Information Systems Outputs (photos 2–14)

The outputs of an information system display facts, text, figures, comparative data, trends, and illustrations. In the final analysis, the purpose of these outputs is to communicate business information among a group of workers and decision makers. Information systems produce many types of outputs to facilitate this communication. These outputs are displayed on computer screens, printed, plotted, and often electronically transmitted. In recent years, desktop publishing has enabled business professionals to produce their own high-quality documents that combine text, graphics, and illustrations.

Computer-to-Computer Communication (photos 15–26)

Local area networks (LANs) allow computers within a few thousand feet of one another to communicate and share mail, documents, databases, and other resources. Modems allow personal computer users to communicate with more distant computers over the telephone or other similar communication lines.

Some businesses develop worldwide computer communication networks to support their operations. For example, a large conglomerate sells to customers on the European continent, processes those orders in Ireland and New York, and ships goods from sources all over the world. To support these operations, it has constructed a worldwide communications system (composed of hardware, programs, data, procedures, and people).

Computer-to-computer communications may occur over microwave lines, via satellite, or through optical cable, some of which is buried undersea. Large communications networks require sophisticated control centers with a staff of professional operators.

International Business (photos 27–38)

Banking, finance, manufacturing, and many other industries have become international in scope. Such business is conducted today by large multinational corporations that support international offices and operations and also by smaller companies that develop alliances with organizations in local economies. Computer-supported communications and information systems have played major roles in the development of international business.

The computer industry itself is international in scope. Computer chips are manufactured worldwide, particularly in Japan and Taiwan. Computers are assembled from components manufactured in Europe, North and South America, and the Far East as well.

Computer programming is accomplished worldwide; international teams of programmers often work together to modify a program written for one country so that it will meet the needs of another country. Chinese and Japanese characters pose particular problems for such localization.

International business is conducted by telephone, fax, teleconferencing, and international travel. All of these media are supported by computer systems and technology.

2   Outputs from information systems are used to facilitate human communication about business situations, problems, and opportunities.

3   A wide variety of graphics can be produced by computer systems.

4 *Communication via an information system report.*

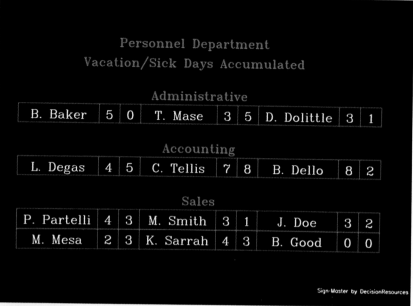

Personnel Department Vacation/Sick Days Accumulated								
Administrative								
B. Baker	5	0	T. Mase	3	5	D. Dolittle	3	1
Accounting								
L. Degas	4	5	C. Tellis	7	8	B. Dello	8	2
Sales								
P. Partelli	4	3	M. Smith	3	1	J. Doe	3	2
M. Mesa	2	3	K. Sarrah	4	3	B. Good	0	0

Sign-Master by DecisionResources

5 *Communication via text.*

the register mark
san francisco

6 *A company logo—communication via computer illustration.*

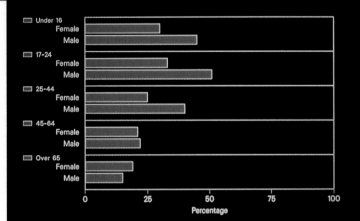

Percentage of Injuries Annually in U.S.

7   Bar graphs communicate comparisons.

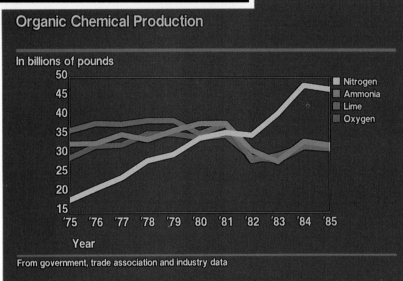

Organic Chemical Production

In billions of pounds

From government, trade association and industry data

8   Line graphs communicate trends and comparisons.

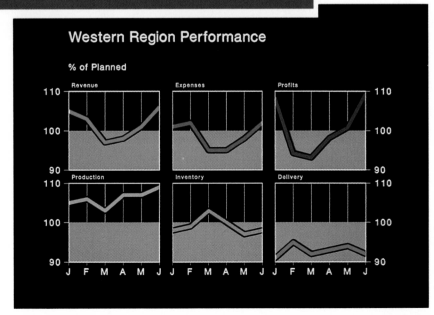

Western Region Performance

% of Planned

9   Line graphs separated for clarity.

4   Communicating with Computer Systems

10 *Three-dimensional bar charts displayed on a computer screen.*

11 *Computer graphics can also be printed.*

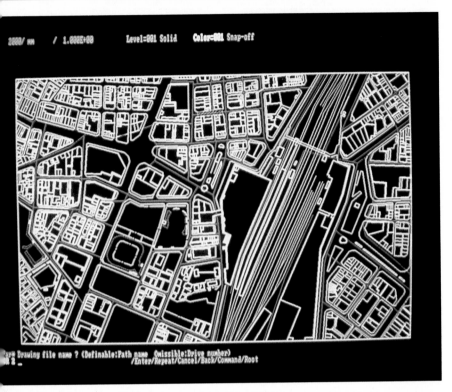

12 A city map displayed on a computer screen.

13 Desktop publishing combines text, graphics, and illustrations.

14 With desktop publishing, business professionals can prepare high-quality documents on their own.

15 *Local area network facilitates communication among personal computer users.*

16 *Modems allow personal computer users to communicate with other computers over telephone and other analog lines.*

17 *Salesperson on the European continent places an order for produce with clerks in Ireland . . .*

18 *Clerks enter order. Order data is transmitted to company headquarters in New York City . . .*

19 *At company headquarters, the order is processed and shipping instructions are transmitted to farmers in Australia . . .*

20 *Farmers in Australia ship goods to customer in Europe.*

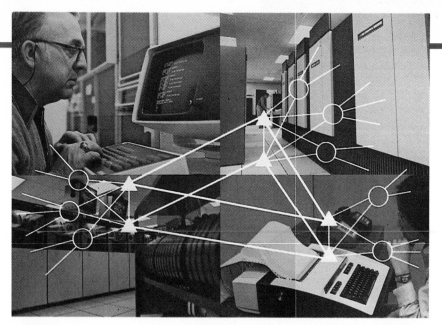

21 Computer-to-computer communication requires all five components: people following procedures instruct hardware processing programs to communicate data.

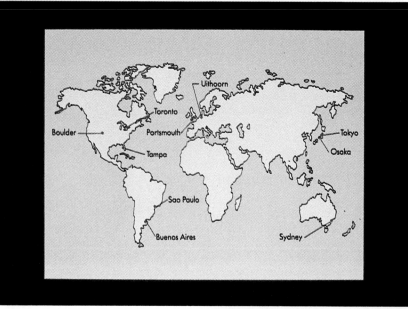

22 Example of computer network: IBM worldwide computer installations.

23 Data communications via microwave transmission.

24   *Data communications via satellite.*

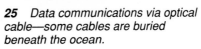

25   *Data communications via optical cable—some cables are buried beneath the ocean.*

26   *Data communications network control center.*

27 Automated teller machines support international banking.

28 International check processing.

29 With major markets in Europe, North America, and the Far East, stock trading occurs 24 hours a day.

30 *The computer industry is an international business—a computer chip fabricated in the Far East.*

31 *The components of many computers are manufactured and assembled worldwide.*

32 *International team of computer programmers.*

33 *Chinese keyboard.*

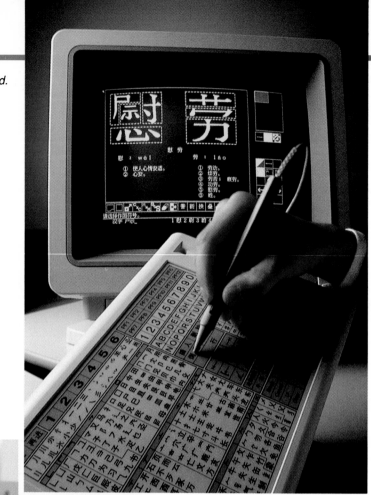

34 *Computer trade show in the Far East.*

35 *International communication can be conducted by fax . . .*

36 *or by teleconferencing . . .*

37 *or by international travel.*

38 *Computer systems are the backbone of the international travel system.*

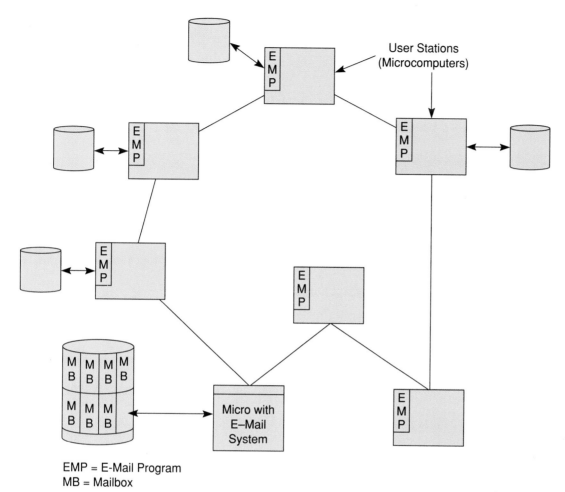

EMP = E-Mail Program
MB = Mailbox

Figure 9-2
Schematic of E-mail system

E-mail systems can be **active** or **passive**. An active system interrupts the user when mail arrives. It informs the user that mail has been put in the mailbox. A passive system just deposits the mail in the mailbox and expects the user to periodically examine it for mail. The system in Figure 9-2 is passive.

Data Sharing Systems

Data sharing is the third reason for multiuser systems. Data sharing systems are the oldest and most common form of multiuser system. Examples include an airline reservation system, an order entry system, and a bank's teller processing system. Because of their prevalence and importance, we will discuss such systems in detail in the next chapter. To appreciate the discussion in this chapter, however, it is important for you to understand one of the significant characteristics of shared data systems: the need for **controlled sharing**.

To be effective, multiuser data sharing systems must allow users to access the same data, but only in a manner that is carefully coordinated

Questions

9.1   What is the significant limitation of personal information systems?

9.2   Explain why this chapter does not describe business information systems. What does it describe?

Figure 9-3
Typical E-mail message entry form

FROM: Marian O'Sullivan		TO: Dept-List-A
DATE: Jan 7, 1991	TIME: 10:47 A.M.	

There will be a department meeting tomorrow, Friday, 8 Jan at 2:00 P.M. Jason will present the findings of the customer survey, and I will summarize the ADARSN Conference proceedings. Also, we can welcome our two new employees, Fred Carsons and Sally Smathers. We will meet in A-207.

9.3   List three purposes of multiuser systems.

9.4   Describe an example hardware sharing system.

9.5   Explain the difference between the Nike method and a local area network for hardware sharing.

9.6   What is electronic mail?

9.7   What advantages does it have over regular mail?

9.8   Give an example of a data sharing system.

9.9   Explain what the term *controlled sharing* means in reference to data sharing systems.

and controlled. Controlled sharing prevents one person's work from interfering with another's.

For example, consider a word processing group. One operator may enter a document that is modified by a second operator on the next day, and by a third operator on the day after that. To make this possible, all three operators must have access to the pool of documents currently in process. Thus, that pool must be shared. But if two word processing operators modify the same document simultaneously, trouble will result. Thus, while the information system must allow the operators to access a shared pool, it must do so with caution.

Additionally, controlled sharing also involves security. Often, not every user needs or should have access to all of the system's information resources. In these cases, the information systems must provide passwords, account numbers, and other forms of security to restrict the access and activity.

We will address the topic of controlled sharing in more detail in the next chapter. For now, understand that the need for controlled sharing places a burden on the components of data sharing systems.

Multiuser System Architectures

There are three fundamental architectures used for multiuser systems. They are teleprocessing, distributed, and hybrid.

Teleprocessing System Architecture

The first, and oldest, is **teleprocessing** or (as it is sometimes called) **centralized architecture**. With this architecture, a centralized computer is connected to a number of terminals, as shown in Figure 9-4. The terminals are just monitors and keyboards (not microcomputers) and are sometimes referred to as **dumb terminals,** since all the processing is performed by the centralized computer.

If teleprocessing users need microcomputers for other purposes (personal information systems, for example), the micros are made to emulate, or perform like, dumb terminals. This is done to reduce the costs

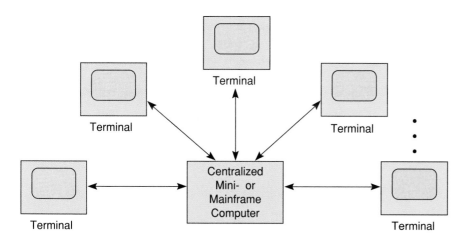

Figure 9-4
Teleprocessing, or centralized, system
architecture

of having both a terminal and a microcomputer, as well as to reduce the amount of user workspace for computer equipment.

The term *teleprocessing systems* is used for these systems since all processing is conducted somewhere away from the user (the prefix *tele-* means "at a distance"). The distance may be short or long. Terminals may be connected directly to a nearby computer, or they may be connected via telephone or other communications lines to a computer hundreds or thousands of miles away.

Since all processing occurs at one site, the single computer can maintain tight control over processing. It can carefully manage accesses and changes to data, dictate the order of processing, and provide extensive security.

Teleprocessing systems are most commonly used for organizational transaction processing applications (for a review, see Chapter 3). At one time, teleprocessing systems were used for workgroup transaction processing (systems that facilitate departmental operations, for exam-

9.1 INCREASING YOUR PERSONAL PRODUCTIVITY

Worldwide ATM Market

Visa U.S.A. Inc. and Plus System Inc. have completed the physical link between their automated teller machine (ATM) networks. Now individuals can use Visa cards bearing the "Plus" logo to withdraw cash from any of the 20,000 Plus System ATMs worldwide.

The unified ATM network allows Plus System cardholders to get cash from Visa's 25,115 worldwide ATMs.

The alliance helps both firms compete for bank business against Mastercard International, which recently acquired the only other nationwide ATM network operator, Cirrus System Inc., according to Plus System officials. Visa officials said ATMs linked to both the Visa and Plus ATM networks should get more use and earn more money for the banks that own them. Banks typically receive a fee of 50 cents per transaction when either card is used in one of their ATMs.

	Characteristics	Control Philosophy	Primary Application
Teleprocessing, or Centralized	• Intelligence centralized on a single computer • Dumb terminals or micros that emulate dumb terminals	• Centralized control of all activities	• Organizational TPS for older systems, limited workgroup TPS
Distributed (primarily LAN)	• Independent micro-computers communicate via LAN or other medium • File server provides data librarian and disk management	• Independent processing on microcomputers • Central control of data when residing on file server	• Workgroup information systems
Hybrid	• Mixture of microcomputer LANS, minicomputers, or mainframe computers	• Hybrid control	• Organizational information systems

Figure 9-5
Multiuser system architectures

ple), but such systems are gradually being replaced by distributed or hybrid architectures. The characteristics of teleprocessing systems are summarized in the first row, first column of Figure 9-5.

Distributed System Architecture

The second type of multiuser system architecture is **distributed**. With this type, multiple, independent CPUs are connected to each other via communications lines. Local area networks (LANs) are the most common form of distributed system in business today, and the discussion in this chapter is devoted primarily to them. Although other types of distributed systems do exist, most businesses do not use them.

A LAN connects independent microcomputers using cables and processor cards that are inserted in the expansion slots of the micros. For some systems, the cables are telephone-type wire; with others, coaxial cable (like that used for cable TV) is required. In general, the microcomputers must reside within several thousand feet of each other.

The LAN shown in Figure 9-6a connects five user microcomputers with a specially-designated microcomputer called a **file server**. The file server contains the database (or other data) on its disk and processes that database in accordance with requests from the other microcomputers. It also schedules and supervises the processing of requests for the plotter.

A more complex network, called a **wide area network**, is shown in figure 9–6b. A wide area network is basically a network of LANs. In general, the system is designed so that micros that need to communicate frequently are attached to the same LAN. In addition, a micro on one LAN can communicate with a micro on another LAN. The computers that connect the LANs together are called **gateway computers**.

Consider an example. Suppose a company maintains three warehouses in geographically separate locations. All of the micros in a particular warehouse are connected to each other via a LAN. Most of the time, the users need only communicate with other micros at the same site. On occasion, however, it is necessary for a user in one warehouse to communicate with a user in a different warehouse. The wide area network addresses that need.

A third network alternative is the **private branch exchange (PBX)** shown in Figure 9-6c. A modern PBX is an extension of the older telephone-oriented switching systems. Since PBXs allow for the transmission of data as well as voice signals, they provide a means for microcomputers to communicate. Most PBX systems provide far less data transmission capacity than a LAN, so they currently are used for low-volume applications such as electronic mail.

Distributed networks, unlike teleprocessing systems, distribute control throughout the network. Since each microcomputer possesses its own microprocessor, it can conduct considerable processing independent of the file server and the other computers. A user on one of the

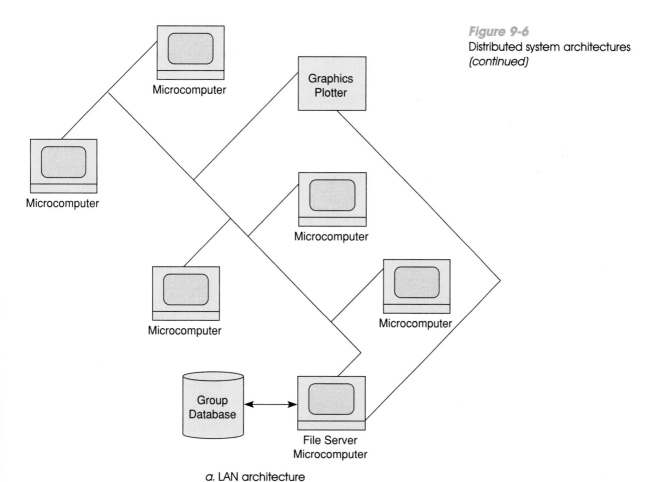

Figure 9-6
Distributed system architectures
(continued)

a. LAN architecture

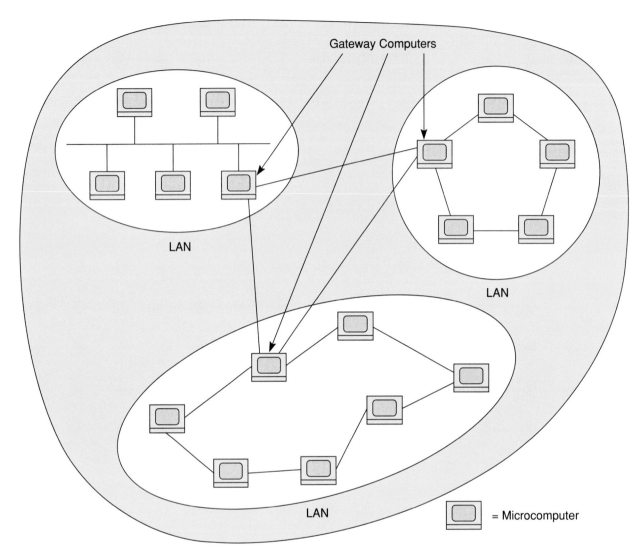

b. Wide area network

Figure 9-6
(Continued)

micros can run a spreadsheet application against a file it received from the server two or three weeks previously, and the file server will not be aware of it. The advantage of this characteristic is that users have more independence and more control over their own processing. The disadvantage is that processing on the several microcomputers can quickly become uncoordinated and chaotic.

Hybrid System Architecture

The third multiuser system architecture is **hybrid**. As you would expect from the name, this architecture is a combination of teleprocessing and distributed. For example, in Figure 9-7a, a local area network is connected via a communications line to a centralized mainframe com-

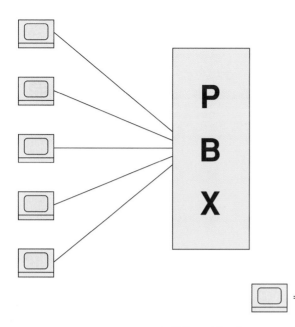

Figure 9-6
(Continued)

= Microcomputer

c. PBX architecture

puter. As with wide area networks, the computer which connects the LAN to the mainframe is called a gateway computer.

Another hybrid example is shown in Figure 9-7*b*. Here, microcomputers communicate with each other and with a mainframe computer via a PBX. The PBX serves two functions. First, it enables intermicro communication, as discussed previously. Additionally, it consolidates input from the micros into a single stream of input for the mainframe.

Questions

9.10 List three multiuser system architectures.

9.11 Sketch a teleprocessing system.

9.2   *INCREASING YOUR PERSONAL PRODUCTIVITY*

Network Security

PC LANs currently provide little inherent security. Companies commonly use log-on security, although security experts contend that log-ons provide limited protection. And frequent password changes and encryption procedures all impact the way people do their work.

Another way to limit security threats is to restrict access to PC LANs to normal business hours and only to users with a need to know certain information.

Hardware protection, such as physically isolating PCs, is just as important as protecting software. Each physical network node is an access point. These access points include not only the PC but also servers, bridges, gateways, modems, network printers and cabling.

Raymond Humphrey, director of corporate security for DEC, says that eliminating bulletin boards, knowing the origin of software and getting rid of remote documentation

and public networks can all help secure a system.

Some companies protect themselves by not using out-of-office disks, limiting the transmission of executable programs over networks, not booting hard-disk systems from a floppy unless it is the original, not executing programs of unknown origin, not using network file servers as workstations and never adding data or programs to system master disks.

Figure 9-7
Hybrid system architectures

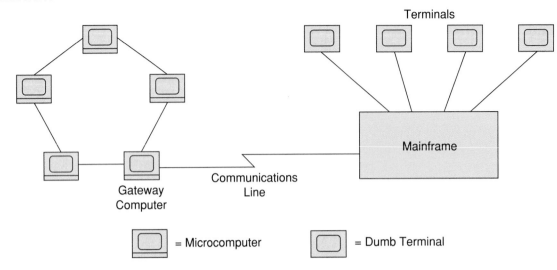

a. Hybrid system architecture with LAN and mainframe

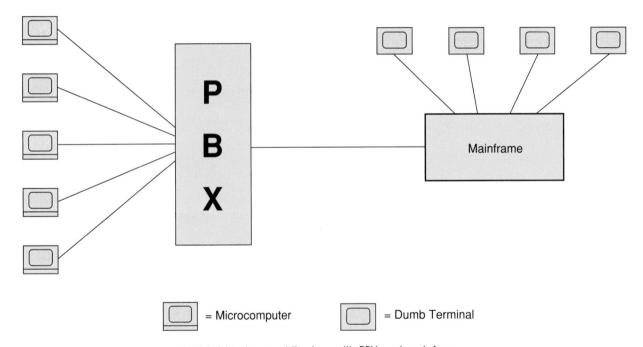

b. Hybrid system architecture with PBX and mainframe

It also routes output from the mainframe back to the appropriate microcomputer.

The hybrid architecture entails hybrid forms of control. For the system in Figure 9-7*b*, for example, the mainframe controls all of the interactions that it has with the microcomputers. However, it does not control any of the message passing that occurs between micros via the PBX.

9.12 Explain the difference between a dumb terminal and a microcomputer. Which is used for teleprocessing? Why?

9.13 Why is tight control possible with teleprocessing systems?

Figure 9-5 summarizes the characteristics, control philosophies, and primary applications of the three types of multiuser system architectures.

Advantages and Disadvantages of System Architectures

Figure 9-8 summarizes the relative advantages and disadvantages of the three architectures just described. The major advantages of teleprocessing systems are that they provide centralized control and that they use established technology and vendors; as a consequence, they involve less technical risk. On the other hand, teleprocessing systems entail a high initial cost; they require highly trained personnel to install and, to a lesser degree, to operate them; and they offer no possibility for local, independent processing. Such systems are also only as reliable as their central processor. If it fails, the entire system is inoperable.

The major advantages of distributed systems are low start-up costs, greater flexibility in tailoring and scaling a system to meet processing requirements, the ability to support local processing, and higher reliability since multiple computers are involved. If one fails, the others can still carry out at least part of their function.

The disadvantages of distributed systems are a lack of centralized control, problems due to multiple vendors (typically the LAN, the LAN operating system, and the base hardware come from different vendors), and rapidly changing technology that can quickly make obsolete the investment in equipment. Further, it is difficult for personnel to stay current with changing technology. Finally, both LAN and PBX applications can have a sharp performance cap. A LAN, for example, may support 10 micros well, support 14 marginally, and not support more than 16 at all. If the workload expands so that 20 micros are required,

9.14 Summarize the characteristics of teleprocessing.

9.15 What is the difference between a distributed system and a local area network?

9.16 Sketch a local area network.

9.17 What restriction exists on the location of computers in a LAN?

9.18 What is a file server?

9.19 What is a wide area network? What roles does a gateway computer fulfill?

9.20 What is a PBX? What function can it serve in a distributed system?

9.21 Summarize the characteristics of a distributed system.

9.22 Sketch an example of a hybrid system.

9.23 Summarize the characteristics of a hybrid system.

9.24 Summarize the advantages and disadvantages of teleprocessing.

	Teleprocessing, or Centralized	Distributed	Hybrid
Advantages	• Centralized control • Established vendors and technology • Low technical risk • High capacity for TPS	• Low start–up costs • Tailorable, scalable • Local, personal computing possible • Reliability	• Greatest capacity • Hybrid control • Most tailorable and scalable
Disadvantages	• High initial cost • Highly trained personnel for development and, to lesser extent, operations • No local personal computing • Vulnerable to one CPU	• Lack of centralized control • Multiple vendor problems • Rapidly changing technology • Sharp performance cap	• Complicated • Expensive • Difficult to set up • High technical risk • Some technical problems unsolved

Figure 9-8
Advantages and disadvantages of multiuser system architectures

9.25 Summarize the advantages and disadvantages of distributed processing.

9.26 Summarize the advantages and disadvantages of hybrid architecture.

the users may be just out of luck. Another LAN or a wide area network may be required. While teleprocessing systems also have performance caps, they tend to peak out more gracefully.

Hybrid systems have the greatest capacity and provide the possibility of both centralized and distributed control. They are the most flexible and tailorable to an organization's requirements. On the other hand, hybrid systems are the most complicated and expensive to develop and operate. They can be difficult to set up and involve considerable technical risk. In fact, some of the problems of more sophisticated hybrid systems do not yet have technical solutions.

We will now consider teleprocessing and distributed systems in more detail. As stated at the beginning of this chapter, we are concerned here only with processing environments that support multiuser systems. As a consequence, we will consider just the hardware and program components.

Teleprocessing Systems—Hardware

The subject of teleprocessing hardware is very technical. The technology is complex, there are a number of fundamentally different strategies, and there are dozens of types of equipment and many options for each. Developing any but the simplest teleprocessing system requires the services of a highly trained professional. In this section, our goal is to define and explain several terms that you will need to understand in order to work with such professionals.

Teleprocessing systems involve three categories of hardware: end-user hardware, communications lines, and processing hardware. We will consider each in turn.

End-User Hardware

With teleprocessing, since all applications processing occurs on the centralized computer, little intelligence is required in **end-user hardware.** Thus, the user can access the teleprocessing system from either

---

9.3 INCREASING YOUR PERSONAL PRODUCTIVITY

The Versatility of PC Networks

▶ They make it much easier for employees to communicate by computer

▶ They thus save time by cutting down on meetings and enabling several employees to concentrate on the same problem

▶ They make it easier to digest larger amounts of information, letting a company react faster and generally be more competitive

▶ They improve the return on investment in computers by combining the use of the machines in new ways to solve problems

▶ They can cut software costs by eliminating duplicate purchases of programs a dumb terminal (a device with keyboard and screen, but no central processing unit), or from a microcomputer. Micros are not necessary and would probably not be used for this purpose at all except that the users already have them on their desks. But even if they do not, the cost of a microcomputer is not that much greater than that of a dumb terminal.

If a dumb terminal is used, the connection to the communications line is built into the terminal. If a microcomputer is used, a communications card must be installed in one of the micro's expansion slots. These cards are similar to those used for local area network connections.

In the future, dumb terminals are likely to fade from use. As they are replaced by micros, the intelligence of the micro will be used to manage more and more sophisticated user interfaces. Graphical user interfaces such as those on the Macintosh and in Microsoft Windows will become the norm, as will color monitors.

Communications Lines

Communications lines can be classified according to their speed, mode, and type.

9.4   INCREASING YOUR PERSONAL PRODUCTIVITY

How to Choose a Network

Decide if You Need One   If your employees spend more time swapping disks and trying to locate data than working on their spreadsheets, you need one. Networks won't only improve communications between employees. They'll also boost the return on your computer investment. Coca-Cola Foods in Houston noted a surge in PC use once its network was installed. A network doesn't have to be a huge expenditure. A 20-workstation PC network will run about $95,000, including operating system software and some applications software. Training costs are additional.

Just Buy What You Need   If all you need is communication among workers in the same department or office, buy a local network. If you need to communicate off-site, you'll want a wide-area network. Aetna Life & Casualty, for instance, has both. Whatever network you buy, be sure

that several dozen independent software companies write programs for it—so you can get more sophisticated software later on.

Get the Right Software   Buying network versions of the software you use now can save money. For instance, if you have a 20-person network, but only six workers simultaneously use Lotus 1-2-3, you'll pay for six copies even though all 20 employees can use the program. You'll want one standard program for each application, such as word processing or accounting, so files can be exchanged. You'll also need programs that can find files that are lost or damaged.

Make Sure Someone's in Charge   You'll need a network administrator who can do day-to-day housekeeping, monitor the system's security, provide backup and recovery, perform maintenance, and establish

training procedures. If a network becomes a political issue because of tensions over who controls the corporate data, you may want to hire from the outside. But you'll also need a high-level executive to monitor issues such as network security. That's why some companies have created the chief information officer position.

Teach Employees to Use the Network   Without good training, you have nothing. Beyond that, identifying a proponent within each workgroup and giving that person time to work with others will improve acceptance of the system and may lead to good ideas on how to use it. A teller at Richmond Savings Credit Union in Richmond, B.C., customized the institution's software so employees on any of 250 workstations get immediate access to the financial records of the credit union's 40,000 customers.

Line Speed   **Voice-grade** lines are communications lines like those used in telephone lines (hence their name). Their speeds vary from 300 to 9600 bits per second, or bps.[2] The most common voice-grade line speeds are 1200 and 2400 bps. A line speed of 9600 bps requires that the line receive special tuning, called **line conditioning**.

Wideband lines have much greater capacity. Their speeds can be 500,000 bps or more. Such lines are commonly used in satellite communications and in communications between or among computers. Local area networks also usually operate at wideband speed. In most situations, wideband lines require special cabling such as coaxial or other insulated and protected cable.

Line Mode   There are two line modes, analog and digital. **Analog lines** carry a smooth, wavy signal. The sounds of a siren and those of a symphony are analog signals. **Digital lines** carry a choppy signal that represents bits (0s and 1s). The sounds of a barking dog and of an ax chopping wood are digital signals.

Now we come to a problem—one that is due to a historical mismatch. The most common communications lines are telephone lines. They are analog lines; they were designed to carry the sounds of a human voice, which is an analog sound. Computers, however, operate with digital data. Thus, to use analog lines for computer communication, they must be made to carry digital data.

To do this, some means must be devised to encode bits into a continuous analog signal. One way is to define a certain signal frequency as *0* and another as *1*. Figure 9-9 shows a scheme in which a lower-frequency signal is to be interpreted as a 0 and a higher-frequency signal is to be interpreted as a 1. A corresponding digital signal is shown for comparison.

Figure 9-9
Analog and digital line modes

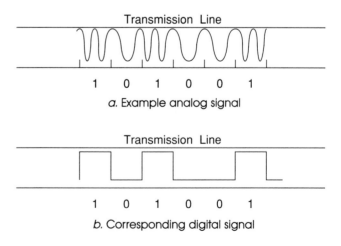

a. Example analog signal

b. Corresponding digital signal

2. You will sometimes hear the term *baud* as a measure of line speed. Baud refers to the rate at which a line can change state. The speed of the line in bps is often greater than the speed of the line in baud. Thus, bps is a better term to use.

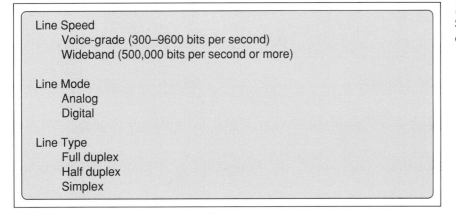

Figure 9-10
Summary of communications line classifications

A device which encodes digital bits into analog signals and decodes analog signals into digital bits is called a **modem** (for modulator/demodulator). Modems are required whenever an analog line is used to transmit digital data.

Line Type   There are three line types, full duplex, half-duplex, and simplex. **Full-duplex** lines are the most common. These lines allow traffic to be transmitted on the line in both directions at the same time. One way in which this is done is to reserve the frequencies above a certain level for traffic in one direction and the frequencies below that level for traffic in the other direction.

Half-duplex lines are rare, but you may encounter them. Such lines allow traffic to be transmitted in both directions, but not simultaneously. Such lines are like the reversible lanes on a freeway. Traffic can go either direction, but only one direction at one time. **Simplex lines** are one-way only. They are seldom used today and most likely you will never encounter one.

The communications line classifications are summarized in Figure 9-10.

Connections to Communications Lines   As stated, the physical connection from the end user to the communications line depends on whether a dumb terminal or a microcomputer is used. In the case of a terminal, the line connection is built in; in the case of a microcomputer, the line connection is made via an adapter card inserted into an expansion slot.

At the other end of the line, the attachment to the processing computer is made via a **communications port**. Such a port is the processing computer's equivalent to an adapter card; it is simply a physical connection to the line. Large mainframes have dozens or even hundreds of communications ports.

Most users cannot keep a communications line consistently busy. For short periods of time, such as during the transmission of a graphic image, a user may keep the line very busy. But much of the time, when the user is contemplating his or her next action or entering data, the line will be idle. For example, a human typing 60 words per minute

Figure 9-11
Terminals or micros sharing the same
communications line

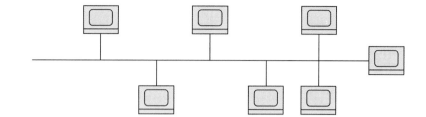

Figure 9-11
Terminals or micros sharing the same
communications line

Questions

9.27 List the three categories of hardware used for teleprocessing systems.

9.28 Explain how the user's hardware is connected to a communications line in a teleprocessing system.

9.29 Why are dumb terminals likely to fade from use in the future?

9.30 In what three ways can communications lines be classified?

9.31 Explain the difference between voice-grade and wideband lines.

9.32 What is line conditioning?

9.33 Explain the difference between analog and digital lines. Which are used for computer systems?

9.34 What is the role of a modem?

9.35 Explain the difference between a full-duplex and a half-duplex line.

9.36 What is a communications port?

9.37 Explain polling.

9.38 What is a front-end and what purpose does it serve?

9.39 Explain multiplexing.

9.40 What is a critical difference between polling and multiplexing?

(which is typing very fast) is transmitting about 60 × 10 characters per word × 8 bits per character, or 4800 bits per *minute*. On a 1200 bps line, the transmission will take 4 seconds, leaving 56 seconds of unused line capacity! And, as you know, some lines are much faster.

Since one user cannot keep a line busy, businesses often connect several or even dozens of users to the same line, as shown in Figure 9-11. When this is done, some means must be created to prevent the traffic from one user from being confounded with the traffic from another.

Several alternatives exist. One is contention, in which the line is managed like a polite human conversation. We will discuss this technique when we describe local area networks later in this chapter.

A second approach is called **polling**. With this approach, the processing computer asks each terminal (or micro), in round-robin fashion, if it has anything to send. If so, the message is sent. If not, the computer asks the next terminal, and so forth. Periodically, the processing computer sends messages back to the terminals, again in round-robin fashion.

The advantage of polling is that no intelligence is required in the end user's hardware. The disadvantage is that CPU cycles on the centralized computer (which is probably already very busy) are required to perform polling. Because of this, some processing computers are assisted by **front-end computers** that perform this and other communications services on behalf of the processing computer.

Another alternative is **multiplexing**. With multiplexing, messages from the terminals are interleaved with one another, as shown in Figure 9-12. A time slot is granted to each terminal. If the terminal has something to send, it fills its time slot with data. If not, that slot remains empty. At the computer end, the signal must be demultiplexed, that is, the messages must be separated out according to their time slots.

Observe a critical difference between polling and multiplexing. With polling, the line that carries the signal operates at the same speed as the line from the terminal or computer. With multiplexing, the communications line is much faster than the lines from the terminals or computers. In fact, if *n* computers are to be connected to a multiplexer, then the communications line must be *n* times faster than the lines from the terminals or computers.

Connections to wideband lines are always made via a computer. Such computers are sometimes called **concentrators**, since they concentrate the signals from many users into one signal. Concentrators also provide a number of other services such as error detection (and correction), character conversions, and data encryption.

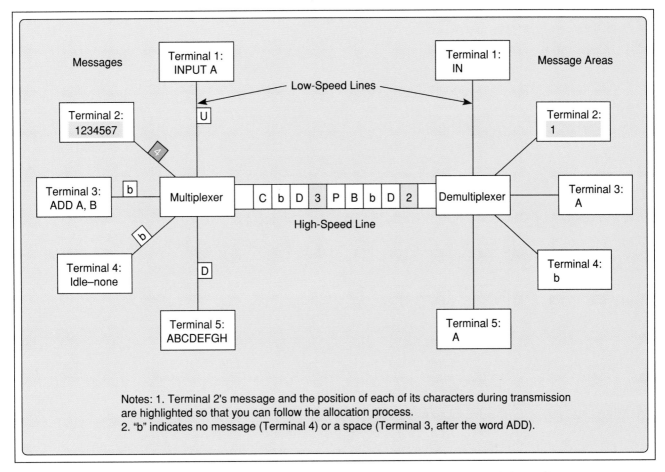

Notes: 1. Terminal 2's message and the position of each of its characters during transmission are highlighted so that you can follow the allocation process.
2. "b" indicates no message (Terminal 4) or a space (Terminal 3, after the word ADD).

Figure 9-12
Example of multiplexing

Figure 9-13 shows yet another alternative, this one involving a private branch exchange (PBX)—a privately owned, computer-based telephone exchange. In Figure 9-13, the PBX serves as a concentrator to route communications traffic between the user stations (connected to telephone jacks) and a high-speed line. As with other types of concentrators, the PBX combines the multiple signals from the lower-speed lines into a single signal for the higher speed line.

9.41 What is a concentrator and what purpose does it serve?

9.42 How can a PBX be used in a teleprocessing system?

Processing Hardware

The third hardware component of teleprocessing systems is the computers that process the applications and the databases. In a teleprocessing system, all applications processing is done on a single processing computer. Although there may be other CPUs (in a concentrator or PBX), these CPUs do no applications processing. In Figure 9-14, for example, the mainframe, the front-end, and the concentrators all possess CPUs. However, only the mainframe does applications processing.

The earliest teleprocessing systems used a mainframe as the central processing computer. As minicomputers gained prominence they were

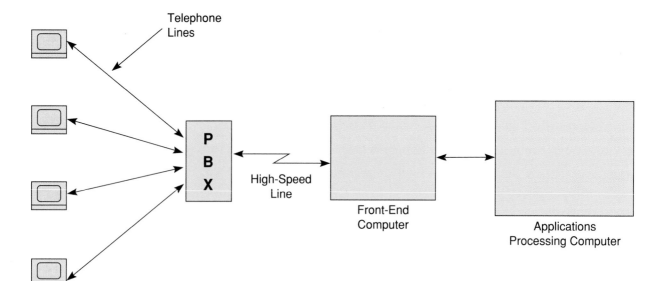

Figure 9-13
PBX as concentrator

used as well. Today, microcomputers have more power than the mainframes of ten years ago, and they could also be used. But this is not done. Micros are used more commonly in local area networks.

Teleprocessing Systems—Programs

Business information systems that involve teleprocessing require both system programs and application programs. Since this chapter is describing only the teleprocessing environment, we will consider just system programs. Application programs will be discussed in the next two chapters.

System Programs

As with hardware, the subject of system programs for communications processing is exceedingly complicated and involved. As system software, they are acquired either from the CPU manufacturer, from the vendor of the operating system (possibly as part of the operating system), or from a specialty software house. The subject is so complicated that most MIS departments allocate their most technically accomplished programmers to the tasks of maintaining and, occasionally, modifying the communications programs.

The Need for Communications Control

To understand the role of communications programs, consider Figure 9-14 again. Suppose the computer shown here resides at a bank and that there are over two hundred terminals connected to a dozen communications lines. Further suppose that terminals submit transactions that are processed by one of seven different programs (demand deposit

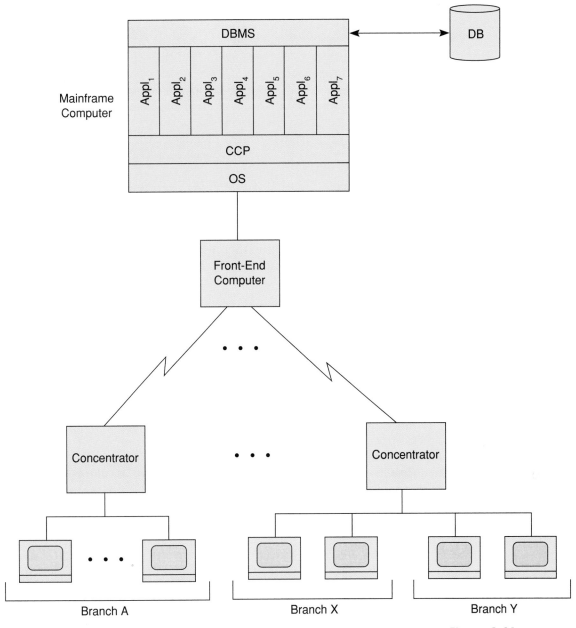

Mainframe Computer

Branch A

Branch X

Branch Y

Figure 9-14
Example teleprocessing system

accounting, loan payment, line of credit activity, credit card payment, etc.).

Now, assume the communications hardware operates correctly and that messages are accepted from the terminals, combined and transmitted over the high-speed lines, delivered to the central computer site, deconcentrated or otherwise processed as necessary, and correctly deposited in the main memory of the processing computer. Now what?

Each message is a transaction for one of the seven application programs. Each must be delivered to the appropriate program. That in itself is tricky enough, but consider this: each one of those programs is processing many other transactions concurrently. The program most likely will be busy when the new message arrives. Not only might it be busy, but there might also be a line, or *queue*, of messages already waiting for it. This message needs to be placed in line with all of the others, and processed in turn. And all of this activity must occur fast enough that the customer notices no delay.

The necessary coordination tasks are handled by a computer program called the **communications control program (CCP).** This program keeps order among the transaction processing programs, their inputs, and their outputs. **CICS** (Customer Information and Control System), licensed by IBM, is the most popular add-on CCP.

Curiously, with mainframe computers, the CCP is an add-on product. It must be licensed (and paid for) in addition to the operating system. With minicomputers, the CCP is built into the operating system. This anomaly arose because, historically, teleprocessing was an add-on to the batch processing typical of most mainframes. Minicomputers, however, were designed from the start to perform teleprocessing. Be aware that in both cases, the functions of the CCP must be performed; CCP functions simply are included in the operating system of most minicomputers.

Protocols

Consider the thousands of activities underway at any time for the teleprocessing system in Figure 9-14. Truly, this situation would degenerate into chaos without very careful coordination of activity among the hardware, the operating system, the CCP, and the application programs. This coordination is even more critical when you consider that the concentrators and the front-end are themselves computers that have operating systems and their own version of a CCP as well.

To provide the necessary coordination, all of the components of a communications system must agree to a set of communication standards. Such standards are called **protocols**. Briefly defined, a protocol is a standardized method of packaging and handling communications messages.

Consider an analogy. When you send a letter, you place it in an envelope, write the receiver's name and address in the center of the envelope, and place your name and return address in the upper left-hand corner. In doing this, you are following a simple protocol. It is standardized because everyone knows that the address in the center of the envelope is the *to* address and the address in the corner is the *from* address. Further, you end each address with a five- or nine-digit number. Everyone understands that this number is a zip code, and everyone agrees that if the *to* zip code is 90007, then the letter should be sent to downtown Los Angeles and not to Enumclaw, Washington. They agree to follow the same standard definition of zip codes.

Consider what happens when your letter reaches the post office. It is placed in a pouch with all of the other mail going to Los Angeles. A tag is attached to the pouch indicating the postal destination (Los Angeles) and the originating destination. When the pouch arrives at the airport, it is placed in a still larger container, the container of goods that is placed in the cargo compartment of the airplane. This container is also labeled with the source city and the destination city.

Everyone in the mailing system agrees to conventions about the meaning of the labels. For example, airline personnel know how to interpret the portion of the tag that indicates flight number. By a world-wide standard, UA167 means United Airlines Flight 167 and nothing else. Any baggage handler in the world would know to place a container with that label into the airplane that is flying United Flight 167.

This is an example of a three-level protocol. At each level, the letter is enclosed in a new package with a new to and from address. Computer communication follows a similar strategy. The terminal addresses its message for a particular program. It passes the message to the concentrator, which adds more packaging and addresses the message to the front-end. In actuality, there are several more levels than we have described here. The International Standards Organization, in fact, has defined a protocol that has seven levels. At each level, there are standard ways of packaging the message, standard meanings for the labels (analogous to flight number or zip code), and standard ways of handling the message.

As a business user, you need not be concerned with any of the details of a protocol. You should, however, understand what the term means and also realize that all communications hardware and programs must adhere to the same protocol. Components of the communications system cannot mix and match protocols.

9.43 Explain the need for communications control in the context of the system shown in Figure 9-14.

9.44 What is a protocol?

9.45 Give an example of a three-layer protocol.

Distributed Systems—Hardware

As with teleprocessing systems, the technology of distributed systems is quite complicated. Again, your goal should be to understand the important terms. If your organization implements a network system, your company will probably employ a professional to design and install it. In that case, you need to be an informed consumer of that person's services.

Local Area Networks (LANs)

A local area network is a federation of microcomputers directly connected to one another within a few thousand feet. LANs exist to facilitate the sharing of hardware, data, and other resources as well as to provide a base for group communication.

Local area network hardware consists of microcomputers, communications lines, controller boards, and peripheral equipment. The purpose of the **controller board** is to connect the microcomputer to the LAN. A LAN controller board is a circuit board placed in one of the expansion slots of each microcomputer in the network; the communications lines are then attached to the controller board. Such boards decode line signals when receiving messages and encode messages for transmission. Controller boards also coordinate message processing with the other processing activities of the local CPU.

Peripheral equipment to be shared among the microcomputers is connected to the LAN. Usually such equipment is expensive, special-purpose hardware like a graphics plotter or a fast, high-quality laser printer. A shared device also has a controller board.

In a typical LAN, one (or more) of the microcomputers is designated a *server*. This microcomputer stores the data that will be shared on the LAN. A **dedicated server** serves the needs of the network and nothing else. No user processing is done on a dedicated server. **A concurrent server** both services the network and performs processing for a user.

LAN Topology

As shown in Figure 9-15, there are three possible configurations of computers (called *topologies*) in a LAN: bus, ring, and star. With **bus topology**, the computers are connected to a cable like clothes along a clothesline. The advantages of this topology are that it is easy to install and that it is cheap. One line is run through the work group and the microcomputers are attached to the line where needed. Adding new computers also is easy; the new computer need only clip into the line. The cost of a bus connection can be less than $500 per computer or **node**, as the computers in a network are sometimes called.

The major disadvantage of a bus topology is poor performance. In most cases, bus topologies cannot match the performance of other topologies. In fact, in busy commercial applications, current technology allows the bus topology to be used for LANs connecting only a small number of microcomputers, say less than fifteen.

Ring is the second type of LAN topology. With this arrangement, the computers are connected to a line that is closed in a circle or loop. A continuous path exists from any one computer through all the other computers and back to the first computer. The advantage of a ring is performance; a continuous flow of data can pass around the ring at a

Figure 9-15
Three basic LAN topologies

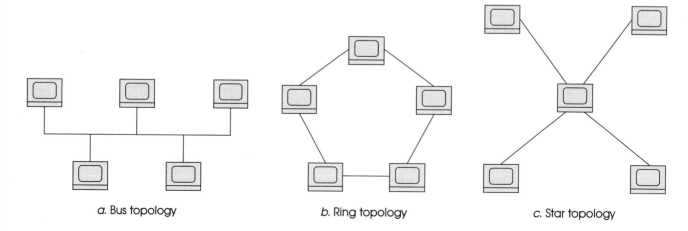

a. Bus topology   *b.* Ring topology   *c.* Star topology

very high rate. The disadvantage is dependency among the computers. If one is inoperable, the LAN is inoperable. If one is slow, all will be slow. Further, due to the need to have a closed loop, more cable is required than with a bus topology.

Star is the third type of LAN topology. One microcomputer is placed in the center and lines run out from it to the others like the arms of a star. The central computer operates as a clearinghouse for LAN traffic. It receives messages from a sending node and directs them to the receiving node. Do not confuse this arrangement with teleprocessing. The essential difference is that with a star LAN topology, the nodes are microcomputers; with teleprocessing, the nodes are dumb terminals. Also, with teleprocessing, the central computer has control; with star-topology LANs, the central computer simply acts as a message switcher.

The advantage of the star configuration is ease of installation and cabling. The disadvantage is dependence on the central computer. It can become a performance bottleneck and, if it fails, the network will fail as well.

The bus topology is used in many commercial applications; neither the ring nor the star are much used in their pure forms. Instead, a combination of ring and star has become popular. This hybrid form consists of a central microcomputer which contains a circular line within itself; and lines radiating from this ring to the other microcomputers. See Figure 9-16. A continuous flow of data circulates through the ring, and data to and from the micros is transmitted along the arms of the star. This topology has the performance advantage of a ring without having the expense of duplicated cables.

IBM, as well as other manufacturers, has published a standard cabling configuration guide that implements this hybrid topology. When publishing this guide, IBM made a commitment to its customers that this topology would be supported for some time. IBM told its customers that they would be safe to follow this guideline when wiring their new or reconstructed buildings.

LAN Transmission Media

Three types of transmission media, or cables, are used on a LAN: twisted pair, coaxial, and optical. **Twisted pair line** is cheap but has the lowest capacity. The wires typically used for telephone lines are an example

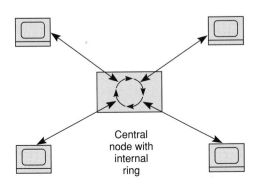

Central
node with
internal
ring

Figure 9-16
Hybrid ring/star topology

9.5 INCREASING YOUR PERSONAL PRODUCTIVITY

How to Select a Data Communications Package

In considering your needs and in selecting a data communications package, remember that you are dealing with two separate, related technologies. The special needs of each of the technologies—communications and computing—must be considered. You need a coordinated system that deals with both requirements.

When you buy a data communications package, you must install both hardware and software components. Further, these components must be compatible in terms of both the computer system and the communications link to be used. Factors to consider in package evaluation include speed, transmission mode, data format, protocol, and operating characteristics.

Transmission speed, the rate at which data are sent and received, usually is measured in baud, roughly equivalent to bits per second (bps). For microcomputers, available packages have transmission rates ranging from 300 to 9,600 baud. In general, costs of packages increase with baud rates. Also, the prospect and potential loss of data through electrical interference on lines increases at higher baud rates. Often, a decision to transmit at higher speeds leads to extra line costs to assure needed signal quality. The most common rates selected by microcomputer users are 1,200 and 2,400 baud. Some modems have fixed rates for transmission and receiving. On others, baud rates can be varied, either through use of switches or through software entries. One factor in selection of transmission speed lies in the volume of data that you want to transmit. Another factor is the rate established for the stations to which you want to transmit. The sending and receiving stations must operate at the same speeds.

Transmission modes are synchronous or asynchronous. Both sender and receiver must be set for the same mode. Most microcomputers operate in asynchronous serial mode. Formats and protocols have settled into a *de facto* standard, established by Hayes Microcomputer Products. Hayes introduced the first successful and widely accepted modem for microcomputer use. The great majority of manufacturers in this field have elected to build products compatible with Hayes standards. For microcomputer users, it is a safe practice to insist that any package proposed for data communications be Hayes compatible.

Most microcomputer users communicate over telephone lines. Therefore, important considerations in package selection lie in ease of connection between the computer and the telephone network. Also, most software packages now available provide capabilities to dial numbers from a directory maintained on a stored file. A communications package also should be able to answer and prepare itself to receive transmissions automatically, without user intervention. These features make for convenience of use.

As with any other tool for computer use, you should start your procedure for selecting a data communications package by determining what you want to do, then check packages to find the one that meets your needs best—at the most reasonable price.

of twisted pair media. **Coaxial line** is more expensive but has greater capacity than twisted pair. It also has greater reliability since it is better insulated. **Optical transmission media** is very expensive but has exceptionally high transmission capacities.

Twisted pair and coaxial are the most frequently used cables for LAN applications. In general, optical is too expensive and its high capacity is not usually needed. The IBM cabling standard allows for all three types of transmission media to be used.

You may hear about two styles of transmission: baseband and broadband. Baseband transmission is slower and cheaper than broadband. With baseband, signals are broadcast on a single frequency; with broadband, several frequencies are used. This means many signals may be carried simultaneously on a broadband network. Also, with broadband both voice and data signals may be carried on the same line.

Private Branch Exchanges

A *branch exchange* is a switching system that enables telephones to be connected to each other. A *private branch exchange* (PBX) is such a system owned by the using organization rather than by a telephone company.

PBX systems grew out of the telephone switchboards of 25 years ago. As microprocessors were installed in PBX systems, vendors were able to add more and more functions and capabilities. Today, PBX calls can be automatically forwarded, numbers can be periodically redialed, busy stations can be *camped on* so that the waiting call is put through the moment the present call is ended, and so forth. Additionally, PBX systems monitor telephone use for budgeting and cost control purposes. They also can be interfaced with a billing system so that telephone charges are automatically charged to specific accounts.

Most PBX systems today allow for data as well as voice communication. Thus, computers can connect to one another across the PBX. One advantage of this is that no special wiring is required for computer communication. The computers can be connected into the telephone system so that an office wired for telephones is also wired for computers. This is not the case with LANs, where special wiring is required.

Most PBX applications are used in what is called *serial mode*. In this mode, they operate in the range of 56,000 bits per second, which is slow for LAN. Computers interfaced on such a PBX are thus restricted to relatively low-volume applications such as electronic mail.

Local Area Networks—Programs

The basic categories of programs for local area networks are system programs and application programs. In this chapter, we will consider only system programs. Application programs will be examined in greater detail in the next two chapters.

Figure 9-17 shows an example of relationships between programs for a local area network of four microcomputers and a dedicated file server. For this example, three of the micros (A, B, and D) are processing a shared database on the file server. The fourth (C) uses the file server's disk for storage but does not process the shared database.

The figure shows the programs stored in the main memory of each computer. Each computer has a local operating system program (labeled OS) and a LAN operating system program (LAN-OS). Computers A, B, and D have a database management system program ($DBMS_u$—"u' indicating "user"). The file server runs a special file server's version of the DBMS ($DBMS_{os}$). That version contains control procedures not present in the user versions of the DBMS. Finally, computers A, B, and D have application programs (AP) that access the DBMS. The remaining

Questions

9.46   Define *local area network.*

9.47   What hardware is involved in a local area network?

9.48   List three types of LAN topology and sketch an example of each.

9.49   Explain the differences between, and the respective advantages and disadvantages of, twisted pair wire, coaxial cable, and optical media.

9.50   What role can a PBX serve in a distributed system?

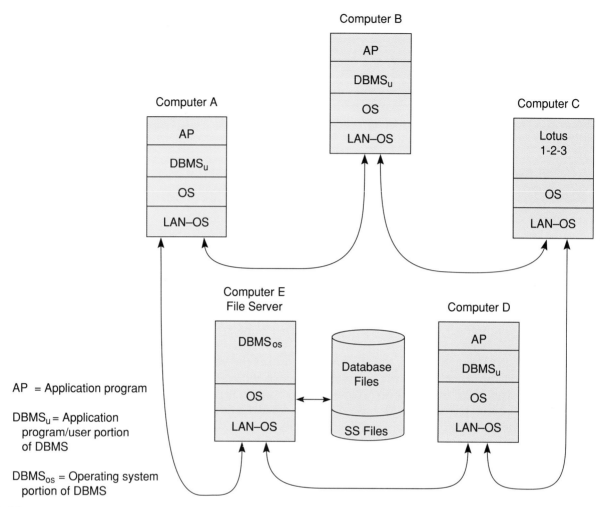

AP = Application program

DBMS$_u$ = Application program/user portion of DBMS

DBMS$_{os}$ = Operating system portion of DBMS

Figure 9-17
Relationships of programs in a LAN

micro, C, is running a spreadsheet program (Lotus 1-2-3); it stores and retrieves spreadsheet (SS) files from the file server.

LAN Systems Programs

As shown in Figure 9-17, two operating system programs are required for each microcomputer in a local area network: one for the micro and one for the LAN. The **LAN-OS** (LAN operating system) is an extension of the local operating system; it supports LAN processing, controlling and coordinating communications traffic (as described under "LAN protocols" below).

In most cases, the LAN-OS is licensed from the vendor that produces the LAN hardware. IBM, Novell, and 3COM, for example, are vendors of LAN hardware; they each license a LAN-OS for the hardware that they sell.

The functions of the LAN-OS are summarized in Figure 9-18. First, it must provide processing control over the traffic on the network. The

- Interfaces with network hardware
    Processes protocol:
        Contention
        Token passing
        Other

- Expands OS constraints
    DOS 640,000-bit memory limit, 32-megabyte disk limit
    Better memory management
    Better disk management

- Provides greater security
    Passwords
    File attributes limit access/update
    User is limited to directories

- Provides printer and peripheral spooling

Figure 9-18
LAN-OS functions

LAN-OS formats transmissions to be sent across the network in accordance with the network's protocol. The LAN-OS also receives transmissions and unformats them for delivery to the user or program. The LAN-OS processes the network using contention, token passing, or some other method (described later).

In addition to these basic functions, the LAN-OS also extends the capacity of the local operating system in a number of ways. First, the LAN-OS is a more sophisticated program and eliminates some of the limitations of the operating system; for MS-DOS, for example, several LAN-OS products eliminate the 640K program limitation, and the 32MB limitation for a disk. The LAN-OS generally provides better memory and disk management as well. Additionally, LAN-OSs provide security features not found in DOS. Finally, most LAN-OSs provide printer and other peripheral **spooling**. This means that requests for printing or other services placed in a queue are dispatched in a first-come-first-served or other orderly process.

For a number of reasons, the local operating system (labeled OS in Figure 9-17) used in a LAN is normally the same as the operating system used for single-user, non-LAN systems. First, using the same operating system enables application programs to run without changing them. The application sees the same interface in a LAN application as it does in a single-user application. Second, there are many features and functions in the operating system that need not be changed for a LAN-OS. By using standard DOS, the vendors of LAN-OS save themselves (and their customers) considerable expense. Finally, using standard DOS reduces the amount of learning and training that people must have.

Newer operating systems that consolidate the LAN-OS and the OS into a single operating system are already emerging. An example is IBM's OS/2 operating system. When such operating systems become common, you will not need to be aware of the differences described here.

The DBMS on a LAN is considerably different from the single-user DBMS products you learned about in Chapter 6. We will discuss this further in the next chapter.

LAN Protocols

Regardless of their topology or transmission media type, all LANs share a common problem: competition among the microcomputers for access to the LAN. Two or more microcomputers may want to use the LAN at the same time. A variety of strategies have been developed to manage this competition.

These strategies are sometimes called protocols. As stated earlier, a protocol is a standard method for packaging and processing communications messages. Two protocols are common for LANs: contention and token passing.

With **contention**, each message is addressed with the identity of the sender and the receiver. Each node listens to the line; when it detects a message addressed to it, it accepts the message. All other messages are ignored. When a node wants to transmit a message, it first listens to the line. If the line is unused, the node sends its message. If the line is in use, the node waits for a certain time, then listens again. It repeats this procedure until the line becomes available.

This strategy has a defect, because it is possible for two nodes to attempt to use the line at the same time. When this occurs, there is a standard procedure to resolve the problem. First, both nodes stop broadcasting. Each one waits a period of time, and then makes another attempt to transmit its message. Obviously, the nodes must each wait a different period of time, otherwise they will be in perpetual lockstep.

Contention is like a polite human conversation. People wait their turn to talk, and if two or more people begin speaking at the same time, they stop and somehow arrange for a single person to speak. The contention protocol formalizes this process.

The advantage of contention is that it is simple and easy to implement. The disadvantage is that considerable excess capacity must exist on the line—otherwise nodes wait inordinate amounts of time to send their messages.

An alternative protocol is **token passing**. This protocol is normally used with a ring topology (or one of its variants). A continuous stream of fixed-length packets, or *tokens*, revolves around the ring. Each packet contains system data, a flag to indicate whether the packet is in use, the identities of the sender and the receiver, and space for user data.

You can think of packets as thousands of little dump trucks revolving around the ring. Some are full, on their way to a destination, and some are empty. Empty trucks travel around the ring until a node needs them.

Each node examines all of the tokens as they pass by. If the token contains data, the node examines it to determine if the data is for that node. If so, the node accepts the data, and marks the packet as empty.

- Contention
      Nodes listen to line
      Send when line is available
      Stop when multiple signals occur; wait and resend

- Token Passing
      Continuous stream of tokens revolves around ring
      Messages loaded on available tokens
      Messages may be disassembled (and later reassembled) if more
      than one token is required

Figure 9-19
Two LAN protocols

When a node wants to send a message, it finds an available token, marks it as used, fills in the sender and receiver data, loads its message into the token, and sends it on its way. If the message is too large to fit into one token, the node breaks the message into token-sized pieces and loads them on available packets as they come by. The receiving node must reassemble the message from the pieces in the packets.

With token passing, a very high percentage of the available line capacity can be used. There is no need for the excess line capacity required for contention. The disadvantage of token passing is complexity. Examining each token and assembling and disassembling messages are more difficult than the actions required for the contention protocol. Still, both protocols have seen considerable commercial application. The two LAN protocols are summarized in Figure 9-19.

Operating System Interface to Application Programs

Application programs vary in the degree to which they are aware of and use the facilities of the network. Most single-user, horizontal application programs such as Lotus, Word, or WordPerfect, can run on a networked computer without change. If the program uses only local disk for storage, then the program is not even aware that the network exists. If the file server is used for storage, then the only difference is that the user must employ the file designator for the file server instead of a local file designator.

Consider an example. Suppose the spreadsheet user on computer C in Figure 9-17 is running Lotus 1-2-3. She can operate this program in the same way on the LAN as she would in a single-user application. Lotus, in turn, interfaces with the operating system in the same way as it does in a single-user application. The difference occurs between the OS and the LAN-OS.

Suppose the user wants to obtain a spreadsheet file from the file server. The user has been told to use a **special file designator** for the file server; suppose that designator is the file g:. To open a Lotus spreadsheet named sheetabc, the user will ask Lotus to open spreadsheet g:sheetabc.wks. The OS will not know where file g: is located, but the LAN-OS will. In this case, the LAN-OS intercepts the request for file

Questions

9.51 Explain the role of the LAN-OS in a local area network.

9.52 Why is the local operating system in a LAN normally the same as the operating system for a personal computer application?

9.53 Explain how contention is used to manage LAN communications.

9.54 Explain how token passing is used to manage LAN communications.

9.55 Explain how a single-user horizontal application program (like Lotus 1-2-3) can access a file stored on the file server.

g: and takes over processing. It obtains and presents the data to Lotus just as the OS would have done; Lotus does not know that the data came from the file server. The particulars of this process are beyond the scope of this text.

This strategy assumes that only one application is using the data at a time. If the access is to be shared, then a number of changes and extensions to the application program must be made. That is the subject of the next chapter.

Summary

Personal information systems are effective, but they have an important limitation: they are independent and isolated. Business often requires the coordinated activity of several or many people. For these situations, multiuser systems are required.

This chapter discusses two environments that support multiuser systems. These are the teleprocessing and distributed processing environments. Since this chapter addresses supporting environments and not information systems, it considers only the hardware and program components. The next two chapters address all five components of multiuser systems that utilize teleprocessing and distributed processing.

Multiuser systems serve three fundamental purposes: to share hardware, to facilitate communication, and to share data. Hardware sharing systems allow users to share access to expensive hardware that they cannot justify for their applications alone. Laser printers, plotters, and large-capacity, fast disks are often shared in this way.

There are a number of different multiuser systems that facilitate communication. Electronic mail (E-mail), the most popular such system, provides a means for creating, editing, and disseminating messages electronically. Each user is allocated a mailbox and a set of programs for creating, transmitting, and reading mail. Messages can be sent to specific people or to all those on a designated distribution list. E-mail systems can be active or passive.

Data sharing systems, the oldest form of multiuser systems, allow users to access the same data, but in a manner that is carefully coordinated and controlled so that one person's work does not interfere with another's. Additionally, the system must provide security so that users can access only the data they need.

There are three types of multiuser architectures: teleprocessing, distributed processing, and a hybrid of the two. With teleprocessing, a centralized computer is connected to a number of terminals, which can either be dumb terminals or microcomputers that emulate dumb terminals. All applications processing is performed on the centralized computer.

Since all processing occurs at one site, the central computer can maintain tight control over processing. Teleprocessing systems are most commonly used for organizational transaction processing.

The second multiuser architecture is distributed. With it, multiple, independent CPUs are connected to each other via communication lines. Local area networks (LANs) are the most common form of distributed systems. A LAN connects independent microcomputers using cables and processor cards. A file server is a microcomputer on a LAN that processes a database or other data on behalf of the other microcomputers.

A wide area network is a network of LANs. A gateway computer is a computer that connects one LAN to a computer on another LAN. Sometimes microcomputers are connected together using a PBX (private branch exchange). Such systems have lower capacity than a LAN.

The hybrid system architecture combines teleprocessing with distributed processing. Often a LAN is connected to the centralized computer via a gateway microcomputer. The characteristics of the three types of architecture are summarized in Figure 9-5. Their advantages and disadvantages are summarized in Figure 9-8.

There are three categories of teleprocessing hardware: end-user hardware, communications lines, and processing hardware. End-user hardware can be either dumb terminals or microcomputers. Communications lines are classified according to speed, mode, and type. Common speeds are voice grade and wideband. The two line modes are analog and digital. The three line types are full duplex, half duplex, and simplex.

Communications lines are connected to the processing computer via a communications port. Since most users cannot keep a line busy, lines are usually shared. Contention, polling, and multiplexing are all used to coordinate traffic on shared lines. Concentrators and PBXs also are used. Processing hardware is usually a mainframe or minicomputer.

Systems programs for teleprocessing are exceedingly complicated. Their primary responsibility is to coordinate the processing of transactions within the centralized computer. The communications control program (CCP) must be licensed as an add-on for mainframe computers but is included as part of the operating system for minicomputers.

A protocol is a standardized method for packaging and handling communications messages. Protocols have levels; the ISO standard protocol, for example, has seven. For communications to occur, all hardware devices must operate in accordance with the same protocol.

A local area network is a federation of microcomputers directly connected to one another within a few thousand feet. Hardware components of a LAN are microcomputers, communications lines, controller boards, and peripheral equipment. The controller board connects the computer to the LAN. In a typical LAN, one of the microcomputers is designated as a server; this computer stores and processes data that is shared on the LAN.

Three types of LAN topology exist: bus, ring, and star. The bus topology is common, as is a hybrid combination of ring and star. The three types of LAN communications media are twisted pair wire, coaxial cable, and optical cable. Optical generally is not used because of its expense.

Private branch exchanges (PBXs) are extensions of local office telephone exchanges. Such systems today allow for both voice and data communications and can serve as a means for connecting microcomputers within an office. They generally have lower speed than a LAN, and so must be used for low-volume applications.

Two versions of the operating system are needed for a LAN. The local operating system (OS) is the same as the operating system used for personal computer systems. The LAN-OS is an add-on that supports communications and other services on the LAN. New operating systems in the future may combine these two functions.

Two communications protocols are used for LANs. With contention, traffic is managed like a human conversation. With token passing, packets continuously circulate around the network; messages are passed via the packets.

Application programs vary in the degree to which they are aware of and use the facilities of the network. Most single-user applications can run on a networked computer without change. If they use a file on the file server, they can access that file using a special file designator. This assumes that applications access the data one-at-a-time. If shared access is necessary, then a number of changes must be made as discussed in the next chapter.

Word List

hardware sharing system	line speed	CICS (Customer Information and Control System)
diskless workstation	voice-grade line	
Nike method	line conditioning	protocol
local area network (LAN)	wideband line	controller board
electronic mail	line mode	dedicated server
mailbox	analog line	concurrent server
active electronic mail	digital line	bus topology
passive electronic mail	modem	node
controlled sharing	line type	ring topology
teleprocessing architecture	full-duplex line	star topology
centralized architecture	half-duplex line	twisted pair line
dumb terminal	simplex line	coaxial line
distributed system architecture	communications port	optical transmission media
file server	polling	LAN-OS
wide area network	front-end computer	spooling
gateway computer	multiplexing	contention
private branch exchange (PBX)	concentrator	token passing
hybrid system architecture	communications control program (CCP)	special file designator
end-user hardware		

Discussion Questions and Exercises

A. Identify a company (it could be your university) that uses teleprocessing. Interview personnel in that company. Describe the general characteristics of the system. How many user stations are there? Are these dumb terminals or microcomputers? What communications lines exist? What is the processing computer? What CCP is in use? What applications does teleprocessing support?

How long has the system been in operation? Why was this approach chosen over a distributed system? How satisfactory has this system been? Would a distributed system have been a better choice?

B. Identify a company (it could be your university) that uses a local area network. Interview personnel of that company. Describe the general characteristics of the LAN. How many micro-computers are there? What communications media are used? What topology is used? How are the lines managed? What LAN-OS is in use? How were these decisions made? What applications are supported? Why was this solution chosen over teleprocessing? How long has the system been in use? How satisfactory has the system been? Would teleprocessing have been a better choice?

CHAPTER 10

Shared Data Systems and Database Processing

This chapter deals with multiuser data-sharing systems. Such systems use the teleprocessing and distributed processing environments described in the last chapter; concepts from that chapter will also appear in the present chapter.

There are a number of different types of shared data systems. Until recently, the term *shared data system* almost always referred to database processing. Databases still represent the bulk of such systems; however, with new technology emerging, other shared data systems are coming to the fore. We will begin with a short description of these newer systems and then turn to shared database processing. After that, we will address each of the five components of shared data systems.

Shared Data Systems

Consider Figure 10-1, which is an adaptation of a figure developed by Felician.[1] Data can be either **coded** or **noncoded**. If it is coded, then particular bit patterns represent letters or numbers, as described in Chapter 2. If the data is noncoded, then it consists of a stream of bits which cannot be interpreted directly as a letter, number, or other symbol. Most graphics, images, illustrations, audio signals, and the like are noncoded data.

Coded data can be either **structured** or **nonstructured**. Structured data is data organized into spreadsheets or database tables. Nonstructured data consists of streams of text and numeric data. It does not have a tabular or any other regular structure.

Any of these types of data can be shared. Bit streams representing illustrations can be shared among a group of graphic artists using desktop publishing. Document files can be shared among a group of word processing operators; spreadsheets can be shared among financial analysts. Database data is frequently shared. Here we will consider shared text, spreadsheet, and database applications.

Text-Sharing Systems

Text-sharing systems allow users to gain concurrent access to text data. In this context the term *text* is broadened to include graphics, drawings, illustrations, and other forms of image data. The written text itself can include multiple type fonts, multiple type sizes, and special features like underlining, boldface, and italics.

There are two major types of text-sharing systems. **Shared word processing systems** are an outgrowth of personal word processing. **Hypermedia systems** are based on an approach quite different from traditional word processing. We will consider each in turn.

---

[1]Leonardo Felician, "Image Base Management System: A Promising Tool in the Large Office System Environment," *Data Base* Vol. 19, No. 1 (Fall/Winter 1987/88): p. 30.

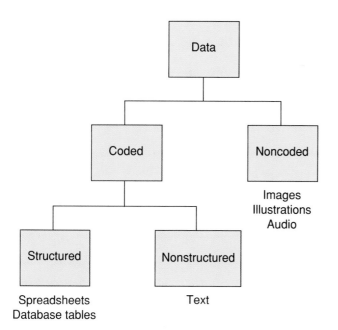

Figure 10-1
Types of data

Shared Word Processing Applications One of the simplest and most straightforward shared data applications is shared or concurrent word processing. Figure 10-2 shows a schematic of such a system. Word processing operators share access to a disk of centralized word processing data. This disk contains boilerplate documents, form letters, lists of customers, routing lists, documents in process, indices of documents, and the like.

The advantage of this system is that operators obtain all their data from a common source. With this arrangement, it is easier for the word processing group to provide a standardized product. All operators, for example, work from the same boilerplate memo format. Further, with centralized document storage, documents are easier to locate (they can be in only one place), so that the group can exercise better security and control than it could if the documents were stored on separate computers.

In addition to the operational word processing data, the system maintains data about the performance of individual operators and of

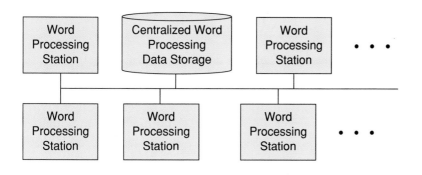

Figure 10-2
Example shared word processing system

Figure 10-3
Example management report from
word processing workload statistics

Word Processing Department
Workload Summary Report

Date	Number Attorneys	Number/ Average Documents Created	Number/ Average Pages Printed	Number/ Average Edit Jobs
1Q 90	35	587 16.8	36,849 1,052.8	2,843 81.2
2Q 90	38	654 17.2	42,461 1,117.4	2,880 75.8
3Q 90	40	660 16.5	40,720 1,018.8	3,092 77.3
4Q 90	41	713 17.4	46,389 1,054.3	3,305 80.6
1Q 91	44	752 17.1	53,050 1,105.2	3,582 81.4
2Q 91	48	840 17.5	53,376 1,112.0	3,917 81.6

the group. For example, word processing applications can monitor operator performance and store the number of documents, number of keystrokes, and elapsed time for each operator. Furthermore, applications can combine the statistics for individuals into group performance records. In this way, a manager can compare performance in the current period to performance in prior periods.

As an example, Figure 10-3 shows a summary of the word processing workload for six quarters. The partnership has been adding attorneys during this period, and the workload has increased. Observe, however, that the workload per attorney has remained relatively constant.

This report can be used for planning and other management purposes. For example, once the managing partner tells the word processing manager how many attorneys there will be in the next quarter, the word processing manager can use this data to estimate the number of operators that will be required.

The administration of shared documents and other text is usually accomplished by a combination of programs and procedures. Programs that support group word processing normally include features and functions to check out or otherwise allocate documents to individuals. In most offices, however, these features and functions are augmented by manual sharing procedures. Such augmentation is required to implement control and security provisions that go beyond the capabilities of the product.

Figure 10-4
Characteristics of hypermedia and
hypertext applications

- Information modeled as chunks called notecards, frames, or nodes. Hypertext chunks hold text; hypermedia chunks hold text, graphics, images, illustrations, audio, animation, etc.

- Frames displayed in windows. Particular format depends on hypermedia (or hypertext) system.

- Frames are connected via links that users navigate.

- Users have commands to create, change, and possibly delete frames.

- In shared hypermedia systems, users can concurrently access hypermedia data. Data may be distributed across multiple computers. Granularity normally a frame.

Hypermedia Applications **Hypermedia** and **hypertext** applications are designed to help professionals organize their knowledge, either as individuals or in groups. Figure 10-4 lists the five characteristics of a hypermedia system as defined by Akscyn, McCracken, and Yoder.[2] First, information is stored in chunks which are referred to as notecards, frames, or nodes. In this text, we will use the term **frame.** Hypertext frames may contain only text. Hypermedia frames may contain text, graphics, images, illustrations, audio, animation, and other forms of recorded knowledge.

Second, frames are displayed in windows; the way in which windows are presented on the screen depends on the particular hypermedia system. Third, frames are connected to one another via **links.** Users **navigate** a hypermedia document using the links. For the frame in Figure 10-5, for example, every item marked with an asterisk is linked to a related frame. To cause the related frame to be displayed, the user employs a mouse to click on an asterisked item.

Fourth, users have commands to create, change, and possibly delete frames. In addition, they can add, change, and possibly delete links. In this way, users can create personalized or special-purpose documents within a collection of frames. Finally, in shared hypermedia systems, users can concurrently access hypermedia data; this data may be distributed across multiple computers. In shared systems, **granularity** is normally at the frame level; that is, the unit of information accessed by a user is the frame—each user accesses one frame at a time.

Hypermedia systems can be used for a multitude of tasks. Akscyn, McCracken, and Yoder report a surprising variety of applications, including electronic publishing, on-line manuals and help, electronic mail and bulletin boards, project management, financial modeling and accounting, and software engineering.[3] Figure 10-6 shows example

[2]Robert M Akscyn, Donald L. McCracken, and Elise A. Yoder, "KMS: A Distributed Hypermedia System for Managing Knowledge in Organizations," *Communications of the ACM* Vol. 31, No. 7 (July, 1988): p. 820.

[3]Ibid., p. 821.

Figure 10-5
Sample hypermedia screen

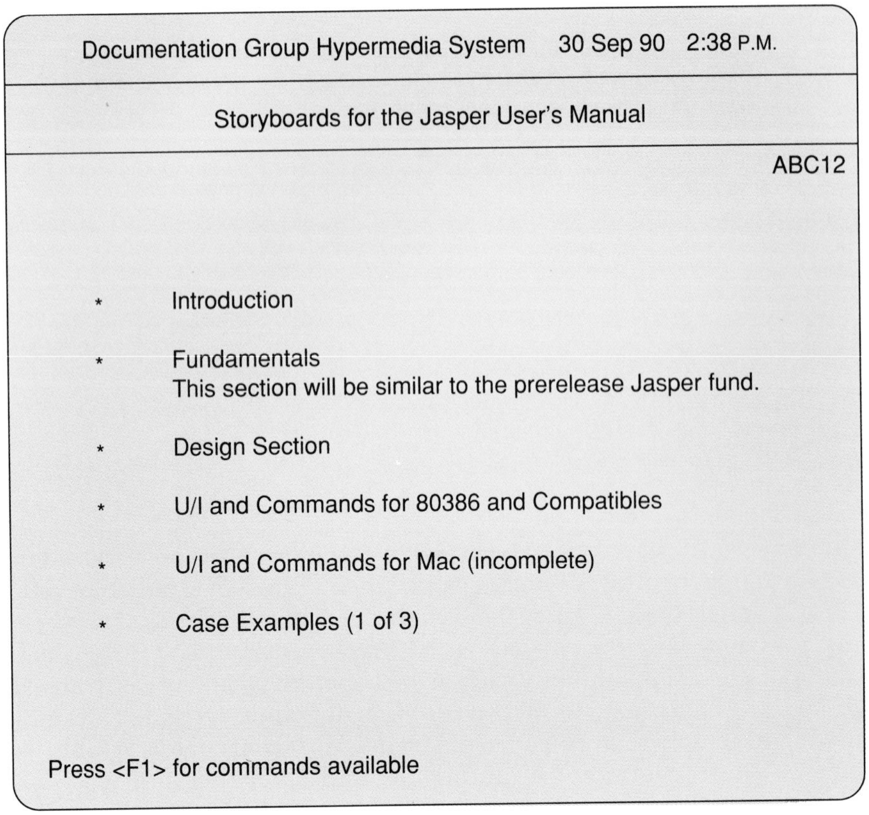

```
┌──────────────────────────────────────────────────────────┐
│   Documentation Group Hypermedia System    30 Sep 90   2:38 P.M.  │
├──────────────────────────────────────────────────────────┤
│           Storyboards for the Jasper User's Manual         │
├──────────────────────────────────────────────────────────┤
│                                                   ABC12     │
│                                                            │
│                                                            │
│      *      Introduction                                   │
│                                                            │
│      *      Fundamentals                                   │
│             This section will be similar to the prerelease Jasper fund. │
│                                                            │
│      *      Design Section                                 │
│                                                            │
│      *      U/I and Commands for 80386 and Compatibles     │
│                                                            │
│      *      U/I and Commands for Mac (incomplete)          │
│                                                            │
│      *      Case Examples (1 of 3)                         │
│                                                            │
│                                                            │
│   Press <F1> for commands available                        │
└──────────────────────────────────────────────────────────┘
```

screens for bulletin board and electronic mail applications for a system called KMS.

Shared Spreadsheet Applications

Some departments share spreadsheet data. A group of budget analysts, for example, might share the fundamental format for the corporate budget. Such a format is called a **template**. A template is to a spreadsheet application as boilerplate is to a word processing application. The template contains the structure of the spreadsheet, the independent and dependent variables, the formulas, and other parts of the spreadsheet structure. For example, if a company includes food, lodging, transportation, and miscellaneous travel expenses in its budget, then the budget template will contain just those items as part of the travel expense formula.

Large and complicated spreadsheet applications become unmanageable in a single spreadsheet. In this case, the total spreadsheet can be divided into subsidiary spreadsheets which are then combined into higher-level spreadsheets. In some applications these subsidiary spreadsheets can be managed by a single individual. In other cases, there is more work and complexity than a single individual can handle. If so, then the spreadsheets are allocated to several workers on different computers. They are integrated into a departmental spreadsheet.

```
                                              KSIworld56
            Knowledge Systems
              Bulletin Board

  ▪ We are going to try for March 15 as the
    release date for Version 6A. Task schedule
    attached.   [Don 2/1/88]

  ▪ Latest version of the "Getting Started" tutorial
    is ready for review. Everyone please feel
    free to make comments.   [Elise 2/4/88]

  ▪ Friday's party is now ON again. Please bring
    the things you signed up for   [Gloria 2/5/88]

  ▪ Results of recent user statistics analysis.
    [Richard 2/8/88]



                  @Previous messages


  Save Exit Reset Prev Next Home Goto Info Disp Linear Print Fmt...
```

a.   Bulletin board frame

```
  Elise's New Mail               KSIworld4

    Rob—Have we heard back from Dolly about
    the PHTC reprints yet? I thought they were due
    yesterday.   [Elise 2/7/88]
    Yes, they're to arrive tomorrow.   [Rob 2/9/88]

  ▪ Elise, here's my latest of the Action Language
    Reference Manual. Please make any revisions
    you see fit.   [Don 2/10/88]

  ▪ Discussion: Whether to provide only on-line
    versions of the reference documents   [Rob
    2/10/88]

  Old Mail

  ▪ Report for Week of Feb 8   [Rich 2/12/88]

  ▪ Bold-Italic font done   [Rich 2/3/88]



  Save Exit Reset Prev Next Home Goto Info Disp Linear Print Fmt...
```

b.   Mailbox frame

- People come to the frame and make their contribution, usually "signing" it with their name and the date.

- A bulletin board entry may be linked to another frame. In the example above, there are entries linked to a task schedule, an on-line tutorial document, and an analysis of user statistics.

- This example shows one person's mailbox frame. People place their messages directly on the frame.

- As with the bulletin board, messages may be linked to other documents, or to a frame elaborating on the message. (Confidential information usually is placed on a protected frame that is linked to the message.)

- Messages can be passed back and forth, with a new response appended each time. After 2 or 3 messages are appended, the people involved usually create a discussion frame for that topic. (In this example, one item is linked to the discussion frame at the right.)

Figure 10-6
KMS frames for communication (from Akscyn, et al. [see footnote 2]. © ACM. By permission of the authors. (*continued*)

Consider an example. Specialty Chemicals is a large, multidivision corporation. There is a departmental spreadsheet application in use in the centralized corporate plans and budgets department. In this department, three levels of spreadsheet exist. Individuals work on spreadsheets for functions and departments within a division. These departmental spreadsheets are combined into total division spreadsheets. These are then rolled into the total corporate spreadsheet. To

Figure 10-6
(Continued)

Discussion: DocDiscuss72

**Should we provide only the on-line versions
of the larger reference documents?**

I tend to think this is a good idea. They can print the
documents out themselves if they want hardcopy. On
our end, we don't have to keep re-printing when
documents get out of date.   [Rob 2/2/88]

I like it—especially the part about not needing to reprint
the documents all the time. But I'm wondering if
people will be disappointed if we don't give them
hardcopy. Lots of people prefer to use hardcopy
anyway, and they expect that's what they'll get with the
system.   [Elise 2/3/88]

We could give them the option of receiving hardcopy,
for an extra charge (we could put it on the order form
for them to mark off)   [Rob 2/9/88]

Additional Benefit—Customers would always have
access to the most recent version of the documents.
[Rob 2/10/88]

Save Exit Reset Prev Next Home Goto Info Disp Linear Print Fmt...

---

c.   Group conference frame

- A discussion frame is similar to a bulletin board
  frame. People place their comments directly on
  the frame. Prior comments are read in context
  since the history of the discussion can be read on
  the frame. People exploit this context by responding directly to earlier comments as if they were
  holding a conversation.

ensure compatibility, all of these spreadsheets are developed from a
common set of templates.

Users in the plans and budgets department share spreadsheet templates and other standard data via a departmental information system.
Additionally, when a subgroup of users within the department finishes
a portion of the budget, it makes this portion available to other analysts
via the shared spreadsheet system. These capabilities are supplemented by an electronic mail system.

Shared spreadsheets can be implemented in several ways. For one,
a spreadsheet program can reside on multiple microcomputers connected via a LAN. For another, a single spreadsheet program can reside
on a mini- or mainframe computer, and multiple users can access shared
data through a multiuser interface to that program. For a third alternative, personal computer spreadsheet programs can transfer data to
and from a shared mini- or mainframe computer spreadsheet.

10.1   INCREASING YOUR PERSONAL PRODUCTIVITY

What Does Relational + Object Equal?

A relational DBMS handles data in terms of keyed tables that contain simple data types. This supports traditional data processing applications.

An object-oriented DBMS handles data as separate entities of complex types with various relationships, such as text, graphics, pictures, and abstract data.

Researchers are working on ways to allow the two models to interact. These include opening tables to complex data, or applying relational techniques to object systems.

Multiuser Database Systems

As stated in Chapter 6, the purpose of a database application is to keep track of something. This is done by managing tables of coded, structured data.

To review, a database contains a group of tables of data; the tables are related by common values. A row in the CUSTOMER table, for example, is related to a row in the ORDER table if the value of the Customer# column in CUSTOMER matches the value of the Customer# column in ORDER.

Now, although it was not mentioned in Chapter 6, there are actually four types of databases, as shown in Figure 10-7. Databases can support one or many users and they can support one or many applications. An example of a multiapplication database is one that contains customer, salesperson, and order data and is used for order entry, customer relations, and sales commission applications.

Personal database applications fall in the first column of Figure 10-7, since they support a single user. Further, most personal database applications support only one application. You saw examples of this type of database application in Chapter 6. (Although single-user, multi-application databases are possible, they are rare, and we will not consider them further.) Moving across the top row of this figure, as we

	Single User	Multiple Users
Single Application	Personal Database Applications	Workgroup Database Applications
Multiple Applications		Organizational Database Applications

Figure 10-7
Database types and levels of database applications

progress from single-user systems to multiuser systems we cross an important boundary. As soon as we allow multiple users to access the same data, we encounter a host of problems.

Many businesspeople are unaware of this situation. A common scenario is that a small business or department is operating a single-user database application and, as business expands, the department finds that it does not have enough time available on its single computer to enter all of the data. So a second computer is installed and connected (usually via a LAN) to the same database. Unfortunately, a number of significant (and expensive) changes must be made in the DBMS, the application programs, and the procedures, to support the multiple users. If these changes are not made, chaos is certain. Since the managers seldom know about the need for these changes, chaos often does occur.

A similar situation occurs when the transition is made from a single-application, multiuser database to a multiapplication, multiuser database. Here, problems occur because users view the data differently. A user of one application will want to delete data in a way that is unacceptable to a user of a different application. In Chapter 1, Elizabeth deleted the data relating to plants that she no longer wanted to purchase—but other users still needed that data for inventory and billing purposes. Thus, during the transition from a single-user to a multiuser system, users need to adapt their activities to the needs of a *community*. We will discuss these issues later in this chapter. First, however, consider a typical multiuser database application.

Hack 'n Sack Video Rentals

Hack 'n Sack Corporation is a national retailer of low-cost sundry merchandise. Two years ago, as video recording equipment became more prevalent, Hack 'n Sack decided to enter the video rental business.

The goal in offering rentals was to bring customers into the stores. The rental movies were located in a back corner so that customers, especially parents and children, would be forced to walk through or around the toy and miscellaneous food sections. On average Hack 'n Sack expects to sell $10 of merchandise for every movie rented. To accomplish this purpose, they price video rentals as low as possible and operate only the video department on a break-even basis.

One of the keys to keeping the rental price low is to keep the video administration costs low. To do this, they developed a rental-processing database application for the video rental department.

The system operates as follows: When renting the first movie, a customer fills out an application form. At that time, the customer is assigned a customer number and given a UPC (Universal Product Code) strip that contains that number. Customers are asked to place the strip on the back of one of their credit cards. A similar code strip, containing a movie ID, is placed on the slipcover case of each movie. When a customer rents a movie, both bar codes are read with a light pen. The system allocates the movie to the customer, computes the rental charge, and prints an invoice. Money is collected when movies are returned; additional charges are made for late movies. Depending on store vol-

Questions

10.1 What is the difference between coded and noncoded data? Give an example of each.

10.2 What is the difference between structured and non-structured data? Give an example of each.

10.3 Explain the meaning of the word *text* in the context of text-sharing systems.

10.4 Name two types of text-sharing systems.

- Track rental volume by
  - Time
  - Day of week
  - Date

- Estimate number of customers drawn to store
  - Project incremental revenue generated

- Track station use and idle time

- Manage inventory
  - Identify losers and winners
  - Eliminate losers
  - Add winners

- Summarize costs and revenues; produce profit and loss statement

Figure 10-8
Management application of video rental data

ume, from one to seven movie checkout stations are installed at each store. These stations share a common pool of customer and movie data.

This system, as far as we have described it, is a transaction processing system that tracks customers and movies. While processing transactions, however, this system gathers data that can be used to manage the video rental department.

Figure 10-8 summarizes the management application of the video rental data. First, a report is generated that shows rental volume by time, day of the week, and date. This information is used in staffing the rental department. It also is used to estimate the number of people drawn into the store (*estimate*, because an unknown number of the movie customers would have come to the store even if it did not offer video rentals). A second report shows the utilization rate at each station. From this the manager can decide whether there are too many or too few such stations.

Other data can be used in managing the video library. The system computes the checkout rate for each movie; it also identifies movies that have been very popular and movies that have not been rented. This data is used in deciding which movies to sell or otherwise dispose of, and in deciding which movies are popular enough to justify buying additional copies.

Still another report summarizes revenues, costs, and contributions to profit and overhead. This report shows the amount of revenue generated per pay period, the cost of labor, and the estimated cost of carrying the inventory. Revenue minus these estimated costs yields the contribution to profit and overhead.

Summary of Data-Sharing Applications

To summarize, all of the data types shown in Figure 10-1 can be shared. Text sharing includes text data as well as graphics, illustrations, photos,

10.5 Describe an example of a shared word processing application.

10.6 What is the difference between hypertext and hypermedia?

10.7 List the characteristics of hypertext and hypermedia systems.

10.8 What is a spreadsheet template? What templates might be shared?

10.9 Give an example of a shared spreadsheet application.

10.10 In a database, how are rows related to one another? Give an example relating rows from the CUSTOMER and SALESPERSON tables.

10.11 Describe the four types of database.

10.12 What problems can occur when expanding a single-user database into a multiuser database?

10.13 What problems occur when the transition is made from a single-application to a multiapplication database?

and the like. Spreadsheet data also is shared. The bulk of data-sharing applications, however, involves databases.

Next we will consider the five components of data-sharing and database applications. The discussion will concentrate on database applications because they are the most common type of shared data systems.

Hardware

The two most common hardware environments for data-sharing systems are teleprocessing and local area networks. Teleprocessing is the older of the two, and has been used for many years to support multiuser database applications. Local area networks are newer and typically support systems with fewer users, usually less than fifty.

As a general rule, databases that support the needs of a single department reside on a local area network. Such systems are operated by personnel within that department, and often are called workgroup systems. Databases that support the needs of users in multiple departments usually reside on a teleprocessing system or on a wide area network. These systems are almost always operated by professionals within the company's MIS department.

Teleprocessing Hardware

Figure 10-9*a* shows a teleprocessing system that supports a multiuser, single-application database. Here, customer support representatives answer queries from customers about the status of their orders. To do this, they access a database that contains order data extracted from an order entry TPS application and a production TPS application.

The customer support database is a single-application database because it is used only for answering customer queries. All customer support representatives follow the same procedures to process the same application. They use dumb terminals and access the centralized processing computer via communications lines. This is a typical teleprocessing system, as described in Chapter 9.

Figure 10-9*b* shows a second teleprocessing system. This one supports a multiuser, multiapplication database. Observe that there are groups of users: salespeople, purchasers, production personnel, and accounts receivable personnel. Each of these groups processes a different application on the database. Salespeople need to know product prices and availability. Purchasers need to know inventory levels and future needs. Production personnel need to know inventory item locations and usages, and accounts receivable personnel need to know the status of orders, amounts due, and payments received.

The hardware used for such a multiapplication database is the same as that for single-application databases. Users employ dumb terminals to access the centralized processing computer via communications lines. The differences between these two types of system are in the programs, data, and procedures more than in the hardware, as you will see.

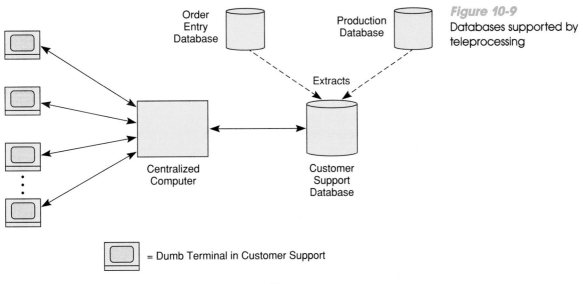

Figure 10-9
Databases supported by
teleprocessing

= Dumb Terminal in Customer Support

a. Single-application, multiuser
teleprocessing database

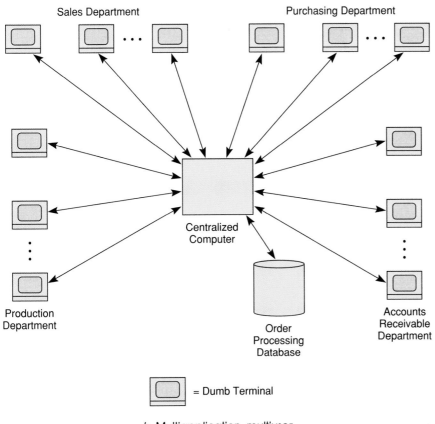

= Dumb Terminal

b. Multiapplication, multiuser
teleprocessing database

Questions

10.14 Describe the two common hardware environments for shared data applications.

10.15 In general, what hardware is used to support databases within a single department?

10.16 In general, what hardware is used to support databases that are used by multiple departments?

10.17 How does the hardware differ between single- and multiapplication database systems?

10.18 Explain the conditions under which the microcomputers in a local area network play a role not much different from that played by a dumb terminal.

10.19 What is the advantage of downloading data on a LAN?

10.20 What restriction applies to the processing of downloaded data?

Local Area Network Hardware

Figure 10-10a shows a LAN that supports the same type of customer support database application as the one shown in Figure 10-9a. Observe that the file server has taken over the role of the centralized processing computer. It receives the data extracts from the order entry and production TPS applications. It then accesses data in accordance with the requests from the users across the LAN.

Although there are microcomputers in this system, these micros are playing a role not much different from dumb terminals. All of the processing is done by the file server and the intelligence in the micros is going largely unused. Figure 10-10b shows an alternative LAN system that takes advantage of the microcomputers' intelligence. In this alternative, the file server obtains the extracted data from the other applications on a regular basis, say every four hours. The file server then sends the updated order database down to the microcomputers on the LAN. The micros then process this downloaded database locally.

The advantage of this alternative is improved performance. The micros can process a local database and thus avoid the delay required to communicate and coordinate with the file server. The disadvantage is that users do not have the most up-to-date data. Their data is up to four hours old. However, that is not likely to be a problem for this application.

The alternative shown in Figure 10-10b is feasible only because the users do not modify the database data. If they did modify the data, it would not be possible to download the database to each micro because it is likely that, at some time, two users would change the same data in different ways. The independent user changes would be uncoordinated.

Figure 10-10c shows a LAN used to support an order processing

Figure 10-10
Databases supported by LANs

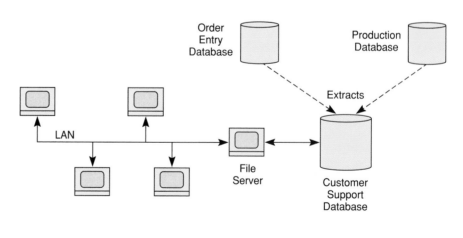

= Microcomputer in Customer Support

a. Single-application, multiuser, LAN-supported database

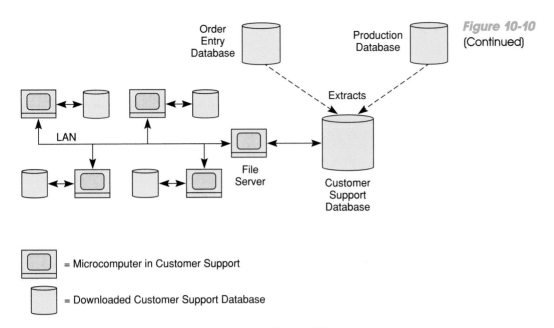

Figure 10-10
(Continued)

= Microcomputer in Customer Support

= Downloaded Customer Support Database

b. Single-application, multiuser, LAN-
supported downloaded database

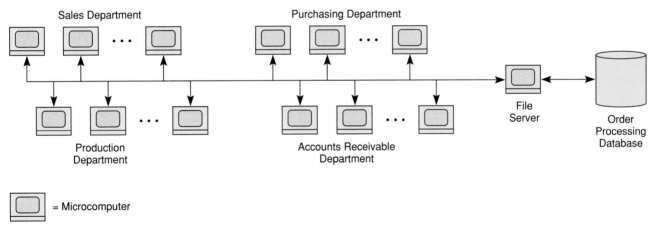

= Microcomputer

c. Multiapplication, multiuser, LAN-
supported database

system. Once again, the file server plays the role of the centralized processing computer. Users do modify data in this system, so it is not possible to download the database to the microcomputers. Thus, the micros in this system must limit their activity to sending requests to the file server for processing.

Any of these hardware arrangements is feasible for the applications described. The choice among them would depend on specific requirements and costs.

Programs

The programs required for multiuser database applications will vary, depending on whether the database resides in a teleprocessing or LAN environment.

Programs in a Teleprocessing Environment

Figure 10-11 shows the programs required to support a database in a teleprocessing environment. The categories of programs are the same whether they support a single- or multiapplication database. The difference is in the number and type of application programs required. In a single-application system, only one (or a few) application programs are required.

The programs shown in Figure 10-11 are those required to support the multiapplication system of Figure 10-9*b*. As described in Chapter 9, the CCP (communications control program) controls and coordinates the communications traffic within the processing computer. As part of this function, the CCP routes transactions to appropriate application programs.

The application programs process database data in accordance with the users' requests. For the purchasing application, for example, the application programs access and change inventory records in accordance with purchase transactions being recorded. Other application programs process other applications. All of these programs call upon the DBMS to gain access to the database.

The functions of the DBMS are listed in Figure 10-12. The first function is to store and retrieve data on behalf of application programs. The second, related, function is to interface directly with users via a query or query/update facility. Such a facility allows users to access the database on an ad hoc basis, without the need for an application program. The DBMS calls upon the operating system to actually read data from and write data to the disk.

The third function is to provide programs, sometimes called **DBMS utilities**, to define and modify the database structure. The fourth function is to provide utility programs to facilitate the creation and maintenance of database application components such as menus, forms, and reports.

Figure 10-11

Programs required for database processing in a teleprocessing environment

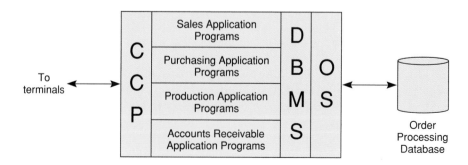

- Store and retrieve data at request of application programs

- Provide query or query/update facility

- Provide utilities to define and update database structure

- Provide utilities to create and maintain application components (menus, forms, reports)

- Provide utilities to support database administration

Figure 10-12
Functions of a DBMS

The final function is to support the administration of the database. When people share any resource, conflicting needs, goals, and objectives often cause coordination problems. The goal of database administration is to address and solve such problems. We will consider this function when we consider the people component later in this chapter. For now, realize that the DBMS provides utility programs to facilitate such administration.

DBMS products used in teleprocessing environments typically cost considerably more than those for microcomputers. DBMS software for a personal computer might cost from $500 to $5,000. The licensing fee for a minicomputer DBMS may be $10,000 or more. The same fee for a DBMS for a mainframe computer may exceed $100,000. These fees do not mean there is that much more complexity and logic involved. Rather, they reflect the smaller numbers of units that can be sold (there are fewer mainframes than minis, for example) and they also reflect the greater utility that can be obtained by supporting more users. A DBMS on a mainframe, for example, supports hundreds or thousands of users.

Teleprocessing systems assume that users use dumb terminals. Thus, menus and forms are created by the application programs and the DBMS that reside on the centralized processing computer. The terminals just display what is created on the centralized computer.

Programs in a Local Area Network Environment

The situation for programs in a local area network is shown in Figure 10-13. There is no CCP; the LAN-OS fulfills the role of coordinating transaction flow across the network. Also the application programs reside on the users' microcomputers. Users that perform purchasing functions run purchasing programs on their computers; those that perform accounts receivable functions run accounts receivable programs on theirs.

This situation with the DBMS on a LAN is considerably different from one in a teleprocessing environment. The DBMS is the liaison between the application program and the operating system. As shown in Figure 10-14, one portion of the DBMS (the application program or user interface, $DBMS_u$) processes requests submitted by the application program and translates those requests into appropriate actions for

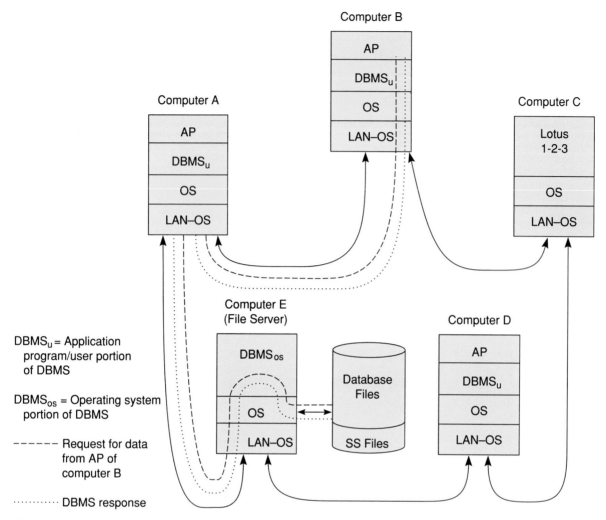

DBMS$_u$ = Application program/user portion of DBMS

DBMS$_{os}$ = Operating system portion of DBMS

– – – – – Request for data from AP of computer B

·········· DBMS response

Figure 10-13
Programs required for a LAN

the operating system. To do this, it obtains commands from the application programs, checks them for errors or inconsistencies, and, possibly, formats data entry forms, reports, and menus. Another portion of the DBMS (the operating system interface, DBMS$_{os}$) sends requests for reading and writing of data to the operating system. This portion formats read and write requests, packs and unpacks data for storage, and so forth.

In a LAN system, the DBMS is split and only the portions that are needed are stored on a particular computer. In Figure 10-13, for example, computers A, B, and D have the program interface portion of the DBMS, since those computers are processing application programs. Computer E, the file server, has the operating system interface portion of the DBMS, since this computer is managing the data. (Computer C does not access the database.)

To understand this arrangement, suppose the application program on Computer B needs the names and addresses of all customers in the

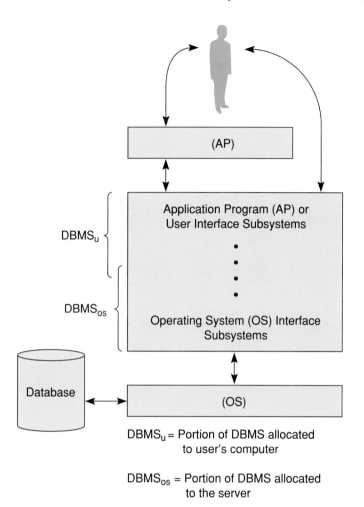

Figure 10-14
Allocation of DBMS programs on a
LAN

$DBMS_u$ = Portion of DBMS allocated
to user's computer

$DBMS_{os}$ = Portion of DBMS allocated
to the server

zip code 98117 area. The application program sends a command to the DBMS on computer B to obtain this data. The DBMS checks this command for accuracy and so on, and, if it is valid, formats a request for the DBMS on the file server. This request is passed to the operating system on computer B, which in turn passes the request to the LAN-OS on computer B. The LAN-OS formats the message for the LAN-OS on computer E and sends it over the network.

When computer E receives the request, the LAN-OS passes it to the OS, which in turn passes it to the DBMS programs on computer E. The DBMS programs determine where the desired data is located on the disk and request the operating system to read that data. The read is done and the operating system hands the data back to the DBMS on computer E. At this point, the processes reverse. Messages are formatted and passed so that the desired data ultimately is delivered to the application program on computer B.

The DBMS is split in this way so as to move as much work as possible to the users' microcomputers. The goal is to achieve as much simultaneous processing as possible.

10.21 Name the programs required to support a shared data system in a teleprocessing environment.

10.22 Sketch the arrangement of programs in the centralized processor for a teleprocessing-based multiuser database system.

10.2   INCREASING YOUR PERSONAL PRODUCTIVITY

The Crucial Steps to Automation: The U.S. versus Japan and Europe

Many U.S. companies tried to hopscotch their way to computer-integrated manufacturing. Most stumbled, but that hasn't deterred some from trying again. Two new technologies, artificial intelligence and object-oriented programming, could lift U.S. competitiveness. But Japanese noses are catching the scent, too.

1. Simplify and reorganize the shop floor for optimum efficiency—with no automation, or at least no new automation. Only then will further steps yield maximum benefits.
   STATUS: *Often poorly implemented in the U.S. Done widely and rigorously in Japan. Western Europe lags behind both.*

2. Create "islands of automation" with robots, flexible manufacturing cells, computer controls, and other advanced shop-floor systems.
   STATUS: *Widely implemented in both the U.S. and Japan, but much more effectively in Japan. Just beginning in Europe.*

3. Link the islands of automation to each other and to computer-aided design (CAD) through a shared data base, either hierarchial or object-oriented.
   STATUS: *Adopted by many major U.S. manufacturers and being implemented at a growing number of smaller companies. Japan is slightly ahead. Europe is far behind.*

4. Use artificial intelligence (AI) and object-oriented software to integrate some operations with CAD and to automate such complex steps as production scheduling and diagnostics.
   STATUS: *Now the cutting edge among progressive U.S. companies. Rare in Japan, but done more effectively. Almost nonexistent in Europe.*

5. Extend AI and object-oriented techniques to all decision-making steps, from product planning to customer service. This is the "computer-integrated enterprise."
   STATUS: *Under way at only a couple of U.S. companies. So far not implemented in Japan, but many Japanese companies could do so rapidly. Nonexistent in Europe.*

10.23 Explain the difference in licensing fees for a DBMS on mini- and mainframe computers.

10.24 Sketch the arrangement of programs in a LAN-based multiuser database system.

10.25 Explain how and why the DBMS is split in a local area network environment.

Observe that there is a considerable difference between a DBMS designed to support multiuser processing on a LAN, and a single-user DBMS that resides on the microcomputers of a LAN. With multiple users, the DBMS is coordinating all of the activities across the LAN. With a single user, the DBMS products and applications are oblivious to one other. The latter situation would result in chaos if the database were used by more than one user.

The licensing fee for a DBMS for a local area network falls in the range of $2,000 to $5,000. This compares to $500 or so for the single-user version of the same DBMS.

Data

In this section, we will address three considerations for the data component of a shared data system. First, we will consider means for preventing problems that can occur when multiple users process the same data at the same time. Next, we will discuss the processing of multi-application databases and the reasons why different users need to have different views of the data. Finally, we will discuss the downloading of databases on more than one computer.

10.3   INCREASING YOUR PERSONAL PRODUCTIVITY

The Relational Model

In concept, the relational data model is very simple. A *relation* is a two-dimensional table, and, in fact, relations are often called *tables*. The data in a table concerns a single theme or entity. For example, a STUDENT table contains data about students. A CUSTOMER table contains data about customers. Each row of the table represents one instance of the table's theme. A row of STUDENT, for example, holds data about a particular student. Rows are sometimes called *records* or *tuples* (rhymes with couples).

The columns of a table represent properties of the theme. For example, the first column of STUDENT might be Student-name, the second column Student-id, and so forth. Columns are sometimes called *fields* or *attributes*.

The essence of the relational model is that, as far as the user is concerned, relationships among the rows of tables are *represented in the data*. For example, a GRADE row is related to a particular STUDENT row if the value of Student-id in GRADE matches the value of Student-id in STUDENT. This characteristic is used to process the tables. For example, using the query language SQL (the most popular query language), the following command will display the names and grades of all students:

```
SELECT    Student-name, Class-grade
FROM      STUDENT, GRADE
WHERE     Student-id.STUDENT =
          Student-id.GRADE
```

Observe that Student-name arises from the STUDENT table and that Class-grade arises from the GRADE table. The SQL command has caused data from two tables to be combined on the basis of matching Student-id values.

Although there is considerable debate among experts as to what constitutes a true implementation of the relational model, the essence of this model can be stated in three rules: (1) multiple relations can be stored in a single database; (2) relationships are stored in the data; and (3) the DBMS provides a language by which any data can be accessed by table and column name. This last point means that any column can be used to identify data.

The relational model is only one of several ways of structuring and processing database data. We discuss it here because it has gradually become the most popular model and has been endorsed by the American National Standards Institute (ANSI).

Preventing Problems in Multiuser Database Processing

Data that is processed by two or more users at the same time is said to be processed **concurrently**. In a teleprocessing system, this occurs when two users attempt to process the same record at the same time. For example, two users may each read the same inventory record with the intent to change it. In a LAN environment, concurrent processing occurs when two users read the same data from the file server and process it on their local computers during the same period of time.

Data can be shared without being processed concurrently. For example, two users might agree that one of them will process data in the morning and the other will process data in the afternoon. The users share the same data, but, by agreement, not concurrently. In nonconcurrent data sharing, at the end of the agreed-on time period users must restore all of the data they have been processing. Otherwise, the data sharing is concurrent.

When designing a shared-data application, the developers must first decide whether data is to be concurrently shared. If not, the data must be organized so as to allow sharing but not allow concurrency. If concurrency is allowed, data and procedures must be developed; otherwise chaos will result.

Nonconcurrent Data Sharing   To share data in a nonconcurrent mode, the processing of the data must be partitioned. Two fundamental ways are to partition the data or to partition the processing. If the **data is partitioned,** then it is divided into groups, each of which is processed by a single user. For example, the accounts receivable department may process past due accounts. These accounts could be partitioned into groups by company name. One account representative could be assigned companies with names A–J, another with names K–S, and a third with names T–Z. In this way, the accounts receivable data is shared, but it is shared in such a way that one user's actions cannot interfere with another's.

Preventing concurrency by data partitioning is not always feasible. For example, if an order entry department accepts telephone orders, then a data partitioning of the inventory file is infeasible. Such a partitioning would assign some products to one operator and other products to a second, and so forth. A customer who wants to place a multiple-item order could conceivably be transferred to a different operator for each item. Clearly, this is impractical.

A second mode of nonconcurrent sharing is to **partition the processing.** With this mode, all of the data is assigned to a single person for processing, but only for certain periods. Thus, one user might be authorized to access all of the data in the morning, and a second authorized to access all of the data in the afternoon. Both data and processing partitioning allow data to be shared without concurrency. In some circumstances, neither of these modes is acceptable. Thus, data must be processed concurrently.

Concurrent Data Sharing   Concurrent data sharing occurs when two or more users process the same data during the same period of time. The nature of the shared system depends, in large degree, on the amount of data allocated to a particular user, or the granularity involved.

As stated earlier, the term *granularity* refers to the size of the units of data that are shared. For example, the granularity of a shared word processing system could be a document. If so, this means that an entire document is checked out to an individual for processing. Alternatively, the granularity might be larger or smaller than this. A system might be designed to allocate an entire floppy disk to a word processing operator. In that case, the level of granularity is the collection of documents on that disk. For yet another alternative, the level of granularity might be major sections within a document. In this case, only a portion of a document is checked out to a particular user.

The level of granularity influences the throughput of the shared system. The larger the level of granularity, the greater the chance that there will be delays due to contention, but the easier it is to administer the system. On the other hand, the smaller the level of granularity, the less chance there is of contention but the greater the cost of administering the shared resources. You will see the role of granularity in some of the examples that follow.

Typically, database applications share data at the record (or table row) level of granularity. Other structured, coded data applications, such as spreadsheets, share data at the file level of granularity. Non-structured and noncoded data is always shared at the file level. First we will discuss record-level sharing.

Record-Level Sharing   There are three fundamental cases of record sharing: (1) read/read, where two users concurrently read the same record; (2) read/update, where one user reads while a second user updates records; and (3) update/update, where both users update records.

No problems will arise in the first case. Both users can concurrently read the same record without interfering with each other.

The second case may or may not be problematical, depending on the needs of the applications. There is no problem as long as the user who is reading understands and accepts that the data he or she is viewing may be inconsistent.

Consider an example at Jenson-Kehrwald, the company introduced in Chapter 1. Suppose that one user is producing a summary report about the number of proposals generated by each salesperson during the past week, while the rest of the company users continue their normal database processing. Salespeople continue to generate proposals and database data is updated at the same time the report is being generated. In this case, the user of the summary report must realize that it is based on changing data. A salesperson whose last name starts with *A* may have fewer proposals in the report than a salesperson whose last name starts with some other letter; the difference may be due to the fact that proposals were added while the report was in preparation. Under these circumstances, the report is not a fair comparison, but, depending on how the report is used, that may not be important.

If, however, the user needs an exact report of the number of proposals at a particular point in time, then the concurrent changes do present a problem. For example, if the report is used to compute bonuses for sales representatives, then it must be accurate.

Consider another example of problematical read/update concurrency. The actions of two users are summarized in Figure 10-15. User A wants to count the number of a certain product, say, Adonidia palms, in Warehouses 1, 2, and 3. User B, concurrently, is transferring three such palms from Warehouse 1 to Warehouse 2. Because of the order in which the reads and writes are processed by the file server, User A concludes there are three fewer palms in inventory than there actually are. This is sometimes called the **inconsistent read problem**. Before discussing means of preventing this problem, we will consider the final type of concurrency.

Update/update concurrency occurs when two users attempt to update the same data concurrently. Such concurrency is always a problem. Figure 10-16 shows an example of the **lost update problem** in which two users read and change the same data. Changes made by the first user are lost due to an update made by the second user.

In general the solution to problematical concurrency situations is for each user to lock data that is read with the intent to update. A **lock** prevents any other program from using the data until the lock is released. Thus, in both Figures 10-15 and 10-16, reads for updates must be pre-

		Data			
User A	W_1	W_2	W_3	User B	
1. Read count for Warehouse 1 (4)	4	10	7	2. Read count for Warehouse 2 (10)	
	4	7	7	3. Decrement count by 3 (7)	
				4. Write count for Warehouse 2 (7)	
5. Read count for Warehouse 2 (7)				6. Read count for Warehouse 1 (4)	
7. Read count for Warehouse 3 (7)				8. Add 3 to Warehouse 1 count (7)	
				10. Write count for	
9. Total 18 (should be 21)	7	7	7	Warehouse 1 (7)	

Figure 10-15
Example of inconsistent read problem

ceded by lock requests. Locks prevent the inconsistent read problem because the reading user cannot obtain the data until the update is complete. Similarly, locks prevent lost updates.

Locking solves one problem but introduces another. Suppose two users are running application programs to process orders. Suppose User A's program obtains a lock on the record for diamond necklaces while User B's program obtains a lock on the record for plush black velvet boxes. Now, suppose that User A requests the record for plush black velvet boxes. User A cannot lock that record because User B already has it locked. So User A must wait. Next, User B requests the record for diamond necklaces. User B cannot lock that record because User A has it locked. User B must wait as well. This situation, called **deadlock** or **deadly embrace**, can be overcome only by canceling one of the transactions and starting it over.

This circumstance occurs rarely, but it does occur. It becomes apparent to the user only because the system will issue a message like, "System contention error," and then ask the user to start the order over.

The locking and unlocking of data is done by the application program or by the DBMS. Users are never asked (nor trusted to remember) to place locks before accessing data. You should know, however, that such locks are being placed, and that on rare occasions users may be required to restart transactions.

File-Level Sharing The second major type of concurrent data sharing is at the file level of granularity. This type occurs in information systems in which **monolithic files** such as word processing documents, spreadsheets, publications, and graphic images are shared across the department.

These files are called monolithic because they are not structured into records as databases are. Such files must be processed as one unit.

		Data			
User A (Remove 3 units from inventory)	W_1	W_2	W_3	User B (Remove 2 units from inventory)
1. Read count for Warehouse 1 (4) 3. Decrement by 3 (1) 5. Write count for	4	10	7	2. Read count for Warehouse 1 (4)
Warehouse 1 (1)	1	10	7	4. Decrement by 2 (2)
	2	10	7	6. Write count for Warehouse 1 (2)

Figure 10-16
Example of lost update problem

Using the terminology introduced at the start of the chapter, most monolithic files can be classified either as noncoded data (bit stream images, for example) or as nonstructured data (text files, for example). Spreadsheet files are an exception; they are normally processed as monolithic entities, but they consist of coded, structured data.

The concurrent sharing of monolithic files is not as regimented as concurrent sharing of database data. Control tends to be spotty, and determined as much by the adequacy of manual procedures as by controls in programs.

Most CCP products and most LAN-OSs provide facilities to control shared files. When first accessing a file, the application program or user can stipulate whether or not the file is to be shared with others. If not, the CCP or LAN-OS will not allow any other entity to open the file while it is being processed. Unfortunately, however, these facilities are not always used.

Horizontal application programs that are developed specifically for multiuser applications usually take advantage of these features. A shared word processor, for example, will lock a document file as nonshareable as long as someone is editing the document. For other products, it is less certain. A paint or draw program, for example, probably does not pay attention to these issues. In this case, it will be up to the user, following manual procedures, to ensure that the file is locked.

This is an undesirable state that probably will change as more and more shared-use products are developed. For now, be aware of the need for controlling the sharing of monolithic files. Also be aware that manual procedures may need to be developed to fill in for the deficiencies of some products.

Processing Multiapplication Databases

Multiapplication databases integrate data from different departments in a company. They allow all employees to share the same data values. The goal is to increase consistency in business operations. For example, no business wants to establish one price at the time of a sale and then bill with a higher (or lower) price at the time of invoicing.

To increase the likelihood of consistent behavior, businesses choose to develop a single database that supports multiple applications rather than multiple databases that support a single application. The chief advantage of a multiapplication database is that data item values are recorded once, and all changes of all departments occur to that one instance of the data item. Thus, multiapplication databases increase the likelihood of appropriate and consistent responses. Or, as one analyst put it, "A single database makes it possible for all of us to read from the same sheet of music."

In a typical company, salespeople, purchasers, production workers, and accounts receivable personnel all have interactions with the customer, and to produce appropriate and consistent behavior each department must refer to (and maintain) data about its interactions with the customer. Also, when appropriate, each department would like other departments to know about significant interactions with the customer after they have occurred.

Data Views

Unfortunately, even though departments often need to share data, they seldom need to share exactly the same data. Usually, one department will need some of the data items used by another department, plus other data items. A grouping of data items from one or more tables is called a **view.** For example, Figure 10-17 shows two different views of customer data. Figure 10-17*a* shows the customer data required by salespeople. This data helps sales personnel to decide which customers to call on and when. Figure 10-17*b* shows the customer data required by the accounts receivable department. This data helps receivables clerks decide on a customer's creditworthiness. The organizational information system that is used for order processing must be able to support both of these views.

Examine Figure 10-17 more carefully. Company Name, Contact, Phone, and Credit Status are shared by both departments. The other data items shown are used by one department but not the other. Furthermore, each customer may have many orders and many payments.

Figure 10-18 shows the structure of a database to support the views in Figure 10-17. Each rectangle represents a table of data. The CUSTOMER table has one row for each customer. The ORDER table has one row for each order and the PAYMENT table has one row for each payment. The columns of the tables contain the data required for the views shown in Figure 10-17. The forks on the lines between the tables indicate that a row in CUSTOMER can correspond to many rows in ORDER and that a row in CUSTOMER can correspond to many rows in PAYMENT.

This database is a simple example. Constructing a database to support many different views of many different departments often involves considerably more work.

The important point for you to learn from this example is that the data you process may be stored in a manner and format that is considerably different from what you see. Since this is so, there may be restric-

Figure 10-17
Different views of data

Company Name: _____

Contact: _____

Phone: _____

Last Order Date: ____/____/____   Last Order Amount: $_____

Credit Status: _____   Last Contact Date: ____/____/____

a. Salesperson customer contact report

Company Name: _____   Credit Status: _____

Contact: _____   Phone: _____

Date	Order	Payment	Balance
10 Oct 89	100		100
18 Oct 89	200		300
8 Nov 89		100	200
20 Nov 89		200	0
11 Dec 89	350		350
14 Dec 89	400		750
29 Dec 89		350	

b. Accounts receivable customer payment report

tions placed on your activities that do not appear to make sense, at least based on the data you see. In such a circumstance, if you need clarification, ask personnel from the organization's MIS Department for an explanation.

Processing Downloaded Databases

Even though there are significant advantages in maintaining a single database that supports multiple applications, there are times when it is appropriate to duplicate portions of that database. Consider the following example.

XYZ Company's information systems support order processing. These systems integrate the activities of the sales, purchasing, production, and accounts receivable departments, as was shown in Figure 10-9b.

The XYZ salespeople use an order entry application to enter their orders. Once an order is entered, production uses that data to plan its activities and to decide what materials to remove from inventory for which jobs. Similarly, purchasing uses the data to determine what items need to be ordered. Accounts receivable also uses the data.

Questions

10.26 What is concurrent data processing?

10.27 Explain how data can be shared without being processed concurrently.

10.28 Describe two ways in which data is shared without being processed concurrently. Give an example of each.

10.29 Define the term *granularity*. How does granularity impact performance in a shared-data system?

10.30 List the three cases of record-level sharing. Which are problematical?

10.31 Give an example of the inconsistent read problem.

Figure 10-18
Structure of customer data in database

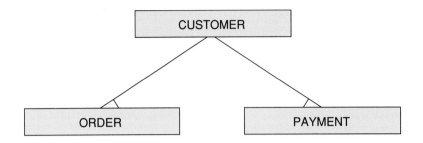

The salespeople travel extensively to meet with their customers. Ideally, before they make a presentation, they would like to know the customer's purchasing habits, payment history, and even personal data such as the names of the customer's spouse and children. All of this data is stored in the order processing database, but the salespeople cannot take that database with them.

However, each salesperson has been allocated a laptop computer. Before leaving on a trip, salespeople extract customer data from the order database and store it on their computers. Then, on the road, they access this downloaded database to obtain the customer information they need.

In doing this, the salespeople create a potential problem. They have duplicated a part of the company's centralized database. If they change this database, they will have a different version of the data. This is called a **data integrity problem**.

To prevent data integrity problems, the company imposes two limitations. First, salespeople are not allowed to change data and return it to the order database. If they believe data is incorrect, they must follow a procedure to have someone else change the data via the order entry application program and then obtain the correct data when they next download customer data.

Second, no attempt is made to keep the salespeople's databases current with the operational database. By agreement, the salespeople get the data that is current as of the time they extract it. Two milliseconds later, massive changes may be made to the data they just extracted, but they will not see these changes until the next time they download the data.

These limitations are workable because the salespeople do not need the most up-to-date data. Changes that are made most often involve new sales, and the salespeople can accomplish their job function by saying that "this data was current as of Monday morning," or something similar in their sales call. If this were not the case—if the salespeople needed the most current data—then this database architecture would not be feasible.

In this system, the salespeople are part of an **organizational information system** designed with the understanding that salespeople will not change data. The salespeople are expected to be responsible members of their organization; once they agree to this limitation, they must adhere to it. The other departments in the company depend on the salespeople's compliance; if the salespeople do not comply, errors, inaccuracies, and misconceptions can result.

Procedures

As described in Chapter 2, every information system must include procedures for people to follow. Recall that there are four categories of procedure: user procedures for normal processing and for failure recovery, and operations procedures for these two stations. We will consider these four categories of procedures in turn. First, however, we will consider special procedural requirements for shared-data information systems.

The Need for Coordination Procedures

A shared-data information system serves a community of users. Procedures need to be developed to coordinate user processing to ensure that one user's actions do not interfere with another's. In the last section you learned how record locking can be used to control concurrent access to record-oriented data. Little user involvement is required for such locking; locks are placed by programs in behalf of the user.

As you have seen, however, the situation is different for the concurrent sharing of monolithic files. Here, concurrency control is often up to users, since there is little support for concurrency control in programs. Such control must be provided by manual procedures.

To understand the need for coordination procedures, consider several examples:

- In a law firm, several attorneys are making changes to different sections of the same document. They submit work to three different word processing operators. All three operators must access the same document from a file server on a LAN.
- In the plans and budget office at Specialty Chemical Corporation, several financial analysts combine their individual work into a common, corporate spreadsheet. The analysts share this spreadsheet via a LAN.
- In the publications department of a major manufacturer, product specifications are produced using a shared desktop publishing system. One group within this department is responsible for drawings, a second for text, and a third for bringing text and drawings together to form documents. For each product, a number of different versions of specifications exist, corresponding to versions of the product. When changes are made to update text or graphics, the changes must be incorporated into the appropriate documents.

The first two examples illustrate the need for control over concurrent data access. The principle here is the same as the one for record locking. Users must lock data before they change it. Unfortunately, few LAN-based products provide this level of locking. Therefore, departments must institute manual procedures to prevent the inconsistent read problem and the lost update problem on monolithic files.

In the law firm situation, for example, the word processing operators must have a procedure for "checking out" a document for the purpose of changing it. Other operators who attempt to access the document while it is checked out must be informed of its status. The operators can then coordinate their activities. However, it is essential that they be informed that others are working on the same document. Without this knowledge, they will not know of the need to coordinate work.

The third example illustrates a different type of shared-data problem. Here, the department is coordinating its efforts to produce product specifications. They need to ensure that the correct version of a drawing, for example, is matched with the correct text and placed in the appropriate publication. This work group needs a configuration control system for its documents. The general considerations for shared data system procedures are summarized in Figure 10-19.

We will now survey each of the four types of procedures as they pertain to shared-data information systems. Keep in mind that, as stated in Chapter 8, procedures must not only be developed, they must also be clearly and completely documented.

User Procedures for Normal Processing

First, users need to know how to initiate access to the processing computer or the LAN. Typically, there is a series of commands that must be issued. With some systems, those commands are gathered together into a program procedure which the user initiates.

Next, users need procedures for accomplishing their work. The specific nature of these procedures depends on the type of application in use. Procedures for a shared text application differ from those for a shared database application; both need to be developed and documented, however. The third important component of procedures is a description of the constraints on processing (like the ones for the database stored on the XYZ salespeople's portable computers). Users are more likely to comply with the constraints if the description includes the rationale for the constraints.

The fourth type of procedure concerns security and control. With a shared system, all of the users have a responsibility, not just to themselves but also to each other, to ensure that data and other resources are appropriately protected against mistakes in processing, inadvertent losses, and intentional malfeasance. A summary of control proce-

Figure 10-19

Major goals for shared-data system procedures

- Control concurrent access (especially for monolithic files)

- Control data merged into workgroup documents

- Establish and enforce workgroup standards

dures is presented in more detail in Module C of this text. Finally, users need procedures to backup their data for protection against systems failure.

Operations Procedures for Normal Processing

First, operations personnel, even more than users, need procedures for starting the system. These include procedures for starting the computer or file server and related hardware as well as initiating the operating systems, the DBMS, and other programs. Next, most communications systems have a number of adjustable features that are set depending on the work to be done. The adjustment is sometimes called **tuning** the system. Most systems produce performance statistics to facilitate such tuning. Operations personnel need procedures to obtain and interpret such statistics as well as procedures for making specific adjustments.

Shared data systems sometimes require periodic maintenance. Such maintenance is obviously required for hardware (cleaning a printer or changing the printer's toner cartridge); maintenance may also be required for programs and data. Periodically, it may be necessary to reload data, to adjust files in directories, to clean up unused space, and so forth. The third type of procedures that operations personnel need is procedures for maintenance activities.

Fourth, operations personnel need control and security procedures. These procedures should specify when the system is to be operational, who is authorized access to the physical network facilities, how the network is to be shared, and so forth. Fifth, most file servers maintain a log of activity. This log should be examined periodically for unauthorized or suspicious activity. A separate manual log may need to be kept as well. Finally, operations personnel need procedures for backup activity. Periodically, the shared disk space should be backed up and the backups stored in an off-premise facility.

The user procedures and operations procedures for normal processing are summarized in Figure 10-20*a*.

User Procedures for Failure Recovery

First, there need to be procedures for correcting errors and detecting system failures. These procedures are needed so that, when unexpected system behavior occurs, the user has criteria for determining if the problem was caused by user error or by a system failure.

Next, users need procedures that specify what to do when the system has failed. For example, in an order entry system, customers will continue to place telephone orders even though the local area network that processes the customer database has failed. How should the representatives proceed? What orders should they accept? What data should they gather? What restrictions should they place on their activities? All of these questions need to be answered long before the failure occurs.

Finally, users need procedures to follow after the system has been recovered. They need to know how to determine how much of their workload needs to be reprocessed, and they need to know how to go

Figure 10-20
Summary of shared-data systems
procedures

- User Procedures for Normal Processing
    Initiating access to LAN (network)
    Accomplishing work
    Placing constraints on processing (with rationale)
    Maintaining security and control
    Maintaining backup

- Operations Procedures for Normal Processing
    Starting hardware and programs
    Monitoring and tuning system
    Periodically maintaining hardware, programs, data
    Maintaining security and control
    Maintaining activity log and other record keeping
    Maintaining backup

a. Procedures for normal processing

- User Procedures for Failure Recovery
    Correcting errors and detecting failures
    Maintaining business operations during failure
    Implementing postrecovery measures

- Operations Procedures for Failure Recovery
    Detecting failures
    Steps to take in case of failure
    Initiating recovery activities
    Maintaining failure logs and other record keeping

b. Procedures for failure recovery

about reprocessing it. They also need procedures to help them check that the reprocessed work has been correctly entered into the system. Other procedural needs depend on the particular type of application.

Operations Procedures for Failure Recovery

Operations personnel, like users, need to know how to detect that failure has occurred. In some cases, the failure is obvious, but in others, it is difficult to determine whether the problem was caused by user action, power variances, or other factors. Next, operations personnel need procedures that specify recovery activities in the event of a failure. What should the operator do? Whom should he or she call for assistance? What users need to be contacted? What should they be told? These and other similar questions need to be answered.

Third, operations personnel need procedures that stipulate actions to take once the system problem has been resolved. Files may need to be recovered from backups, saved workload may need to be reprocessed, and other actions will need to be taken. Such procedures need to be carefully thought out well in advance. Finally, operations personnel need a standard procedure and format for keeping records of failures and recovery activities. These records serve a number of purposes, including documentation for complaints to vendors and even for potential litigation.

The user procedures and operations procedures for failure recovery are summarized in Figure 10-20b.

This has been a brief survey of the types of procedures that need to be developed and documented for shared data information systems. It is by no means exhaustive. The goal here is to make you aware of the most essential procedures and to illustrate typical situations. When you work with such a system, remember the importance of procedures. Do not fall into the mistaken belief that information systems eliminate the need for manual procedures. Instead, such systems make the presence of complete procedures, consistently applied, even more important.

People

The final component of shared data systems is people. As with other information systems, there are users, operators, and development personnel. With the exception of operators, the jobs and their descriptions are similar to those discussed in Chapter 2.

Operations Personnel

In personal systems, the user is also the operator. With shared data systems, however, this is often not the case; there are too many activities for users to perform on their own. So a group of people needs to be identified as the system operators.

If the system is used only within a department, some departmental employees are given special training to operate the LAN (or centralized computer) and associated equipment such as file servers. These people are trained in the procedures listed in Figure 10-20. They know how to start and stop the system, how to respond to routine problems, and whom to call in case of nonroutine problems or failures.

Systems that cross several departments usually are operated by professionals in the MIS department. These people will be trained in procedures and operations. Unlike departmental user/operators, MIS department operators normally perform operations as a full-time job.

Data Administration Personnel

The users of a shared database have a variety of different needs, objectives, and goals. Because of this, they sometimes have different ideas about how the data should be processed. Also, from time to time, two users want to take actions that are inconsistent, or make conflicting changes to the system. This situation gives rise to the need for a new function, data administration, and a new job title, **data administrator.**

The functions of the data administrator are to guard and protect the data. Without a data administrator, shared data has no owner other than the community of users. Consequently, no one will consider it his or her responsibility to protect the data. When a problem occurs, members of the community will accuse one another. "I thought YOU were going to make the backup!" and so forth. Additionally, from time to time, users will have disagreements about how the data should be processed, and who has the right to perform what actions on the data, and when.

The data administrator ensures that backup and recovery procedures exist and that they are followed. Additionally, this person (or office in the case of a large database) provides a focus for discussions about the structure, use, and meaning of the data. The administrator is a focal point for questions, problems, and concerns. Absent an administrator, issues about the care, control, and processing of the data go unaddressed. These tasks fall into the category of tasks that should be done but no one ever has time to do. Assigning a person to these tasks increases the usefulness and reliability of the data.

For a departmental database, data administration can be a part-time job. For databases that span several departments, data administration is probably a full-time job. And, as mentioned, for very large databases there may be a staff or office of data administration.

Questions

10.47 In what situations do users serve as their own operators for shared data systems? What training must they receive?

10.48 In what situations are professional operators required for shared data systems?

10.49 Describe the general nature of data administration.

10.50 Under what conditions is data administration a part-time job? A full-time job? A job for a staff of people?

Summary

This chapter examined several types of shared-data systems. Shared-data systems involve multiuser access of coded and noncoded data, and structured and nonstructured data.

Text-sharing systems involve the sharing of text, graphics, drawings, illustrations, and so forth. Two types of text-sharing system are shared word processing and hypermedia systems. Shared word processing systems allow multiple users to access a disk of centralized word processing data. Hypermedia applications organize information in chunks of text (hypertext) or chunks of text, graphics, and other data (hypermedia). They allow users to navigate through the stored knowledge using links.

Shared spreadsheet applications allow multiple users to share spreadsheet templates and data. Large and complicated spreadsheets can be organized into subsidiary spreadsheets, which are integrated in a shared teleprocessing or LAN system.

The oldest and most common type of shared-data system is the multiuser database system. There are four types of database, as shown in Figure 10-7. There are important differences between single and multiuser databases; these differences are not always understood and appreciated. Multiuser access must be carefully coordinated and controlled to keep the actions of one user from interfering with those of another. Similarly, the transition from a single-application database to a multiapplication database can cause problems because the users view the data differently.

Shared-data systems can reside in either a teleprocessing environment or a local area network environment. If the application requires tight control over data changes, the microcomputers on a LAN must be restricted in their processing, sometimes to the point that they perform not much differently than dumb terminals. On a LAN, if users do not need to update data, the database can sometimes be downloaded to the users' microcomputers to increase performance.

Programs for multiuser database processing vary between teleprocessing and LAN environments. With teleprocessing, transactions and other communications are managed by the CCP. Application programs process transactions and, in the process, generate requests for service from the DBMS. The DBMS, in turn, issues requests for data reading and writing to the operating system. In multiapplication systems, there are multiple application programs.

On a LAN, the LAN-OS manages communications. Application programs issue requests for service to the application program interface component of the DBMS. The LAN-OS, the applications programs, and the application program interface portion of the DBMS all reside on the users' microcomputers. The balance of the DBMS and the portion of the operating system that processes changes against the shared database reside on the file server computer.

Data that is processed by two or more users at the same time is said to be processed concurrently. Data can be shared without being concurrently processed by partitioning the data or by partitioning the processing. *Granularity* refers to the size of the data units that are shared. The larger the granularity, the greater the chance of contention, but the easier it is to administer the database. The smaller the granularity, the less the chance of contention, but the harder it is to administer the database.

Record-level sharing involves three types of sharing: read/read, read/update, and update/update. Read/read sharing is never a problem. Read/update may or may not be a problem, depending on the requirements for the application. Update/update is always a problem. Problematical sharing situations can be avoided by record locking. Unfortunately, record locking introduces the possibility of deadlock.

File-level sharing is used to process monolithic files such as text documents, spreadsheets, and so forth. In such systems, the entire file is allocated to a single user for processing. The support for such locking in horizontal market application programs is currently sporadic. Therefore manual procedures must be developed to prevent problems.

Companies develop multiapplication databases to increase the likelihood that employees and departments will respond consistently with one another. Users of multiapplication databases often have different views of the same data. Such views must be accommodated by the system. Because of the need to support multiple views, sometimes database data is stored in a manner and format that is considerably different from the way it appears to the user.

In some situations, it is desirable to download data to users' computers. When this is done, restrictions normally are placed on the activity that can be performed on the downloaded data. It is most important that users follow these restrictions.

Shared data systems require that procedures be developed and followed to facilitate controlled and coordinated sharing. These procedures fall into four categories: user procedures for normal and for backup and recovery processing, and operations procedures for normal and for backup and recovery processing.

The type of operations personnel varies for shared data systems. For LAN-based systems that support a single department, some users are given special training and serve as the system operators. Teleprocessing systems and wide area networks are usually operated by professionals who work for the company's MIS department.

Users of shared data systems have different needs, objectives, and goals. Consequently, they have different ideas about how data should be processed and how the system should evolve. The database administrator manages and protects the database and serves as a focal point for the resolution of such problems. Depending on the size of the system, this can be a part-time job or a full-time job, or it can require the services of a staff of people.

Word List

coded data	navigation	lock
noncoded data	granularity	deadlock (deadly embrace)
structured data	template	monolithic file
nonstructured data	DBMS utility	view
shared word processing system	concurrency	data integrity problem
hypermedia application	data partitioning	organizational information
hypertext application	processing partitioning	system
frame	inconsistent read problem	tuning
link	lost update problem	data administrator

Discussion Questions and Exercises

A. Suppose that you work in a department that operates a single-user database application that keeps track of the company executives' automobiles. The application is run on a microcomputer in your department. Each auto is allocated to an executive for an indefinite period of time. When executives join or leave the organization, assignments are altered accordingly. Now and then older autos are replaced and new assignments are made. Periodically, reports are printed about the auto inventory, about particular autos, and about the individual assigned to a particular auto. Suppose the application satisfies its requirements except that the auto inventory has grown so large that not all of the data can be input and changed in an eight-hour shift. Your department decides to acquire a LAN and use it to connect a second microcomputer to the database that resides on the first one, thus creating a multiuser database application. List the problems that you think might occur when this is done. What actions should be taken to prevent or correct the problems you've identified? What alternatives exist besides creating the multiuser database? Would any of your alternatives offer a better solution? Explain why or why not.

B. Assume that you are a consultant to a company that promotes its product via direct mail advertising. The sales department keeps lists of customer names and addresses and income levels. They send different sales catalogues and other materials to customers depending on income level. Orders from the catalogue and other mailing pieces are taken both over the telephone and by mail. Order data is keyed into an order processing system which maintains customer and other data. Company managers are divided in the way they think this data should be stored and processed. Some believe that there should be two totally separate databases that support these applications. Others believe that all customer data should be stored in a single database and that DBMSs should support the two different applications. Summarize the advantages and disadvantages of having two separate databases. Summarize the advantages and disadvantages of a single multiapplication database. Which alternative do you think is more appropriate?

C. Locate a department that operates some type of shared-data system. Interview employees in that department. What functions does the application serve? What type of shared-data system is it? What data is shared? Is the data concurrently shared or not? If not, how is the sharing controlled? If so, what is the granularity of sharing? What special procedures exist to support this system? What special training have employees received? Is someone called a data administrator? What are the strengths of this system? What are the weaknesses? How satisfied is the department with this system?

CHAPTER 11

Information Systems and Management

CHAPTER OUTLINE

In this chapter, we will consider the relationship between information systems and management. First, we will define the term *management information system (MIS)*. As you will learn, this term refers to information systems that serve not only managers but also people at other levels in an organization. MISs are used by individuals, groups of people, and entire organizations. Next, we will consider how information systems are used to support decision making, specifically to support unstructured decision making. Finally, we will address the organization and functions of the department that is responsible for a company's information systems and information systems technology: the MIS department.

Management Information Systems

Before proceeding, we need to clear up two sources of potential confusion. Both involve the definition of the term *management information system (MIS)*. First, as stated in Chapter 3, there are two meanings for this term. One refers to a type of information system that produces regular and recurring reports. This definition is a narrow one, and it is not the one we are using in this chapter.

Here we use a broader definition of MIS. Even in its broad sense, the term *management information system* does not accurately communicate what most professionals mean when they use the term. Peter Keen, one of the leaders in this discipline, defines management information system as "the effective design, delivery, and use of information systems in organizations."[1] Observe that this definition includes the word *organization* but does not include the word *management*.

Thus, the subject of MIS is broader than the words *management information system* imply. This subject includes managers, but it also includes all of the other people in an organization, and the structure and design of the organization as well. A better term would be **organizational information system**, but the term *management information system* has become established and accepted.

In this discussion, we will alter the Keen definition as follows: ***MIS is the development and use of effective information systems in organizations.*** The essence of the definition is unchanged; we are simply substituting the word *development* for design and delivery, and placing the emphasis on *effective* information systems.

Now, given this definition, there are a number of questions that arise. What makes an information system effective? How do information systems relate to organizations? How are information systems developed? We will address the first two of these questions now. The answer to the third question is the subject of the entire next chapter.

1. Peter G. W. Keen, "MIS Research: Reference Disciplines and a Cumulative Tradition," in *Proceedings of the First International Conference on Information Systems*, ed. Ephraim McLean (Philadelphia, Pa.: ICIS Conference), 1980.

Effective Information Systems: Competitive Advantage

In the final analysis, information systems are effective if they provide a competitive advantage. Even in nonprofit and service-oriented organizations, information systems can be judged effective if they enable the organizations to provide more service or better quality service than they would otherwise provide.

Ives and Learmonth argue that information systems can create a competitive advantage by providing benefits to the organization itself (internal use of information systems) and by providing benefits to customers (external use).[2] We will consider both types of benefits in turn.

Benefits to the Organization

Considering the use of information systems inside the organization, a number of researchers have identified three levels or types of activity that can benefit. One of the earliest of such observations was made by Simon:

> An organization can be pictured as a three-layered cake. In the bottom layer we have the basic work processes—in the case of a manufacturing organization, the processes that procure raw materials, manufacture the physical product, warehouse it, and ship it. In the middle layer, we have the programmed (structured) decision-making processes, the processes that govern the day-to-day operation of the manufacturing and distribution system. In the top layer, we have the nonprogrammed (unstructured) decision-making processes, the processes that are required to design and redesign the entire system, to provide it with its basic goals and objectives, and to monitor its performance.[3]

These same three levels were identified by Robert Anthony in a subsequent publication. Anthony defined the levels as **operational control**, "the process of assuring that specific tasks are carried out . . .";[4] **management control**, "the process by which managers assure that resources are obtained and used effectively . . .";[5] and **strategic planning**, "the process of deciding on objectives of the organization, on changes in these objectives, on the resources used in attaining these objectives. . . ."[6]

Gorry and Scott Morton built upon these foundations to establish a two-dimensional framework, which is summarized in Figure 11-1.[7] The columns of this figure show the three layers identified by Simon and Anthony, and the rows identify the degree of structure involved in the

2. Blake Ives and Gerard P. Learmonth, "The Information System as a Competitive Weapon," *Communications of the ACM* Vol. 27, No. 12 (December 1984): p. 1197.
3. Herbert A. Simon, *The New Science of Management Decision* (New York: Harper and Row, 1960), p. 40.
4. Robert N. Anthony, *Planning and Control Systems: A Framework for Analysis* (Boston: Harvard University Graduate School of Business Administration, 1965), p. 69.
5. Ibid., p. 27.
6. Ibid, p. 24.
7. G. Anthony Gorry and Michael S. Scott Morton, "A Framework for Management Information Systems," *Sloan Management Review* (Fall 1971): pp. 55–70.

Figure 11-1
Gorry and Scott Morton systems classification

	Operational Control	Management Control	Strategic Planning
Structured			
Semistructured			
Unstructured			

process. By *degree of structure* is meant the amount of human judgment and evaluation required in the activity. **Structured activity** requires little judgment, evaluation, or insight; in structured activities, much of the decision making can be automated. **Unstructured activity** requires considerable judgment, evaluation, and human creativity, and is very difficult to automate.

Simon viewed business activity along one dimension—the three layers of the cake. He contended that activity became less structured moving from operational, to management, to planning activities. In this view, Figure 11-1 would have no rows; activity simply becomes less structured while moving from left to right across the columns. In contrast, Gorry and Scott Morton postulated that there are actually two dimensions: type of activity (the columns) and degree of structure (the rows). According to their model, operational control can be structured or unstructured, as can management control, and strategic planning.

Both of these points of view have merit. While there may be both structured and unstructured decision making at the operational level, there is no doubt that most decision making at that level is structured. Similarly, there may be both structured and unstructured decision making at the strategic planning level, but most decision making at that level is unstructured.

Business Activity and Information System Types In Chapter 3 you learned about five types of information systems: transaction processing systems (TPSs), management information systems (MISs), office automation systems (OASs), executive support systems (ESSs), and decision-support systems (DSSs). We are now in a position to show the relationship of these system types to the business activities. Figure 11-2 uses the Gorry and Scott Morton grid to show the approximate domains of each system type. TPSs are used primarily for structured operational and, to a lesser degree, management control applications. MISs (narrow definition) are used primarily for semistructured management control applications, although MISs overlap into the operational and strategic planning realms as well.

DSSs are used primarily for unstructured decision making, whether that occurs at the operational, management, or planning levels. ESSs are used primarily for structured management and strategic planning applications. Finally, OASs, used for office correspondence and communication, are used in all the domain.

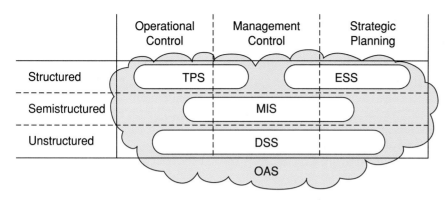

Figure 11-2
Domains of information system types

An Order Processing Example   Consider the example of order processing depicted in Figure 11-3. There are three levels of decision making in this organization. Here are some examples of *operational* decisions. A salesperson might ask, "Is this my customer?" A packer in the order processing department (warehouse) might ask, "Do we have six widgets in stock?" An accounting clerk might ask, "Have we received the Ajax payment?" Such operational questions are most likely answered by TPS applications.

Management decisions for this system concern allocation and use of resources. A regional sales manager or the vice president for sales might ask, "Are the territories defined appropriately?" A warehouse manager might ask, "Is our inventory too large (or too small)?" The accounts receivable manager or chief financial officer might ask, "Are we receiving payments fast enough from our customers?" Such questions are most likely addressed by MIS and, to a lesser extent, DSS applications.

Strategic planning questions involve objectives. A high-level manager, vice president, or CEO might ask, "Should we add (or dispose of) a product line?" or "Is our advertising program appropriate?" or "Should we change the terms on customer orders to encourage faster payment?"

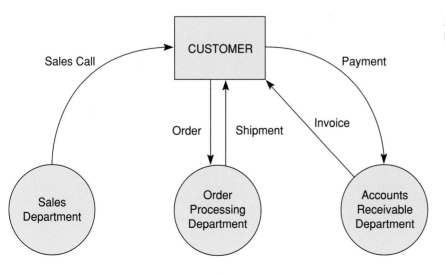

Figure 11-3
Information flow in order processing

These questions, which are primarily unstructured, are best supported by DSS applications.

ESS applications support high-level executive management control and planning. They deal with questions about the status and activity of the business, but at a very high level. They involve structured questions, but the questions are asked for management and strategic reasons, not for operations. Thus, the CEO may use an ESS to determine the company's checking account balance, but he or she does not want to know this balance in order to write a check. The CEO uses that balance as an overall measure of the success of corporate management and planning.

Finally, OAS applications underlie all of the activities in order processing. OASs can be used to address operational issues such as a salesperson informing order processing that a large order is on its way.

11.1   INCREASING YOUR PERSONAL PRODUCTIVITY

The Right User for the ESS

by Kelly Shea

Before you go off and set up an executive support system—no matter what type it is—be acutely aware that not every executive is going to be the perfect candidate for using one. Some people are just naturally more inclined than others to use an ESS. What makes a good ESS user and what constitutes an executive who may be less successful using one?

Computerworld talked with IS [information systems] professionals implementing ESSs and found that while the distinction between a good and bad candidate is not cut and dried, two requirements are evident: The executive must want to have an ESS in the first place; and, contrary to what might seem obvious, the successful ESS user need not be computer literate.

So say several ESS developers, including Tom Holmes, worldwide manager of executive information systems and office technology at Du Pont Co. in Wilmington, Del. "It takes an executive who has an appreciation for the value of information and an appreciation for the role that information technology plays in the organization," Holmes claims. He adds that executives who are successful with ESS "don't have to be comfortable with computers, but they have to believe that using computers is important to the success of the organization and that there is a business need for the system."

IS pros stress that upper level executives will be the most successful with these systems. "The higher up you get in the organization, the more information needs to be summarized, and that's what the ESS can do," says Dave Burton, manager of advanced applications at Dow Chemical Co. in Midland, Mich.

He and others add that executives whose style of management is more hands-on—those who feel more comfortable with the personal touch in managing—would probably be less inclined to use an ESS to full advantage than those whose style is to work more with numbers. The latter group has a need for the kind of review and support that an ESS can provide.

Alan McClurg agrees. Vice-president of support systems at Society Corp., a bank holding firm in Cleveland, McClurg says that "the more intuitive the individual is, the less receptive he's going to be to an ESS. The more analytical an executive is, then the idea of working with the machine is going to be more acceptable." But he points out that in no case can you push an ESS on any type of person. At Society, McClurg tries to get a system into the senior vice-president level before pushing it at the executive vice-president level. "As it gets into the organization and is accepted and used by those who do want it," McClurg explains, "those who weren't so sure they wanted one become more interested in it."

A final characteristic of successful ESS users is that they should be willing to help IS develop the system. "They can't get a good product unless they share their needs with the person providing it," Holmes says. If ESS users give IS their time and expertise during the development of the system, it will come out the way they want it. And that really is the bottom line for IS.

They also can be used for management control questions, like disseminating to the corporation's officers and key managers a report of inventory status over the last six months. OASs can be used similarly for DSS and ESS applications.

Improvements to the Organization's Product

Information systems can improve a product in two basic ways. They can improve the quality of the product, or they can improve the delivery of the product.

Improving Product Quality   Every product possesses both physical and information components. Even a product as basic as cement has an information component (how long it will be before the cement sets). Other products have information components that concern their use, maintenance, and repair. As Porter and Millar state:

> Historically, a product's physical component has been more important than its information component. The new technology, however, makes it feasible to supply far more information along with the physical product. For example, General Electric's appliance service data base supports a consumer hotline that helps differentiate GE's service support from its rivals'.[8]

Consider the definition of *product*. If you buy a clothes washer, what are you buying? What is the product? Certainly it includes the machinery that washes your clothes.[9] However, the product also includes documentation about how to use and maintain the machine and how to diagnose problems. Moreover, as indicated in the quotation above, the product includes information systems that improve customer support, that catalogue and identify replacement parts, and that facilitate the delivery of such parts on a timely basis. Since the product includes service, it also includes the training and knowledge of repair personnel.

Porter and Millar state that information systems enable organizations to differentiate themselves from their competitors. This, in the long run, creates a new product standard. Companies must match or exceed one another's product-oriented information systems. Thus, during your career, information systems will become a new arena for competition.

Improving Product Delivery   Information systems not only improve the quality of products, they also improve the means by which products can be delivered to the customers. One of the most common and obvious examples of this are airline reservations systems. To a buyer with a

---

8. Michael E. Porter and Victor E. Millar, "How Information Gives You Competitive Advantage," *Harvard Business Review* Vol. 63, No. 4: p. 154.

9. Today, this machinery is likely to contain a microprocessor or other computer-based device. We will not consider such applications of computer technology in this discussion. While important, such applications fall outside of the definition of MIS as the development and use of information systems in organizations.

Figure 11-4
Functions of information systems

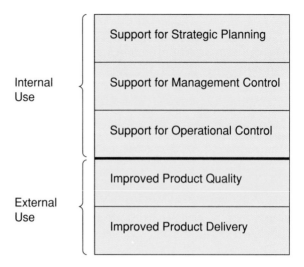

credit card, a reservation and ticket to any destination in the world is no more than a telephone call away. That is good product delivery.

There are many other examples. Some companies support in-home computer-based shopping; banks provide automated teller machines; and corporations order parts or raw materials through automated corporate purchasing systems. Avis has developed a portable computer terminal that car lot attendants carry on a hip belt. When a customer returns a car, the attendant keys in the car license plate number and the portable terminal accesses a central computer that computes the amount due. The attendant's unit prints the invoice and the customer is on his or her way without entering any buildings or standing in any lines.

Figure 11-4 summarizes the functions of information systems in organizations. Internal uses include support for operational control, management control, and strategic planning. External uses include improving product quality and improving product delivery.

Information Systems and Organizations

Now, consider the definition of MIS again: the development and use of effective information systems in organizations. How do information systems relate to organizations? Take a moment and imagine a large company, say Procter & Gamble, or IBM, or Boeing. Think about the information systems in one of those companies. Imagine the myriads of ways in which people, groups, departments, and divisions share information. It is truly mind-boggling to consider this picture.

Clearly, to make sense out of the question of how information systems impact organizations, we will have to divide and conquer. Daft and Steers provide a clue for organizing the study of information systems: "As social systems, organizations are composed of systems at different levels. . . . Organizational scientists generally think of three levels of

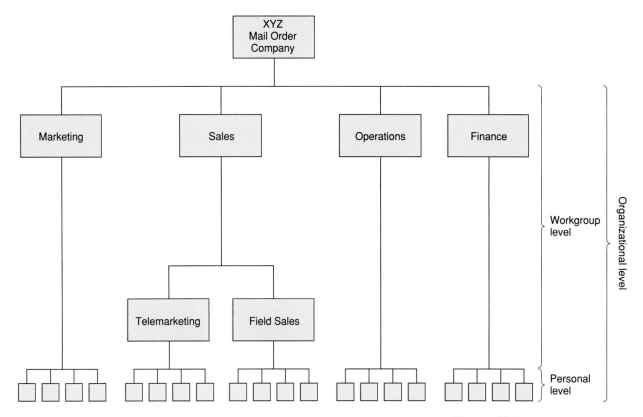

Figure 11-5
Three levels of information system

analysis—the individual, the group or department, and the organization itself."[10] We will use this approach in the present text, and study information systems at these three levels.

Three Levels of Information Systems

Consider Figure 11-5, which shows a portion of an organizational chart for an order processing company. This could be a mail-order catalogue company, for example. The chart shows four major departments: marketing, sales, operations, and finance and accounting.

Organizational Level   At the organizational level, there is a revenue generation system. This system tracks and reports on every activity that affects the company's finances. As a result, all departments use this system. (See Figure 11-6*a*.)

Group or Department Level   Look again at Figure 11-5. Within the sales department, the telemarketing group operates at the workgroup level. This group calls prospective customers on a rotating basis. They try to contact every active customer at least once per quarter. The

10. Richard L. Daft and Richard M. Steers, *Organizations, A Micro/Macro Approach* (Glenview, Ill.: Scott, Foresman, 1986), pp. 7–8.

Questions

11.1 Explain the difference between the two meanings of the term *management information system*.

11.2 State the definition for MIS that is used in this chapter.

11.3 What three questions arise from the definition in question 11.2?

11.4 What makes an information system effective?

11.5 In what two ways can information systems create a competitive advantage?

11.6 How can an organization be pictured as a three-layered cake?

11.7 List the three levels of business activity identified by Anthony.

11.8 Sketch the framework developed by Gorry and Scott Morton.

11.9 Using the sketch from your answer to question 11.8, show the domain of each of the five types of systems defined in Chapter 3.

actions of the telemarketing representatives need to be coordinated. While the group does not want to miss any customers, it does not want to duplicate calls either. Furthermore, some calls require follow-up. The telemarketing group does not want to drop the ball even if the particular representative who promised to follow up is not working at the appointed time.

To meet these needs, the telemarketing group has developed a workgroup information system (see Figure 11-6*b*). This system maintains a file of customers and assigns customers to representatives on a rotating basis. It also keeps track of the need for follow-up calls and assigns these calls to representatives.

Just as the corporate system coordinates the activities of the individual departments, so, too, the workgroup system coordinates the activities of the individual sales representatives within the department.

Personal Level In addition to the telemarketing group, the XYZ Company employs a field sales force (see Figure 11-5). Field salespeople are each assigned a particular territory, and they operate independently. Salespeople are paid on commission; they want the highest productivity, making the most sales in the shortest time.

Salespeople can use personal information systems to gain higher productivity. Each salesperson can have his or her own system: the systems do not interface with one another (see Figure 11-6*c*). For example, a salesperson could use a mail/merge word processing system to generate personalized form letters and to prequalify customers. Or the salesperson could keep track of sales calls and resulting sales to determine which customers are the most responsive. Or the salesperson could use an information system to identify potential contacts, and so forth. These are all uses of personal information systems like those you studied in Chapters 5–8.

Figure 11-6
Examples of systems in the XYZ Mail Order Company

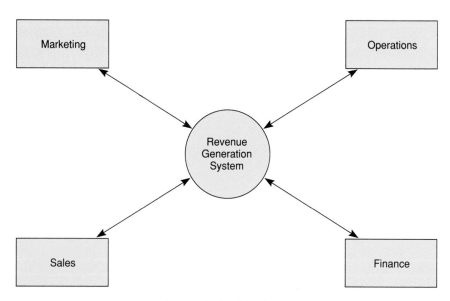

a. An organizational-level system

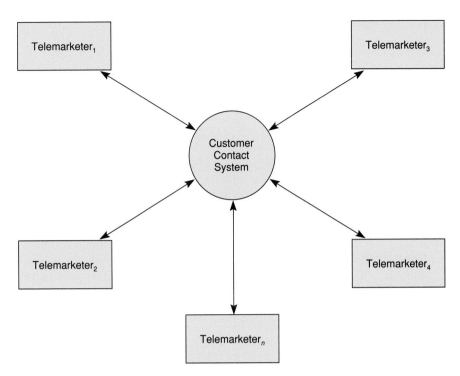

b. A workgroup-level system

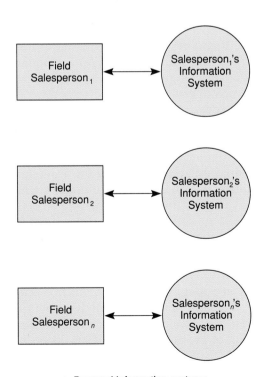

c. Personal information systems

Questions

11.10 Give an example, other than order processing, that illustrates Anthony's levels of business activity and the five types of information systems defined in Chapter 3.

11.11 In what two ways can information systems improve an organization's product?

11.12 Name two components of a product. Which of these can information systems improve?

11.13 Explain how information systems can improve product delivery. Give an example.

11.14 List three levels of organization that are important to information systems.

11.15 Give an example of an organizational information system. Give an example of a benefit of this system corresponding to each of the functions listed in Figure 11-4.

11.16 Give an example of a workgroup information system. Give an example of a benefit of this system corresponding to each of the functions listed in Figure 11-4.

11.17 Give an example of a personal information system. Give an example of a benefit of this system corresponding to each of the functions listed in Figure 11-4.

Benefits at All Three Levels

Earlier in this chapter, we considered the benefits of information systems to organizations (summarized in Figure 11-4). In fact, these benefits apply to all three levels of organization.

Consider a department. Departments are workgroups that have operations, that have management, and that perform strategic planning. Information systems can facilitate all three of these types of activity. Departments also have products. The product of the accounts receivable department, for example, is collections. Information systems can be used to improve the information component of the product (for example, who owes which money, for how long, and how this differs from their payment history in the past). Information systems also can be used to improve the delivery of the product. For example, having available the information when it is needed to make collection calls.

Now consider the benefits of information systems to individual employees. Internal uses are those that facilitate activities within the individual's job sphere. These are actions that no one but the individual knows about. For the salesperson, these are the activities that she undertakes to plan, execute, and follow up sales calls. External uses are those that help to improve the products that the individual produces. These products may be generated for people in horizontal relationships, either within the organization or outside of the company, or for vertical relationships (with bosses or subordinates). For a salesperson, the product consists of sales calls, follow-up calls, and sales letters.

You may be asking yourself, Why does this matter? The answer is that the framework shown in Figure 11-4 provides a means for thinking about the role of information systems at all three levels of organization. Whether you are considering an information system for an individual, for a workgroup (either a group or department), or for the entire organization, you can use this framework to help you understand and organize the benefits of the potential system. Also, when wondering if an information system is appropriate for a situation, you should consider the types of benefit shown here.

To review, MIS concerns the development and use of effective information systems in business. An effective information system is one that provides a competitive advantage in terms of the functions listed in Figure 11-4. Information systems are used at three levels of organization: the organizational level, the group or departmental level, and the personal level.

Decision Support Systems

In this section, we are going to change orientation and perspective. In a large measure, the functions shown in Figure 11-4 are related to business processes; they concern the processes of operations, management, and planning of the organization. They concern doing, measuring, and responding. Systems that facilitate such processes tend to be structured, because the processes themselves are structured.

Some business situations, however, are not as process oriented. Such situations center on particular decisions—how to respond to an unanticipated opportunity or problem. Company decision makers ask, "What should we do?" The process of answering this question tends to be less structured and more open-ended. Decision support systems (DSSs) were developed to support managers in such situations.

You were introduced to DSSs in Chapter 3. Here we will expand on that discussion to show the role of DSSs in business management. DSSs cut across the personal, workgroup, and organization-wide information system categories and are used at all three levels. Further, although early DSSs were developed for use by an individual, today attention is focused on both individual and group applications.

What Is a DSS?

There are many definitions of a DSS. One of the earliest was developed by Gerrity: "an effective blend of human intelligence, information technology, and software which interact closely to solve complex problems."[11] This definition identifies the basic character of a DSS; but many other types of information systems also address complex problems. A more precise definition is: "an interactive computer-based system which facilitates solution of unstructured problems."[12] The keywords in this definition are *facilitate* and *unstructured*.

Decision support systems facilitate the decision-making process; they do not make decisions. People make decisions. In fact, the word *system* may be misleading. DSSs are not rigid, structured systems with fixed, standardized interfaces, as menu-driven TPS applications are. Rather, a DSS provides a set of capabilities for managers to use to assist decision making. As stated in Chapter 3, a better term might be *decision support facility*, since the DSS is actually a set of tools, data, models, and other resources that managers and analysts use to understand, evaluate, and solve problems.

Additionally, DSSs address unstructured problem domains; this is what most distinguishes DSSs from other types of information systems that you have studied. Consider an example.

Suppose a grocery store chain faces an extended labor strike, and needs to determine the impact of reduced operations on the company and its financial position. There is no fixed, predefined set of rules and procedures for producing this information. No existing TPS or MIS was designed with such a question in mind. The problem statement itself is vague, involving nonspecific terms like *extended*, *impact*, and *reduced*. Further, when the answer is developed, it will be difficult to know how accurate it is, whether a better answer could have been developed, or whether the process used was the best or even a good one.

11. T. P. Gerrity, "Design of Man-machine Decision Systems, An Application to Portfolio Management," *Sloan Management Review* Vol. 59 (Winter 1971): p. 314.
12. Beradine DeSanctis and Brent Gallupe, "Group Decision Support Systems: A New Frontier," *Data Base* Vol. 16, No. 2 (Winter 1985): p. 3.

11.2   INCREASING YOUR PERSONAL PRODUCTIVITY

Judging the Value of an Executive System

Cost justification is only one factor in determining the value of a system designed specifically for executives. In the following excerpt from their book *Executive Support Systems, the Emergence of Top Management Computer Use,* John F. Rockart and David W. DeLong identify six criteria for evaluating executive information systems.

1. *How much time does the executive spend using the system?* This superficial criterion is often used by executive support system (ESS) developers to judge a system's success. If the manager never uses the computer, it is hard to argue that the system is contributing to organizational effectiveness, unless hands-on use has been delegated. But use alone doesn't mean increased effectiveness because there's no direct relationship between time at the terminal and executive performance.

2. *Does the system save the executive time and allow more work to get done?* This is a question of increased efficiency or logistical support. To some, this is what executive support is all about. For others, a system that focuses only on increasing the efficiency of top management is selling short the technology's potential.

3. *Does the ESS change how the executive thinks about using and managing information technology?* Educating top management about computer technology and its expanding capabilities to provide competitive advantage is an objective of some ESS advocates. Although part of this educational objective may be realized, the ESS will languish when its applications are not focused on a significant business need. Education is a measurable but secondary criterion for success, often a by-product of an effective ESS.

4. *Does it change the way the organization utilizes technology?* This is a result of the change in mindset just described. Seldom a criterion to justify ESS, increased technology utilization by the organization is often a major benefit of a system installed for top management. Once educated, executives are more likely, for better or worse, to accelerate the use of information technologies in the organization.

5. *Does the system improve the executive's understanding of and control over the business?* This intangible benefit is an explicit or implicit criterion for success in the minds of several executives interviewed. These executives are striving to reduce the uncertainty they feel about their environment or to make sense of equivocal information. An effective ESS will enhance their mental model of the business and competitive environment by creating a better understanding of cause and effect relationships.

6. *Does the system improve the organization's planning and control process?* This is one of the most tangible measures of ESS effectiveness. Providing more timely and better-quality information to top management can have a major impact on an organization's management processes. But it can also generate the most resistance from other parts of the firm during the implementation process. Changing information flows within an organization alters the power structure, and this can be extremely upsetting to subordinate line managers and staff alike.

DSS Task Environment

Ariav and Ginzberg define three dimensions to the tasks that DSSs are designed to accomplish: degree of structure, level of application, and phase of the decision process addressed.[13] We will consider each of these, plus a fourth, recurrency.

Degree of Structure   DSSs are designed to address unstructured problem environments. As Ariav and Ginzberg point out, however, the degree

13. Gad Ariav and Michael J. Ginzberg, "DSS Design: A Systemic View of Decision Support," *Communications of the ACM* Vol. 38, No. 10 (October 1985): p. 1046.

of structure is not a property of the problem to be solved as much as it is a property of the way humans perceive the method for solving the problem.[14] Thus, the appropriate question is not how structured is the problem, but rather, how structured is the decision-making process.

Consider weather prediction. Weather is a very fluid and unstructured phenomenon. Most weather prediction, however, is accomplished by a well-known, predefined, and highly structured process. Thus, weather prediction would not fall into the unstructured problem environment, even though the problem itself is unstructured.

Level of Application   *Level* refers to the type of management activity, conceived in terms of Simon's three-layered cake and Anthony's dimensions discussed in the last section. These levels are operational control, management control, and strategic planning. Early development of DSS theory and technology assumed that DSSs would be used only for strategic planning and upper-level management control applications. While there is no doubt that DSSs do have application at these levels, more recent research indicates that DSSs can be applied to problems at all three levels of activity.[15]

Thus, DSSs can be used at the operational control level when decision-making at that level requires an unstructured process. Production scheduling is a good example. Accelerating a critical job is an operational control issue; yet to do this, the production manager is required to adjust and adapt the week's production activities using a very unstructured process.

Phases of the Decision Process   Often, the decision process is defined as involving three primary phases: intelligence gathering, alternative development, and choice. DSSs can be used for all three phases.

DSSs can be used to investigate, understand, and discuss the problem and its environment. They can be used to produce information statements that reveal the key elements of problems and the interrelationships of those elements. DSSs can be used to identify, create, and communicate alternative courses of action and other decision alternatives. And they can be used to facilitate choice by estimating costs and benefits, by projecting other outcomes of decisions, by determining the sensitivity of outcomes to decision variables, and by communicating these projected results to decision makers.

Observe that the purpose of DSS applications is not only to generate information statements, but also to facilitate communication about those statements among the personnel involved in the problem. Thus, a specific function of a DSS at all levels and in all phases is to generate documents, reports, tables of data, graphs, slides, and other outputs. This role is particularly important for group decision support systems (GDSSs), as you will see.

14. Ibid.
15. Ibid., p. 1046.

Recurrency   Another dimension to the tasks addressed by DSSs is task **recurrency.** Some DSS applications are developed to address one-of-a-kind, never-to-occur-again problems. The labor strike at the grocery store is an example. At the other end of the recurrency continuum are tasks that recur regularly. Scheduling production is an example. It must be done every day, every week. In between these extremes are intermittent tasks; these tasks recur, but not regularly. The need to assemble a construction crew for an offshore drilling operation is an unstructured problem that recurs, but at irregular intervals.

Organizations respond to the recurrency dimension in different ways. Permanent DSS applications are established for regular and recurring needs. These applications are supported and maintained just as other types of information systems are.

To support the development and use of DSSs for intermittent applications, some organizations have decided to establish centers of DSS resources. These centers are staffed by personnel with DSS expertise and with access to programs, models, and data.

Such centers or departments are like internal consulting companies. They exist to assist the development of DSS applications as the need for them develops. No one knows what needs for DSSs will occur, but, it is known that *some* needs will occur. Thus, the organization creates a permanent DSS department to facilitate the construction of DSS applications for whatever needs develop as the future unfolds.

In other cases, where the need for the DSS is temporary, the MIS department will set up an ad hoc team to build the DSS to meet that particular need. For the strike situation at the grocery store, for example, the MIS department might staff a temporary team to build and use a DSS to compute estimates of the financial impact of the strike.

Amalgamated Mining

Consider the case of Amalgamated Mining, a multinational corporation that operates mines throughout the world. From time to time, Amalgamated opens or closes a mine. In the process, hundreds of decisions must be made regarding the acquisition or disposition of equipment and the relocation of personnel.

The Need for a DSS   In the spring of 1990, Amalgamated closed one of its largest copper mines. In planning this closure, Amalgamated needed to decide which equipment to sell, which to move, and which to abandon. Further, it needed to make personnel decisions consistent with the equipment decisions. Because of the interrelationships among components that are inherent in mining operations, this reduction was exceedingly difficult to plan.

Consider, for example, the consequences of eliminating 50 bulldozers. Clearly, if the bulldozers are removed, then the drivers of the bulldozers will not be necessary. But if the drivers are unnecessary, then the trainers of the drivers also are unnecessary. In addition, the personnel required to hire both the drivers and the trainers are not needed. Furthermore, if the bulldozers are removed, then the bulldozer trailers also need to be removed; and, if they are removed, then the trucks that pull the trailers also can be eliminated. But if the trucks are removed, then the truck drivers are not necessary, nor are the truck driver trainers, nor are the personnel who hire the truck drivers and truck driver trainers. Additionally, the people who maintain the bulldozers and the trailers and the trucks will not be needed (along with their trainers and support personnel).

Now, given the reductions in personnel, fewer people need to be supported. Since Amalgamated's mines are located in remote locations, this has a substantial impact on operations. With the closing of the mine, fewer cooks, food buyers, builders of baths and showers, and people to maintain warehouses of tissue and toilet paper will be needed . . . and so forth.

This, clearly, is a complicated problem. It also is an important one. Amalgamated wants to make its cutbacks and reductions in a sensible manner. It does not want to cut operational capability when closing the mine only to find out later that useless parts of some systems remain (truck drivers who have no trucks, for example).

An Example DSS Figure 11-7 shows the fundamental structure of a DSS program.[16] Users interface with the **dialogue management** component, which is a set of programs that manage the display screens, obtain inputs from and send outputs to the users, and translate the users' requests into commands for the other two components.

The **model management** component maintains and executes models of business activity. Examples of models are spreadsheets, operations research models, financial models, and process simulations. The model management system is used to create, store, modify, and retrieve models.

The **data management** component maintains the DSS database. It also interfaces with other sources of data such as TPS databases and data utilities.

Figure 11-7 is a generalized structure. An example of this structure for the DSS application at Amalgamated Mining is shown in Figure 11-8. Amalgamated keeps a model of mining operations that pertains to all types of mines, in all locations. It also keeps models that pertain to particular types of mines, and other models that pertain to mines in particular locations. In addition, it keeps data concerning the level of activity at each mine in the DSS database.

When a user wants to perform an analysis on a particular mine, he or she indicates the type of analysis to be performed, the type of mine, and the location of the mine. These inputs enable the model management component to load and invoke the correct models. Then the user indicates the specific mine to be analyzed, and the data management portion of the DSS fills the models with the appropriate data. The models are executed and results are displayed to the user, stored in the DSS database, or both.

---

16. Ariav and Ginzberg, "DSS Design," p. 1047.

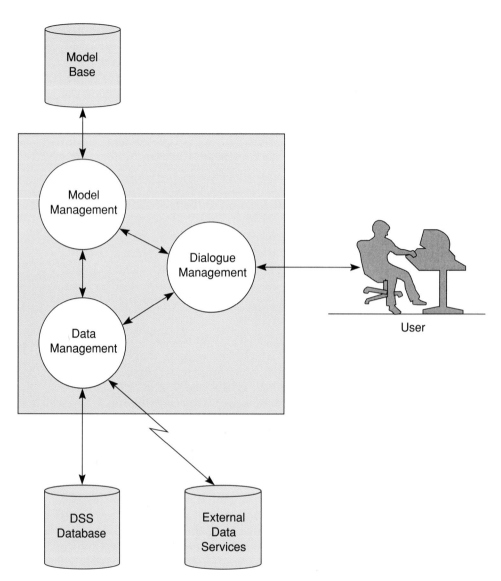

Figure 11-7
Fundamental DSS program structure

Group Decision Support Systems

Initially DSSs were seen as tools for individual decision makers or analysts. The notion was that the results from an individual's DSS session or sessions would be printed, graphed, or otherwise documented, and those results would then be used for the individual's decision or would be taken to a meeting in which the results would be discussed.

Recent work in DSS, however, has moved DSS applications into the group decision environment. Here, the members of the group employ the DSS, as a group. This form of DSS is known as a **GDSS (group decision support system).** As shown in Figure 11-9, the user interface is expanded to include computers that are connected together in some

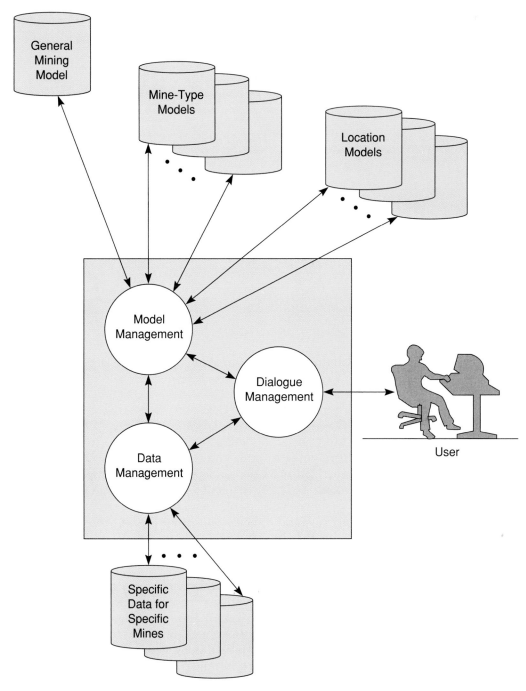

Figure 11-8
DSS for Amalgamated Mining

manner.[17] In this way, members of the group can communicate via their computers with the DSS or with other members of the group. If the group meets in one location, they share a public screen for input and output. If they are geographically dispersed, they each have a window at their computer that displays the public screen.

17. DeSanctis and Gallupe, "Group Decision Support Systems," p. 4.

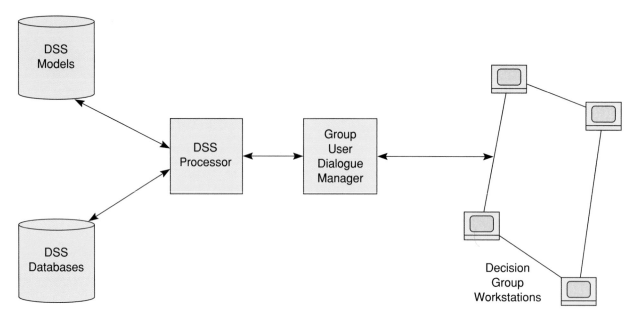

Figure 11-9
Architecture of group DSS

A number of different architectures for supporting GDSSs have been developed. The architecture to be used depends on the recurrency of the DSS and the geographical location of the users. Figure 11-10 shows the alternatives recommended by DeSanctis and Gallupe for various combinations of recurrency and geographic proximity.[18] For limited, ad hoc, and intermittent group DSSs, whose members can meet in the same physical location, DeSanctis and Gallupe recommend a **decision room** environment. Here, group members each have a computer station that they use to communicate with one another, to obtain stored data, and to alter the display on the public screen.

For limited, ad hoc, and intermittent group DSSs, whose members are geographically distributed, DeSanctis and Gallupe recommend **teleconferencing**, with different meeting rooms connected via video displays.

Next, for recurring group DSSs whose members are in the same physical location, they recommend microcomputer workstations connected via a local area network (LAN). The recurring need for GDSSs justifies the expense of maintaining a permanent LAN connection.

Finally, for recurring group DSSs among geographically dispersed users, DeSanctis and Gallupe recommend "uninterrupted communication between remote 'decision stations.'"[19] Their article, which appeared in 1985, recognized that at that time there were few such systems. Today, wide area networks are the preferred architecture for this combination, but such networks did not exist, for practical purposes, in 1985.

18. Ibid., p. 6.
19. Ibid., p. 7.

Figure 11-10
Alternative GDSS architectures

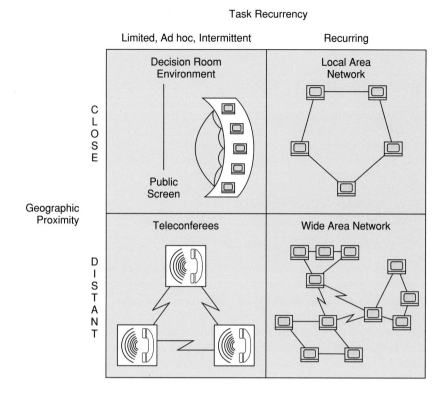

Task Recurrency

For the remainder of this chapter, the term *DSS* will be used to refer to both individual and group DSSs. When we need to refer specifically to group DSSs, we will use the term *GDSS*.

Functions of DSS Applications

Figure 11-11 lists the major functions of DSS applications. First, DSSs can be used *to become familiar with the problem domain*. For large problems, it is often not clear what is dependent on what. A DSS can be used to identify relationships among key elements of the problem.

For Amalgamated Mining's budget reduction problem, for example, a DSS can be used to identify what equipment and personnel are required to support a bulldozer, either directly or indirectly. It is likely to be easy for the analysts to determine direct support; the number of personnel and the skills required for the bulldozer crew are well documented. What is less obvious are questions like: How many trainers are needed to support 100 bulldozer crews? What facilities are required to train 100 such crews? How much training is required for the trainers? How long does it take for a trainer to become qualified? Clearly, indirect support for a bulldozer is not easily determined. One purpose of the DSS is to help people determine what is dependent on what.

A second DSS function is *to determine the sensitivity of results to changes in decision variables*. For example, it may be that eliminating ten bulldozers from the budget saves $1 million in logistic support

Figure 11-11
Major functions of DSS applications

- Becoming familiar with a problem domain

- Determining sensitivity of results to changes in decision variables

- Identifying patterns

- Predicting decision outcomes

- Developing models of business processes

- Computing optimum mixes

- Facilitating group communication

11.18   Explain how the orientation and perspective of DSS applications differs from those of TPS applications and MIS (narrow definition) applications.

11.19   State the second definition of DSS. Explain the key words *facilitate* and *unstructured*.

11.20   List the four dimensions of the DSS task environment.

11.21   Explain the statement that "degree of structure is not a property of the problem to be solved."

11.22   List the levels of application for DSSs.

11.23   List the phases of the decision process for which DSSs are applicable.

11.24   Explain how task recurrency influences the ways that organizations support DSS applications.

11.25   List the three major components of a DSS program.

costs. Or it may be that the elimination of these ten bulldozers saves $10 million in support costs. Or it may be that support costs are fixed over the relevant period, and the elimination of ten bulldozers saves nothing at all.

Obviously, the difference is important. Knowing which decision variables have the greatest impact on the outcome enables the decision makers to focus attention on the important matters. You may be surprised to learn that it is very easy and quite common for business leaders to focus considerable attention on unimportant matters and not enough attention on critical ones.

A third DSS function is *pattern identification*. The DSS application can, using both statistical techniques and the visual display of quantitative data, help the analysts to identify patterns in either the input data or the results. For example, a plot of sales data on a map can reveal differences in market size, penetration, or sales effectiveness. The same plot repeated over successive time periods can help to identify trends.

Another DSS function is *to predict decision outcomes*. For example, a DSS can be used to estimate the impact on sales of doubling the size of the sales force, or increasing the advertising budget, or introducing a product in a new market. All such predictions rely on models that relate outcomes to input variables. This leads to the next DSS function.

A DSS can be used *to develop models of business processes*. Such models may consist of one or more equations that relate outputs to inputs. One example is an equation that relates sales to the number of sales personnel, or sales to advertising, or both. The DSS can include statistical programs that estimate the parameters of such equations.

Computing optimum mixes is another DSS function. Consider, for example, the problem of allocating people to jobs. Suppose that Amalgamated eliminates 50 bulldozers, and as a result 500 employees become available for assignment to other positions. Now, some of the personnel will have other skills and training and some will not. Some of the skills the personnel have will be in demand and some will not. If there is no match between personnel skills and available jobs, then some people will need to be retrained or laid off. Amalgamated's problem in this case may be to allocate personnel to jobs so as to minimize retraining and moving costs. Operations research techniques like linear programming can be used to compute the optimum solution.

The last major function of a DSS is *to facilitate group communication.* Problems that require DSS applications nearly always involve a group. Seldom does one individual make the decisions. More often, decisions are made by group consensus. Even when the decision is made by a single authority, that authority relies on the input of other team members. All of this means that the group must have a common understanding of the problem, of the available solutions, and of criteria for choosing among those alternative solutions. Individual DSSs can facilitate the group communication first by producing outputs that can be easily copied and shared, and also by producing overhead transparencies, 35mm slides, and even video images and animation.

The Management of Information Systems

In this section we will consider a third dimension of information systems and management. This dimension concerns the management of the information systems themselves and the acquisition and use of information technology.

Both systems users and information systems professionals have a role in the management of information systems. We will begin by discussing the role of end users in the management of information systems. From that, we will examine the organization of the MIS department, the department that specializes in information systems. Finally, we will consider the special requirements of decision support systems.

User Departments

Although the wording in this text would seem to indicate that users are a homogeneous group, this is not the case at all. Users differ in their education, experience, job title, job level, and interest in and desire to learn about information technology. Consequently, users differ in the amount of training, documentation, and other support that they need.

Additionally, users' attitudes about information systems vary considerably. Some users could care less about the role of the information system to the organization while others need to understand how each component relates to the others. Some users want to be taught only how to perform a particular function and then to be left alone. Others are constantly searching for unknown features, functions, or capabilities in the system.

As a result of these differences, users typically differentiate themselves with regard to the system, quite often on an informal basis. One user will become intrigued by computer technology and begin to learn more and more. Over time, his or her co-workers will come to recognize that person's special skills and knowledge and will bring new, difficult,

11.26 Explain the function of the dialogue management component.

11.27 Explain the function of the model management component.

11.28 Explain two functions of the data management component.

11.29 How do GDSSs differ from DSSs?

11.30 Explain the meaning of each of the cells in Figure 11-10.

11.31 List and explain the functions of DSS applications.

11.3 INCREASING YOUR PERSONAL PRODUCTIVITY

What Is Artificial Intelligence?

The term "artificial intelligence" means different things to different people. Academics take the narrow view that true artificial intelligence (AI) seeks to develop computer models of human intelligence. Developers of business software are less dogmatic, and often inappropriately put the AI label on any product that may arguably be considered "smart," or possessed of an advanced level of computing power.

Ignoring such marketing hype, commercial AI products generally fall into one of three categories: expert systems, natural-language systems, and neural networks.

Expert systems are by far the most plentiful type of commercial AI program. They are also called rule-based systems because they follow a set of rules to reach conclusions. To create an expert system, a "knowledge engineer"—the AI programmer—interviews experts in a particular field and distills their knowledge into a series of if/then rules.

Following the rules, an expert system running on a personal computer, workstation, or mainframe can analyze a problem and advise people on how to solve it. The idea is to make the experts' knowledge available to novices.

The knowledge represented in an expert system is restricted to a narrow field, ranging from the relatively mundane (how to fix a car engine) to the esoteric (deciding where to drill for oil). AI purists scoff at these systems, arguing that experts use a lot more than if/then reasoning when making decisions.

Natural-language programs come closer to representing human cognition. They grew out of AI research into how people derive meaning from language—how do we understand, for example, that a reference to New York in a sentence refers to the city or the state? Natural-language software consists of powerful programs that let people tap into a database using plain-English commands instead of computer language.

Neural networks, the most ambitious form of artificial intelligence to date, are still in the research lab, especially at Princeton and the California Institute of Technology. Developers aim to recreate in silicon the complex network of neural pathways in the brain to build a computer that would mimic human thought. The technology is promising, but a long way from commercial use. So far, researchers have simulated the nerve structure of the eye's retina and the ear's cochlea, and AT&T has created a computer copy of the brain of a garden slug. It's something to think about.

or anomalous situations to that person's attention. Over time such a person becomes an informal, internal systems consultant and manager.

Some organizations have recognized this situation and created a new job title. It has a variety of names: key user, information systems liaison, even computerist, are typical names. Here, we will employ the term *key user*.

A **key user** is a person who holds a job in an end user department—say, accounting—who, because of an interest in computers and information systems, has gained specialized expertise. This person becomes a local broker of information systems knowledge. Other end users go to this person when they have problems or need help.

The key user, who often has received special training from the MIS department, answers all of the other users' questions that he or she can, and calls on the MIS department for help with questions beyond his or her knowledge. In this way, users have someone local whom they trust to go to with their questions; they do not need to display their ignorance to the strangers in the MIS department, who may not understand their plight. At the same time, the MIS department is not plagued with simple and routine problems or requests.

The MIS Department

The MIS department is responsible for the development, maintenance, and security of the information systems. The organization of the MIS department is important to you for two reasons. First, you may decide on an information systems career; if so, many of the jobs that you might want are located in this department. Second, you need to know about the organization of the MIS department so that as an end user you can be an effective consumer of that department's services and resources.

Organizational Placement   Figure 11-12 shows a high-level organizational chart of a typical corporation. User departments are supported by the MIS (or information services or information technology) department. As shown in this figure, the vice president of MIS reports directly to the chief executive officer. This arrangement reflects the importance of information and information systems in business.

In the past, the MIS department often reported to the VP of finance. (Early business computer systems were nearly completely financial.) This structure eventually proved to be unworkable, primarily because organizations need other information systems besides those of concern to finance. The organization in Figure 11-12 enables the MIS department to serve the needs of the overall organization as opposed to the needs of the finance (or any other) department alone.

Function of the MIS Department   The MIS department is the organization's primary source of information technology and is responsible for ensuring that the organization uses such technology to best accomplish its goals and objectives. That responsibility breaks into two major functions. One is to develop, operate, maintain, and manage organizational information systems. The second is to acquire technology and to help end users apply it appropriately.

The nature of this second function was summarized by Cash, McFarlan, and McKenney in a description of three broad objectives of information systems management control: "1. Facilitate appropriate communica-

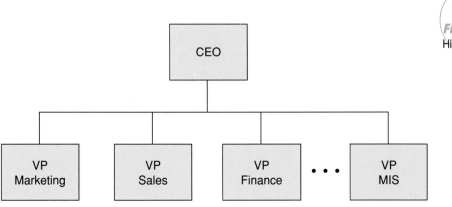

Figure 11-12
High-level corporate organization

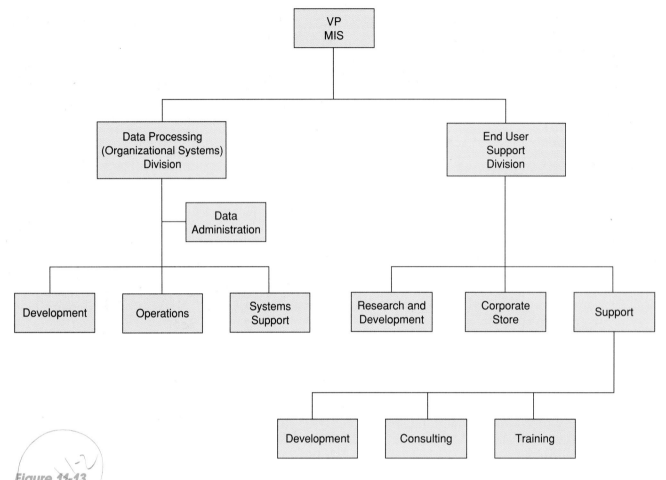

Figure 11-13

Organization of a large corporate MIS department

tion between the user and the deliverer of information technology services and provide motivational incentives for them to work together. . . . 2. Encourage the effective utilization of the [MIS department's] resources and ensure that users are educated on the potential of existing and evolving technology. . . . 3. Provide means for efficient management of information technology resources and give necessary information for investment decisions."[20]

Today, the organization of MIS departments recognizes these dual roles. Consider Figure 11-13, which shows the organization chart of a typical MIS department for a large corporation. This organization has two major divisions. The data processing division develops and operates the organizational information systems. The end user support division helps end users apply computer technology for personal and work-group information systems. We will consider each of these divisions in turn.

20. James I. Cash, F. Warren McFarlan, and James L. McKenney, *Corporate Information Systems Management* (Homewood, Ill.: Irwin, 1988), pp. 135–136.

Information Systems Provide a Competitive Advantage

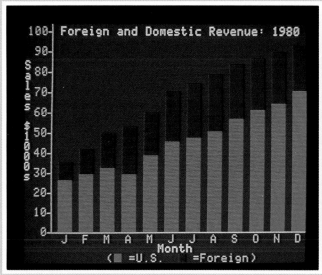

1 Analysis of foreign and domestic sales helps marketing develop product needs.

2 Analysis of product sales performance helps marketing develop product plans.

Information systems can provide a competitive advantage not only by facilitating the organization's internal operations but also by improving the quality and delivery of the organization's products. Such improvements occur through better product marketing, conceptualization, design, manufacturing, and support.

Product Marketing (photos 1–5)
One of the major functions of product marketing is to develop a plan of action that will accomplish the overall financial goals and objectives of the organization. This plan includes a description of the products and services to be sold, their sales and marketing plans, quotas for those products, and their budgets.

To accomplish this function, product marketing evaluates past company performance, analyzes changes in the size and composition of the market, and determines the importance of certain product functions and features.

Product Conceptualization (photos 6–11)
Based on this research, product marketing works with engineering to develop conceptual product designs. These include the product's characteristics, its physical appearance, and the development of product models and mock-ups. In some cases, simulations of the product's usage are conducted.

Detailed Design (photos 12–21)
Once a product has been approved for development, a detailed design must be created. CAD (computer-assisted design) systems are used to generate the design, to display it, and even to perform analyses such as stress analysis. Both two- and three-dimensional displays are used, and parts are often shown in conjunction with one another so as to check part interfaces and tolerances. CAD systems also produce design documentation such as circuit diagrams or blueprints.

Manufacturing (photos 22–35)
Computer-assisted manufacturing (CAM) provides many different types of service to the manufacturing process. CAM systems vary from machines whose operation is directed by programs (called NC or numerically controlled machines) to sophisticated integrated manufacturing systems that coordinate and control the activities of humans, NC machines, and robots on an entire shop floor or in a factory.

Programs for NC machines are developed using CAD/CAM systems. Robots can be directed by prewritten programs, or they can be trained by human operators to perform their activities. In the latter case, the robot "memorizes" the motions it is led through. Robots can also be directed by humans using remote control.

Computer systems also have a role in quality control. Computers can be used to test products, to gather the results of test procedures, and to display test results. In some cases, quality control information is used to adjust equipment in the production process automatically.

Product Support (photos 36–37)
Computer-based information systems are also used to increase the quality and delivery of product support. Computer-based systems can be used to produce more accurate and timely product documentation. Such systems can also facilitate the training of personnel and improve the quality of customer service and support.

1

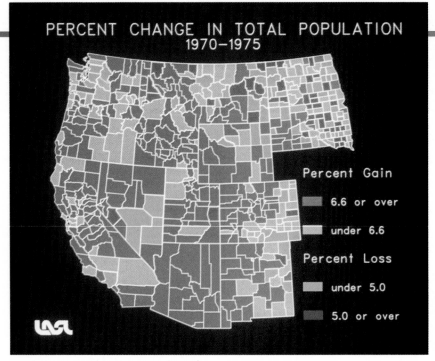

3 Analysis of trends in demographic data is used to forecast market size and characteristics.

4 Analysis of specific market projections is used to forecast sales potential.

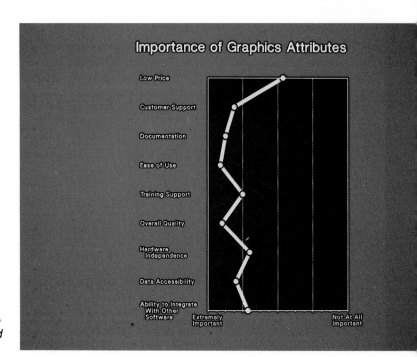

5 Survey data is used to help determine product features and functions.

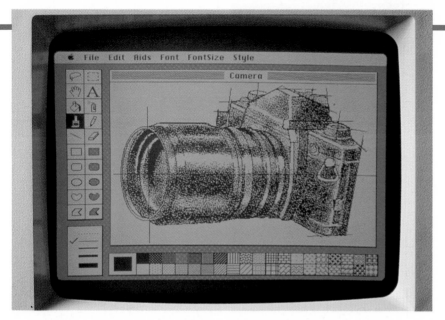

6 A graphics system is used to create a conceptual design of a camera lens.

7 Marketing and engineering personnel work together to develop a conceptual design of an automobile.

8   *A conceptual automobile design shown in an environmental setting.*

9   *A computer simulation of use of a conceptual automobile design.*

10 *A conceptual design of a software product being tested in an IBM software usability laboratory.*

Enter name of screen display file to save:PROJECT.003_

11 *A conceptual design of an apartment building.*

12 A CAD (computer-assisted design) system used for detailed design of an electronic circuit.

13 A CAD system used to analyze stresses in bridge design.

14 *A CAD system for detailed architectural design.*

15 *A CAD system for design of a multicomponent product.*

16 *Checking tolerances using a CAD system.*

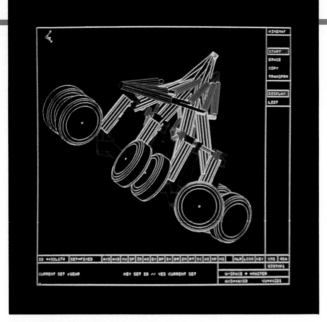

17 *A CAD-supported design of aircraft landing gear.*

18 *A three-dimensional picture of an automobile exhaust manifold.*

19 Checking tolerances using three-dimensional graphics.

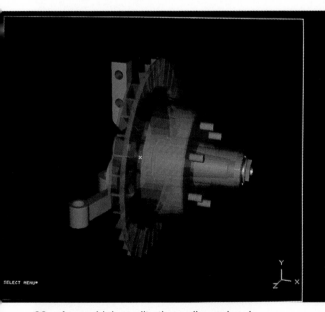

20 A very high quality three-dimensional visualization of a part design. Observe simulated shadows.

21 A circuit diagram drawn by a computer system.

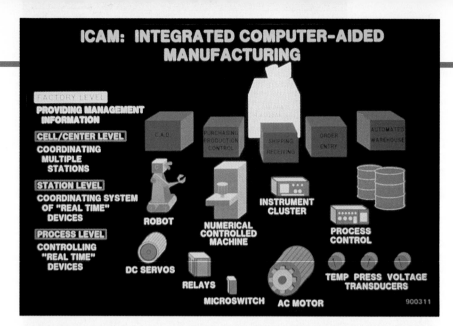

22 Example roles for information systems in computer-assisted manufacturing (CAM).

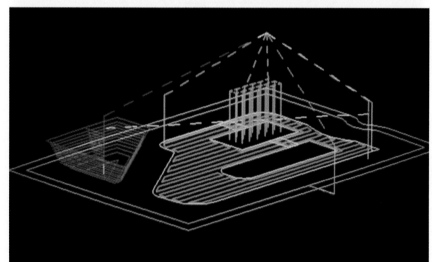

23 Using a CAM system to plan the order of activities of a numerically controlled (NC) cutting machine.

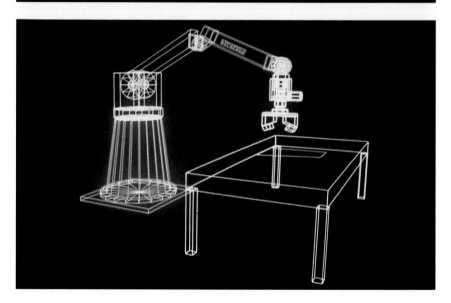

24 A CAM system portrays the configuration of an NC cutting

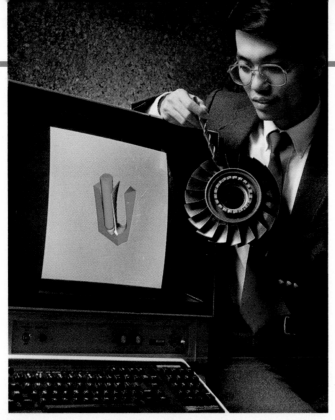

25 *A computer system simulates the action of an NC-controlled cutter. This system is used to verify correctness of NC programs.*

26 *A numerically controlled machine making a spot weld.*

27 *Robots are trained by a human operator to pick up and pass an object.*

2

28, 29, 30 *A robot used to assemble an IBM portable computer.*

29

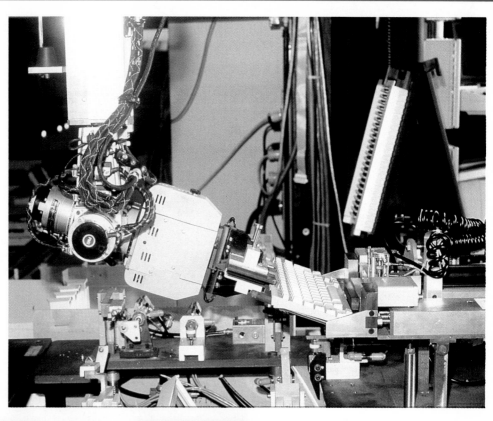

30

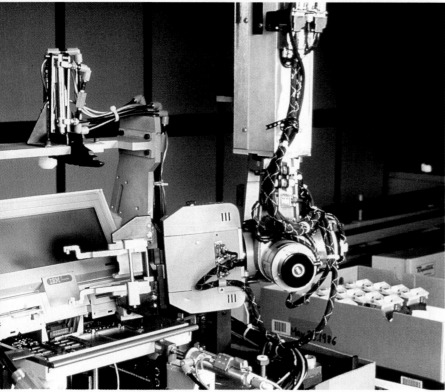

31 An assembly line of welder robots.

32 Robots can be used in environments that are too uncomfortable or hazardous for human workers.

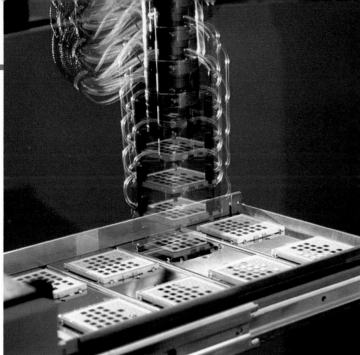

33 A robot tester subjects electronic components to repeated impacts.

34 A CAM system used to record completion of a production task and to determine the next task in manufacturing a Boeing 747.

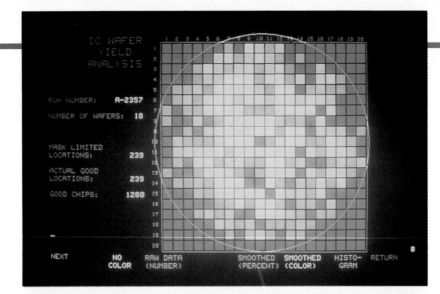

35 *Graphical display of quality assurance data.*

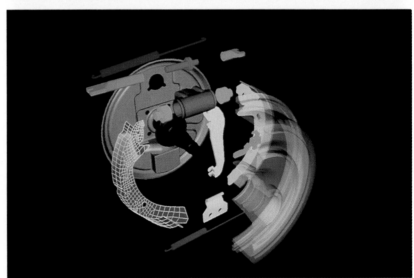

36 *A computer-drawn schematic used for repair documentation.*

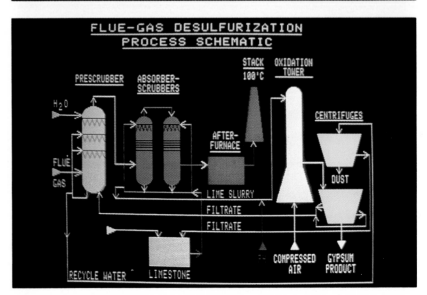

37 *A computer-drawn schematic documents an industrial chemical process.*

The Data Processing (DP) Division The **data processing division,** or as it is sometimes called, the organizational systems division, has the responsibility for developing, operating, and maintaining organizational information systems. As shown in Figure 11-13, this division normally has a development group, an operations group, and a systems support group. Then, too, there is generally a data administration group that provides a staff function to the DP director.

The **development group** consists of systems analysts and programmers who work with users to create organizational information systems. Normally, a senior systems analyst is the leader of a systems development project, although in some cases, a senior end user is the leader.

The systems analysts guide the project through all five of the stages described in Chapter 8. Systems analysts are responsible for ensuring that all five components of an information system are properly developed.

Programming personnel, on the other hand, are concerned only with the program components and possibly with data and hardware as they relate to programs. As you know, application programs can be purchased from a vendor or they can be written in-house. If they are written in-house, there will most likely be a team of from two or three to several dozen programmers creating the programs.

In addition to creating the system, the development group typically is responsible for maintaining the system. This term may conjure up an image of people in bib overalls holding a dripping oil can over a hot machine, but that is not what it means. Instead it refers to the process of changing the system to meet new requirements (or to make the system do what the users really wanted to begin with). In some organizations, more people and resources are used for system maintenance than for system creation.

The **operations group** runs the computer hardware. This group normally consists of several shifts of computer operators. It may also include a data entry group if the organization requires one, and several data control clerks who control the receipt and dispersement of data to and from the data center. Operations normally manages the tape or other data library as well, and sometimes it includes a hardware maintenance group.

The **systems support group** consists of highly technical programmers who select, install, tune, and otherwise maintain systems software. This software includes the operating system, the communications control program (and other teleprocessing software), the DBMS, systems utilities, and other programs. Normally, the programmers in this group are very talented; often they have advanced degrees in computer science (systems analysts and application programmers normally have degrees in information systems).

We discussed the need for data administration in the last chapter. As mentioned there, all shared data systems require such administration. For group or departmental systems, the administration is normally done from within the group. For systems that span several departments, this arrangement is unworkable. Usually such data administration is done by the MIS department.

Figure 11-13 shows the **data administration group** as a staff function under the DP director. This group acts in the role of custodian or trustee of the organization's data. Its functions include establishing data conventions and standards, managing the configuration of organizational databases, ensuring that adequate backup and recovery procedures exist and are followed, ensuring that adequate security controls and procedures exist, and performing any other tasks needed to protect the organization's data asset.

Data conventions and standards are required for data consistency. While there may be many views of data, and while data may occur in many different systems, the organization needs a standard set of data definitions and formats. Consider, for example, a product number. The organization needs to have one standard set of product numbers with one standard set of meanings. If several different product-numbering schemes are allowed to develop, chaos will result. One department or function will be unable to communicate with another. Sometimes it is not possible to gain consistency. In these cases, the inconsistencies should be defined and documented.

Organizations are dynamic; they change in response to both external and internal stimuli. As they change, it is often necessary to alter the structure of organizational databases. Since such databases are shared, however, this change must be accomplished so as to minimize the consequences on other systems and applications.

Data administration is an important function. Much has been written about it; see Lyon[21] in particular.

The End User Support Division   The purpose of the **end user support division** is to help end users employ computer technology to solve their own problems. Whereas the DP division creates, maintains, and operates systems *for* users, the end user support division helps end users to help themselves to create and operate both personal and group-level applications.

You learned in Chapter 8 that end users can develop many of their own personal information systems. It is less likely, however, that they will develop their own departmental or other group-level systems. For such systems, end users typically obtain the support of an outside consultant or a professional within the MIS department. If the former approach is taken, then the end user support division will often help in selecting such a person or company. If the latter approach is taken, then normally someone from end user support provides development expertise and, when necessary, personnel from the development group in the DP division get involved.

End user support divisions are organized in many different ways. The organization shown in Figure 11-13 is one arrangement; you may encounter others. Here, there is a group doing research and development. The function of this group is to keep pace with the rapid growth in technology, products, and services available from the microcomputer and end-user support industries. This group typically evaluates new

21. John K. Lyon, *The Database Administrator* (New York: John Wiley, 1976).

releases and new products and determines if they offer potential benefits to the company. They also have a crucial role in setting organizational standards.

Many MIS departments operate their own company microcomputer store. Large companies are often able to negotiate dealer status with many vendors. The advantage of this is that the MIS department is then able to buy products at the same price as dealers can. Large companies might buy as many copies of, say, a spreadsheet program as a small dealer would. Since this is the case, they want the same price breaks as a dealer gets.

The third group shown in Figure 11-13 is the support group. This group provides consulting and training services to end users. It may also provide a limited amount of development service. For example, an accounts payable department may be able to get along perfectly well with the standard features of a spreadsheet program for all but 5 percent of its workload. For that 5 percent, however, personnel in that department need specialized programs or macros. Rather than involving DP development personnel, many companies use personnel in the end user support group to provide this service. Custom development is generally restricted to a few hours or workdays of labor.

Information Centers

As indicated earlier in this chapter, the character of DSS applications is considerably different from that of other information systems. Because of this, some companies have a special DSS support organization. This organization is often called an **information center**.

11.4   INCREASING YOUR PERSONAL PRODUCTIVITY

Opportunities for Expert Systems

Expert systems are still uncharted territory for many IS managers. The following are a few pointers from managers with first-hand expert systems experience on how to identify and manage opportunities for the technology.

- Identify project needs ahead of time, and specify exactly what it is the system is supposed to do. Don't start with a blue-sky idea and hope the expert system can do most of it.
- Appoint someone to be in charge of expert systems technology for the organization. It's important enough and com-

plex enough an area to warrant a full-time position at larger organizations.
- Don't proceed without a solid and well-thought-out commitment from the highest levels of the organization, otherwise, projects could be torpedoed by erratic funding or by disappointed executives with unrealistic expectations.
- Do extensive pilot testing and validation of the expert system's knowledge base. Even experts don't yet fully understand all the ways in which an expert system can go wrong.

- Do a standard cost/benefit analysis of all projects. Although payoffs will be harder to predict as precisely as those from conventional projects, don't build all your justification around vague, serendipitous benefits.
- Select only projects that have an unusually high payoff-to-cost ratio. As with all young technologies, expert systems are likely to be far less expensive to build in just a few years, so it makes sense to put off all but a few low-risk projects for now.

An information center provides facilities to support the development, operation, and maintenance of DSS applications. Such a department may operate its own mini- or mainframe computer or it may support users in acquiring their own hardware resources. Additionally, information centers provide DSS programs and libraries both of models and of other DSS data. Such centers also provide a professional staff.

The staff in an information center is analogous to the staff in an organizational MIS department. There are personnel involved in supporting DSS operations, others for developing and supporting programs, and still others for data administration. There are also consultants who assist users in the utilization of the information center's resources.

Questions

11.32 Explain why users are not a homogeneous group.

11.33 What is a key user and what functions does such a person serve?

11.34 Why should the MIS department report to the CEO rather than to the VP of finance or any other VP?

11.35 What are the two major functions of the MIS department? What are the two major divisions of the MIS department?

11.36 What is the function of the data processing division? What groups does it normally contain?

11.37 Sketch the organization of the data processing division.

11.38 Explain the functions of the data administration group.

11.39 What is the function of the end user support division?

11.40 Give an example of the organization of an end user support division.

11.41 What is an information center? What function does it serve? How do information centers relate to DSSs?

11.42 Summarize the issues involved in the organizational placement of an information center.

11.43 How does the organization of the MIS department in a smaller company vary from that in a larger company?

Organizational Placement of the Information Center The relationship between the information center and the corporate MIS department is an interesting one. In some companies, the information center resides within the MIS department. In that case, the information center is a smaller MIS department within the MIS department.

There are two problems with this arrangement. First, transaction-oriented and decision support applications are antithetical. They are like oil and water; the first focuses on control and the second focuses on flexibility. This difference creates a number of difficult management problems. Second, when the information center is located within the MIS department, it tends to lose its value to its customers; the DSS management becomes more responsive to the needs of the MIS department than it is to the needs of the DSS users.

Because of these problems, many companies pull the information center out of the MIS department and establish it as a staff function under the president or CEO. Figure 11-14 shows the arrangement of the MIS and DSS functions for Amalgamated Mining.

The problem with separating the two functions is that they tend to step on one another's toes. There is a continuing turf battle over which department has the authority to perform which services. The MIS department tends to wage an insidious battle to pull the information center inside.

It is impossible to say unequivocally which arrangement is better, since the answer depends on the company, the roles of the departments, and the personalities of key personnel. It is true, however, that the information center and the MIS department are often at odds, and if the DSS manager reports to the MIS manager, the losers in the battle tend to be the DSS customers. Therefore, in many circumstances, a separation of the two is preferred.

DSS Personnel in the Absence of an Information Center If the organization does not have a separate information center, then selected personnel within the MIS department are sometimes identified as DSS experts. They form the core of teams created to develop or operate DSS applications. The same job descriptions exist as described in the last section; the personnel would be taken from a number of departments within MIS for the duration of the DSS project.

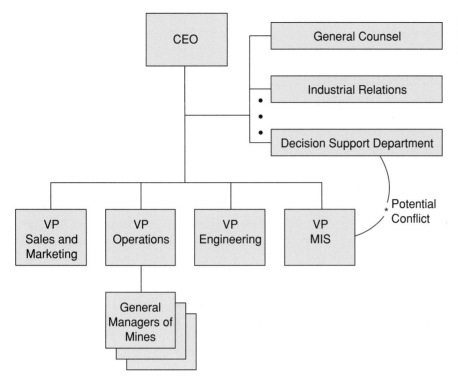

Figure 11-14
Organizational relationship of Amalgamated Mining's DSS and MIS departments

MIS Organizations in Smaller Companies

As mentioned at the start of this section, the organization shown in Figure 11-13 is typical for large organizations. For smaller companies, some of these functions will be combined as shown in Figure 11-15. For example, in the DP division, the data administration and systems support functions may be performed by one group. For reasons of control, however, it is never a good idea to combine the operations and development groups.

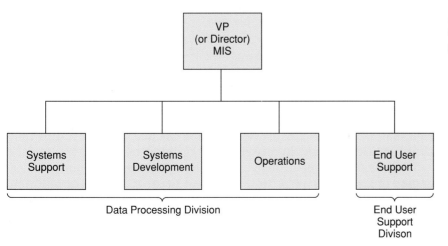

Figure 11-15
Organization of MIS department in a smaller company

In the end user support division, smaller companies do not operate their own computer store. Further, the research and development group may be combined with the support group. In very small organizations, the functions of the entire end user support division may be performed by the development group in the DP division. In this case, the MIS department and the DP division become one and the same.

Summary

The term *management information system* has two meanings. The narrow one refers to a type of information system that produces regular and recurring reports. The second meaning, and the one used in this chapter, refers to the development and use of effective information systems in organizations.

Information systems are effective if they provide a competitive advantage. They can do this by facilitating internal and external operations. With regard to internal operations, information systems can facilitate three levels of activity: day-to-day operations, management control, and strategic planning. Figure 11-1 shows a grid of activity versus degree of structure. Different system types satisfy different business situations, as summarized in Figure 11-2.

Information systems can facilitate external operations by improving the organization's product. This can be done by improving the quality of the information component of the product or by improving the delivery of the product. The benefits of information systems are summarized in Figure 11-4.

MISs deal with the role of information systems in organizations. Three levels of organization are important. Information systems operate at the organization-wide level, at the workgroup (or department) level, and at the personal level. At each of these levels, the benefits shown in Figure 11-4 apply. This framework is important because it provides a means for thinking about the role of information systems at all three levels of use.

The functions shown in Figure 11-4 are, in large measure, related to business processes, that is, doing, measuring, and responding. Some situations are more decision oriented; they require responses to unanticipated opportunities or problems. Decision support systems support managers in such situations.

A DSS is an interactive computer-based system which facilitates the solution of unstructured problems. DSSs are sets of capabilities that assist decision making in unstructured problem domains.

We considered four dimensions in the DSS task environment. The degree of structure refers to the amount of structure in the solution process and not the amount in the problem itself. The level of application can be operational, management control, or strategic planning.

The phase of decision process can be during intelligence gathering, alternative development, or choice. Finally, recurrency refers to the number of times the DSS is used. On one end of the recurrency spectrum are DSSs that are used only once, to solve a particular problem. On the other end of the spectrum are DSSs that are used for regularly recurring situations.

There are three major components to DSS programs: user dialogue management, model management, and data management. Dialogue management maintains the interface with the user. Model management maintains data and programmatic representations of the business. Data management maintains the DSS database and interfaces with other sources of data such as TPS databases and data utilities.

Group decision support systems (GDSSs) are employed by users, as a group. A number of GDSS architectures have been developed. The architecture used depends on the recurrency of the DSS and the geographical location of users, as shown in Figure 11-10.

The functions of DSS applications include becoming familiar with the problem domain, determining the sensitivity of results to changes in decision variables, identifying patterns, predicting decision outcomes, developing models of business processes, computing optimum mixes, and facilitating group communication.

Both users and information systems professionals have a role in the management of information systems. Users have a variety of attitudes about information systems. Some wish they would go away; others are content to learn the minimum they need to know to perform their job; still others take an active interest in systems and become key users.

MIS professionals work in the MIS department. The functions of the MIS department are to develop, operate, maintain, and manage organizational information systems and to acquire technology and facilitate its transfer to appropriate applications. This department should report directly to the CEO. Reporting at lower levels tends to bias the information services provided.

There are two major divisions within the MIS department. The DP division has responsibility for developing, operating, and maintaining organizational information systems. This division normally has development, operations, system support, and data administration groups. The end user support division helps end users employ computer technology to accomplish their jobs. This division can be organized in many ways. One feasible organization has a research and development group, a microcomputer store, and a support group.

An information center is a department that supports the development and use of DSS applications. The information center can reside within the MIS department or it can be separate from it. Neither alternative is superior to the other in all cases.

The MIS organization described in this chapter pertains to large organizations. Small companies combine the departments shown in Figure 11-13, resulting in an organization like that shown in Figure 11-15.

Word List

management information
   system (MIS) (*two definitions*)
organizational information
   system
operational control
management control
strategic planning
structured activity
unstructured activity
recurrency
dialogue management

model management
data management
group decision support system
   (GDSS)
decision room
teleconferencing
key user
data processing (DP) division
system maintenance

development group
operations group
systems support group
data administration group
end user support division
information center

Discussion Questions and Exercises

A. Suppose you are hired as a consultant by Valley Swimming, a company that runs your local community swimming pool. Valley Swimming (VS) operates an indoor pool year-round and an outdoor pool between May 1 and September 30. The company staffs these pools with attendants and lifeguards. It also runs a swimming instruction program and offers classes for people of all ages. In addition it sponsors a swimming league.

Construct what you think would be an appropriate organization chart for VS. Describe examples of operational, management control, and strategic planning activities for this organization. List the products produced by VS.

Describe an organization-wide information system, a workgroup (or departmental) information system, and a personal information system that might be used at Valley Swimming. Describe the benefits that would accrue from these systems in terms of the framework in Figure 11-4.

B. Suppose that Valley Swimming (in question A above) is considering opening another pool facil-

ity just like one it already operates. VS wants to know whether or not it should do this. List the issues that should be considered in answering this question. Give an example of DSS facilities that could be used to address these issues. Describe the degree of structure, level of application, phase of decision process, and recurrency of your DSS. Summarize how your DSS might be used to accomplish each of the functions for a DSS described in this chapter.

C. Reread the section on user departments under the heading "The Management of Information Systems." Also, review Figures 11-13 and 11-15. With this context in mind, describe three different jobs that involve information systems technology. Explain the functions of each of these jobs and describe the knowledge you think a person would need in order to be successful in these jobs. Would you be interested in these jobs? Why or why not?

CHAPTER 12

Developing Multiuser Information Systems

CHAPTER OUTLINE

This chapter deals with the development of multiuser information systems. It extends the discussion of systems development presented in Chapter 8 to the multiuser setting. In the first part of this chapter, we will reconsider the five stages in the systems development process and see how those stages are different for multiuser systems development than they are for personal systems development. Next, we will consider the use and development of two tools: dataflow diagrams and prototypes. Such tools are exceedingly useful for understanding, modeling, and documenting the requirements and the flow of activity in a department or organization. Finally, we will introduce CASE, or computer-assisted systems engineering, a set of methodologies and tools that facilitate systems development, especially the development of larger, more complicated systems.

As you read this chapter, place yourself in the role of a manager or other key participant in the development activity. Assume that someday you will participate in the creation of a multiuser information system. When that occurs, you need to know what to do. Continually ask yourself, How would I do that? How would I proceed?

As with the discussion in Chapter 8, this chapter sets out one possible system development process. There are many such processes; the one described here is not necessarily the best one. It is simply one process that works.

The Five-Stage Systems Development Process

The process used to develop a multiuser information system is not fundamentally different from the process used to develop a personal information system. Some of the stages are more complicated, and some need to be more carefully documented and reviewed, but the fundamental actions remain the same. Thus, in this chapter, you need only augment the knowledge you gained from Chapter 8.

As in that chapter, we will consider each of the stages in order. We devote most of our discussion to the definition and requirements stages since those are the stages in which you are likely to have the largest role.

Problem Definition Stage

As described in Chapter 8, there are three major tasks in the definition stage: define the problem, assess feasibility, and build a plan.

Problem Definition Problems are harder to define in multiuser information system settings than in personal information system settings. There are two reasons for this. First, a problem is a perceived difference between what is and what ought to be. Since there are many people in a multiuser setting, there can be many perceptions. In most cases, at the onset of the project there will be several, if not many, different perceptions of the problem. Unless the developer is very lucky, a system designed to solve one perceived problem will not solve the other perceived problems. In such a situation, when the developer has finished and is waiting for the applause, he or she may receive, instead, catcalls from those people whose perceived problems remain unsolved.

Thus, when developing multiuser information systems, the developer must obtain a definition of the problem that is understood and accepted by the entire community of users, or at least by the influential people in that community. This means that the problem definition will need to be documented, presented to key people for feedback, and, if necessary, adjusted. If this is not done, the entire development effort may be directed toward the wrong goal.

The second reason why problem definition is more difficult in multiuser than in personal settings is that the business systems themselves are more complicated. There are more people involved, there are more activities, and there is typically more data, not just in volume but also in variety. This complexity means that it will be more difficult to determine both what is and what should be. Problem definition will thus be harder and more time-consuming.

Dataflow diagrams are one way of expressing the fundamental nature of a business system in a manner that can be readily comprehended. Such diagrams can express both what is and what should be. You will see examples of this later in this chapter.

Feasibility Assessment   The second major task in the definition stage is assessing feasibility. In Chapter 8 we discussed three dimensions of feasibility: cost, schedule, and technical. These three dimensions apply to multiuser information systems development just as much as they apply to personal information systems development. An additional dimension of feasibility must be considered in relation to multiuser systems: political feasibility.

Cost and schedule feasibility may be more difficult to assess for multiuser systems than for personal systems, because the scale of the system is larger. There are more cost factors to consider and, with regard to schedule, there are more people and activities to be coordinated. Still, the fundamental activities are the same as presented in Chapter 8. This is also true for assessing technical feasibility.

In a multiuser information system, the assessment of political feasibility must address the social dynamics of the group or groups involved. Influential personnel must endorse the project. So often in groups, people can make of a system what they want to make of it. If the system is considered positively, people will tend to make it work. If it is considered negatively, the system will fail, no matter how well designed it is.

Group norms often dictate members' response to the new system. Developers need to pay attention to such norms and to work within them, as much as possible. In conflicts between system use and group norms, the norms always win, sooner or later.

Finally, do not assume that a system judged politically feasible by management is politically feasible to employees. Often management does not understand the dynamics of the group. The best way to assess political feasibility among group members is to ask them.

Figure 12-1
Considerations for definition stage

- Problem Definition
    Harder for multiuser system than for personal system because
        a. Several perceptions of the problem may exist
        b. Business systems more complicated
    Need to set realistic expectations

- Feasibility Assessment
    Cost, schedule, and technical feasibility components harder to
        assess because multiuser system scale is larger than personal
        system scale
    Political feasibility must address social dynamics of the group

- Build Project Plan
    Multiuser system plan more complicated than personal system
        plan because of larger scale
    Must allow more time for review and discussion

Project Plan   The third task in the definition stage is to build a project plan. Here again, the work is not different from that for personal information systems, it is just more complicated. There will be more people involved and more activities to coordinate. This means, by the way, that having a project plan is all the more important.

In constructing the plan, far more time will need to be allowed for review, discussion, and possible rework. To be successful, a system must be understood, accepted, and supported. This means that key people will be given a chance to comment on and influence the development of the system. Such activity takes time and should be built into the schedule and plan. Considerations for the definition stage in the development of a multiuser information system are summarized in Figure 12-1.

Requirements Definition Stage

The tasks in the requirements stage are the same for multiuser information systems development as for personal information systems development, except that the tasks need to be expanded to account for the number of system users. The types of requirements to be identified were listed in Chapter 8 as output, input, system size, and constraints. These are summarized in Figure 12-2, together with an additional task that is needed for multiuser systems: documentation of the requirements.

Output Requirements   We determine output requirements by assessing what information people need to do their jobs. Different users have different jobs; they will have to make different decisions or commitments. A word processing operator, for example, might have to make a decision like, Can I finish this document and have it printed by four o'clock? To make this decision, the operator may want a system that

- Output
    - Recognize report differences that vary with amount of development activity required
    - Use prototype reports

- Input
    - Use standard forms to guide input requirements definition

- System Size
    - Assess degree of concurrent use of hardware and programs
    - Set response time requirements

- Constraints
    - Establish constraints on user duties and authorities
    - Do not allow new system to contravene established control procedures

- Documentation
    - Recognize need for user understanding, acceptance, and support of requirements
    - Allow time for review and discussion

Figure 12-2
Considerations for requirements stage

shows him or her what other work needs to be done, what jobs are in the print queue, and what other jobs in process will soon be in the print queue.

The shift supervisor, on the other hand, might need to make a decision about the competency of an employee. To do this, he or she wants the same system to show how much work has been done by each operator in a shift. The word processing department manager, meanwhile, needs to make a commitment to next year's budget. To do this, he or she wants the system to summarize the work done this quarter and compare it with a similar summary from prior quarters.

In developing output requirements, different system users need to be identified and interviewed. Further, their specific requirements in terms of menus, output displays, and reports need to be documented. Prototypes are especially useful, as you will see later in this chapter.

Input Requirements   In one way, the development of input requirements for a multiuser information system is easier than for a personal information system. Since there are many people in a multiuser system setting, the organization is more likely to use standard forms to control and coordinate its activity. These forms are a rich source of requirements for input data.

Consider the form in Figure 12-3. It is completed when an attorney leaves work to be done by the word processing department. Whoever designed this form considered that each of the data items is important. Unless the form is poorly designed, somewhere in the department, at

```
┌──────────────────────────────────────────────────────────────────────────┐
│                        Word Processing Work Request                        │
│                                              Job #:  _____    │
│                                                                            │
│   Date: _____        Requested by: _____  │
│                                                                            │
│   Time: _____          Phone: _____  │
│                                                                            │
│   Related Job Numbers: _____ │
│                                                                            │
│   Date Needed by: _____   Completed: _____   │
│                                                                            │
│   Description: _____ │
│                                                                            │
│            _____ │
│                                                                            │
│            _____ │
│                                                                            │
│            _____ │
│                                                                            │
│            _____ │
│                                                                            │
│   Operator: _____     Supervisor Approval: _____  │
│                                                                            │
│   Special Equipment: _____ │
│                                                                            │
│   Number of Pages: _____   Number of Copies: _____   │
└──────────────────────────────────────────────────────────────────────────┘
```

Figure 12-3
Example of a standard form

some time, each data item in this form will be needed. Thus, standard forms can be used to develop a list of candidate input data items.

Standard forms also can be used to check the completeness of output requirements. If the department collects data on an input that does not show up on any of the output requirements, then that omission might indicate that either (1) some outputs were missed, or (2) the input is not actually needed, or (3) the data is needed by another system.

Sources of input documents and forms can be identified in several ways. Dataflow diagrams are most commonly used for this purpose; they will be discussed in the next section of this chapter.

Estimates of System Size All of the considerations for estimating the system size or **processing scale** of a personal information system also pertain to multiuser information systems. In addition, since multiuser systems involve multiple users, estimates of the degree of **concurrent workload** also need to be made, that is, estimates of how many users will be simultaneously using the hardware. Such hardware could be a LAN and its associated file server, or it could be a mini- or mainframe-based teleprocessing system. In fact, for some projects, it is not known at the time requirements are developed whether the system will involve LANs or teleprocessing.

In any case, part of the processing scale requirement is to determine the distribution of the number of concurrent hardware users. Questions like the following need to be answered: How many concurrent users will there be? How long will their sessions last? Over which hours of the day? On which days of the week? What will be the average number of users? What will be the maximum number of users?

Constraints The constraints described for personal information systems also pertain to multiuser information systems. There can also be additional constraints on procedures and on personnel that do not exist for personal applications.

Restrictions on duties and authorities are an example of the type of constraints that apply in a multiuser setting. In a department that produces negotiable instruments (like checks), usually one person authorizes payments while another person produces checks. If a single employee were allowed to both authorize payments and generate checks, a control weakness would exist. For example, the employee would be able to authorize and write checks to fictitious people. Thus, to strengthen control, duties and authorities are separated.

When such procedural restrictions are in place, the multiuser information system must support (or at least not counteract) them. Consequently, such constraints need to be made part of the requirements. We will discuss controls and the need for them in Module C.

Requirements Documentation and Review As stated, to be successful, a multiuser information system must have the understanding, acceptance, and support of the user group. To gain these, influential members of the user community must participate in requirements development. If such users are involved in requirements specification, then the requirements will be more accurate, and the users will be more committed to the project.

Once the requirements have been determined, they must be documented and reviewed. The particular form of the requirements documentation varies from project to project. Usually, the requirements are presented in the form of text descriptions, dataflow diagrams, prototype forms, reports, and menus, and any other descriptions or examples that illuminate the users' needs.

If the project will involve products or services from an outside vendor (and this is often the case), then the approved and accepted requirements are put in the form of a **request for proposal (RFP).** The RFP sets out the background of the project, the specific requirements (output, input, scale, and constraints), the overall schedule and dates, selection criteria, and other information that will be helpful to a vendor in preparing a proposal. Depending on the size and nature of the project, it is sometimes appropriate to have the corporation's legal counsel review the RFP. The characteristics of a good RFP are summarized in Figure 12-4.

Figure 12-4
Characteristics of a good request for
proposal (RFP)

- Clearly written

- Consistent

- Complete

- Describes
    Background, context, and processing environment
    Specific requirements
    Constraints on system
    Constraints on procurement process
    Needs, *not* solutions (unless a particular solution is required)
    General description of evaluation criteria
    Response dates
    Single point of contact for questions

Evaluation of Alternatives Stage

Most users do not play a substantial role in designing and implementing a multiuser information system. Instead, they provide guidance and direction and approve the initiation of work and the disbursement of funds.

This fact is a key difference between the development of a personal information system and the development of a multiuser information system. With a personal information system, you may perform your own design and implementation. For example, for a spreadsheet application, you might select the hardware and software yourself, learn how to use the software, design your own file directories, and build and implement your own spreadsheet applications.

With any but the simplest multiuser information systems, this is too much to expect of yourself. To build such a system yourself you would have to be an information systems professional, instead of a business professional in some non-MIS discipline.

Thus, when developing a multiuser information system, you will most likely employ a professional or a group to design and implement your system. This group might be employees of the MIS department of your own corporation, or it might be an outside contractor, or both.

Development with In-House Personnel If your project is developed in-house then a development team of users and MIS professionals design and implement the system (a team similar to this may already have been formed for the requirements stage). The users on this team serve as experts in the domain of the application; they clarify requirements and test various components of the system as the development proceeds. Users, who are the ultimate beneficiaries of the system, are responsible to ensure that the system is being developed effectively. If

Questions

12.1 List the five stages of the multiuser systems development process.

12.2 List the three major tasks of the definition stage.

12.3 Why is problem definition more difficult for multiuser systems than for personal systems? Give two reasons.

12.4 List the four dimensions of feasibility.

12.5 What crucial issue is involved in assessing political feasibility in a multiuser system?

12.6 What special consideration should be given to developing a project plan for a multiuser system?

12.7 List four kinds of requirements that need to be documented.

12.1 INCREASING YOUR PERSONAL PRODUCTIVITY

A Properly Planned Interview Can Be an Analyst's Best Tool

While the methods of obtaining useful information from the user vary greatly, the personal interview will bring the best results and best understanding, if conducted properly. The properly planned interview can be the analyst's best business tool in the tool kit.

An important key to excellent interviewing skills is the ability of the analyst to prepare to deal with the different personalities and attitudes of the people being interviewed. If the analyst can modify personal style to complement the personality of the interviewee, then a channel of communication will be established that will allow ideas to be effectively communicated and the needed information to be obtained.

Studies indicate that verbal messages convey 7%, intonations convey 38%, and body language conveys 55% of the total message. Body language is the key factor, and the alert and well-informed analyst and interviewer should take advantage of this fact during the interview.

Listening has specific goals as they relate to the interviewee as an employee:

1. To raise the level of employee motivation.

2. To increase the readiness of subordinates to accept change.
3. To improve the quality of all managerial decisions.
4. To develop teamwork and morale.

Active listening is characterized by a nonjudgmental attempt on one person's part to explore a problem. Use of body language that encourages openness and acceptance should motivate the employee to participate in the interview more fully, and this should be the interviewer's goal in obtaining information. As with other attitudes, openness encourages similar feelings in others.

---

it is not, then during development they need to bring to the attention of the professional developers any problematical issues.

During the evaluation stage, the development team assesses various approaches and architectures for the potential system. They then evaluate the alternatives and select one. Normally, the alternative consists of a brief specification of each of the five components of the information system. Sometimes the alternative is less detailed.

Development with Outside Vendors   If your project is being developed by an outside vendor, then you need to accomplish three major tasks. First, you must locate qualified vendors, describe your needs, and ask for a proposal. This is usually done via an RFP. Second, once you have the responses, you must evaluate them and select one. Finally, you must negotiate and sign a contract. Normally this involves the assistance of your organization's counsel or of outside counsel.

When working with outside vendors, it is a good idea to build review dates into your contract. It is even better to tie vendor payments to the successful completion of these reviews. During these reviews you have an opportunity to verify that the project is on track and on schedule. Tasks for the evaluation stage are summarized in Figure 12-5.

Design Stage

The evaluation stage is the transition stage. From that stage on, during both design and implementation, you become the manager (or involved user) and the consumer of someone else's expertise. Your responsibility

12.8 Why do users have different kinds of output requirements?

12.9 What documents facilitate the determination of input requirements in a multiuser system?

12.10 Explain what estimates need to be made concerning concurrent workload.

- In-House Development
    Form development team
    Assess alternative
        approaches and
        architectures
    Select one alternative

- Outside Vendor Development
    Identify qualified vendors
    Describe needs
    Request proposals (RFPs)
    Evaluate proposals
    Select a vendor
    Negotiate and sign contract

Figure 12-5
Tasks during evaluation stage

Figure 12-6
Considerations for design stage

- Manage as technical project
    Assess people
    Follow intuition
    Get help when necessary

- Procedures
    Check for completeness and feasibility
    Ensure data-entry and conversion procedures are appropriate

- People
    Review draft of new or altered job descriptions
    Prepare for personnel training

- Develop systems installation plan

Figure 12-6
Considerations for design stage

12.11 Give an example of a constraint that might exist for a multiuser system.

12.12 Why is it important to interview influential users? Why should they be involved in requirements reviews?

12.13 How does the user's role differ between the development of a personal information system and the development of a multiuser system?

12.14 Explain activities during the evaluation stage assuming the system is developed by in-house personnel.

12.15 Explain the activities during the evaluation stage assuming the system is developed by an outside vendor.

12.16 What is the user's responsibility during the design stage?

12.17 What should users do with regard to the design of the data, procedures, and people components?

12.18 What should users do with regard to the data, procedures, and people components during the implementation stage?

in these stages is to ensure that you are receiving what you want and need on a timely basis.

Thus, you will not develop the design. In fact, there are aspects of hardware, program, and data design that you need not even understand. But it is crucial that your developer understand them. Therefore, you should manage this activity as you manage the activity of any other technical effort. Assess people and their competency. When you suspect problems are developing, follow your intuition, involving someone who understands the technical details, if necessary.

Representatives of the user community should be given an opportunity to review and approve the design of the user interface. This includes menus, data entry forms, report layouts, and command sequences. While some of these components will have been established during requirements definition, it is important to verify that the developer has understood and incorporated these requirements. New elements of the user interface should receive thorough review.

You should understand the design of the procedural and people components. It should also be clear to you from the design how procedures will be established and maintained. You should be given a draft of the user job descriptions and an outline of user procedures. Review them to ensure they are complete and realistic. Take corrective action if they are not. Review the plans for personnel training. The system developers may view personnel issues as *your* problem. Manage this activity so as to cause it to become *our* problem.

Finally, during the design stage, your developer should begin a systems installation plan. Work with the developer to create this plan. Do not take the plunge approach. Instead, investigate the pilot, piecemeal, and parallel strategies. In a multiuser setting, probably the parallel method is the most frequently used. You should have the basic installation events decided by the end of the design stage. Considerations for the design stage of the development of a multiuser information system are listed in Figure 12-6.

Implementation Stage

As with design, during the implementation stage you are the manager of others' activities. As stated in Chapter 8, each of the five components is obtained, installed, and tested separately, then the system is integrated and tested. Finally, you convert to the new system.

Hardware is installed and tested first, followed by programs. You should ensure that this activity takes place as scheduled. If schedule delays develop, do not allow test procedures to be abbreviated so as to make up lost time. Better to be late than to accept defective components that will cause operational problems once your department has become dependent on the system.

During implementation, data is entered and verified. Here again, manage this activity to ensure that it occurs on a timely basis. Do not let verification procedures be abbreviated.

Procedures are documented during this stage. As this is done, review the procedures yourself and with key members of your staff. Ensure that the procedures are realistic and that you have scheduled sufficient training for users to learn the procedures.

Finally, you should hire and train new employees (if necessary) and ensure that existing employees are receiving adequate training. Again, check that the quality of the training is appropriate. If not, take corrective action. Follow up on these items while the system is in development. Do not wait for problems to develop after installation. The best way to solve a problem is not to let it occur!

Once each of the five components has been installed and tested, the system is ready for a dress rehearsal. Your job as manager is to make certain that the rehearsal occurs on schedule, to ensure that adequate time is allocated to it, and to evaluate the results of the rehearsal. From this evaluation you make the decision either to implement the system or to rework some of the components.

Once you are satisfied with the results of the dress rehearsal(s), you can initiate your systems installation plan. This installation plan should have been developed during the design stage and modified as the components were installed. Again, for most situations, the parallel method of installation is preferred. The tasks for the implementation stage are summarized in Figure 12-7.

- Hardware
    Install
    Test

- Programs
    Install
    Test

- Data
    Enter
    Verify

- Procedures
    Document

- People
    Hire
    Train

- Dress Rehearsal
    Run system with all five
        components
    Repeat, if necessary

- Installation
    Use parallel, piecemeal,
        or pilot, *not* plunge

Figure 12-7
Tasks during implementation stage

Dataflow Diagrams

Multiuser information systems are more complicated than personal information systems because they involve the interaction of many people who maintain complex relationships with one another. This complexity makes it difficult to define the problem to be solved and to develop the system's requirements. **Dataflow diagrams** are tools that can be used to document the business activity and the interaction among employees. Obviously these diagrams do not make the system any less complex. They do, however, provide a means for developers to deal with this complexity.

In this section, you will learn how to create dataflow diagrams. This modeling skill will benefit you in the development of multiuser information systems applications and in any other activity that requires you to understand and model the flow of data (and work) within an office.

The Need for Dataflow Diagrams

The purpose of a dataflow diagram is to identify and record the essence of office processing by representing the flow of data among departments, functions, and people. A dataflow diagram is a snapshot of the data movement in an organization (or department).

Dataflow diagrams do not show logic. They are unlike flowcharts, pseudocode, and other tools used for documenting program logic. For example, consider the portion of a dataflow diagram shown for a credit union in Figure 12-8. Among other things, this diagram indicates that two forms are produced by a process labeled Credit Evaluation. One form is labeled Loan Acceptance and the second is labeled Loan Rejection. The dataflow diagram indicates that both items flow out of the process and go to a Customer. But the dataflow diagram does not show the conditions under which either form is sent. That is not the purpose of the dataflow diagram.

Imagine a snapshot of the trains and subways in Manhattan at 5:00 p.m. Suppose the picture shows two trains emerging from a tunnel. The snapshot shows the trains emerging, but it does not show why. The snapshot simply documents the fact that two trains leave the tunnel at that time of day. Dataflow diagrams are like this snapshot, but they show the movement of data.

Dataflow diagrams are a popular tool used by professional systems developers. There are many rules and constraints in the construction of these diagrams. Some people believe it is important to be quite rigid and compulsive in following these rules and constraints. For professional systems developers, this may be true.

You, however, are not a professional systems developer, and this discussion is not aimed at making you one. Instead, we will present the essence of dataflow diagramming and show you the symbols and enough of the methods and rules so that you can document the activity in your office or review a dataflow diagram someone else drew. Be aware that

Figure 12-8
Portion of a dataflow diagram

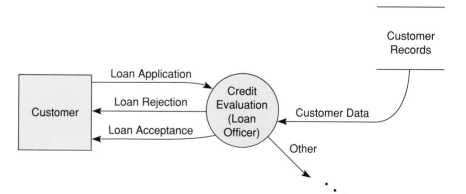

the diagrams you construct with this knowledge may not be "pure." They will be useful, however, and to teach you all of the rules would take more space than is appropriate in this text. You can learn more about this technique by taking a systems development class.

The Basic Dataflow Symbols

Figure 12-9 is an example dataflow diagram. This diagram shows the flow of data in the customer support department of a software publisher (such as Microsoft or Lotus). Observe that there are four types of symbols in this diagram: rectangles, circles, arrows, and pairs of horizontal lines.

Rectangles represent offices, departments, companies, or people that are *external* to the department or office being modeled. Such entities are called sources and sinks. A **source** is an external entity that produces a dataflow. A **sink** is an external entity that absorbs a dataflow. Besides their name and the dataflows they produce or absorb, nothing else needs to be documented about sources and sinks.

The second symbol type is a *circle*. Circles represent offices, departments, processes, or people that are *internal* to the department or office being modeled. Circles are sometimes called **bubbles.**

Figure 12-9
Dataflow diagram customer support department

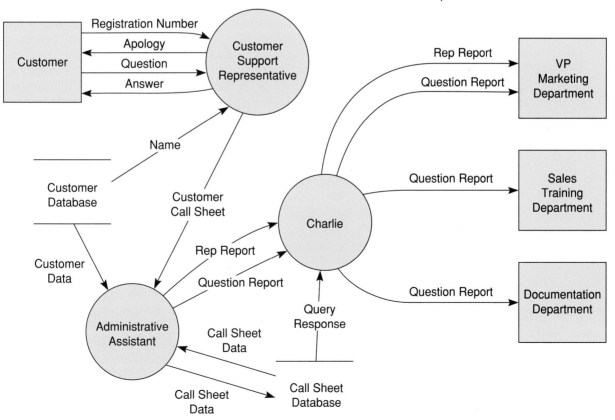

Bubbles can be general, like Customer Support Representative, or specific, like Charlie. To purists, a chart should have only one type of bubble. Charts that have only generalized titles are called **logical dataflow diagrams;** those that have only specific titles are called **physical dataflow diagrams.**

We will mix and match bubble types, using whichever is most appropriate in each case. Thus, in Figure 12-9, we do not name the customer support reps, although we do name the manager (Charlie). We do this because it best represents how the workers in this office understand their environment.

Some people believe that bubbles should contain only processes. Thus the bubble Customer Support Representative should be labeled Customer Support Process. Sometimes relabeling bubble names with process names does, in fact, improve the meaning of the chart. Other times it does not matter. As you name bubbles, be aware of this distinction; when you label a bubble with a job title, ask yourself whether the chart would be more understandable if you used the name of a process instead.

The third symbol type is a *labeled arrow*, representing a dataflow. In the upper left hand corner of Figure 12-9, there is an arrow labeled Registration Number. The arrow emerges from the Customer rectangle and flows into the Customer Support Representative bubble. The arrow means that a data item, registration number, is provided by the customer to the customer support representative. The medium of the flow is not shown. This number could be provided verbally over the telephone, in writing on a request form, or in some other manner. In general, no media are shown in dataflow diagrams.

Sometimes dataflows are single data items such as a registration number. Sometimes they are forms or documents. The dataflow going from the circle labeled Charlie to the rectangle labeled VP Marketing Department represents a report. At times we even show the flow of physical entities, such as shipments, on dataflow diagrams. Strictly speaking, such physical items do not belong on dataflow diagrams; however, we include them when their presence adds to the clarity and communicative value of the diagram.

The fourth and last symbol type is a *pair of horizontal lines* with a file name between them. This symbol represents a **file,** that is, an entity in which data is stored. All the processes that read and write a file might not appear on one page. As a consequence, a file may appear to be read-only or write-only.

In Figure 12-9, the file Customer Database appears to be read-only— the only dataflows are out of the file. From this single diagram it appears that data is being spontaneously generated; actually, it is not. This situation simply means that the process that writes to the file is shown in some other dataflow diagram. Similarly, all dataflows in a particular diagram may flow into a file. In such a case, the process that reads the file will be shown in some other dataflow diagram.

The four symbol types are summarized in Figure 12-10. These are all of the symbols used in dataflow diagrams. This modest set is actually

Symbol	Meaning

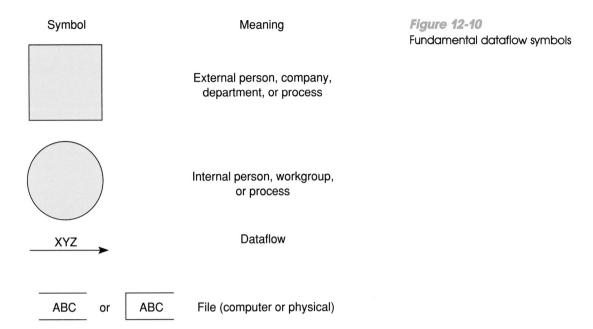

Figure 12-10
Fundamental dataflow symbols

External person, company, department, or process

Internal person, workgroup, or process

Dataflow

File (computer or physical)

quite powerful; it can be used to model a great many different offices, activities, and situations. We will now consider the process of creating dataflow diagrams.

Building Dataflow Diagrams

Creating a dataflow diagram is an artistic process. We cannot specify a set of rules which will enable you to create an accurate and communicative diagram every time. What we can do is discuss a number of principles and illustrate them with examples. From these you will gain a sense of how to proceed.

First, building a dataflow diagram is an iterative process. Start with lots of paper and expect to make mistakes. Plan on doing four or five or six different versions of the same diagram. The human mind is iterative in its processing, and you won't know exactly what to do until you have learned what not to do. Be patient with yourself.

Second, start anywhere. Work until you do not know what to do next, then start again someplace else. Keep working until you have connected all of your different starts. You can work from the top down (from the big picture to the detail level), or from the bottom up (from the detail to the big picture), or both, in alternation.

Third, do not expect to get everything into a single diagram. It will not fit. Instead, consider the levels of the company, and work level by level. Figure 12-11 shows a very high-level chart of Jenson-Kehrwald Company (JKC), the landscape design company first discussed in Chapter 1. The chart depicts the relationship of JKC to its customers and its vendors. While this is not too informative, it is a start. Since this diagram depicts the dataflow at the highest level, it is labeled Level 1.

Figure 12-11
Level 1 dataflow diagram

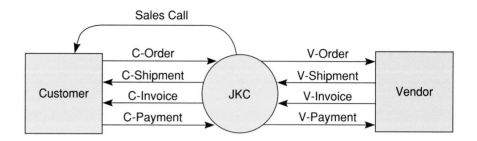

We will now blow up the JKC bubble and show departments within the company. This next diagram will be called Level 2, since it shows the dataflow at the next level down. The process of exploding a bubble in this way is called **leveling**.

Figure 12-12 shows the processes or bubbles involved in the purchasing function at JKC. The processes are Salesperson, Purchasing, Accounting, Receiving, Order Processing, and Showroom.

Figure 12-12
Level 2 dataflow diagram

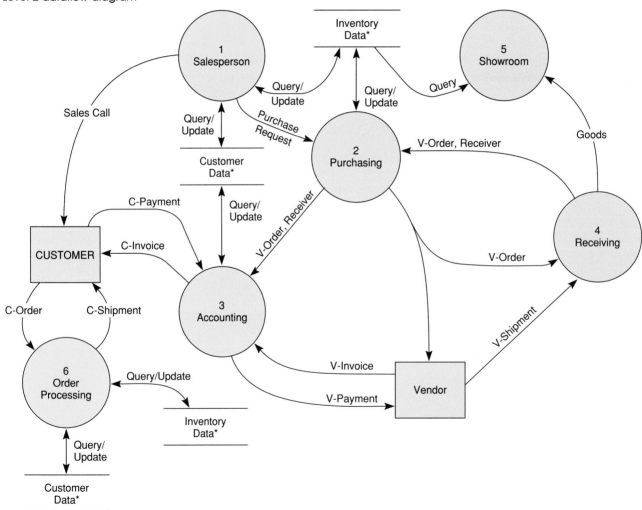

Figure 12-12 shows the dataflows among these bubbles. Observe that this diagram also includes Customer and Vendor, external entities from Level 1. Observe further that the dataflows into and out of Customer and Vendor are the same as they were at Level 1. (Customer receives Sales Calls, generates C-Orders and C-Payments, and accepts C-Shipments and C-Invoices. Vendor accepts V-Orders and V-Payments and generates V-Shipments and V-Invoices.) This makes sense. No dataflows to externals should disappear or be created just because we have expanded the bubble.

In fact, you can use this phenomenon as a way of checking your work. When you have finished a lower-level diagram, check that your diagram includes all of the dataflows in and out of the higher-level bubble. If not, you missed something. If there are new dataflows, then you should add them to the next-higher-level diagram. (There is one exception to this. Some dataflows that have to do with rare and unusual cases are sometimes shown on the detailed dataflow diagram and not on the higher-level diagram. This is done since the higher-level diagram is intended to show the normal flow of work; if all exception conditions are shown at higher levels, then the diagram can become crowded and confusing.)

Figure 12-13 shows a Level 3 diagram that is an explosion of the Purchasing bubble in Figure 12-12. Observe the numbers on the bubbles. In Figure 12-12, Purchasing is labeled as process 2. At the next level down, in Figure 12-13, the bubbles within Purchasing are labeled 2.1, 2.2, and so forth. This numbering system is carried down to the

Figure 12-13
Level 3 dataflow diagram

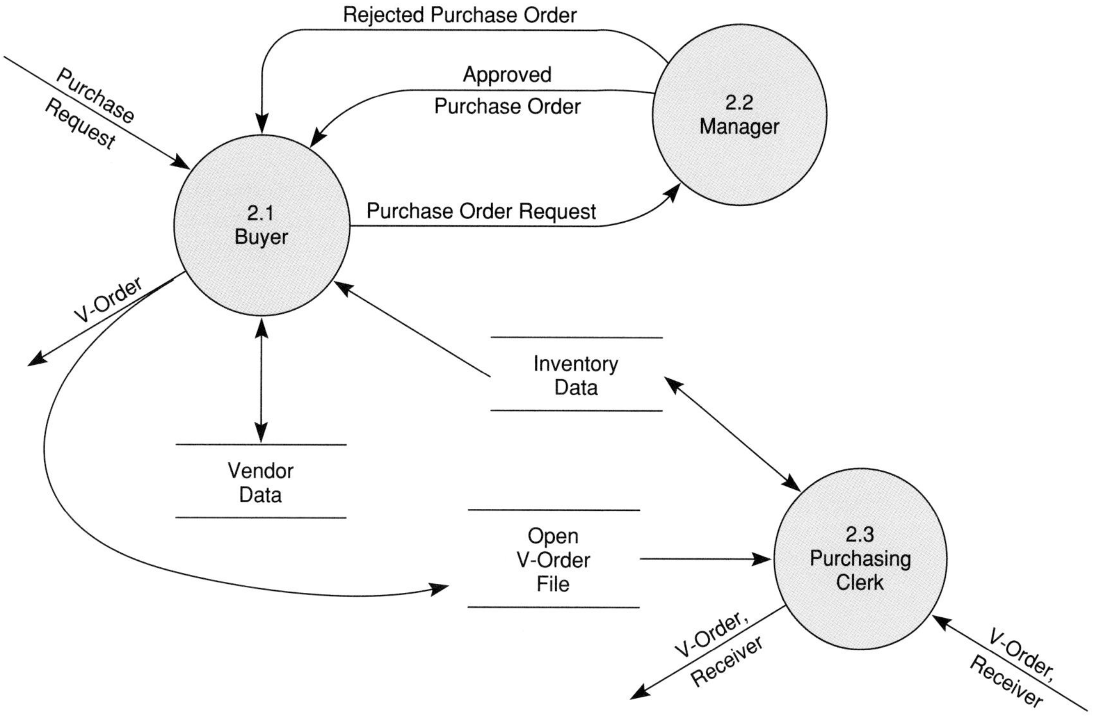

lowest-level diagram. Thus, the number of digits corresponds to the level of the diagram: zero digits at Level 1, one digit at Level 2, and so on.

Also, notice that two files appear in Figure 12-13 that have not appeared before. These files exist entirely within the Purchasing bubble and they are not visible until that bubble is exploded. If a file were to be used by, say, both Purchasing and Receiving, then it would have been documented between those two bubbles in Figure 12-12. Thus, files appear only at the level where they are shared by two or more bubbles.

In general, no dataflow diagram should have more than seven to nine bubbles. If a diagram needs more than that, some of the bubbles should be merged and then shown separately on a lower-level diagram.

Making Your Own Dataflow Diagrams

You now have enough knowledge to make your own dataflow diagrams. Take an example that is close to you—say the recording of grades—and work through it. The best way to learn how to make dataflow diagrams is to do it. The discussion questions and exercises at the end of this chapter provide a number of suggestions.

Dataflow modeling is useful in other situations besides developing information systems. Whenever you want to understand the flow of work in a complicated office situation, consider making dataflow diagrams. They are useful both for developing your own understanding and for communicating that understanding to others.

Documenting Dataflows with the Data Dictionary

Although we have chosen names for dataflows in these diagrams that suggest the meaning of the data items, this is often not enough. In Figure 12-13, for example, what exactly is a Purchase Order Request?

Dataflow diagrams are given meaning if they are accompanied by a description of the dataflows. Such a description is sometimes called a **data dictionary**. This dictionary is a file or database that documents data requirements and explains, in detail, the meaning of each dataflow. There should be one entry in the data dictionary for every dataflow on every dataflow diagram.

The specific contents of a data dictionary are beyond the scope of this discussion. Just be aware that dataflow diagrams are always accompanied by data dictionaries.

Questions

12.19 What is the purpose of a dataflow diagram?

12.20 Dataflow diagrams do not show logic. Describe what they do show.

12.21 List the four basic dataflow diagram symbols and explain their meaning.

12.22 What is the difference between a logical dataflow diagram and a physical dataflow diagram?

12.23 What is leveling? Why is it used?

12.24 How can the inputs and outputs be used to verify the accuracy of two leveled dataflow diagrams?

12.25 Explain the circumstances under which a file in a dataflow diagram appears to be read-only.

12.26 What is the purpose of a data dictionary?

Prototyping

In its general sense the word *prototype* means a sample, a pattern, an example, or the first thing of its kind. As applied to systems development, a **prototype** is a simulation, a demonstration, a piece of a system, or the first instance of a system. Usually prototypes are limited to hardware, programs, and data. While there is no reason for prototypes not to involve the procedural and people components, they usually do not.

Why Prototype?

Prototypes are used for a number of reasons. For one, prototypes are used to demonstrate a concept and to sell or market an idea. It is often difficult for management or end users to understand the benefits of a new product by reading a description of the product and its specifications. A prototype *shows* the benefits. Within an organization, prototypes are used to generate enthusiasm for a concept or to obtain access to financial or other resources. Startup software companies use prototypes to raise money for product development.

Another use of prototypes is to demonstrate the feasibility of an idea or an approach. Such prototypes are sometimes called **proof-of-concept prototypes**. With these, the essence of the idea is developed sufficiently in the prototype to demonstrate its technical feasibility. Such a demonstration might be required to show that the idea works at all, or to show that it works with acceptable performance, or to show that it works within the constraints of a particular hardware configuration.

Another use of prototypes is to better understand requirements. Users and professional systems developers come from two different cultures. Often, after an exchange of words, the two parties wonder whether or not they have understood one another. One way to check on the clarity of the communication is for the developers to build a sample of the entity being discussed, say a report, and show that sample to the users. The users can then approve the sample, or they can better describe what they want by referring to the sample.

Yet another use of prototypes is to determine requirements. It may be that users and developers agree that they do not know what is required. One way to learn more about the need is to build a prototype and then apply it to the problem to be solved. The deficiencies of the prototype will then lead to more questions and further understanding of the requirements.

The reasons for building prototypes are summarized in Figure 12-14.

Components Suitable for Prototyping

The most frequently prototyped component of a system is the user interface. For example, prototypes are used to demonstrate the structure and processing of menus and other user commands. They are also

- Demonstrating and selling concept or idea

- Demonstrating feasibility

- Improving understanding of requirements and improving communication between users and developers

- Determining requirements

Figure 12-14
Reasons for building a prototype

built to represent data entry forms. Often such prototypes simulate the user's action in processing the form. Users can try out the prototype with some sample data and see how well it works. Awkwardness in processing steps and missing features often are identified using prototypes.

Similarly, prototypes of reports are often constructed. Here, the users employ the prototype report in a realistic situation and evaluate its effectiveness. From such firsthand experience they can better comment on the appropriateness and usefulness of the form's design.

Prototypes are also used to evaluate an algorithm or processing method. Here the essence of the algorithm is programmed and tested and sample data are submitted to it. Then the performance of the system is measured to determine technical feasibility. Performance is measured in terms of CPU cycles used, main memory required, disk accesses needed, and the like.

Finally, prototypes are used to test system interfaces. A new system may need to obtain data from or send data to another information system or even another computer. The only way to know for certain that the system interface works is to build a prototype and try it. If data can be exchanged in the manner expected, the likelihood of surprises in the interface is greatly reduced.

Types of Prototypes

There are a number of different types of prototypes. The simplest is a **simulation**, or **slide-show**, **prototype**. This type is most often used for prototypes of user interfaces. With it, dummies of menus, data entry forms, or reports are constructed. The user then uses the keyboard as he or she would with the actual system. Behind the scenes, a program reads files of predrawn screens and data to simulate what would happen with the actual system.

The advantage of simulated prototypes is that they are quick to develop. They also can provide a realistic-feeling impression of what the user interface is like. Usually, however, this type of prototype is restricted to a canned script, or only minor variations from a canned script. This means that users cannot perform realistic tests against such a prototype.

When, as a business professional, you use or review a prototype, be certain to ask what type it is. If it is a simulation or slide-show type, keep in mind that none of the actual work in building the system has been done, and that the prototype only indicates the nature of the idea, it does not indicate that the interface being demonstrated can actually be built.

A second type of prototype was mentioned previously, the **proof-of-concept prototype.** Such prototypes are developed when there is substantial risk that the proposed design will not work. Building the prototype reduces the dollars and other resources that must be placed at risk.

Proof-of-concept prototypes typically have a very rough user interface (unless, of course, the user interface is the concept being proved).

Little time is spent developing program instructions to accept data or return results. Instead, the programming activity is focused on the particular aspect of the problem whose feasibility is unknown.

Most end users and managers are not qualified to evaluate a proof-of-concept prototype. Instead, the prototype should be evaluated by competent information systems professionals who are disinterested in the results of the evaluation. Those whose idea is being tested are obviously not disinterested, nor are opponents of the concept.

A third type of prototype is a **partial-function prototype**, in which a part of the actual system is partially developed and tested. Such prototypes are constructed to demonstrate a key feature of the system. Unlike simulations and proof-of-concept prototypes, the assumption behind a partial-function prototype is that the programs that are written will become part of the actual system. Thus, the programs, even though they only partly implement a part of the system, are written with the same care and control as the operational system.

The advantage of such a prototype is that it need not be thrown away; the work invested in it saves work later. The disadvantage of such prototypes is that they are slower and more expensive to develop than either simulations or proof-of-concept prototypes.

The final type is **pilot prototypes**, in which a part of the operational system is fully developed. All the features and functions, the entire user interface, all error processing, and all other aspects of some piece of the system are developed. As with partial-function prototypes, the prototype programs are expected to become part of the system. Thus, the prototype is not thrown away.

The advantage of such a prototype is that users can truly test the system for adequacy. The disadvantage is that considerable time and expense are required to develop the prototype. The four types of prototypes are summarized in Figure 12-15.

Problems with Prototyping

While there are substantial advantages to building a prototype, there are also important disadvantages. First, the rapid development of a prototype may create an expectation in the users' minds that the system can be developed faster than it can. A complete system must not only process all of the features and functions, but also handle exceptions and errors. It almost certainly takes more time to develop the program code for the complete system than for the prototype.

Second, the prototype may gloss over important issues. It may not reveal what turn out to be the most critical and difficult-to-accomplish requirements. It may make the system appear to be easier to develop than it is and thus generate a false sense of optimism.

Third, prototypes can lead to a false sense of how much has already been accomplished. Particularly with simulations and slide shows, if the reviewers do not understand that they are seeing a mock-up, they may believe that the technical challenges have already been overcome. They will later be surprised to learn that problems have been encountered in building something they thought already existed.

- Simulation, or slide-show, prototype
- Proof-of-concept prototype
- Partial-function prototype
- Pilot prototype

Figure 12-15
Types of prototypes

Questions

12.27 What is a prototype?

12.28 Describe four reasons for building prototypes.

12.29 What is a simulation prototype? What is it used for?

12.30 What is a proof-of-concept prototype? What is it used for?

12.31 What is a partial-function prototype? What is it used for?

12.32 What is a pilot prototype? What is it used for?

12.33 Describe three potential problems in using prototypes.

Computer-Assisted Software Engineering (CASE)

In this section we will consider CASE, a methodology and set of tools used to facilitate the development of information systems. While CASE could be used for the development of any type of system, it is most frequently used for the development of larger, organization-wide systems.

CASE is an acronym that has two interpretations. Sometimes it stands for **computer-assisted (or -aided) software engineering**; sometimes it stands for **computer-assisted (or -aided) systems engineering**. In this text, we will use *CASE* to stand for the second meaning. It will refer to the process of using information systems (having the five components) to build information systems (having the five components).

CASE technology developed as information systems professionals sought ways to use computer technology to improve their own produc-

12.2 INCREASING YOUR PERSONAL PRODUCTIVITY

CASE Has Not Delivered on Its Promises: Pro and Con

PRO Even though CASE tools are commercially available, hyped in the media and heavily marketed, why is it that the technology has been implemented by less than 10% of mainframe users in North America? (CASE usage is drastically less among non-mainframe users.)

CASE hasn't caught on for several reasons. A major factor is business' limited ability to manage organizational change. When a pilot team is selected to experiment with a glamorous new technology, time schedules, deadlines and expectations generally go out the window.

Another factor concerns what CASE is capable of doing vs. market expectations. The market is pursuing a goal of improved productivity, yet CASE, for the most part, increases the amount of effort expended in building a system. In the short term, productivity is actually decreased. What CASE does is increase the *quality* of the resulting system. Until the U.S. market learns that productivity is a by-product of improved quality, CASE is bound to bring disappointing results. There are far too many shops

abandoning the use of CASE because they were unaccustomed to the higher level of effort required during the early stages of the application development life cycle. They were left waiting for code. Quickly, they reverted to the old, familiar ways of building systems, leaving the CASE tool to become another victim of the shelfware syndrome.

CASE tools alleviate the drudgery of drawing the graphical representations of system specs, which is the primary attraction of CASE technology today.

But there are still significant hurdles to overcome for CASE to become a success.

CON The promise of CASE cannot be oversold. No other technology answers today's critical need for a better way to develop computer systems.

Successful users of computer-aided software engineering are not only cutting down on bugs and backlogs, but they are also building strategic information systems that give them a competitive edge in developing engineering applica-

tions too complex to tackle any other way.

True, CASE technology's payback is not immediate, and some vendors neither prepare customers for the necessary CASE implementation period nor support them through it. Reaping the benefits of CASE requires education, training, organizational commitment and adoption of standards—and vendors that can provide comprehensive support.

The proper implementation of CASE is an undertaking that in itself delivers far-reaching organizational benefits: introducing discipline and engineering methods to the systems development process; enabling integration of CASE offerings with existing software tools, hardware platforms and development methods; promoting an evolutionary adoption of new technology; and accommodating long-term systems development planning.

Once the implementation issues are addressed, computer-aided software engineering can begin to deliver on its full potential.

tivity. Some professionals found it ironic that there were so many people in the computer field attempting to increase others' productivity but ignoring the potential for improving their own.

While many of the ideas that form the foundation of CASE have existed for quite some time, it was not until advent of the microcomputer that CASE technology began to see widespread use. Today there are dozens of CASE products and almost every major corporation is experimenting with, if not using, CASE products and methodology.

CASE, however, is more than a set of computer programs. It is an information system that includes all five components. There is *hardware* and there are CASE *programs*, which are sometimes called **CASE tools**. As CASE is used to develop systems, CASE *databases* of system descriptors and other system parameters are also developed. Further, there are *procedures* for using CASE, which are sometimes called the **CASE methodology**. Finally, CASE requires a staff of CASE-trained systems development *personnel*.

It is a mistake to think of CASE as a set of programs. Technology without methodology is a waste of money. Organizations that have acquired CASE programs without changing their methodology have found little benefit from the tools.

We will now survey the important components of CASE methodology and then discuss the capabilities of CASE tools.

CASE Methodology

While there is no single step-by-step CASE methodology, there is general agreement about the stages and basic activities that need to take place for developing systems using CASE tools.[1] This generally agreed-on process is a variation and extension of the five-stage process you studied in Chapter 8 and earlier in this chapter.

Consider Figure 12-16, which summarizes this process. It begins with **strategic systems planning**. In this preliminary stage, the organization decides which information systems to build and what order to build them in.

This stage is necessary because there are normally many more systems that could be developed than there is time or money available to develop them—so projects must be prioritized. The prioritization is complicated, however, because information systems coexist. They feed inputs and outputs to one another; for example, sometimes a database is created by one system and used by another. The result of this stage is a prioritized list of systems to be developed.

Next, a development process is followed for each of the systems on the list, in accordance with the established priorities. In Figure 12-16 two systems are being developed, A and B.

In the first stage of the development process, a *system analysis* is performed: requirements are developed, including dataflow diagrams and data dictionaries. Figure 12-16 shows an arrow labeled Shared

1. Greg Boone, *The CASE Experience*, CASE Product Profiles, Publication No. PP-10688) (Bellevue, Wash.: CASE Research Corp., 1988).

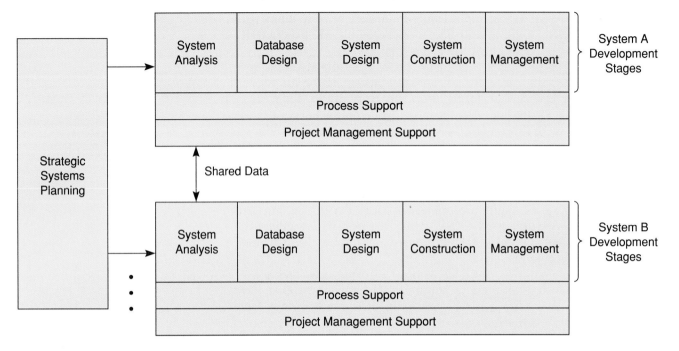

Figure 12-16
CASE methodology

Data.[2] This means that, with some CASE tools, requirements developed for one system can be used as input to others. This is useful when an office or department is common to both systems. In this situation, the dataflow diagrams and data dictionary that have been developed for one system can be used as a starting point for the analysis of a second.

The next stage is **database design**. In this stage, the data dictionary data is used to develop a design of the database. Next, **system design** is undertaken. In CASE literature, the word *system* in this context refers to programs, user interfaces, forms, and reports. It does not generally include hardware specifications, procedures, or job descriptions.

The next stage is **system construction**, that is, the creation of programs, user interfaces, forms, and reports. The last stage is **system management**. During this stage the system is monitored, and changes are made to it in a controlled fashion. Versions of programs and other system components are managed so that configuration of the system is always known and under control.

Two activities underlie the development of the system. **Process support** refers to activities that ease the development process and ensure that it complies with the MIS department's development standards. It includes support for group communication; the creation, editing, and review of work; the provision of security; backup and recovery; and compliance with quality assurance standards. **Project management support** refers to activities carried out to plan, schedule, allocate resources, and control the development project.

2. Be certain you understand that the data referred to here is data about a system and not user data. What is being shared is a data dictionary, or data that describes a system.

The process described here is similar to the five-stage process you learned previously, but it emphasizes different aspects of the development effort. With larger, organizational systems, much more time must be placed on the coordination of the new system with existing systems. Also, since such systems are typically far more complicated than personal or departmental systems, this methodology places greater emphasis on design activities. Also, since the systems are larger, it places more emphasis on system management.

But it is not incompatible with the five-stage concept. The definition stage occurs during strategic systems planning; the requirements and evaluation stages occur during system analysis, the design stage occurs during database and system design, and the implementation stage occurs during system construction and management.

CASE Products

The goal of CASE is to use computer technology to facilitate the development of information systems by automating or at least improving human productivity for each of the activities in Figure 12-16.

Figure 12-17 shows the general architecture of a **CASE product**, which is a collection of CASE tools plus a database of systems development data. The database, shared among all of the tools, is often called the **CASE encyclopedia**. The advantage of sharing the database is that the results from one stage of development are automatically available to tools in a subsequent stage of the process.

Not all CASE products have all of these tools, though most CASE vendors are developing a complete set, or are cross-licensing tools with other vendors to form a complete set. Not all CASE products have the same strengths. One product may have a particularly good system analysis tool, while another product has a particularly good database design tool. Consequently, some organizations mix and match tools from different products. They use a tool from one product for one stage and a tool from a different product for another stage.

Unfortunately, there is a problem with using multiple CASE products: there is no standard structure for the encyclopedia. The data in the encyclopedia for one product may be incompatible with the data in the encyclopedia for another. Different products have different data standards. For example, one product restricts data element names to ten characters; another product allows them to be 30 characters. Names from the second product cannot be input to the first. Organizations that plan on using several CASE tools must therefore restrict their encyclopedia data to the lowest common denominator.

There are CASE tools for each of the activities shown in Figure 12-16. Some tools store, organize, and present the results of a strategic planning analysis. Using these tools helps to organize the presentation of the strategic plan as well.

There are dozens of CASE tools that facilitate the creation of data-flow diagrams. These tools are graphical and driven by mice. They provide a standard set of symbols that can be placed and moved about the screen, and they allow the input of both text and drawings. Using

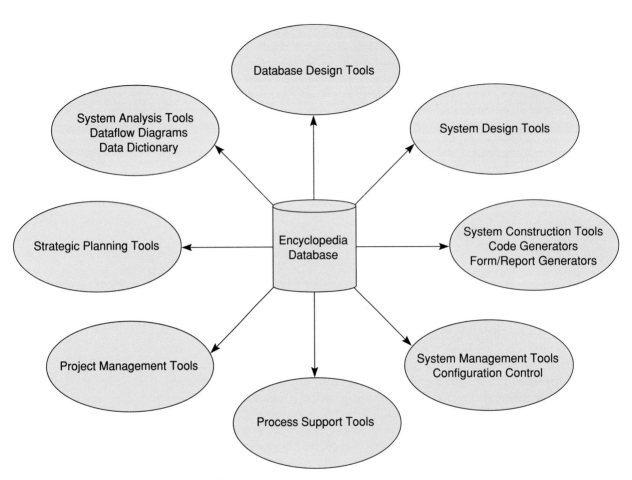

FIGURE 12-17
General architecture of a CASE
product

them, dataflow diagrams can be developed with far greater ease and productivity than when they are drawn by hand. In addition, these tools provide automatic validation checking. For example, they ensure that as a dataflow process is expanded to another level, no inputs or outputs are left out nor are any extraneous ones added.

Analysis tools also provide capabilities for creating the new system's data dictionary. Each dataflow, file, and process can be defined, as described earlier in this chapter. These definitions are then carried forward into the design and construction processes.

CASE products generally include a database design tool, although the capabilities vary widely. Some such tools are simply graphical systems that help people to document the design. At the other end of the spectrum are tools that will construct a database design from data descriptions recorded in the encyclopedia. Generally, there are problems with automatically generated designs, however, and usually such designs serve only as a starting point for human designers.

CASE products also include systems design tools to facilitate the design of programs, menus, forms, and reports. By the time the systems design tool is used, the data dictionary data and the database design will be stored in the encyclopedia. The systems design tools can access

12.3 INCREASING YOUR PERSONAL PRODUCTIVITY

Laying the CASE Groundwork

Barbara Bouldin, author of *Agents of Change*, gives the following advice to lay the groundwork for computer-aided software engineering:

- Assess the need for CASE. Many companies bring in new technologies without a firm understanding of the corporation's needs for that technology.
- Evaluate the computer-aided software engineering product carefully, possibly in a pilot project, before it is formally integrated.
- Present the product to upper level management and show what it can do. Bouldin says senior management has come full circle on CASE in the '80s, going from skeptical to overly enthusiastic and back to skeptical. Showing is believing.
- Present the product to users and show how they will derive direct benefits from CASE. Afterward, go back and canvass users on their thoughts and ideas for improvements on CASE policy.
- Look for potential agents of change. CASE doesn't always have to involve just IS staff, Bouldin maintains. Valuable CASE support can come from other personnel, including users and senior management.
- Plan how CASE should be introduced to the corporation. At this stage, according to Bouldin, IS should have the representation and understanding of people from those areas of the company that will be affected by CASE.
- Introduce CASE quickly but incrementally once the skids have been greased, so to speak. CASE should be aimed at software projects that will have a direct impact on user/programmer productivity. Quick, hard results will establish long-term corporate support for CASE.

---

this data to make it easy for the human designer. For example, the human need only specify the name of a table when designing a report, and the systems design tool can obtain the names of all columns of that table and guide the designer through the process of locating the columns on the form.

CASE products vary widely in their support for system construction. Some provide little, if any, support. Others provide tools that generate application program code, menus, and form and report descriptions. Many products produce large sections of source code that application programmers then move into the programs they write. This saves considerable time and eliminates the need for much of the programming work that is boring and repetitive.

There are also CASE tools to facilitate system management. Many of the tools are used for configuration control over programs and database structures. Changes are made to programs or database structures either to correct errors or to adapt the system to changes in system requirements. Either way, it is important to know what changes were made when, for what reason, and by whom. Such records are also important for control reasons, as discussed in the previous chapter.

Concerning process support, many CASE tools include word and other text processing programs, paint and draw programs, as well as a limited version of electronic mail. They also include facilities to control concurrent processing by development personnel, and to protect the database against accidental, unauthorized, or criminal losses.

Finally, many CASE products include project management tools. These include programs for developing plans and budgets, for sched-

Questions

12.34 What are the two possible interpretations of the acronym *CASE*? Which is used in this text?

12.35 What are the two components of CASE?

12.36 Explain CASE methodology as depicted in Figure 12-16. How does this methodology differ from the five-stage system development process?

12.37 Explain the role of the encyclopedia in Figure 12-17.

uling system development tasks, and for allocating resources. These tools are used to organize and control the project and to report on progress to management.

From this discussion, you can see that CASE is exactly what it sounds like. It is computer *assisted* systems engineering. CASE is not automated systems development. Instead, it is a methodology and a set of tools for increasing the productivity of people who develop systems.

Summary

The process for developing multiuser information systems does not differ, in any fundamental way, from the process used to develop personal information systems. The same five stages apply, although some of them are more complicated and difficult.

During the definition stage, the problem is defined, feasibility is assessed, and a plan is created. Problem definition is more difficult for multiuser systems because there are usually many differing perceptions of what problem is to be solved. Also, the underlying business systems are usually more complicated.

Feasibility assessment consists of cost, technical, and schedule dimensions, as with personal information systems development. In addition, there is a political dimension which concerns the social dynamics of the group or groups involved. Group norms have a major impact on the success or failure of the system.

In constructing the project plan, time needs to be allocated for review, discussion, and possible rework. Group understanding, acceptance, and support for the project as documented in the plan is essential.

The tasks during the requirements stage are the same for multiuser systems development as for personal information systems development, except that they need to be expanded to account for the multiple users and types of users. Categories of requirements that need to be identified and documented are: output requirements, input requirements, estimates of processing scale, and constraints. Requirements should be determined by interviewing each type of system user.

To maintain user acceptance of the system, influential users must be allowed to participate in the development of the requirements. Once requirements have been determined, they must be documented and reviewed. If the project will involve products or services from an outside vendor, then the approved and accepted requirements are put into the form of a request for proposal (RFP).

The tasks in the evaluation stage depend on whether the system is being developed by in-house personnel or by an outside vendor. If it is developed in-house, a development team is formed and various systems alternatives are evaluated; one of these is selected. If it is developed by an outside vendor, the RFP is given to vendors, their responses are evaluated, and eventually a contract is negotiated and signed.

During both the design and implementation stages, you become the manager (or involved user) and the consumer of others' expertise. You might not understand the details of the hardware, program, and portions of the data design. You should, however, review the design of the user interface. You should also understand and have an opportunity to review the procedural and people components.

During implementation you should hire new personnel as necessary, and ensure that future users receive adequate training. Also, once the five components have been installed and tested, the system will be given a dress rehearsal. You participate in this dress rehearsal and have a voice in the decision to implement (or not implement) the system. In most cases, the parallel style of implementation is recommended for multiuser systems.

The purpose of dataflow diagrams is to identify and record the essence of office processing by representing the flow of data among departments, functions, and people. A dataflow diagram is a snapshot of the data movement in an organization. Dataflow diagrams do not show logic.

The four basic dataflow symbols are: a rectangle, which represents external entities; a circle, which represents an internal process, department, or person; a labeled arrow, which represents a dataflow; and a pair of horizontal lines, which represents a file.

Building dataflow diagrams is an iterative process. Mistakes are normal. The diagram can be begun anywhere, with dataflows being traced as far as possible, then restarted somewhere else. Continue working until all of the separate flows have been connected. A single diagram cannot represent an entire business (or even an entire process). Dataflow diagrams need to be leveled so that no diagram contains more than seven to nine bubbles.

Dataflows are often accompanied by a data dictionary that explains the meaning of each data flow. The data dictionary is contained in a file or database.

A prototype is a simulation, a demonstration, a piece of a system, or the first instance of a system. Prototypes are used to demonstrate and sell an idea, to demonstrate the feasibility of an idea or an approach, to clarify and better understand requirements, and to determine what requirements might exist.

One use of prototypes is to demonstrate the user interface. Another is to evaluate an algorithm or processing method. A third use is to test a system interface. One type of prototype is simulations, also called slide shows. Other types are proof-of-concept prototypes, partial-function prototypes, and pilot prototypes.

Prototypes do have disadvantages. They may create unrealistic expectations in the minds of the users about how fast the system can be developed; they may gloss over important issues; and they may lead to a false sense of how much has been accomplished.

In this text, *CASE* refers to computer-assisted (or -aided) systems engineering. CASE was developed as MIS professionals sought ways to use computer technology to improve their own productivity.

CASE consists of a methodology and a set of tools. Trying to use the tools without the methodology is a waste of time.

CASE methodology consists of the following stages: strategic systems planning, system analysis, database design, system design, system construction, and system management. These activities are facilitated by process support and project management support.

A typical CASE product maintains a database of systems data called the encyclopedia. Components of CASE products are shown in Figure 12-17.

Word List

processing scale	leveling	CASE methodology
concurrent workload	data dictionary	strategic systems planning
constraint	prototype	system analysis
request for proposal (RFP)	proof-of-concept prototype	database design
dataflow diagram	simulation (slide-show)	system design
source	prototype	system construction
sink	partial-function prototype	system management
bubble	pilot prototype	process support
file	CASE (computer-assisted (or	project management support
logical dataflow diagram	-aided) systems engineering)	CASE product
physical dataflow diagram	CASE tools	CASE encyclopedia

Discussion Questions and Exercises

A. Suppose that you are a member of a department that is in the process of developing an information system. The manager of the workgroup does not have a particularly strong personality or management style. The manager does not understand the problem to be solved, either. Several of the more outspoken members of the group have different interpretations of the problem; they each lead a subgroup within the workgroup that supports their position. A $100,000 contract has been awarded to a consulting company to develop the information system. You have been with the group for about 18 months and have the respect of most of the department. You have not joined any of the three factions. What do you do?

B. Suppose that you are a member of a department that is in the process of developing an information system. The manager of the department has a very strong and domineering management style. The manager has, almost single-handedly, defined the problem and requirements and selected a vendor. You believe that a significant issue has been left out of the problem definition and that a number of critical requirements have been omitted. Further, you believe that a number of influential members of the group intend to subvert the development activity. A $100,000 contract has been awarded for the development effort and the vendor is scheduled to begin work in a week. What do you do?

C. You manage a department that is about to begin the development of an information system. You are talking with a manager who runs a department in a different functional area and who has just completed a development effort. That manager advises you to hide your project from the corporate MIS department. That group, he says, will only slow you down with meetings, paperwork, and endless requests for justification. You believe that your department information system will require data from the corporate database. How should you proceed?

D. Suppose you are the manager of the sales department at a company that manufactures paper products. Your company has $40 million per year in sales. The salespeople desperately need an order tracking system. The MIS department and the steering committee agree to initiate the development of that system but it will be nearly 12 months before the system will be finished. The MIS department offers to build a simulation prototype and show it to the salespeople at your national sales meeting next month. How do you respond to this offer? How certain are you that the new system will be done in 12 months? What can you do to improve your confidence? What can you do to help the sales force in the meanwhile? Suppose you start losing a substantial number of sales because of lost or untracked orders. What should you do?

E. Consider the situation in question D. Suppose that you complain loudly about the delay in the schedule, so loudly that your needs come to the ears of the board of directors. One of the directors manages a company that has drastically reduced its systems development time by using CASE technology. That director tells your CEO about CASE, and the CEO directs the MIS director to employ CASE technology on your project. The MIS director resists, claiming that CASE is inappropriate for your project. You perceive that your project has become a political football between the MIS director and the CEO. What do you do?

F. Suppose you own and manage a small pottery shop. You sell your product over the counter for cash; you also accept checks and Visa and Mastercard. You deposit cash, checks, and charge-card receipts with your bank. You purchase clay, paint, glazes, and equipment from a number of different vendors. Occasionally you must have kilns and pottery wheels repaired. You pay two part-time helpers an hourly wage. Draw a dataflow diagram of your business.

G. You manage the purchasing department for a business that has $10 million in sales. Your staff consists of three purchasing agents plus yourself. Your department receives purchase orders (POs) from other departments in the company. The agents check each PO for completeness and accuracy and then check the corporate budget to determine if sufficient unencumbered funds exist to pay for the purchase. If so, the agents choose, from departmental records, an appropriate vendor(s) and order the item(s). When items are received in the shipping department, the shipping personnel generate a receiver document and send a copy of that document to your department. When all items have been received, the agent closes the PO. Periodically, you review open POs to ensure that work is being completed on time. Generate a dataflow diagram for this department.

H. Interview a department in an actual business. Pick a department that is large enough to require a two-level dataflow diagram but not so large or complicated that you cannot understand its basic flow in an hour or two. Develop a dataflow diagram for the department. If possible, obtain copies of paper forms used in this business. Develop entries for a data dictionary to describe each form. Create a policy statement for one of the bubbles in your chart. Review your work with a member of the department for accuracy and make changes as necessary. Describe any errors or misconceptions that you had.

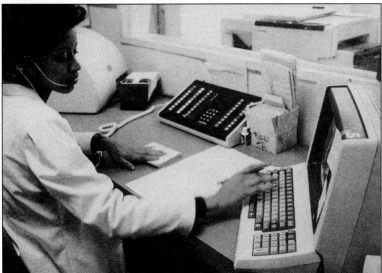

PART FOUR

Special Topics

In this part we present four special topics. They may be assigned as supplementary reading, or they may be incorporated into the course itself.

Module A outlines the history of computing, which dates back farther than you might suspect. As you will see, some mistakes made early on are still being made today.

Module B presents a brief but comprehensive discussion of binary and hexadecimal representation and computer arithmetic. If you have mathematical leanings, or if you like to know more about what goes on inside of things (like computers), you might find this module to your liking.

In Module C we discuss some topical issues: computer crime, security and control, and ethics. As a user, client, and owner of computer systems, what are your responsibilities? Is it enough to know what is legal and illegal? Are there behaviors that are legal but unethical?

In the appendix we present a brief introduction to BASIC programming. The appendix covers some of the BASIC instructions, just enough to get you started. You can use the lessons in the appendix to learn BASIC on your own. Having mastered this fundamental material, you might decide to study BASIC further, using one of the many tutorials on the subject.

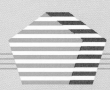

MODULE A

History of Information Systems

The history of computing began thousands of years ago when people first started to count on their fingers. In fact, fingers and toes were probably (who knows for sure?) the earliest computational devices. As business and commerce developed, however, a need arose for a calculator that could count higher than 20.

The **abacus** shown in Figure A-1 is an early form of such a calculator. Different versions of it were used for centuries by people of many nations and areas of the world. The abacus was used even before numbers were represented in writing. Other computational devices were constructed throughout the centuries. The numerical wheel calculator (Figure A-2) was the predecessor of the adding machines and manual calculators that commonly were used before the electronic calculator. The slide rule (Figure A-3) was another type of computational device.

Charles Babbage and His Machines

As far as we know, **Charles Babbage** is the father of computing. This amazing man was far ahead of his time. He developed the essential ideas for a computer over 100 years before the first computer was constructed. He was so advanced that practically none of his contemporaries appreciated him. In addition to computing, Babbage made contributions to mathematics, optics, underwater navigation, railroads, industrial engineering, mechanics, and other fields.

Many of the mistakes that Babbage made continue to be made today, and so it is worth considering his life's activities in some detail.

Figure A-1
Abacus

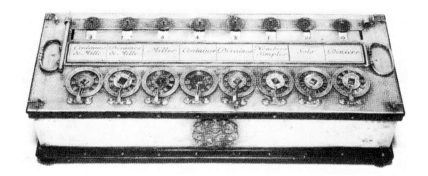

Figure A-2
Numerical wheel calculator

Babbage's Life

Babbage was born in England in 1792 (George Washington was still alive). His father was a wealthy banker who left him a sizable fortune. Babbage says he suffered from high fevers, and so he was sent to a private tutor "with instructions to attend to my health; but, not to press too much knowledge upon me: a mission which he faithfully accom-

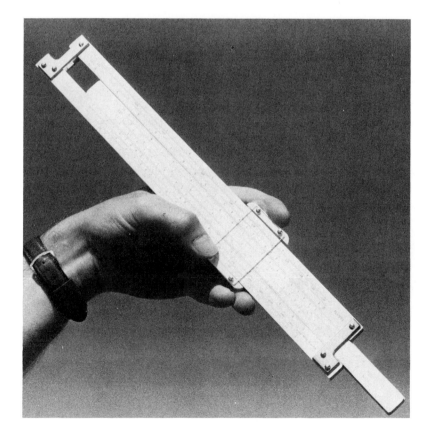

Figure A-3
Slide rule

plished.[1]" Babbage relates, "My invariable question on receiving any new toy was, 'Mamma, what is inside of it?' " Apparently, if she couldn't answer, he tore it apart.

Sometime prior to 1822, Babbage and his friend John Herschel were checking data calculated for the Astronomical Society. In frustration, Babbage remarked to Herschel, "I wish to God these calculations had been executed by steam." (Steam engines were common.) In 1822, Babbage proposed the design of a **difference engine** composed of gears and wheels (see Figure A-4). This engine would automatically compute functions of the form

$$y = a + ax + ax^2 + \ldots + ax^n$$

In 1823 the British government granted Babbage money to build the engine. The first government-sponsored computer project was on. Like most of those to follow, the project fell behind. By 1833 the government had invested 17,000 pounds ($85,000 at the 1833 rate of exchange), and only part of the difference engine was completed. Meanwhile, Babbage's active mind had been extending the possibilities of automated

1. Philip Morrison and Emily Morrison, eds., *Charles Babbage and His Calculating Engines* (New York: Dover Publications, 1961).

computing. By 1834 he had developed the idea of an **analytical engine.** The analytical engine would compute *any* mathematical function. It embodied most of the concepts that early computers did.

In 1834 Babbage asked the government whether it wanted him to finish the difference engine or start on the analytical engine. After eight years of frustrating correspondence, Prime Minister Robert Peel told Babbage that the government was going to abandon the project. This case may have established a record for governmental delay.

The analytical engine had a main memory that Babbage called the *store.* It was to have room for 1,000 variables of 50 digits each. It had an arithmetic and logic unit that he called the *mill.* Programs for the mill were written on punched cards. The engine would drive a type-setter. It had logical capability and could ring a bell or take other action when a variable passed zero or exceeded the capacity of one of the words. All of these operations were to have been implemented mechanically.

People had a hard time understanding the concept. Mathematicians asked Babbage how the engine would use logarithms. He told them that it wouldn't need logarithms because it could compute any function. Some people didn't believe this claim, so he showed them how it could be programmed to ask an attendant to supply a logarithm from a library of cards. Furthermore, it would check for the correct logarithm.

Ironically, Babbage got more attention from outside England than from within. He had two automated devices in his home: a clockwork woman who danced and a part of the difference engine. He reported that his English friends would gather about the dancing lady, whereas an American and a Hollander studied the difference engine. In fact, a Swedish printer, George Scheutz, built the only complete version of the difference engine (except for one made recently by IBM). Babbage was delighted and helped Scheutz explain it.

We know about the analytical engine largely from a paper written by an Italian, L. F. Menabrea. This paper was written in French and translated into English by **Ada Augusta, the Countess of Lovelace.** There is interesting social commentary here.

Ada Augusta was the only legitimate daughter of the poet Lord Byron. She was an excellent mathematician and understood Babbage's concepts perhaps better than anyone. In 1842, when she translated Menabrea's paper of 20 pages, she added 50 pages of "notes." Babbage wanted to know why she didn't write a paper of her own. "I never thought of it," she replied. In fact, she didn't sign her translation or her notes, but used the initials *A. A. L.* instead. Apparently, ladies didn't do such things.

However, ladies could go to the race track. The Countess loved racing, and it may have been inevitable that she would use the difference engine to determine horse bets. Apparently, it didn't work too well. She lost the family jewels at the track. Her mother, Lady Byron, had to buy them back.

The Countess died of cancer at the age of 36, just ten years after reading Menabrea's description. Her death was a big loss to Babbage and perhaps to the world. The programming language Ada is named after Ada Augusta Lovelace.

Babbage was a fascinating person. Charles Darwin reported lively dinner parties at Babbage's home. Another person complained of barely being able to escape from him at 2:00 in the morning. Babbage once said that he would be glad to give up the rest of his life if he could live for three days 500 hundred years in the future.

Lessons We Can Learn from Babbage

Many of the errors Babbage made have been repeated again and again in the computer industry. For one, Babbage began with vague requirements. "Let's compute numbers by steam" sounds all too much like "Let's use a computer to do billing." Much more precise statements of requirements are necessary.

Second, it appears that Babbage started implementing his plans before his design was complete. Much work had to be redone. His engineers and draftsmen often complained that they would finish a project only to be told the work was wrong or not needed because the design had been changed. The same complaint has been made by countless programmers since then. Another mistake Babbage made was to add more and more capability to his engines before any of them was complete. As his work progressed, he saw new possibilities, and he tried to incorporate them into his existing projects. Many data processing systems have remained uncompleted for the very same reason.

Work on the difference engine was set back considerably by a crisis over the salary of Babbage's chief engineer, Joseph Clement. Clement quit, and Babbage had little documentation to recover the loss. Further, Clement had the rights to all the tools. Who knows how many systems projects have failed because indispensable programmers quit in the middle? Working documentation is crucial for successful system implementation.

Even Lady Lovelace's losses at the track have a lesson. Systems ought not to be used for purposes for which they weren't designed. The computer industry has experienced much inefficiency because systems are applied to problems for which they weren't designed.

There was no electronics industry to support Babbage's ideas. All of the concepts had to be implemented in mechanical components, and the tolerances were so fine that they could not be manufactured within the limitations of nineteenth-century technology. Furthermore, Babbage's plans were grandiose. Building a computer with 1,000 50-decimal-digit numbers was a large task. He might have been more successful if he had completed a smaller computer first and then built credibility with his government and solidified his funding before starting on a larger one. Many government-sponsored projects fail today because of a lack of technology to support grandiose plans. The lessons we can learn from Babbage are summarized in Figure A-5.

We do not know what impact, if any, Babbage's work had on future development. One pioneer, Howard Aiken (discussed later in this chapter), reported that he worked for three years before discovering Babbage's contributions. We do not know about the others.

Babbage's Mistakes

Vague problem definition and requirements
Implementation started before design was complete
Requirements added during implementation
Working documentation not complete
Dependency on one person
System used for unintended purposes
Grandiose plans that exceeded existing technology

Herman Hollerith

In the late nineteenth century, the U.S. Census Bureau had a problem. The bureau was supposed to produce a census of the U.S. population every ten years. However, the 1880 census took seven and a half years to finish. By the time the census data was processed, much of it was no longer useful. Furthermore, at the rate that the population was growing, the Census Bureau was afraid that the 1890 census would not be finished before the 1900 census was due to begin.

In 1879, the bureau hired **Herman Hollerith** to help them. He worked for the Census Bureau for five years and then started his own company. Hollerith designed and managed the construction of several punched-card processing machines (see Figure A-6).

In 1889, the bureau held a contest among Hollerith and two competitors to determine whose system was the fastest. Hollerith's system required only one-tenth of the time needed by his nearest competitor. Using this equipment, the first count of the 1890 census took only six weeks! However, the final, official count was not announced until December 1890.

Hollerith's equipment was an extension of the work of the Frenchman Joseph Marie Jacquard. Jacquard designed looms in which punched cards controlled the pattern on woven material. In Jacquard's looms, needles fell through holes in the cards. The needles lifted threads so as to produce a pattern. This technique had been used in the weaving industry since 1804.

Hollerith extended this concept by using the cards to control electric circuits. Data was punched on three-by-five-inch cards and fed into a machine that moved the cards over a group of pins. If there was a hole in a card, the pin would fall through the hole and touch a pan of mercury. This contact closed a circuit and registered on a meter. Apparently, the machine worked so well that the humans became exhausted. There is a story that occasionally someone would pour all of the mercury into a nearby spittoon. The machine would stop, and everyone would rest.

Hollerith decided he had a marketable idea. He sold his equipment to railroads and other large companies that had computational prob-

Figure A-6
Hollerith's punched-card machines

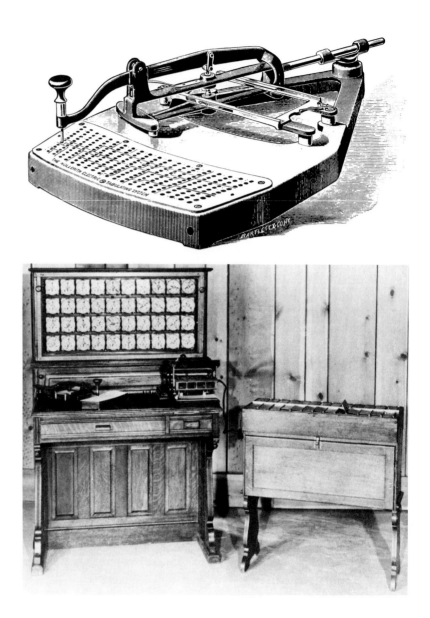

lems. This step represented the start of the punched-card industry. Hollerith built up his business and then sold it to the company that later was to become IBM (International Business Machines). Hollerith didn't know it, but he was setting the pace for many entrepreneurs to come. Hundreds of computer people have done the same thing he did. They have taken a good idea, developed it, formed an attractive company, sold it, and enjoyed many trips to the bank. Perhaps you can do the same.

The punched-card industry was the beginning of automated data processing. The earliest business computer systems were developed around punched-card technology. Companies found that to use this new technology successfully, they needed to build systems composed of hardware, programs, data, procedures, and trained personnel.

Programs? Well, sort of. As the punched-card equipment became more sophisticated, it became possible to change the wiring of the equipment to make it do different things. People who changed the wiring were doing an elementary form of programming. Programming as we know it today did not exist until stored-program computers were developed in the middle of the twentieth century. However, the concepts used in business computer systems started evolving with the 1890 census. The idea of developing systematic procedures to direct machines to turn data into information was born in that year.

Early Computers

In 1937, **Howard G. Aiken** proposed the use of electromechanical devices to perform calculations. He was a professor of applied mathematics at Harvard at the time, and the IBM Corporation gave him a grant to pursue his ideas. IBM was active in the punched-card industry.

In 1944, Aiken and IBM completed an electromechanical calculator called the **Mark I.** This computer had mechanical counters that were manipulated by electrical devices. The Mark I could perform basic arithmetic, and it could be changed to solve different problems (see Figure A-7).

At about the same time, the U.S. government signed a contract with the University of Pennsylvania to develop a computer that would aid the military effort during World War II. As a result of this contract, **John W. Mauchly** and **J. Presper Eckert** developed the first all-electronic computer, called the Electronic Numerical Integrator and Calculator, or **ENIAC.** Unlike the Mark I, ENIAC had no mechanical counters; everything was electronic.

Figure A-7
Mark I computer

Figure A-8
The ENIAC, a first-generation computer

Although Mauchly and Eckert are often given credit for developing the first electronic computer, this apparently is not completely true. Their work was based in part on work that had been done by **John V. Atanasoff.** Atanasoff was a professor at Iowa State University, and in 1939 he had developed many ideas for an all-electronic computer. In 1942, he and a graduate student, Clifford Berry, completed an electronic computer that could solve systems of linear equations.

ENIAC (the Mauchly/Eckert machine) was used to perform many different calculations. It had 19,000 vacuum tubes, 70,000 resistors, and 500,000 soldered joints (see Figure A-8). The ENIAC could perform 5,000 additions per second. It used 150,000 watt-hours of power a day— so much that, when it was turned on, the lights in one section of Philadelphia dimmed. Unfortunately, it was inflexible. Changing its program meant rewiring the machine and thus required considerable time and resources. Since it could be changed, it was programmable; however, it was not programmable in the sense that we understand the term today.

In the mid-1940s the mathematician **John von Neumann** joined the Mauchly/Eckert team. Von Neumann proposed a design for a computer that stored programs in its memory. He also developed other concepts that were to become the foundation for computer design for 30 years. Two computers evolved from this work: the **EDVAC** (Electrical Discrete Variable Automatic Computer) and the **EDSAC** (Electronic Delay Storage Automatic Calculator). Both machines stored programs. EDSAC was completed in England in 1949 and EDVAC in the United States in 1950.

At the time, the potential of these machines was not understood. Atanasoff couldn't get support from Iowa State. The administration

Figure A-9
UNIVAC I

thought that there would be a need for only three or four of these devices throughout the United States. Furthermore, in the late 1940s none of the ENIAC-EDVAC staff was promoted to full professor at the Moore School of Engineering. People didn't seem to feel the work was going to be very important.

Another social commentary: The first programmers for the Mark I and the ENIAC were women. U.S. Navy Rear Admiral **Grace Hopper** programmed the Mark I, and **Adele Goldstine** programmed the ENIAC. Both of these women were talented mathematicians. Their presence undoubtedly helped to establish women's strong position in the computer industry.

John Mauchly and Presper Eckert decided to follow in Hollerith's entrepreneurial footsteps, and in 1946 they formed the Eckert-Mauchly Corporation. This ripe young company was purchased by the Remington-Rand Corporation. Their first product was **UNIVAC I** (Universal Automatic Computer). It was the first computer built to sell. The Census Bureau took delivery of the first one in 1951, and it was used continuously until 1963. It now resides in the Smithsonian Institution (see Figure A-9). Sperry Rand still manufactures a line of computers under the name *UNIVAC*, although these computers are a far cry from the UNIVAC I.

Meanwhile, other companies were not idle. IBM continued development on the Mark I computer and eventually developed the Mark II through Mark IV, as well as other early computers. Burroughs, General Electric, Honeywell, and RCA also were busy with computer developments.

IBM took an early lead in the application of the new computer technology to business problems. The company developed a series of business-oriented computers and sold them to their punched-card customers. Because IBM had a virtual monopoly on punched cards (which they had been unsuccessfully sued for by the U.S. government in the 1930s), they were in a strong position to capitalize on the new technology.

Furthermore, IBM had an extremely effective marketing philosophy. They emphasized solving business problems. They developed products that were useful to businesses, and they showed businesspeople how to use those products. IBM provided excellent customer service and good maintenance.

This philosophy paid off. Some other companies had better computers, but their computers weren't packaged to provide total solutions to business problems. IBM was the first company to understand that wise businesspeople don't buy the best *computer*; they buy the best *solution* to their problem. Today, many vendors have adopted this philosophy. They sell solutions to business problems, not just computers. However, the fact that IBM understood this first has much to do with the company's strength in the computer market today.

The computers manufactured in the 1950s are often called **first-generation computers.** Their major components were vacuum tubes. Most of them used magnetic drums as their primary storage devices. Main memory as discussed in this book did not exist at that time.

Because of the number and size of the vacuum tubes, these computers were huge. Furthermore, they generated tremendous amounts of heat, were expensive to run, and experienced frequent failures. A large first-generation computer occupied a room the size of a football field. It contained row upon row of racks of tubes. A staff of a half-dozen people was required just to change the tubes that burned out.

Computers in the 1960s and 1970s

In the late 1950s and early 1960s, vacuum tubes were replaced by transistors. This development led to **second-generation computers.** These computers were much smaller than vacuum-tube computers, and they were more powerful. A new type of main storage was developed. It was called **core memory** because it used magnetized, doughnut-shaped cores. The term *core* is still used today. Some people use core synonymously with *main memory*, but this usage is incorrect, because most main memories today do not contain magnetic core.

The first high-level programming languages were developed during this stage. First-generation computers were programmed in **machine code,** but second-generation computers were programmed in **assembly language** and English-like **high-level languages,** such as FORTRAN and ALGOL. Further, primitive operating systems were installed on second-generation machines. Operating system programs controlled the use of the computer's resources.

Most second-generation computers could run only one program at a time. Therefore, to speed things up, certain input and output operations were done off-line. For example, punched cards were read and

their contents copied to tape without the computer's involvement. Then the tape was read into the computer and processed, and the generated output was written to tape. The tape was then dismounted and printed on a separate machine. This process was followed because tape units could read and write much faster than card readers or printers could operate. Figure A-10 shows the IBM 7094, a typical second-generation computer.

Most of the business computer systems at this stage were designed for accounting. The computer was used to produce checks for payroll and accounts payable and to keep track of inventories. General ledger was also computerized. However, processing was done in batches. Inputs were gathered into groups and processed, and outputs were produced. Applications such as order entry that required interaction could not be handled.

In the 1960s, the **third-generation computers** became available. In these computers, **integrated circuits** were used instead of transistors. An integrated circuit is a complete electrical circuit on a small chip of silicon (see Figure A-11). Because of these chips, third-generation computers are smaller and more powerful than second-generation computers. Figure A-12 compares the sizes of vacuum tubes, transistors, and integrated circuits.

Vast improvements were also made in programming for third-generation computers. Sophisticated operating systems were developed. These systems allowed many programs to be executed concurrently. Slow input and output operations such as card reading or printing could be performed in the background: one job would be in processing while another was being read and the output of a third was being printed. The computers ran programs and every now and then took a

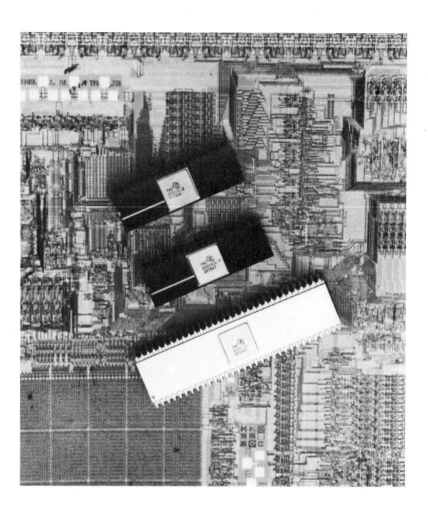

little time to handle slow I/O operations. This arrangement eliminated the need for the off-line processing typical of second-generation computers. Figure A-13 shows a typical third-generation computer.

Third-generation computers also supported interactive, **on-line processing.** Users could interact with the computers to perform functions like entering orders or making airline reservations on-line. Although some on-line processing had been done by earlier, military systems, these applications were very specialized and not economical. The third generation of computers allowed on-line processing to be a standard operation.

Minicomputers appeared in the mid-1960s. Initially, minis were small, special-purpose machines designed for military and space applications. Gradually, however, the capability of these machines has increased to the point that the more powerful minicomputers and the less powerful mainframes have overlapped. Figure A-14 shows a Digital Equipment VAX minicomputer, a very powerful machine that exceeds the capability of many so-called mainframes. Thus, it now is hard to distinguish between the two categories of computers.

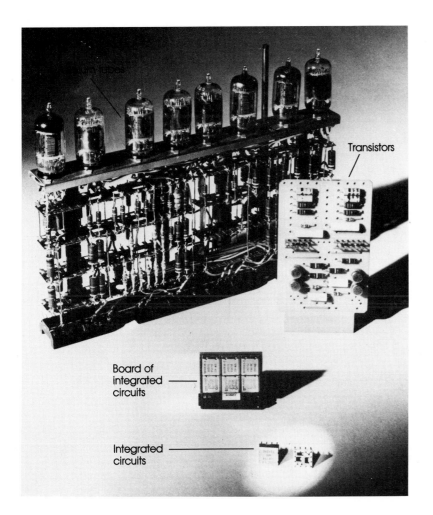

Vacuum tubes

Transistors

Board of integrated circuits

Integrated circuits

Figure A-12
Three generations of hardware components

Figure A-13
A third-generation computer: the Honeywell 6000

A.1   INCREASING YOUR PERSONAL PRODUCTIVITY

The Computer Age: 1946 A.D. to 2000 A.D.

1946 J. Presper Eckert, John Mauchley and a team of 50 complete the Electronic Numerical Integrator and Computer (ENIAC), the first large-scale electronic digital computer, at the University of Pennsylvania's Moore School. Weighing 30 tons, standing two stories and covering 15,000 square feet, ENIAC operates at 357 multiplications per second. Sponsored by the Army, the $500,000 project is aimed at designing a computer for the rapid calculation of military ballistics tables.

1947 Grace Hopper documents the first computer bug, a dead moth found in a cabinet of the Mark II. She immortalizes the insect by pasting it in her logbook beside a note about the incident.

1948 Jealous of ENIAC's success and miffed at Howard Aiken, who snubbed IBM at the Mark I dedication, Thomas J. Watson, Sr., orders built an ENIAC-like computer, the Selective Sequence Electronic Calculator (SSEC). With more than 12,000 vacuum tubes, SSEC becomes the target of cartoonists and motion picture makers, who use its huge size and flashing lights to illustrate the outlandishness of computers of the period.

1949 Maurice Wilkes of England's Cambridge University builds the first stored-program computer, the Electronic Delay Storage Automatic Computer (EDSAC). A student at Eckert's and Mauchley's Moore School lectures, Wilkes works with a copy of John von Neumann's draft on the Electronic Discrete Variable Automatic Computer (EDVAC) to beat out the Americans.

1950 Von Neumann's EDVAC is finally complete. Having lost the distinction as the first stored-program computer, it is still the first to use binary or digital mathematics.

1951 The Universal Automatic Computer, UNIVAC I, made by Remington Rand and operating at a rate of 2,000 computations a second, is delivered to the U.S. Bureau of the Census as the first American commercially produced computer.

1953 IBM introduces the first magnetic tape device, the Model 726. It can pack 100 characters per inch and move at 75 inches per second.

1954 FORTRAN, or Formula Translation programming language, is developed by John Bakus at IBM.

1956 The term "artificial intelligence" is coined by Dartmouth College Assistant Professor John McCarthy, who organizes the Dartmouth Conference in Hanover, N.H., with the help of Marvin Minsky of MIT.

1958 Seymour Cray builds the first fully transistorized supercomputer for Control Data Corp., the CDC 1604.

1959 Jack Kilby of Texas Instruments and Robert Noyce of Fairchild Semiconductor develop "the monolithic idea," creating the integrated circuit, a breakthrough that will allow the dream of smaller and more affordable computers to become a reality.

COBOL, for Common Business-Oriented Language, based on Grace Hopper's FlowMatic, is created by CODASYL, the Committee on Data Systems Languages. Hopper invents a compiler that makes COBOL run on many types of computers.

1960 The first modern computer generation ends as vacuum tubes, punched cards and machine codes give way to second-generation transistors, magnetic tape and procedural languages in computer design and operation.

1963 CDC ships the first supercomputer using silicon transistors to Lawrence Livermore National Labs in California.

1964 In the first computer crime involving criminal prosecution, *Texas v. Hancock*, a programmer who stole $5 million worth of his employer's software is convicted and sentenced to five years.

1965 Beginner's All-Purpose Symbolic Instruction Code (BASIC) language is created by Tom Kurtz and John Kemeny of Dartmouth.

1966 Texas Instruments offers the first solid-state hand-held calculator.

Operation Match computer dating service opens in Cambridge, Mass.

1967 The third generation is under way, with integrated circuits, floppy disks and nonprocedural languages becoming prominent in computer construction and usage.

1968 Gordon Moore and Robert Noyce found Integrated Electronics (Intel) Corp.

1969 The Intel 4004 becomes the first microprocessor.

1970 The first robot supermarket, Telemart, opens in San Diego. The idea was that shoppers would use their Touch-Tone phones to call into a computer that would help them select their groceries and have them delivered. The supermarket closes because so many shoppers call that the computer can't handle the orders.

1971 Intel markets the 4004 microprocessor, which paves the way for the micro revolution.

The floppy disk is introduced to feed instructions to the IBM 370.

1971 Pascal, named after the famous mathematician, is developed by Niklaus Wirth of Switzerland as a programming language for systems development.

1975 The Cray-1 supercomputer is introduced as the fastest computer on earth, performing a million more calculations per second than ENIAC in a space a thousand times smaller.

Microsoft Corp. is founded by Bill Gates and Paul Allen after they adapt BASIC to the Altair microcomputer.

1977 Apple Computer, founded by Steve Wozniak and Steve Jobs, introduces the Apple II personal computer.

Originally developed for computerized astrology by Gary Kildall, CP/M is marketed by Digital Research as a standard control program for personal computers.

1978 Dan Bricklin and Bob Frankston create VisiCalc, electronic spreadsheet software.

1979 Micropro International releases WordStar, one of the best-selling word processing programs.

1980 Shugart Associates introduces the Winchester disk drive, which stores 30 times more data than a small floppy.

1981 The IBM Personal Computer debuts, and Microsoft's MS-DOS becomes its standard operating software.

"Factory Robot Kills Worker" reads the headline about the first reported death caused by a robot: Kenji Urada, 37, is killed when a self-propelled robot cart in a Japanese factory runs him over as he tries to repair it.

Osborne Computer introduces the Osborne I, the first portable computer.

1983 Lotus' 1-2-3 takes VisiCalc's place as the popular spreadsheet program marketed by company founder Mitch Kapor.

Hewlett-Packard offers the first touch-screen personal computer, the HP-150.

1985 Technological trends and innovations include the use of IBM PC-DOS and Unix operating systems as standards, the start-up of fault-tolerant computer firms and the invention of the one-million-bit random-access memory chip.

1988 Computers containing a million processors are set to work solving complex problems.

1990 The advent of parallel processing and greatly increased processing power is expected to make this truly the year of artificial intelligence.

2000 Experts predict that computers containing a billion processors will be technologically feasible, exceeding the power of the human brain.

Figure A-14
The DEC VAX minicomputer

The Fourth Generation

The fourth generation of computers is characterized by **very large-scale integration (VLSI).** With VLSI, thousands of transistors and other components can be placed on a single quarter-inch silicon chip. In fact, an entire CPU can reside on a single chip. The computer that may have occupied a football field in 1952 is today less than half the size of a penny.

VLSI chips can be mass-produced, which means that they can be manufactured and sold in quantities of thousands. Because so many are sold, the costs of research, development, and tooling are spread over many items. Thus, VLSI chips are extremely cheap. A circuit that might have cost $50,000 ten years ago can now be purchased in quantity for $10 or less. Thus, VLSI technology has caused a tremendous decrease in the price/performance ratio of new computers.

A computer on a chip is called a **microprocessor.** When the chip is installed with electronics to perform input and output processing and other functions, it is called a **microcomputer.**

Microprocessors were not designed with forethought. They just happened. The companies that manufacture silicon chips found ways to put more and more circuitry on the chip. They were increasing the circuitry to support other products. For example, the Intel 8008, a microprocessor, was originally intended to be the controller for a CRT terminal. For a variety of reasons, the chip was not used for this purpose.

Because Intel had developed the product, however, they put it in their catalog. To their surprise, apparently, it sold very well. The company saw the demand, put a design team together, and a year later introduced the Intel 8080 microprocessor, shown in Figure A-15. This product has become one of the most popular microprocessors. Other manufacturers quickly followed suit. Today there are dozens of microprocessor products to choose from. While there was no such thing as a microprocessor in 1969, by 1975 750,000 microprocessors were in use and by 1984 that figure had exploded to 100,000,000.

All of this development means that computers have become cheaper and cheaper. Some experts believe that the cost of computer CPUs will soon be essentially zero. At least, the cost will be negligible compared to that of other components of a business computer system.

These inexpensive microprocessors may well lead to entirely new computer architectures. Since microprocessors are so cheap, it becomes feasible to develop and market **supercomputers,** or computers that are banks of many microprocessors. For example, a supercomputer could be a 100 × 100 array of microprocessors. It boggles the mind to consider the power of such a machine.

Computers in the 1980s

During the 1980s there have been some exciting developments both in the large mainframe environment and in the area of microcomputers. All of these developments have affected business in some way.

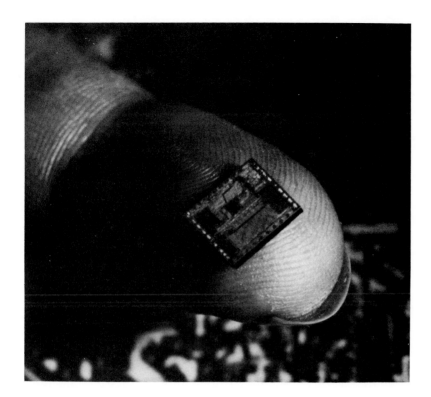

Off-the-Shelf Programs   The most significant cost of business computer systems is the cost of the development process itself. A lot of money and time must be invested to develop a new business computer system. One significant development in the 1980s is the acceptance of **off-the-shelf software,** even by large corporations. Recall from Chapter 2 that the two ways of acquiring programs are to write them yourself or to buy packaged software. Until recently, many companies were distrustful of any software that was "NIH" ("not invented here"). As software development costs continue to rise, new development projects continue to be backlogged; and as high-quality software packages become available, more data processing managers are turning to off-the-shelf software to satisfy at least some user needs.

Prototyping   Another significant development in the area of system development is the concept of **prototyping,** discussed in Chapter 12. Recall that a prototype is a skeletal system that users can work with very early during system development. This hands-on experience enables users to more accurately define their requirements and to reject unsatisfactory features of a system while it is easy and inexpensive for the developers to make changes.

Fourth-Generation Languages   A third improvement for developers of mainframe systems is **fourth-generation languages (4GLs).** 4GLs are *nonprocedural* languages (unlike COBOL, BASIC, Pascal, and hundreds of other languages). Some are easy enough for users to learn and use, though the more powerful 4GLs are too technical for use by an ordinary businessperson. In the hands of a skilled programmer, a 4GL can increase programming productivity by as much as 200 percent.

What impact will the use of fourth-generation languages have on software development? If the biggest deterrent to custom programming is the time and cost of developing programs (and maintaining them later), then will 4GLs eliminate the problem? Rather than settle for off-the-shelf programs that almost (but not quite) meet their needs, will users insist on custom programming? Will fourth-generation languages eventually be developed that *any* user, even an inexperienced one, can easily learn and implement? What impact will such a development have on the people currently in data processing? Of course, we do not have the answers to these questions. Only time will tell what systems development will be like in the 1990s. But the changes just described are probably indicative of what is to come.

The Microcomputer Explosion

The most exciting recent developments have taken place in the area of microcomputers. When microcomputers first appeared during the early 1980s they were almost immediately snubbed as playthings for the computer hobbyist. But their sophistication, power, small size, portability, and software rapidly changed the minds of even the cynics. The 1980s have seen almost every type of business, large and small, embrace the microcomputer as an important piece of equipment.

A Brief History of Microcomputers   The first microcomputer was a kit computer called the Mark-8, which was designed by Ed Roberts in 1974. He followed the Mark-8 with a machine called the Altair, named for the destination of the starship Enterprise on a *Star Trek* episode. The Altair sold for $397 in 1975. The bank that had financed Roberts' company, MITS, hoped he could sell 200 computers. In April of 1976, MITS reported at a meeting of the Homebrew Computer Club (a pioneering microcomputer club) that 4,000 Altairs had been ordered.

Two computer programmers in Boston, Paul Allen and Bill Gates (then a Harvard freshman), learned about the Altair and convinced Roberts to adopt their BASIC interpreter. Allen and Gates subsequently established Microsoft, now one of the world's largest software publishers.

The Tandy Corporation began as a leather business in 1927. In 1962 the owner's son suggested buying a chain of mail-order electronics stores in Boston called Radio Shack, which was losing four million dollars a year. By August 1977 the TRS-80 microcomputer was announced. Within a month the Tandy Corporation had sold 100,000 units.

The story of the Apple computer is an interesting one. Stephen G. Wozniak built an addition-subtraction machine for a local service firm in 1962. By 1971 he had built his own computer from spare electronic parts. Wozniak knew about the Altair computer, but he couldn't afford one at the time. So he and a high-school friend named Steve Jobs (pronounced "jobs" with a long "o"), another electronics buff, decided to

A.2   *INCREASING YOUR PERSONAL PRODUCTIVITY*

Beyond the Laptop—True Pocket Size

How small can computers really get and still be useful? With the Wizard, Sharp has tried to answer that question—with mixed success. The Wizard is clearly not intended as a replacement for a desktop computer. Instead, it's designed as a true *personal* computer. It can help you with day-to-day tasks that require more than just a calculator in a near-pocket-sized package: 3.7-by-6.4-by-0.85-inches. The Wizard weighs 8 ounces and includes calendar, scheduler, phone book, searchable memo pad, local time, world time, and calculator functions. Results are displayed on a flat LCD in either eight lines of 16 characters each or four lines of 10 characters each.

Credit card-sized (3.4-by-2.1-inch) software cards are available to expand the Wizard's capabilities. Also available are a time/expense manager, a dictionary/thesaurus, and an eight-language translator. Sharp has designed a clever touch-pad area into the Wizard where brightly colored legends on the software card define new keys specific to the application, making these add-in programs especially easy to use. The software cards can store your own information as well as the program and retain that information using a wafer-thin lithium battery installed in the card. For example, the time/expense manager will store your expense record and calendar right on the card. You can even transfer your calendar and expense information to another Wizard by transferring the card. All the information in the Wizard can be protected against unauthorized access through your assignment of a personal password.

What can make the Wizard truly useful is the complement of peripherals Sharp has provided. With these accessories, you can print your calendar or expense reports and even send them to another computer, where they can be incorporated in documents, databases, and spreadsheets. It's also possible to enter information on a PC and then download it to the Wizard. If you need to coordinate with someone else owning a Wizard, you can exchange information directly between two Wizards. Sharp also provides a cable for storing data to and retrieving it from a cassette recorder.

All this power in your pocket doesn't come cheap. The basic Wizard is priced reasonably at $299, but adding the extras can be expensive. The hand-held printer costs $169.99; the cassette recorder costs $99.99; the dubbing cable for connecting two Wizards is $30; a combination of software and cable for interfacing with a PC costs $149.99; and software cards range from $99.99 to $129.99. Nonetheless, the Wizard is a viable miniature computer and may be worth the expense if you're looking for pocket pyrotechnics.

develop a BASIC interpreter to run on the 6502 chip, and to build a computer to run it. Wozniak dubbed the result the Apple. (Some say he named it after the Beatles' record label, others say the inspiration came from visiting Steve Jobs in Oregon, a state famous for apple orchards.)

In February 1977, the Apple Computer Company opened its doors in Cupertino, California. The Apple II computer was unveiled a few months later at the first West Coast Computer Faire.

IBM entered the microcomputer market on August 12, 1981, with its announcement of the IBM Personal Computer, or IBM PC. IBM's computer was built from parts available to the general public. Other computer manufacturers scrambled to build their own "IBM look-alike" computers. An entire industry has grown up around the IBM PC and compatible computers.

Recognizing IBM's importance in the microcomputer field, the Apple Computer Company took out a full-page advertisement in the *Wall Street Journal*. "Welcome IBM," the ad said. "Welcome to the most exciting and important marketplace since the computer revolution began 35 years ago."

In 1982, the COMPAQ Corporation began to sell its own version of the IBM Personal Computer—a computer that was *IBM compatible*. COMPAQ's computer was small, portable, and high quality. It became an overnight success. Within three years COMPAQ had grown to over $500 million in sales per year!

Meanwhile, Apple had become a billion-dollar-a-year company, but Steve Jobs encountered problems in dealing with the management team he had helped to assemble. He was forced out in 1985 by John Sculley, whom Jobs had himself hired two years before. He was able to take with him, however, stock worth about $100 million at the time.

Apple went on to turn its Macintosh series of computers into a resounding success, largely because it was able to make inroads against IBM in major corporations. Many had predicted this feat would be impossible because such accounts had been IBM's bread-and-butter for several decades. The Macintosh, however, had a vastly superior user interface than IBM and IBM-compatible computers. This interface made the computer much more approachable for first-time users.

Meanwhile, Jobs invested some of his proceeds from Apple into another start-up venture. This venture's first product is a computer called NeXT. NeXT uses much state-of-the-art technology, including an optical disk for large-capacity storage, sophisticated graphics, high-quality synthesized sound, and a new programming methodology called object-oriented programming. Whether NeXT will gain widespread acceptance is not yet known. Jobs has gained the support of investors like H. Ross Perot and the strong support of Businessland as a chain sales outlet.

Still, today the microcomputer industry is largely dominated by the IBM, COMPAQ, and Apple corporations. Other companies such as Zenith, Hewlett-Packard, NEC, and Toshiba also have a presence, but a much smaller one.

Special-purpose microcomputers called **workstations** are used primarily by engineers. These computers have high-quality graphics and fast processors. They are used in all types of industries for engineering applications such as design and drawing. Sun, Apollo, and Hewlett-Packard are the leading workstation manufacturers.

Microprocessors Although over a hundred different microprocessors have been invented, only a few have had importance in the commercial world. Early important microprocessors were the Intel 8080, the MOS Technology 6502, and the Zilog Z-80. The 6502 was the basis for the Commodore PET and Apple II computers. The Z-80, which is a variation on the 8080, was the basis for the TRS-80 microcomputer.

Since those early years, two families of microprocessors have dominated the market. The Intel family has been the basis for the IBM (and compatible) line of personal computers that were first introduced in late 1981. Intel microprocessors include the 8088, the 80286, the 80386, and the i486. This last microprocessor has over one million transistors on a single chip. The second line of microprocessors was developed by Motorola. The Motorola 68000 is the most important Motorola microprocessor and is the basis for the Apple Macintosh family of computers.

Standardization As indicated, in the early 1980s, there were a large number of different microprocessors and microcomputers being sold. This was a disadvantage, however, because a different version of software packages had to be created for each different hardware platform. Software companies found that supporting many different versions of each product was too expensive, and they gradually restricted their programs to the best-selling hardware. Users, too, wanted to have more simplicity in the computers that they purchased and supported.

Hence, from about 1984 on, the industry settled on two standard personal computer platforms. One was the IBM or IBM-compatible hardware architecture with the MS-PC/DOS operating system. The second was the Apple Macintosh with its own operating system. Today, almost all commercial microcomputers are a version of one of these.

Recently, IBM began shipping a new operating system called OS/2. This operating system, which runs on the PS/2 and compatible computers, overcomes many of the important limitations of DOS and is likely to see considerable use in the future. See Chapter 4.

The Impact of the Microcomputer

The microcomputer has had a tremendous impact on business and society, in the United States and throughout the world. Since we are still in the midst of a revolution in information processing and communications, it is difficult to assess what the true impact of the microcomputer has been.

For example, laser printers and desktop publishing programs enable the ordinary person to produce exceedingly high-quality documents. What is the impact of such capability in the long run? Consider not only the impact on business, but also the impact on government and politics. State control over newspapers becomes nearly impossible. In a similar vein, consider the experimental personal newspaper developed at MIT. This newspaper allows people to use microcomputers that communicate with a news source to tailor their own newspaper. No paper is involved. What impact will such a facility have on business, society, governments, and politics? We simply do not know.

Some impacts are easier to identify. One obvious one is that there has been a tremendous increase in computer usage and literacy. Between 1980 and 1986, for example, some 9.6 million people learned how to use a microcomputer. Today there are more than 25 million micros in use worldwide.

Presumably, most of these micros are being used for some productive purpose. This might be one of the applications you learned about in Chapters 5–7—word processing, spreadsheets, database processing, graphics, or some other application. These applications are changing the way business is conducted. For example, many more what-if analyses can be conducted using a spreadsheet than can be conducted by hand. Such changes lead to changes in expectations and in the way that business is conducted.

Another significant impact is that the microcomputer has been the impetus for the creation of new lines of business. Computer stores and retail chains, distributors of both hardware and software, consulting companies, and computer repair companies have all come into existence as a result of the microcomputer and its popularity. Bookstores and publishers have felt the impact of the microcomputer as well. Hundreds of how-to books have been written to answer some of the public's questions about the microcomputer.

Probably the most obvious impact of the microcomputer is that so much more information is being produced. One would assume this means that better decisions are being made. Or, in terms of the model in Chapter 11, that there is an improvement in operations, management control, and strategic planning, as well as improvements in products. On the other hand, it's not clear that all of this information is needed, nor is it clear that the neighborhood swimming pool schedule needs to be produced in a slick format complete with graphics of local children.

As stated, the microcomputer has certainly caused much more information to be produced. You will undoubtedly participate in this production process during your career. As you do so, you might contemplate Otto Rank's observation: "For the time being I gave up writing—there is already too much truth in the world—an overproduction which apparently cannot be consumed."[2] It is certainly reasonable to ask from time to time whether the information your system produces is truly needed.

Summary

Questions

A.1 Explain what people can learn today from the experiences of Charles Babbage.

A.2 What role did the U.S. Census Bureau play in the development of computers?

A.3 Explain the contribution to the development of computers made by each of the following individuals:
Charles Babbage
Herman Hollerith
Howard Aiken
John Mauchly
J. Presper Eckert
John V. Atanasoff
John von Neumann
Rear Admiral Grace Hopper

Although the history of computation began thousands of years ago, the development of computers is a recent phenomenon. In the early 1800s, Charles Babbage developed many of the design concepts used in today's computers. However, these concepts were not implemented at that time. Many of the mistakes that Babbage made are still being made today.

In the late 1800s, the U.S. Census Bureau had a problem. They hired Herman Hollerith to develop automated ways of computing census data. This led to the development of punched-card equipment and the beginning of the punched-card industry.

Computers were not actually developed until the mid-1940s. Early computers were produced through the cooperation of universities, government, and industry. There have been four generations of computers so far. First-generation computers had vacuum tubes, and main storage was a magnetic drum. These computers were huge and very hard to maintain. Programs were written in machine code.

Computers in the second generation used transistors and had main memory made of magnetic core. They were smaller and still very expensive. High-level languages were developed for programming, and rudimentary operating systems were invented.

2. Jessie Taft, *Otto Rank* (New York: Julian Press, 1958), p. 175.

The third-generation computers have integrated circuits on silicon chips. These chips are used both for the arithmetic and logic unit and for main memory. Third-generation computers are much smaller and cheaper than first- or second-generation computers.

Today computers are in their fourth generation. They have become significantly cheaper and more powerful. In the near future, the cost of a CPU will be essentially zero. We may see the development of super-computers that are banks of microprocessors.

Unfortunately, the costs of developing programs has increased during this same time period. To compensate for these increases, businesses have turned to packaged programs and fourth-generation languages. It is possible that users will one day be able to do all of their own programming using 4GLs.

Microcomputers had a profound impact on business in the 1980s. They are widely accepted as an important piece of business equipment, and millions of people have learned how to use them in only a few years. They have made information more available, through technology such as communications. New businesses have appeared which sell and service hardware and software, and teach people how to use microcomputers. More information than ever is being produced, at least partly because microcomputers make it easy to produce information.

A.4 How did Herman Hollerith set the pace for computer entrepreneurs?

A.5 What was the IBM marketing philosophy in the early days of computing? How did it help the company?

A.6 Characterize the machines and programs of each of the four generations of computers.

A.7 Explain why computers are becoming inexpensive.

A.8 Why has the cost of developing computer programs not decreased as the cost of hardware has?

A.9 Name and describe two ways businesses have found to decrease the cost of acquiring programs.

A.10 Which microprocessors currently dominate the personal computer market?

A.11 What are the two standard personal computer platforms?

A.12 Describe three ways in which microcomputers have affected business or society.

Word List

abacus
Charles Babbage
difference engine
analytical engine
Ada Augusta Lovelace
Herman Hollerith
Howard G. Aiken
Mark I
John W. Mauchly
J. Presper Eckert
ENIAC
John V. Atanasoff
John von Neumann

EDVAC
EDSAC
Grace Hopper
Adele Goldstine
UNIVAC I
first-generation computers
second-generation computers
core memory
machine code
assembly language
high-level language
third-generation computers
integrated circuit

on-line processing
minicomputers
fourth-generation computers
very large-scale integrated (VLSI) circuits
microprocessor
microcomputer
supercomputer
off-the-shelf software
prototyping
fourth-generation language (4GL)
workstation

Discussion Questions and Exercises

A. The rate of computer technology development has been astronomical in the last thirty years. What impact do you think this growth has had on industry? How do you think a company can best cope with this type of growth if it continues in the future?

B. What impact do you think the rapid change in technology has had on education? How do you think education will change as computers become less and less expensive?

C. Judging from the past, what do you think is going to happen in computing? What impact will computers of the future have on business? How will business in the year 2000 use computer technology?

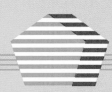

Numeric Representation and Computer Arithmetic

In this module, we discuss how computers represent numbers and perform arithmetic. This information supplements material in Chapter 2, so be sure to read Chapter 2 before continuing with this section.

Computers represent two basic types of data: **numeric** and **alphanumeric.** Numeric data consists of numbers that can be processed arithmetically, and alphanumeric data consists of numbers, letters, and special symbols such as #, $, and %. Alphanumeric data is not processed arithmetically. Even if alphanumeric data consists entirely of numbers, the computer represents it in such a way that arithmetic cannot be performed on it.

Alphanumeric data is represented by character codes such as EBCDIC. This type of representation was discussed in Chapter 2, and we will not repeat that discussion here. Instead, we will discuss the format and processing of numeric data.

Decimal and Binary Numbers

To understand how numbers are represented in the computer, try to recall your second-grade math. Remember Mrs. Gazernenplatz, your second-grade teacher? When she wrote a number such as 5437 on the board, she said that the 7 is in the ones place, the 3 is in the tens place, the 4 is in the hundreds place, and the 5 is in the thousands place. The number can thus be defined as 5 times 1000, plus 4 times 100, plus 3 times 10, plus 7 times 1.

Later, in algebra, you learned that you also can write 1000 as 10^3 ($10 \times 10 \times 10$), 100 as 10^2, 10 as 10^1, and 1 as 10^0. Thus, each place is a power of 10. The power value starts with 0 and increases by 1 for each place to the left of the decimal point. (See Figure B-1.)

In the computer, numeric data often is represented in binary form. The binary number system has only two digits (or symbols): 0 and 1. Each binary place is assigned a binary digit, or **bit.** Examples of binary numbers are 110110, 01110, 11111, and 00000. The number 0121 is not a binary number, because the symbol 2 is not defined in the binary system. As explained in Chapter 2, computers use the binary system because the symbols 0 and 1 are easy to represent electronically.

Binary numbers are constructed the same way as decimal numbers, but, instead of powers of 10 in the places, powers of 2 are used. Thus,

Figure B-1
Decimal-place notation

5437 Decimal

5 × 1000		5 × 10^3 (thousands place)
+4 × 100	or	+4 × 10^2 (hundreds place)
+3 × 10		+3 × 10^1 (tens place)
+7 × 1		+7 × 10^0 (ones place)

1010 Binary Is 10 in Decimal Form

1×8		1×2^3 (eights place)
$+0 \times 4$	or	$+0 \times 2^2$ (fours place)
$+1 \times 2$		$+1 \times 2^1$ (twos place)
$+0 \times 1$		$+0 \times 2^0$ (ones place)

there is the ones place 2^0, the twos place 2^1, the fours place 2^2, the eights place 2^3, and so forth, as shown in Figure B-2. The binary number 1010 is interpreted as 1 times 8, plus 0 times 4, plus 1 times 2, plus 0 times 1, or 10 in decimal. Figure B-3 shows the first 16 binary numbers.

Humans like to work with decimal numbers, but computers are more efficient when working with binary numbers. Therefore, when many calculations are to be performed, the computer converts decimal numbers to binary form and makes the calculations using binary arithmetic. Results are then reconverted to decimal format before they are printed. We will discuss how these conversions are performed after we discuss binary arithmetic.

Binary Arithmetic

Binary numbers can be added much the same way decimal numbers are added. You add one column at a time and carry when necessary. In binary format,

$$0 + 0 = 0$$
$$0 + 1 = 1$$
$$1 + 0 = 1$$
$$1 + 1 = 10$$

Binary	Decimal	Binary	Decimal
0000	0	1000	8
0001	1	1001	9
0010	2	1010	10
0011	3	1011	11
0100	4	1100	12
0101	5	1101	13
0110	6	1110	14
0111	7	1111	15

Thus, when two 1s are added, a 1 is carried into the next place. The following are examples of binary addition:

		1 ← (Carries) →			1111
0010		1010			1111
+ 0101		+ 0010			+ 0001
0111		1100			10000

Although subtraction can be done in binary arithmetic just as it is done in decimal, computers usually do not do this. In fact (here's an amazing fact), *most computers cannot subtract*! Instead, they find the result of a subtraction by adding in a special way. This technique is called **complement addition.**

Suppose that you want to compute 8 minus 3 in decimal arithmetic. To do this subtraction using complements, you add 8 to the **tens complement** of 3 and throw away the carry. The tens complement of a number is the value you add to the number to get 10. Thus, the tens complement of 3 is 7 because 3 plus 7 is 10. The tens complement of 6 is 4 (6 + 4 = 10), and the tens complement of 2 is 8 (2 + 8 = 10).

Now, to compute 8 minus 3, you add 8 to the tens complement of 3 and throw away the carry. Thus, 8 plus 7 (the tens complement of 3) is 15. Throwing away the carry, you get 5, which equals 8 minus 3 (see Figure B-4). Now you try subtraction. Compute 9 minus 2. The tens complement of 2 is 8. Add 9 and 8 to get 17. Throw away the 1 and you have 7, which is the result of 9 minus 2.

Try another computation. Compute 9 minus 5. The tens complement of 5 is 5 (5 + 5 = 10). Adding 9 and 5 gives you 14. Throw away the carry to get 4, which is the same as 9 minus 5.

What happens if the answer should be a negative number? Suppose that you compute 3 minus 6? The answer should be −3. Using complements, we add 3 to the tens complement of 6. Thus, we add 3 to 4 and get 7, which is not −3.

What happened? Complement addition has one more rule: If the result of the addition leaves no carry to throw away, the answer is negative. When this occurs, take the tens complement of the answer and add a minus sign to get the correct result.

Figure B-4
Subtraction using complement addition

> **To compute 8 − 3,**
>   **a.** Find the tens complement of 3, which is 7.
>   **b.** Add 8 to the complement of 3 to obtain 15.
>   **c.** Throw away the carry to obtain 5, the difference of 8 and 3.
>
> **To compute 9 − 5.**
>   **a.** Find the tens complement of 5, which is 5.
>   **b.** Add 9 to the complement of 5 to obtain 14.
>   **c.** Throw away the carry to obtain 4, the answer.

> **To compute 3 − 6,**
>   a. Find the tens complement of 6, which is 4.
>   b. Add 3 to the complement of 6 to obtain 7.
>   c. There is no carry, therefore the answer is negative. Take the tens complement of 7, which is 3, and add a minus sign. The answer is −3.
>
> **To compute 7 − 9,**
>   a. Find the tens complement of 9, which is 1.
>   b. Add 7 to the complement of 9 to obtain 8.
>   c. There is no carry, therefore the answer is negative. Take the tens complement of 8, which is 2, and add a minus sign. The answer is −2.

Figure B-5
Subtraction using complement addition to obtain negative answers

Thus, 3 minus 6 is computed by adding 3 to 4 (the tens complement of 6), which yields 7. There is no carry, so the answer is negative; take the tens complement of 7 and add a minus sign. The answer is −3, as it should be (see Figure B-5).

Try 7 minus 9. The answer should be −2. Take the tens complement of 9, which is 1. Add 7 and 1 to get 8. There is no carry, so the answer is negative. Take the tens complement of 8 and add a minus sign. The answer is −2. It works!

Computers do the same thing in binary arithmetic. To form the **twos complement** of a binary number, the computer just turns all the 1s to 0s and all the 0s to 1s; then it adds 1. Thus, the twos complement of 0110 is 1001 plus 1, or 1010.

Suppose that we want to compute 1111 minus 0110. The answer should be 1001. To compute this subtraction, we add 1111 and the twos complement of 0110. The twos complement of 0110 is 1001; thus, we add 1111 to 1010.

```
(Carry) →    111
            1111
          + 1010
          1 1001
```

We throw away the carry, and the answer is 1001, as it should be. If there is no carry, the number is negative. Complement the answer by switching 1s and 0s and adding 1.

Thus, computers subtract by adding complements. Forming twos complements is easy, and adding also is easy, so computers can work very fast.

Computers multiply by successive additions. Thus, to multiply 7 times 8, the computer adds eight 7s together. To multiply 1234 times 438, the computer adds 438 1234s together. Division is performed by successive subtractions.

Octal and Hexadecimal Number Systems

Working with binary numbers is easy and convenient for computers, but it is not so easy for people. Adding the binary number 11010101110100 to the binary number 110100100001111101001101011 is a chore. It's also very easy to drop a bit and get the wrong answer. To make errors less likely, people have found a way to shorten binary numbers.

One way is to group the binary symbols into threesomes and to represent each threesome by a number. The table in Figure B-6 shows how to represent three binary digits with a single number. The first column lists all the possible three-place binary numbers, and the second column lists the symbols used to represent them.

Let's use this table to shorten some binary numbers. Group the binary symbols into threes and substitute the corresponding single digit from Figure B-6.

111011 becomes 111 011, or 73
011010 becomes 011 010, or 32
111000 becomes 111 000, or 70
111111 becomes 111 111, or 77

Notice that the symbols 8 and 9 are not used in this abbreviation scheme. The largest symbol is 7. We have created a number system that has only eight symbols: 0, 1, 2, 3, 4, 5, 6, and 7. This system is called the **octal number system** because it uses eight symbols.

Figure B-7 shows the decimal equivalents of some octal numbers. In the decimal system, we have the ones place, the tens place, the hundreds place, and so forth. In the binary system we have the ones place, the twos place, the fours place, the eights place, and so forth. In the octal system, we have places for the ones, the eights, the sixty-fours, and other powers of eight. The octal number 3456 is equal to 3 times 512 ($8 \times 8 \times 8$), plus 4 times 64 (8×8), plus 5 times 8 (8×1), plus 6 times 1, or 1838 in decimal format.

As mentioned, octal format is used primarily as a shorthand for binary format. Converting from octal to binary format is very easy. We just replace each octal symbol with the three binary symbols that it represents. Thus, 234 in octal format equals 010 011 100 in binary format.

Figure B-6
Binary numbers and their abbreviations (octal equivalents)

Binary Number	Octal Equivalent	Binary Number	Octal Equivalent
000	0	100	4
001	1	101	5
010	2	110	6
011	3	111	7

Octal Number	Decimal Form
47	4 × 8 + 7 × 1 or 39
312	3 × 64 + 1 × 8 + 2 × 1 or 202
4057	4 × 512 + 0 × 64 + 5 × 8 + 7 × 1 or 1583

Several manufacturers produce computers that abbreviate binary numbers with octal numbers. Control Data Corporation (CDC), for instance, makes computers that have 60 bits per word. When the binary value of a word is printed by these machines, it is usually shown in octal format. So, instead of printing 60 binary symbols thus:

111111111111111111111111111111111111111111111111111111111111

they print the octal number 7777777777. Such a number is much easier for humans to understand and manipulate.

Sometimes computers print a **dump** at the end of a run that terminated abnormally. This dump shows the values in certain critical areas of main memory. The values in these critical areas will be in binary format, but the computer will print them in octal format so humans can understand them more easily.

Some computers, such as some IBM machines, have 32 bits per word. In these computers, the octal number system cannot readily be used to abbreviate the stored values, because 32 bits cannot be broken into equal groups of three. Thus, the word is divided instead into eight groups of 4 bits each. This division presents a problem, however.

Four bits can represent the decimal values 0 through 15. To abbreviate 4 bits by one character we need 16 symbols. We can use the symbols 0 through 9 to represent the first 10 numbers, but we need other symbols to represent the last 6. Figure B-8 shows a scheme for solving this problem.

Binary Number	Hexadecimal Equivalent	Binary Number	Hexadecimal Equivalent
0000	0	1000	8
0001	1	1001	9
0010	2	1010	A
0011	3	1011	B
0100	4	1100	C
0101	5	1101	D
0110	6	1110	E
0111	7	1111	F

Hexadecimal Number	Decimal Form	
79	$7 \times 16 + 9 \times 1$ or	121
E4	$14 \times 16 + 4 \times 1$ or	228
A1C	$10 \times 256 + 1 \times 16 + 12 \times 1$ or	2588
A14E	$10 \times 4096 + 1 \times 256 + 4 \times 16 + 14 \times 1$ or	41,294
1F7C8	$1 \times 65,536 + 15 \times 4096 + 7 \times 256 + 12 \times 16 + 8 \times 1$ or	128,968

The binary values 0 through 1001 are represented by the decimal characters 0 through 9. The binary value 1010 equals decimal 10. However, we need a single symbol to represent 1010. Hence, we use the letter A. The letter B represents 1011, C represents 1100, and so forth.

This scheme creates a number system with 16 symbols: 0 through 9 and A through F. It is called the **hexadecimal number system.** The places in this system are powers of 16. The places are the 1s place, the 16s place, the 256s place, the 4096s place, and so forth, increasing by powers of 16. As shown in Figure B-9, the hexadecimal number A14E represents 10 times 4096, plus 1 times 256, plus 4 times 16, plus 14, or 41,294 in decimal format.

On computers that use 16- or 32-bit words, the dumps and other binary printouts are produced in hexadecimal format. To convert from hexadecimal to binary format, just substitute the bit pattern for each character from Figure B-8. Thus, A14E in hexadecimal format represents 1010000101001110 in binary.

So far, we have discussed four number systems. Decimal numbers are traditionally used by people. Binary numbers are used by computers, mostly because the binary symbols 0 and 1 are easy to represent electronically. However, working with binary numbers is troublesome for people. Therefore, binary numbers sometimes are abbreviated using either octal or hexadecimal numbers.

Converting Between Number Systems

Sometimes people and computers need to convert a number from one system to another. For example, we may need to know what the hexadecimal number A1A equals in decimal format, what the decimal number 789 equals in octal format, and so forth.

Converting from binary, octal, or hexadecimal format to decimal format is easy. In fact, we have already seen how. Just multiply each symbol by its place value. In the binary system, the place values are powers of 2, in the octal system they are powers of 8, and in the hexadecimal system they are powers of 16.

Figure B-10

Converting from decimal format to binary, octal, and hexadecimal formats

Division	Remainder	Division	Remainder	Division	Remainder
2|37		8|92		16|489	
	1		4		9
2|18		8|11		16| 30	
	0		3		E
2| 9		8| 1		16| 1	
	1		1		1
2| 4					
	0				
2| 2					
	0				
2| 1					
	1				

Answer: 100101 binary	Answer: 134 octal	Answer: 1E9 hexadecimal
a. Decimal 37 converted to binary	***b.*** Decimal 92 converted to octal	***c.*** Decimal 489 converted to hexadecimal

Converting from binary to octal or from binary to hexadecimal format also is easy. Just use the table in Figure B-6 or in Figure B-8. To convert from decimal to binary, octal, or hexadecimal format, however, is not so easy.

Such conversions can be done by the **division/remainder method.** This method uses successive divisions by the base number. For example, to convert from decimal to binary format, the decimal number is successively divided by 2. To convert from decimal to octal format, the decimal number is successively divided by 8. As the divisions are done, the remainders are saved; they become the transformed number.

Examine Figure B-10. Three conversions are shown. In the first, the decimal number 37 is converted to binary format; 37 is repeatedly divided by 2 until the quotient is 0. As the division is done, the remainders are written on the right-hand side. The equivalent binary number is read from these remainders, from the bottom up. Thus, 37 in decimal format equals 100101 in binary format.

In the second example, the decimal number 92 is converted to octal format; 92 is repeatedly divided by 8 until no whole division is possible. Then the number is read from the remainders. Thus, 92 decimal equals 134 octal.

In the third example, 489 is converted to hexadecimal format; 489 is repeatedly divided by 16 until no whole division is possible. The remainders are kept on the right-hand side. Note that the remainder of 14 is represented by the hexadecimal symbol E, not by 14. The number 489 decimal equals 1E9 hexadecimal. In practice, such conversions are done by special hand calculators.

Floating-Point Numbers

The binary format just described is only one of the ways that computers represent arithmetic numbers. Another format is called **floating point.** This term is used because the decimal point of the number is allowed to move, or float. The same form can represent 0.45 or 4500. The advantage of this form is its flexibility. It can represent very large and very small numbers, including fractions.

Floating-point numbers are represented in **exponential** or **scientific form.** The decimal number 1257 is represented in exponential form as 0.1257 times 10^4. This notation means that 1257 equals 0.1257 times 10,000 ($0.1257 \times 10 \times 10 \times 10 \times 10$). Numbers from other number systems can be represented similarly. Thus, the binary number 1011 equals 0.1011 times 2^4 ($0.1011 \times 2 \times 2 \times 2 \times 2$). Similarly, the octal number 765 equals 0.765 times 512 ($0.765 \times 8 \times 8 \times 8$).

In each of these cases, the fractional number is called the **mantissa** and the power of the base is called the **exponent.** The mantissa of 0.1257 times 10^4 is 0.1257, and the exponent is 4.

Scientific notation can represent fractions as well as whole numbers. The decimal number 0.0123 is 0.123 times 10^1. The number 0.000345 is 0.345 times 10^{-3}. In this latter case, the mantissa is 0.345 and the exponent is -3.

Floating-point numbers use exponential notation. Each computer word has two sections: one section holds the exponent, and the other holds the mantissa. On IBM computers, for example, the first 8 bits of a word hold the exponent (a power of 16), and the remaining 24 bits hold the mantissa (see Figure B-11).

On Control Data computers, the first 12 bits hold the exponent (a power of 8), and the remaining 48 bits hold the mantissa. Because more bits are used to represent the mantissa on CDC computers than on IBM computers, greater precision is possible. The mantissa can have a larger number of characters.

Both the mantissa and the exponent have a sign. The sign of the mantissa indicates whether the number is positive or negative. The sign of the exponent indicates whether the number is greater or less than 1.

The particular method of representing floating-point numbers is beyond the scope of this book. You should know that they exist and that

Figure B-11
Floating-point word formats

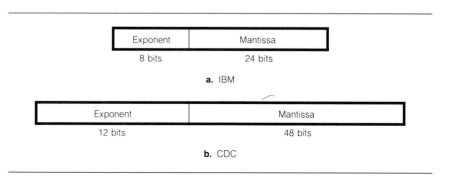

a. IBM

b. CDC

they are represented in a special way in the computer. You should also be aware that, because of the special format, extra instructions (and time) are required to process floating-point numbers.

Some small computers use only one type of number. Some micro-computers use only integer numbers and integer instructions; others have only floating-point numbers and instructions. Make sure that your computer has floating-point capability if you need it. Otherwise, you will have to program your own floating-point capability, and that is a chore.

Fractions and Round-Off Errors

Fractions can be represented in two ways. The first is floating-point format, as just described. The second way is **fixed-point binary format.** For this format, numbers are represented in binary format, but a binary point is assumed to exist. (A binary point, like a decimal point, separates the integer part of a number from the fractional part.) For example, a binary point could be defined as being to the left of the third bit in a word. Then the binary number 110111 would be interpreted as 110.111 (see Figure B-12 for other examples). When using this format, the program defines where it wants the point to be, and all operations are based on that definition. Note that in this case the binary point cannot float; every number has the same number of places to the right of the point.

There is a curious fact about fractions. Exactly representing a fraction that can be represented exactly in one number system may not be possible in another system. For example, the decimal fraction 0.1 cannot be evenly represented in the hexadecimal (or binary) system. It is slightly more than hexadecimal 0.199.

The fact that 0.1 cannot be evenly represented in the binary system is very important in business. For instance, the dollar value $12.10 does not have an even binary representation, nor does $1.1 trillion.

Fixed-Point Format	Binary Number	Is Interpreted As
XXX.XX	11101	111.01
	10011	100.11
	10001	100.01
X.XXXX	11101	1.1101
	10011	1.0011
	10001	1.0001
.XXXXX	11101	.11101
	10011	.10011
	10001	.10001

Figure B-12

Examples of fixed-point binary numbers

Assume that you ask the computer to add the value $0.01 one hundred times. If 0.01 is represented in binary format, you may not get $1.00. Instead you may get $0.99999999999999. This problem, called the **round-off error,** can be inconvenient and embarrassing to computer personnel. Sometimes it makes the computer appear unable to add.

Decimal Numbers

Questions

B.1 Which of the following are valid binary numbers?
a. 1101
b. 1200
c. 9812
d. 0000

B.2 Decimal places have values of ones, tens, hundreds, and so forth.
a. What are the values of binary places?
b. What are the values of octal places?
c. What are the values of hexadecimal places?

B.3 Add the following binary numbers:
a. 110 + 001
b. 110001 + 001110
c. 111111 + 0000001
d. 11101 + 00011

B.4 How do most computers perform subtraction?

Because of this problem (and for other reasons as well), some computers have the ability to perform arithmetic in decimal format. With these computers, the inputs are never converted to binary format, and the round-off error does not occur. Unfortunately, decimal arithmetic is slower than binary arithmetic. Therefore, decimal arithmetic is only done when calculations are simple and few. In business, such calculations often are required. Many business systems need only perform simple additions or multiplications. Therefore, the decimal form of data often is used in business.

Figure B-13 shows decimal digits represented in the EBCDIC code. Two hexadecimal, or "hex," characters are used to represent each decimal digit: F1 represents 1, F2 represents 2, and so forth. Note how inefficient this scheme is. Two hex characters, or 8 bits, are needed for each decimal character. In binary form, these 8 bits can represent all of the numbers from 0 to 255. In decimal form, they can represent only the numbers from 0 to 9.

Using the code shown in Figure B-13, the decimal number 287 is represented by F2F8F7. Other examples are shown in figure B-14. This format is sometimes called **unpacked** (or **zoned**) **decimal format.**

In Figure B-13, the first hex character for each of the digits is F. To reduce the storage space consumed by decimal numbers, all but one of the Fs can be removed. This is called **packed decimal format.** Thus, in figure B-14, the decimal number 287, which has unpacked decimal notation F2F8F7, has the packed decimal notation 287F. All but one of the Fs has been removed, and the remaining F is put at the end of the number.

Figure B-13
EBCDIC code for decimal numbers

Decimal Number	EBCDIC Code (Hexadecimal)	Decimal Number	EBCDIC Code (Hexadecimal)
0	F0	5	F5
1	F1	6	F6
2	F2	7	F7
3	F3	8	F8
4	F4	9	F9

	Decimal Form		
Decimal Number	Unpacked	Packed	Signed
287	F2F8F7	287F	287C (+287)
			287D(−287)
1492	F1F4F9F2	1492F	1492C(+1492)
			1492D(−1492)
77	F7F7	77F	77C(+77)
			77D(−77)

Figure B-14
Unpacked, packed, and signed decimal data formats

In many applications, numbers must have signs. These can be positive or negative. In packed decimal notation, the last hex position is used to denote a sign. This format is called **signed decimal format.** If the last character is a hex C, the number is positive. If the last character is a D, the number is negative. Thus, 287C represents +287. 287D represents −287. The notation 287F is still valid. It just means that the number 287 is unsigned. Figure B-14 provides other examples.

Summary

Computers represent two types of data: numeric and alphanumeric. This module described the representation and processing of numeric data. The binary number system is most often used to represent numeric data. The binary system uses only two symbols: 0 and 1. In the decimal system, the place values of a number are ones, tens, hundreds, thousands, and so forth. In the binary system they are ones, twos, fours, eights, sixteens, and so forth.

Binary numbers are added just like decimal numbers are. However, instead of carrying when the sum of two numbers exceeds nine, we carry when the sum exceeds one. Subtraction is usually done by computers in complement form. The complement of the number to be subtracted is added to determine the answer.

Two other number systems are used to abbreviate binary numbers. The octal number system has eight symbols; each octal symbol represents three bits. The hexadecimal number system has 16 symbols; each hex symbol represents four bits. Octal format is used when the computer's word size is a multiple of three bits. Hexadecimal is used when the word size is a multiple of four bits.

Floating-point numbers allow the decimal point to shift. They represent both very large and very small numbers. They can also represent fractions. In addition to floating-point format, fractions can be repre-

B.5 Perform the following subtractions using complements:
a. 9 − 4 (decimal)
b. 1101 − 0001 (binary)
c. 1111 − 0101 (binary)
d. 4 − 9 (decimal)
e. 0011 − 0100 (binary)

B.6 What are octal numbers used for?

B.7 Convert the following numbers to decimal format:
a. 1101 binary
b. 1110101 binary
c. 453 octal
d. 7671 octal
e. A21 hexadecimal
f. ABC hexadecimal

B.8 What are hexadecimal numbers used for?

B.9 Convert the following numbers to binary format:
a. 789 decimal
b. 1234 decimal
c. 643 octal
d. 77777 octal
e. CE4 hexadecimal
f. FEBCAD hexadecimal

B.10 What causes the round-off error? Why is it important in business?

B.11 How can the round-off error be eliminated?

B.12 What are the unpacked and packed decimal formats of each of the following numbers?
a. 12345   b. 484930
c. 23   d. 1

B.13 What is the signed decimal format for each of the following numbers?
a. −19
b. 7345
c. −78965
d. 0

sented in fixed-point binary format. In this format, a fixed location of the binary point is assumed.

Decimal fractions are not necessarily represented evenly in binary format; for example, 0.1 does not have an even representation in binary format. This means that computers can make round-off errors. To eliminate this problem, some computers can perform decimal arithmetic. With these computers, decimal numbers are not converted to binary format, and arithmetic is done in decimal form. Data is carried in packed decimal format.

Word List

numeric data	dump	exponent
alphanumeric data	hexadecimal number system	fixed-point binary number
bit	division/remainder method	round-off error
complement addition	floating-point number	unpacked decimal format
tens complement	exponential form	zoned decimal format
twos complement	scientific form	packed decimal format
octal number system	mantissa	signed decimal format

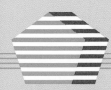

MODULE C

Computer Crime, Control, and Ethics

In this module we will consider the important topics of computer crime, control, and ethics. As you will see, information systems are vulnerable to a number of types of threat. Such threats can be mitigated with proper controls. Additionally, computer communications and networks introduce special risks, such as unauthorized network access, unauthorized data access, and the damage and disruption caused by computer viruses. Further, the openness of most networks necessitates that users learn and practice ethical behavior. We address all of these topics in this module.

Harold Johnson, Computer Criminal

Harold Johnson applied for a systems analysis/programming job at Modern Record Distributing Company (MODREC). Harold was young, only 25, but he had an impressive background. He had had major responsibility in the development of three different computer systems at his prior place of employment. His reason for leaving was that he believed the major challenges were over, and he wanted something new.

In fact, Harold was very bright and eager for new opportunities to apply his problem-solving skills. He was highly motivated and willing to spend many hours solving difficult problems. Furthermore, he was courageous and would stand up to anybody when his ideas were disputed. He was also creative and adventurous, and he enjoyed challenges. In short, he had all the skills and traits needed to be a superior systems developer.

MODREC was a spinoff company. It had been a division of a large, traditional record manufacturer. The separate company was created when MODREC's sales exceeded $5 million, and the directors of the parent company thought forming a subsidiary made sense. MODREC specialized in distributing rock music of interest to people under 30.

MODREC's first president was the son of one of the parent company's directors. He was promoted to his position through influence and not ability. Consequently, MODREC's sales began to slip, personnel morale fell, and MODREC lost many opportunities in the marketplace.

MODREC's small data processing department was managed by the chief accountant. The accountant meant well, but he was uneducated about data processing. When Harold Johnson applied for the systems analysis/programming job, the chief accountant was delighted. He made Harold an excellent offer, and Harold came to work for MODREC.

In his first year, Harold made many contributions to data processing. There was a vast improvement in the level of service. Salespeople were given better information about their customers. The time required to deliver an order was cut in half. Sales went up. Further, the accounting systems were improved, and the chief accountant had better information than ever.

Unfortunately, Harold began to feel discontented. Nobody paid attention to him. He felt that no one recognized the contributions he made. He probably would have gone to another company, but after a year, MODREC gave him a substantial pay increase. He thought that he would have trouble earning as much money elsewhere.

As Harold worked with the accounting systems, he began to notice MODREC's large profits. These profits were possible in spite of ineffective management, because MODREC's products had a very high markup. Harold concluded that MODREC was "ripping off" its customers.

One day Harold mentioned this to Joan Everest, the manager of a neighborhood record store that ordered from MODREC.

"Harold," said Joan, almost in jest, "why don't you reprogram one of those computers to offer special discounts to my store? Perhaps I could share the savings with you."

Harold was never quite the same. He was bored at work, and the technical challenge of programming such "special discounts" excited him. Additionally,

he was angry with the way MODREC had treated him, and he believed that it was unfair for the company to make so much profit. Joan needed the financial help, and MODREC could easily afford to lose $40,000 to $50,000 per year. In some ways he felt he was playing Robin Hood—stealing from the rich and giving to the poor.

Once Harold decided to cooperate, the technical aspects of his task were easy. In fact, Harold was disappointed at the lack of challenge. He changed the pricing program to look for Joan's customer number and to reduce her prices by 85 percent. He was the only one to see the special copy of the program. The unchanged version was kept in the program documentation library for appearances.

Harold Johnson is a typical computer criminal. He also was caught. We will explain how as this module progresses.

What Is Computer Crime?

No one knows for sure how many **computer crimes** have occurred or what the total losses have been. Computer crime statistics are difficult to obtain, and most sources claim their statistics are unreliable. One expert estimates that $300 million is lost per year through computer crime. He estimates the average loss per crime at $450,000. Compare this to the $10,000 that is typically lost in a full-service bank robbery, or the $19,000 that is lost in the average conventional bank embezzlement.

Figure C-1 presents computer crime data published by the Bureau of Justice Statistics.[1] From 1958, the year of the first reported computer crime, to 1979, a total of 669 cases were reported. In many of those cases, the amount of the loss was undetermined (companies are reluctant to state their losses). The average of the known losses was $1.658 million per crime. According to the National Institute of Justice (NIJ), the theft of *information*—usually done with the aid of a computer—

1. *Computer Crime: Criminal Justice Research Manual* (Washington, D.C.: Bureau of Justice Statistics, 1979).

Figure C-1
Computer crime statistics

Year	Total Cases	Total Known Losses	Average Known Loss
1958	1		
1959	1	$278	$ 278
1962	2		
1963	2	2,081	1,040
1964	6	2,600	1,300
1965	8	126	63
1966	3	28	9
1967	4	10	5
1968	12	12,454	2,075
1969	20	3,011	376
1970	38	19,353	967
1971	59	16,137	849
1972	73	14,524	518
1973	75	233,066	6,474
1974	73	8,162	247
1975	84	98,312	2,006
1976	59	52,601	1,461
1977	87	67,853	1,330
1978	42	15,207	633
1979	20	200	200
Totals	669	$546,001	$1,685

(Losses in thousands of dollars)
Source: *Criminal Justice Research Manual*

costs business as much as $20 billion a year. NIJ estimates that the average computer theft nets $400,000 and can be committed in less than three milliseconds. In 1983 alone, somewhere between $70 million and $100 million were stolen from the nation's banks by automated teller machine fraud.

The data shown in Figure C-1 is old; it refers primarily to crimes committed before the advent of the microcomputer and the extensive use of computer communications. Today, many smaller crimes are committed and they often involve viruses and worms (discussed later in this module). Figure C-2 shows more recent crime statistics. The study from which this data is taken also indicated that crimes against banks decreased from 18 percent of all crimes in 1986 to 12 percent in 1987, but that crimes against other commercial organizations increased from 23 percent of all crimes to 36 percent in that same time frame.

Pacific Telephone

Jerry Schneider was a child prodigy who developed his own telecommunication system at the age of ten. By the time he was in high school, he had started his own electronics company. While he was a part-time

Total estimated losses (5096 cases):	$555,464,000 930 person years 15.3 computer years
Average loss:	$109,000 365 person hours 26 computer hours

Figure C-2
Computer crime during 1987
Source: National Center for Computer
Crime Data and the Recal Corporation, Los
Angeles. Quoted in *Communications of the
ACM* Vol. 32, No. 6 (June 1989): p. 657.

college student, he found a way to steal electronic equipment from the Pacific Telephone Company. He used a terminal in his home to order parts without being charged for them. He learned the correct account numbers, passwords, and procedures by taking old computer printouts and other documentation from a telephone company trash container.

Jerry had expensive telephone components delivered to his home and other locations. He got bored with the project and, to add more excitement, had the company deliver a $25,000 switchboard to a manhole cover at the intersection of two streets. The company delivered, and he picked up the switchboard in the telephone truck that he had bought at a telephone company surplus auction.

Much of the equipment that he stole in this way he resold to Pacific Telephone. In fact, he used their own information system to determine what they were low on so he could know what to steal.

Schneider was caught when one of his own employees informed on him. The employee wanted a pay raise, and Jerry refused. When he was apprehended, Pacific Telephone refused to believe that he had stolen as much inventory as he claimed. He said he had stolen $800,000 to $900,000 worth; they said $70,000.

Penn Central Railroad

Another famous computer crime concerned the Penn Central Railroad. In the early 1970s, someone modified a freight-flow system to send boxcars to a small railroad company outside Chicago. There, the box cars disappeared. Apparently, they were repainted and sold to or used by other railroads. Estimates vary, but somewhere in the vicinity of 400 boxcars disappeared. Somehow, the computer system was modified so that it would not notice that railroad cars were missing.

The Penn Central case is mysterious. Although a Philadelphia grand jury was convened to investigate the case, and although some stolen boxcars were found, Penn Central refused to acknowledge the affair. For some reason, it was in Penn Central's interest to minimize attention to the crime. No criminal action was ever taken. There were rumors that organized crime was involved.

Equity Funding Corporation

A third famous case occurred in 1973. This large fraud involved the Equity Funding Corporation. Over 20 people were convicted on federal charges. Estimates of loss are as high as $2 *billion*.

Equity Funding was a conglomerate of companies that specialized in investments and insurance. Top-level management distorted the company's financial situation to lure investors. They also created artificial insurance policies.

Although the media described this crime as a modern computer fraud, there is some debate about whether it can be blamed on the computer. Most of the criminal activity did not involve the computer. All of the phony accounting was done manually.

The Equity Funding case is very complex. Over 50 major lawsuits were filed. Basically, the fraud was accomplished by inflating the company's reported income. This misrepresentation was done in two ways. First, the company's officers declared income and assets that didn't exist, simply by writing them into financial statements. The firm's auditors were severely criticized for not detecting this activity.

The second way income was inflated did involve the computer. Massive numbers of phony documents were generated by a computer system. These documents were supposed to be valid insurance policies. In fact, they were computer fabrications. The phony policies were sold to other insurance companies for cash.

In retrospect, it is amazing that these documents were accepted at face value. The system was audited, but it was designed to print only valid policies at the times audits were being done. Further, insurance industry personnel believed in computer-generated documents. It didn't occur to them that the computer could produce phony data.

Types of Computer Crime

These three short stories represent only a few of the ingenious ways that people have found to commit crimes with computer help. Most computer crimes fall into one of the five categories shown in Figure C-3. Sometimes, the *input to the computer is manipulated*, as was done in the Pacific Telephone case. Other crimes are perpetrated by *changing computer programs*, as Harold Johnson did.

A third type of computer crime is to *steal data*. Such data might be the names and addresses of a company's customers. It might be proprietary designs or plans. Fourth, *computer time can be stolen*. The criminal either uses the time or sells it to others who may not be aware that the time is stolen. For example, a computer communications system may be used to transmit unauthorized data. In one case, a company's message-switching system was used daily to broadcast racing results.

Finally, *computer programs can be stolen*. Computer programs are very expensive and time-consuming to produce. They can give a company a competitive edge in its marketplace. Therefore, stealing programs is a criminal act.

The theft of computer data and computer programs is very hard to detect. It can be done simply by copying the computer files that hold the data or programs. Since the original copy is not missing, companies have difficulty knowing a crime was committed.

Many computer crime experts think the cases we know about are only the tip of the iceberg. Some companies have been victims of crimes

Type of Crime

Manipulating computer input
Changing computer programs
Stealing data
Stealing computer time
Stealing computer programs

Figure C-3
Types of computer crime committed

C.1   INCREASING YOUR PERSONAL PRODUCTIVITY

Taking a Byte Out of Crime: Some Guidelines on Computer Theft Prevention

Warning Signals   "Several red flags can signal alert managers that a fellow employee could be a 'wolf in sheep's clothing,'" says Louis Scoma, founder and CEO of Houston-based Data Processing Security, Inc., which has aided over 650 companies with their computer security systems since 1970. Consider the following:

- Does one of your employees consistently come in early and stay after hours—with no visible results from the extra hours of work?
- Have you recently fired an employee who had access to sensitive information? Do you have any such workers on staff who are disgruntled with the company for any reason?
- Do any of your employees with access to sensitive data tote personal microcomputers to and from the office in order to do "extra work"?
- Did an employee you transferred from headquarters to a branch office come back to "clean out his desk" or "visit old friends" even though he knew the security codes had been changed?
- Has your company experienced a recent increase in data processing needs, while you have not upgraded your security system to accommodate the change?

"If you have answered yes to two or more of these questions," says Scoma, "double-check your security system and the people responsible for keeping it intact. If you don't, you could be headed for high-tech trouble."

An Ounce of Prevention   According to the Better Business Bureau, the vast majority of computer crimes are preventable. Although the following measures may seem like common sense, consider them in light of your company's own practices. How many are fully followed?

- *Employee hiring.* Conduct thorough background checks on all potential EDP employees. Check with former employers: get references—both professional and personal. Verify technical skills, and check credit histories.
- *Controlling access to facilities.* Maintain a logbook with times and names of all who have access to the computer facilities. Allow only employees who work with the computer to sign in. Confirm and verify any service calls, and have a company employee accompany any technician to the worksite.
- *Physical security.* Separate computer facilities from other departments, in a secure, isolated area with few windows or doors, adequate lighting, secure locks, and, if possible, a security guard at each entrance. Provide the appropriate personnel with proper identification that can be verified at the entrance, such as photo or fingerprint IDs.

- *Protective devices.* Take advantage of all the security devices built into the computer system. Have the company that sold or leased you the equipment explain how password rotation, security codes, and code scrambling devices can control access. Electronic security, such as closed-circuit television and sound sensitive listening devices, might also be worthwhile investments.

Computers can "stall" after wrong passwords are entered, disconnect after a certain number of wrong guesses, record attempts to penetrate, and even trace phone calls. Take advantage of these features.

- *Storage procedures.* It is essential to have a duplicate set of all vital tapes, software, and company data stored in a secure, isolated storage space accessible to only a few top EDP executives.
- *Audits.* Conduct periodic security checks both internally and independently. Many auditing firms now will attempt to defraud your company's system, to determine whether security is sufficient.

"Keeping in mind that some computer crimes are so sophisticated that they may take months, even years, to detect and unravel, management should be constantly on the alert for possible indications of wrongdoing," warns the Better Business Bureau.

and have not acknowledged it because they want to avoid adverse publicity. A bank that lost money by computer crime will not want its customers to know it. Further, businesses do not want to advertise their vulnerability. They may not know how to prevent similar crimes in the

C.2 INCREASING YOUR PERSONAL PRODUCTIVITY

Computer Crime: Who's Responsible?

by Ann Dooley

Personal computer network security is everybody's business. Unfortunately, few companies see it that way. To be effective, information security has to be part of the corporate business plan, not just the responsibility of information systems professionals. Although a recent study of chief executive officers by *Computerworld* showed that 91% of those top executives consider corporate data security to be a major concern to them personally, they don't act on that concern. Security issues are left to the IS staff.

That's not all bad, of course. IS managers have the know-how to implement security measures. But in many cases, they lack the political clout and authority to make sure that information and networks in daily use by end users are kept secure. According to security experts and IS professionals, what companies need is education and a mandate from the top that end users must treat information in a responsible

and ethical manner. Instead of viewing network security as a computer problem of hardware, software and communications, companies must see it as a business problem. The organizations that see it that way will have more effective security, experts agree.

One priority to consider before implementing security procedures is to assess how much security is actually needed. The trade-offs between productivity, cost and convenience can be monumental if the information involved doesn't have to be secured in the first place.

The only way to make a network totally secure is not to use it, one IS manager maintains. A more practical solution is to change people's attitudes toward security issues through corporate mandate. Employees can almost always find a way to break into a network, so it is up to IS management with top executive backing to make sure employees are aware that tampering with

a network is wrong and to explain the risks and repercussions of such an action.

The challenge is to maintain an effective flow of information along a network without restricting users. With PCs, the user becomes the programmer, operator and security officer. Companies can protect against specific entry points and specific types of invasion, but they can't protect it all, or it would be impossible to get any work done, one IS executive complained.

A major problem is that organizations are installing PC networks so rapidly that many of the orderly development processes are being overlooked. As one IS manager states, "It's hard enough keeping up with the various networks that are popping up all over the company, let alone trying to implement security. What's really needed is a concerted effort if we want to keep our information safe."

future, and they certainly do not want the crime advertised in the newspapers. Therefore, they do not prosecute suspected computer criminals.

For this reason, computer criminals often are not penalized. Further, when they are, they typically receive light sentences. Jerry Schneider spent only 40 days in jail and lost just $8,500 in a court battle.

Here are 12 warning signals indicating that the potential for computer crime exists:

1. The computer seems to run the company; management just reacts.
2. Management expects computers to solve major existing problems.
3. Management does not (cannot) communicate with the MIS staff.
4. Users are told how their systems will be designed.
5. There are no documented standards for the development of new applications or the maintenance of existing ones.
6. Technical management is actively involved in programming and troubleshooting.

7. Programmers are uncontrolled; they can do what they want with the computer.
8. MIS staff have easy access to data and to program libraries.
9. Errors occur so frequently that adequate investigation is not possible.
10. Auditors treat the computer like a mysterious black box.
11. Management fails to implement audit recommendations.
12. No computer audits are performed.

These signals are characteristics of companies in which crimes have occurred. Let's hope that, in the course of your business career, you will not work for a company that demonstrates many of these signs. However, if you do, you should be aware of the possibility of computer crime.

Most of the characteristics listed above indicate poor data processing management. Except for the items concerning audits, every one of these characteristics is a violation of a principle discussed in this book. Thus, good data processing management is needed to build and use systems that are less susceptible to computer crime.

Preventing Computer Crime

Unfortunately, there is no such thing as a completely secure data processing installation. First, computer manufacturers do not provide completely secure computers. An ingenious programmer can find a way to modify the operating system. Once such a modification is made, computer security features such as passwords and account numbers are ineffective.

Second, many, if not most, data processing departments are so busy just keeping up with the business and with changes in computer technology that they do not take the time to consider computer security adequately. Inputs to the computer are not as well controlled as they should be. Outputs are not checked for accuracy and completeness. Furthermore, security issues often are only superficially considered when systems are designed or when programs are written. Most companies have the attitude that computer crime "won't happen here."

Finally, effective security can be costly. Building a secure system takes time and resources. Additionally, the system may be more expensive to operate because of security features. If a user must spend half of each working day verifying output, then in a year half of the person's salary is spent for security. Good computer security also means that programs operate more slowly. More instructions must be processed for security functions. Thus, more computer power is required.

Most companies must strike a balance between no security at all and as near-perfect security as possible. How much security is needed depends on the potential loss and the level of threat. An accounts payable system probably needs more security than a system that produces company telephone lists.

One aspect of computer crime is both surprising and distressing: most computer crimes are caught by accident. In some cases, the computer failed, and irregularities were discovered while someone was fixing it. In other cases, people consistently spent more money than they were earning, and the source of the additional money was traced back to a computer system. The Internal Revenue Service (IRS) has caught some of these people for not paying taxes on their criminal earnings. In other cases, the Federal Bureau of Investigation (FBI) caught them in illegal gambling activities.

The distressing part of this statement is that few crimes are caught as a result of controls in the business computer system. Apparently, few systems provide protection against computer crime. However, this vulnerability need not exist; systems can be designed to thwart unauthorized activity. We will see how in the next section.

Computer Auditing and Controls

The American Institute of Certified Public Accountants has recognized the possibility of computer crime or other unauthorized activity. This organization has issued an official statement (called SAS-3) directing certified public accountants (CPAs) to pay special attention to business computer systems. As a result of this statement, auditors are paying more and more attention to data processing departments and personnel.

Further, groups of auditors and data processing personnel have worked together to develop recommended procedures or *controls* over data processing operations. In the remainder of this module, we will discuss these controls. To show the usefulness of them, we will relate each control to the MODREC case introduced at the start of this module.

The term **EDP controls** originated with the accountants and auditors. (*EDP* is an accounting term that means *electronic data processing*.) EDP controls are features of any of the five components of a business computer system that reduce the likelihood of unauthorized activity. Here is a list of the basic categories of EDP controls:

- Management
- Organizational structure
- Data center resource
- Input/processing/output
- Data administration
- Systems development

Harold Johnson was dissatisfied with the management at MODREC. He felt underappreciated. Because his boss was only the chief accountant, Harold was buried in the finance department. Consequently, neither he nor *anyone else in data processing had access to top management.*

Top management did not have access to Harold or data processing either. They knew little of what he was doing, and they had only a limited idea of how data processing operated. They spent considerable money on data processing operations, but they did not know how the money was

spent. In short, there was a large gulf between top-level management and data processing.

Management Controls

Over the years, professionals have learned that a management situation like the one at MODREC is an invitation to trouble. Senior managers of a company should take an active part in the management of the data processing function. They do not have to be walking the machine floor, mounting tapes. However, they should recognize the importance of data processing to the company, and they should set the direction for, and be actively involved in, data processing plans. In other words, **management controls** need to exist.

It may seem surprising that this statement even needs to be made. However, in the past, too many managers have washed their hands of data processing. They have stayed as far away from the computer as possible. Perhaps they didn't understand computing, perhaps they were afraid of it, or perhaps the data processing personnel used a strange language. In any event, data processing went its own way. In some cases (like Harold's), data processing personnel felt disassociated from the company. They felt rejected and underappreciated, and computer crime was the result.

Senior managers can handle data processing in several ways. First, they can demonstrate an appreciation for and an interest in the data processing function. Occasional visits to the computer staff, recognition of them in the company newsletter, and references to data processing in the year-end report are examples of showing their interest.

Senior managers can recognize data processing in another significant way as well. They can place the data processing function high in the organizational structure. Instead of burying data processing somewhere in accounting or finance where none of the senior managers ever sees or hears of it, they can make it a department on a par with other business departments. Figure C-4 shows two ways that data processing can be raised from the company bilges to gain the attention it deserves.

Next, senior managers can understand the company's vulnerability to computer crime. Once they do, they can communicate the importance of controls to the entire organization. As we will see, controls on the data processing function involve more than just the data processing department. To encourage other departments to cooperate, management needs to be very positive about the need for controls.

Another responsibility for management is to form a steering committee which controls data processing development efforts. The committee receives reports about project status and makes go/no-go decisions as appropriate.

Finally, management can take a role in data processing by requesting and paying attention to periodic operations reports. Management should know how well the computing resources are being used, how happy or

Figure C-4
Two organizational structures recognizing the information systems department

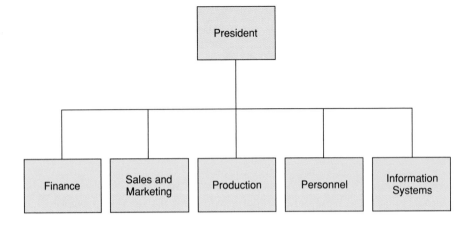

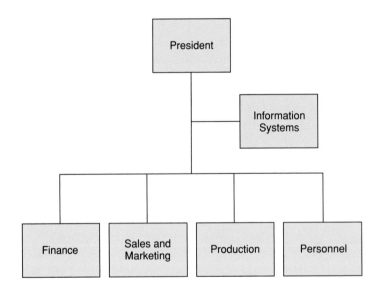

unhappy the users are with the data processing function, and what the major data processing problems are. These reports increase the amount of communication between data processing and senior management. Management control responsibilities are summarized below:

1. Data processing is placed at high organizational level.
2. Senior management demonstrates knowledge and good attitude toward data processing.
3. Data processing steering committee takes active role in DP.
4. Management requests and reviews periodic reports.

Harold Johnson had free access to the computer and all of its resources. When Harold needed a tape file to determine Joan's account number, he walked into the tape library and got it. When he wanted to obtain the pricing program, he instructed the computer to print a copy of it. After he made the changes,

Harold put the changed program into the standard program library. No one checked Harold's authority to do these things.

Organizational Controls

Organizational controls concern the organizational structure of the company. We have already mentioned that data processing should be organizationally on a par with other functions of the company. In addition, the company should be structured so that authorization and duties are separate.

The MODREC case is a good example of what can happen when no separation exists. Data processing employees had unlimited access to the computer. MODREC should have at least two categories of data processing personnel: operations and development. These groups should provide checks and balances on each other. The operations group should control the equipment and the production program library. The development group should develop new programs in accordance with requirements. They should not have access to the tape library or to the production programs.

If this were the case, authorization and duties would be separated. Only the programmers could develop program changes, and only the operations department could change the production library. Further, making changes to the program library would require a supervisor's authorization.

Separating authorization and duties provides checks and balances in the system. In general, the more people and the more levels of management that are involved in authorizing and performing duties, the less susceptible the system is to unauthorized activity.

After Harold Johnson changed the pricing program to give Joan special discounts, he wanted to test it. After all, he didn't want to make a mistake and give the discounts to the wrong customer. However, to test the change, he needed to mount the customer and price files on the tape drives. To avoid suspicion, Harold stayed at work after hours the next week.

Since none of the managers paid any attention to data processing, they didn't ask what Harold was doing. In fact, nobody asked Harold what he was up to. Harold took his time, and after three short nights, he had fully tested his program. Not only was he sure it would work, he was also sure no one could trace the changes to him.

Data Center Resource Controls

Data center resources controls also should be implemented. Use of computer equipment should be restricted to authorized personnel. Processing should be controlled by schedules, and records of use should be reviewed. Therefore, access to the computer must be controlled. Only authorized personnel should be allowed in the computer room. This restriction not only protects the equipment from damage, but also helps to ensure that outputs are delivered only to the right people. Furthermore, limiting access to the machine room allows a quieter working environment and helps eliminate operator errors.

Computer operations should be controlled as well. Procedures and job schedules should be documented and followed. A supervisor should examine operations to ensure that the procedures are followed, and records of all computer activity should be kept. These records should be reviewed. It should be very difficult for operators to deviate from the established schedule and procedures.

In addition to protecting computing resources during normal operations, plans and procedures should exist to recover from problems. All files and libraries should be backed up by copies stored in secure, off-premise locations. Further, recovery procedures should be well documented, and the staff should be trained in their use.

The company also should have a disaster recovery plan that explains what to do in case of fire, flood, earthquake, or other disaster. The company should consider having backup hardware and programs available in other locations. The procedures and data necessary to use the hardware should be available in the backup location. Resource controls are summarized below:

1. Access to computer center is controlled.
2. Operating procedures are documented.
3. Program libraries are secure.
4. Backup and recovery procedures exist.
5. There is protection from natural hazards.
6. There are documented emergency procedures.

Harold Johnson did not have to modify program inputs. He found a way to provide special discounts by changing the processing. This process changed the outputs. If anyone had ever examined the invoices generated by the pricing program, they would have seen that something was amiss. Luckily for Harold, MODREC did not have a policy of examining outputs.

Input, Processing, and Output Controls

In general, **input, processing, and output controls** should be used. First, the authorized form of input data should be documented. The operations personnel should be trained not to accept improper input data. Second, data processing personnel should be trained not to make changes to input data. Such changes should be made by the system users.

Where appropriate, control totals should be used. For example, when the users send the weekly payroll to data processing, they should calculate (independently) the sum of the hours worked or a similar total. The payroll program should be written to calculate the total number of hours worked and to print this total on a summary report. The report should be examined by the payroll department after the payroll run to ensure that the manually prepared total and the computer-generated total match.

Similar totals can be kept on changes to master files, number of accounts payable checks to be issued, and so forth. Users must be trained to compute these totals and to treat them seriously. Often they are the most important control in the computer business system.

Input to teleprocessing applications are harder to control. A program can be coded to accept only certain input from certain users or certain locations. However, it is possible to fool such a program. Therefore, the use of terminals must be limited to certain individuals and to specified times. Further, the supervisors of these individuals need to be trained to review their subordinates' terminal activities.

There must also be controls over the processing of data. As stated earlier, all operations procedures should be documented and followed. The performance of the operators should be monitored periodically. The operations department should keep records of all errors and system failures. The corrections for each of these should be documented. These records should be reviewed periodically by data processing supervisory personnel to determine whether or not the failures are related to unauthorized activity. The records can also be used to determine whether or not there is a need for additional training, as well as to assess employee performance.

Finally, the output of all data processing activities should be controlled. Procedures for disseminating output should be documented and followed. Output should be given only to authorized users, and these users should examine the output for completeness and accuracy. Control totals produced by programs should be reconciled against input control totals.

Output from on-line systems is hard to control. Where data is changed on-line, tracing the sequence of activities can be very difficult. For example, a price might be changed several times with no written record generated. The absence of records can make the job of the auditor impossible. Consequently, on-line programs often are programmed to log transactions on computer tape or disks. These logs are saved and used for error correction or audits. Figure C-5 summarizes input, processing, and output controls.

Other EDP Controls

Some EDP controls are not oriented toward preventing criminal activity. Instead, their purpose is to encourage effective use of EDP systems. Data administration controls are one example. Controls over systems development are another. We will not discuss these controls in this module. They are important to systems designers and auditors, and if you make either of these professions your career, you should learn more about them.

Harold Johnson and Joan Everest were able to continue their crime for 18 months. During that period, they obtained $150,000 worth of records for $22,500. The crime would have gone on longer,

Figure C-5
Input/processing/output controls

Category	Type of Control
Input	Documentation of authorized input format
	Separation of duties and authorities
	Verification of control totals
	On-line system input controls
Processing	Documented operating procedures
	Reviews of processing logs
	Adequate program testing
Ouput	Documented output procedures
	Control over disposition of output
	Users trained to examine output

except for a change of management at MODREC.

A new president was hired, and he expected better performance from the entire company. As part of his improvement program, he required the sales force to increase sales. When one of the new sales managers reviewed the performance of the region containing Joan's store, he detected something suspicious. It seemed that the volume of sales should have netted larger income. He examined the sales invoices for the past year and saw what had been going on. He contacted the new president, and the game was up.

Harold was actually relieved. The strain of perpetrating the crime had begun to wear on him.

Furthermore, he was frustrated. He liked to brag about his creations, and he wanted to tell his friends about the crime. He thought it was clever, and he wanted credit for it.

MODREC threatened to sue for damages, but a settlement was made out of court. Harold and Joan paid MODREC $50,000, and Joan turned over a sizable part of her record inventory. Surprisingly, Harold had saved all but a few hundred dollars of the money Joan had paid him. He really didn't participate for the money.

Criminal action was taken. Since both Harold and Joan were first-time criminals, they received light sentences. They each spent 60 days in jail and were fined $5,000.

Network Security and Viruses

Computer communication and networks, established to facilitate the exchange of information, are vulnerable to unauthorized, criminal, and unethical activities.

Two recent events point out the vulnerability of computer networks to such illegitimate activity.

Infiltration of Military Network

On March 2, 1988, West German police arrested five people in Hanover, Hamburg, and West Berlin. The charges were illegally gaining access to computer systems in Germany, France, Switzerland, and the United States; and stealing information. The information obtained was reportedly sold to the KGB for cash and drugs.

The crime was committed by connecting to university computers in Germany, then to France, and then to a network operated by a military contractor in the Washington, D.C., area. From there, computers all over the United States were accessed. The criminal reportedly would search system files for names of other files that indicated that their contents might contain information related to military activities. When files with such names were found, the files would be copied and the information later sold.

The criminal was first detected by an alert systems manager at the University of California at Berkeley. This manager observed that an account had been opened for which there was no billing address. Checking further, he found other activity that eventually led him to believe that someone was trying to infiltrate the network for unauthorized activity.

At first he thought that it was someone in the local Berkeley area. As he continued to investigate, however, he learned that the activity was originating in Washington, D.C. Eventually, a number of different law enforcement and security agencies were involved in identifying the responsible group. The criminals had used dozens of computers in hundreds of different communications paths.

The story of the detection of this activity is fascinating. Thanks to the work of the systems administrator, the violation of a simple control in an accounting system led to the unravelling of an incredibly complicated and sophisticated crime.[2]

The Morris Worm

In November 1988, Robert J. Morris created and introduced a worm on a national computer network called Internet. A **worm** is a computer program designed to infiltrate computer systems by taking advantage of security flaws in operating system programs. Worms also reproduce themselves on the local computer and spread to other computers over the network. Other, similar, programs are called **viruses**. Unlike a worm, a virus actually changes some of the operating system instructions in the systems it infects.

Ultimately, the Morris worm infected some 6,000 computers. Additionally, many more systems that were not infected were affected in that they had to be tested for the presence of the worm and preventive measures had to be applied.

---

2. *Communications of the ACM* Vol. 31, No. 5 (May 1988).

C.3   INCREASING YOUR PERSONAL PRODUCTIVITY

Technology: Invader or Protector of Privacy?

The high-tech revolution is regarded with apprehension by a sizable element within our society; many of these people are themselves members of the high-tech community. They fear that the electronic genie is fast taking control of our lives—that we may have glimpsed Pandora's secrets without fully understanding their ramifications. Our very privacy is at stake.

There is reason for concern, especially as computers increasingly take over our daily lives. For example:

- Computers perform more than 100,000 calculations each second for every man, woman and child in the U.S.
- Our names pop up in some computer at least 40 times a day.
- Federal, state and local governmental agencies keep more than 35 files on each one of us,

while the U.S. Bureau of the Census collects more than five billion facts on us.

Privacy and civil liberties are one and the same—one cannot survive long without the other. But privacy is fast becoming a thing of the past in our computer society.

- The NSA's* computers eavesdrop 24 hours a day, seven days a week, on all overseas communications. NSA also occasionally monitors communications within the U.S.
- Much of the confidential data stored in the computer systems of financial institutions, retailers and manufacturers is vulnerable to unauthorized tapping.
- The computerization of our telephone system makes it very vulnerable to electronic snooping.

- As computer systems are linked to national and international networks, it will become even easier to track a person's movements.
- By using a device called an addressable converter, cable companies can now keep track of what programs a customer watches.

Rep. Robert W. Kastenmeier (D-Wis.) observed that "the essence of personal privacy protection is the assurance that private communications are protected." Sadly, this is not the case today. Our massive data banks and instant retrieval systems make George Orwell's telescreens seem ancient by comparison. All that is now missing is a giant network that would link all private and governmental computer systems into one. That, too, may be in the offing.

*National Security Administration's

The intent of the author of the worm is unknown, although it is known that the worm was not malicious. It did not modify or destroy data or other resources, nor did it attempt to intercept private mail or steal other data. The worm did, however, tie up valuable system resources and force the closure of communications gateways between nationwide research networks. "This action led to delays of up to several days in the exchange of electronic mail, causing some projects to miss deadlines and others to lose valuable research time."[3]

Some of the popular press described this worm as a work of creativity and insight, and said it was useful because it helped professionals learn about security flaws and weaknesses. This view is disputed by the Cornell Commission, a group of professionals formed to investigate the incident. They report:[4]

3. Donn Seeley, "Password Cracking: A Game of Wits," *Communications of the ACM* Vol. 32, No. 6 (June 1989): p. 702.

4. Ted Eisenber, et al., "The Cornell Commission: On Morris and the Worm," *Communications of the ACM* Vol. 32, No. 6 (June 1989): pp. 707, 709.

Although the worm was technically sophisticated, its creation required dedication and perseverance rather than technical brilliance. The worm could have been created by many students, graduate or undergraduate, at Cornell or at other institutions, particularly if forearmed with knowledge of the security flaws exploited or of similar flaws. . . .

Contrary to the impression given in many media reports, the commission does not regard this act as an heroic event that pointed up the weaknesses of operating systems. The fact that UNIX, in particular BSD UNIX, has many security flaws is generally well known, as indeed are the potential dangers of viruses and worms in general. . . . It is not an act of genius to exploit such weaknesses.

Although this event was not heroic, a number of important lessons were learned from it. First, it exposed the vulnerability of large computer networks. If so much disruption could be caused by a program that "could have been created by many students, graduate or undergraduate," how much disruption could be caused by sophisticated professionals with bad intentions? Consider this thought in light of the infiltration by the German group discussed above. What if they had written this worm, and what if it had been purposely written to be harmful?

Second, this event pointed out the importance, once again, of all five of the components of an information system. Authentication and other manual procedures and the interaction among the "old boy" network were cited as key elements in understanding and stopping the worm.[5] Also, software tools were not as important as expected. The primary resources used were skilled people, a simple program, and a hardware architecture manual.[6]

A third consequence was that knowledge about passwords that had been relegated to obscure technical journals became more widely known. In fact, it is known that there are a number of significant patterns in the way that people assign passwords. For example, Grampp and Morris had determined that in a survey of 100 password files, between 8 and 30 percent of the passwords could be guessed by using the account number and a few variations.[7] These and other patterns were used by the Morris worm. Thus, users need instruction in better selection of passwords.

Another result of this situation is the need for more instruction about computer ethics. Networks, especially academic networks, are designed to be open and available. To maintain this character, users need to be taught responsible and ethical behavior. Preventing events like this by making networks closed and difficult to use is too costly a way to prevent such problems. At least this is the case for academic networks. Networks that support the international financial system and the military probably need to be made more secure.

5. Jon A. Rochlis and Mark W. Elchin, "With Microscope and Tweezers: The Worm from MIT's Perspective," *Communications of the ACM* Vol. 32, No. 6 (June 1989): pp. 696–697.

6. Ibid., p. 697.

7. F. T. Grampp and R. Morris, "UNIX Operating System Security," *AT&T Bell Laboratories Technical Journal* Vol. 63, No. 8, Part 2 (October 1984): p. 1649.

Figure C-6

Elements of unethical behavior
Source: National Science Foundation,
Division of Network, Communications
Research and Infrastructure. Quoted in
Communications of the ACM Vol. 32, No. 6
(June 1989): p. 710.

A user is behaving unethically if he or she

- Seeks to gain unauthorized access to the resources of a computer network or other system
- Disrupts the intended use of a computer network or system
- Wastes resources (people, capacity; computer) through such actions
- Destroys the integrity of computer-based information
- Compromises the security of users

Computer Ethics

As a result of the Morris worm, a number of institutions have established guidelines for ethical behavior. A professional group, the Computer Professionals for Social Responsibility, has established a Statement of Ethics,[8] as has the Internet Activities Board.[9] The essence of these statements is shown in Figure C-6.

Users of computer networks should know and understand each of the elements listed in Figure C-6. Furthermore, each network should establish procedures to ensure that ethics guidelines are followed and that appropriate action is taken when any of them is violated.

The list shown in Figure C-6 is concerned with unethical behavior on networks. It does not mention one important breach of computer ethics, **software piracy**. Computer software is not sold. When you or your company purchase software, you actually are purchasing a *license* to use the software for a particular purpose in a particular way. You do not buy the software; you buy the right to use it.

The implications of this are that when you purchase this license, you are expected to read the licensing agreement and to abide by its restrictions. If you choose not to do this, you can return the software, disk package unopened, for a refund. If you open the package, you are deemed to have accepted the licensing agreement.

Most licensing agreements stipulate that only one person or one computer can use the software at a time (with the exception of multiuser products for which a multiuser license is written). Copying the software for additional computers or for additional users is normally forbidden. You are expected to obey these stipulations yourself and to take reasonable care to ensure that others do not violate them either.

Copying software is theft. And copying software documentation is a copyright violation. Laws concerning these issues are clear in the United States, Europe, and some countries in the Far East. Other nations, however, either do not endorse or do not enforce these laws. According

- People's Republic of China
- Saudi Arabia
- Korea
- India
- Philippines
- Taiwan
- Indonesia
- Brazil
- Egypt
- Thailand
- Nigeria
- Malaysia

Figure C-7

Nations that are the worst offenders in copyright piracy
Source: International Intellectual Property Alliance, Washington, D.C. Quoted in *Communications of the ACM* Vol. 32, No. 6 (June 1989): p. 657.

8. Gary Chapman, "CPSR Statement on the Computer Virus," *Communications of the ACM* Vol. 32, No. 6 (June 1989): p. 699.

9. Vint Cerf, "Ethics and the Internet," *Communications of the ACM* Vol. 32, No. 6 (June 1989): p. 710.

to a report by the Intellectual Property Alliance in Washington, D.C., software piracy in the 12 nations that are the worst offenders costs the U.S. software industry $1.3 billion in revenue per year. These 12 countries are listed in Figure C-7.

In the United States, most corporations have taken their responsibility very seriously. In addition to the ethical matters involved, the consequence of not following licensing agreements is substantial financial penalties. Thus, when you purchase or use software, read the licensing agreement and follow it. Also, learn any additional policies and practices established by your organization and follow them. Failure to do so is not only unethical, it places both you and your organization in danger of financial and other penalties.

Summary

Computer crime is an important issue. Millions of dollars are lost each year. There are five types of computer crime: manipulating input, changing programs, stealing data, stealing computer time, and stealing programs.

The characteristics of companies that are vulnerable to computer crime are known. Most of these characteristics reflect bad data processing management and violate the principles of effective data processing discussed in this book.

To prevent crime, companies need to develop better controls within their business computer systems. These controls involve several areas: management, organizational structure, data center resources, input/processing/output, data administration, and systems development. EDP controls will not guarantee that crime is eliminated, but they will reduce the likelihood of crime.

Computer networks are vulnerable to illegal and unauthorized access as well as to the damage and destruction caused by worms and viruses. Computer professionals need to address these issues to reduce vulnerabilities. All five components, especially trained personnel, are required to protect against and solve such problems. Users need better information about how to assign passwords and they need to be educated in computer ethics.

Examples of irresponsible, unethical behavior for information systems users are summarized in Figure C-6. In addition to avoiding these, users should know and follow the restrictions in the licenses for the software that they use.

Questions

C.1 How much money is lost due to computer crimes every year?

C.2 Describe five types of computer crime.

C.3 List 12 indications that an organization is vulnerable to computer crime.

C.4 How have most computer crimes been discovered?

C.5 What are EDP controls?

C.6 List the categories of EDP controls described in this module.

C.7 Describe management controls.

C.8 Describe organizational controls.

C.9 Describe data center resource controls.

C.10 Describe input/processing/output controls.

C.11 How was the infiltration of the military network detected?

C.12 Explain why the Cornell Commission concluded that the Morris worm was not a work of genius.

C.13 According to the text, what four lessons can be learned from the Morris worm incident?

C.14 Summarize the elements of unethical computer activity.

C.15 What responsibilities do users have with regard to the licensing agreement for software that they use?

Word List

computer crime	organizational controls	worm
EDP	data center resource controls	virus
EDP controls	input/processing/output controls	software piracy
management controls		

Discussion Questions and Exercises

A. What organizations or industries do you believe are particularly vulnerable to computer crime? If you worked for one of these companies, what would you do to reduce the likelihood of computer crime?

B. What would you do if you believed computer crime was happening at a company for which you worked? Would you report it? If so, to whom? Suppose you didn't report it, but later someone found out that you knew about it all along? What might happen? Could the company hold you accountable because you never reported the crime?

C. How can computer crime be detected? What role do you think accountants and auditors have in the detection of computer crime?

D. Find out more about SAS-3. (Ask an accounting professor.) What does it mean to public auditors? What does it mean to data processing professionals? How do you think you should respond to an EDP auditor?

E. Are existing laws sufficient for prosecuting computer crimes? Are special laws needed? What laws are currently in effect at the federal level? What laws are being considered by Congress concerning computer crime? What are the strengths and weaknesses of the laws being considered?

F. Summarize what you think are the important elements of ethical computer behavior. Describe why you think each of these elements is important. How would you go about teaching users to follow these behaviors? How would you enforce them? What consequences would you establish for people who do not follow this set of standards?

BASIC Programming

APPENDIX OUTLINE

In the mid-1960s, two college professors developed a programming language that they used to teach the fundamentals of programming to beginners. The language, called **BASIC** (for Beginners' All-purpose Symbolic Instruction Code), has become a very popular one, especially for personal computer users. BASIC was not standardized for a long time, so many versions of the language exist. This means that the BASIC programs written for, say, an Apple Macintosh will not work on an IBM-PC without modifications. However, the bulk of BASIC is similar enough from one computer system to another for a programmer to make an easy transition. In this text we use Microsoft BASIC, run under MS-DOS.

With the abundance of personal productivity tools such as spreadsheet programs and database management programs, it is unlikely that as a user you will ever need to develop a program in BASIC (or any other programming language). Still, an understanding of programming—even in a simple language like BASIC—can help you to understand and appreciate the effort that goes into developing application software. And who knows—maybe you will be intrigued enough with programming to consider studying it in more depth. Maybe you simply will find it fun.

To learn BASIC you need to do the exercises and examples here with a computer as you read. You need to have a computer that runs BASIC, a diskette containing the DOS operating system, and a blank formatted diskette. If you do not know how to format a diskette, consult with your instructor or a lab assistant.

Getting Started

When you write a program in BASIC, the instructions you write must be translated into machine language by a translator program. Consequently, you need to load a copy of the BASIC translator into your computer's main memory before you write any programs. This is called "loading BASIC."

Loading BASIC

The steps needed to load BASIC vary from one computer to another. If you use Microsoft BASIC (also marketed as IBM PC BASIC), then follow these steps.

1. Insert the DOS disk into diskette drive A.
2. Power on your computer.
3. At the A> prompt, type **BASIC** or **BASICA**, and press the Return key. (BASICA accepts more instructions than BASIC, but you can use either for purposes of this appendix.) The operating system will load the

BASIC translator, and you will be ready to begin. The BASIC prompt—the indication that BASIC is loaded and ready to be used—is **OK**.

4. Remove the DOS diskette from drive A. (Most people do not store programs on a system disk.)

If you use another version of BASIC or another computer, write in the box provided here the sequence of instructions your instructor gives you for getting started.

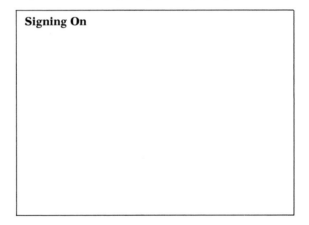

Signing On

BASIC Modes

BASIC can be run in two modes, direct and indirect. In **direct mode,** each BASIC instruction you type is executed by the computer as soon as you press the Return key. This is sometimes useful. For instance, you might want to use the computer as a calculator. To calculate a 9 1/2 percent sales commission on a sale of $6,732.98 you could type the following instruction, then press Return:

```
PRINT .095 * 6732.98
```

(Note: In this text we use uppercase letters for all commands and statements, but BASIC accepts both uppercase and lowercase letters.) The computer executes the computation and displays the answer:

```
639.6331
```

More often, you will run BASIC in **indirect mode.** This means that you will write a group of instructions, called a program, and execute them as one entity. To use indirect mode, you assign each instruction a line number between 1 and 99999. Regardless of the order in which you enter instructions, they will be executed in sequence according to their line numbers. (There are some exceptions, because you can change the order of execution with certain BASIC statements such as IF and GOTO—we'll discuss them later.) Line numbers do not have to be consecutive. Most programmers number their lines in increments of ten, to make inserting instructions easier. Here is an example of BASIC in indirect mode:

```
10  PRINT .095 * 6732.98
20  PRINT "All done."
```

Type those instructions just as you see them, pressing the Return key at the end of each line. (You should press Return after each instruction; we will not explicitly tell you to do so from now on.) Notice that the instructions are not executed as soon as you enter them. They are being stored as a program and will not be executed until you give the command to run the program. Now type RUN. This time the computer displays

```
639.6331
All done.
```

BASIC Commands

BASIC commands perform various kinds of program maintenance, such as loading and saving programs. Commands (when not preceded by a line number) are executed as soon as you enter them. The commands you will use most often are LIST, NEW, LLIST, RUN, SAVE, and LOAD. The format notation used in this text appears in Figure D-1.

LIST. The **LIST** command allows you to review a BASIC program by listing all or part of the program on the computer screen. The format of the LIST command is

```
LIST [line number] [-line number]
```

If you specify a line number, that line will be listed on the screen. If you do not specify a line number, the entire program will be listed. Two line numbers separated by a hyphen (-) tell the system to list a **range** of lines, beginning with the first line number and ending with the second one.

If the program to be listed is too long to fit on one screen, it is **scrolled**, like the credits at the end of a movie. Find out from your instructor how to stop the scrolling and restart it, so you can read the program before it whizzes by. Record how to do this in the box provided here.

```
┌─────────────────────────────────────┐
│ Controlling Scrolling                │
│                                      │
│                                      │
│                                      │
│                                      │
│                                      │
│                                      │
└─────────────────────────────────────┘
```

If the two-line program that you just typed is still in the computer's memory, type LIST and see what happens. If the program is not in memory, enter those two lines first and then type LIST.

NEW. The function of the **NEW** command is to clear the computer's memory when you want to enter a new program. If you do not issue this command, your new program statements may be interspersed with whatever hap-

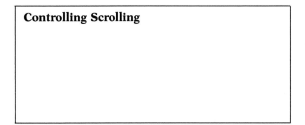

Figure D-1
Format notation for BASIC statements

[ ]	*Italics*	. . .	CAPS	Punctuation	Spaces
Square brackets indicate that the entry inside is optional.	*Italics* indicate that you must enter the data. For example, RUN *program-name* means you have to enter the name of the program you want to run.	Ellipsis points indicate that an entry may be repeated.	Capital letters indicate parts of a BASIC statement that must be entered exactly as shown.	All punctuation, such as commas, quotation marks, parentheses, and equals signs, must be entered exactly as shown.	Spaces are used to separate words, items in a list, and other entries. Wherever one space is required, several may be entered.

pens to be in the computer's memory at the time you enter the program. The format of the NEW command is

```
NEW
```

Type NEW, then type LIST. There are no program statements remaining in memory, so no listing appears.

LLIST.   The function of the **LLIST** command is to print your program listing on paper. For lengthy programs, some people prefer to work with printouts, or **hard copy**. As you enter and modify your program, you should occasionally print your program as a backup. The format of the LLIST command is

```
LLIST [line number] [-line number]
```

Two line numbers specify a range, just as in the LIST command format.

RUN.   The function of the **RUN** command is to execute all or part of a program. The formats of the RUN command are

```
RUN [line number]
```

and

```
RUN "program name"
```

Use the first format when you want to run a program that already has been loaded into main memory. When you specify a line number, program execution begins at that line. Type the two-line program into memory once more:

```
10   PRINT .095 * 6732.98
20   PRINT "All done."
```

Now type

```
RUN 20
```

This time, the only output is

```
All done.
```

because the program started running at line 20.

The second format of the RUN command is used when you want to execute a program stored on disk. (In some versions of BASIC the quotation marks are optional.) When you specify a program name, the operating system will find that program on disk, load it into the computer's memory, and begin executing it. We'll illustrate this format after discussing the SAVE command.

SAVE.   The function of the **SAVE** command is to store a BASIC program on disk or diskette. Every saved program needs a unique name. If you are working on a program

that you already have saved on disk, then saving it again with the same name will erase the old version of the program, replacing it with the new one. Be careful when saving programs. Most computer systems do not warn you if you are using a program name that already exists—you could inadvertently erase a good program. Keep a handwritten list of the programs you already have saved, and a brief description of each one. The format of the SAVE command is

```
SAVE "program name"
```

Program names should not exceed eight characters.

With the two-line sample program in memory, save it on disk:

1. Insert a formatted diskette into drive A.
2. At the BASIC prompt (OK) type

```
SAVE "TEXT1"
```

Now that the program is saved, erase it from memory by typing NEW. To be certain it is gone, type RUN. Now run it from disk by typing RUN "TEXT1". The system responds by displaying

```
639.6331
All done.
```

If those are not your results, trace through the steps above again.

LOAD.   The function of the **LOAD** command is to place into memory a copy of a BASIC program stored on disk. This is useful when you want to work on a program without running it. The format of the LOAD command is

```
LOAD "program name"
```

The six BASIC commands you will use frequently are summarized in Figure D-2. Commands are not preceded by a line number, so they are executed immediately. The formats of these commands may be slightly different on your computer system. If so, note the appropriate formats in the margins of this text.

BASIC Statements

BASIC statements are instructions preceded by a line number. They become part of a program. One BASIC statement you have seen already is PRINT. You will learn several more BASIC statements throughout this module. Each of the following lessons introduces one or more BASIC statements. In some instances, you will learn new formats for statements you have already learned.

Command	Function	Examples
LIST	Displays program on screen	LIST LIST 20–100
NEW	Clears memory for new program	NEW
LLIST	Prints hard copy of program	LLIST LLIST 20–100
RUN	Executes BASIC program	RUN RUN 100 RUN "TAXES"
SAVE	Stores BASIC program on disk	SAVE "GRADES"
LOAD	Places BASIC program into memory	LOAD "GRADES"

Figure D-2
Frequently used BASIC commands

Lesson 1

In this lesson you will learn formats for the INPUT, PRINT, and CLS statements, about string and numeric variables, and how to insert and delete BASIC program statements.

With your computer on and BASIC loaded into memory, type the following program:

```
NEW
10 PRINT "THIS PROGRAM WAS WRITTEN BY"
20 PRINT "CINDY BIRDSONG"
RUN
```

The output is

```
THIS PROGRAM WAS WRITTEN BY
CINDY BIRDSONG
```

INPUT

Of course, unless your name happens to be Cindy Birdsong the program just told a lie. (Actually, the programmer is the malfeasor. Keep that in mind the next time someone tells you 'The computer made a mistake.' People, not computers, make the mistakes.) To allow you (or anyone using the program) to enter his or her own name, change the program this way.

```
10 INPUT "NAME"; N$
20 PRINT "THIS PROGRAM WAS WRITTEN BY"
30 PRINT N$
RUN
```

The **INPUT** statement displays whatever is in quotation marks as a prompt, then waits until the user types a response and presses the Return key. In response to the NAME prompt, type your name, then press Return. The program output is

```
THIS PROGRAM WAS WRITTEN BY
your name
```

Notice that your name appears exactly as you typed it, using uppercase and lowercase letters, even typographical errors. When you type input data, BASIC distinguishes between upper- and lowercase letters; it does not distinguish between them when you enter instructions.

Now type RUN again, but enter someone else's name at the NAME prompt. Because you can vary the value, N$ is called a **variable**. Variables contrast with constants. A **constant** is a value that does not change during program execution. Anything enclosed in quotation marks is a constant, as is any number. If you wanted to enter your age in this program, you could do it this way:

```
10 INPUT "NAME, AGE "; N$, A
20 PRINT "THIS PROGRAM WAS WRITTEN BY"
30 PRINT N$
40 PRINT "WHOSE AGE IS"
50 PRINT A
RUN
```

At the first prompt (NAME, AGE), type your name, then a comma, then your age in years. When you press Return, the output is

```
THIS PROGRAM WAS WRITTEN BY
your name
WHOSE AGE IS
your age
```

Numeric and String Variables

BASIC (and computer programs in general) distinguishes between **numeric variables** (ones that contain numeric data) and **string variables** (ones that contain alphanumeric data). In BASIC, the variable name chosen by the programmer identifies the type of data. The strictest standards for variable names are the ones we will use here. They are:

1. All variable names must start with a letter.
2. Variable names can be one letter or one letter followed by a digit.
3. String variables, in addition, must end with a dollar sign.

Using these rules, the following are examples of valid variable names: A, X, A1, X7, P0, A$, and T3$. Notice that A$ and T3$ are string variables; the others are numeric variables. Using the same rules, the following are examples of invalid variable names: 8A, XXY, BB, X12, and AB$.

Many versions of BASIC allow you to use extended variable names, having, say, eight characters (instead of two, as we described above). If you can use extended names, then by all means do so. Extended names can be more descriptive—for example, TAX, COST, SCORE, NAME$, and BALANCE. Ask your instructor about the rules for variable names for the computer you use.

As you can see from the program on your computer screen, you are expected to input one alphanumeric string (N$), then a number (A). What happens if you enter two strings instead of a string and a number? Try it and find out.

PRINT

You can print more than one entity on the same line by listing the items (constants and variables) separated by semicolons (;). Change the sample program by typing

```
20 PRINT "THIS PROGRAM WAS WRITTEN BY";
   N$
40 PRINT "WHOSE AGE IS"; A
30
50
RUN
```

Now the output looks like this:

```
THIS PROGRAM WAS WRITTEN BYyour name
WHOSE AGE ISyour age
```

Notice that no space separates your name from the word BY or your age from the word IS. This happens because BASIC accepts whatever appears between quotation marks

just as it appears. Change line 20 by putting a space between the letter Y and the quotation marks. Change line 40 to put a space between the letter S and the quotation marks. Run the program, and observe the results.

Deleting a Line

Typing a line number with no BASIC statement deletes it from the program. If you had not typed 30 and 50 in the last program, those lines would have remained in the program. Type LIST to look at the current version of the program. It should look like this:

```
LIST
10 INPUT "NAME, AGE"; N$, A
20 PRINT "THIS PROGRAM WAS WRITTEN BY ";
   N$
40 PRINT "WHOSE AGE IS "; A
```

Inserting a Line

Now insert two more lines into the program by using line numbers to indicate where you want them to be:

```
5 CLS
25 PRINT "A BRILLIANT PROGRAMMER"
RUN
```

CLS

This time the program started by clearing the computer screen and positioning the cursor in the upper left corner, called the **home** position. The BASIC statement that clears the screen this way is **CLS.** You inserted that statement on line 5. Also, you added an editorial comment about yourself on line 25. The program now looks like this:

```
5 CLS
10 INPUT "NAME, AGE"; N$, A
20 PRINT "THIS PROGRAM WAS WRITTEN BY ";
   N$
25 PRINT "A BRILLIANT PROGRAMMER"
30 PRINT "WHOSE AGE IS "; A
```

Now move CLS from statement 5 to statement 15, then run the program:

```
5
15 CLS
RUN
```

This time the input prompt appears on the next line on the screen, but the output is on a clean screen. This is true because in the new program you cleared the screen only *after* you got the input variables. As you can observe, the order in which statements are executed is significant.

Lesson 1 Exercises

D.1.1 What is a variable? What is the difference between a numeric variable and a string variable?

D.1.2 Give examples of five valid variable names. Give examples of five invalid variable names. Explain why they are invalid.

D.1.3 Write a program to input one numeric variable, the wholesale cost of a product; to print the words "COST IS"; and to print the value of the variable on a second line. The retail price is 150 percent of the wholesale cost. Calculate the retail price and print it with an appropriate heading.

D.1.4 Do the same as in exercise D.1.3, but print the values on the same lines as the words.

D.1.5 Do the same as in exercise D.1.4, but clear the screen before prompting for input.

D.1.6 Write a program to input one string variable, to print the words "WINNER IS", and to print the value of the variable on a second line.

D.1.7 Do the same as in exercise D.1.6, but print the constant and the variable on the same line.

D.1.8 Write a program to input a salesperson's name and amount of sale, to print the words "SALESPERSON AND AMOUNT OF SALE", and to print the variables on a second line.

D.1.9 Do the same as in exercise D.1.8, but print the constant and variables on the same line.

D.1.10 Do the same as in exercise D.1.8, but print only one line containing the word "SALESPERSON", then the name of the salesperson, then the word "AMOUNT", and then the amount.

Lesson 2

In this lesson you will learn another way to prompt a user, the END statement, the REM statement, how to perform calculations, and the USING option of the PRINT statement.

Prompting for Input

With your computer on and BASIC loaded into memory, enter the following program:

```
10 PRINT "TYPE YOUR NAME"
15 INPUT N$
20 PRINT "THIS PROGRAM WAS WRITTEN BY ";
   N$
99 END
RUN
```

When you run this program you see that the prompt message is printed on one line, then a question mark appears on the next one where the input is entered. An INPUT statement that does not include a prompt message displays only a question mark. If you use this form of the INPUT statement, always precede it with a PRINT statement that tells the user what to enter.

END

The physical end of a program is the last instruction (the one with the highest line number). Often (but not always), this is also the logical end of the program, that is, the last one executed. If no explicit instruction to stop is given, the program stops when the last physical instruction is executed.

Most programmers prefer to state explicitly when the program should stop. To do this, they use the END statement. Line 99 contains an **END** statement for this sample program. Using a high number such as 99 allows the programmer to insert other lines easily, if needed. The format of the END statement is simply

```
END
```

When the END statement is encountered during program execution, the application program is terminated and control returns to the BASIC system. The END statement can appear anywhere in a program, but by definition it is always the last one executed.

REM

Just as labeled prompts make a program easier for a user to understand, comments within a program make the program itself easier for a programmer to understand. In BASIC, program comments are made with the **REM** (for "remark") statement. REM statements can be placed anywhere in the program. When the translator program encounters a REM statement, it bypasses it. Therefore, you can write anything in a REM statement and it will be ignored. It will be printed when you LIST or LLIST the program.

In the following example, we use the REM statement to add a program comment that stands out in the listing, making it easy to read. With the program that you last wrote in memory, add these statements:

```
5 REM ********************************
6 REM *   THIS IS A VERY SHORT PROGRAM   *
7 REM ********************************
```

Now list the program. You get

```
5 REM ********************************
6 REM *   THIS IS A VERY SHORT PROGRAM   *
7 REM ********************************
10 PRINT "TYPE YOUR NAME"
15 INPUT N$
20 PRINT "THIS PROGRAM WAS WRITTEN BY ";
   N$
99 END
```

Run the program, and notice that the remarks have no effect on it. Remarks are useful for explaining complex parts of programs, identifying the author, indicating when a program was updated and by whom, and for other situations in which comments are helpful.

Performing Calculations

BASIC programs often include arithmetic operations. These are accomplished by means of the **LET** statement. The format of the LET statement is

```
[LET] variable = expression
```

Notice that the word LET is optional. You need only the equals sign to indicate a LET statement. For illustrations of the LET statement, clear your computer's memory and enter this program:

```
NEW
10 REM HERE ARE EXAMPLES OF LET STATEMENTS
20 INPUT "ENTER ITEM PRICE ", P
30 X = P * .075
40 PRINT "SEVEN AND ONE-HALF PERCENT TAX
   IS "; X
50 T = P + X
60 PRINT "TOTAL IS "; T
99 END
```

This program accepts an item price (P), computes $7\frac{1}{2}$ percent sales tax (X), displays the tax, computes the total price (T) for the item, and then displays it. (Notice that $7\frac{1}{2}$ percent is written .075. Numeric constants contain no punctuation except a decimal point if necessary.) Run the program several times with different item prices.

The two LET statements are in lines 30 and 50. They could be written as follows:

```
30 LET X = P * .075
50 LET T = P + X
```

As mentioned earlier, the word LET is optional. Although LET statements look like equations, they are not. The equals sign should be read "be made equal to." Thus, line 30 is read "Let X be made equal to P times .075." Line 50 is read "Let T be made equal to P plus X." When a LET statement is executed, the expression to the right of the

equals sign is evaluated, and the value is placed in the variable on the left of the equals sign. The expression can be an arithmetic expression, another variable, or a constant. For example, you could set a variable to represent the sales tax rate, R, to 7.5 percent by writing

```
R = .075
```

or

```
LET R = .075
```

Arithmetic Expressions

An arithmetic expression can contain numeric variables, numeric constants, arithmetic operators, and parentheses. The **arithmetic operators** are symbols we use to indicate which operations we want performed on the data. The operations are addition ($+$), subtraction ($-$), multiplication ($*$), division ($/$), and exponentiation ($\hat{}$ or $**$). The **operands** in an arithmetic expression must be either numeric constants or numeric variables. The computer cannot perform arithmetic on string data. Here are some examples of LET statements that perform calculations:

```
A = B / C
A = B / 10
A = B + C
A = B + 10
A = B * C
A = B / C
A = B + C - 30
A = B * C / D
```

Order of Arithmetic Operations

As you can see, an arithmetic expression can be a combination of operations. When several operations are included, the computer follows a specific order, or **hierarchy**, to perform operations (see Figure D-3). Thus, for example, multiplication and division are done before addition and subtraction. Operations at the same level are performed from left to right. Sometimes you want the expression evaluated in an order different from the standard one; in this case, use parentheses around the part of the expression you want done first. For example, suppose you wanted to find the average of two test grades, T1 and T2. Clear your computer's memory and enter this program:

```
NEW
10 INPUT "TEST SCORES ", T1, T2
20 A = T1 + T2 / 2
30 PRINT "AVERAGE IS "
40 PRINT A
99 END
RUN
```

Symbol	Operation
( )	Parentheses
^ or **	Exponentiation
* and /	Multiplication and division
+ and −	Addition and subtraction

When prompted, enter the scores 100 and 80. The average, obviously, is 90. But this program says, incorrectly, that it is 140. That's because it first performed the division (T2 / 2 = 40) then added T1 (100) to the result, yielding 140. Now change line 20 this way:

```
20 A = (T1 + T2) / 2
RUN
```

Enter the scores 100 and 80 again. Note that this time the scores are first summed (100 + 80), then the total (180) is divided by 2, yielding the correct result (90). Use parentheses whenever you want to supersede the normal hierarchy of arithmetic operations.

Now change lines 10 and 20 so you can find the average of three test scores, as follows:

```
10 INPUT "ENTER SCORES ", X, Y, Z
20 A = (X + Y + Z) / 3
```

Lines 30, 40, and 99 remain the same. Run the program several times, entering different sets of scores.

PRINT USING

When prompted, enter the scores 65, 85, and 90. Notice that the average is several decimal places long. Sometimes this level of precision is desirable, but in other cases it is not. A teacher, for example, might be satisfied with just one decimal place. In order to round the average to the nearest tenth of a point and print the answer you need to use the **print format** option of the PRINT statement. Change line 40 as follows:

```
40 PRINT USING "##.#"; A
```

Notice that we have added the word USING followed by a print format, which is enclosed in quotation marks. Each number sign (#) indicates a digit position. Digit positions are always printed, except for leading nonsignificant digits. A decimal point, if you need one, may appear anywhere in the format. If all the digits to the left of the decimal point are zeros, then only one zero will print—the rest of the positions will be filled with blanks. If there are more digits to the right of the decimal point than your print format can accommodate, the number will be rounded when it is printed. Figure D-4 contains several examples of formatted numbers.

Now change line 40 in the program using different print formats. Run the program with the same data, and observe the results.

Lesson 2 Exercises

D.2.1   What is the purpose of the REM statement?
D.2.2   What is the difference between a LET statement and an equation?

Print Format	Data	Displayed Results
"##.##"	15.78	15.78
"##.##"	.78	b0.78
"##.##"	.786	b0.79
"#,###.##"	2365.86	2,365.86
"#,###.##"	2365.8	2,365.80
"#,###.##"	.892	bbbb0.89

Note: b indicates a blank print position.

D.2.3   In an arithmetic expression, which operation is evaluated first, multiplication or subtraction? Multiplication or addition? Exponentiation or division? Exponentiation or an operation inside parentheses?

D.2.4   Write a program that accomplishes the following:
- Include your name, the date, and the exercise number in remarks (do this for all subsequent exercises in this and all future lessons).
- Prompt the user to enter the number of cases of soda pop he or she wants to buy.
- Display the price of the pop, figured at $6.99 per case.

D.2.5   Do the same as in exercise D.2.4, but print the answer with only two decimal places.

D.2.6   Write a program to do the following:
- Prompt the user for the number of people who will be attending a dance.
- Prompt the user for the cost of each ticket to the dance.
- Calculate and display the expected gross proceeds from the dance, using an appropriate print format.

D.2.7   Do the same as in exercise D.2.6, but add the following features:
- Subtract the cost of the disc jockey ($500.00).
- Compute and subtract the cost of refreshments ($1.50 per person).

D.2.8   The campus student center needs new carpeting, and some student groups are trying to raise money to have it replaced. Write a program to do the following:
- Prompt the user for the dimensions (width and length) of the area to be carpeted.
- Prompt the user for the price per square yard of the carpet.
- Use a fixed price of $2.00 per square yard for the carpet pad (which is required for installation).
- Compute and display the total cost of installing the new carpet.

D.2.9   The same campus student center needs to be repainted. Write a program to do the following:
- Prompt the user to enter the number of square feet of wall space to be painted.
- Note that one gallon of paint covers approximately 500 square feet, and costs $12.50. (This paint can be purchased in whole gallons only.)
- Compute and display how many gallons of paint will be needed and how much the paint will cost. Note: To round up to a whole gallon, do the following: Compute the number of gallons needed (it probably will include a fraction); add 0.5 to this answer; print the new answer using this print format: "###".

D.2.10   The President of the United States is coming to visit the campus, so the students are mobilizing volunteers to paint the student center. They estimate that it takes one student two hours to prepare, paint, and clean up a 500-square-foot area. Write a program to do the following:
- Prompt the user to enter the number of square feet of wall to be painted.
- Compute and display the number of student-hours required to paint the student center.
- Compute and display the number of volunteers that will be needed for the job if each volunteer agrees to work for 4 hours. Note: you cannot have fractional volunteers, so round this answer up using the same method as described in the previous exercise.

Lesson 3

In this lesson you will be introduced to program design, and you will learn about program loops and the IF and GOTO statements.

The programs you have been studying and writing until now have been relatively simple. Each one consists of several statements, executed from beginning to end, one time through. If you want to execute a program more than once, you have to run it again. Sometimes that is not adequate. Sometimes we want to control execution of a program from *within* the program.

Loops

Consider the flowcharts in Figure D-5. The flowchart in D-5*a* shows a series of instructions that are carried out just once. The flowchart in Figure D-5*b* shows those same instructions, but in this case they can be repeated if the user wants them to be.

Here is the program that matches the flowchart in Figure D-5*a*:

```
10 REM THESE INSTRUCTIONS ARE EXECUTED ONLY
20 REM ONCE EACH TIME THE PROGRAM IS RUN
30 INPUT "ENTER ITEM PRICE ", P
40 X = P * .075
50 T = P + X
60 PRINT "TAX IS "; X
70 PRINT "TOTAL IS "; T
99 END
```

Here is the program that matches the flowchart in Figure D-5*b*. Modify the existing program so it looks like the following, then run it.

Figure D-5
Program logic with and without loops

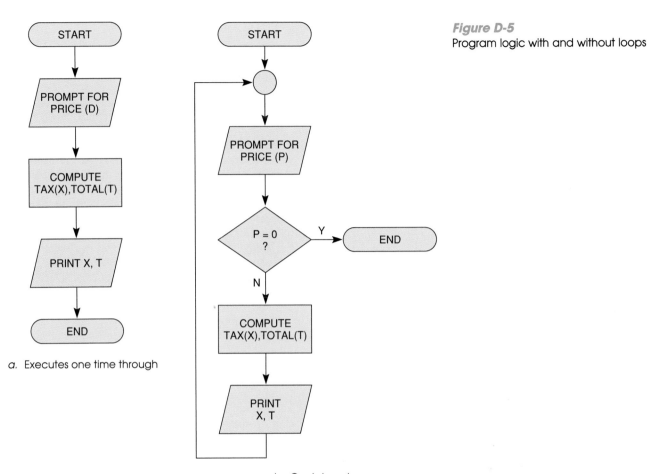

a. Executes one time through

b. Contains a loop

```
10 REM THIS PROGRAM CONTAINS A LOOP
30 INPUT "ENTER ITEM PRICE, OR 0 TO
   QUIT ", P
35 IF P = 0 THEN END
40 X = P * .075
50 T = P + X
60 PRINT "TAX IS "; X
70 PRINT "TOTAL IS "; T
80 GOTO 30
```

Notice that the program "offers" to be executed again. In fact it will stay in this loop until you enter a price of zero.

Many new things are being introduced to you at once. Let's examine each one individually, starting with program design.

Program Design with Flowcharts

Before writing a complex program, programmers design the logic that the program will follow. **Logic** simply means the sequence of instructions including transfers of control

that change the ordinary sequence. Remember, a program ordinarily executes in the order of its line numbers *unless you tell it to do otherwise.*

Program logic can be illustrated using a variety of techniques. A commonly used one is the **flowchart**, a graphic diagram that uses symbols to indicate the type of operation being performed. In the flowcharts in Figure D-5 several symbols are used. The oval ⬭ indicates the starting and ending points of the program. A parallelogram ▱ indicates an input or output operation. A rectangle ▢ indicates an operation. A diamond ◇ indicates a condition being tested. And arrows indicate the flow of control from one operation or decision to another—hence the name flowchart. Trace the logic in the flowcharts in Figure D-5 and see if you can easily follow it.

GOTO

Let's turn our attention to the program now in your computer. Two new statements are introduced here, in lines

35 and 80. Let's look first at line 80, which says GOTO 30. The format of the **GOTO** statement is

```
GOTO line number
```

The GOTO statement is an unconditional transfer of control. This means that when a GOTO statement is encountered during program execution, control is transferred immediately to the line number specified and program execution continues there. By transferring control to an instruction that already has been executed, we produce a **loop**. Because of this loop, you do not need to run the program several times to input different data.

The IF statement in line 35 plays an important role. It terminates the loop when the user wants to quit—that is, when the user enters a price of zero. Whenever you put a loop into a program, make sure there is a way to stop the loop. Sometimes programmers make errors in a program that result in an endless loop, one that has no achievable end condition. In that case some outside intervention is needed, such as pressing the control key and the C key at the same time. Find out from your instructor how to interrupt a program during execution, and write the instructions in the box provided here.

```
Interrupting Program Execution



```

Now delete line 35 from the program and run it. Notice that you are in an endless loop: the program has no built-in means of terminating. Interrupt the program following the instructions you wrote in the box above. Then put statement 35 back into the program:

```
35 IF P = 0 THEN END
```

IF ... THEN ... ELSE

The format of the IF statement is

```
IF condition THEN statement(s) [ELSE
statement(s)]
```

The function of the **IF** statement is to make a decision regarding program flow based on the result of a test condition. When an IF statement is encountered during program execution, a condition is tested. If the condition is true then the statement or statements following the word THEN are executed, but not the ones following the word ELSE. If the condition is false, then the statement or statements following the word ELSE are executed, but not the ones following the word THEN. If the path taken does not include a GOTO, then program execution resumes at the next sequential instruction following the IF statement. The statement(s) following the word THEN (or ELSE) can be any BASIC statement, such as LET, GOTO, END, or even another IF (you'll learn about this possibility in Lesson 4).

Notice from the format that the ELSE part of the IF statement is optional. Leaving out the ELSE simply indicates that something will be done only if the condition is true. Nothing special happens when the condition is false. This is sometimes referred to as a null ELSE.

A **condition** is a logical expression composed of variables, constants, and relational operators. **Relational operators** are used to compare two values. Figure D-6 shows the relational operators and their meanings.

Here is an IF statement that gives a bonus of 5 percent to anyone whose salary (S) is more than $30,000, and a bonus of $500 to anyone earning $30,000 or less:

```
IF S > 30000
    THEN B = S * .05
    ELSE B = 500
```

For the sake of readability, the condition and each of the two actions were written on separate lines. *Note that some*

Figure D-6
Relational operators

Operator	Relation Tested	Example
=	Equality	= 30000
< >	Inequality	< > 30000
<	Less than	< 30000
>	Greater than	> 30000
<=	Less than or equal to	<= 30000
>=	Greater than or equal to	>= 30000

versions of BASIC do not allow this format. Consequently, the entire IF ... THEN ... ELSE statement must be typed before pressing the Return key.

Here is an IF statement that sets the tax rate (X) at 8 percent for sales made in the state (S$) of Connecticut:

```
IF S$ = "CT"
     THEN X = .08
```

Notice that the above IF statement has a null ELSE.

The following IF statement displays an error message if the parent's age (P) is less than or equal to the child's age (C):

```
IF P <= C
     THEN PRINT "AGE ERROR. REENTER AGES."
```

Now let's examine line 35 of the sample program.

```
35 IF P = 0 THEN END
```

Each time this statement is encountered, P is compared to zero. If it is equal to zero (meaning the user just typed in a 'price' of zero), the statement following THEN is executed. In this case, it stops the program (END). If P is not equal to zero (the user typed in some other number) then nothing special happens because the statement has a null ELSE. Instead, control passes to the next instruction following the IF statement, in this case, line 40.

Consider another example. Suppose you wanted to determine someone's average grade for an unknown number of tests. You would need to sum all the test scores and divide them by the number of tests. The flowchart for this program appears in Figure D-7. Examine it now. When you are sure you understand it, clear your computer's memory and enter this program:

```
10   REM T IS TEST SCORE
20   REM S IS SUM OF TEST SCORES
30   REM N IS NUMBER OF TESTS
40   REM G IS AVERAGE GRADE
50   REM
100  CLS
110  INPUT "ENTER TEST SCORE ", T
120  S = S + T
130  N = N + 1
140  INPUT "DO YOU HAVE MORE TESTS
     (Y / N)? ", A$
150  IF A$ = "Y" THEN GOTO 110
160  G = S / N
170  PRINT "THE AVERAGE IS "
180  PRINT USING "###.#"; G
999  END
```

Run the program using the scores 75, 83, 60, 40, and 99. You should get the answer 71.4. If you do not, carefully compare your program to the one in the text and correct

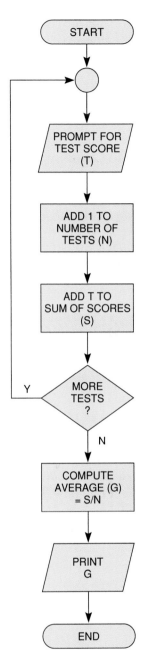

Figure D-7
Logic for program to find test average

any differences. Note: when the program prompts DO YOU HAVE MORE TESTS (Y / N)? only a response of uppercase Y will enable you to enter another score. Lowercase y or any other input causes the program to leave the loop, calculate the average, and stop. As an exercise, can you modify the program so it will accept lowercase y also?

Line 120 means "Add to whatever the accumulated score is so far (S) the value of this test (T) and put the new answer back in S." S is called an **accumulator**.

Line 130 means "Add 1 to the total number of tests so far (N) and put the new answer back in N." N is called a **counter**.

Change the program to allow the user to find the average of another set of scores (this would be useful to a classroom teacher). Add these statements:

```
190 INPUT "PRESS Y IF YOU WANT TO ENTER
    ANOTHER SET ", B$
200 IF B$ = "Y" THEN GOTO 100
```

Now run the program, entering these test scores: 50, 100. The average you get is 75. When prompted to go again, answer Y (use an uppercase Y). This time, enter only one score, 95. The average you *should* get is 95 (95 / 1 = 95); but the program says the average is 81.7. That obviously is incorrect. How did that happen?

Resetting Accumulators and Counters

Well, 81.7 is the average of 50, 100, and 95. As you recall, 50 and 100 were the test scores you entered for the previous student. When the program was done with those scores it had a value of 150 in variable S and a value of 2 in variable N. The variables act just like calculators: the first time you use them they have already been set to zero; if you want to use them again from the beginning, you need to zero them out, or **reinitialize** them. In this program you can accomplish this by making the following program changes:

```
105 S = 0
107 N = 0
```

Now when you loop back to line 100 to enter the next set of grades, you start off by resetting S and N to zero. With those changes, run the program again with two sets of grades, first with 50 and 100 (giving an average of 75), then with just 95 (this time giving a correct average of 95). If you do not get those results, compare your program with the one in this text and correct any discrepancies.

Lesson 3 Exercises

D.3.1 What is a loop?
D.3.2 What is an endless loop? How do you prevent it? How do you stop it if your program goes into one?
D.3.3 What happens when a GOTO statement is encountered during program execution?
D.3.4 Write the IF statement that counts the number of people whose age (A) is under 25.

D.3.5 Write a program to do the following:
- Identify yourself, the date, and the exercise number in remarks, as usual.
- Prompt the user to enter a loan amount.
- Calculate and display the simple interest on the loan (9.9 percent).
- Allow the user to repeat the process.
- Quit when the user enters a loan amount of zero.

D.3.6 Write a program to do the following:
- Prompt the user to enter his or her net earnings for the past five years.
- Calculate and display the average earnings.
- Allow the user to repeat the process using any method of your choice to stop the loop.

D.3.7 Do the same as in exercise D.3.6, but allow the user to enter any number of years' earnings.

D.3.8 Write a program to compute batting averages. Note: a batting average is the ratio of the number of hits to the number of times at bat, expressed as an integer. A batter who gets two hits out of four times at bat has a batting average of 500. A batter who gets 3 hits out of ten times at bat has a batting average of 333.

D.3.9 Write a program to count the number of excellent customers, and calculate their average purchase amount. Include the following:
- Prompt the user to enter a customer name and two purchase amounts.
- If the sum of the purchases is $300 or greater, print the message "*customer name* IS AN EXCELLENT CUSTOMER."
- When the user has entered all the customer data, compute and display the average purchase amount *for excellent customers only*. Print the number of excellent customers.

D.3.10 Write a program to calculate employee pay amounts for an undetermined number of employees.
- Prompt the user to enter the number of hours an employee worked and the employee's hourly pay rate.
- Compute regular pay for the first 40 hours.
- Compute overtime pay as time-and-a-half for all hours worked over 40 (there may be none).
- Calculate total pay: regular pay plus overtime pay.
- Enable the user to repeat this process; stop the loop using any method you choose.

Lesson 4

In this lesson you will learn about nested IF statements and the TAB function of the PRINT statement.

Nested IF Statements

Consider this problem: A program needs to be developed to accept sales data, then count the number of sales up to $300.00, the number between $300.01 and $600.00, and the number over $600. Examine the program logic illustrated in the flowchart in Figure D-8. Trace the logic. One of the conditions (S > 300?) is tested only if the previous one (S > 600?) was false. Here is the program that matches that flowchart. Enter it on your computer and run it.

```
10   REM COUNT SALES
20   REM A IS COUNT OF SALES OVER $600.00
30   REM B IS COUNT OF SALES BETWEEN
     $300.01 AND $600.00
40   REM C IS COUNT OF SALES  UP TO
     $300.00
100  INPUT "ENTER SALE AMOUNT OR ZERO TO
     STOP ", S
110  IF S = 0 THEN GOTO 140
120  IF S > 600 THEN A = A + 1 ELSE IF S >
     300 THEN B = B + 1 ELSE C = C + 1
130  GOTO 100
140  PRINT "OVER $600: "; A;
     "BETWEEN $300.01 AND $600: "; B;
     "UP TO $300: "; C
999  END
```

The **nested IF statement** is in line 120. As stated earlier, BASIC requires that the entire IF statement exist on one line (that is, with a single line number). The IF statement may be longer than one screen line, and BASIC automatically continues it on the next line. But the programmer does not press Return until the end of the entire statement. The structure of the nested IF statement can be seen more clearly if it is written like this:

```
IF S > 600
THEN A = A + 1
ELSE IF S > 300
     THEN B = B + 1
     ELSE C = C + 1
```

With this indentation it is easier to see which THENs and ELSEs go with which IFs. Obviously, nested IFs can get very complex and confusing. Therefore, try to limit yourself to only one or two levels of indentation—that's what we have used in the example.

Consider another example. Excise taxes for electronic equipment manufactured in the country of Circuitoria are levied at different rates. Products are categorized into computer and noncomputer equipment. Excise tax for noncomputer equipment is 15 percent. Computer equipment is further classified into laptop computers and desktop computers. Laptops are hit with an excise tax of 22 percent, and desktops are taxed at the rate of 28 percent.

A program to determine the appropriate tax rate and then compute excise tax might be designed as illustrated in Figure D-9. Note that this flowchart contains a nested IF.

Here is the BASIC program that matches the flowchart. With your computer on and memory cleared, enter this program:

```
10   REM CALCULATE EXCISE TAX
100  R = 0
200  INPUT "ENTER PRICE "; P
210  INPUT "ENTER CATEGORY: N, L, OR D ",
     C$
220  IF C$ = "N" THEN R = .15 ELSE IF C$
     = "L" THEN R = .22 ELSE IF C$ = "D" THEN
     R = .28 ELSE PRINT "INVALID CATEGORY. "
250  T = P * R
280  PRINT "EXCISE TAX IS "; T
300  INPUT "DO YOU WANT TO GO AGAIN? (Y) ",
     A$
310  IF A$ = "Y" THEN GOTO 100
999  END
```

Notice that in this example we are checking for valid categories (that is, either N, L, or D). In case the user makes a mistake when entering the category (say she enters an R instead of a D), this program will tell her an error was made. Suppose we had written line 220 like this instead:

```
220  IF C$ = "N" THEN R = .15 ELSE IF C$ =
     "L" THEN R = .22 ELSE R = .28
```

What would happen if the user entered an incorrect category such as R or B or &? If you said that the excise tax rate would be set to 28 percent then you have correctly interpreted the IF statement. Programs that accept input data from a user need to perform extensive verification procedures to prevent bad data from entering a system, and to give users an opportunity to correct bad data at the beginning. In fact, some estimates indicate that in some programs as much as 80 percent of the instructions exist just to verify the input data while only 20 percent are used for actual processing.

PRINT and PRINT TAB

Let's take another look at the first program example in this lesson:

```
10   REM COUNT SALES
20   REM A IS COUNT OF SALES OVER $600.00
30   REM B IS COUNT OF SALES BETWEEN $300.01
     AND $600.00
40   REM C IS COUNT OF SALES  UP TO $300.00
100  INPUT "ENTER SALE AMOUNT OR ZERO TO
     STOP ", S
110  IF S = 0 THEN GOTO 140
```

(continued on page 482)

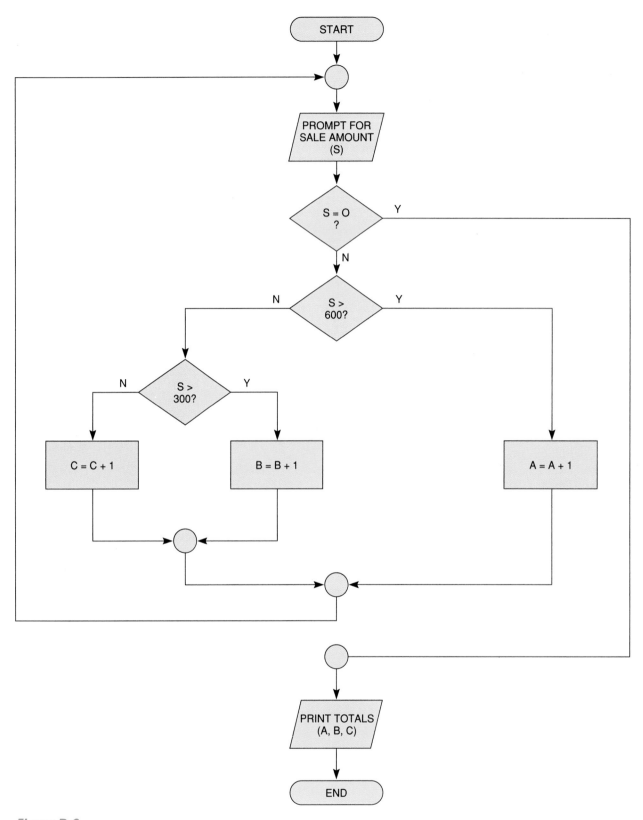

Figure D-8
Program logic with nested IF
statements

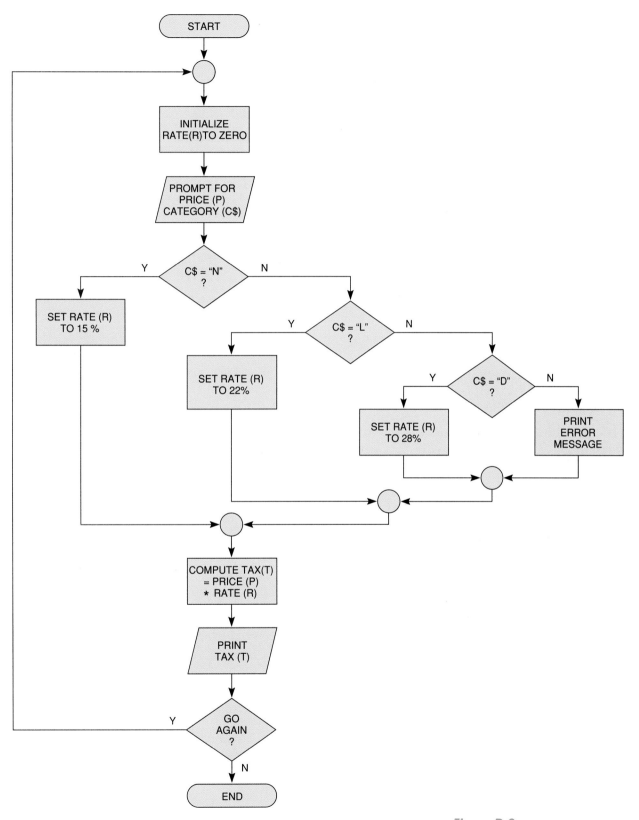

Figure D-9
Logic for program to determine
excise tax

```
120 IF S > 600 THEN A = A + 1 ELSE IF S >
    300 THEN B = B + 1 ELSE C = C + 1
130 GOTO 100
140 PRINT "OVER $600: "; A;
    "BETWEEN $300.01 AND $600: "; B;
    "UP TO $300: "; C
999 END
```

Previously we were concerned with the nested IF logic in the program. Now let us turn our attention to the output produced by this program. Examine line 140:

```
140 PRINT "OVER $600: "; A;
"BETWEEN $300.01 AND $600: "; B;
"UP TO $300: "; C
```

By stringing several items together in the same PRINT statement and separating them by semicolons, we produce output that looks like this:

```
OVER $600:  3 BETWEEN $300.01 AND $600:
8 UP TO $300:  4
```

Although it may be correct, the presentation of the results is not very easy to read. It can be made more readable by separating items. Their locations on the printed line are specified by means of the **TAB** function of the PRINT statement. So if we wanted to print the word "OVER" beginning in position 1, the word "BETWEEN" beginning in position 25, and the word "UP" beginning in position 50, we would change the PRINT statement as follows:

```
140 PRINT TAB(1) "OVER $600: "; A; TAB(25)
    "BETWEEN $300.01 AND $600: "; B; TAB(50)
    "UP TO $300: "; C
```

The result is a printed line that is easier to read and interpret. Enter the program with the updated line 140 and try it. Change the TAB positions and see what happens. Put TAB positions in front of the variables, A, B, and C, then print the line and observe the results. Using TAB gives you more control over the design of your output.

Finally, you may want to leave some space on the screen before printing the output line. You leave space by printing blank lines. The format for printing a blank line is simply

```
PRINT
```

Add this line to your program:

```
135 PRINT
```

Now run the program and observe the results. If you want to print multiple blank lines, issue multiple PRINT statements, like this:

```
135 PRINT: PRINT: PRINT
```

BASIC allows you to put more than one statement on one line by using a colon to separate the statements.

Lesson 4 Exercises

D.4.1 What is a nested IF?

D.4.2 Write a program to accomplish the following:
- Prompt the user to enter a student's grade level (freshman or sophomore, using whatever codes you choose), and grade point average (a number between 0 and 4.0).
- Count and display the number of freshmen and the number of sophomores who are eligible for tuition rebates. Freshmen with GPA of 3.0 or higher and sophomores with a GPA of 3.2 or higher are eligible.

D.4.3 Do the same as in exercise D.4.2, but add this feature:
- Calculate and display the percentage of freshmen, the percentage of sophomores, and the overall percentage of students eligible for tuition rebates.

D.4.4 A landscaping company sells live plants, silk flowers, and pottery. Handling charges for live plants are 10 percent of the cost, for silk flowers 13 percent, and for pottery 8 percent. Write a program to do the following:
- Prompt the user to enter the price and classification of each item a customer buys.
- Compute the total cost of the customer's order, including the handling charges.
- Display subtotals for items and for handling.
- Display the total cost for the order.

D.4.5 Employees earn vacation time based on the number of hours they work each week. Anyone who works 50 hours or more earns 1/2 day vacation; between 35 and 49 hours, 1/4 day; between 24 and 34 hours, 1/8 day; and below 24 hours, 0 days. Write a program to do the following:
- Prompt the user to enter the number of hours worked by each employee in a department.
- Compute and display the number of vacation days earned by the entire staff.

D.4.6 Do the same as in exercise D.4.5 but add this feature:
- Compute and display the ratio of vacation hours earned to hours worked. A vacation day is equal to 8 hours.

D.4.7 A survey is being made of salaries earned by male and female employees. Write a program to do the following:
- Prompt the user to enter details on each employee: gender (F or M), work status (executive, administrator, or clerical), and annual salary.
- When all employee data has been entered, compute and display the following: number of men and women in each work status category, average

salary in each category, average salary for each gender in each category, average overall salary for men, and average overall salary for women. Be sure that your output is clearly labeled and is easy to read and interpret.

Lesson 5

In this lesson you will learn how to make program loops using the FOR and NEXT statements.

FOR and NEXT

Looping, or the repetition of instructions, is common in computer programs. We have seen examples of programs that obtain a set of data, process it, produce outputs, and repeat for the next set of data (that is, we issue a GOTO to go back to the input instructions). This procedure is called the input/process/output cycle. Other loops occur in programs also. Besides the GOTO statement, BASIC has another technique for handling loops. In this section you will learn about the FOR and NEXT statements.

To introduce these statements, we will consider a very simple grade school problem. We will write a program to count by 5s from 5 to 25. The flowchart for this program appears in Figure D-10*a*. Also, Figure D-10*b* shows a BASIC program using statements you already know.

At the top of page 484 is another version of this algorithm, or program design, using the **FOR** and **NEXT** statements. Load it into your computer and run it.

Figure D-10
Counting by 5s to 25

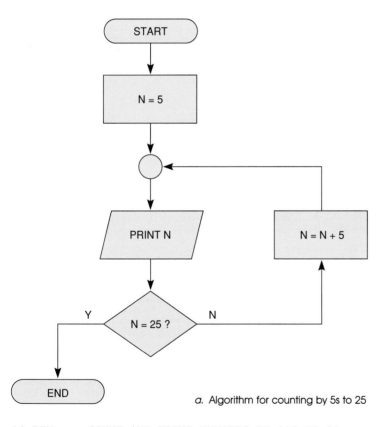

a. Algorithm for counting by 5s to 25

```
10 REM     COUNT AND PRINT NUMBERS BY 5'S TO 25
20    N = 5
30    PRINT N
40    IF N = 25 THEN 70
50    N = N + 5
60    GOTO 30
70    END
```
b. BASIC program for counting and printing numbers by 5s to 25

```
10 FOR N = 5 TO 25 STEP 5
20   PRINT N
30 NEXT N
40 END
```

The meaning of these statements is as follows. At line 10, set the variable N equal to 5. Process all statements until the statement NEXT N is reached (line 30). When NEXT N is reached, go back to the FOR statement (line 10). Add 5 to N and check to see if N is greater than 25. If it is not, repeat the loop. Continue repeating the loop until the value of N exceeds 25. Then skip over the loop and continue execution at the statement following the NEXT N statement (in this case, line 40).

Thus, the FOR statement sets up a variable that serves as an index over the loop. When the value of the index exceeds some specified amount, the loop is terminated. The format of the FOR statement is

```
FOR index = start TO end [STEP increment]
```

The index is the name of the variable. The start value is the value to which the index is set the first time the loop is entered. The end value is the value that the index is compared to in order to terminate the loop. The increment is the number added to the index each time. Specifying the increment is optional; the default is 1 (that is, the increment will be 1 unless a different value is specified).

The format for the NEXT statement is

```
NEXT index
```

When a NEXT statement is encountered during program execution, control is returned to the appropriate FOR statement, at which point the index is incremented and tested for the terminal value. FOR and NEXT statements always are used as a pair.

Here is another application for the FOR and NEXT statements. This program prompts the user for exactly five test scores, then computes and displays the average. Enter it into your computer and run it.

```
100 FOR I = 1 TO 5
110   INPUT "ENTER TEST SCORE ", T
120   X = X + T
130 NEXT I
200 A = X / 5
210 PRINT "AVERAGE IS "; A
999 END
```

The next program is a variation of the previous one. In this version, the program prompts the user first to enter the number of tests (N). Then it executes the loop up to N times, and finds the average of N scores.

```
90  INPUT "HOW MANY TEST SCORES? ", N
100 FOR I = 1 TO N
```

```
110   INPUT "ENTER TEST SCORE ", T
120   X = X + T
130 NEXT I
200 A = X / N
210 PRINT "AVERAGE IS "; A
999 END
```

One pair (or more) of FOR-NEXT statements can be nested within another pair of FOR-NEXT statements. Consider the problem of producing a multiplication table like the one shown in Figure D-11.

To compute this table we need two variables: one to indicate the column (C) and one to indicate the row (R). To compute the first row we let R = 1 and let C go from 1 to 5. For each value of C we compute R times C and print the result. To do just that much we would use these BASIC statements:

```
10 R = 1
20 FOR C = 1 TO 5
30   P = R * C
40   PRINT R; " TIMES "; C " EQUALS "; P
50 NEXT C
999 END
```

Enter that program and run it. The results should be:

```
1 TIMES 1 EQUALS 1
1 TIMES 2 EQUALS 2
1 TIMES 3 EQUALS 3
1 TIMES 4 EQUALS 4
1 TIMES 5 EQUALS 5
```

This is the equivalent of the first row of the table. It does not use the same format as the one in Figure D-11, but the values are the same. Printing the second and sub-

Figure D-11
A multiplication table

sequent rows is done by following the same order of operation, but this time letting R be equal to 2, 3, and so forth.
Change your program by replacing line 10 and adding line
60, as follows:

```
10 FOR R = 1 TO 5
20   FOR C = 1 TO 5
30     P = R * C
40     PRINT R; " TIMES "; C " EQUALS "; P
50   NEXT C
60 NEXT R
999 END
```

Notice how we use indentation to make the program logic
easier to discern. Now run this program and observe the
results. This time, all twenty-five entries are printed.

Note that the FOR and NEXT statements for variable
C are enclosed between the FOR and NEXT statements
for variable R. BASIC requires this format. See what happens when you switch the order of the NEXT statements
(you should get an error message).

The start value, end value, and step value for an index
do not have to be stated as numeric constants; they also
can be variables. Consider the following example. A program will begin by asking the user to enter the number
(N) of patient weights that will be entered. Then the program will perform its input/process/output loop N times
before printing the average weight and stopping. Here is
the program:

```
100 INPUT "HOW MANY PATIENTS THIS TIME? ",
    N
110 CLS
200 FOR X = 1 TO N
210   INPUT "ENTER WEIGHT IN POUNDS ", W
220   T = T + W
290 NEXT X
400 A = T / N
410 PRINT "AVERAGE WEIGHT IS "; A
999 END
```

Enter and run the program, and observe the results.

Lesson 5 Exercises

D.5.1   Explain the actions the computer will take for each
of the following sets of BASIC statements:
```
a. 10 FOR J = 1 TO 9 STEP 2
   20 PRINT J
   30 NEXT J
b. 10 FOR J = 1 TO 10 STEP 2
   20 PRINT J
   30 NEXT J
```

```
c. 10 FOR J = 1 TO 3
   20 PRINT J
   30 NEXT J
d. 10 FOR J = 1 TO 4
   20 PRINT J
   30 FOR K = 1 TO 3
   40 PRINT K
   50 NEXT J
   60 NEXT K
```

D.5.2   Write a BASIC program that will produce a division table for the values 20 through 26 divided by
2, 3, and 4. (Hint: start by figuring it out manually,
so when you print results you'll know if they're
correct.)

D.5.3   Write a BASIC program that will prompt the user
for the number of shipment weights to be entered.
Then accept that many weights, expressed in
pounds; convert each weight into its metric equivalent, expressed in kilograms; print each weight.
When all weights have been entered, print the
average weight in pounds. Note: One kilogram is
equal to approximately 2.2 pounds.

D.5.4   Write a BASIC program to print a multiplication
table that finds the product of 3 times any consecutive numbers the user chooses. Prompt the
user for the starting and ending numbers. (Hint:
when you run the program, keep the range of
numbers small so the table will fit on one screen.)

D.5.5   Write a program that will calculate and print 10
numbers in a series, starting at 1, such that each
successive number is the sum of the previous two
numbers, like this:

1   2   3   5   8   13

(This is known as the Fibonacci sequence.) The
programming logic for this program appears in
Figure D-12. Be certain you understand the logic
before you try to write the program.

Lesson 6

In this lesson you will learn how to define and use arrays.

Arrays

An **array** is a table that has rows and columns. People use
arrays, or tables, all the time, and they are very useful
data structures within programs. Consider, for example,
a table you could use to look up shipping and handling
charges to add to customer order totals. Each of the six

Figure D-12
Program logic for Exercise D.5.5

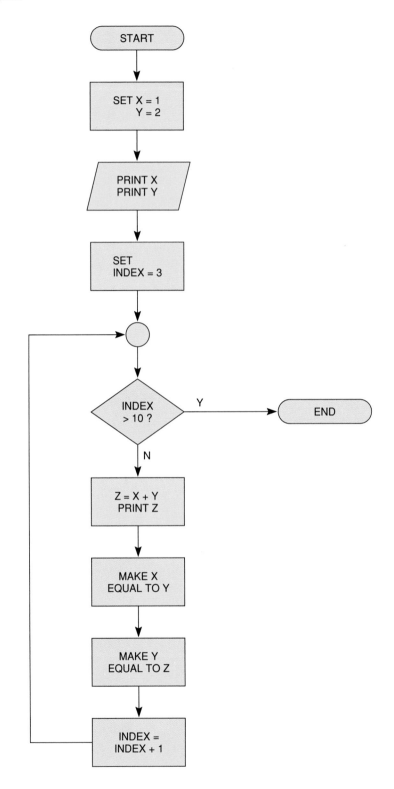

postal zones has a fee associated with it. The table looks like this:

```
ZONE     FEE
1        10.00
2        13.00
3         8.00
4        16.00
5        14.00
6        12.00
```

Thus, if a customer lived in zone 2 she would have to pay $13.00 for shipping and handling; if she lived in zone 6 she would pay $12.00 for shipping and handling.

In a BASIC program you could determine the shipping and handling fee by writing a series of IF statements, like this:

```
210 IF Z = 1 THEN F = 10:  GOTO 400
220 IF Z = 2 THEN F = 13:  GOTO 400
230 IF Z = 3 THEN F = 8:   GOTO 400
240 IF Z = 4 THEN F = 16:  GOTO 400
250 IF Z = 5 THEN F = 14:  GOTO 400
260 IF Z = 6 THEN F = 12:  GOTO 400
270 PRINT "INVALID ZONE. TRY AGAIN ";
    GOTO 200
400 etc.
```

Notice that the true evaluation of each IF statement causes two statements to be executed. In BASIC you can incorporate more than one statement on a line by separating them with colons (:). Consequently, line 210 reads: If zone is 1, set the fee to $10.00 and then skip down to line 400, bypassing all the rest of the IF statements. The other IF statements are interpreted similarly. Now, back to the problem at hand.

The program is an awkward one. What happens if we suddenly expand the business and include fifty more zones? Do we need to write fifty more IF statements? What about a table containing 1,000 entries? Fortunately there is a way to handle tables in BASIC. We will start with some terminology. Because we will be referring to the items in the table we need to give each one of them a name. First, let's call the table T. We also need to name the rows and columns. We can call the first row, row 1, the second row, row 2, and so on. Similarly, we name the columns column 1 and column 2.

Now to identify a particular item we state the table name, the row name, and the column name. Thus, the value 1 is found at table T, row 1, column 1. The value 8 is found at table T, row 3, column 2. This naming is cumbersome, so we can use shorthand. To reference a particular table location we'll put the row and column numbers in parentheses after the table name. So T(1,1) refers to table T, row 1, column 1 (which contains the value 1);

T(3,2) refers to table T, row 3, column 2 (which contains the value 8). The names of the rows and columns are called **subscripts**.

Tables can vary in size. They can have one or many rows and one or many columns. The shipping and handling table we are using for an example has six rows and two columns. The number of rows and columns are called the **dimensions** of the table. The dimensions of the shipping and handling table are 6 by 2.

Before we use a table in BASIC we must define it. This is accomplished by naming the table and giving its dimensions. The system then can reserve space in main memory for all of the values. The BASIC statement used to define a table is **DIM**, which is short for dimension.

DIM

The format of the DIM statement is

```
DIM tablename(subscripts)
```

The subscripts are the numbers that define the maximum value of the dimensions of the array. The rules for creating a table name are the same as for a variable name. To define the shipping and handling table we would code:

```
100 DIM T(6,2)
```

This statement tells the system to reserve enough storage for a table with six rows and two columns. You can visualize the table as a grid, six rows down and two columns across, whose values are all initialized to zeros. Once the table is defined, we must put data into it.

We could do it with a list of LET statements like this:

```
10 T(1,1) = 1
20 T(1,2) = 10
30 T(2,1) = 2
40 T(2,2) = 13
```

and so forth. But this approach is tedious and would be even worse if the table dimensions were, say, 100 by 100. Also, what if we wanted to input the table values from the user? In this case we might code:

```
10 INPUT "ZONE, FEE "; T(1,1), T(1,2)
20 INPUT "ZONE, FEE "; T(2,1), T(2,2)
30 INPUT "ZONE, FEE "; T(3,1), T(3,2)
```

and so forth. When line 10 is executed, the user is expected to provide two values. The first value will be put into position 1,1 of T; the second one will be put into position 1,2 of T.

We can employ the FOR-NEXT statements to make the programming easier. Consider this program for defining and filling the shipping and handling table:

```
10 DIM T(6,2)
20 FOR I = 1 TO 6
30   INPUT "ZONE, FEE"; T(I,1), T(I,2)
40 NEXT I
```

The FOR-NEXT loop causes the INPUT instruction to be executed six times. The first time it is executed, I has the value of 1; the second time, I has the value of 2, then 3, then 4, then 5, and finally 6.

This approach has even more appeal when you consider what would happen if the table dimensions were 100,2. Without the FOR-NEXT loop it would take 100 INPUT statements to fill the table. However, with the FOR-NEXT instructions it can be filled with just two changes, as follows:

```
10 DIM (100,2)
20 FOR I = 1 TO 100
30   INPUT "ZONE, FEE "; T(I,1), T(I,2)
40 NEXT I
```

Using an Array

Now let's return to the problem of adding the shipping and handling charge to a customer's order total. The logic for this program is shown in Figure D-13. Study it carefully; it may seem a little confusing at first. The program starts by establishing the table: defining it and prompting the user to key in the values.

Next, the user is prompted to enter the customer's subtotal and postal zone. The index (J) is initialized to 1 and the loop begins. First, check to see if the customer's postal zone matches the subscripted table entry. If it does match, add the appropriate shipping and handling fee to the subtotal and print the results.

If the customer's postal zone does not match that table entry, then add 1 to J. At this point, one of two things can be true: either there are no more entries in the table to search (J > 6), meaning that the user typed in an incorrect postal zone; or the customer's postal zone needs to be compared to the next table entry. Eventually, we will exit from the loop, either because a match was found or because we exhausted all the table entries unsuccessfully.

Now, with your computer on and memory cleared, enter this program:

```
05   REM LINES 10 THROUGH 40 ESTABLISH THE
     TABLE
10   DIM T(6,2)
20   FOR I = 1 TO 6
30     INPUT "ENTER ZONE AND FEE SEPARATED
       BY A COMMA ", T(I,1), T(I,2)
40   NEXT I
100  INPUT "ENTER SUBTOTAL AND ZONE,
     SEPARATED BY A COMMA ", S, Z
```

```
120 J = 1
130 IF Z = T(J,1) THEN GOTO 400
140 J = J + 1
150 IF J > 6 THEN PRINT "INVALID ZONE.
    TRY AGAIN.": GOTO 100
160 GOTO 130
400 G = S + T(J,2)
410 PRINT "TOTAL: "; S; " + "; T(J,2);
    " = "; G
500 INPUT "GO AGAIN? ", A$
510 IF A$ = "Y" THEN GOTO 100
999 END
```

Notice that the fee extracted from the table—T(J,2)—is used like any numeric variable. It is an operand in the calculation in line 400. It is printed as output in line 410.

Run the program several times, using both valid and invalid zones. When you have seen how the program works, answer N to the prompt. Then run the program again. Notice that you have to load the table again (in fact, the way the program is right now, the table needs to be loaded by the user every time it is run). In the next section you will learn an easier way to fill the table with data.

READ and DATA Statements

Using the INPUT statement to fill a table may not always be appropriate. It can be time consuming and error-prone. If a user enters incorrect table data, then the program results also will be incorrect. Building the table values into the program would be better, because then no user intervention is needed to fill the table.

The **READ** statement works similarly to the INPUT statement, except that the program does not look to the keyboard for input; rather, it looks through its own instructions for a **DATA** statement. When one is found, values are taken, one at a time. In the following example, values are assigned to variables A, B, and C:

```
40 READ A, B, C
50 DATA 10, 20, 30
```

When line 40 is executed, the value 10 is assigned to A, 20 to B, and 30 to C. Although DATA and READ statements do not need to be adjacent in a program, organizing them that way makes the program more readable. Consider this program:

```
10 DIM A(3)
20 FOR I = 1 TO 3
30   READ A(I)
40 NEXT I
50 PRINT "THE VALUES OF A ARE  "
60 PRINT A(1), A(2), A(3)
70 DATA 10, 20, 30
99 END
```

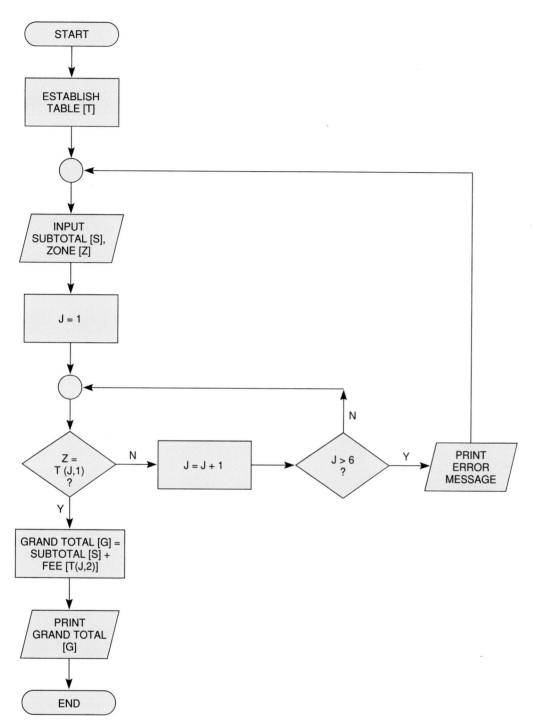

Figure D-13
Program logic for adding shipping
and handling fee to customer order
total

READ statements can be executed repetitively. If this is done, however, sufficient data must be provided in one or more DATA statements. In the following program, the READ statement is executed three times. The first two sets of data are taken from the DATA statement in line 50, and the third set is taken from the DATA statement in line 60.

```
10 FOR J = 1 TO 3
20   READ A, B
30   PRINT A, B
40 NEXT J
50 DATA 9, 8, 7, 9
60 DATA 5, 6
99 END
```

Output from the program is:

```
9    8
7    9
5    6
```

Now let's reconsider the program for adding a shipping and handling fee to a customer's order total. In the following version of the program, the table is filled from DATA statements within the program itself. This ensures that no incorrect table data is used.

```
05   REM ** THIS SECTION ESTABLISHES THE
     TABLE**
10   DIM T(6,2)
20   FOR I = 1 TO 6
30     READ T(I,1), T(I,2)
40   NEXT I
50   DATA 1, 10
51   DATA 2, 13
52   DATA 3,  8
53   DATA 4, 16
54   DATA 5, 14
55   DATA 6, 12
90   REM ** THIS SECTION PROCESSES
     CUSTOMER ORDERS **
100  INPUT "ENTER SUBTOTAL AND ZONE,
     SEPARATED BY A COMMA ", S, Z
120  J = 1
130  IF Z = T(J,1) THEN GOTO 400
140  J = J + 1
150  IF J > 6 THEN PRINT "INVALID ZONE.
     TRY AGAIN.": GOTO 100
160  GOTO 130
400  G = S + T(J,2)
410  PRINT "TOTAL: "; S; " + "; T(J,2);
     " = "; G
500  INPUT "GO AGAIN? ", A$
510  IF A$ = "Y" THEN GOTO 100
999  END
```

Using READ and DATA Statements

READ and DATA statements are appropriate in situations where the input data doesn't change very often, such as the shipping and handling fees in the example above, and income tax tables. Although fees may change occasionally, they remain the same much of the time. Income tax tables change once a year.

READ and DATA statements are inappropriate when input data values change frequently. Consider, for example, a table of currency exchange rates, which can change daily. In that case, it would be better to prompt the user to enter today's rates than to build them into DATA statements. The other option is to teach users how to go into a BASIC program and change DATA statements themselves—but most users are not interested in getting involved in programming. Furthermore, even experienced programmers make mistakes when modifying programs. Making program changes should be avoided whenever possible.

Lesson 6 Exercises

D.6.1 Explain what the following statements mean:
   a. 10 DIM R(50,50)
   b. 10 DIM X1(1000)

D.6.2 Which of the following statements are valid references for question D.6.1.a?
   a. INPUT R(23,4)
   b. T = R(−2,17)
   c. Z = R(23,4)
   d. Q = R(40,2)

D.6.3 Which of the following statements are valid references for question D.6.1.b?
   a. INPUT X1(200)
   b. X1 = 75
   c. T = X1(−5)
   d. INPUT X1(1001)

D.6.4 What will happen when the following statements are executed?
```
10 READ A, B
20 PRINT A, B
30 END
40 DATA −10, 400
```

D.6.5 Describe the output produced by the following program:
```
10 FOR J = 1 TO 2
20   READ K, L, M
30   PRINT K, L, M
40 NEXT J
50 DATA 10, 20, 30
60 DATA 40, 50
70 DATA 60
80 END
```

D.6.6 Write a program to calculate and print a multiplication table. The table should show the product of odd numbers from 1 to 9. Thus, rows and columns of the table are 1, 3, 5, 7, and 9. Use a one-dimensioned array to calculate and print one row of the table at a time.

D.6.7 For a major cross-country meet, runners are being assigned to starting groups based on their times at an earlier qualifying run. The group assignments are made as follows:

Previous Time	Group Assignment
35 minutes or less	1
36 to 40 minutes	2
41 to 50 minutes	3
51 to 60 minutes	4
over 60 minutes	5

Develop a program to make the group assignments. Your program should prompt the user to enter the runner's name and previous time. It should output the runner's name and group assignment.

D.6.8 Develop a program to compute gross pay and taxes. Input the employee name, hourly pay rate, and number of hours worked. Give the employee time-and-a-half for work in excess of 40 hours. Compute taxes on the basis of the table given below.

Your program should output the employee name, gross pay, taxes, and net pay. Also calculate and print the total payroll, total taxes, and total net pay. Hints:
- Use a table with three columns.
- Use READ and DATA statements to fill the table.
- Test the program for correct results. Show that it works for all possible values.

If Gross Pay Is		
Greater than or Equal to ($)	But Less than ($)	Then Taxes Are
0	200	10% of gross pay
200	600	$20 + 15% of the amount over $200
600	1000	$80 + 20% of the amount over $600
1000	1500	$160 + 40% of the amount over $1000
1500 or greater		$360 + 60% of the amount over $1500

Word List

BASIC
direct mode
indirect mode
LIST command
range
NEW command
LLIST command
hard copy
RUN command
SAVE command
LOAD command
INPUT statement
variable
constant
numeric variable

string variable
home
CLS statement
END statement
REM statement
LET statement
arithmetic operator
operand
hierarchy
print format (PRINT USING statement)
logic
flowchart
GOTO statement
loop
IF statement

condition
relational operator
accumulator
counter
reinitialize
nested IF statement
TAB function
FOR-NEXT statements
array
subscript
dimensions of a table
DIM statement
READ statement
DATA statement

Credits

Increasing Your Personal Productivity

1.1 (page 18) *Infoworld*, February 13, 1989 **1.2** (page 20) *Business Week*, October 14, 1985 **2.1** (page 60) *Hartford Courant*, June 16, 1989 **4.1** (page 105) *San Jose Mercury News* **4.2** (page 111) *San Jose Mercury News* **4.3** (page 114) *Syllabus* **4.4** (page 117) *PC Magazine*, August 1989 **5.1** (page 140) *Personal Computing* **5.2** (page 141) *Infoworld*, March 6, 1989 **5.3** (page 150) *Infoworld*, May 29, 1989 **6.1** (page 174) *Communications of the ACM*, September 1989 **7.1** (page 201) *PC Magazine*, June 13, 1989 **7.2** (page 206) *PC Today*, September 1989 **7.3** (page 212) *Infoworld*, March 13, 1989 **7.4** (page 213) *PC Magazine*, June 27, 1989 **8.1** (page 240) *San Jose Mercury News* **9.1** (page 267) *Computerworld*, June 7, 1989 **9.2** (page 271) *Computerworld Focus on Integration*, June 5, 1989 **9.3** (page 274) *Business Week*, June 5, 1989 **9.4** (page 275) *Business Week*, June 5, 1989 **9.5** (page 286) *San Jose Mercury News* **10.1** (page 305) *Computer Decisions*, March 1989 **10.2** (page 316) *Business Week*, May 8, 1989 **11.1** (page 340) *Computerworld*, July 10, 1989 **11.2** (page 348) *Infoworld*, May 15, 1989 **11.3** (page 358) *High Technology Business*, May 1988 **11.4** (page 363) *Computerworld Focus on Integration*, June 5, 1989 **12.1** (page 377) *Data Management* **12.2** (page 390) *Computerworld Focus on Integration*, June 5, 1989 **12.3** (page 395) *Computerworld Focus on Integration*, June 5, 1989 **A.1** (page 418) *Computerworld* **A.2** (page 423) *Infoworld*, June 5, 1989 **C.1** (page 449) *Management Review* **C.2** (page 450) *Computerworld Focus on Integration*, June 5, 1989 **C.3** (page 460) *Computerworld*

Photo Essay: Computer Systems Extend Human Capabilities

1, 18, 19, 26, 38 IBM Corporation **2, 12, 25, 40** Ramtek Corporation **3** NASA **4, 7** Regents of the University of California **5** Los Alamos National Laboratory **6** Hewlett-Packard **8, 33** Tektronix, Inc. **9, 35** Nelson L. Max / Lawrence Livermore Laboratory **10** Chuck O'Rear **14** Evans & Sutherland **15, 16, 17** Chuck O'Rear / West Light **21** Cray Research, Inc. **22, 24** Texas Instruments **27** Woods Hole Oceanographic Institution **23, 28** General Electric Research and Development Center **29** Mary Jo Dowling / The Robotics Institute, Carnegie-Mellon University **30, 31** GMF Robotics **32** Apple Computer, Inc. **37** Vibeke Sorensen **39** Toyo Links

Photo Essay: Hardware: More and More for Less and Less

1–3, 6–8, 14, 17, 20, 21, 23, 24, 26, 27, 29, 31, 33, 36, 37, 44 IBM Corporation **4** Four Phase **5** American Airlines **9** National Semiconductor Corporation **10, 19, 28, 35, 38–40** Hewlett-Packard **11** Lite Pen Company **12** Bergen-Brun **13** Calcomp Inc. **16** Greenleigh Photo **18, 32** Apple Computer, Inc. **22** Sun Microsystems **25** Tandy Corporation **30** Paul Shambroom **41** Texas Instruments Inc. **42** Carol Lee **43** Federal Bureau of Investigation

Photo Essay: The Chip: The Heart of the Computer

1–5, 10–12, 15, 16, 19, 29 Chuck O'Rear **6, 31–33, 39** Hewlett-Packard **9** IBM Corporation **13, 17, 18, 20–27, 30, 32, 37** Intel Corporation **28** Honeywell, Inc. **35** Battelle Memorial Institute **38** John Greenleigh / Apple Computer, Inc. **40** Apple Computer, Inc.

Photo Essay: Communicating with Computer Systems

1, 5, 11, 14 Hewlett-Packard **2, 20, 37, 38** NCR Corporation **3, 10, 17, 19, 22, 26–29, 31–34** IBM Corporation **4** Decision Resources, Inc. **6** New England Technology Group **7** ISSCO **8** 3M **12** Hitachi, Ltd. **15** Apple Computer, Inc. **16** Hayes Microcomputer Products **21, 23** AT&T / Bell Labs **25, 36** AT&T **30** Chuck O'Rear / West Light **35** Lanier Worldwide Inc.

Photo Essay: Information Systems Provide a Competitive Advantage

1, 2, 6 Apple Computer, Inc.   **3, 7, 12, 15, 17, 20, 28–30, 33–36** IBM Corporation   **4** 3M   **5** ISSCO   **8, 13, 16, 19, 21, 35** Hewlett-Packard   **9, 24** Evans & Sutherland   **10** Los Alamos National Laboratory   **11, 23** Computervision Corporation   **18** Tektronix, Inc.   **22** Intel Corporation   **25** General Electric Research and Development Center   **26** Automatix Inc.   **27** Iowa State University   **31** Chrysler Corporation   **32** The Robotics Institute, Carnegie-Mellon University

Text Photos

Most photographs of hardware equipment are courtesy of the manufacturers, whose assistance is gratefully acknowledged. Figures 2-1(a), 2-14, and 2-17 are © Chris Gilbert.

Access arm Mechanism on a disk drive that holds read/write heads and moves to access disk areas.

Accounts payable system A business system concerned with recording, scheduling, and paying a company's debts.

Accounts receivable system A business computer system concerned with recording and reporting a company's receivables (debts owed to the company) and income.

Ada Programming language developed for the Department of Defense as a standard for all armed services. It is patterned after Pascal, is highly structured, and very complex.

Aiken, Howard Pioneer in using electromechanical devices to perform calculations; developer of the MARK I computer.

Algorithm A statement of the steps to be followed in solving a problem or performing a process.

Alphanumeric data Another name for textual data.

American National Standards Institute (ANSI) A group that develops programming language standards for use by industry and computer manufacturers.

American Standard Code for Information Interchange (ASCII) A standard bit pattern using seven bits per byte, traditionally used on smaller computers.

Analog signal Continuous sound signal having a variety of frequencies, like those found in a voice or in music.

Analog transmission mode A technique for sending data that uses a continuous smooth wave instead of sharp peaks and valleys. Contrast with digital transmission mode.

Analytical engine Machine developed by Charles Babbage in 1834 that could mechanically compute any function. It had a memory unit and an arithmetic/logic unit.

Animation Rapid display of slight variations of an image in order to simulate motion.

ANSI *See* American National Standards Institute.

Application development team A group of programmers and systems analysts who work together on large projects.

Application package A group of documents including a computer program with related manuals, a user's guide, and run instructions.

Application program Program written for a particular user's need—for example, payroll, inventory, or scheduling.

Arithmetic/logic unit The part of the processing hardware that performs calculations and logical comparisons.

Arithmetic operation Computer processing operations involving adding, subtracting, and other calculations.

Artificial intelligence (AI) The ability of a computer to learn from experience by storing information and applying it to new situations.

ASCII *See* American Standard Code for Information Interchange.

Assembler Software that translates assembly language code into machine language.

Assembly language Machine language instructions written mnemonically to aid programmers.

Assignment statement (BASIC) A LET statement that assigns a value to a memory cell.

Atanasoff, John V. Pioneer who developed some of the theory behind the first all-electronic computer.

Automated office A business office where operations such as mailing, typing, copying, and scheduling are done on interrelated computerized equipment.

Babbage, Charles Considered the "father of computing"; developer of analytical and difference engines.

Backup An extra copy of data on a disk or tape that is kept for use in case of emergency.

Backup and recovery procedures That portion of a business computer system concerned with saving data and restoring it in the event of a problem or disaster. See also procedures.

Bar code Machine-readable stripes found on consumer products that are read by a scanner and used for pricing and inventory.

Bar graph (graphics) A graphic that shows data values as differing lengths of bars. A bottom scale indicates what each bar means, while a side scale shows the measurement of the bars. Different shading often distinguishes the bars.

BASIC *See* Beginner's All-purpose Symbolic Instruction Code.

BASIC command An instruction in BASIC that the computer interprets and processes immediately after it is input by the user.

BASIC statement A single instruction found in a BASIC program.

Batch processing Processing data in large groups to keep the computer as busy as possible.

Baud A term used to describe the speed of a communications line. It measures the number of times a line can change state in a second. A different and more informative term for business people is bits per second. Line speed in baud is less than or equal to line speed in bits per second.

Baud rate The maximum speed at which a modem can change the status of a signal.

Beginner's All-purpose Symbolic Instruction Code (BASIC) A programming language developed in the 1960s at Dartmouth College. It is used extensively on microcomputers and in education and small businesses.

Berry, Clifford Graduate student who worked with John V. Atanasoff on the theories for an all-electronic computer.

Binary A number system having two symbols, 0 and 1. Place values are based on powers of two. Binary is used by computers because zeros and ones are easily represented electronically.

Binary code The bit pattern for each instruction in the computer's memory.

Binary digit (bit) The basic building block for data, consisting of a 0 or a 1.

Bit *See* binary digit.

Bits per second (BPI) Measurement for the rate of data transmission.

Boot, booting To load the operating system into the memory when turning on a computer.

BPS *See* bits per second.

Bug An error in a computer program.

Bus topology A network where several nodes are connected through a single cable.

Business computer system A collection of computer hardware, programs, data, procedures, and trained personnel that interact to satisfy a business need.

Byte A group of bits that represents one character.

Bytes Per Inch (PBI) A term used to describe the recording density of magnetic tape. Common tape densities are 800, 1600, and 6250.

C A high-level programming language used for systems and communications software.

CAD/CAM *See* computer-aided design/computer-aided manufacturing.

CAM *See* computer-aided manufacturing.

Card reader Computer hardware that puts input data into the computer by sensing the holes on punched cards.

Cassette tape Storage medium, similar in operation to magnetic tape reels, used on microcomputers.

Cathode ray tube (CRT) A televisionlike screen used to display information, also known as a VDT.

CD *See* compact disk.

CD-ROM (Compact disk with read-only memory) Laser disk whose surface can only be written on once, but read many times.

Cell (spreadsheet) A location on a spreadsheet, at the intersection of a row and a column, that holds a single piece of data.

Central processing unit (CPU) The computer hardware that contains the processor (arithmetic, logic, and control/communications) and memory.

Character A single letter, digit, or special symbol.

Character printer A printer that writes a full character. Contrast with dot-matrix printer, line printer, and serial printer.

Chip Another name for integrated circuit.

Clientele of system The people for whom a system exists; the consumers of the system's services. The clientele of the class enrollment system are students. Clientele for an airline reservation system are airline passengers. Contrast with users.

CLS (BASIC) Command to clear the screen without erasing memory.

COBOL *See* Common Business-Oriented Language.

Code Actual statements written in a computer programming language.

COM *See* Computer output microfilm.

Command An instruction that a computer follows immediately.

Common Business-Oriented Language (COBOL) A programming language designed in the 1950s to handle business applications. It is the most widely used programming language.

Communications channel Medium (like cable, satellite) over which data are transmitted.

Communications software Programs that coordinate data communications between networks and check for transmissions errors.

Compact disk A small laser disk primarily used for storing music.

Compatibility The ability of software or peripherals to work on a variety of systems.

Compiler A systems program that translates an entire high-level program into machine language. The program is not run, only translated.

Complement addition The process by which machines subtract in binary.

Components of a business computer system There are five: data, hardware, programs, procedures, personnel.

Compute (spreadsheet) Command to process formulas entered into a spreadsheet.

Computer Equipment used to store and process data according to the step-by-step directions of a program.

Computer-aided design/computer-aided manufacturing (CAD/CAM) The utilization of computers to aid in the design and manufacture of a product.

Computer-aided manufacturing (CAM) Use of computers to control manufacturing equipment.

Computer application Any use for a computer.

Computer center The physical location of the computer system, housing the computer hardware, both input and output, and related personnel.

Computer operator Person responsible for the working of the computer and related equipment, who is also capable of handling minor equipment emergencies and repairs.

Computer output microfilm (COM) Output data produced as microfilm.

Computer professional Person who works directly with the operation or development of computers.

Computer program A set of computer instructions followed in sequence that is designed to control the input, processing, output, and storage performed by a computer. Also known as software.

Computer programmer *See* programmer.

Computer system A collection of five components (people, data, hardware, programs, and procedures) that interact to satisfy an input, processing, output, or storage need.

Concentrator Hardware that saves data transmissions and sends them out as groups.

Concurrent processing The process by which the CPU executes several programs. For example, it may allocate a short amount of time (say 10 milliseconds) to each program in round-robin fashion. Portions of the programs are executed sequentially, but the process occurs so fast, it appears to humans the programs are executed simultaneously.

Concurrent update problem Difficulties that occur when concurrently executing programs attempt to access and modify the same data.

Contention line management A way of controlling traffic on a communication line. When a line is unused, terminals are allowed to broadcast at will. If two terminals initiate messages simultaneously, they must stop and retransmit again, at different intervals.

Contract programmer Programmer hired by an organization to write a specific program. He/she is not a regular employee of the organization.

Control program Part of the operating system that manages the flow of data and programs through the computer.

Control total Total calculated independently of a computer to see if output is correct.

Controls Procedures that help reduce illegal or accidental access or changing of data.

Conversion Changing from an old to a new computer system or from a manual to a computerized system.

Copy (spreadsheet) The process of duplicating the contents of a cell, row, column, or block of text to another location.

Copy command Operating system command to transfer files to a second disk.

Copy protection Software instructions or device put on some programs to prevent illegal copying.

Core memory An early type of memory unit using small ring magnets.

CPU *See* central processing unit.

Crash Computer failure.

Cray, Seymour Early designer of supercomputers.

Create command (spreadsheet, database) The command used to establish a new file and allocate storage space for that file.

CRT *See* cathode ray tube.

Cursor The flashing box or line on a CRT that shows where the next character will appear.

Cursor control (word processing) The use of arrow keys to move the cursor up, down, left, or right through the document. Movement can be one character, word, line, or paragraph at a time.

Data Facts and figures; unprocessed information.

DATA (BASIC) A statement that provides for the security and correctness of data.

Data communications Transmission of data over long distances. Also called data telecommunications.

Data dictionary A systems development tool in which are stored the names and structures of all records and files.

Data encryption Scrambling the code used to store data on disk.

Data entry operator A person who enters data into the computer or onto a machine-readable medium.

Data management services The portion of the operating system that provides data access services to application programs. Data management is concerned with creating, accessing, modifying, and deleting data.

Data manipulation language (database) A series of commands that control the database program, allowing manipulation of files and data.

Data model (database) A plan used by the computer for storing and accessing data items from a database.

Data processing Using computers to convert data into useful information.

Data storage and retrieval Keeping data in an organized file and later accessing them for processing.

Data telecommunications *See* data communications.

Database A collection of files integrated together for cross-referencing, it is under the control of a database program.

Database administrator (DBA) The person in charge of designing, implementing, and managing the ongoing operation of a database.

Database management system (DBMS) A special application program that allows data in a database to be accessed and maintained.

Dataflow diagram A systems development tool that shows processes, dataflows, and files, and their interfaces.

DBA *See* database administrator.

DBMS *See* database management system.

Debugging Finding and eliminating logic and syntax errors in a computer program.

Decimal numbers A number system having ten symbols. Place values are based on powers of ten. Humans usually work in decimal. Computers can work in decimal, but they are not as efficient as when they work in binary.

Decision support system (DSS) A subsystem of the management information system that combines data with models and graphics to answer a decision maker's questions about the data.

Decision symbol Flowcharting symbol, shaped like a diamond, indicating where in a program a logical decision is made. In BASIC it is shown as the IF...THEN statement.

Default Values that, unless changed by the user, are assumed each time a program is run.

Delete A command used to erase a figure, letter, block of text, or a whole file from disk.

Demodulation The process by which an analog signal is converted to a digital one.

Design The fourth stage of systems development in which specifications for hardware are developed, program logic

is specified, data formats are constructed, procedures are defined, and personnel requirements are determined.

Desktop publishing Application package that allows a user to combine word-processed text, graphics, and digitized images into a professional document or brochure. When printed on a laser printer, the document is considered camera-ready.

Difference engine A machine developed by Charles Babbage that used a steam engine to compute linear equations.

Digital signal A noncontinuous sound signal used in data transmission; it has a limited number of frequencies.

Digital transmission mode A technique for transmitting data in which messages are sent as digital (choppy) signals. Contrast with analog transmission mode.

Digitizer An input device that scans graphic material and converts it into digital data that can be read on a CRT screen.

Direct access The ability to retrieve and process records immediately from a file regardless of their order. Also called random access.

Direct-connect modem A modem connected to phone lines through the wall jack, instead of a phone receiver. It is often housed within the computer itself.

Disk A circular platter with concentric tracks that is used as a machine-readable medium.

Disk cartridge High-capacity, removable disk storage used on microcomputers.

Disk directory A list on a disk of all the files kept on it. This list is updated and available every time the disk is used.

Disk drive The hardware that spins a disk, it includes an access mechanism and read/write heads for storing and retrieving data.

Disk operating system (DOS) A series of systems programs that aid the user in storing, copying, and finding programs on disk, as well as managing the work of the control unit.

Disk pack A collection of hard disk platters stacked together to allow access and storage of large amounts of data.

Disk track   One of the concentric circles on a disk holding data as a stream of bits.

Diskette   *See* floppy disk.

Distributed processing   Several computers that send/receive data over communication lines, as well as processing local jobs.

Documentation   Written support for a system, including manuals and a user's guide.

DOS   *See* disk operating system.

DOS utility   One of several programs available on DOS to perform common disk maintenance functions. DOS must be in the system drive to start a utility.

Dot-matrix character   Print character made up of tiny dots.

Dot-matrix printer   A printer that forms characters made up of small dots.

Download   Transfer of a program or data from a host computer to another computer.

DSS   *See* decision support system.

Dumb terminal   Input/output hardware containing a keyboard and screen. It has no processing capabilities.

EBCDIC   *See* Extended Binary Coded Decimal Interchange Code.

Eckert, J. Presper   Codeveloper with John W. Mauchly of the all-electronic computer (ENIAC) and the first commercial computer (UNIVAC I).

Edit   (word processing) To update a text by adding, deleting, changing, or moving words, lines, and/or paragraphs.

Editing   Having the computer check for errors in the input data.

EDP   *See* electronic data processing.

EDP auditor   An auditor who specializes in reviewing a company's financial records and procedures that are kept on a computer.

EDP controls   Procedures used to prevent any illegal or accidental misuse of any component of a computer system.

Electronic bulletin board   A computerized version of a bulletin board that allows users to post messages for others.

Electronic data processing (EDP)   An early term for computer processing, used by accountants and auditors.

Electronic mail (E-mail)   Using personal data files to send and store messages in an office.

Electronic mailbox   The personal file or area on disk used to store messages in an electronic mail system.

Electronic Numerical Integrator and Calculator (ENIAC)   Built by John Mauchly and J. Presper Eckert, it was the first all-electronic computer.

Electronic spreadsheet   An application package that allows the user to input rows and columns of data, which can be manipulated and updated through use of spreadsheet functions and commands.

END   (BASIC) A statement that marks the end of the program run.

End-user computing   Applications where the user is responsible for all aspects of processing: data entry, operations, and using the output.

ENIAC   *See* Electronic Numerical Integrator and Calculator.

Enter   (spreadsheet, database) A command to allow data, numeric and alphanumeric, to be input into a spreadsheet or database.

Error recovery procedure   Rules people follow after processing errors occur.

Evaluation stage   The third stage of the systems development process in which alternatives for all five components are identified, and one of the alternatives is selected.

Exception report   A document that lists, in report form, only those records of a file that fulfill certain requirements.

Execute   Following the program code that has been translated into machine language.

Executive   The highest level of management, responsible for making long-term decisions.

Expansion card   Circuit boards that are added to a computer's motherboard to increase memory or processing power.

Expansion slot   Area on the computer's motherboard set up to connect expansion cards to the processor and memory.

Expert system   A computer system containing a knowledge base and inference engine that can draw new conclusions from data and add them to the knowledge base. Also known as a knowledge-based system or knowledge engineering.

Exploded pie chart   (graphics) Pie chart in which one piece is separated from the whole for emphasis.

Exponentiation   Raising a number to a power or multiplying a number by itself several times; that is, $2^3 = 2 * 2 * 2 = 8$.

Extended Binary Coded Decimal Interchange Code (EBCDIC)   A standard bit pattern, traditionally used on larger computers, having 8 bits per byte.

Facsimile machine   Hardware that scans an image, digitizes it, and transmits it to a remote location.

Feasibility evaluation   The evaluation of the possibility of satisfying a business need with a computer-based system. Cost, schedule, and technical dimensions are considered.

Feasibility study   Report to management on the possibility of a new systems development project's success based on requirements in finances, personnel, and time.

Field   A group of characters that represent a single piece of data. A customer's name, address, and phone number are all separate fields.

File   A collection of related records; all information about a subject. For example, a student file is all the information about students in a school.

File management system   A series of programs that control and manage files, as opposed to a database.

First-generation computer   Computers manufactured in the late 1940s and early 1950s containing vacuum tubes, having no memory units, and using magnetic drums as storage devices.

Fixed disk   A disk pack permanently installed within a drive.

Fixed-point constant   Numerical data that contain a decimal point.

Floating point numbers   Numbers represented in scientific form. The value of the exponent determines the location of the point; hence the term *floating point*.

Floppy disk   A small, flexible disk used to store data. Also known as a diskette.

Floppy disk drive   Hardware used to store and retrieve data to and from a floppy disk. The dtaa are accessed through a window in the disk's cover.

Flowchart   A tool used by programmers to design the logic of a program, it is composed of boxes containing descriptions and arrows indicating flow.

Font   The style of character type for a printed document.

FOR...NEXT   (BASIC) Statements that allow a series of instructions to be repeated a number of times with a variable taking on specified beginning, ending, and incrementing values.

Format   (spreadsheet) Enables the user to change the characteristics of a spreadsheet from the default values.

Formatting   (word processing) Functions of a word processor that allow manipulation of a document's appearance (for example, spacing, centering, and margins).

Formula (spreadsheet) Calculations that can be entered into a spreadsheet cell, and later replaced by the result.

Formula Translator (FORTRAN) A high-level programming language developed for scientific and engineering applications.

FORTRAN *See* Formula Translator.

Fourth-generation computer Computers with processing hardware characterized by very large scale integrated circuits such as a microprocessor. The fourth generation is used in data communication networks.

Fourth-generation language (4GL) High-level programming languages that use nonprocedural techniques to help users specify program requirements. Also known as program generators.

Free-drawing graphics Using the computer to create drawings, much as an artist does on a canvas.

Full-duplex line Synonym for duplex line. Messages can be transmitted both ways, simultaneously.

Full-duplex transmission Data transmission that occurs in both directions at the same time over a communications line.

Function key Programmable key that replaces several keystrokes with a single keystroke.

Gigabyte A measurement of computer memory or disk capacity equal to one billion bytes.

GIGO (garbage in, garbage out) Rule in data processing that correct output depends on complete and correct input.

Global replace (word processing) Automatic replacement of all occurrences of a word or phrase in a document.

Goldstein, Adele Programmer for the ENIAC.

GOTO (BASIC) A statement that transfers control of the program to another statement.

Graphics package Application program that allows a user to present data as graphs or charts, and/or do original drawing.

Half-duplex line A type of transmission line in which messages can be sent in both directions, but not simultaneously.

Half-duplex transmission Data communications occurring in both directions, but only one way at a time.

Hard copy Output data or information in the form of a printed report.

Hard disk A large type of disk, consist-ing of one or more inflexible platters, used for storing data.

Hard disk drive Hardware used to read and write information on a hard disk. The drive accesses hard disks through access arms containing read/write heads.

Hardware A general name for computers and associated equipment.

Head crash A malfunction of a disk drive, where the read/write head touches the surface of a hard disk.

Hexadecimal number system A number system having 16 symbols. Place values are based on powers of 16. Used to abbreviate binary data.

High-level language A people-oriented programming language, such as COBOL or BASIC, that must be translated into machine language before it can be used by the computer.

High-resolution graphics A way of displaying graphic output using a large number of pixels per screen area that is effective for drawing precise lines and curves.

Hollerith, Herman An inventor who applied punched card technology to census data, thereby starting automated data processing.

Hopper, Grace A mathematician and programmer for the MARK I computer.

Host Main or controlling computer in a network.

Hybrid topology Network arrangement containing some combination of the star, ring, or bus topologies.

Icon Picture representing data or the function of the program.

Icon-driven operating system Operating system that works when the user enters or points to an icon, rather than typing in commands.

IF...THEN (BASIC) Statements used to perform actions based on the value of a given condition.

Impact printer A printer that produces output by having a hammer strike the paper through an inked ribbon.

Implementation stage The fifth stage of systems development during which the system is constructed, tested, and installed.

Infinite loop A form of the repetition structure in programming that continues indefinitely unless stopped.

Information Knowledge derived by processing data, usually in the form of a printed report or CRT display. Also known as output data.

Information center An organization designed to support end-user computing and provide decision support.

Information utility A company that provides references and consumer information at standard rates to individuals and companies.

Ink-jet printer Printer whose mechanism involves small nozzles squirting ink dots to form characters.

INPUT (BASIC) A statement that assigns incoming data to a variable name.

Input data Data read into the computer for processing.

Input hardware Equipment used to put data into the computer for processing, such as a keyboard or bar code reader.

Input/output (I/O) Characteristic of hardware or operations involving input and output of data.

Input symbol Flowcharting symbol, shaped like a parallelogram, indicating where in a program data must be input.

Installation Systems development step involving the set-up and testing of a new system.

Integer constant Numeric data that do not have a decimal part.

Integrated circuit A complete electrical circuit on a small silicon wafer, it is the basis for processing in third-generation computers. Also known as a chip.

Integrated manufacturing System that uses CAD, CAM, robotics, materials resource planning and/or data communications to manufacture goods.

Integrated software Programs capable of sharing data with other programs.

Intelligent copier A copy machine that can accept and reproduce input from a word processor.

Intelligent terminal Input/output hardware consisting of a keyboard, CRT or printer, and memory to do preliminary data error-checking.

Interactive Characteristic of hardware or operations involving real-time processing of data and instructions.

Interactive mode (BASIC) A method of accepting data through a keyboard or from a file one item at a time. In a BASIC program this is done with the INPUT statement.

Interface A device that converts data signals between different types of equipment.

I/O *See* input/output.

Jacquard, Joseph Marie Developed use of punched cards to identify weaving patterns on a loom.

Job management The portion of the operating system concerned with starting and stopping jobs, and the allocation of the computer's resources.

Jobs, Steve The man who started the Apple Computer company with Steve Wozniak.

Just-in-time inventory Raw materials arrive in a manufacturing plant just before they are used. This saves storage costs.

Justify (word processing) To align the right and/or left margins of a document.

K *See* kilobyte.

Key *See* key field.

Key field A field in each record of a file that uniquely identifies that record. Also called a key.

Key-to-disk equipment Hardware that allows an operator to type on a key-board and have data put directly on disk, usually a floppy disk.

Key-to-tape equipment Hardware that allows an operator to type on a keyboard and have data put directly on tape.

Keypunch Hardware that punches holes in punch cards by typing on a keyboard.

Kilobyte (K) A measurement of computer memory or disk capacity that is equal to 1024 bytes.

LAN *See* local area network.

Language translator System program that translates high-level language code into machine language.

Laser disk Very high capacity disk storage, where bit patterns are burned, as small holes, onto the disk surface. Laser disks can store pictures and sound as well as traditional data forms.

Laser printer A nonimpact printer that uses a laser beam to write dots on a drum coated with a light-sensitive material that transfers ink to paper.

LET (BASIC) A statement allowing an internal value to be assigned to a variable name.

Life cycle Organization of a systems development job into small, organized steps.

Light pen Penlike input hardware that is used to draw directly on a CRT. Its movements are recorded as data.

Line graph (graphics) A graphic that shows trends in the data. The graph has two scales: The bottom one shows passage of time, while the side measures money or quantity. Different trends are shown as separate lines containing unique symbols.

Line number (BASIC) A number before each statement in a BASIC program identifying the order in which the statements will be carried out.

Line printer Printer that sets up and prints an entire line of output at one time.

LIST (BASIC) A command that causes the computer to display all or part of a program that is stored in the computer's memory.

LLIST (BASIC) A command that prints on paper program code presently in memory.

LOAD (BASIC) A command that instructs the computer to copy a program for tape or disk into the computer's memory.

Local area network (LAN) A network of personal computers within one building or small area.

Logical operator (BASIC) Symbol that indicates the type of comparison to be made in an IF...THEN statement.

Loop *See* repetition.

Lovelace, Ada Augusta Mathematician who helped explain the theory of the analytical engine and conceptualized the binary number system.

Low-resolution graphics Displaying graphic output by using a small number of pixels on a CRT screen. The display quality is rather limited when drawing curved lines.

LPRINT (BASIC) A statement that displays output on a printer.

Machine code *See* machine language.

Machine language Instructions used by the computer itself. All instructions are reduced to bit patterns. It is not commonly used for application programming. Also called machine code.

Macro (spreadsheet) A small program built into a spreadsheet that performs a series of instructions. A macro is started by pressing just a few keys.

Magnetic ink character recognition (MICR) Characters used by the banking industry that allow input hardware to read information directly from a check.

Magnetic tape A medium for recording data sequentially. Data is recorded as magnetized spots.

Main memory A portion of the CPU that contains data and instructions. Programs must be brought into main memory before they can be run, and data must reside in main memory before it can be processed.

Mainframe A large computer used by big businesses and organizations.

Maintenance Ongoing inspection and repair of computer hardware to ensure continuous reliability.

Maintenance programmer A person who modifies programs already in use in order to reflect a change in law or policy.

Management information system (MIS) A collection of business systems, not necessarily computer-related, that provides information to business people.

MARK I A computer having mechanical counters controlled by electrical devices, developed in 1944.

Materials requirements planning (MRP) Computer applications where current inventory and production schedules determine purchase and delivery of additional raw materials.

Mauchly, John W. Codeveloper with J. Presper Eckert of the ENIAC (first all-electronic) and UNIVAC (first commercial) computers.

MB *See* megabyte.

Megabyte (MB) A measurement of memory or disk capacity consisting of one million bytes.

Memory The part of the processing hardware where the program and data are stored before and after processing. Also known as memory unit or primary storage.

Menabrea, L. F. Wrote a paper disseminating Babbage's theories on development of a computng machine.

Menu A list of available program options, it appears on the screen and makes program control much easier.

MICR *See* magnetic ink character recognition.

MICR reader An input device that reads the magnetic ink characters at the bottoms of checks. Also known as an MICR scanner.

Micro *See* microcomputer.

Microcomputer A small computer, used in homes, schools, and businesses, with processing hardware that is based on a microprocessor.

Microfiche Output data photographically reduced and put on a sheet of film for storage.

Microprocessor Processing hardware combining many processing circuits on a small silicon chip. It is the basis for the processing power of the microcomputer.

Microsecond One-millionth of a second; used to measure speed of operations within the computer's processor.

Millisecond One-thousandth of a second; used to measure speed of operations within the computer's processor.

Minicomputer A medium-sized computer often used in research or to monitor a specific manufacturing process.

MIPS Abbreviation meaning million instructions per second; a measurement of processing speed for computers.

MIS *See* management information system.

Mnemonic A memory aiding device, such as using letters to represent bit patterns, that is the basis of assembler languages.

Mode Classification of transmission line. Transmission lines can be analog or digital.

Model A mathematical simulation or plan representing an area requiring a managerial decision.

Modem *See* modulator-demodulator.

Modulation The process of converting (or de-converting) a digital signal into an analog one.

Modulator-demodulator (modem) A device used to connect a computer or terminal to a telephone line for data communication. It translates between analog and digital signals.

Monochrome A screen display limited to one color and black.

Motherboard A circuit board containing a microcomputer's RAM, ROM, clock, and other circuitry.

Mouse Small input hardware with a rotating ball underneath used to input data by rolling on a flat surface.

MRP *See* materials requirements planning.

MS-DOS Disk operating system designed by the Microsoft Corporation.

Multiplexer Hardware that merges signals from several incoming sources or separates signals, sending them to different destinations.

Multiprocessing The execution of complex computer applications by simultaneous use of several linked computers.

Multitasking, multiprogramming Capability of a computer to store more than one program at a time while working on the program with the highest priority.

Nanosecond One-billionth of a second; used to measure speed of operations within the computer's processor.

Narrowband A slow-speed transmission line, capable of 45 to 150 bits per second.

Network Collection of computers connected by communication lines.

Network topology Models of arrangements for computers and communication channels for handling data communications. The four types of network topologies are bus, ring, star, and hybrid.

NEW (BASIC) A command that clears the program and data from the computer's memory.

Node A communication station, such as a computer or terminal, within a network.

Nonimpact printer A printer that produces characters through electrostatic, heat, or other means not involving striking the paper.

Numeric data Data that contain only numbers, decimal points, and signs.

Numeric variable name Variable name in BASIC consisting of one or two letters or a letter and a number that identifies numeric data.

OCR *See* optical character recognition.

Office automation Networking office equipment together to facilitate word processing, electronic mail, and electronic filing.

Octal number system A number system having eight characters and place positions based on powers of eight. Used to abbreviate binary numbers.

Online Direct input and processing of data by a computer.

Online processing The characteristic of being in direct communication with the computer.

Online thesaurus (word processing) Feature that allows a user to call up synonyms for a word indicated in a document.

Operating procedure Rules people follow to turn the computer on and off, and do standard functions for maintaining files.

Operating system System programs that control the use of the computer's resources (that is, memory or input/output hardware).

Operational decision Decision on day-to-day activities in an organization, usually made by front-line management.

Operations personnel People involved in the day-to-day working and maintenance of computer equipment.

Optical character recognition (OCR) The ability of an input device to read characters that are also readable by people.

Optical disk A form of secondary storage that uses lasers.

Optical mark Mark made by a pencil on a designated area of paper, usually an answer sheet, that can be read by a scanner.

Optical mark recognition (OMR) Ability of a scanner to read a pencil mark. The most common application is an answer sheet.

Optical scanner An input device that uses light to read optical marks, bar codes, and optical characters.

Output Results of computer processing—an image on a CRT, a printed document, and so on.

Output hardware Equipment that provides the processed information to the user, such as printers or display screens.

Page printer Printer that sets up and prints an entire page at a time.

Paintbrush (graphics) Function that allows the user to draw lines on the screen in a variety of widths.

Palette (graphics) An icon display of different colors, shapes, and line sizes available in a graphics package.

Parallel installation A style of systems installation in which the new system is run in parallel with the old one until the new system is shown to be correct and fully operational.

Parallel port An input/output plug that allows the entire bit pattern for a single character to be sent at one time.

Pascal A high-level, highly structured programming language that was developed in the 1970s.

Pascal, Blaise Inventor, in the 1640s, of the first mechanical adding machine.

Passwords Keywords, phrases, or numbers that must be specified before the system will allow an action to take place.

PC-DOS Disk operating system developed by the IBM Corporation.

Peripheral Any online input, output, or storage hardware used in a computer system.

Personal computer A microcomputer system used to meet personal needs.

Personal productivity software General-purpose programs that have wide appeal and help us work with words, numbers, graphics, and large groups of data.

Personnel One of the five components of a business computer system. Categories of personnel are systems development, operations, users, and systems clientele.

Phased installation A style of systems installation in which the system is broken into subsystems, and these subsystems are implemented one at a time.

Picosecond One-trillionth of a second; used to measure speed of operations within the computer's processor.

Pie chart (graphics) A graphic circle divided into slices, each representing a single component's relation to the whole. Each slice is labeled with the component name and the actual percentage. Percentages for the entire chart add up to 100.

Pilot installation A style of systems implementation in which the using organization is divided into groups, and the system is installed one group at a time.

Pitch Number of characters printed per inch of document.

Pixel One of an array or matrix of dots that makes up a visual display.

Pixel graphics Graphics that are formed by rows and columns of small dots. Also known as bit mapping.

Plotter Output hardware that draws continuous images by movement of pen on paper.

Plunge method of implementation A seldom-justified style of systems implementation in which the old system is abruptly discontinued and the new system replaces it. This is a high-risk style of implementation.

Point of sale (POS) A terminal combining a cash register with a machine-readable source document scanner that is connected to a computer.

Polling A style of line management in which the computer, or concentrator asks each terminal on its polling list if the terminal has a message to send. If so, the message is transmitted.

Port A plug or connector on a computer where input or output devices are attached. Also known as an I/O port or input/output port.

POS *See* point of sale.

Presentation graphics A productivity software package used to prepare line charts, pie charts, and other information-intensive images.

Printer Output hardware that produces information as typed images on paper.

Problem definition The first stage of systems development. During this stage, the business problem(s) to be solved are identified and documented.

Procedure Systematic courses of action used by people when they are involved with a computer system.

Processing The action of a computer on data as it performs calculations or comparisons.

Processing hardware The equipment that performs calculations and comparisons upon input data. Also known as a computer.

Processing unit *See* processor.

Processor Hardware that interprets a program, controls data flow in memory, and performs both logical and arithmetic operations. Also known as a processing unit.

Program *See* computer program.

Programmer A person who writes instructions for a computer according to set requirements.

Programmer/analyst Person who determines the users' needs and writes the appropriate programs.

Programming language A vocabulary for instructing the computer. Programming languages vary from low-level binary machine code to high-level, English-like languages such as COBOL.

Prompt A short explanation to the user about what kind of data should be input.

Protocol The set of rules two computers follow when communicating with each other.

Prototyping A systems development alternative whereby a small model, or prototype, of the system is built before a full-scale systems development effort is undertaken.

Public domain software Free programs available to the general public.

Pull-down menu A menu that, when pointed to by keyboard or mouse, expands to show all available options.

Query language (database) High-level commands that direct the search operations, making it easier to access the database.

Query/update utility A general-purpose program for accessing and modifying database data.

RAM *See* random access memory.

Random access *See* direct access.

Random access memory (RAM) The type of computer memory where programs and data are stored temporarily. RAM can be cleared and reused.

Range (spreadsheet) Option listing the beginning and ending cells to which you want a function applied.

Range check An edit check to ensure input data is within established bounds.

Read-only memory (ROM) Type of computer memory where preset instructions (such as control programs and interpreters) are permanently stored.

Read/write heads The mechanism in a tape drive or at the end of a disk drive access arm that picks up or records data.

Reasonableness check An edit check to verify that input data is reasonable.

Record A collection of related fields.

Relational model (database) Organization in which data are organized into tables. Rows represent records, while columns represent fields. Other tables index the data tables, allowing access to single fields or records.

Removable disk Hard disk module containing an access arm and read/write head in a protective case that can be removed from the drive.

Repetition One of the three structured programming patterns. A sequence of instructions is repeated until a condition is met.

Report Program Generator (RPG) A high-level programming language first developed for producing standard reports and now expanded for general business applications.

Report writer (database) A program that allows users to create hard copy report formats for data output. Users can set up margins, headings, footings, and so on. The report writer also does some calculations, such as totals and averages.

Request for proposal Formal bidding procedure for an organization's new computer system: System specifications are sent to vendors, who send bids to the organization.

Requirements stage The second stage of systems development. During this stage, the project team is formed, the problem is defined, feasibility is assessed, and specific needs of the system are determined.

Resolution The sharpness of the images on a display screen.

Response time Time elapsed between a user's request and the computer's response.

Retrieve (word processing, spreadsheet) To load a previously existing document into the computer's memory.

Ring topology Network model where each node is connected to two other computers in a ring formation.

Robotics Technical area involving use of programmable machines to do repetitive movements.

ROM *See* read-only memory.

RPG *See* Report Program Generator.

Run A command that instructs the computer to follow, one instruction at a time, a program already loaded into memory.

Save (word processing, spreadsheet) Command to store a file on disk.

Scanner Input hardware that can read characters, marks, and bar codes as data.

Scroll The rolling of text up, down, and sideways on a screen for viewing long or wide documents.

Search and replace (word processing) User enters phrase or word to be found and a corresponding replacement text. In a global replace, all occurrences of the phrase are found and automatically replaced. In a discretionary replace, replacement of each occurrence of the word is decided by the user.

Second-generation computer Computer developed in the late 1950s that used transistors as part of the processing hardware. It contained core memory, used an operating system, and was programmed in high-level programming languages.

Secondary storage General term meaning storage other than the computer's memory—that is, disks and tapes.

Sequential access Retrieving records in the order they are found in a file, first to last.

Sequential file Method of organizing data by putting all records in key field order—access can be slow.

Serial port An I/O port that allows only one bit to be sent at a time.

Serial printer Printer that outputs one character at a time.

Service bureau Company that specializes in providing data processing services for other organizations.

Service technician Person responsible for repairing and installing computer equipment.

Shapes (graphics) Function that allows the user to draw standard shapes, such as a circle, oval, square, or rectangle.

Shareware Software available through the public domain whose author requests a donation if it is used. For that money, the user will receive updates and manuals.

Simplex line A type of communication line in which messages can flow only one way.

Simulation A program that models or mimics a real-life situation, allowing the user to react without endangering life or property.

Software *See* computer program.

Sort Command that places data into order by a key field identified by the user.

Source The file or disk to be transferred when using the DOS copy command.

Source document Form on which data are collected for computer input.

Speech-generated output Sound output in the form of computer-generated words.

Speech generator Output hardware that generates recognizable human speech.

Spelling checker Part of some word processing packages that highlights spelling errors in a text and may display suggested correction.

Spraypaint (graphics) A method of spreading color or a pattern over a large area. As with a can of paint, the color or pattern gets darker the more the spraypaint function is used over an area.

Stacked bar chart (graphics) A bar chart where each bar represents more than one measurement, each in a different color or pattern.

Statement (BASIC) Each numbered line of code in a program. It is not acted on by the computer until the program is run.

Status line (spreadsheet) A line on the screen that displays which spreadsheet function is currently being used.

STEP (BASIC) Part of the FOR...NEXT statement that identifies the value by which the counter will be incremented.

Storage hardware Equipment used to record data for later use—that is, tape and disk drives.

Storage medium Material (disk or tape) used to save data for later processing.

Strategic decision Long-term decisions made by top management.

Stretch (graphics) Function that lets the user pull out or stretch standard shapes, such as increasing the length of a rectangle.

String Data that are combinations of letters, numbers, symbols, or spaces. Also known as a string constant.

String constant *See* string.

String variable A string value that can change each time a program is run.

String variable name Variable name in BASIC consisting of one or two letters or a letter and a number. It is always followed by a dollar sign. It identifies string data.

Style sheet (word processing) Standard formats available for a variety of common correspondence, reports, and other documents. Style sheets are often used with desktop publishing software.

Summary report A document, in the form of a report that lists totals and trends.

Supercomputer A high-capacity computer used by large organizations to handle volumes of scientific computations.

Supervisor One of the control programs of the operating system. It is usually the first program loaded in when the computer is turned on. It allocates memory and coordinates peripheral activity.

System A group of elements working together to solve a specific problem.

System programs A class of computer programs that includes operating systems, compilers, utilities, and database management.

System test Trying all parts of a computer system under the conditions you expect it to work.

Systems analyst A person who puts together the computer system components by identifying needs, formulating requirements, and helping the user understand how the new computer system works.

Systems development project The design, development, and implementation of a system, usually done in organized steps called a life cycle.

Systems maintenance The implementation of changes and additions to equipment and programs that keep a working system functional and efficient.

Systems programmer A person who writes systems programs for an organization.

Table A matrix of data organized into rows (fields) and columns (records); used in a database.

Tactical decision Decision about short-term managerial problems, made by middle-level management.

Tape A machine-readable medium in which data are stored as magnetic patterns on strips of plastic coated with a metal oxide.

Tape drive Storage hardware used to access information on tape. It runs the magnetic tape over a read/write head.

Task management One of the major portions of the operating system. Task management controls executing programs; it allocates the CPU's resources.

Technician A person with on-the-job training and minimum educational background who works with instruments, assembles parts, or oversees a manufacturing process.

Telecommunications Long-distance communications of data, voice, or any other signal.

Telecommunications software Programs that aid in linking computers together over communications lines.

Teleconferencing A conference held between several parties at remote sites through telecommunications.

Teleprocessing Transferring data between remote system components and a single host computer using communication lines.

Template (spreadsheet) A partially completed spreadsheet containing labels and formulas. The user copies the template and fills it in with different data each time the same application is needed.

Terminal A keyboard and printer or CRT that is connected by communication lines to a computer and is used for input and output only. It can contain a limited memory but no control unit or arithmetic/logic unit.

Testing The important process of verifying that systems do what they are supposed to do.

Textual data Data that contain letters, numbers, and symbols organized into words and sentences.

Third-generation computer Computer developed during the 1960s that uses integrated circuits as the basis of processing. It normally has multiprogramming and online capabilities.

Time slicing A process by which the CPU allocates small portions of time to programs.

Tool box (graphics) A graphics package feature that contains a variety of tools to let the user choose the type of drawing tool, make common shapes, color the drawing, and manipulate what is on the screen.

Top management *See* executive.

Touch-sensitive screen A screen that uses grids to locate the user's touch and translates that into data.

Track Storage area on a disk or tape holding a single bit of data.

Transaction An exchange of value, usually recorded as data.

Transaction Processing System (TPS) A type of processing in which the impact of events occurring in the organization is recorded in stored data.

Transistor A small electronic component that can alter a signal in a predefined way. It is the basis of the second-generation computers.

UNIVAC I *See* Universal Automatic Computer.

Universal Automatic Computer (UNIVAC I) The first commercial computer, developed in 1950 by John W. Mauchly and J. Presper Eckert.

Updating The operation of adding, deleting, or changing records in a disk or tape file.

User Anyone utilizing information generated by a computer.

User-developer Users who design and write programs for their own applications.

User friendly Software that is self-explanatory and easy to use.

Utility software Operating system programs that perform common functions such as sorting and merging files, copying files, and so on.

Vacuum tube A glass tube containing circuitry, which was the processing basis for first-generation computers.

Variable Names given to data values that can change.

VDT *See* video display terminal.

Video disk Laser disk that stores and plays pictures as bit patterns.

Video display terminal (VDT) A screen that is used as an output device.

Virtual memory The use of secondary storage space (a disk) to expand primary memory. A large program is broken into pages that are swapped between the disk and memory as needed.

Voice grade transmission line A medium-speed transmission line capable of 1800 to 9600 bits per second.

Voice recognition device Input hardware that accepts spoken words as data.

Volatile memory Memory whose contents are erased when power is lost.

Von Neumann, John Mathematician who developed the design for the first computer with the program stored in memory.

Wideband transmission line A high-speed transmission line capable of 500,000 bits per second or more.

Winchester disk A nonremovable, high-capacity storage unit containing a single hard disk and drive.

Window A section of the screen divided to help the user organize all of the different program activities.

Word processing Using computer technology to prepare letters, memos, and other documents.

Word processing program A program that lets a user write, edit, store, and print text in any needed form.

Word wrap (word processing) A document is entered without carriage returns. The word processor senses margins and moves the cursor to the next line when necessary.

Workstation A name given to a microcomputer when it is connected to a mainframe.

WORM (Write Once Read Many) Laser disk whose surface can only be written on once, but read indefinitely.

Wozniak, Steve Started Apple Computer company with Steve Jobs by building and marketing the Apple computer. Later they formed Apple Corporation.

Write protect notch Cut-out area on the side of a diskette used to prevent erasure of the data and programs it contains. When the notch is covered, the disk is write protected.

WYSIWYG (What You See Is What You Get) Feature of word processing and other software that shows on the screen exactly what will be printed.

Index

Note: Page numbers in bold type refer to pages on which terms are defined. Page numbers in italic refer to pages on which relevant figures or "Increasing Your Personal Productivity" extracts appear.

Abacus, **404**
Accounting, 72, 87–88
Accounts payable system, **87**
Accounts receivable system, **87**
Accumulator, **478**
Active E-mail system, **265**
Adapter card, 277
Ad hoc query, **171**–172
Ad hoc question, 169, 171–172, 176–177
Aiken, Howard G., 408, 411, *418*
Alphanumeric data, **430**
ALU. *See* Arithmetic/logic unit
Amalgamated Mining vignette, 350–351
American Standard Code for Information Exchange (ASCII), 53–54, 204–205
Analog line, **276**–277
Analytical engine, 407
Apple computer, *419*, 422–423
Application developer, 178
Application development, 182–185, *185–191*
Application programs, **42**, 48–51, *172–173*, 252
Application user, 178
Archives, 39
Arithmetic/logic unit (ALU), **27**, 104
Arithmetic operators, **472**–473, *473*
Array, **485**
Arrow in dataflow diagram, 382
Artificial intelligence, *358*, *418*, *419*
ASCII, 53–54, 204–205
Assembly language, **414**
Assumption, **150**
Atanasoff, John V., 412
ATM. *See* Automated teller machine
Augusta, Ada, 407
Automated document production, 219
Automated teller machine (ATM), 29, *267*
Automatic recalculation, **129**
Automation, *316*

Babbage, Charles, 404–409
Babbage's mistakes, *409*
Background program, **110**, 111, 112
Backup, 7, **39**, 44, 117, 221
Backup software, *117*
Bar graph, 148
Baseball league vignette, *185–191*
Baseband transmission, 286
BASIC, *418*, **466**–490
BASIC commands, **467**–468, *469*
BASIC statements, **467**, 468–490
BASIC translator, 466
Basketball statistics vignette, *156–160*
Batch transaction processing, **67**–68, 415
Baud, 276 n

Billing system, **87**
Binary numbers, 430–433, 436, 437, 439
Bit, 37, **52**–53, 104, 276, **430**
Bits per second (bps), 276
Boilerplate document, **219**
bps (bits per second), 276
Broadband transmission, 286–287
Bubble in dataflow diagram, **381**
Bug, 50, 155
Bulletin board, electronic, 301–302
Business computer system, **24**–27, *27*, 51
Business information system, 51. *See also* Business computer system
Bus topology of LAN, **284**, *284*, 285
Byte, **28**, 54

Cables for LAN, 268
CAD/CAM, **94**
Calculations area of spreadsheet, 153
Camera-ready copy, **206**
Capital expenditure analysis, **89**
CASE (computer-assisted systems engineering), **390**–396, *390*
CASE encyclopedia, **393**
CASE groundwork, *395*
CASE methodology, **391**, 391–393, *392*
CASE products, **393**–396
CASE tools, **391**
Cash planning application, **89**
Caterer vignette, *176–177*
Cathode-ray tube (CRT), 33. *See also* Terminal
CCP. *See* Communications control program
CD-ROM, **39**
Cell in spreadsheet, **125**, *142–143*
Centralized system architecture, **266**, *268*, 273–274, *273*
Central processing unit (CPU), **27**–28, *28*, 43, 420
Channel, **105**
Character, 54
Character-based interface, **103**, 108
Charts with spreadsheet program, 130, 146–148
CICS. *See* Customer Information and Control System
Clientele of system, **59**
Clip art, **214**
CLS statement in BASIC, **470**
Coaxial line, **286**
Coded data, **298**, 321
Color monitor, 33
Column in database table, 166. *See also* Field
Column in spreadsheet, **123**
Column names, glossary of, 182, 184

Command structure, 138–141
Communications control program (CCP), **282**, 312, 321
Communications devices, **40**–41
Communications lines, 19–20, 275–279
Communications package, *286*
Communications port, **277**
Communications software, **47**
Communications systems, 263–265
Company computer store, 363
Compatible data, **115**
Competitive advantage, 337
Compiler, 42, **45**
Complement addition, **432**
Computer-assisted design (CAD), **94**
Computer-assisted manufacturing (CAM), **94**
Computer-assisted systems engineering. *See* CASE
Computer-based information system, 10–14
Computer codes, 53–54
Computer crime, *418*, 445–452, *449*, *450*, 459
Computer crime vignette, *444–445*, *452–453*, *454–455*, 455, 456, *457–458*
Computer ethics, 462–463, *462*
Computerization, 14–17
Computers, history of, 404–426, *418–419*
Computers and privacy, *460*
Computer security, 451–452
Computer system, 24
Computer usage, 425
Concentrator, **278**–279
Concurrent data sharing, **317**, 318–321
Concurrent server, **284**
Concurrent workload, **374**
Condensed print, **143**
Condition, **476**
Conference presentation vignette, 194, *207–208*
Configuration of bits, 53
Constant, **469**
Constraint, **176**, 181, 184, **240**–242, 375
Contention, **290**–291, *291*, 318, 320
Context switching, **109**–110
Continuous-tone art, **212**–214
Controlled sharing, **265**–266
Controller board, **283**–284
Control panel of spreadsheet, **138**
Control unit, **27**
Coordinates in spreadsheet, **125**
Coordination procedures, 325–326, *326*
Core memory, **414**
Corporate (organizational) information system, 324, 336, 343, 346, 361
Cost feasibility of system, **235**, 371
Counter, **478**
CPU. *See* Central processing unit